Pelican Books
An Eye to India

David Selbourne was born in London in 1937. He was
educated at Manchester Grammar School, Balliol College,
Oxford, and the Inner Temple. He has been Tutor in
Social and Political Theory at Ruskin College, Oxford,
since 1967, and visited India as Aneurin Bevan
Memorial Fellow (1975–6).

His work as a playwright, which includes *Class Plays*,
The Two-Backed Beast, *Samson* and *Dorabella*, has been seen
at the Traverse Theatre, Edinburgh, the NUS Drama
Festival, the Edinburgh Festival Fringe, the Crucible
Theatre, Sheffield and the Everyman Theatre,
Liverpool. His previous political writing includes *Brook's
Dream*, an essay on the politics of the theatre, and *An
Eye to China*. He has also contributed to the *Guardian*,
Harper's, *Tribune*, and other journals.

David Selbourne

An Eye to India

The Unmasking of a Tyranny

 Penguin Books

Penguin Books Ltd, Harmondsworth,
Middlesex, England
Penguin Books, 625 Madison Avenue,
New York, New York 10022, U.S.A.
Penguin Books Australia Ltd, Ringwood,
Victoria, Australia
Penguin Books Canada Ltd, 2801 John Street,
Markham, Ontario, Canada L3R 1B4
Penguin Books (N.Z.) Ltd, 182–190 Wairau Road
Auckland 10, New Zealand

First published 1977
Copyright © David Selbourne 1977

All rights reserved

Made and printed in Great Britain by
Richard Clay (The Chaucer Press) Ltd,
Bungay, Suffolk
Set in Linotype Plantin

Contents

List of Tables

WITHDRAWN

India is a vast and diverse country that has something to offer to everyone. The beauty of the Taj Mahal by moonlight, the finest monument to love ever created; the beat and rhythm of folk dances which have come down the ages almost unchanged; crowded, colourful bazaars contrasting with the peace and grandeur of snow capped mountains, the quiet backwaters of Kerala fringed with coconut palms – these are a few of the countless facets of India which are timeless in their appeal.

Department of Tourism, Government of India, 1975

The face of truth is covered with a golden disc. Unveil it, O Pūsan, so that I who love truth may see it.

Īsá, 15

Preface

The passage of events during the emergency in India is recorded in this book. I have tried to show what the roles of its architects and protagonists were; and the illusions and cruelty, lies and violence to which India was subjected. But this could not be an end in itself, nor has it been my main purpose.

For the emergency was part of a continuum in the history of India since independence. It is a history which cannot be perceived as a simple trilogy: that is, as a pre-emergency democracy ('the world's largest'), an emergency dictatorship, and a post-emergency democratic restoration. Moreover, the emergency served – as no previous sequence of events has done in modern India – to make manifest the nature of the political economy of India, the nature of the state, and the condition of the Indian people. Finally, the Indian emergency, as a response to political and economic crisis, constitutes a paradigm case, an object lesson, whose implications cannot be confined to India.

This is true also of the nature and source of the support, inside and outside India, which was given to the assaults on the people and institutions of India during the emergency, a brutal and ignominious period in the history of the nation. Attempts by some to dignify the emergency, from whatever standpoint and whether in terms of utilitarian necessity or as a form of 'socialist' progress, can now be seen in focus. Others, eyes closed and ears stopped, saw and heard little or no evil. For them, the trains ran on time also. It is for this reason, and because the record of the crimes committed against the Indian people requires to be made safe from cancellation by denial and evasion, that almost every emergency event and statement referred to in the text has been given its attribution. But for the reader who does not choose to check or follow these authentications, the book may be perfectly well read without them.

I have been concerned, too, with questions of method, a search for those forms which would enable me to establish the truth about India. This has led me in chapter 2, for instance, to bring together observed life with the empirical and quantitative measure of it; indeed, I have attempted this synthesis in the text as a whole, believing that only a combination of perceptual and rational knowledge can carry the reader to the heart of the matter. Indeed, the setting of the book and its continuous theme is the condition of the people; a condition, with other factors, propelling India towards revolution, surviving the succession of one faction by another, and one illusion by another – the last, and perhaps greatest, that of the transformation of India by election.

I owe apologies in advance for any mistakes there may be in the transcription and transliteration of names from faded or badly typed documents, some of which had a rough passage from India. There may be other mis-hearings and mis-readings where information was orally transmitted, or was partially suffocated by the censor. But what was happening in emergency India was clear at the time, and has since merely become clearer. In the last analysis, therefore, the shortcomings are my own; varieties of censorship and intimidation, and other restraints, cannot be blamed for them.

I would like to thank Peter Preston and Malcolm Dean of the *Guardian*, Dick Clements of *Tribune*, Lewis Lapham of *Harper's*, and Paul Sweezy of *Monthly Review* for having given me opportunity on different occasions to speak of the circumstances of India; Neville Maxwell for encouraging me to write this book; my wife, whose own work at the Centre for Contemporary Cultural Studies in the University of Birmingham on problems of ideology and historical method led to helpful discussions at all stages of this text's writing, but who bears no blame for any of its errors of judgement; Sybil Brooke for typing from the manuscript with great skill, care and speed; and the library staffs of the Indian Institute and the Institute of Commonwealth Studies in Oxford for their assistance.

Above all, I am indebted to those who – often at risk to themselves – provided me with facts and assistance during a long journey through emergency India. I have chosen not to name them here; but they are the real authors of this work, just as the condition of the Indian people, and not the eye of the beholder, is its subject.

David Selbourne, 19 April 1977

1 From Crisis to Crisis

In exercise of the powers conferred by clause (1), article 352 of the constitution, I, Fakhruddin Ali Ahmed, President of India, by this proclamation declare that a grave emergency exists, whereby the security of India is threatened by internal disturbances.

26 June 1975

The President has proclaimed emergency. This is nothing to panic about.

Indira Gandhi, Prime Minister, 26 June 1975

The Indian arena measures 3,280,483 square kilometres. It is the seventh biggest country in the world. Within this area are 600 million people. It is the second largest society, after China. India is rich; to the World Bank, with its own perspectives and vocabulary, 'rich in potential but slow to develop'.[1] It is in the United Nations' fourth division of polities, those which are known to possess great riches, but remain poverty-stricken and immobile.

Thus, Mrs Gandhi's Finance Minister C. Subramaniam declared, perhaps with a certain ingenuousness, in the Lok Sabha (Lower House) of the Indian Parliament, 'We should find out why the backwardness is persistent.'[2] He was referring specifically to Bihar, the richest and poorest state of India. It is the richest in resources, and the poorest in the condition of its people. 'As far as land resources are concerned,' he continued, and on the terrain of fact, 'it has got the richest soil. As far as water resources are concerned, no other state is its equal. With regard to minerals it has got a rich mineral wealth also.[3] Why this backwardness?' he demanded of his audience. 'Is there no remedy for it?' he inquired of them.

India is a rich country, which is poor. It is rich in minerals and power, in coal and iron; rich in oil resources;[4] rich in its rivers. It has the most extensive cultivated alluvial plain in the world, and the potentially highly productive volcanic soils of the Deccan; it has 'vast ground water-resources'.[5] According to the American Overseas Development Council, India even 'has a natural endowment for food production very close to that of the United States', with a per capita availability of arable land similar to that of France, New Zealand and Yugoslavia,[6] and a density of population not only lower than that of Germany, Holland, Japan and the United Kingdom, but also of Bangladesh or Sri Lanka.[7] It is said to be 'possible for India to double and treble her food production'.[8] It has a potentially cultivable land area at least comparable with, and probably exceeding, that of China – no less than 100 million acres being uncultivated, fallow or 'not available for cultivation'[9] – but with three quarters of China's population. In other words, and as the Indian government has incautiously admitted itself, India is actually capable of economic self-sufficiency.*[10]

But India's rural millions – more than 450 million live in the countryside, dependent upon its impoverished agriculture – are universally known to be poor and indigent. Less known is that 75 per cent of the land under crops is without irrigation;†[12] under-fertilized; the net area of rural India sown and cropped barely rising in a decade;[14] half its cultivable land either threatened with erosion, or in need of soil and water conservation.[15] A portion of its land resources is lost each year to desert and dereliction. The better, or 'bumper', harvests, which temporarily alleviate hardship, and lead to temporary falls in prices, also

---

* Until I began to inquire into this question in detail, I was unaware of the facts. I can now put in balance the views of the deputy managing director of the Metal Box Company in Calcutta, that 'one third of India's population (sc. 200 million)' was 'hopeless', and 'would have to be exterminated if the other two thirds was to survive';[11] a view which, as I will show in chapter 7, must also be linked to the politics of emergency India.

† The disjunction between Indian planner and producer (between theory and practice) may be illustrated in a preliminary fashion as follows: 'One can *imagine* the misery of a hot summer day without a drop of water to drink, or of having to *look at* parched fields devoid of rains'[13] (my emphases). Moreover, it contains part of the answer to Subramaniam's rhetorical questions, just cited.

lead to storage problems and landlord hoarding; the average to suffering and hunger; the worst lead to famine. It is a country of summer drought, and monsoon inundation. But one quarter of India's exports is food;[16] grown and harvested by the hungry, and the chronically undernourished.

At least 40 per cent of rural workers are entirely landless – just under fifty million being euphemistically classed as 'agricultural labourers' in the last (1971) census,[17] a figure which is rising[18] as rural bankruptcy increases, and which itself understates the volume of landlessness; or have tiny landholdings inadequate for domestic self-sufficiency; a huge total, and, with the dependent families of the landless added to it, certainly more than one hundred million. All the most up-to-date indices reveal, despite fluctuations, a stagnant rural economy, presided over by the landlords and a minority of rich peasants who can be termed kulaks; of mountainous inequalities; an order of magnitude in which 50 per cent of all landholdings are marginal, and account for a meagre percentage of the total cultivable area of India.[19]

These 'agrarian relations', arguably (to put it modestly) responsible for the chronic lack of growth of the rural economy, are predominantly 'pre-capitalist'. That is, they are a complex compound of feudal structures of land tenure, large landholdings, precarious tenancy, cruel and extortionate rents, sharecropping, and an army of indebted and bonded serf-labour. Together they point to the awesome sorrows and hard labour of rural India, and what the Finance Minister in an outbreak of candour (which the reader should retain) described as 'a serf society, responding to pressures'.[20] With it is a smaller 'capitalist' rural sector employing 'free' agricultural labour, earning subsistence or less than subsistence wages. There is a growing and unquantifiable number of rural and urban unemployed and under-employed,[21] a 'long-run stagnation'[22] (with intermittent rises and falls, the better results relentlessly offset by the worse) in overall agricultural and food-grain production,[23] and accompanied over the last decade by sharp rises – doubling and tripling in the case of cereals, rice, wheat and pulses[24] – in prices.

Perhaps even less known is that, in all this period, the feeding of the hungry and the clothing of the near-naked and ragged have not prospered. The per capita availability of cereals has fluctuated within a general stagnation: the same in 1966 as it had been in 1955; the same in 1975 as in 1956, but less than it was in 1953;[25] while there has been an overall fall – 23 per cent in the last decade[26] – in the per capita avaliability of cloth to the people of India. Its output in volume now is only what it was in 1944, with a 10 per cent drop in 1975 alone.[27] And if there has been a minuscule increase in overall per capita income – it was less in 1973, for instance, than it had been in 1970, and the same in 1972 as in 1964[28] – it is of little real significance. For the truth says that 'when we have produced more, we have increased our cash by a little; but then our pockets have been picked by the rising of prices'.[29]

It is overshadowed, also, by the increasing absolute and relative number of those living below a poverty line which is itself drawn at the very margins of subsistence, a total of humanity always cited as more than two hundred million[30] even in official pronouncements. It is overshadowed by the slow decline in per capita consumption of calories and proteins;[31] and by sharp inflation in food prices, higher during the last decade in the prices of food grains than in other food articles.[32] The latter bears hardest on the poorest – for the lower down the income scale the higher the proportion of income spent, under the laws of poverty, on basic foodstuffs.[33] It is overshadowed by a sharp drop, in the last decade, in the production and availability of pulses,[34] the protein food of the very poorest, who in India stand waiting upon the perimeter of starvation.*

These are merely the barest lineaments of a precarious balance between life and death for millions of the people. For them a small erosion of purchasing-power from inflation – let alone the very large rise in prices between 1972 and 1975[36] – puts at risk access to the means of survival in an exchange economy; it may then push them from chronic malnutrition towards, and into, starvation. These are the millions of India with nothing to sell and no savings, and already deeply in debt; with little or no land; and whose labour is intermittent or unwanted. For them, and

---

*Or, if you prefer, 'In the extent of its coverage and efficiency, the public distribution system for food grains in India stands unrivalled in the world.'[35]

others, monsoon- and crop-failure immediately arouse the scything spectre of famine. Most serious – though there were lesser famines in other years – were the famines in 1943–4, when perhaps four million in Bengal died;[37] in 1966–7; and in 1972–3, when famine passed from Orissa through West Bengal to Bihar, and stalked in and round the Rajasthan desert in the West, and in other parts of India also.*[38] But 'famine' is arguably a term of art; some hold that it signifies in India nothing more than an appreciable, or even unappreciable, increase in the normal patterns of the death rates of the rural (and urban) poor.

This is – despite some of the best arguments offered by apologists for India's social and economic progress since independence – the rural India left behind by its succession of conquerors; its indigenous economy held by some historians to have been uprooted or distorted in its development, its land exhausted, an economy impoverished by empire and yet still tied now to its economic order.

It is also a country which needed but never got, and could not generate on its own account, the capital to create its own industrial revolution; and yet which has, since independence, launched the development of an urban free enterprise economic order upon a sea of urban misery and squalor.

Here is that classical division of labour which is represented as the 'mixed economy'. That is, the private sector, dominant in the industrial economy, is itself dominated by a handful of indigenous and growingly prosperous (as well as corrupt) monopolists, who are in turn supported by a state patronage which they have the political and economic power to manipulate. But the 'public' sector, while providing the costly infrastructure for the activities of private capital, takes only a 16 per cent share of the domestic product;[40] and both sectors are wedded to, and therefore considerably dependent upon, foreign capital and foreign aid, both western and Soviet.†

*Or, if you prefer, 'no one was allowed to die [sc. during 1972 and 1973] due to non-availability of food'.[39]

†Basically, western capital – principally British, American, German and Japanese – is invested in the private sector, Soviet in the 'public', or 'state capitalist' sector;[41] see appendix, p. 431.

This edifice rests, as it must, upon the backs of Indian industrial labour, itself surrounded by a huge and growing reserve army of the unemployed, the registered unemployed alone increasing four-fold in the last decade,[42] though the population in the same period grew by about one fifth.[43] They are underpaid when employed, and without unemployment insurance or other forms of effective social security, when jobless. As T. A. Pai, Mrs Gandhi's Minister of Industries, put it, again with somewhat laconic candour, in the Rajya Sabha (Upper House) of the Indian Parliament, 'we have a growing unemployment problem'.[44] Moreover, there has been no statistically significant increase[45] – on the contrary, some official sources record actual falls, and even steep falls*[46] – in real industrial wages during the last decade and a half of India's independence.

The daily life of the rural and urban millions, to be confronted in detail in the next chapter, presents a continuous spectacle of inequality, hard labour, and injustice. Furthermore, the people may be perceived as citizens of a client state of the richer bourgeoisie and landlords, which is itself in turn deeply mortgaged. That is, the state itself is encumbered by international indebtedness while struggling to assert its national autonomy, as might a fly in a web; and all presided over, from independence in 1947 to defeat in 1977, by a single ruling party, the Congress. Since the 1960s in particular it had been supervising and administering the social and economic effects of this stagnation, punctuated by uneven short-term development, within a context of long-term deterioration, and compounded latterly by severe inflation and recession.

This is arguably the social stasis of India, a barely moving pyramidal structure of inequality, uncorrected by economic distribution. It was what the Minister of Industries T. A. Pai memorably called 'the weakness in our society of a big proces-

---

*For instance, a report from the W. Bengal Labour Ministry, released in March 1976, showed that 'the real earnings of the working people in the state have been steadily falling since 1961. In 1961, the consumer-price index was 101, money earnings 102, real earnings 101·67 (base 1960). In 1974, they were respectively 279, 288 and 103·47;[47] and see appendix, p. 422.

sion, with only a few of us in the front, and with a big gap in between, and a large section of our population limping behind'.[48] Alternatively, it was a situation in which, according to Indira Gandhi, 'the people are much better off now than ever before'.[49]

It will be well to remember also, as context for what is to follow in this text, that in these circumstances there could have been no qualitatively or absolutely *new* crisis, or 'emergency', for the Indian people as a whole. That is, without profound structural change, there was nothing which could intervene in the deepening of those processes which both the official indices, and the naked eye, will conjointly reveal to the observer.

A further and egregious feature of the Indian political economy with which it is necessary to come to terms early, is that the development of an indigenous Indian capitalism, together with its consequent steepening of existing inequalities given the soil in which it was planted, has been carried out since independence in the name of 'socialism', albeit of a special kind.* The degree of inequality which characterizes this 'socialism' is of Himalayan proportions. The Finance Minister, in his speech of 4 August 1975 from which I have already quoted, can be safely regarded as having been an authoritative source of information (which can be fully substantiated from official Indian data) upon the order of magnitude of this inequality. 'The standard of living of the topmost people,' he said, 'is much higher than that of the topmost people in the developed countries. They are able to exploit the cheap labour; they can have any number of servants; two servants in the kitchen, and another two servants in the drawing-room. The disparity is much more here than in the capitalist countries.'[50]

Congruently, a succession of 'land reforms' since independence appears to have touched less than one per cent of India's total arable land area. There are more than 400 million acres of arable land in India[51] (of which no less than fifty-two million are fallow).[52] Of the total, sixty million acres have been estimated to be recoverable as landlords' 'surplus', under 'ceiling' legislation,

*For a fuller discussion of this in context, see chapter 3; and thereafter, *passim*.

which ostensibly limits the extent of private land ownership;[53] but only a tiny proportion of it[54] had been distributed up to 1975, after more than a quarter-century of independence, and with state power uninterruptedly in the hands of a 'reforming', and even 'socialist', party. Not only have these programmes of reform made a very small statistical impact on concentrations of land ownership,[55] but while the cruelties of rural indebtedness among the landless poor have deepened, landlord wealth and income have almost entirely escaped taxation. The incidence of direct taxes on agriculture is extremely low; amounting to less than one per cent of the net domestic product from agriculture.[56] In addition, anti-eviction acts, rent-reduction acts and minimum wages acts have, as we shall see later, gone unimplemented.

The attempted imposition of nominal 'land ceilings' on the huge concentrations of rural ownership has been continuously defeated; by the political power of a rural landlordism embedded in the structure of the political system, by blatant evasions of the law, by collusion between bureaucracy, revenue staff and landlords, and of course by institutionalized violence. As briefest instance, 'the ease with which a landlord's mercenaries gunned down women workers in Marachi,' wrote Arun Sinha on 6 December 1975,[57] 'shows the power of the feudal landlords'. The youngest was Saraswati Kumar, aged fourteen, for whom these few lines will serve as insufficient memorial, described by the landlords as a 'looter'. Her brother came running from the field, saying '*daiya khatam*', 'sister is no more'. In this case, according to Sinha, the landlord owned hundreds of acres of land, even though the limit on landholding under the Bihar Land Ceiling Act is, nominally, eighteen acres per family of five. Such concentrations of landownership have survived efforts at reduction, such as they have been; efforts not merely cosmetic, but palliatives dictated by successive rural rebellions, a real-politik of response to the accelerating – or to use the West Bengal government's own term, 'unusual'[58] – increase during the last two decades of landless labour. Properties have in further response been promptly divided *within* landlord families; tenant peasants, far from benefiting, have been evicted in the process of division, swelling the number of landless; so that a small minority continues to own a disproportionately vast part of the land area of India, after nearly three decades of a 'progressive' independence.

Explanations offered by the state have varied; lack of 'proper land records' has been one. In reply has come:

> 'Give land to those who have no land!'
> Who has prevented you from doing it?
> 'Complete the land registers!'
> Who has prevented you?
> In Bihar, there is no land register at all.
> And in Bihar, ever since independence, it is
> your ministry which is functioning.
> Who has prevented you?

> *N. G. Goray, to the Rajya Sabha, 22 July 1975**

Lack of 'political will' has been another; or 'limited availability of land';[59] vested interest blaming vested interest, perhaps the most familiar to those with knowledge of India. Alternatively, as the Minister of Industries put it to the Rajya Sabha on 28 July 1975, 'our programmes of land reform have failed. They have failed because somehow [sic] there has not been a strong public opinion which supports their implementation.'[60] Or we may choose between Mrs Gandhi's 'who stopped us? I shall not say that any person stopped us or any group stopped us. The *atmosphere* stopped us';[61] and Krishan Kant's declaration in the Rajya Sabha on 21 July 1975 (and himself a member of Mrs Gandhi's faction of the Congress Party, until expelled from it) that 'nobody[62] stopped the Congress Party from carrying out the radical restructuring of the economy of the country and taking measures to eradicate poverty. Besides passing some legislation on paper and making some amendments to the constitution, what else have we done?'[63]

Beyond such Socratic dialogue and rhetorical questioning,

---

*For a further excerpt from this speech, see appendix, pp. 387–8. After the emergency's imposition of censorship on press reporting of parliamentary proceedings (see chapter 5), such speeches as this had to be privately circulated, though they continued to be published in the official record of debates in India's Parliament.

beyond the empirical data and the evasions, stand the accusing poor; in millions. They speak another language.

'Years ago we had no land. And today we have no land. For years and years we have lived and worked on these fields, and yet not a portion of it is ours.' The women of Kovilpathu have never heard of land ceilings. They knew that their master then, and their master now – Desikar of Valivalam – had all the lands. O yes, he leased out lands to the tenants, strictly in accordance with the law. It was irrelevant to the law that the tenants themselves did not know that they were tenants. But there was one new duty they had to perform for him – make periodic trips to the Co-operative Credit Society to get loans in their own names, and then hand them over to him.[64]

The 'green revolution' which attempted in the 1960s, and according to the admissions of the government's own pre-budget Economic Survey of March 1976 failed,[65] to achieve an artificially induced free enterprise solution to the problem of rural stagnation and immiseration, was typically set within the matrix of that progress towards 'socialism', to which I have referred. But the provision – financed by foreign capital and foreign aid – to certain landlords and rich peasants, whom corruption selected – of credit, machinery and high-yielding seeds led instead to increased disparities and inequalities both regional and local, and between rich landlords and poor smallholders. The latter experienced a 'serious absolute and relative deterioration in their economic position'.[66] Poor tenants, moreover, were often evicted as landlords consolidated their holdings in pursuit of 'economies of scale'. Such growth as was achieved under these schemes – and there was some until, as the Economic Survey put it, 'it became clear that the initial impetus had been exhausted'[67] – was neither reflected in any significant overall increases in the per capita availability of food grains, nor in the real wages of the 'agricultural labourers' who brought in these harvests.[68]

The real *net* effect of the political and economic policies of India's last decade is visible in the official data, compilations, digests and yearbooks, without even considering the verdicts of critics. It is visible whether 'achievement', and distortion or exaggeration of 'achievement', are admitted or discounted, and whether the fallibility of statistics be ignored or emphasized for the sake of argument. Comparisons between the growth rates of India and properly comparable countries such as China or Nigeria, and even Pakistan or Sri Lanka, reveal what has happened, or not happened, in India.[69] We can see, for instance, that there has in some states even been an actual decline in the *absolute* total of the employed during the last ten years.[70] That there has been a general accentuation of poverty in the rural areas is not in question; the fatal nexus between inequality and backwardness remains unbroken; 'economic and social development [has been] stalled for a whole decade in the country as a whole'.[71] Or, if the testimony of power and the language of Machiavelli were to be preferred, 'the country has made enormous progress in the past decade',[72] 'the success achieved by India spectacular by any standard, either western or eastern, or developing or developed countries'.[73]

India's is a political economy in which the poor are (not unusually) held in a vice-like grip; held not only by the exigencies of poverty and structural destitution, but by functional political necessity. That is, one section of the ruling classes must resist the agrarian revolution which is needed by another for the development of capitalism; has no choice but to hold down the rural poor in preservation of their own political and economic interests. The other seeks to build, and partially succeeds in building, an indigenous capitalism, while itself held in near thraldom (circumscribed by shortages of resources, insufficient investment and its inherited position within the international division of labour) to the world economy, with its disorderly succession of slumps and recoveries, inflation and recession, and its control of both capital and market. These are also the first intersecting and colliding circles of dependency, instability and potential violence, played out upon the suffering body politic of India.

There is thus a violence latent not only in the barest recital of the Indian data of deprivation, as I shall show more clearly in the following chapter; there are also those varied species of violence latent in any dependent and impoverished economy, which compound the historical violence of an India mythically supposed to be both pietist and pacific.

The political economy of India since independence has been a battleground; not only a battleground between the classes, but between the shifting economic and political oppositions and compromises within the ruling classes. There has been vacillation and irresolution in reform (and the capacity to 'plan' only a backward and dependent economy). There has been an oscillation between paternalism, parliamentarism and savage reprisal against the people and their organizations, particularly at times of rebellion in the vortex of acute social, political and economic crisis. There has been alternation, in foreign and trading relations, between appeasement of India's paymasters and belligerent assertions of a largely illusory political and economic independence of them.

These are the fluctuations and volatilities of a polity which is externally dependent, and because internally unreformed socially, inherently unstable; with little leeway to offer concessions; and which is continuously threatened by its people's discontents and the organizations which against great odds express them. The precarious and difficult pursuit of industrialization, and the accumulation of capital to achieve it – since the capitalist road is being 'independently' travelled in India – cannot easily withstand the pressures of opponents, trade union demands, fissiparous tendencies, and nationalist movements in its states or among its minorities. It cannot tolerate the claims of any form of revolutionary upsurge, whether from left or right. Moreover, the humiliations of external economic dependency, from which they nonetheless cannot afford to alienate themselves, drive its government and ruling classes – divided as they additionally are in India – at one moment towards 'clipping the wings of foreign investors',[74] and at the next towards giving them free access to their domestic market. And in the latter case, they are admitted to take full advantage of cheap labour and raw materials, at increasingly profitable rates of return in India during the last decade.[75] They are permitted to export both raw materials and the resulting manufactured products, while returning an increasingly larger portion of the profits to the foreign metropolitan economy.*

The history of post-independence India has not only been a stagnant and unstable one, but also a humiliating and bloody one, belying both its 'independence' and its supposed 'non-violence', as well as its reiterated professions of 'non-alignment'. It has been doubly humiliating, because India has been increasingly subjected to two international divisions of labour, not one; both the western, and the Soviet. As the *Hindustan Times* put it euphemistically, when the new five-year accord between India and the Soviet Union was signed on 15 April 1976, 'there has been a dovetailing of certain sectors of the two economies for meeting the Soviet Union's demand';[76] the *Hindu* asserted that 'the Soviet willingness to set up projects in India, where labour is cheap, will be the application on the ground of the theory of "division of labour" in relation to developing countries'.†[77]

It is additionally humiliating for a largely dependent economy, such as India's, that its more powerful trading partners can increase or decrease India's exports much as they please. They can import what they wish to import at prices they choose to pay (for instance, by manipulating their exchange rates against the rupee), taking the very primary products, foods and raw materials, which India can least afford to export. And while the terms of trade are in constant deterioration against the 'underdeveloped' economies, every rise in exports will be offset in value by imports.[79] To meet the cost of provision to India of both

* Thus, for instance, by 31 March 1974, there were 752 corporate bodies in India controlled by foreign enterprises, the value of their assets 30 per cent of the entire private corporate sector in India. *Times of India Directory and Year-Book*, Bombay, 1976, p. 588.

† There are, of course, other views of this process. For instance, the pro-Moscow Communist Party of India (hereafter CPI)[78] sees the Indo-Soviet relation as a catalyst to take backward India to industrialization by a non-capitalist path to socialism; alternatively, to the managing director of Simpson's, a big industrial conglomerate in Madras, 'because of India's ties with Russia, India can offer to US investors both cheap Indian labour and access to the Russian market' (in conversation with the writer, Madras, January 1976). Whether both views are equally false is another issue; see chapter 6.

needed and unneeded, obsolete or poor quality technology, they can lend the impoverished economy the money with which to pay for it, as 'aid', debt upon debt being heaped upon the national economy – that is, upon the people – as debt upon debt is heaped upon the threadbare domestic economy of the poor peasant of India.

It is not surprising that, whatever may be the residual illusions about it, the social history of post-independence India has been both cruel and violent. And in foreign affairs, the pivotal position of 'non-violent' and 'non-aligned' India in south Asia, located in the midst of the interplay of relations and oppositions between the United States, the Soviet Union, China, Pakistan and India, has brought it, at one end of the spectrum, to successive military hostilities with China in 1962, Pakistan in 1965 and 1971, and, at the other, to what was described in *The Times* as the 'takeover of Sikkim'.[80] It has been in an almost continuous 'state of emergency' since 1962*; in its 'non-alignment' it has come, or been driven, to successive alignments, first with the United States and subsequently with the Soviet Union. The Indian state has been violent in its internal struggles with its own national minorities, such as the Nagas, the Mizos and others. It has been capable, above all – shattering widely held notions about its pacific state policies – of a barbarous cruelty, authoritatively as well as fully documented, in dealing with successive peasant uprisings and armed rebellions since independence, with oppositional party forces in India, and with the organized labour movement.

This 'social' history is not only well documented, but much grimmer than can be encompassed merely by the assertion that 'beneath the forms, democracy in India has never been much more than government of the shallow political class for its own benefit and privilege, and for the maintenance of the social order upon which the parliamentary forms have been an alien transplant',[81] true though that may be. Moreover, it is not sufficient to explain what has happened since independence simply in terms of a Constitution whose provisions establish a poten-

---

*The *penultimate* emergency was declared on 3 December 1971 because of 'external aggression', also by invoking article 352 of the Constitution.

tially unitary, and strongly centralized, state – despite its nominally federal structure – with draconian reserve powers available to those who can command them. The same is true of the fact that democratic and fundamental rights conferred by the Constitution on the citizens of India can be suspended by decree and ordinance, whenever the 'security of the state' is held to be threatened. For these are rights, and limitations upon rights, which are not unique to India.

Instead, what has to be noted, for example, is the cumulative history since independence of the subversion or displacement, by the centre, of the political and electoral processes in the states of the Indian Union. It has included the overthrow by decree, and by less savoury methods – as Amnesty International reports have shown, by the occupation or sacking of political offices, the harassment and intimidation of opponents, ballot-rigging and violence against both politicians and voters[82] – of duly elected incumbent state governments, when they came to be dominated by parties opposed to the ruling Congress Party. These governments came to power, particularly in the last decade, in response to deepening economic crisis, the process beginning as early as 1957 in the state of Kerala; or because of the growth of an increasingly radicalized politics of opposition to an entrenched and corrupt ruling party at the centre, as in Bengal in 1967, 1969 and 1971; or because of the assertion of a separatist or regionalist state politics, as in Tamil Nadu in 1967 and 1971; or as the result of a complex combination of these factors. In some cases, single opposition parties came to office in these state governments with large majorities over the Congress Party. In others, coalitions were formed which established a sufficiently strong conjoined opposition to form a majority and a united front government, as in Kerala from 1967 to 1969, and Gujarat in 1975.

The result of such varied electoral defeats, in the states, of the party which was in continuous command at the centre of the 'federal' system, particularly when combined with the economic deteriorations over which it was presiding, and with or without the accompaniment of spontaneous and organized outbreaks of rural insurrection and industrial conflict, was an extensive use of

reserve powers – such as 'presidential rule' – under the Constitution, and often unmitigated police terror, against both political
and trade union opponents.* These activities of the state – in
which strong evidence had come to light of participation by the
Congress Party organization itself, and its youth wing, the Youth
Congress[84] – rested not only upon extra-legal violence, but also
upon the continuous invocation and intermittent refinement of
preventive detention regulations. Though these were devised
originally by the British (such as the Defence of India Rules)
they were used before independence with substantially less
severity. The refinements have included most notably the 1971
Maintenance of Internal Security Act (MISA) providing for
detention without trial, subsequently refined still further by
amendment, and the particular cruelties of long periods of incarceration without redress in India's jails. In fact by 1974 it was
being openly argued, rightly or wrongly, that 'in its treatment of
those who pose a political threat to it, the government of India
has nothing to learn from the most repressive régimes in the
world',[85] a comparison which would take me outside this text's
scope if it were to be followed.

When Jawaharlal Nehru published his autobiography in 1936
he wrote – having been imprisoned himself under the same
Defence of India Rules which have been in continuous use since
independence – that 'political imprisonment was a frequent
occurrence in India'.[86] The 'social' history of post-independence
India, its reverence for life (which co-exists with the maintenance
of capital punishment) notwithstanding, its philosophy of
ahimsa – or non-violence towards people and nature – its pieties
and passivities notwithstanding, and whatever the claims which
may be made for it as being the 'world's largest democracy',
encounters and must encompass these continuities. Such a
social and political history, when it comes to be written by
future historians, must also face certain alternatives of perspective : either what the parliamentarian H. N. Mukherjee des-

---

*Thus the evidence of the Centre of Indian Trade Unions (henceforward
CITU) to the International Labour Organization, and the subsequent
ILO reports, are couched in the language of 'stabbings', 'beatings' and
'killings'.[83]

cribed in August 1973 as that 'political enormity in India, the phenomenon of unprecedentedly heartless treatment of political prisoners, large numbers of whom have been beaten up and killed, inside and out of jails, without anything like a judicial process, without conformity with routine regulations regarding *post mortem*, and other investigations';[87] or the claim of 'India's scrupulous adherence to the Western concept of democracy, a democracy which gives pride of place to civil liberties'.[88]

Within the politico-economic context I have already sought to define, the incidence of uprising, revolt, opposition and dissent since independence has ranged widely in geography, in scale, and therefore in order of cruelty of state response. It has included peasant rebellions: such as that of Telengana, in the state of Andhra Pradesh, between 1946 and 1950. There, a form of revolutionary government based upon wholesale land-seizures and rural 'soviets' was brought to hundreds of villages and hundreds of thousands of peasants, until defeated by irresolution and crushed by police and army, in what was a putative agrarian revolution. It has included similar but smaller-scale uprisings in Bengal, Kerala and Tanjore during the same period; and in East Thanjavur, between 1967 and 1969. There, three miles west of Kilvenmani in early January 1969 landlords and their agents, who were arrested and later released without trial in a special dispensation of mercy, rounded up and burned to death in their wretched huts forty-four landless agricultural labourers, women and children.[89] It has included the 'naxalite' peasant uprisings, from 1967 onwards,[90] which broke out in Naxalbari in rural West Bengal, Gopiballabpur in the same state, and Srikakulam in Andhra Pradesh. A spreading rebellion of poor peasants, it brought with it landlord dispossession, land-seizure and large-scale rural violence, and was led from 1969 by the then recently constituted CPI–ML.[91] In its train came, inevitably, mass-reprisal and state counter-violence – including the death in custody of that party's general secretary* and long-term detentions without trial. According to the West Bengal Home Minister, there were 17,782 prisoners 'held as naxalites'[92] in one state alone, in 1973.

*Charu Mazumdar was arrested on 16 July 1972, and died ('of a heart attack') twelve days later, on 28 July 1972.

Large numbers of the detained were to remain in jail, untried. Large numbers of those assumed by the government to be 'naxalites' and denoted as such, were young people and students,[93] who were engulfed in the orgy of violence and counter-violence, variously arrested, beaten and killed in that panic-stricken crescendo of cruelty and counter-cruelty which marks the insurrection of the dispossessed. 'Is it not true,' asked Goray, addressing himself to the Upper House of the Indian Parliament, and himself no 'naxalite', 'that in West Bengal the finest flower of youth has been liquidated under the pretext that they belonged to the "naxalites"?'[94]

It has included the 1972 mutiny in the Indian navy, suppressed not only by force but by the press also; and the 1972 state police revolt in Uttar Pradesh, crushed by the special police forces and the army.[95] It has included the general railway strike of May 1974, provoked by demands from the huge 1·8 million-strong and underpaid work-force – 600,000 of them classed as 'casual', earning about £5 per month, without provident funds, sick leave entitlement or social security – for industrial worker status in conformity with the 1919 ILO convention, for an eight-hour work day and a need-based minimum wage. It was met with a reported 20,000 arrests, both under the preventive detention regulations I have mentioned, and others; with 25,000 dismissals; with the intervention of the territorial army, the regular army, the Central Reserve Police, and even the navy at Cochin. It was met as well with assaults on railway workers' families, and eviction of railway workers from their homes in the 'railway colonies'.[96]* Alternatively, 'the railways have been able to achieve progress, mainly because of the industrial peace [which] has for long been the hall-mark of labour relations in the railways'.[98]

In West Bengal, an opposition government led by the CPI–M[99] had been three times elected to power in the space of four years. Consequently overthrown by, and then ruled from,

---

*'They used the military to raid our houses; there were terrible beatings. We were dragged from our beds in the night and taken away to the lock-ups. Armed militias were let loose against us; in some places our women even were raped and assaulted. There were clubbings with *lathis*, and then killings.'[97]

the centre during 1970 and 1971, both domestic[100] and international[101] sources have documented the scale of the terror and
violence in the state, and the volume of arrests under MISA.[102]
They both preceded and followed the re-installation in 1972 of a
Congress Party-led state government, which was subsequently
to use 'the toughest of strong-arm methods to cow and destroy
its opposition',[103] and to set an example for the future. It perhaps
constitutes too an example of the political consequences of the
entry, however misguided, on to the field of parliamentary
practice of political parties demonstrably attempting to represent the interests of the working classes. Should they go beyond,
or merely seek to go beyond, mere palliatives, it is often the
signal for the jettisoning of the rules of parliamentary democracy by its erstwhile proponents.

So that this period had been noted clearly as one marked by
the murder of the opponents of the Congress Party – political
party workers and trade unionists – of deaths in custody, of the
fettering and manacling of prisoners, and of torture. Throughout it, there was also that familiar litany of explanations for the
'disappearance' of prisoners, which included denial of initial
arrest, the asserted 'release' of prisoners of whom there was no
subsequent trace, and the 'shooting of prisoners while trying to
escape'.[104] These events were documented and described throughout the whole period both inside India and outside it, and were
raised with the Indian government by Amnesty International for
instance, without result, on 15 March 1973, 19 October 1973, 14
June 1974 and 1 December 1974.[105]

It will be important for social and political historians of India
in the future, with a duty to reconstruct the truth of the period
under review shorn of all illusion and unharassed by the urgency
which informs this text, to take note of the speed and comprehensiveness with which much of the history of the decade has
been elided from official memory. It was also to be selectively
re-written with that classical combination of *suppressio veri*
and *suggestio falsi* in which (as I shall show later) India's
emergency rulers appeared to specialize. 'The CPI–M,' said the
Prime Minister, for example, in the Lok Sabha on 22 July 1975,
'formed a government in West Bengal, and everybody knows

what was the situation there. Could people walk in the streets after dark? Anybody who wants to read the newspapers of that period can see how many murders were committed, and what was happening when their government was there.'[106]

In fact, a reading of the newspapers of that period, whether they were those supporting the Congress Party or those opposed to it, proves a daunting experience. The *Economic Times* speaks of 'more than two hundred and fifty trade union leaders and activists alone [who] have been killed, several hundreds arrested and detained, a large number wounded, and thousands of family members of the workers beaten up and locked behind bars without trial. The [police] authorities have so far failed to explain why no fruitful investigation of these murders has been possible.'[107] The *Hindustan Times*, more circumspectly, declares that 'the Congress victory would have been more welcome but for the reports of violence by youth groups and toughs who rallied round the Congress'.[108] The *Economic and Political Weekly* states that 'in West Bengal, as successive reports from our Calcutta correspondent have shown, the CPI–M Party has been subjected to organized political terror with the connivance of a pliant governor's administration'.*[109] The evidence of violence was consistent and repetitious in its unanimity, whether retrospectively denied or conceded, responsibility admitted or displaced on to the opposition.

There are in fact two broad facets of the Indian prism of judgement and description of its own past and experience, to which it is necessary to refer, and to place early in this book. One is more particular, the other more universal, in its features. The first illustrates one of the special characteristics of Indian corruption, and takes it outside some of the familiar parameters of political excess committed in the defence or recovery of the privileges of power. The speech to which I have just referred provides a convenient preliminary example of it. For the *suppressio veri* it contained had been immediately, and typically, preceded in the same speech by the assertion that 'democracy

---

*The *Economist* ('Indira calls on the toughs to win back West Bengal') reported 'tough political warfare by the youth wing of the Congress Party while the police stood idly by or even actively assisted them'.[110]

... implies that once representatives are chosen and government comes into being with the approval of the majority, it functions freely to bring about the social and economic changes that it promised to the people'.[111] The invocation of democratic principle in order to justify undemocratic practice is of course not unique, but only a reconstituted Indian history of the decade could redeem India from the structured illusion of the period.

The second offers contrast, and will be given attention in the next chapter. In judging the verities of Indian cruelty, it is the appeal of the victim, his own testimony, which must be admitted. It is evidence indispensable to any discovery of the meanings of political event in India, and not only India. It will give a deeper sense to what, with reserve, may be called the increasing recourse during the period under review to extra-legal and extra-parliamentary political methods.

The growth in the last decade, in particular, of the paramilitary arm of central authority – the Central Reserve Police (CRP), the Border Security Force (BSF), the Central Industrial Security Force, the obliquely described Research and Analysis Wing (RAW) of the security police – has been described as 'one of the most significant creations' of India's recent history.[112] Here we confront a paradigm for other similarly degenerating political systems in the 'third world'. But in India's case, it lodged itself within an increasing, rather than diminishing, obeisance to democratic and 'socialist' theory; and aroused not the hopes but the fears of the people in ways which in the last analysis only they can express, as lived experience.

Further, democracy notwithstanding, the Defence of India Rules and the Maintenance of Internal Security Act had been 'increasingly used to detain political opponents, members of trade union movements, as well as participants in widespread disobedience movements'.[113] In the crescendo of reprisal which had afflicted dissent and opposition before the new emergency, there had also been a series of attempts to extend the preventive detention laws. The attempt, for example, to amend Article 17A of MISA in order to increase the period of detention to twenty-one months was declared illegal by the still independent

Supreme Court of India on 19 April 1973.[114] On 16 November 1974, a presidential order was issued in a move ostensibly directed at 'economic offenders', to remove their right of appeal to the courts against illegal detention, contrary to the provisions of the then unamended part three of the Constitution.[115] On 8 May 1975, a Bill was introduced into Parliament only six weeks before the declaration of the new June emergency – but it was resisted by the opposition and withdrawn – to increase the period of detention without trial to two years. Detention was not to be subject to review by an advisory board, contrary to Article 22 of the Constitution.[116] These were not straws in the wind, but part of a progress: towards a further dénouement and declaration, about to express itself in more vivid political forms, of the nature and condition of India.

The fraction of the Congress Party led by Indira Gandhi had supervised the fortunes of India during most of the period under review. It was constituted, after a factional split in 1969, under the title Congress (R) – for Requisitionist, because it had requisitioned a special party session – to distinguish it from the other, defeated but still extant, Congress fraction, Congress (O) – for Organization. Mrs Gandhi was chosen to succeed Lal Bahadur Shastri in 1966, whose prime ministership of about eighteen months, cut short by sudden death, had represented the only gap in the otherwise uninterrupted rule of India by the Nehru family since independence.

By 1969, she had consolidated her position despite the disabling 1967 electoral reverses for the Congress Party in several states' elections.* She was variously perceived as the victor in a 'power struggle' conducted within the chronic factionalism of the ruling party, during which attempts were made to oust her;[118] as the doughty keeper of the true socialist faith of Congress; or as a leader of the whole people, above party, in combat with 'conservative and vested interests', 'right-reactionary ele-

---

*This period was reconstructed analytically by official emergency 'history', viz: 'In the 1967 elections, power came to be distributed among a large number of heterogeneous parties and groups, and this led to instability.'[117] For an interpretation of the political theory underlying this judgement, see chapter 3.

ments' within the Congress Party, and 'a group of calculating politicians who used the party as a tool for grabbing power, rather than for rendering service to the people'.[119] She was seen both as spuriously progressive, always of the right, but 'taken onto populist ground and encouraged to do so by the people's response', in the effort to 'divide her opponents';[120] and as 'rejuvenating the soul of Congress, wresting it from the clutches of the experts of the politics of manipulation, and restoring to it its democratic character and vitality'.[121]

Whichever interpretations are chosen, and in whatever permutation, whether the reconstituted party and its leadership was or was not rejuvenated or senescent, corrupt or democratic, moribund or vital, the voice of radicalism or reaction, is a question I shall return to. What is beyond doubt, is that the conjunction of suffering, inflation and recession, and the cyclical collision of mounting opposition from right, left and centre to the misgovernment of India, and the draconian intolerance of such opposition began to deepen and quicken.

The extent of opposition to the Congress régime throughout 1974, and thence 1975, was both one of a predictable and familiar mass discontent, and unusual in its variety, range and eclecticism. It was a multiple discontent confronting a régime typically and necessarily circumscribed in its possible responses by the narrow political options of the kind of state earlier characterized. That it was essentially inchoate (and often incoherent) is also true; that it was another of the many expressions of the potentiality in India for a future revolution has also been asserted.

Equally important to the present purpose was the fact that it was disparately organized, as well as unorganized, and heterogeneous therefore in its composition, traversing both the political and the class spectrum through left, right and centre. It directed our attention not towards a gathering proletarian revolution – and somewhat less still towards a 'fascist conspiracy' of 'right-reaction' being led into battle against a progressive government by the CIA's 'dark forces',[122] as official historical reconstruction was to insist subsequently – than towards a volatile populism. Especially in messianic and usually short-lived forms, such populism has historically accompanied deepening mass distress in other societies also.

This distress expressed itself in different ways. It expressed itself impartially in the language of left and right, the Hindu nationalist Jan Sangh, amongst the latter, speaking of the need for 'people's struggles'.[123] It expressed itself in the self-sustaining rhetoric of plangent moral demands – heard throughout the whole period of modern India – to reconstitute and regenerate the body politic with a Utopian programme, at once naïve and impassioned, popular and populist, and above all vulnerable to repression. This was the call, for decentralized political power, non-violence and non-cooperation with the corrupt Caesarism of India's rulers, which the veteran 'Gandhian' (variously described also as 'non-party', 'socialist' and ultimately as 'fascist') J. P. Narayan represented. It expressed itself in fierce protests in Bihar and Gujarat against the corrupt incumbent governments, put down in many places with great force and bloodshed.*

Unexceptionally, it found its focus also in traditional socialist forms of protest, organized, among others, by the Socialist Party (SP) and the CPI–M. Much of the industrial unrest – including the previously mentioned railway strike – expressed itself through the opposition trade union movement. It was an unrest propelled by anger at the soaring prices of food and the traditionally cruel forms of landlord and merchant hoarding, carried on under the aegis of regional governments and corrupt officials. It expressed itself in CPI–ML-led peasant disturbances, a response to rural distress and the excesses of landlordism in parts of Bihar and Andhra Pradesh tormented by poverty and hunger. The counter-response to such varied motions of economic grievance by central and state governments – as the reaction to the railway strike had foreshadowed – was, unsurprisingly, increasing state violence.

These various expressions of economic distress which must accompany – particularly in an aroused populace – deteriorations

---

*Or, in the words of the Prime Minister, 'democracy was murdered in Bihar and Gujarat'.[124]

in an impoverished marginal economy, and which instantly herald the onset for the poorest millions of an insufferable degree of additional fear and deprivation, did not constitute the lineaments of any revolution. Threatening to a corrupt and unstable régime though mass popular discontent must be, this was not, in my judgement, what political theory might wish to diagnose as a revolutionary class-movement of peasantry and proletariat, or a Chinese revolution in process, led by a 'vanguard party' of the left, whether armed with the weapons of war, or the weapon of theory.

There are three other points to be briefly made on this question. First, that Narayan's politics of *panchayat raj* (an association of village republics), *ahimsa* (non-violence), *satyagraha* (non-violent resistance) and *sarvodaya* (communal welfare), whatever else they may be, were not the politics of the 'dictatorship of the proletariat', even less of Hitler's 1920 Munich programme, and least of all recognizable evidence of the CIA's brand of forward politico-economic planning. Second, Narayan's appeal was strong precisely in those areas where the opposition working class movement was weakest. Third, and most important, it began to take shallow root in some traditional strongholds of the Congress Party, and thus appeared to be threatening its hegemony.

The popular language or rhetoric of the movement around Narayan, a 'mass movement' which must be called evanescent (and whose evanescence was to be proved subsequently by its rapid evaporation), was alternatively the passionate language of freedom, and of disgust with corruption. It contained a vocabulary of revolt and non-cooperation; of civil disobedience, 'de-recognition of government' and 'total revolution';[125] of appeals for an end to dictatorship, and to army and police brutality; and that 'Gandhian' oratory of moral revival familiar enough to students of Indian history. Like Mahatma Gandhi before him, his lexicon of invocations included enjoining upon police and army that they should not obey illegal orders to commit violence against the people, an injunction subsequently to be used itself to justify the overturning of the rule of law and the Constitution.

I pay attention to this first because of the disparate amount of emphasis placed upon this invocation in the subsequent barrage of justifications for what followed. More important, the former Chief Justice of the High Court of Bombay, Minister of Education in the Indian government, and Indian Ambassador in Washington, M. C. Chagla, made it clear – if it were necessary – that 'it is not incumbent upon a police officer or an army officer to carry out an order which is illegal ... Narayan was merely enunciating a legally sound proposition, and he was moved to do so because he found in Bihar policemen and soldiers shooting down innocent people'.[126] Narayan's other verbal targets – if they can be pieced together coherently – included corruption, electoral malpractice, increasing political violence, the erosion of civil liberties, black-marketeering, rising prices, economic mismanagement as a whole, and the long barren rule of Congress; that Gordian knot of privilege and cruelty, Indian poverty and riches, stagnation and misery.

But if there was in the events of this period a rising scale of seriousness in the portents for the continuing rule of the Congress Party, what I have so far described must be placed low on the list. Far more serious than the political theories and practices of the 'JP movement', were near-simultaneous political, electoral, legal and institutional developments, in a conjuncture compressed into a time-span of days and weeks, though they had been unfolding in Indian file through the years of a decade or longer. Only with the greatest difficulty – not itself an obstacle – could they be made the ingredients of 'conspiracy' by *ex post facto* rationalization. Instead, each represented merely a further descent in that pedigree of instances, some of which I have already mentioned.

The substantial defeats of the ruling Congress faction both in by-elections and in the mid-term elections for the Gujarat State Assembly (announced in Ahmedabad on 13 June 1975), during the campaigning for which, as Mrs Gandhi told me with asperity, 'stones were thrown at me, even by children so high; they even flew black flags to greet me,'[127] were far more ominous. They presaged defeat in the general elections due in March 1976, and therefore were much closer to the reasons for the constitutional *coup d'état* which was approaching.* Similarly serious in scale of gravity and almost stimultaneous (as classical instance of the complex historical moment) was the Prime Minister's conviction, announced in the Allahabad High Court on 12 June 1975, for electoral corruption and malpractice. This was a minor malfeasance in any register which includes the blatant and violent delinquency of her party's earlier electoral practice in the West Bengal elections I have mentioned, but it was a major reverse at this moment, accompanied as it was by a disqualification from holding office for six years. A stay of sentence, though it permitted her to continue in office, barred her from voting in Parliament. There must also be added to the texture of explanation of the nature of the hegemonic crisis, and because it will be instructive later, the Court's findings as to the continuously unreliable and contradictory nature of the Prime Minister's evidence.[128]

The conviction itself drew from constitutionalists arguments far removed from, but concurrent with, the desperate clamour of the poor for the redress of their grievances, and the accelerating rhetoric of moral denunciation. The constitutional arguments were couched in the language of jurisprudential disquisition and legal rectitude, anomalous though it might be in a political culture of murder and equivocation; there was a 'constitutional impropriety'[129] in the Prime Minister continuing in office; 'political decorum'[130] required immediate resignation.

Juxtaposed with such finely poised arguments were the escalating threats, inherent in the social crisis, to an already embattled junta. The opposition parties were also gathering in unwonted and precariously temporary solidarity; to try to coordinate their parliamentary practice in a united front which would command a majority in Parliament; to call for Mrs Gandhi's resignation;[131] and to create a united opposition to fight the March 1976 elections which, if achieved, might bring Congress Party rule to an end across wide swathes of India. At the same moment, the political leadership of the Congress Party in general – and of the Prime Minister in particular – was being

*The Gandhi government's White Paper, '*Why Emergency?*', which contains the fullest official pre-history of the emergency, in its exclusion of all references to this defeat, tends to confirm this analysis.

subjected not, as was subsequently to be maintained, to violent coercion for its removal, but the force of those moral demands (at public rallies) which the distress and anger of a people can mobilize against its rulers. It is a force which has little in common with that which would herald the 'seizure of state power'.

Instead, meetings; between 21 June and 25 June 1975, of a cross section of opposition parliamentarians, including Narayan, gathering in Delhi.[132] More serious for the ruling faction of the Congress Party, some of its own members were moving closer to the ranks of the newly forming opposition, a dissident faction within a faction, of quickly growing size. Here was the chronic fissiparousness – evinced throughout the whole of the period under review – of a ruling party of the minority classes dividing (in the accelerations of the hour) into its several sub-factions and competing vested interests. As many as one hundred or more of the Prime Minister's own group of Members of Parliament were reportedly ready to demand her resignation and replacement – after more than a quarter century of family rule – by a different faction-leader of the ruling party.[133]

Concurrently, and in the heat of the moments of disintegration of that 'shifting compromise' within a party ruling over a political economy such as India's, arose the magnified threat not of a *coup d'état* from left or right, but of further 'Gandhian' pressures from Narayan. These were familiar during the so-called 'raj', and by it popular discontent was designing to express itself. Announced on the fatal day of 25 June 1975,[134] they included a peaceful *dharna* before the Prime Minister's house from 29 June to 5 July 1975, and a 'people's awakening week' in the same period, through demonstrations and public rallies. There was the spectral promise also of an all-India convention on civil liberties; a civil disobedience campaign to begin on a date not yet fixed; and a meeting to be held on 6 July 1975 in Delhi to demand the re-convening of the recessed Parliament, the summoning of which had been 'inexplicably delayed'.[135]

Such a programme of action confirmed the disjunction between this kind of opposition political practice, and anything known to 'fascist' or CIA procedures. Moreover, a judicious assessment of the nature, combinations (and mutual oppositions) of the forces then opposed to the ruling party – including the dissident faction within it – does not reach those totals required for subversion of *state power*. This is so whether the mathematics of addition or multiplication is employed; the latter always preferred by conspiracy theorists, and much in use when the falsified accounts of this darkening period were later presented.

Instead, on the verge of the emergency, the case might appear as follows: a semblance of unity involving only part of the parliamentary opposition; the 'JP movement', 'in difficulties long before Mrs Gandhi's emergency was imposed';[136] the far right, despite its prominence in the subsequent official demonology, absurdly impotent to challenge the state power;* and the right opposition, the Jan Sangh, constrained both by its own ideology, and the competition of rival populisms, from becoming the vanguard party of the hour. As for the left opposition, the Socialist Party, the CPI–M and the CPI–ML were divided from each other. The CPI–M, whatever its political and industrial strengths, was insufficiently aware, as it turned out, of what was impending.† The 'naxalites' had been decimated by half a dozen years of imprisonment and murder. The CPI, obeisant, was tactically committed to its belief in the progressive role of the Congress Party in bringing 'socialism' to India.

'She said,' stated Chagla later, 'that there was a conspiracy to bring about a deadlock in the country, to ask the army to revolt, to bring about a situation where there would be chaos in India. Now let me say one thing,' continued the former Bombay Chief Justice, 'and I say it with confidence, not an iota of evidence has been produced that there was any such conspiracy ... The conspiracy was by the Prime Minister.'[139]

However that may be, there then followed the now familiar mass-arrests under MISA; not a qualitative, but certainly a

---

* *Link*, the pro-CPI weekly, in its issue of 27 June 1976 made the mistake of pointing out that, after the declaration of emergency, 'not only did the "total revolution" collapse totally, but also the serried ranks of the RSS[137] vanished into thin air'. This was not true, but its implications helped to undermine official rationalizations for the emergency.

† 'We were completely taken by surprise by this sudden development.'[138]

quantitative change from precedents well established. The first arrests – including those of leading political figures of the opposition – caught their victims by surprise, took place on the night of 25–6 June 1975 before the emergency's public proclamation, and were carried out by police and para-military forces acting under powers which I have shown were already available to deal with conspiracy whether real, putative or imagined. Taken away were politicians of left, right and centre and of no party; critical and dissident members of Mrs Gandhi's own ruling faction; her past accusers in court and in Parliament; newspapermen and academics; trade unionists and student leaders. For just as the opposition to Mrs Gandhi had spread across the political spectrum, so accordingly did the target broaden;[140] to all in the political arena save (unsurprisingly) those who supported her, and much more important, therefore, the arrests were conducted without reference to a selectivity based on political principle. Though they included the left and right, they also excluded it; excluding not only the parliamentarians and politicians of the CPI but also that section of the extreme right, the Shiv Sena, which supported Mrs Gandhi.

Disappearing into India's already overcrowded jails both before and in the wake of the President's declaration of emergency at 7.0 a.m. on 26 June 1975 (proclaimed under duress and without prior Cabinet approval) went J. P. Narayan* and Morarji Desai, the former Deputy Prime Minister; L. K. Advani, president of the Jan Sangh; Jyotirmoy Basu, deputy leader of the CPI–M; Raj Narain, the socialist, who brought the charges of corruption against Mrs Gandhi, and was also her constituency opponent in the 1971 general election; Piloo Mody, the Member of Parliament who, on 26 May 1971, had demanded explanations for the deaths of those said to have been involved with Mrs Gandhi in the extraction from the State Bank of India of millions of rupees, allegedly 'back money' for party uses;† and Kuldip Nayar, the editor of the *Indian Express.*

---

*cf. 'The arrest of Jayaprakash Narayan is unfortunate. I do not know what speech has brought him within the law . . . if he is guilty of violence, violence should be proved.' Mahatma Gandhi, in *Harijan*, 16 March 1940.

† This and related issues will be discussed in chapter 3.

More important, there were thousands of others – all to be declared unnameable under the censorship which was immediately imposed upon press, radio and television – less well-known, or worse, unknown; whose lack of prominence and lack of name were to deprive (and always will deprive) of the protections of a public reputation.

There were to follow, in defence of the encircled ruling fraction of the Congress Party, not only drastic institutional changes but also a sequence of contradictory and insecure obfuscations, whose examination – irksome though it has proved – is decisive in understanding part of the process of ideological degeneration in a political system.

I take the preliminary 'explanations' of the CPI first, because they can be disposed of more quickly. They were, to put it mildly, extravagant.[141] A 'pre-emptive' – or 'stunning' – 'blow had been struck against counter-revolution'. 'The main edge of the emergency' was directed against 'neo-colonialist, reactionary, communal and fascist forces',[142] though they were 'by no means routed, and desperately trying to regroup', or 'waiting for a chance to strike again at the opportune moment'.[143] Moreover, if the Prime Minister had not taken 'the courageous step of enforcing the emergency', 'India would have been turned into another Chile'.[144] This proposition of course rests upon a political equation between Mrs Gandhi and Salvador Allende, and arguably passes beyond the threshold of understanding.

From the plethora of alternative, or contradictory, assertions offered by the ruling party and Prime Minister, it is similarly difficult at first sight to make sense; they tempt instead to a quick withdrawal. But contradiction has its own resonance and signification; there may even be a pattern of coherence in incoherent explanation. (In the last analysis, it will yield a clear enough structure of political meaning.)

Thus, for economic context, the emergency was either declared at a period 'while the country was passing through a period of galloping inflation',[145] or 'when a galloping inflation had been checked through firm steps, even before the emergency'.[146] The range of the political context was also a wide one. Thus the emergency was declared not only because of 'a campaign in the name of democracy'[147] to 'take advantage of the difficulties of the people';[148] but also because of opposition plans to 'paralyse the national economy',[149] to 'weaken us at a time of delicate alterations in international power relations and structures'.[150] And for industrial context, the railway strike, for instance, had 'nothing to do with the declaration of emergency';[151] or, the declaration of emergency was necessary 'because the opposition attempted to paralyse the economy through strikes such as the railway strike'.[152]

This opposition was constituted (in some versions) of 'political parties with fascist leanings combining with a set of frustrated politicians',[153] 'undermining the nation's self-confidence';[154] as well as being alternatively engaged in a quite different programme of 'loot, arson, vandalism, strikes and violence'.[155]

The opposition's 'frustration' was explained in terms which necessarily involved the reconstruction of preceding and recorded event; that passage in India's history otherwise described by a former chief economic adviser to the government of India, as 'a massive discontent, stemming from economic failures, threatening to sweep [Mrs Gandhi] away'.[156] Instead, 'the opposition had very little chance of winning an election because the people believed in our programme'.[157] Additionally, an extra historical gloss, 'Mrs Gandhi's tremendous popularity with the people and their unstinted faith in her leadership were the main stumblingblocks in their way of capturing power.'[158]

The 'prime target'[159] of an opposition which was 'fascist', 'neocolonialist' or 'frustrated', was thus either Mrs Gandhi herself personally, in a 'deliberate campaign against her of vilification and hatred',[160] or the more general attempt to 'distort democratic functioning at all levels';[161] politically somewhat different charges.

Its crimes and concerted violences were, on the one hand, programmatic, deliberate, 'conscious',[162] where they were not 'sinister'[163] and a 'conspiracy'.[164] On the other, the opposition 'did not want crime, but somehow [sic] the shelter they gave to all kinds of groups and individuals and the call to revolt, led to permissiveness',[165] rather than elsewhere to the subversion of state power in the larger magnifications.

Last, a mass movement, an 'all-India movement', at one

moment 'threatening the whole economy with paralysis', 'holding the country to ransom', bringing in its train 'anarchy and chaos',[166] 'a deep and widespread conspiracy'[167] – 'brewing ever since I began introducing progressive measures of benefit to the common man and woman of India'[168] – was elsewhere, and for other ideological purposes, transmuted into 'the work of just a few mischief makers lacking the support of the people'.[169]

This discordant and, at first sight, fatally flawed chorus of explanation accompanied the procession of many thousands into India's jails ('it was not an easy decision to take, because by nature I am a person who does not believe in restricting people').[170] It accompanied also the rapid and often simultaneous deteriorations in what remained of the integrity of India's political, legal and administrative apparatus, which I shall discuss later.

For the acute economic and social crisis of India, compounded by personal and party disarray, a large number of victims had been found. To hasten the classical process of state response – again a paradigm case of it – the extra-legal was being made lawful. To describe it, there was to be increasing (and increasingly complex) recourse to newspeak. What was actually signified by this in terms of the particular nature and compulsions of the Indian political economy is the critical, or analytical, issue; the deciphering of what it was actually to mean and not to mean to the victims, is deeply implicated within it.

To attempt an understanding of either, it is necessary to begin to search for, and to represent, the condition and circumstances of the long-suffering Indian people. And to do so, I must now employ a new method.

2 On the Condition of the People

It is not difficult to 'sell' India as a land of dreams, a land full of mysteries and grandeur, snow-capped mountains, golden beaches, age-old monuments, colourful festivals, traditions and ancient religions.

> *Raj Bahadur, Minister for Tourism and Civil Aviation, 6 March 1796*[1]

The progress of a country like India cannot properly be judged in terms of the gross national product.

> *Indira Gandhi, 20 February 1976*[2]

The success achieved by India has been spectacular by any standard, either west or east, or developing or developed countries.

> *Indira Gandhi, 13 April 1976*[6]

They are already awakening from their dreams, here, wrapped in rags, grey-clouted like the sheeted and phantom dead, against the dull cold dawn; grey-on-grey. Men in ragged greatcoats and broken shoes are huddled, like down-and-outs, in the hillocked, hummocked rough beside the Delhi road, waiting for the first light. Brown thin hands are purple brown with cold, or mittened; with numbed and blown finger-ends; breath funnelling from turned-up collars, and tousled scarved heads. At small heaps of cracking, crackling twigs ('O Agni, showerer of sparks, O Agni, bring us riches!'), are thin-tongued spitting fires, and stick-like arms and legs, crouching before the whorls of smoke in sackcloth and ashes.

In the dawning cold light of day, grey-upon-grey, the poor, lapped and swathed in rags, and risen from their pavement hearths and pallets, begin to stalk the streets like beasts. 'Dawn awakens every living creature,' says the *Rigveda*, 'each to his different vocation.' Cows and men stand, in rumination, beside the lean-to shanties, the shacks, and sheds; home-made.

A pale grey light shines in all these gaunt and brittle bodies, moving figures upon a bare ground; walking, standing, crouching, eating; or sleeping, cheeks sunk and mouths open. In the early morning's chill halo, the sickly babe-in-arms lies on the pavement, too, swaddled and quiet, yellowing in the rags of its burial, and the first sunlight.

This is Uṣā, another dawn, '*parāyatinām, anveti, pātha āyatinām prathamā śāśvatīnām*', 'best of the mornings that have gone, first of the endless mornings that are to come'. When the sun is full risen, it will give its warm light to the flowers, to the chirping birds and the large-leafed trees; to the living, and the dying.

In the dark-domed shadows cast upon the grey river Jumna by the white-turbanned Taj, "the finest monument to love ever created', built in white marble (inlaid with jasper, agate, lapis lazuli and bloodstone) with the labours of twenty thousand, teeth snap like secateurs; the pariah-dogs – as if grinning or grimacing – tug and rend the corpse, pulling at skin and sinews, stretching open a white and purpling underbelly; shaking their heads, muzzles dripping, backs bristling and furring; teeth clenched and biting, worrying and nuzzling the flesh of a child, cast-away in the waters. And on the high parapet above the river, a lissom and fashionable pose (much in vogue) is struck; with dieted cheek-bones, and a thin smiling, a model performance such as this commands its own price and figure. In dark polaroids, and silk headscarf, she stands for the New York and London fashion plates; or index-finger to chin, cameras clicking, in the *kasbah* or purdah of her own imagination; or, a sphinx in a bazaar, with natives.

But on the Bihar night-platform, the illuminated weighing-machine blacks out, and flashes; the curled-up, ravaged body, feet in a gunny sack, pressed against its black cast-iron.

This is a mortified and wasted figure, a body forced into a corner, in the wall's dark angle. 'O', truly says the sage in the *Taitirrīya Upaniṣad*, 'beings here are born from bliss; when born, they live by bliss; and into bliss, when departing, they enter.' His drawn face, in alternations of livid light and shadow, is wracked, black fingers (one with a silver ring, tarnished) clutching the flashing scales' base; in a hacking coughing and spitting, back and sides of his crouching breathless body pulsing, in spasm.

The metal track (disappearing into darkness), sleepers, and pulverized gravel, are lit yellow, blacking out and flashing. On cracked station concrete, his killing sputum, slimy, glistens; and small pinched twists and scraps of torn paper, with the night's wiped-up spittings. 'You will not waste away,' says the *Atharvaveda*, 'the Ādityas and Vasus, Indra and Agni, will raise you into well-being; the powers that furnish strength will breathe upon you; the mourning women will not wail over you, with their hair dishevelled.'

But this is a racking coughing, his huddled body ... these things being so (if they are so), conceding that 'there are still some undeveloped pockets of India',⁴ as the Minister for Chemicals put it, we should instead ... buttocks, in rags, contracting, turning his arching back as if hiding, coughing and heaving as if crying; a stubbled face, pillowed on iron; mouth tormented, and struggling to catch his breath ... we should instead call a halt to such description ... tuberculous blood at lips and chin in a red illuminated trickle; a slight figure, bleeding to death beside the Try-your-Weight scales in a pool of light, blacking out and flashing. Yet, say the gods of India, 'he who is alike in cold and heat; and contented with anything whatever; he who is homeless' – feet in a gunny sack, kneeling in a corner – 'and to the gods devoted, will be dear to me for ever'.

Walking the dark platform, are rags flapping; torn hanging jackets; bodies leaning against each other, heads resting upon each other's shoulders; stretched-out bare feet, hardened and blackened; hunger, on the rack, and mortification; bodies sleeping and beggared; a sunken mortal wreckage; a standing mass of camp-rags and bitter-cold staring; a fearful and mesmerized rage.

This is the avenging, cadaverous fury of the stricken; India-in-Bihar weighed in the balance; fighting dark faces, driven wild; a shawl-wrapped woman with a shrivelled child; the unwanted, dead or alive.

But, knowing that in other moods, and on other occasions, India's leaders acknowledge that 'there are still some people amongst us who are extremely rich, and many who are very poor',[5] we should call a halt to such description. Alternatively, despite what has been asserted and is widely known about India's political economy and its laws of causation, we should hold fast to the view that India and poverty are indissolubly one, the first being the classical and exemplary instance of the second, according to an irrefragable law of physical and human nature.

We should, instead, turn away from the old woman, rump and leg-stumps (bandaged and matted) just clearing the ground; quickly working her weight forward along the soft and dusty road-verge, in a sitting and swinging motion, weight taken in a heaving exertion and propulsion upon scrawny bird-wrists and clawing fingers, the stringy sinews of her withered arms taut and straining. It is better to look to something more grateful than the mutilated men and boys sitting and twisting for coins, ravaged with wanting and whining.

Better to turn from, and pass by on the other side, the old man – foundered by the roadway – on his bed propped by two bricks at each corner of the wooden bed-frame, his stick lying alongside it, a blanket and old coverlet folded on the pavement. In any case, he cannot be dying. Avoid, by crossing over, the thin hair and misted cataracted eyes, the match-like legs at the kerb's side, of the begging child. Treat merely as local colour the plaited straw hovels and the sack awnings; the peasant swineherds rushing their swine through the streets of the city, *rus in urbe*, switching their flanks with sticks; or the man squatting to empty a nostril into the dereliction, or pissing a dark trickle into the dust; or the black beeves sitting in a mulch of street-waste, lipping and cropping the trodden detritus.

Overtake (in the warmth of your own well-being and with a spring in your stride) the wrapped load, bent back, bowed and bandy legs, and wrinkled buttocks, bared in the movements of hanging rags and tatters, trudging the gutter, beneath its possessions.

Watch instead the silken bangled women passing by in their graces, shining hair black as jet, and flowered, swaying to some unheard but palpable rhythm; hands in gold and silver, folded for greeting, sari's silk end thrown over a soft shoulder, your eye to the red spot in the middle of their foreheads, and their eyes' deep mooning, with a purple-and-white smiling, as if swooning.

For it is written in the First Khanda of the Third Mundaka of the *Mundaka Upaniṣad* that two birds may very well cling to the same tree, one of them eating the sweet fruit, and the other looking on without eating; grieving. The poor hungry bird's grief will surely pass away, as it is written, when he sees the other bird's contentment and knows his glory.

And you can fly over it all – flight – if you wish, dreaming to Indian muzak; hostess's face as full as the moon, type of all beauty, *sitar* arpeggios plucking the perfumed air. But under the deep green trees, a little girl, head-loaded with a heavy cloth-wrapped bundle, thin arms raised to hold it, stops to adjust its weight with weary staring eyes, on this fragrant morning. And the dust at your feet is hand-printed by the crippled woman's passing; through the tiny litter of often-sifted and winnowed trifles, and the flecks of cinnamon-red brick-dust, you may see the spoor of her fingers and the press of her palms upon the dun-pink ground.

But none of this is necessary; and, if it is, better the data and index of it only, for there is safety in such numbers, or an analytical caution, and a careful weighing in the calculus of the accountant. There was, moreover, Mrs Gandhi's consolation of India's 'steady transformation to modernity';[6] of that rural India (thin women sitting under the ox-carts' awnings, their feet henna-painted; passing slowly along the rutted road to the sound of straw rustling, the creaking wooden axle, and the ox-step) which was 'today humming with development activities'.[7] There was that India, not of 'mysteries and grandeur', but where 'moving about the countryside as I do, I can clearly see that the poor are not poorer';[8] that India where there was 'a long-range technological strategy for the improved consumption of our energy-resources',[9] 'a programme for the rapid re-orientation of rural job-patterns',[10] and 'new technology data-banks, to accelerate the interplay of knowledge inputs'.[11]

Unhappily, reality stands on its own feet; not raised on the stilts of illusion, but at ground-level. There, in that vast 'undeveloped pocket' which is most of rural India, the village, stockaded like a kraal, is hedged with rustling wind-breaks in scrub, rubble and dust. The yellow-grey sands, drifted and streaked by wind, are desert, dry as a picked bone. In a bare landscape stand the thorn-marked boundaries of near-barren fields, dry-ochre. The draught animals and hump-backed cattle are walking carcases, moving hoops of rib and leather, too scarred for a tanner; flanks sunk and skinny; tails flicking the flies away. Beside the tumbled dry-stone walling are boars, in a tusked smiling, bristling like porcupines. The grey carts, standing in dust, are wooden-axled; laden with flattened cow-pats, hand-kneaded for fuel, and finger-printed; the ox, standing tethered, stock-still.

At the straw stockades, beside the ragged thatch and faded adobe, and perched on broken walls, are Krishna's peacocks, kingly emblems (*Pavo cristatus*), blue-crowned, and blue-black necked, with bronze-green backs, gawking, drily pecking and scraping for grain-specks, or running quickly; each feather a purpling eye, with a deep-blue heart-shaped iris in a dark-green pupil, and long eye-lashes of green and copper, dragging their trains (through dust) behind them, or fanning them out, and stalking the hard rubble, Argus-eyed and elevated to the purple. And in the sky soar the fork-tailed kites; or land, scavenging like pariahs, common as muck and shameless; bill-hooked, and claws black on the sand, or sunk and crouching on a dung-heap.

To the naked eye, there is no sign or token of cultivation (neither irrigation, nor 'energy resources', neither 'new technologies', nor 'data-banks'); beyond the caked and dry tumble of walls, neither truck, nor tractor; and in explanation, neither mystery, nor grandeur.

There are, however, naked children ('the gaily clad women

and children smile at the passing traveller from the wayside');[12] pot-bellied in a dazed looking and staring; four child cowherds to a cow, and one stick for its flanks between them. There are birds here also, bandy as any bowed Indian; a buff dog scratching at his mangy and scabbed neck, bent-leg-to-ear, and twisted into a fakir's yoga position; and in a cluster by the endless roadside, hawkers at a shack-stand, skin of their knees and elbows worn and rubbed into grey and dusty wrinkles.

And in the tracts of parched scrub and stunted thorn in the sand-wastes, are solitary figures beneath a remote blue sky; bending, looking, and straightening, back-breaking; picking for gleanings, with pinching fingers in furrows and billows as shallow as a beach's rib-cage, after the tide has turned and gone. There are scarecrow men in beaked turbans (peaks like a cock's comb), with mattocks and wicker baskets for the stalks raked from the cracked ground; and straight-backed women, walking in a wilderness for water, brass water-pots and beakers catching the eye of the sun, and glittering.

On a bare ground, they are stately in saffron or yellow, and silver anklets; or in skirts of pink and scarlet; and, from a distance, are delicate as flamingoes, walking; but near at hand, are wasted birds-of-paradise; far away, thin statistics, nearer, veiled and biblical Salomes; nearest, face to face, their faces become skulls before you, and turn to a wild-eyed emaciation, heads held high, but gaunt and ravaged as scything Time; or Death, with his sickle, gleaming. Here, there are no 'colourful festivals' in progress, nor sung hosannahs in celebration; only the peacock's crying, like the sound of women screaming.

But, in a decade of 'rural progress', and a 'green revolution' – with the facts temporarily discounted for the sake of balance – in a countryside 'humming with development', this must either be atypical; or, if not that, an example of that undenied poverty 'in pockets', which 'can still be seen in some rural areas', and which should be set in some broader and more generous context. And, why are there no countervailing observations here of the poor's embellishment (secular and sacred) of their immiseration? That decoration which conceals a life of hardship with a flourish or a flower? The painted horns of cattle; the sides of the rolling cart and the hood of the rickshaw; the flanks of mule and pony, and the women their faces and bodies?

But the true condition of rural India's more than four hundred and fifty millions admits of no illusion; misfortune, alike, for the salesman of dreams, and the purveyor of political falsehood. For the eye of the observer and the mathematics of the observed corroborate one another, and will not be resisted.

To begin, at random, in the welter of quantifications, the numbers of unemployed resist precise measure. It is subject to an unknown margin of errors, and the difficulty of assessment in a huge agrarian household economy, permanently impoverished and on the margin of survival. But the eye reveals what the mind cannot fully fathom; that long after the sun has risen, and the day has come to its best light and zenith, the poor are lying still; crouching, squatting, or sleeping; doing nothing, because there is nothing doing. With magnitudes which are 'gigantic' and 'trends' which are 'alarming',[13] estimates of rural 'surplus labour', unemployed and 'seriously underemployed' come within the range of nineteen to twenty-one million, and in some academic estimates are more than double that figure.*[14]

In rural (and urban) India, this is 'the forest of uplifted arms demanding work', which 'becomes ever thicker, while the arms themselves become ever thinner';[16] and here commences the construction of that context both of quantity and theory demanded by the observations of an eye directed at the face of India; for the meanings in the faded adobe, and the bare landscape, for the naked children, or the distant figures.

Moreover, on the question of the poverty of over 450 million in the 550,000 villages of India, the consensus of study, analysis, and glib or unguarded government pronouncement (again in different moods, and for different purpose) is decisive. If the rural 'poverty line' is set, as it has been variously in the last decade, in a range between fifteen and twenty-five rupees *per*

---

*It has been asserted, with ill-concealed irony, that *because* no precise estimates are available of the huge figure of the unemployed, to the state 'the problem of unemployment does not exist'.[15] The paucity – near to exclusion – of reference to it both in the Fifth Plan and subsequently in the '20-point programme' (see chapter 6) lends some support to this proposition.

month of 'disposable per capita income for consumption, at 1960 to 1961 prices' – and the implications of such a standard I will explain in a moment – then, by 1970, at least half and probably more than half of the rural population, in a pattern varying in intensity from poor state to poorest, was below, and even substantially below, this subsistence or lower than subsistence figure.[17] And in every instance, it is a deepening figure, both absolutely and relatively, whatever time-span is taken.[18]

And what does this criterion, for the economic analysis of poverty, itself mean? It means that the academic discussion about what constitutes 'poverty' in India – albeit more rational and more 'scientific' than the real-politik of 'I can clearly see that the poor are not poorer' – is confined to the grim business of definition of a biological minimum. It is a calculation not for life, but for existence; to be precise, a calculation of the minimum level of nutrition, and the 'disposable' income which will purchase it. And what is this nutritional norm – itself inaccessible to over half the rural population and an estimated 40 per cent of the urban[19] – set by the Indian econometrician's slide-rule, and found in the Indian index? It is 2,250 calories per day,[20] itself in excess of the actual 'average intake', which has been estimated at less than 2,000 calories.[21] This figure, in the 'calorie requirement charts' of the dietitians' handbooks of another – our own – culture, is held to be appropriate to children of eight.[22] It is the 'quick slimmer's diet' of Paris and London, in which the 'moderately active man between eighteen and sixty-five', let alone the toiling field-hand, 'requires 3,000'; and the breast-feeding mother, 2,700, for the well-being of herself and her children.[23]

Moreover, poverty's magnitudes in India, and their accompanying minima, are not only clear but have grown clearer. Whether the poverty-line be drawn at fifteen, twenty, twenty-five, thirty, or even forty rupees (just over £2 or $3.40) per head, per month, to the Minister for Revenue and Banking, '220 million of the people in the country'[24] were below the 'poverty-line', and to the Director of the Indian Council of Medical Research, 'over forty per cent of the population'.[25] Even in the judgement of the government's Fifth Plan, which used the highest datum-line of disposable monthly income (forty rupees, at 1972 to 1973 prices), 30 per cent of the total population were below it. To yet other commentators, '300 million people'[26] stand below that 'line' which is itself drawn at the very base of Indian existence.

If I am to continue to be persistent in a search for the real meaning of such quantities, what is meant by having fifteen rupees to 'dispose of for consumption' per month; or fifty paise per day? The latter is the price, perhaps, of an egg, or two tomatoes; insufficient for a rice-diet; too little for a half-pint of milk; perhaps enough for boiled millet, and a little pickle, to fuel the body for survival, or for 'moderately active' hard labour. Upon this, the procession of the millions of field-hands trudges to work at dawn; working upon this until sundown.

And when this single fact is replaced within the broader context from which it was first extracted, the subject becomes too awesome to encompass in this text. It is the real condition of the landless, or of those with minuscule plots unable to produce a sufficient subsistence, let alone a surplus; while the average per capita income stands motionless, stated officially in October 1975 to be 2.30 rupees daily.[27] This 'works out at less than two rupees a day for more than three fourths of the population living in the rural areas', in the words of India's official sourcebook of economic information.[28] And if the official figure be discounted, whether because it has no meaning, is too low, or is steadily rising, it is always eclipsed in a period of inflation by the doubling and tripling in the prices of some of the foods of the poorest. Moreover, the 'fixed' minimum wage rates for rural employment are unenforced and therefore not paid, and are themselves inadequate to meet the actual (as distinct from the putative) calorie requirements for labour.*[29]

Here is not the accident but the anatomy of pauperization. It is a matter of complex, insecure and oppressive tenurial relations, rack-renting, and share-cropping. As Myrdal has shown,

*They ranged on 30 September 1974, from sixty-two paise per day (4p) in Tamil Nadu, to three rupees (17p) per day in Punjab, for the 'unskilled male worker'; *PBLS*, p. 40. They have been raised by a little since; see chapter 6, pp. 207–8.

it is a matter of rents raised for higher output;[30] and of the making over to landlords, in lieu of rent, of a 'tithe' – which is asserted by common knowledge sometimes to reach 50 to 90 per cent – of the peasants' harvest.[31] Here, too, is that 'low output', as the agricultural economist puts it (or 'inertia', the callow critic of 'human nature'), which is itself product of such agrarian relations, low wages, hunger and exhaustion of land and body. Here is hard labour, conjoined with less labour – the number of days of rural work to be found per annum by the agricultural worker falling through our decade of rural progress[32] – and with no labour at all for the millions. Here are debt and dispossession and the lengthening shadow of the money-lender (himself often the landlord, in his other persona) falling across plough and furrow. Here, 'production is compelled to proceed', as an earlier political economist put it, 'under ever more pitiable conditions', 'impoverishing the mode of production and, instead of developing, paralysing the productive forces';[33] here, are the very lineaments and dead-weight of rural bankruptcy, the land of India bankrupted by its owners.

Different modes of perception can be brought to bear upon any of the immanent social consequences. One is arrived at by taking the already disclosed path of immediate observation; another, say, by the route of the official blandnesses of state government surveys. They reach the same destination, that of inescapable conclusion, and (if in a different dialect) speak a common language. In rural West Bengal, for example, it means 'the movement of landless agricultural labourers from one landlord to another' and an average of only five to fifteen days under each employer. It means from 6 to 12 per cent literacy in surveyed areas,[34] a figure which contains (in microcosm) the history of social stasis in 'post-independence India'. It means 90 per cent 'unaware of the minimum wage-rate'; but it also means the 70 per cent who 'possess significant political awareness', a point to shed light on the closing paragraphs of this chapter.

There are mountainous ranges of the data of rural misery to traverse, only some of which can be attempted. The agricultural labourer bends not merely to his labour, but beneath a heavy burden of debt also; and to the accompaniment of a litany of official government, and Reserve Bank of India statistics. The estimated total of debt, rising like every other both relatively and absolutely, stands at from 40,000 to 60,000 million rupees.[35] The causes are built into the very structure and fabric of the agrarian system. The circumstances of inescapable debt are embedded both in the struggles of daily life, and in the columns of official surveys. The latter reveal that the overwhelming majority of poor domestic economies (rural and urban) are always in deficit, with the minimum monthly family expenditure exceeding monthly earned income in every one of the sample of fifty-eight 'factory, mining and plantation' centres across the face of India.[36] This is a chronic condition of life which other economic indices clearly suggest has subsequently deteriorated. Thus, as the *Times of India* reported of Bihar for instance,[37] 70 per cent of *working* households are driven to take loans for consumption, at varying rates of interest paid to the landlord/ money-lender, with a common – perhaps the commonest – rate being 25 per cent to 30 per cent, but known to rise as high as 80 per cent or higher.[38] And, quite apart from the millions of destitute unemployed and working landless who are indebted, so also are perhaps 65 per cent to 70 per cent of small and marginal landholders (though in India the categories overlap), with an average debt of from 250 to 500 rupees.[39]

The extent of exploitation involved, especially when resumed or replaced within the full social and economic context of rural indigence and hardship, has been rightly described as 'stupendous'.[40] Debts compound into totals (of interest alone) which become unpayable; but compound also into other totals, and another mathematics : into rural revolts of the dunned and debt-fettered against the money-lending landlord, as in the bitter histories of every such unreconstituted agrarian economy as the Indian. This history is also, again characteristically, marked by formal efforts to avert (as well as to crush) attempts at mass-escape and reprisal. It is marked by palliative and pacificatory law and ordinance, to relieve – with pen-strokes – the indebted from that power of rural landlords which is beyond all such sanction, and who are the real untouchables of India. It is a history of nugatory legislation extending from the colonial mid nineteenth century to the Uttar Pradesh Debt Relief Ordinance of 1974, for example, which 'would break the chains of slavery and serfdom', according to the Chief Minister, and 'release the dormant energies of the poorest and weakest sections* of society'.[45] It would include, say, the Bihar Debt Relief Act 1974 and the Bihar Moneylenders Act 1974, which have served merely to 'push usury further underground', according to the *Times of India*, and 'enable the money-lender to drive harder bargains'.[46]

'And how,' inquired the Finance Minister of himself – with loans for consumption and the demands of daily necessity known to be the major compulsions towards indebtedness – 'do these people get indebted?'[47] The 'real answer' was not, above all, for food, or to repay other loans, or to borrow further to pay interest on existing debt to the same lender, or to marry a daughter.[48] 'They get indebted,' the Finance Minister told himself, 'because they want to imitate the rich ... it is the educated who spoil the poorer sections by their own wasteful expenditure.'[49]

And then, whether from such desire for emulation, or from poverty and the contiguous compulsions of feudal and customary relations, the tenant, the share-cropper, the landless and the 'marginal' landholder, become what is variously termed 'attached', 'unfree', 'bonded', or serf labour. This is a prohibited, 'illegal', 'abolished' – and periodically re-abolished – form of agrarian relation. It is a 'cognizable offence' under section 386

---

* This term – about the continuous use of which more will be said in chapter 3 – should be applied first to the perhaps thirty million 'tribal' people, or 'aboriginal' *adivasis*. They are held to be the autochthonous inhabitants of India. Their dispossessed social and economic condition – reperceived during the emergency as one 'steeped in ignorance'[41] in which they 'do not even know that the Prime Minister, Mrs Indira Gandhi, has emerged as their liberator',[42] or as one in which they are 'ill-equipped to understand the mechanics of a monetized economy',[43] and who thus suffer exploitation, expropriation and violence[44] – is analogous with those of other 'aboriginal' peoples in other continents, such as those other Indians of the 'new world'. With the outcastes, or *harijans* – transformed to 'scheduled castes' by the signature of the law – they may constitute as many as 20 per cent of India's total population. To be indebted, 'bonded' (q.v.), an *adivasi*, or of a 'scheduled caste' is often, therefore, in economic terms synonymous.

of the Indian penal code and unlawful under the Constitution, but also the fixed basis of the hierarchy of agrarian relations, the barely moving political, economic and social foundation of all the pyramidal gradations of landlord power superimposed upon it, in a countryside 'humming with development programmes'. It is variously called '*jeetha*' '*mat*' and '*sagri*', '*gothi*' '*sonkia*' and '*hali*', '*begar*' '*sanjayat*' and '*khundit-mundit*'.[50]

It is perceivable as 'a social agreement between a debtor and a creditor under which the debtor agrees to render labour or personal services to the creditor without remuneration in lieu of the debt's satisfaction'.[51] Or it may be seen in the form of the poor peasant of Rangakol, 'indebted for two generations, with no knowledge of how much money was originally borrowed, and whose son is working in the fields of the landlord/money-lender', in return for two poor meals a day and clothing,[52] 'rendering his labour', with no fixed working hours per day or working days per annum, to the creditor. It may be understood as

interest on a principal loan of say 200 rupees at 25 per cent per annum, or 50 rupees a year, in lieu of which, if the debtor puts in twenty days of labour a month for ten months, he works for 200 days; and if an average labourer is paid three rupees daily, the debtor ought to have been paid 600, which is more than twice the amount he borrowed plus interest; yet at the end of the year, the bonded labourer has repaid only the interest, the principal remaining.[53]

It may also be understood as assault and intimidation, the continuing phenomenon of child-sale and the use and abuse of poor peasant women in part-repayment.

It is, in sum – this question of the rural condition – the decade's 'green revolution', the slow growth and stagnation, and at noon the tin-box with dry maize *chapatis*, salt, and raw onion, of the labouring landless at their poor commons. It is both the 'spectacular success of India', and a little girl tending the cattle, lips cracked and dry, skirt blowing, in a ragged veil, holding up a younger sister, noses running, with the dirty unkempt hair of the poverty-stricken. You can hear the silent thin child's speaking-voice, within its coughing; head lolling, not seeing;

'*mrtyu-pāsán puratah pranodya*', 'the bonds of death tied, here, before dying'. The cow also watches, with a weeping eye; the men bending and digging at dusk; between their legs, knots, folds and hangings. The wind blows the dust of no green revolution into a gritty swirling before you; gaunt women – in orange, blue and scarlet – mesmerized with exhaustion at the day's end; in that country, like any, which (additionally) should not be judged 'in terms of the gross national product'. It is better, now, that night coming quickly should fall on this scene; and also, for the time being, leaving to one side the question of what harvest will be reaped from the condition of rural India, and the labours of its millions.

In any case, we should turn from the country, for a while, and enter the city, with its illuminations. We should take our places in that long unending procession, and rising proportion of the village poor, increasingly unemployed and landless, who therefore make the same journey in search of their fortunes in the factory, or in the streets, on the shop floor, or on the pavement: what has been described well as 'the entry of the village into the city'.[54]

The city is the metropolis of hope and desire, and universal variety of movement. It is the urban world of India's industrial proletariat of about fifty million,[55] with 60 per cent of India's industries concentrated in the four biggest cities of India, Calcutta, Bombay, Delhi and Madras.[56] It is the focus of the potentially productive mingling of classes and commerce; of enterprise and achievement, whose range of success and failure follows what is regarded by some, though not by others, as the uneven capacities of human nature.

The 150 millions of the cities (or about one quarter of India's population, a rising proportion throughout the last decade)[57] present a teeming heterogeneity for observation. It is a world of suede jackets and black moustaches, plump sweating chins and sun-glasses; of pigeon-chests and square high shoulders; of coughing; black quiffs of brilliantined hair, and nostrils flaring with effort; of red mouths, red tongues, red teeth, red gums, *pan*-stained, as if bleeding; man-and-dog, lying on their sides, in the same attitudes, in twin pools of shadow; shoes without socks and no shoe-laces; ordure of animals, pig and dog, cow and ox, and the stumping of beggars; broken-down cars, honking and pinking, or knackered; the dead passing and jolting on their bamboo stretchers, feet protruding, draped with white flowers; dogs and hogs in packs, browsing, barking or grunting; battered and smashed taxis, and rusting cabs, drivers waiting for custom, sleeping; scraps of grey rag in the dusty clottings of the gutters; banana-peel and brick-shards, and hanging udders, calves trotting.

There is: red forehead spot, nostril pearl or floret, and centre-parted hair; pale face a fine oval, in a gossamer pink sari; black plaits, raven-headed, with red toe-nails, necklace and silver anklets; a gold green fringe and a fluttering red sari; with rings on their toes, and eyes *kohl*-darkened; gold glinting, and the flash of flesh passing; cardigan, ear-rings and bangles, and slapping golden sandals; on dusty pink, yellow and ochre, the sandalled footprints; saris of silk, pink, blue and green, red and purple and yellow.

There is: cap, stubble and scarf; hollow cheeks and thin ridged noses; men sitting upright in rigor, or heads bowed, *in extremis*; the blind old woman, with socketed eye-holes, and stalks of uptufted ragged hair, eating; her pursed fingers placed in a blind mouth, carefully as if hand-feeding a baby; bandaged Egyptian mummies, walking.

And the police have always stood so, against the landscape of the city; the officers with their swagger sticks and corrupt glances, the constable with his *lathi*; or with the white crash-helmets of outriders, jackboots, and bulging bellies, black eyes and clipped black moustaches; legs apart, pent-up, and eyes blazing or thin as any victim, walking; or striking the pavings, stalking the city; or arms akimbo, smiling and waiting.

And there are limping lepers, stumps gleaming, or burnt-out cases; and men tramping; parked rickshaws in ranks, waiting; black turbans, saffron turbans, shiny trousers and dusty shoes, sharp-pointed; the faces of poverty, workshop-labour, and power in the blast of a furnace; and the calendar of Indian divinities, many-armed, multi-coloured, and many-headed.

Amid such a standing army of the people, encamped in the

city, we can be lost, or lose ourselves; the features and detail of its activity, disparity and poverty inaccessible in the flux of the crowd's passage. Alternatively, from another vantage-point, another street-corner, it is poverty dwarfed by the richness of its detail. Or, the measured quantities pale before the magnitudes of the misery to which they point; of the '45 per cent' of the urban 150 million living in the worst forms of deprivation;[58] of the estimated quarter of urban India living in slum shacks, and on the pavements;[59] of totals rising, as from 500,000 in 1968 to 800,000 in 1975, out of the 2·5 million population of Madras city, living in '1,200 slums'.[60] This was itself a 'conservative estimate', for it did not take into account those who live on pavements, and in blind alleys'.[61]

Or : of Bombay's population of about eight million, 1·1 million live in '262,000 huts', 200,000 'live on the footpaths',[62] while '77 per cent of Bombay's citizens live in one-room tenements'.[63] Of Calcutta's roughly estimated nine million, three million are said to live in its *bustees* and shanties, and an incalculable and growing number on its pavings;[64] in Delhi's slums, from '500,000' to 'over 700,000' of its four or five million;[65] in Agra, city of the Taj Mahal, 46 per cent of its population.[66]

But these quantities of immiseration must not be shirked; nor must their causes and consequences, if a correct judgement is to be made, later in this text, of the perceptions brought to this particular form of Indian suffering. Of 'the entry of the village into the city', and its propulsions, I have already spoken; of the patterns of urban response and reaction developing through the decade (and of course before it), to this flight from country to city, and outlines require to be established.

On the one hand,

even those to whom the figures are meaningless, have watched with awe the proliferation of the city's poverty; have noted year after year the huts spring up on every bit of the city space; in 'residential' areas, on the thin stinking river-banks, on waste-land, near factories, around railway overbridges, warehouses and cremation grounds ... and have seen the thousands left shelterless on the pavements.[67]

On the other, as forewarning for what was to come later, the 'alarming migration',[68] or flight from rural bankruptcy, is increasingly seen in this period as a pollutant of the city. What is, in fact, the 'misery of village life pushing the impoverished peasant and landless labourer to the city', the 'last ditch in the struggle for existence' (and 'in this ditch, lie millions')[69] is seen, when the kaleidoscope of social relations is shaken, as the steady erosion of urban values. Whether they are expressed economically in terms of property-value, or 'socially' as an 'irrational' and 'irregular', or 'disorganized' and 'unauthorized' violation of normal land-use,[70] they are either adjacent or identical arguments, expressing themselves in different terminology.*

But standing, in significance, far above all the other irreducible facts of urban and industrial India of which account must be given – such as its crimes and violences, the compressed densities of population, the preying upon the urban poor by the omnipresent money-lender and his gangs of thugs or '*goondas*'[73] – are two others. One is that the majority of the slum-dwellers, the denizens of its shanties, are not the 'feckless', the beggarly and the 'lumpen', or the sweepers and scavengers of the city. In Bombay, for example, 60 to 65 per cent of slum-dwellers are workers; 'the backbone of the Indian economy',[74] according to the state government's Minister of State for Housing, and including among them, in Bombay, 'forty thousand textile workers and five thousand policemen'.[75]

The other and complementary fact, its implications lodged in the very interstices of the structure of India's industrial progress, is the discovered rate of indebtedness, again not among the 'work-shy' or the huge army of urban jobless, but the settled and employed proletariat. As instance, over 90 per cent of the 'relatively better-paid' textile workers, this time in a big textile mill in Ahmedabad (a long-established industrial centre), were found

---

* Not only is the rootedness of this judgement evident in the decade's debate on the subject; so has been the response to it. It has consisted in random 'dismantlings', 'removals', and 'destructions' of the shelters of the homeless – usually without alternative resettlement – 'in order', in the words of the Mayor presiding over one such social action in the 1960s, 'not to encourage more people to come from outside the city'.[71] This social history of urban planning (in fact, driving the poor from the centre of the city) has been retrospectively seen as 'an improvement of our slums throughout all these years', though 'on an *ad hoc* basis'.[72]

to be 'neck-deep in debt', with average debts of over 3,000 rupees (£175, $300). They were spending 70 per cent of their earnings on food, and 90 per cent on the basic necessities of existence;[76] a statistic of proportional expenditure and indebtedness consonant with what has already been said in this text on the subject, and familiar to every inhabitant (and student) of the political economy of India.*

But, what if the power which commands the lives of labour and the forces of production does appear to be neither respecter, nor provider, of the conditions due to the employed Indian proletariat? What if such numbers of the 'better-paid' textile workers of Bombay or Ahmedabad (together with the guardians of the law and order of inequality and injustice) do live in a wretchedness of debt and squalor not qualitatively dissimilar from that of the general condition of the Indian people? Would it not be juster to set it all within that utilitarian and practical calculus which would bring gain and loss into balance?

That is, we must balance the moving engines of growth and development, generating the capital to fuel India's ultimate social and economic progress, or to create that surplus upon which socialism and democracy depend – the latter a specious, and sometimes vicious, argument to which I will give attention later – against the unavoidable necessity that men, women and children must work long hours, for low wages, and in bad conditions. Such labour is not only to eat, but – so the argument runs – to provide the material resources of an arduously earned, but growing, prosperity both for individual and nation. Britain, Ger-

---

*And beneath the 'better-paid' is a veritable miasma. It reproduces the forms of rural life, in urban and other variants; among the pitiable army of itinerant, and often highly skilled, unorganized labour ('they are more easily cheated when they are away from their own districts'[77]); among the artisans – to go no further – of the slums and pavements of the northern city; among the weavers, say, paid eighteen rupees for the weaving of the sari which will fetch a thousand. It is visible in the 'picturesque' fishermen on the 'golden beaches' of the eastern and southern travel brochure; who 'can never hope to own a catamaran or a drift-net'; 'fishing marked by a ferocious rate of exploitation by middlemen and merchants'; 'hiring themselves out'; 'attached to a master'. They, too, are 'deep in debt, and at the mercy of the owners of nets and catamarans, who are themselves the money-lenders'; 'they are like bonded labour'.[78]

many, America, Japan – China, also – were, so the argument continues, thus in sequence built; India is, and can be, no exception.

Moreover, the violence of industrial practice – the killings, the hired thugs, the breaking of militant trade unions by detention and intimidation, the conditions of work – might be seen, let us say for the sake of argument (before approaching closer), as a permanent feature of some 'asiatic mode of production'. And if not that, we could fall back on that violence, planned or random, which is a 'natural' characteristic of poverty and deprivation, whether it expresses itself in the industrial or any other sector of the Indian social order. Or better still, if we can extract the Indian economy entirely from its particular matrix, its determining features, and the facts of stagnation, such violent practice as greeted the 1974 rail strike could be an expression of the speed and urgency of India's decade of industrial progress.

After all, America's and Britain's early phases of industrial history were also a passage through varying degrees and species of violence. They too knew 'trade-union-as-conspiracy', union- and strike-breaking, and resort to thuggery both organized and random; and other forms of criminality both licensed and unlicensed. What else, then, can you expect in India but alternations of sullen quiescence and similar violence under the pressures of capital accumulation (within the particular frame of reference I have already provided in this portrait) and in a race against time, a rising population and a falling standard of living?

We should not be surprised, therefore, that ILO reports, press accounts, or police 'charge-sheets' coincide; speaking concurrently of management, police and inter-union violence generated at the point of production, and not contained there, but often spreading to workers' homes and into the streets of the city. But we must be generous in our definitions of industrial violence, and here I break loose from the parameters of the apologists' special pleading. It has not been confined to the widespread use of assault and murder,* consistently and particularly

---

*e.g. 'in the night, in the village, the house of the local trade-union leader [of the opposition CITU] was broken open. The hired Congress thugs entered, gagged him and tied him; his wife also was gagged, and then they

directed against unions and work-groups opposed to the Congress Party's trade union movement, INTUC;[80] nor to the smaller beer of often brutal forms of strike-breaking, the use of black-legs, and the attacking of pickets.

For the worker there are multiple forms of violence, particularly acute in India. There is the violence of underpayment and over-work in bad conditions; the simultaneity of indebtedness and full-time employment; the continuous fear of dismissal (with or without blacklisting), and its consequences. There is the violence of unprotected unemployment and indigence, often as the single income-earner responsible for a family, which may be largely or entirely dependent on the employed family-member's labours; where strikes, for whatever just causes, are circumscribed by the fear of further pauperization ('strikes can mean fear, and debt, and a fearful crisis in the lives of the worker'),[81] and which therefore constitute either an act of heroism or folly, depending on the vantage-point of the observer. There is all that unnameable violence against the person, that grievous bodily harm unknown to the law of India, or any other country, of malnutrition and exhaustion; and at the day's end, relief from labour spent in a shack, for shelter.

The events revealed (or partially revealed) by the typical industrial 'charge-sheet', or related in individual testimony, often refer to unholy alliances between police, management and corrupt trade unionism against workers. They indicate the violences of internecine and factional trade union struggles; of reprisal and counter-reprisal, often between the so-called 'stooge unions'[82] and their opponents. They refer to the consequences of stoppages and strikes, and other forms of industrial action; the structured violence of modern industrial production transplanted to a largely subordinate and dependent economy; or all these woven together.

---

raped her in his presence. They told her "your husband is being taken to the police station. Tomorrow, you will be able to see him." In the early morning, with all shame and sorrow, she went to the police station, and was told that her husband was not there. The police officer directed her, smiling, to search for him in a nearby paddy-field. There she saw him; first his hands, then his head, and after his legs, separated.'[79] (See, also, ILO and Amnesty Reports, op. cit.)

British Leyland's 'plant' at Madras, known as Ashok Leyland – with its work-force of about 4,000 ('where they dump used and surplus machinery on us at exorbitant prices')[83] – furnishes appropriate contextual illustration of Indian industrial practice, of the consequences of a strike, and the processes of reprisal. It also helps to illustrate the installation in India of forms of industrial existence with which the repetitious analysts of caste or faction seem to be unfamiliar, to say nothing of those who still see India through the lorgnettes of a Victorian perception. Nor is it exceptional. With other similar events in the summer of 1972 in Madras (but it might be Bombay or Calcutta), it has passed as a detail into the industrial history of urban India, as well as into the historical record of international capital; both of which remain to be written.

The personal testimony of Ashok Leyland workers, for all its fallibilities, and with whatever reductions made in its force to reduce the risk of excess, is damning. 'They [sc. hirelings, 'professional thugs'] came into our section, armed with iron bars, cycle chains, and steel hammers'; 'they went straight to the active trade unionists', recently on strike, and opposed to the 'stooge unions'. 'Some were beaten heavily, and fell where they were working'; 'they said to "Bendy" Srinivasan from the sales department, who has a twisted arm, "we will straighten it out for you". They knocked him down, held his arm on the ground and smashed it with a hammer'; 'Jagdeesan from the engine and assembly section was given a wound on his head. We cannot stop at calling it a wound. They sliced off the back of his head'; 'those who were beaten, when they left the premises, running and bleeding, were confronted by armed policemen and arrested, and taken away in police vans; but their attackers passed through the cordon'.[84] Throughout June, the industrial troubles spread in Madras, engulfing Simpson's and other plants. At Simpson's, on 15 June 1972, a worker 'was clubbed to death', another 'cut to pieces';* throughout the month, the trouble did not abate at Ashok Leyland.

*Alternatively, there is the view of Sivasilam, Simpson's managing director, taking a cucumber sandwich from a white-gloved bearer: 'basically, the Indian worker is peace-loving'.[85] (For an informal comparative study;

Police 'charge sheets' and court depositions are revealing of Indian industrial politics at the point of production. However, since the real malefactors, the hirelings – as in the early industrial histories of Britain and America – are not brought to account, but special cases are made out by police and management against the already-victims, a different kind of caution has to be applied to the documents. 'Charge-sheeting' is the term used in the hierarchy of penal sanctions provided by Employment Acts – inherited from the British – for industrial 'indiscipline'. The available procedures range from 'show-cause' notices addressed by managements to 'industrial trouble-makers', demanding reason as to why further action should not be taken against them; to tribunal dismissal, in the course of which the complainant is, at important stages, judge in his own cause; to detention for, say, 'unlawful assembly'.

Over one hundred Ashok Leyland workers were accused before the magistrates' court of Poonandee of an 'unlawful assembly' inside the factory on 31 May 1972; the evidence was expressed in language often reminiscent of Britain's social history of the 1820s. The depositions of the implanted managing director, R. R. Jones, speak of 'attempts to address the workmen'; of 'appeals for peace and order'; from other deponents that 'they threatened the managing director that they would cut up his body, and send it in pieces to London'; alternatively that they 'would drive him out of India'; of stones being thrown, of managers being 'struck on the head with heavy objects'; of tables smashed and windows broken; of 'telephones pulled from the wall', and 'wall-charts pertaining to production torn down, and fallen'; of the whole place 'ransacked and in disorder.' The managing director, in his depositions, speaks of 'authorizing the police to be sent for'; of then 'jumping out through the window'. From other deponents we hear of his 'frequent futile attempts to address the workers', of the workers' ('jeering') re-

---

Ramaswamy, Ashok Leyland director: 'Simpson's were worse affected than we were. This was the fault of the management, and their bad handling of the forces.' Varadarajan, Ashok Leyland works director: 'No, we were more clever.'
Ramaswamy: 'I should not say we were cleverer, but more lucky.')[86]

fusal of offers to translate into Tamil what the English managing director was either trying to say, or saying; of 'threats of revolution'.[87]

'You are responsible,' shouted one of the accused to another managerial deponent, 'for the shedding of the blood of the workers. We will see that your blood is shed here also.' And 'in a torn shirt, he stood on the table before us baring his chest' demanding the dismissal of those in complicity with their assailants. Another of the accused declared, 'you have had people beaten; you have paid people to beat us, and now we will show you what it is to be beaten'. 'They shouted while he spoke,' said one of the last managerial witnesses, of the managing director, 'and turned very violent. They looked at his face, and said they would smash him. They pointed at him, and said they would make him run to London. And pointing at the works manager, "Who the hell do you think you are?" they shouted.' One, last, the personal assistant to the supply manager, said, 'I was sitting at my place, praying to God . . . I do not remember the faces.'

Were this an isolated instance of the nature of the decade's industrial struggles, or of the consequences of the plantation in a dependent economy of the trans-national company – in British Leyland's India, the skilled worker earns approximately one sixth of the wages of his unskilled fellow-employee in Cowley – it would be improper to retain the record of it. Instead, it is a contextual instance of part of the industrial condition of the Indian people; context, not exception.

It is part of the context for the observation of the grimy worker going home; hob-nailed and plodding past the slum huts and the smoking factory chimneys, in a wafted stench, breeze-borne, of the drifting scum of the city; dirty torn shirt flapping, and face blackened; a heavy going. It is the setting for the crowds of workers – and police – milling at the factory gates of Ashok Leyland, dust trampled as in a stampede, or when a fight is gathering; a shift-change. It is context for that history of Indian industrial struggle which has been pitted in revolt not only against the facts of industrial life, but also within the circumstances of a massive and growing 'reserve-army' of the unemployed, and the fear of joining it.

It is also context for, and contrast with, the far worse incidents of the decade's industrial violence, which I might otherwise have chosen to detail, whether as emphasis or example.

For behind it, and beyond, stand other excesses, greater as well as lesser, if there is a scale in which such weights and measures can be scrupulously balanced. To represent them is the veteran opposition union leader, bending forward, shirt rolled up, wrist twisting round to point at the fading purple stab wound, and the blue herring-bone pattern of two hundred stitches hooping his chest and back, like a coil of barbed wire, beneath the dim bulb-light.

By now at least two responses, quite different, may beckon (both reader and writer) and set up their different clamours. One, the more fastidious, might be that industrial India is not the India of which they wished to hear – but, rather, say, the mysteries, subtleties and significances of the caste system; or something of the 'age-old monuments, colourful festivals, and ancient religions'; or some diverting incident culled from India's history, imperial, political or social: the 'mutiny', Clive's story, the 'black hole of Calcutta'. The other, the more 'positive' reflex – as well as corresponding more closely to the process of the Indian ruling mind – would be to go in search of evidences of compensating social progress, to offset admitted shortcomings.

The first, the caste system, however beguiling it may be to follow its ramifications and whatever else it may or may not be, is historically itself an exemplary form of the division of labour; both vertical hierarchy and lateral relation of position and function. It is perceived to be at work both in the social texture and the mind of India, and since the latter is supposedly unfathomable, it is a field rich in infinite speculative possibility; a system of mutual awareness of relation and function; enforced additionally by complex mechanisms of guilt and tradition; and sanctioned equally by privilege, revelation, piety, fear and violence.

It is conveniently integral and unchanging, the fixed lodestar of India; or, in transition, and waning, under the twin pressures of law and social practice. It is alternately source of stability and cohesion in a world which has elsewhere lost its bearings, or source of inequality and violence; or both together. For some, it is the true origin of cabal and faction, an explanation of social inequality without equal; or, a present but increasingly peripheral factor, in complex interrelation with, and corroboration of, the class system, or systems. Or, at the last, it is an evasion of the true nature of the polity of India.

The second response is that we must look to India's social progress, the benign expression and not the frowns and eruptions upon the faces of India's secular gods and goddesses. We must look at the decade's progress in, say, literacy and education, in public health and child welfare, in women's emancipation, in the abating of social and economic inequality;* all of which might conceivably have occurred, despite what we already know of its almost immobilized economic order.

But wherever one turns first, the incubus of both fact and impression bears down upon the realist and the impartial, the optimist and the apologist alike. It is so even with the most scrupulous desire to be moderate towards immoderate injustice, harm and suffering, both gratuitous and reinforced. It is so whether one writes in the light of, or ignores, the worse violence, cruelty and degeneration which was in process of breaking in upon the conditions we are discussing.

What, for example, of education? Against the accumulated weight of economic dispossession, literacy may be considered either an insubstantial bulwark, or a fundamental criterion of social progress; illiteracy an additional vulnerability or measure of further indignity. It may even be partially spirited away, as social fact, in the setting of an 'oral' or 'de-schooled' culture.

But nothing can be done with the accusing Indian facts themselves except to conceal them. In the words of the head of India's Council of Social Science Research, literacy† 'has increased by five eighths of a per cent per annum since indepen-

---

*For the magnitudes of inequality in India, see appendix, pp. 425–7. For the time being, as measure of extremes, the all-India per capita income of 2.30 rupees per day might be compared with, say, the cost of a room for the night (without breakfast) at the Oberoi-Sheraton Hotel in Bombay of 250 rupees in January 1976.

†Whatever other objections there may be to this term, it often denotes only a capacity to write one's name; thus, the statistics for 'literacy' and 'illiteracy' actually understate the magnitude of the latter.

dence, when population has been increasing at more than 2 per cent per year'.[88] The consequences are obvious: 'we have more illiterates in our midst today than we had in 1947'[89] – 71 per cent of the total population, 81 per cent of all women;[90] 'we have the dubious distinction of harbouring more than half the illiterate population of the world';[91] 'we have failed to implement the directive principle of Article 45 of the Constitution, both in letter and spirit'.[92]

Against the high-sounding efflorescence of the decade's official achievements, and the grand totals of 'enrolled' children ('90 million children are going to schools')[93] which are offered to occlude real consequences and meanings, it is necessary to look to the simplicities, or profundities, of the facts as they are. It is necessary also to keep in mind, beyond the span of this page or a paragraph, their social and economic implications.

Thus, the number of illiterate children in the age-group five to fourteen went up from 80 million in 1961 to 97 million in 1971, or by over 21 per cent.[94] Only one third of all India's children, and only one fifth of all girls, between the ages of eleven and fourteen, are 'enrolled' at school,[95] a figure which itself masks the scale of intermittent or complete non-attendance; only 40 per cent of those enrolled in class 1 reach class 5, and only one in four class 8.[96] There is now a total of 52 million illiterate young men between fifteen and twenty-five;[97]* and between 1961 and 1971 the number of illiterate adults over the age of twenty-four rose from 140 million to 163 million.[99]

And in the cascade of statistics can be heard different voices. There is the reassuring, or unctuous, voice of 'breakthrough'; the technologized impenetrability, or drivel, (comparable with the earlier 'rural data banks') of 'cognitive and attitudinal variables', 'the didactic components of learning units', and ' the synchronization of educational inputs';[100] together with the more serious 'anguish and concern' at the 'lowest ever proportional allocation of expenditure', under the Fifth Plan, on education.[101]

And what of 'public health' and its progress since indepen-

---

*Or, as Mrs Gandhi's Deputy Minister of Education, D. P. Yadav, in a post-prandial (and belching) near-coma, put it to me: 'You have seen our Indian boys. They are very happy. It is not education we need, but irrigation.'[98]

dence, in the decades of achievement? The official tone of voice is of reassurance, or silence. Statistics measure unknown quantities of sorrow; the death-rate figure is given officially as '16 per thousand' in 1970, based on a 'sample scheme of registration'.[102] The 'expectation of life at birth' – a dire phrase portending misery for millions – is officially rising. It had risen to 41·2 years by 1961, but the figure discovered by the 1971 census is not given.[103]

But for what is to follow neither causes nor facts are far to seek, and are already obvious. The most important factor in the level of India's public health was, in the words of the Minister of Health himself, the 'widespread malnutrition'[104] of the poverty-stricken. There is, additionally, 'the lack of potable water in 80 per cent of India's villages'[105] (or a 'national programme of protected water-supply benefiting many areas, urban and rural').[106] There is the low average ratio – lowest, as always, in the poorest areas – of 1 : 4260 in 1973 to 1974, of doctors to population.[107] There is the 'meagreness of public health services',* according to the director of the Indian Council of Medical Research, 'from which hardly 15 per cent of the population derive any benefit'.[109] From this base rises the spectral colossus of Indian debility, epidemic and endemic sickness; tuberculosis and malaria, malnutrition's blindness, leprosy and poliomyelitis, jaundice and scabies, anaemia and typhoid, filariasis and *kalazar*, cholera (but not smallpox).

Tuberculosis: is either 'controlled',[110] or in fact extended throughout India, with 'eight million people suffering from it'. There are an 'estimated two million new cases per annum' and two million 'active TB agents', in an 'advanced stage of infection'.[111] It is as prevalent in rural areas as in cities, with a half million deaths each year caused by it;[112] or, seen in microcosm, with 'more than 600 people dying every month in Bombay alone'

* This is, in part, the social expression in the lives of the people of 'democratic' choices, made during the decade, in favour of a falling per capita allocation for public health and education, and rising per capita expenditures on nuclear weapons research and military and para-military forces, presumably in compensation.[108] As Mrs Gandhi rightly put it, 'education and social welfare are the fields where it is easiest to make financial cuts'. *Statesman*, 28 November 1975.

from tuberculosis.[113] There is either 'a vigorous campaign to eradicate it' according to the Ministry of Information and Broadcasting,[114] or, according to the Indian Council of Medical Research, the percentage of patients getting no treatment at all ranges from 67 per cent in Maharashtra to 97 per cent in the state of Orissa, in eastern India.[115]

Or, the associated slow attrition of malnutrition, but with its direst of physical consequence : that easy death which comes to the homeless, the beggarly and undernourished, and takes young and old alike by the hundreds from the pavements, in, for example, Uttar Pradesh or Bihar during every winter's 'cold wave'.* It leaves, in its quiet wake, only the brief notices of 'the hawkers selling biscuits found frozen to death at Bhagalpur',[117] or the unnamed 'beggar' who 'died from the cold wave on the Mokameli Junction pavement'.[118] But perhaps these are small nothings set against malnutrition's slow blindness; against the World Health Organisation's warning that 'there will be 20 million blind people in India by the end of the century, if proper measures are not taken in time';[119] and the 80 per cent of the surveyed 20,000 Madras primary schoolchildren 'prone to diseases', 'a majority threatened with blindness due to gross undernourishment'.[120]

Or, malaria : it has either, officially, also been 'controlled' (and with a similar 'vigorous campaign to eradicate it'),[121] or in the words of the Health Secretary, was 'now threatening the national economy'.[122] The 'national malaria eradication programme', with its inadequate funds misspent, or unspent,[123] itself reported 4·6 million cases in 1975.[124] 'The actual total number', said the *Times of India*, 'is nearer nine million',[125] compared with 100,000 in 1965,[126] at the beginning of the decade of social progress; with no reported deaths from the disease then, but twelve million cases and 40,000 fatalities now projected by the WHO for 1980, at the present levels of malaria's increase.[127]

Or, leprosy : treatable, and curable if treated, was according to the Minister of Health 'very widespread'.[128] In fact there are 3½ million sufferers from it, one third of the world's population

---

*cf. 'Only eighteen chaps disappeared in the last cold wave. It is nothing if you take the percentage.'[116]

of lepers being in India;[129] or, filariasis, a disease caused by the presence of the threadworm *filaria* and its eggs in the bloodstream, cause of elephantiasis of the limbs, and a 'major public health problem which plagues India'.[130]

It is debatable always whether a purpose is served by such detail, knowing its causes, or whether in the service of sensibility and to avoid satiety it is better to draw a halt to it. Or is it better still to try to see even more clearly, but in different focus, the meaning of it in its place; and if to fail, at least to have glimpsed it, however obliquely, from another angle? For here under a hot sun, or in an Indian silence, is that leprosy, which if untreated and uncared for (and only then) becomes a shining liquefaction.

Here, the leper watches and waits in a stationary sunscape, black-shadowed; sound tramped down by heat and dust. Here, freed of the analytical mode, you may also see a humming-bird, the purple sun-bird, back-pedalling in the unmoving air, wings whirring; alighting, the mind's eye quickening to the small flickerings and palpitations of its body. The leper, sitting in the sun, adjusts his stumps and lesions for approaching footsteps, padding in dust, or sandals clacking; the dog chasing a bounding sow, purple-dugged, fierce and heavy, and running away across open ground, sound sun-stopped. He arranges his rags, lips moving, sitting, stumps protruding, back to the wall; sallow, with grey hair; preoccupied; his withered arms, cut off in their prime, like two docked tails, crossed on his chest; a brown skull and scarred crossbones, in black sunshine.

Beside him is a leper woman; lazar of lazars, with no tolling bell for warning, ulcerations gleaming, flesh eaten, and also a cleft lip and palate; cleft in twain, teeth and gums bared in a wide wolfish snarling, maddened eyes shining wild, as if at an unseen horror. Beside the lepers, but standing alone (as if afraid), is the man with elephantiasis; who waits in fear with his gross and swollen elephantine leg, hard and thickened as the hide of an old pachyderm; waits upon its blackened and warted fold on bulging fold, humping it, tugged and lifted with both hands on to a small sqeaking-wheeled wooden trolley, to this station of the cross, dragging his leg through dust.

But 'learned men should not grieve for the living,' says Krishna, in the Second Lesson of the *Gītā*, 'since we shall never cease to be'. 'What is it to be?' asked an Indian sage, simply. 'It is to be one's self, *ātmavān*.' To be one's self, is to be. But here are bodies, palpable, of corrupted flesh-and-bone; being, in dissolution: not into the 'formless *Brahman*', but into this suffering and every sorrow.

Or, if the issue be the decade's progress in child welfare, what might be found? It needs no statistician to confirm impression (in an inversion of method), but still the magnitudes of the harmed must nonetheless be recorded. There are estimated to be 'eighteen million children mentally or physically handicapped [excluding the legions of the illiterate], blind, deaf and dumb', and 'more than one million destitute or orphaned'.[131]

There are also, in India, over ten million child workers and child labourers in countryside and city below fifteen years of age,[132] 6 per cent of the total labour force, and in some states such as Andhra Pradesh, almost 10 per cent;[133] and a proportion which, unsurprisingly now, is itself increasing.[134]

This can and should be otherwise expressed, too; by a child road-gang, and bare feet on broken stone; children walking barefoot on hacked and jagged blue-grey granite, and gingerly, as if on hot coals; ragged little boys and girls, stone-breaking, building a road. Alternatively: in the naïve protests of the traveller 'driving from Madras to Coimbatore' and 'shocked to see gangs comprising solely of children aged between five and twelve years working on highway construction jobs in the hot midday sun'.[135]

This is ingenuous, because these are the small human indices of the economic compulsions driving often undernourished children to labour for a pittance; and families to dependence on the labour of their children for survival. No such naïveté exists in the Ministry of Education, nor in its judgement that the ratification of the 1973 ILO convention, abolishing labour by children under fourteen, is not only 'not feasible' but also 'not desirable at the present state of the country's economic level'.[136]

But within this state practice are both truth and falsehood.

You can either have increasing magnitudes and proportions of child labour and illiteracy; or, statistics of overall national progress in child welfare and education; but not, without contradiction, both together.* The different argument, that men, women and children are working in the interest of an increasingly just and egalitarian national economy, rather than from the bitterest compulsions of survival, fails immediately in the teeth of the now unconcealable facts of economic and social pauperization. But the whole issue of ideology and illusion – such as the description of deepening social failure and paralysis as part of India's progress towards socialism and justice – is reserved for further discussion.

For there can be no further postponement of a collected response (nor quietus for what it reveals) to the facts of women's life and labour in India. Nor is there any rationalization available for the compression of multiple elements of deprivation, dispossession, exploitation, violence and hard labour in the social reality faced by the poor, poorer, and poorest majority of the three hundred million women of India. Neither is there time, space, nor will to encounter the sanctifications (whether by 'tradition', 'custom', or more complex – but not, therefore, more profound – structures of obscurantism and evasion) of the condition and circumstances of women's inequalities and hardships. Fact at once reveals it; observation compounds it.

Ten per cent of India's total female population is 'employed';[138] if paid, paid even less than men (that is, therefore, often almost nothing).[139] Eighty-nine per cent of women workers are illiterate;[140] 94 per cent working in the 'unorganized sector'.[141] Eighty-five per cent of those 'employed' are 'engaged in agriculture', and 2 per cent in manufacturing.[142] The other truths of early marriage, poverty and violence crowd in, but must be held off to let the facts speak for themselves. Both proportion

---

*It could be argued, given the general conditions of Indian childhood, that the view that 'some sort of work for children should be introduced, as a part of their growing' and that 'a child regards working with parents as a thrilling experience',[137] falls to a somewhat lower level of adequacy and coherence.

and even *totals* of women working (despite the rising population) have fallen, each decade more steeply since 1911, from nearly 42 million, and 34·4 per cent of women then, to about 33 million and 10 per cent of women now.[143]

Within these facts, circle within circle, are others. In the last census-measured decade of women's progress and achievement to 1971, the number of women working has fallen by 40 per cent, while the female population has risen by a quarter.[144] Women thus constitute an increasing proportion of the vast army of rural and urban unemployed; and over the last two decades, have been engaged in agriculture increasingly as 'labourers', usually from earliest childhood, rather than as 'cultivators in their own right'.[145] This corresponds exactly to the process of general rural pauperization and land dispossession of which I have already written.

This is also the beginning and merest sample of those unyielding data which speak to the stony condition of women's India.* They are facts avoided by the pieties of 'custom and practice', or, more shamelessly – as we shall see later – by fusing the sufferings and misfortunes of women's life and labour into the single 'evil of the dowry system'.[146]

They are facts which conceal further within them what cannot longer be held at bay: the speaking voice of women, immeasurably burdened with more than the weight and accumulated totals of the statistical tables.

We are the ones who pick up the firewood and the cow-dung. It is we who keep the family going. We are the ones who must feed the children. We try to save a little, to hide it in the salt-pot, or where we keep the tamarind. In a small hut, where else can you hide money? But when the harvest is over, then the men go to town, and are missing. And if they return and find nothing, we are the ones who are beaten.

The facts may be translated into different languages. Moreover, either 'women's problems and working conditions, because

---

*A glimpse of it was perhaps afforded by the governor of Uttar Pradesh, who 'to mark International Women's Year' ordered the immediate release from prison on 22 December 1975 of 'all women prisoners suffering from tuberculosis, leprosy and cancer'. *Press Trust of India*, Lucknow, 22 December 1975.

of excessive hours of work, exceptionally low wages, insecurity of employment, and lack of legal protection' are 'beyond description',[147] behind the impregnable wall of statistics; or we may simply describe them.

We may describe, for example, women getting down to it in the dusty early morning, squatting low beside the wicker baskets, at two rupees a day, eleven pence, or less than twenty cents, whichever way you count it. They are unseen, crouching, beneath notice. They part the veils over their heads, when they turn to speak to a neighbour, and raise their arms to it; or draw the veils across their faces, when the sun strikes them. They move sideways, crouching, with toe-holds in earth, the old women with tired drawn faces. They wear long, torn, yellow or blue skirts and veils; under the sun, they pull and tear at the ground with bony fingers. In the heat of the afternoon, a vein protrudes across the front of a bared and glazed shin, point of stress in a day's crouching. Her ankle is thin, bird-ringed with an anklet, hanging like a loop around it, and resting in dust; stirring with each reaching and planting. Between her knees is a small naked child, swathed in her skirts; she suckles him as she works, in her open-legged crouching; not a madonna with child, but a tired woman working, yet with a faint smile and glitter at her nostril. Her bare feet, silver-ringed, are still planted in earth, at the day's end.

Or, we may perceive the same phenomena in the terms and judgements of the Committee on the Status of Women in India. 'The committee found that 81 per cent of the women in the sample had begun their working life as wage-labourers very early in their childhood'; 'working till the day before delivery of their children'; 'of the 645 children born to the Delhi women of our sample, only 389 were living'; '43 of the Delhi respondents were carrying small children to work with them'. In the cigarette workshops of Kurnool in Andhra Pradesh, wage rates were found to be 2.50 rupees a day (fourteen pence, or less than a quarter) per thousand *bidis* manufactured; the average monthly income of the 45,000 women engaged in the embroidery craft in Lucknow, was 27 rupees (£1.50 or $2.50), with failing eyesight and near-blindness common at fifty.[148]

We may look for the conditions of women's work, to field, factory or plantation; to the 'anaemia which is the curse of women plantation workers, and has taken a heavy toll of pregnant women in particular, since the start of the industry';[149] to the 'steady increase in workload, production of tea going up for "each unit of labour employed", together with chronically low wages'.[150] We can narrow the focus of perception of working conditions to the 'leeches from the soggy plantation ground which get over us [so that] every day we come home swollen all over the body'.[151] Or we can widen the focus, both to anticipate what is to be discussed later, and to admit the World Health Organization's findings that 'the incidence of anaemia in India is the highest in the world, affecting 70 per cent of all pregnant women'.[152]

But we must go further, beyond such relative triviality. We must look at, and not away from, the millions of women of the pavements and the streets. We must look at the consequences of the compulsion of early and forced marriage,* poverty and violence,† upon the bodies of the poor women of India; and not as an attractive social anthropology of the 'lower orders', rooted and ended in empiricism, but as the consequence of specifically analysed causes, and set firmly within the political economy of India. Here too is the ground-bass to the 'harmonies' of the caste system; here, the world of the female pavement-dweller and vegetable-seller, the scavengers and the homeless, the outcaste widow searching in refuse for survival, and the young girl

---

*This is, of course, widely known both as general fact – 'in rural areas, children are still married off at the age of six and seven'[153] – and, equally, as a statuesque sociological phenomenon. Characteristically, it is less often considered in its physical and social consequences for the *actual social reality* encountered by poor Indian women; and least of all can the sound of their own voices be heard.

†For an example of rape of untouchable girls and women, not by their husbands, but by 'officials' (in this instance, police) at Ranipur, see *Times of India*, 17 December 1975. The decade's recorded violence against poor (men and) women of low caste was very various. But it is only in exceptional circumstances that it becomes a matter of public notice – in some cases of murder, aggravated assault or, say, the 'branding with hot iron' of untouchable women in Madhuban village, Saharsa district, Bihar on 6 July 1973. *Indian Express*, 24 December 1973.

come from the countryside to the city brothel. These are separate constituents of women's condition, and not to be confused one with the other. They stand at a common level of indigence and desertion (additionally sanctioned and rationalized as it may be, in India), whose ravages and necessities are one and indissoluble.

Here, too, is the heterogeneity of the city. It may express itself as 'I am 16. I cleaned, washed, did sweeping and stored the water. I looked after the master's children. I came from the countryside and thought, "here at least I have shelter". But he forced me, and his wife beat and kicked me, so I came out to live by the roadside, to find labour.' Or she may say, 'I married at 12. I got up at three in the morning to do the housework. Then I went to the fields for harvest or sowing. Two rupees a day I earned, which my husband took from me, and beat me. He called me filthy names unfitting for a woman. I could go without food, but my children were starving, so I came to the city.' It may be expressed, by observation: of women walking the streets in search of cow-dung for fuel, or sleeping (covered or coverless) on the pavements of the city; or standing, gathered in doorways, as smiling or sullen houris, flowers for sale, in bunches.

In the trample of feet and carts, these last are blown roses, with bare midriffs and brothel saris. Eyes are lowered; poor women, stunned like stalled cattle in a shambles, the strolling fanciers eyeing the made-up faces, and boys selling contraceptives. It is like a floral meat-market, with plump purchasers of this merchandise of poor mata-haris; and hawkers of poor women's bodies; fates not worse than death, but crimes without passion, and to be avenged, not punished.

In the social and economic biographies of these women is a contracted microcosm of the extremities of the female condition, the eye of the storm (with causes as simple, or complex, as it may be wished to make them).[154] Here, too, are the special patterns made by the miseries of Indian poverty, and an attempted escape from it into the lower depths; and into one form of self-abandonment – the *suttee* of modern India – or another.

'I came from the country,' they may say;

my parents died when I was six or seven. I ate food once in a day, or two days only. When I was ten or eleven, a man forced me in the field, and spoiled me. I was bleeding, and could not stop weeping . . . He broke my hand also, and I could not do physical labour. A village woman brought me to the city, and for 500 rupees sold me. I saw the women standing in the doorways, with painted faces. I pleaded, and started crying. She said, 'since you are spoiled already, you should not mind doing this business. Here you can stand and earn your living'. When the first man came to me, I wept bitterly and had the idea of dying. But when I refused to take them, I was beaten.

There is a complete correspondence between such self-description, the socio-economic facts, and studies of the 'genesis of prostitution' in India.[155] They speak to the condition, also, of the poor, 'lower-caste' and 'tribal' women, in that fatal osmosis which occurs between poverty, abuse and caste-ranking. Brought even by their husbands, fathers and brothers, they are sold for varying sums within a range of 300 to 5,000 rupees into city prostitution, as 'victims of extreme poverty';[156] 'to escape from the local money-lender';[157] with 'trade in "tribal" girls widespread'[158] and 'linked up inextricably with the system of bonded labour'.*[159]

Beneath this 'system', are the paid-for but uncountable totals of misery, violence or dull sorrow of the thin ragged girl-children, lost, and wandering the streets of the teeming city. What can be said of them? What must be said, will be said in a moment.

One of the studies of the kind to which I have referred, did well to name the traffickers in rural women.[161] It revealed – unsurprisingly, given the extent of corruption of all forms in India – the continuous implication of local rural bureaucracy in this

---

*Convoluted within the primacy of these facts and their real causations, are also sometimes to be found the sanctions of religion. Most notable is the 'sacrifice' or 'gift' by poor peasants, of their daughters, to the goddess Yellamma; that is, the temple-prostitution of the *'devadasis'*. Large numbers of such dedicatees are to be found, not in temples, but in Bombay's brothels.[160]

human commerce. It describes the working day in a Delhi brothel, which begins at 6 a.m. and ends at 1 a.m. the next morning; the virtual imprisonment of the women; the collection and sharing of earnings between relatives and brothel-owner; the inmates' monthly payments of fixed sums: 'ten rupees for the use of a fan, ten for the laundryman, and fifteen for the combined bribe to the policemen who patrol the area'.[162]

Perception (and comprehension) of such a condition may thus stand between the testimony of experience:[163]

I do not know where I came from. I know only that I lost my eye and was a beggar, in the railway station area. I did not have a mother. I was put down on the pavement somewhere, in the beginning. I had only myself, and was not wanted by another person. Day and night I walked the city. I collected firewood and scraps of paper. This was hard labour for a child, and I could not make a living. I had no one to get me married, and no money for my dowry. So I slept in an empty hut beside the roadway. A man gave me money for my body, but later struck me. It would have been better then for me to die under a train, or in the water. I came to the brothel when I was about eleven, because I had no money, and I was still alone, and without anybody . . .

and the testimony of survey, or index.

There are other correlations between the causes, the social condition of women's poverty and its other worst consequences; raising again the issue of India's perhaps compensating social progress, to which I referred earlier.

I recall to attention, or choose from a wide variety, only those which are here informing. There is the connection between the just over one-in-five, and one-in-ten, of girls between the ages of 11 and 14, and 14 and 17 respectively, 'enrolled' in schools (a figure almost stationary for the last half-dozen years of the decade),[164] and the socio-economic structure of women's condition. There are the connections between women's illiteracy rate – 82 per cent for India as a whole, and variously near, or even over, 90 per cent in Bihar, Kashmir, Madhya Pradesh, Rajasthan and Uttar Pradesh[165] – and family-size, to be considered later; and between women's destitution, violence against children, and child-sale.[166] There are the connections between these, the unquantifiable violence* against women, and the incidence of suicide among (men and) women.† Sometimes accompanied by the desperate homicide of their children, it is response, as in the old China also, to domestic poverty and misery without end or visible solution; in India, often compounded by the woman's fatal, or mortal, assumption of responsibility for the family's economic well-being.

The toll it takes of poor life is registered, briefly, in the pages of the press; or may be observed through the eye of the beholder. At random, it is in 'the young woman who last night committed suicide, taking poison after giving to her three children aged from four to ten years poison also';[170] in the 'extreme poverty and mounting debts'[171] or 'extreme poverty and disappointment',[172] which respectively 'drove a family of five to end their lives by walking into the sea', and another family to 'consume poison'. Or, it is in a young woman lying sleeping on the Madras beach, on soft pink sand, in a faded rose sari, hemmed green and gold at her ankles; wind-blown; her thick black hair untied and streaming. Fishermen are laying out their long grey nets, the beached grey boats weatherbeaten; with ropes coiled, and stacked fish baskets. Fisher-girls, the sea wind blowing their long grey dresses, bare feet in sand and hands on hips, look down at her, talking. There is a rim of washed-up and dried grey wooden flotsam, and seashells; and net-mending, in a sunny silence.

---

*Expressed in common knowledge; in daily experience; in the collocation of press reports; restated in such 'cultural' notions as that 'a woman's skin becomes darker when she is married';[167] and intimately known from the work in progress of the women's movement in India. ('I have stopped asking peasant women if they are beaten. They are all beaten.')[168]

† This has been studied by the Institute of Criminology and Forensic Science in Delhi, revealing that people in the age group 18 to 30 are especially prone to suicide; that 'one hundred Indians commit suicide each day'; that even more men than women take their lives; that the rate is high and increasing throughout India to different degrees in different states, and that its major causes are 'unemployment, poverty and hunger'.[169]

The fine dark fingers of her left hand are pursed; her open right palm and soles a seashell yellow; lying asleep with her feet a little open; the green sari's fringe round her shoulders; unstirring. Her delicate face is dark, tired and thinning, with fine cheekbones glossed and faintly paling, caught thus in the sunlight; mouth a little open, and teeth protruding; feet facing seawards. In the *Upaniṣad* it is written, 'when passions have passed away, you will be tranquil'. 'From abandonment, comes tranquillity', says the *Bhagavad Gītā*.

The gentle breeze ruffles the hem of her sari; broken slivers of mother-of-pearl are iridescent in pink sand; drying to a stiffness in the sunshine, the fishermen's small-fry glitter; in such a place, it is bliss to be alive on such a morning; the sleeping figure's eyes were open, staring.

We may lose, or memorialize, her; it may make no difference; or the event is unexceptional. A line in the local paper about her self-poisoning from poverty adds only minimally to the facts of India. It is something, or nothing; she is either giant, as victim; or dwarfed by the moving mountains of India's social progress, or tidal sea-change; in the people's general emancipation; in the advance of social equality, and the rising levels of public welfare. If that is not possible – and it is not – then we must, alternatively, measure women's work and progress by the poised laughter of educated assurance, by the rustling of parcels, the madrigals of mannered voices, or the richest contentment. Or we must measure it by the relatively less poor's pinched and precarious survival; at the very least, by the surviving graces of the poorest – that is, by a way of walking, not living. Or we must measure it by some other index, which emphasizes the minority of women's condition, not only as balance, but (surreptitiously) as equation; or replaces women, where they belong, within the general condition of India.

So let us start to do so, and try to be done with it; and widen the perspectives and arguments to a more balanced conclusion. Let us dismiss offensive and atypical evidences of the people's rage and anger, and locate them instead within the notorious passivity and quietude of Indian 'human nature' (as was also attempted, albeit with limited success, in the China of the 1930s). Let us restore the inhibitions of caste to their proper primacy and dominion; and, above all, elevate once more, as archetypal figure of India, the stoicism in suffering of the Job, and the dignity in indignity of its people.

Let us go back to that India we knew or heard of, where they 'keep going' in adversity; where the drivers, woken in the small hours, emerge stooping from their low-slung sack-tents at the taxi stands, straighten up, and walk to their cabs, sleepwalking. Or let us follow in a cold red dawn of black girders, funnelling coal smoke and piercing whistles, the girl climbing the iron-rimmed concrete steps of the crowded station footbridge, carrying (without demur) her heavy head-load though her ankle is gashed; and as she climbs the steps in the crush, blood runs from it, and under her heel, staining the worn leather sole of her black sandals with a dark red blood. And passing her arm, raised to the load, you might see the tired face in profile of a young woman going into Calcutta city, in the early morning; but keeping going.

So, too, the old man with a rag cap, string-tied, bent forward under a bulging sack ('visitors are requested to employ coolies with numbered market-badges only')[173] in the sun; dumps it, and straightens, walking quickly with a slight limp and lurch to the right, right slipper scratching or slapping the ground, the left soundless on the stone – the stagger of an old man; but keeping going. Or, the woman in the ambling and jolting cart, blank, and with a baby at her shrunken breast, creaking and jolting past you through the heat of the afternoon village; eyes unblinking, child feeding; she is keeping going.

Bring to the fore, as Homeric hero, the itinerant storyteller, voice hoarsened, in a coat of many colours and black bearded, and with silver ankle bells, singing, feet shuffling and trampling the dust to his rhythm; a thin woman with two wrapped babies sitting on the ground beside him, hungry by sunset, tapping on a stained drum, but singing. He sings and dances, ankle bells jingling; jongleurs, keeping singing. Record the 'true', 'timeless', India; and that sanskrit 'endurance', *Titikṣā,* which is endurance of the merely 'impermanent', of merely external objects, 'coming and going'; '*āgāma paymiah*'. And if men and women, too, should happen to be impermanent, coming and going also, in India (at least) they also keep going.

Let us be done with the statistics, which in face of India's permanences and continuities mean nothing, or little; consider, instead of all the arduously assembled and empirical nonsenses of 'percentage shares in total consumption and disposable personal income by decile groups', or 'rising unemployment among the educated',[174] the beauties of Taj and temple, or the cadences which catch the eye and the resonant gesture of Indian music; sound dancing, and singing movements of mind and body, as quick as thought, or quicker.

Place too in the unfairly tilted scale, order and the fulfilment of duty; not contradiction, struggle and sorrow. Whether the facts be alternately denied or admitted, admit into fact's sombre shadows the light reliefs of the itinerant traveller's familiar comic clichés – the pantomime stand-ins for India. Take the Chekhovian rail clerk, say (albeit on his beam-ends and desk-bound, spending his railway pension in advance, to eke out a present living), perspiring and fraying at the seams and edges as may be, but doing his duty; or keeping his comic station, beneath the sooty shelves and ledges of imperial India, with the other cramped clerks, cuffs rubbed out at the wooden table tops, writing in serge, grit and silence.

Find the details for a book's quick sale and an empty belly-laugh on a joist of the railway office ceiling, head under its wing and hidden in feathers, preferably pecking its toes, a pigeon, shot-green and blue, eye darting. Or, better still, make a joke of the slamming and thudding of official stamps on refunds and requisitions, and the rustling of smudged carbons, the slow transports and looplines around the station office of clerks' communications with each other, in a hand-to-hand traffic. (But if he should write slowly – served from a battered tea tray by a near-sleeping 'peon', in hanging grey *dhoti* – eyes dulled and weary behind scholarly spectacles, forehead gleaming; and finished, look askance, eyes averted; or, from another angle, glittering with desperation and anger, there is nevertheless a jest, somewhere, to distill from his condition.)

Above all, do not listen so attentively and obsessively to the voice of social fact, with all its limitations, nor be beguiled by superficial impression. Attend to the multiple voices of India, and from their cacophony or counterpoint discern and extract not the discord of classes, but the overarching harmony of the unity of India. Against the ugliness of truth, place the truth of beauty. For 'small abandoned boys who are utilized by anti-social elements, who break the boys' legs, cut them off, twist them, and the collection of money they keep, and give a little food each day to the children',[175] read, 'one child has a thousand mothers; (chuckling) they pass it from hand to hand whenever you are coming'.[176] Displace the knees, wrists and ankles, already dislocated and shrivelled and set down upon the pavement, with the pietist's highest moral doctrine of non-injury, or '*ahimsa*'.

And if all else fails, and all this fails, there is a last mode, apart from lying, by which the shaming detritus of destroyed and harmed lives in a decade of progress – on the verge of even faster progress with the aid of mass arrest, and new economic programmes – may be brought to a just summation. Little Mr Kakubhai, the commercial director, with the cream bone buttons on his linen jacket and a check handkerchief in his upper pocket, sitting forward in his cushioned wicker on the green lawn (the wicker creaking), placed his hand on your sleeve lightly, his mouth in an upturned smiling. Balancing on a fine fingertip the massive weight of India's condition, in a precise and jewelled equilibrium, he said: 'the poor have no envy; they think only they should do a better *Karma*, and fulfil their duty, in this life, and the next one'.[177]

But it is no good. First, because in the blocked bowel of the city, the grey-haired woman, looking round quickly, rummages in the congealed gutter for a small gleaning. On the pavement, where she bends, the eyes of a dying child are misted over, like two small beached jelly fish, overcast and whitening ('right from birth, they have resistance to cold, to sun, and even to fire').[178] Deep down in Dante's last circle, women are fighting for slops and waste in the café alley; crusts and droppings are thrust into the front fold of a sari, fangs drawn in the scuffle; and in the very heart of all putrefaction, the poor haunted girl-child stands before you – blood streaking her ragged skirt, sweat marks in the armpits of her torn blouse-top – set in a mulch of filth and sorrow, saying, 'You want? You go? You want go with girl, sahib?'; and shrugging, walks away, turning and staring; pointing to a crucifixion; or a Golgotha.

And, second, because there have been too many other voices in this decade, also; not only the voices of the tormented and degraded arising from the ruin of India and the abyssal condition of millions, but those we have already heard, of outrage, of anger mobilized, of hatred. 'We have sown these fields,' they may say, 'reap them, landlords, if you can. And in the stooks and stubble, you'll find our plan. There are sickles in it, we warn you, and heads will be our harvest; neck and crop to the last man.'[179] There are voices of irreversible knowledge ('it is we who harvest the rice, but we who are given the coarsest grain in payment');[180] and of bitter memory, ineradicable from the lives of the people. 'I come to the fields at seven,' she says, at the field's corner, shading her eyes.

At ten, I have gruel. At one, gruel with rotten egg-plant pickle. I can go home, when I see the sun too is going. With wood picked up at the wayside, I start cooking for my husband and children. Lighting the fire is hard with such fuel. I get pains in the chest from blowing. I eat only at ten or eleven. To clean the hut and fetch water, I must get up at four or five in the morning, and leave something for the children. Then I must walk and walk, to come to the fields at seven.[181]

There are the voices of strength in sorrow. 'She beat,' they say, 'with her bare fists on the doors of the police wagon, crowded with the arrested, and put her baby down in front of the wheel, shouting to the police in fury, "Now you take them; drive over my child, drive over him and take them"';[182] and the sounds of shared suffering, with its familiar accents and universal language. 'The police dealt out terrible beatings and threw tear-gas, but the poor people took in those fleeing, and bathed their wounds, telling them, "I'll say you are my son," and then spread the mat on the ground, saying, "Show you are sleeping, when they come for you".[183]

These voices are all out of reach of illiteracy's index, and demand a different reading. We must now carry forward the full nightmare weight of the real condition of this India, cross the threshold inscribed with 'the success of the policies followed by India', which had become 'such an eyesore to other countries',[184] and enter the ideological dream-world built by power; and measure there the geometries of illusion and violence, theory and practice in widening disjunction, and the compound arithmetic of corruption.

3   The Politics of Illusion

I am sure you are all conscious of the deep and widespread conspiracy which has been brewing, since I began introducing certain
programmes of benefit to the common man and woman of India.

Indira Gandhi, 26 June 1975[1]

Mrs Gandhi's régime is also exceedingly corrupt ... baser elements
usually come to the top in such an environment, which is what
happened both in the Congress Party hierarchy and in the civil
service.

*Ashok Mitra, former Chief Economic Adviser
to the government of India, Economist,
24 January 1976*

Disruptive forces inside the country will be ruthlessly put down.
The Government and Congress Party will fight these forces until
they are eliminated, and the country made safe for democracy.

Indira Gandhi, May Day, 1976[2]

Our passage through the dark labyrinth of the people's condition
thus ends not in the light of progress, but in the resumption of
the analysis of power and its uses with which I concluded the
first chapter. It is necessary now to gather together matters referred to in passing; matters of ideology, theory and practice,
and the politics of Indian illusion.

The latter's range is wide. It includes the familiar alternations of professed innocence and brutal practice. It includes
'freedom of action' unable to extricate itself from the accommo-
dations of economic dependence; building the power of capital
for 'socialism's' progress; asserted autonomy of mind and
sovereign political language, with the long-echoing accents and

humiliations of the colonial era. The observer faces (classically) parties above class, which are in fact class coalitions of vested rural and industrial interest; a 'party of the people' which presided over the fortunes of the few and the misfortunes of millions; and a 'mass party' which had become pyramidally dynastic.

Analysis must embrace the Indian profession of peace, and the practice of aggression; the stepping with caution over the cockroach, and the retention (and continuing use) of the gallows.[3] It must encompass the corruption and moral turpitude in high places which itself then excoriates indiscipline, corruption and licence in others. It is not surprising that power in disarray – under increasing social, economic, and political pressures – should demand order; but in India, it is accompanied by self-lacerating admission and denial (one alternating with the other) of the people's condition. We must likewise come at a history of mass-arrest in the defence of freedom; or the continuous conjunction of restated commitment to parliamentary democracy and social justice, and an increasingly repressive practice to quell the rebellions of the people.

Moreover it is not enough to withdraw in the face of this, and denote it either as hybrid paradox or 'contradiction', terms which can be both exact and just but whose misuse or abuse permits evasion. Nor is it helpful to confuse the issues further with amusing or perceptive discourse on the particularities and continuities of 'Indian human nature'.

Signs and portents of this chapter's subject can be found in many directions, from which it is only possible to make a sample selection. To begin we can look, for example, to the compressed generalization of 'the flag-fall of empire, with the inheritors of the imperial power hastening to adopt the metropolitan political institutions'.[4] Under this rubric, independence movements become the ruling power, and factions within it the satellite political parties; the whole shrinking from 'cabinet to cabal, from cabal to caste or kin-group and thence to family',[5] with, for good measure, 'the astrologers moving from behind the arras to the council table'.[6]

Or, we can go for explanation to the post-colonial class structure of no single strong class, the fundamentally 'weak' state, seeking – acrobatically – to maintain its precarious balance by 'curbing any constituent group that becomes too strong'.[7] Unable to depress such a balance too far for fear of imperilling the ruling coalition, it is also 'driven to make periodic concessions to the exploited',[8] in order to maintain itself on the high wire suspended above the Niagara-roar of the masses.

We can find also in the pre-independence Congress Party features 'in many respects similar to the Chinese Kuomintang ... representing the interests of the bourgeoisie, landlords and *kulaks*'.[9] It can then be seen as an anti-colonial force under the leadership of its own Sun Yat-sen and Chiang Kai-shek; Mahatma Gandhi and Nehru. A nationalist, popular (or populist) movement, led by figures with socialist pretensions analogous to those found in other colonial countries, it struggles for what was expected to be 'freedom' from extraneously imposed imperial rule, while 'sowing ideological confusion in the minds of ordinary men and women'.[10] It produces an incompatible '*ménage à trois*' of revolutionary rhetoric, extreme (even proto-fascist) nationalism, and the colonialized servitude to the 'Westminster model', impossible of consummation. This argument would assert that, in whatever combination or permutation these elements are arranged, they produce the fissures and fusions between utopian ideals, the use of violence, and commitment to civil liberties being played out both in theory and practice within the body politic of India.

We could go back further to what has been described as that 'Janus-like posture'[11] – a bifocal, or cross-eyed, glancing – which, as future inheritor of power, looked up (or appeared to look up) to the colonial mode as archetype of good governance and 'culture'. At the same time, it looked down, then as now, in its guise of indigenous landlordism and urban privilege, upon the submerged rural and urban millions and their structured destitution. So that what was partially lost from ideological view in the embrace of a populism mobilized for national independence, is now re-presented and obfuscated, as one of the 'paradoxes' of India. And built on this is an elaborate debate about Indian 'human nature' which obscures, whether as intellectual detachment or sophisticated diversion, the awareness in the mind's eye of the continuities in the real condition of the people.

Whether what has just been argued is true or false – and I think it is largely true – there are important points which stand beyond the argument, and need stating early. The luxury of intellectual illusion about India can be more quickly dispelled with words here than can the suffering of the people be dissolved by either rhetoric or 'explanation'. Whether India's 'socialism', 'democracy' and 'freedom' are real or false, or indigenous variants peculiar to India, is not the same question or issue as the daily experience of their presence or absence. There is as wide a disjunction latent here as that between India's 'philosophy' and its practice. Similarly, the 'joke' of India's continuous succession of economic and social 'programmes'[12] is no joke to the denizens of India's hovels, or its skeletal figures in the landscape. The anatomy of, say, divisive factionalism in the political process is also nothing compared with the totality and unity of India's immiseration. Finally, the task of analysis must not be insulated within a special 'Indian' context, whether it be of wretched intellectual muddle and treason, self-deception, lack of 'moral courage',[13] or humbug and a limitless capacity for lying, whatever the evidence which points in all these directions.

Instead, we need to be alert to the real meanings of the confluence in the Congress Party's ideology of incompatible elements, which here reflected among other things that shifting compromise of competing interests already referred to. We need to consider also what their effects have been upon the short-term and long-run interests of the people.

This historical confluence was a multiple one. Thus, 'to ameliorate the conditions of the masses',[14] it was considered 'essential to make revolutionary changes in the present economic and social structure';[15] but such a revolution was to be 'based on non-violence and the harmonious cooperation between capital and labour, the landlord and the tenant'.*[16] It was to include

---

*And 'I shall throw the whole weight of my influence,' Mahatma Gandhi added, 'in preventing a class war';[17] 'I shall be no party to dispossessing the propertied classes of their property without just cause';[18] 'capitalists are fathers and workers are children'.[19]

both the 'removal of gross inequalities and rural misery',[20] but not such as would involve the 'large-scale' break-up of existing landholdings, since this 'might give rise to organized forces of disruption'.[21] It demanded that 'the state own or control key industries and services',[22] but 'without interference with individual initiative'.[23] It was a politics which reconciled individualism with the encouragement of collective effort, a dalliance with marxism, but with 'communistic tendencies to be avoided'.[24]

It included centralized 'five-year' planning on a Soviet model – Nehru first visited the Soviet Union in 1927 – and the home-spun handicraft production of a simple, rural (or 'natural') economy. It was to speak later both in the post-war language of American managerialism, and traditional *ahimsa*. It brought together, and not always in collision, apocalyptic, militant nationalism – such as Subhas Chandra Bose's politics of the destiny of the east, at its extremes both chauvinist and racist – and the more fastidious notions and accents of parliamentarism and its procedures. It sought to combine the development, on a 'pragmatic' basis, of industrial capitalism through selective nationalization – that is, a 'mixed' capitalist economy – with the retention of enterprise in Indian hands. These in turn were displaced by the rejection of 'a hard and fast rule in the matter',[25] or were subjected to the moral restraints – advocated by Mahatma Gandhi – of the politics of a paternalist trusteeship to be held by the owners of the means of production, in partnership with the state, on behalf of the people of India. And with all these, 'secularism', shibboleth, and religious obscurantism presided over the marriage of god to mammon.

'Somehow' – to use the frequently employed Indian term – the task was to bring about 'revolutionary changes' without revolution; structural change without real change to the structure; reform without offence to vested interest. Therefore the irruption of the misery of the people, and its expression in rebellion and struggle, was to encounter both paternalist concern for their welfare, and violence. The cause of the poverty-stricken was to be championed, but without real change in their condition; its instrument, the construction of a 'socialist' capitalism, an arduous task but arguably not an ambivalent one. Above all, it came to depend upon two constants: entrenched and therefore corrupted ruling power ('it would require a powerful political microscope to find out how many party units are not dominated by the rural rich in the Indian countryside'),[26] and an almost immobilized people.

The 'discordant explanation', as I termed it in my first chapter, can begin to contain its own harmonies. Ambiguity and contradiction come to stand within a decipherable structure of ideological meaning. It is a structure, moreover, containing reiterated terms whose usage may differ, and whose interpretations may vary, but whose recurrence establishes a sufficient frame of reference for analysis.

'Socialism' is one such recurring term. Commitment to it is repeatedly restated. The available variants of the term's meaning and content, whether as theory or practice or located in the void between them, are admittedly wide, but the form of Congress 'socialism' came to contain a fixed structure of invariable assertion, even if of an indeterminate nature. Nor is it ahistorical. In the emergency's heyday, it was of past, present and future; a dream or a continuum. 'Congress history is the story ... of a commitment to establish a socialist society';[27] the 'dream of establishing socialism evolved in the course of the freedom struggle'.[28] Either 'there will be no deviation from the path of socialism',[29] or 'Congress must become an effective instrument for establishing socialism in India'.[30] What kind of socialism, or how such a 'dream of socialism' should be released and realized – if it had not already been – from the nightmare circumstance it inhabits, is also one of the fixed points on the spectrum of intellectual discourse in India.

It was hard (without further knowledge) to find it on the map of a geography of politics. 'Whatever socialism the party has is not doctrinaire socialism, neither the Soviet, nor the Chinese, nor the Scandinavian type'.[31] Or, 'taking the world as a whole, the socialist bloc does not come into the picture because it is completely a different system altogether.'*[32] Indeed, even 'the

---

*As response to this undisguised renunciation of its own form of 'socialism', the pro-CPI weekly *Link* thought that 'the left outside may not fully subscribe to the theory that the Indian road to socialism would, or should,

world experience holds no solution for us as our situation is complex and unique'.[34] It was a socialism 'designed to meet the demands and needs of the people';[35] 'a dream of making the people live happily';[36] 'our socialism is Indian socialism'.[37]

In sum, this 'Indian socialism' was 'not doctrinaire';[38] that is, 'the party is not a party of theoreticians, but of pragmatic socialism'.[39] 'I have my own version of socialism, and my own vision of what India should be like, and I have been working towards that vision steadfastly. It is a slow movement, but surer.'[40] How slow, and how sure, we have seen, and would see further. Moreover, whether fluctuating as dream of making the people happy, as path embarked upon, as commitment, or already existent realization (or all together) – the symptoms of its recurrence as ideological notion – the placing of this socialism in terms of any cartography of 'left', 'right' or 'centre' was also somewhat difficult. For, at the same time as 'we do not believe in the expressions "right" and "left" ',[41] there was 'no intention to shift to the right';[42] and 'Congress politics will continue to be left of centre'.*[43] Elsewhere, though 'the ideology of the Congress is neither leftist nor rightist',[46] 'if socialism consisted of following leftist policies' (or 'fashionable leftism'), 'then Congress does not go in for such socialism'.[47]

Despite the sterilities of this debate, it represented an historical residuum, the (audible) 'left' and 'right' factionalism within the Congress Party and its opposed perceptions. Above all, these were the thinnest attenuations of the already ambiguous commitments of pre-independence Congress politics. This was also 'pragmatism'. Thus, 'it is not as if we have no ideas about socialism; we have to take into account the peculiar situation in which we are placed', and 'the peculiar conditions which exist today in our country'.[48] And with it, were this pragmatism's

---

in its essentials be different from the path followed by other socialist countries'.[33]

*Thus, despite disclaimer and the shorthand inadequacy of the terms themselves, Congress Party debate during the emergency was often conducted within them; e.g. the Congress Party had 'lurched to the extreme right', according to Ayub Syed, member of the All-India Congress Committee, and Bombay editor of *Current*;[44] or 'I would ask my friends if there is really a swing to the left, or whether it is not in fact a swing to the right.'[45]

many fixed components. They included, and include, acceptance of unalleviated mass suffering, the coercive Benthamism based on wishful thinking of 'making the people live happily', the defence of vested interest, and the sullied aroma of a moral and intellectual corruption often discernible in the very lineaments of the arguments, and in those who argued them.

In other ways, too, the meaning of 'pragmatism' in practice was clearly signified. 'As far as the bureaucracy is concerned,' said the Finance Minister for instance, 'they get accustomed to any sort of programme that we put forward, and they are able to get themselves adjusted.'[49] As strategy for political practice, or 'pragmatism's' self expression, it was manifest in 'when we speak of changes, people are so used to clichés that they think along certain lines ... going further ... more of something else ... I am not saying that it may not be done, or it may be done'.[50] Here, there was also illustration of that intellectual frailty and blankness which can become part of the texture of corruption, as I shall seek to explain later.

This pragmatism could mean taking to the radical tilting ground, jousting with 'the shield of socialism against reaction',[51] as 'champion of the poorest',[52] and with 'the welfare of the people the only touchstone'.[53] It could mean 'taking the bold decision of nationalizing the banks',[54] or 'dumping the nationalization bogey';[55] or scrapping the privy purses of the former princes of India, as pragmatism or 'the people's welfare' demanded. It could mean the theory of 'a socially conscious private sector, accelerating the development process'.[56] It could lead to the denial of demands for equality of opportunity in education (within the context of the mass illiteracy as we have examined) in favour of 'flexibility in the educational pattern',[57] and on the grounds that 'the government does not stand for regimentation'.[58]* It alternatively reminded the CPI of that potentiality for economic and social progress supposedly residing in the Congress Party's philosophy and practice; and others of the Kuomintang, which 'rested in the countryside on the landed gentry', but

---

*This was said after the declaration of the June 1975 emergency, the imposition of censorship, the dispatch to jail of thousands of opponents, and the other features of the pragmatic response to crisis, still to be considered.

nonetheless 'wrote into its law books some of the most progressive legislation ever conceived to alleviate peasant hardship'. But the legislation was 'never applied; it was window-dressing'.[59]

But we can also hear the familiar voices of more realistic forms of utilitarianism. In self-defence against 'the disturbing dimensions of the problem of landless labour',[60] there was argument that 'a section ... should be provided with work so that their frustrations are not taken advantage of by anti-social elements'.[61] Otherwise, 'if a person has a very large property and he is surrounded by poor people who have nothing, and if you are not able to redress this situation, then what happens is what happened in Bengal, where there was a marxist government'.[62]

When this theory-and-practice moves into closer preoccupation, or (worse) actual encounter with the people, ambivalence becomes more acute. It can, as ever, be resolved by recourse to intimidation, bribery, or violence. As ideological presentation, it was equally often expressed in the reflexes of Congress 'socialism' but with its rhetoric become more insistent, or elevated by crisis to closer identification with the working classes. Thus the Labour Minister, 'whose knowledge and understanding of the working class and their problems is as deep as his scholarship in marxism',[63] could speak to a theory of labour whose terms and accents are still recognizable. That is, 'the labourer labours not only for himself but also for his country. The glory of toil lies precisely in the fact that toil produces wealth for society, and for posterity.'[64] And still within the terms, however cynically employed, of a familiar language of political economy, ' "self-centric economism" is a malaise, harms the nation economically and impoverishes the social consciousness of the working classes'.*[65] This 'socialist' mode of address,

---

*This could be translated in two ways; prosaically, to mean that demands for wage-increases above, and not below, the level of subsistence were disallowed. Or, as follows, by a south Indian poet:

> '. . . The audience started to leave.
> The accursed gang, sensing this,
> Shouted "Socialism!"
> Postered the walls, "Socialism!" . . . "Socialism!"
> All over the land, the slogans rebounded.
> But amidst the infernal din,
> The looting of the people went on . . .'

expressing the dependency of class-power, has always been reserved for occasions of appeal to the working class, at May Day rallies, after strikes or industrial disasters. It was also an element in that hegemonic consensus which required the incorporation on its own terms of the radical working-class tradition of India.

But there have been more noticeable ingredients vital to a fuller understanding of Congress 'socialism', its concepts of democracy, freedom and social justice, and its practice. They have included what the former Chief Economic Adviser to the government of India called 'making great play of solicitude for the poor'.[66] Going deeper into the party's special terminology of reference to the Indian people, we reach the habitual description of 'the poorer and weaker sections', whose 'lot' – almost always the term used – was constantly either being attended to, or was improving. In the realm of ideology, however, to diagnose it as incantation is superficial. So, too, is the over-ready ascription to it of non-meaning, even if it was significantly disjoined from reality, inhabited its own self-generating realm of illusion, and inhibited perception of real condition. Alternatively, the people might be perceived as 'the masses', rarely as the 'proletariat', and at the highest gatherings of Congress politicians, as the 'dumb millions' of India.

Here was contained decisive meaning and ramification, with its own political resonance. It needs to be considered in the light and shadow of the previous chapter's expressions of grief, anger and self-knowledge by the 'dumb' victims of India's ruling powers. 'The Congress Party will sacrifice every interest for the sake of the interests of the dumb millions';[67] they were at once 'the sinews of strength of our Congress',[68] but also a 'colossal man-mass'.[69] 'Abolishing poverty is no mere platitude; it reflects our concern and commitment to the dumb millions'.[70] They were, thus, not only the 'poorer and weaker sections' of the solicitude of power, but also part of 'a vast reservoir of human and material resources for national reconstruction'.[71] Slowly unravelling and drawing out the ideological thread which began with ideal aspiration and passes, coloured by rhetoric and illusion, through 'pragmatism' into a dense knot of dependent and interwoven violence, lying and corruption, the suffering Indian people were thus seen as weak, dumb and defenceless, and therefore in need of the protection of the Congress Party. They were also seen as an indistinct and conjoined part of 'our production machinery both in men and industrial capacity, which must be utilized to the fullest extent possible'.[72]

It is not my purpose at this point to determine whether this is the vocabulary of 'state capitalism', 'socialism' or 'fascism'; that must await later discussion. It serves only as extraction from the many components of the presented ideological structure. We must leave for further inquiry the question of whether it was the expression of the resignations of poverty and misery ('difficulties are a part of life'),[73] and the arduous administration of impoverishment in order to meet the needs of the 'poorest and weakest sections'. What it helps to do at once, however, is to establish preliminary familiarity with convoluted but coherent processes of mind. Thus 'the revolution', in the words of the president of the Congress Party's trade union movement (INTUC) could be brought about 'only by the proletariat and not by the upper strata of society'.[74] In the next sentence – and now more assimilable to the understanding – was invoked that 'history of the Congress Party ... of looking after the interests of the dumb masses, since the days of Mahatma Gandhi'.[75] Thus, the yawning chasm between the 'proletariat' and the 'dumb masses' was bridged by a Congress trade union leader with a speed and dexterity a Brunel would have envied.

Implicit in the rhetoric was and is both the latency of violence, and the strategy of pacification. Close at hand are concepts of the 'adoption of rural areas'[76] by state and private agency, and the 'rural uplift' of the 'simple-minded', who 'could do with a little bit of education'.*[77] Even closer to the realities of educational policy in practice, they would then, according to the Minister of Education, 'become more interested in developing their personalities',[79] or 'benefit from the injection of some rational thinking and take new techniques more sportingly'.[80] This is a paternalism which, with whatever adjectival addition – 'benevolent', 'self-interested', 'idealist', 'socialist', and so on –

---

*cf. 'But the fact that Mrs Gandhi won in in 1971 shows that the rural people are also basically intelligent and hard-headed persons'.[78]

expresses in its very terms of perception the actual power of landlordism. The language itself defines the limits (here as 'policy for rural areas') of that fixed arc or pendulum movement between concern and violence, unable to escape the political economy's confinements. It was and is capable only of swinging within its metronome range, sometimes more quickly, sometimes more slowly.

Simply following this single example and etching in further detail, the picture becomes clearer. 'Industry is keen on rural uplift',[81] or 'wishes to get the feel of the problem of rural uplift';[82] 'youth participation is vital in the work of the uplift of the rural masses'.[83] 'I have a soft spot in my heart for the village people';[84] and, in general, 'wherever people are in distress it is my duty to go to them and offer solace. It makes the people happy and also gives me the satisfaction of sharing in their distress',[85] and so on.*

In the 'dumb masses' and the repetitious usage of 'the poorer and weaker sections', resided the distancing by class-power of the 600 millions. In the consolations of paternalism ('I would like to express on behalf of Congress my particular gratitude to the working classes'),[87] resided a complex of responses. They included palliation of the people's anger, and fear by ruling power of that greater power latent in the people. But there was something different also. I would define it as a jealous populism, which helps to explain the violence of the régime's response to that rival populism, dubbed 'conspiracy', of the movement of opposition led by J. P. Narayan.

Nor was this the politics of open-ended utilitarian improvisation. The terms 'non-doctrinaire' and 'pragmatic' all have quite specific meanings in theory, as well as in practice. This was not the politics of a scope for reform limited by the compulsions of poverty, or the inadequacies of administration. It was not a gentle or crusading idealism, defeated upon the stony ground of the

---

*cf. 'On behalf of poor people like me, I have a request to the leaders of the country. If they want to help us, let them do so quietly. I am poor, but I do not like to be pitied. For the sake of some minor material comforts and benefits, I do not want to be told to do what I do not like. I do not want to benefit at the cost of my soul'; another of the voices of India.[86]

facts of India. For it contained specific claims to forms of political exclusivity and monopoly, coupled with determinate notions of democracy. With all the other already mentioned limitations on political manoeuvre and the continuous recourse to violence, they severely circumscribed the ruling party's range of practice.

First, the ambivalent and dangerous possibilities of drawing analogies – historical, geographical, economic, sociological – between this Indian 'revolution' without a revolution, this 'socialism' without redistribution, between this democracy of the dumb masses and the only larger mass agrarian economy in the world, that of China, arouses a complex but specific reaction. In the Indian ruling class, it is a compound of consuming interest, resentment ('Isn't everybody dying to go to China?'),[88] fear, denial and emulation. Thus, 'the Chinese kind of revolution has only brought misery to the common man, and was not the type of revolution Gandhiji contemplated for a peaceful transformation of society'.[89] Or, 'China's economic growth and progress has not been more spectacular than India's, although it is true that class disparities are less visible in China'.[90] Or – said to me by Professor Rashid ud-din Khan after the wave of mass arrests which included both his parliamentary and academic colleagues – 'China is *dirigiste*. We are getting there more slowly, but by the democratic method.'[91]

The complex of such responses was many-layered. It included the attribution to J. P. Narayan and George Fernandes (the railway union and socialist leader) of the *ex post facto* crimes of 'speaking approvingly' of Mao Tse-tung; of 'expressing great respect for him',[92] and 'writing to him',[93] respectively. It included an implicit debate with China, usually avoided directly, which expressed itself obliquely. Thus, 'we cannot afford large-scale farming ... our conditions compel us to provide title to land to more people, to enable them to feel real partners in production ... these social realities cannot be sacrificed at the altar of any economic theory'.*[94] It moved un-

---

*cf. 'Let us stop kidding ourselves ... the fact is that China has achieved both a very much higher rate of growth, and, at the same time, eradicated poverty. The explanation of what China has done, and we have not, is not to

easily from absorptions and representations of the forms of Chinese political vocabulary on street hoardings and in the terminology of 'new economic programmes', to the reservation for the Chinese example of expressions of fear – logical, given the nature of Indian rural insurrections – and hatred. Mao Tse-tung was thus described prominently in the Indian press as 'gape-mouthed', receiving 'senile oaths of fealty', while China itself was facing a 'devil's array of problems',[96] including a 'less spectacular' growth and progress than that of India.

Nonetheless, the notion of the Congress Party as a 'mass-party' with a 'mass-base' – despite having obtained in the past only a minority of the votes cast by the electorate in national elections, and despite its internal factions and divisions – was a large component of its self-image and the form of its presentation to the people as a political monolith. And by this route we can begin to discern further meanings in the political theory of India's ruling classes. It carries us further into the problematic of the 'call for a non-violent revolution in rural India'.[97] It gives significance to the populist '*pada-yatras*', or walkabouts by political leaders – including the former President and Prime Minister – to 'give India's villages a healthier look',[98] 'to make the people part of larger national endeavours',[99] or 'to meet the people face-to-face on a level of physical equality, as had done India's old saints and preachers'.[100]

The issue of the 'national' coalition party of particular class and interest which, in alliance with the working class and its separate organizations, leads a people to at least a nominal political independence, and on this basis lays subsequent claim to monopoly and consensus both as party and movement, is a large one. In its import, it takes us far beyond both the village circuit of a '*pada-yatra*' and the boundaries of the Indian state. But without it, the Indian debate – which the ruling party primarily conducted with itself – about 'democracy' and 'freedom', the 'interests of the nation', 'conspiracy' and 'opposition', lacks a crucial dimension.

---

be sought in economic theory (whether stood on its feet, or its head), but in the political systems of the two countries . . . Clearly what is called for is a change of political systems, not new political slogans, or new economic messiahs.'[95]

As a monopoly, the Congress Party was seen from within as 'the only true representative organization of the people'.[101] During the emergency it was 'an all-India party representing no one sectional interest',[102] in pursuit not only of 'a long cherished ideal of social justice',[103] and engaged in 'an increasing quest for a dynamic and just society',[104] but also 'fostering a political culture in the people'.[105] It was synonymous not only with the government of India, but 'everywhere, in every village, every *taluk*, every division, everywhere in the country',[106] and 'directing state policy towards securing social, economic and political justice to all citizens as enjoined by the directive principles enshrined in the Constitution'.[107] Moreover, it was 'more than a mere organization';[108] 'not a political party in the sense in which a party is commonly understood, but completely identified with the people'.[109] In the words of the party's president, D. K. Barooah (the same reportedly described by J. P. Narayan as a 'court jester'), the Congress Party had 'evolved in its ninety years' not merely into 'an instrument for social and economic change', which might be a tolerable proposition if it had taken place, but was retrospectively synonymous with India's history. Thus, 'the history of India of the last ninety years' was 'the history of the Congress'. Prospectively, also, 'the destiny of India' was 'inextricably intertwined with the destiny of Congress';[110] in other words, past, present and future, state, government, constitution, political culture and people were all compressed into the service of factional party interest.

That the making of such a politics demands not only violence in action (both against the facts and the people) but also corrupt servility and readily available sycophany in its elaboration, will become obvious on closer examination. Distasteful though its excesses were, they are not dismissible. Their role is equally decisive in the construction of a political theory as in its enactment in practice. Nor was it a superficial phenomenon; its extravagances and inversions of reality are as contagious and organic as any of India's epidemic disorders, and demand treatment because of the political corollaries and side effects which follow.

So, 'if the Congress' – structurally riven as it was by dynastic succession and division – 'disintegrates, India will also disintegrate'.[111] 'If Congress is destroyed, India gets destroyed';[112] even 'if the influence of Congress is weakened, India is weakened'.[113] Thus India was Congress, though 'India' gave it, even with the assistance of ballot rigging, only 43·5 per cent of the votes cast in the 1971 general election and 40·9 per cent in the 1967 election before it. And therefore – with 'India and Indira' even made synonymous in a further exquisite contraction[114] – *ipso facto*, opposition to Congress was 'opposition to Indira'.[115]

Until this became the basis for mass arrest – or even torture – of opponents, or the extremer forms of political paranoia in which the politics of delusion joined the politics of illusion, it could be contained. It could be held, at worst, within an understanding of the vocabulary of sycophancy and parody, or, at best, as the common but debased rhetoric of power. But the problem of this particular politics extends much further. For the heavy burden of a corrupted body politic thus came to rest on the shoulders of a people already weighed down under a freight of unmoving misery, want and debt, in their magnitude beyond all parallel. Of course, that an equivalence should be established between pluralism and chaos is no more than an orthodox Hobbesian position. In India, it was perceived as the equation we have already seen between 'instability of government' and the 'distribution' of political power among the opponents of Congress. That the state of a single party should claim a monopoly of wisdom and right was also unexceptional, and given evidences of socio-economic progress and reconstruction would have been both just and necessary. But the establishment of an ideology and practice of 'the one-party state' within a multi-party system, and in the name of a plural liberal democracy, took it some way beyond the bounds of the familiar; arguably, it was a species of intellectual as well as political corruption, which has its own context, and to which I will come shortly.

Such theses therefore about the nature of the Congress Party proposed, and provided, a wilderness for the claims of the opponent, before prison van and paranoia entered the lists to claim their victims. First, and most obvious, because if 'only the Congress can be in charge of India'[116] then the opposition could be ideologically perceived as having nothing to say.* It was 'wholly negative',[118] or 'recalcitrant'.[119] It used 'obstructionist tactics [which were] an impediment to smooth functioning, and [did] not fit into a democratic system governed by the constitution';[120] 'reform was never possible before because we were busy, always busy, fighting the opposition'.[121] Thus, the opposition was not merely 'without a better policy or programme'[122] – the normal language of inter-party contention – but with 'no support from the people'[123] and 'unconcerned with any of the major problems of India'.[124] It was not merely 'divisive and disruptive',[125] but 'trying to break the morale of the people',[126] and 'engineering strikes and generating violence'.[127] And then, one reaches a theoretical nadir in which opposition was perceived to be undermining not a unitary system (in which the argument would be at least theoretically plausible) but 'the democratic system which our people have chosen', and 'which we intend to make a success of by dealing with those forces seeking to undermine it'.[128]

I spend time and space on this, not because of the ease with which the nature of the arguments themselves (and their poverty) can be brought to light, but for two main reasons. First, because the otherwise continuously widening disjunction between social theory and practice was abruptly closed at this point, and within this ideological construct, as the prison doors were closed and bolted in its name on the ranks of the opposition. Second, because compacted by force within this structure of ideas was another notion, to recur in our discussion of its theory of 'democracy' and 'freedom'. It was that the ruling fraction of the Congress Party was not merely the concentration of past and present, distillation both of destiny and history, embodiment of state, government and constitution, and so on, but that, despite the unmitigable nature of the facts, it was the 'protector of the common man from the rapacity of the rich and powerful'.[129] It was therefore not merely opposed in general, but 'opposed by certain vested interests trying to resist social and economic changes'[130]

*Or, in full, as the Prime Minister put it in the wake of both her mid-term electoral defeat and the declaration of emergency, 'no country in the world keeps on electing the same party. Why does it happen here in India? Because the opposition never has anything positive to say.'[117]

(announced to a 'mammoth public meeting' at Rudrapur in Uttar Pradesh) 'who fear attack on their privilege',[131] or were being 'panicked by radical measures'.[132] And this being so, the ruling faction demanded, and had a right to expect, a 'strong and stable centre',[133] a euphemism for the completion of what I designedly called earlier the 'geometries of illusion and violence'.

Now, what the observer is driven to grasp is the instrumental importance to such a theory and practice, of a system of corroborating flatteries and deference. (This was described to me by Mrs Gandhi, as 'perhaps a form of oriental excess, to which I pay no attention'.)[134] It was watchful and calculating because it was based on the insecurities of faction, and made not more secure, but less, by the use of violence and corruption. It was made even more watchful by the related promptings of what should perhaps not be termed 'paranoia' – though I have used, and will use, the word myself – because it was in fact derived from the ideological perception of the nature of opposition *per se*, which we have already encountered. Moreover, it was intricately woven as thread or filament into the spun web and texture, near to defeating analysis, of alternative strands and extremes of cynicism and candour, subtlety and blatancy, blandness and corruption, delicate shadow-play and grim earnest, admision and denial, perception and intellectual frailty, meaning and unmeaning, truth and lying. Thus the (classically employed) phantoms of the ruling Indian political mind, which we will soon consider as they mobilized a sense of menace or danger to the nation, must not be separated from the manoeuvres of intriguing factions, the context of criminality and violence, the betrayal of the truth for the prizes of patronage, the advocacy of law and order by the corrupt, and the worse degenerations which were to come, across the whole spectrum of the political system.

First, let us take the question and role of deference and servility, a complex compound of those connected factors abovementioned, and which I employ here as a necessary, though not inexact shorthand. We can start, for explanation, upon a 'socioeconomic' ground, at the very base of the hierarchical class and caste structure of servilities and service, and which would thus begin to speak in the language of 'widespread disguised unemployment in the tertiary sector'.[135] It would go on to see, as I saw, in the ante-chamber to the Rashtrapati Bhavan, the official residence of the Prime Minister, and in the cluster of function-aries and attendants gathered there, merely the apex of yet another pyramidal edifice. This one begins deep down among the impoverished one million or more 'civil service, class four' bearers, *chaprasis* and peons, the 'functionally redundant' in the vocabulary of studies of the social structure of India.[136]

Alternatively, we can look to that mordant (but conventional) political description which placed 'around the seat of power, within the palace circle ... unprincipled sycophants, rank oppor-tunists and time-servers who [vied] with each other to pronounce their loyalties'.[137]* Or, preferably we can avoid detaching it as a grotesque phenomenon from the context which holds it, and of which it is merely one expression.

Its expression, in fact, was raucous, equally from rival and opponent, as from associate of 'left', right' or 'centre'; from 'in-tellectual' as from hireling, from journalist as from retainer. It required no magnification of volume to become audible. The Prime Minister, for instance, came to be variously possessed of 'superhuman, transcendental strengths and courage'[139] and a 'highly evolved renaissance mind' of 'vast dimensions'.[140] She was both 'the people's Prime Minister'[141] and 'possessed of a dormant serpent-power coiled in sleep at the base of her spine', which was 'carrying her into a higher dimension of conscious-ness, blossoming into genius, whereby the knower transcends the known'.[142] In the religious mode, she was seen as 'Maheshakti, the goddess of strength';[143] or in the secular (befitting its author, a CPI parliamentary spokesman), as 'the greatest lady which this country has ever produced',[144] 'to whom the gods have entrusted the destiny of India'.[145] She was 'a true democrat',[146] 'tough, pragmatic and respectful of democratic values',[147] 'frail'[148] or 'strong and imaginative',[149] 'dynamic'[150] and 'beloved',[151] and 'thanked for the good she has done India'.[152]

* 'It would be pertinent,' added Krishan Kant, 'to recall the advice given by Napoleon. He said "the people to fear are not those who disagree with you, but those who disagree with you and are too cowardly to let you know." '[138]

She was 'filled with valour in fighting the overwhelming odds that confronted her'.[153] She was supremely confident';[154] 'a less confident leader might have fallen to the lethal implications of the Allahabad High Court judgement, and deserted the command post of the country'.[155] She had 'made democracy stable and viable in this country'.[156] She was 'praised repeatedly for her leadership, maturity and foresight', by Jagjivan Ram, earlier the choice of the pre-emergency faction seeking to oust her,[157] and a long-standing aspirant to the throne of faction leader of India. When she spoke, audiences 'marvelled at her style and eloquence as well as her thought's dimensions';[158] when she holidayed in Himachal Pradesh, the whole Cabinet of the state government expressed its 'deep gratitude' to the Prime Minister for 'having chosen Simla for her four-day vacation'.[159]

Her 'deeds' – and their consequences for India – would be 'inscribed in the history books of the future in letters of stone, not of gold, because these don't last'.[160] More obliquely, in the words of Vinoba Bhave, 'India has always respected and worshipped women, and had women saints since the days of the *Vedas*'.[161] More blatantly, 'according to Indian philosophy' (as reinterpreted by the editor of *Blitz*), 'the gods rest within us; it is for us to incarnate them. Can Indira Gandhi have incarnated at least some of them? I see no other explanation.'[162]

There were, of course, other explanations.* But a response to such an extravagant entourage of description must be careful. It must be as cautious and guarded as were the attitudes of which this flattery was itself, often, the expression. It must also be careful not to confine or reduce these sentiments either to the normal exchange of political courtesy, or to a supposedly elaborate ritual obeisance, lacking credence and devoid of meaning; though both were certainly part of the truth. It is necessary to avoid the sometimes spurious outrage of the affronted ('if she

---

*And cf. 'nobody takes this seriously, no one believes it, because it is insulting to our intelligence';[163] 'a lot of people around here believe Indira Gandhi is really a sort of goddess';[164] and the not uncharacteristic combination in the same individual of elaborate praise, followed by 'you have only got to look at this country to know that mental competence and political leadership do not have to be connected'.[165]

must have followers, let them be men, not minions'),[166] because the outrage was often too knowing, itself cynically implicated, or the product of factional exclusion. A dismissive or ironic ridicule will not do either, particularly when set against, say, 'I do not want followers, I want people who will march firmly in step'.[167] For this was part of a complex – if unstable – political interchange. It was the expression not merely of the Machiavellian obviousness of patronage and power, but part of a precarious structure of interdependent and contradictory falsehood. Moreover, it was linked to a whole world of political and intellectual corruption; the servile rhetoric could only point to it, though it pointed in the right direction.

The extravagance of 'flying squads', or 'swinging into action', of 'new eras' (as of 'thrusts' and 'inputs'), and of 'launching programmes for mobilizing the masses' was likewise a world of words, but also of meanings. They too could be located upon a rising scale, from triviality and wishful thinking to the grossest mutilation of truth, which were the ideological correlatives of rising levels of Indian violence to mind and body. There was, and is, a compass range from pole to pole, which includes the flattery of power, luxuriant excess, and the spurious vocabulary of restraint's 'self discipline' and 'stern' self-control. It admits to the same bed (or, to vary the metaphor, lying in the same mouth) not only religious obscurantism and the oracular wisdom of priest, guru and prophet,* but also the furthest reaches of modern managerial jargon. Within this frame of reference, 'the development of mini-polytechnics for girls in small urban centres',[168] or 'the provision of infra-structural agricultural facilities',[169] could be intertwined with invocation to 'the miraculous changes wrought by the emergency in the life of the nation'.[170]

---

*For instance, what was called the 'cryptic message' ('100 + 100 + 100') of the elderly 'sage', Vinoba Bhave, dispatched to the 49th annual session of the (this-worldly) Federation of Indian Chambers of Commerce and Industry. It was not only held to mean, by Shriman Narayan the 'noted Gandhian', that 'there should be 100 per cent private sector, 100 per cent public sector, and that both should be equal to 100 per cent only' – a new mathematics of the mixed economy – but it was also described as 'a feature of the FICCI inaugural session', and, together with its exegesis and clarification, was covered by the *Economic Times*, 2 May 1976.

Likewise, 'the provision of community irrigation resources', or 'the diversification of economic activities in rural areas',[171] might be found together as forms of ideology, excess and illusion, with the celebration of 'the magic of the stabilization of prices'.[172] Nor were they variant forms of absurdity;* instead they are to be placed in the scales of corruption. 'An accelerated programming of inputs for the handicapped'[174] – without such a programme existing – was one with the 'magic effect of the emergency on the performance of the railways';[175] 'the relentless reorientation of individual and national reconstruction',[176] with the 'miracle of evil forces spreading so fast and stemmed so suddenly'.[177] Together they also pointed into the penumbra of the deeper shadows we are approaching.

In the political culture of any insecure power coexist in labyrinthine connections all manner of relations. There are also universal forms of political practice resorted to in the exigencies of the moment. When India's ruling party identified itself, especially at times of crisis, with heterogeneous factions and obscurantist organizations, whether secular, political or religious, these might be construed as no more than the tactical alliances – however indiscriminate – of political compulsion. If commitment to 'secularism' was and is combined with alliance with religious sectarianism, or a monopoly of any other official state virtue in theory is combined with its opposite in practice, perhaps this is the Indian expression of the universal humbug and cynicism of the politician.† And if political leaders suggested (successively)

---

*That some of it seemed risible or daft does not alter the judgement; cf. for nstance, Professor L. K. Mohapatra's 'the new economic programme made everyone sit up and look inside oneself and out into the future. The country as a whole and this state [sc. Orissa] in particular literally turned a corner, opened a new leaf and swung into single-minded action'.[173]

† 'Secularism' (with 'socialism' and 'democracy') constitutes one leg of the tripod upon which official state ideology supposedly rests.[178] Like the others, it is more apparent than real. Space does not permit an account in this text of secularism's manifestation in the disguise of omnipresent religious obscurantism. That India is proceeding towards secularism is equally part of the politics of illusion. This is a different issue from the myth of Indian 'spirituality', though the myth compounds the problem of making a correct judgement. cf. 'Secularism in this country is tomfoolery. Millions of rupees are being spent on the building of new temples';[179] and Mrs Gandhi's

an exclusive preoccupation with, or special attachment to, the interests both of the weakest and the strongest; or of first one interest group and then another; this must have been to display the astuteness of the unifier of a nation.[181]

If a ruling power enters into covert alliance with publicly proscribed enemies of the state, and couples this easily with detention of critical members of its own ruling faction – who have merely made tactical errors of judgement, while sharing a commitment to its theory or practice, or both – this also may not be exceptional.[182] If there is a connection between excess of rhetoric and excess of violence, and between both and the consolidation of an ideology grounded in illusion, there have been other historical examples of it, if you look for them. And if in return for the support of silence, equivocation or approval, there was to be offered immunity from imprisonment and from other forms of torment, it would not have been unique to India.

But deepening political insecurity played other tricks with India's people. Illusion can cast longer ideological shadows than those we have so far examined. We have already caught a glimpse of what lurked there, in 'the deep and widespread conspiracy' already referred to. Here resided also 'dark and threatening forces',[183] 'threats both visible and invisible',[184] 'internal and external intrigues'[185] ('people and countries are after us'),[186] and 'evils weakening the nation'.[187] Here was the habitation of Barooah's 'combination of dark and sinister forces representing pseudo-socialism [sic] and right-reaction',[188] and also the External Affairs Minister's 'dark forces needing to be smashed for obstructing our efforts for social justice'.[189] In these overcrowded quarters were not only those who had 'previously engaged themselves in dark things [and who are] still in India',[190] but hurrying out of the Noah's Ark of seeming paranoia, 'new forces creeping in to weaken society and the country',[191] 'to frighten the government',[192] 'to hinder our fight against superstition',[193] and 'rearing their heads'[194] to 'hatch their fascist designs in India'.[195] These were 'the vultures' of 'Professor' V. P. Dutt (prompted by patronage and intellectual frailty to a poetically mixed meta-

---

'I always try to visit different places of worship, because my visit to these places helps secularism to develop.'[180]

phor) 'hovering in the sky' – whether before or after laying is unclear – while 'black marketeers, landgrabbers, smugglers and racketeers' were all 'lying low for cover'.[196]

Thus were the Indian forces of light arrayed against the alien forces of darkness. The dark forces were frequently denoted 'fascist';* or, to the president of the Congress Party, they might be 'dark forces of neo-imperialism and eastern racial arrogance combining in a sinister attempt to snuff out in this part of the world the light of democracy'.[198] Or, if you prefer it, three weeks later, in the CPI's own distinctively autonomous judgement, they were the 'dark forces of neo-imperialism and reaction combining in a sinister attempt to snuff out the light of democracy in India'.[199] They multiplied in the teeming monsoon rains (even though the 'dark period' was officially proclaimed over in Varanasi on 13 March 1976),[200] into 'increasing external danger from all sides, not as earlier we thought from one direction, but from any direction, from the sea, the plains and over the mountains'.[201] This was interpreted by the president of the Congress Party as the 'increasing belligerence of Pakistan', and 'menacing moves by China';[202] by another spokesman as 'Chinese fascism surrounding India',[203] in a more explicit version of the unnamed 'eastern racial arrogance' just referred to. To the Prime Minister, the circumstance demanded 'unity and alertness',[204] to Y. B. Chavan that 'the nation be alert and wary',[205] to Barooah 'the sharpened vigilance of the people'.[206]

It is important to add that though usually expressing itself in general and unnamed terms (as 'dark' or 'evil' forces), the breeding of phantoms was always controlled by political selection, random though it may seem to have been. On the one hand, it was to mean infrequent reference to the CIA, but included on the other the machinations of Pakistan and China. It also named the 'Socialist International and others'; 'who are the people be-

---

*The term 'fascist' was ill-defined within this ideological structure. For instance, according to the Prime Minister, fascism 'over and above everything' was 'the use of campaigns of whispering'. 'The use of whispering campaigns' was 'the major weapon of the Jan Sangh and the RSS'.[197]

hind them, what are the forces backing them, and from whom are they receiving money?'[207]*

We now have several of the ideological elements generated by Congress rule simultaneously in motion. It is necessary, like the juggler, to try to avoid dropping them – whether it be socialism's 'dumb millions', or seeming paranoia's 'evil forces'; or the disjunction between illusion, the true nature of the political economy and the condition of the people. It is necessary to avoid dropping them, both because there were others in play also (like the continuing and simultaneous rhetoric of 'democracy' and 'freedom'), and because these processes of formation and transformation of ideology are of general, and not particular, importance.

Thus, to begin with, 'democracy is a value we cherish'.[213] 'We believe in the form of parliamentary democracy. We have worked it and found it suitable and successful in this country and we will continue it.'[214] (Or, 'the parliamentary system of government is unsuited to the conditions of our country, to the temperament of our people, and to our historical background').[215] To the CPI, the 'Indian road to socialism differs from others because it is being built through the democratic process'.[216] 'The peace-loving people of India will never tolerate a democracy based on violence';[217] in any case, 'the judicial system would crumble under its own weight if the good of the common man were not subserved by it'.[218] Despite its defects, 'the Congress has put 100 per cent trust in democracy, which as

---

*The reflection of the hallucinatory memory of the 1974 railway strike was another obsessional theme, with continuous reference to it in publications and speeches, particularly as being foreign-financed and inspired. For example: 'with the active and militant support of the CPI–M, George Fernandes' – 'gloating over the ruinous prospect', or 'complaining to Mao Tse-tung'[208] – 'got a free hand in carrying out his designs to effect a complete breakdown of the administrative machinery'.[209] Equally interesting for the purpose of this chapter's analysis was the entry of a recurring *metaphorical* vocabulary into the speeches and publications of the Congress Party. e.g. 'Democracy has been derailed . . . let us put it on the rails again, and give it a new direction, so that it will not get derailed again';[210] 'an atmosphere should be made so that democracy which has been derailed can be put back again';[211] or even 'we need the cooperation of newspapers in putting our system back on the rails'.[212]

everybody knows is a fertile ground for violent and evil-minded forces',[219] which characteristically conflated a theory of democracy, an inversion both of pre-emergency and emergency reality, and a conspiracy theory. What was wanted, as a next step, was 'a democratic system, but one not confined to elections';[220] that it, 'not a farce to be enacted after every five years through general elections'.[221]

What was in fact wanted was both 'a chief executive irremovable and free to govern through a Cabinet of experts',[222] and a democracy in which 'the voice of the peasantry and workers will be heard in its programmes',[223] their dumbness notwithstanding. 'Not elections, nor the press, but the voice of the people is democracy's fundamental basis'.[224] This would be, moreover, 'a democracy which gives the people power, power to govern themselves with social and economic justice ... a meaning kept away from the people, by the forces which had designs to scuttle the democratic process',[225] arguably a doublespeak become quadruple.

And if there was a 'confusion in our minds', despite such definition – and at a superficial level there was, but as ideological illusion and manipulation, none whatever – it was 'because the words democracy and truth have been twisted and misrepresented'.[226] In final clarification, the ruling class-coalition declared that 'any system we have must be democratic';[227] more, 'a democracy for the entire Indian people'.[228] 'Only a democratic system could work in India because of the high sort of individualtistic tendencies of the people',[229] but 'freedom of the individual will not be allowed to come in the way of the freedom of the masses';[230] while 'those who say democracy is not suitable to India, know neither democracy nor India'.[231] But it was to be a democracy which was not more important than the nation.[232] That is – and here we take leave of illusion – it was to be a democracy for the millions consisting of shared inequality, suffering and violence, presided over by landlordism and industrial power, and with continuous dynastic rule at its apex. And it was this democracy which would be 'defended at all costs from subversion',*[233] and 'disruptive forces ruthlessly put down'[235]

---

*Less 'sophisticated', but clearer as to the meaning of the particular theory of democracy under discussion, was the view that 'the Indians are not fit for

by means which much of the rest of this book will follow.

We have already seen that the combination of claims to a one-party monopoly of right, and the less rational exclusivities prompted by notions of conspiracy, must pronounce an anathema – of differing degrees of intensity – against the parties of opposition. That it makes a nonsense of the theory and practice of plural democracy is obvious; while the fact that it created a quagmire of suspicion and compensating compromise infected both parties and individuals, and led in turn to yet deeper political illusion.

The Congress Chief Minister of West Bengal, Siddhartha Shankar Ray – whom we have already obliquely encountered in the reports of violence and torture against political opponents in that state – at the 75th plenary session of the Congress Party not only asserted that 'democracy is our way of life',[236] but proclaimed the equivalence of the Congress Party and India, and the consequent impossibility of any other party 'taking charge of the whole of India'. He then hierarchically categorized the inadequacies of the 'many other political parties of various hues which have been formed in India'.* In particular, he singled out the CPI for 'a low leadership rating'.[238]

From other figures in the ruling faction, emergency blows of denunciation and dismissal ('scathing attacks') fell on the backs of right, left and centre. Their nature and methods, according to the Prime Minister, were various. The Jan Sangh and the 'naxalites', on right and left respectively, sought 'to impose the view of a small number on the majority, through intimidation and terror'.[239] As to the DMK of Tamil Nadu, their 'interest in strengthening the nation' was 'suspect'[240] and 'their faith in democratic methods and non-violence' was 'less than total'.[241] The Socialist Party had 'always tended towards methods of sabotage and underground bravado, abusive language and character-

---

democracy. Some threat must be there. There must be always something heavy on their heads. That is the solution.'[234]

* 'You can have Jan Sangh in charge in a pocket of India or two, the CPI–M in a *taluka* or two, and the CPI in a sub-division or two.'[237]

assassination, dragging public life to a low level'.[242] Indeed, levels of both verbal and physical violence and aggression rose sharply when the target under attack was militant workers' and opposition socialist organizations. This was true whether they were marxist – 'everybody knows the sort of governments that marxists have had. It is known all over the world'[243] – or, non-marxist, as in the case of the Socialist Party just quoted.

I do not question these political judgements here, *per se*. Rather, it is their implication which is of a different order of significance. Moreover, they attracted attention with their euphemism and deception, particularly when they came in the wake of mass arrest and detention. Thus, 'I may tell you what kind of democracy I believe in. It is that the ruling party allows the opposition freedom of expression and freedom of organization ... but also expects the opposition not to come in the way of national programmes.'[244] More important still, they took the CPI in particular – arguably already corrupted ideologically – into the realms of congruent fantasies and equivocations. Driven by various practical and tactical political exigencies, they included the need to corroborate and even outbid the ruling illusions. Only the carrying forward of the full context of the Indian political economy permits access to the ideological meaning of the CPI's dilemma. Its significance is then seen as not at all confined to India, though it presents itself in an excruciating form there.

The task of the 'right-wing' CPI – until delivering itself of its left in the birth of the CPI–M in 1964[245] – was made complex because of the historical claims laid to a socialist aspiration and programme by the pre- and post-independence Congress Party, as we have seen. It narrowed both the practical and ideological ground upon which any Indian communist movement could stand. The CPI in part overcame this in the bitter struggles of revolt and rebellion in the 1950s and early 1960s, but became increasingly implicated in the forms, structures and ideologies of ruling power. This was expressed after the split of 1964 not only in the CPI's alliances with the Congress Party in state government, but also in conjoint (and documented) terrorization of opponents to the left of its coalition.* Moreover, the CPI shared the belligerent national chauvinism of India's foreign relations with Pakistan or China; and, as Neville Maxwell has shown, it gave 'unconditional support for the war effort against China', calling for 'monolithic support for Nehru'.[247] It is expressed above all in its complex relations with the Congress Party's factions and subfactions, grounded, as I have said, in its belief in the ultimately progressive nature of Congress 'socialism'.

But to have been subject, even as ally, to the Congress Party's undisguised recoil from the CPI's long-dissolved communist practice, was a circumstance multiply revealing. It of course speaks much to the nature of the Congress Party's own brand of socialism. The 'alliance' itself becomes visible, through metaphor, as an exhausted marriage to a hostile, fleeing, or even long-divorced partner, or as a shotgun remarriage propelled by the secular demands of Soviet foreign policy. More to our present point was the cohabitation of both Congress and CPI in the one world they undoubtedly shared between them: the void of ideological illusion.

Here, for the CPI too, 'right-reactionary and fascist forces' were 'at work, spinning the web of conspiracy from underground' and 'in collusion with their agents'.[248] 'The fate of the nation, its freedom, its democracy and its future' were 'hanging in the balance'[249] (until brought by force into equilibrium). It was armed with an hyperbole containing a just perceptible ideological variation from that of the Congress Party, in which 'our work and struggle in this period of stormy crisis' would 'determine for decades to come the destiny of our country'.[250] Circumstances demanded a 'spirit of unity and urgency to inflict a decisive defeat on the forces of fascism and counter-revolution'[251] – equally unidentified – and to 'write a new golden page in the long and splendid history of India'.[252]

This political language was capable of a further gaseous and

---

*For example, in the early 1970s, under the Kerala coalition government, despite the CPI's call for the release of 'naxalite' prisoners held without trial, 'naxalites' were allegedly tormented and tortured both in the suburban interrogation centre and the Central Jail of Trivandrum.[246]

ballooning inflation, but without being completely severed from the terms of a recognizable parody of marxist theory, though of a particularly immodest extravagance. 'History' had not merely 'placed a heavy responsibility on our shoulders'[253] – a perfectly ordinary rhetoric – but, according to Mohit Sen, one of the CPI's principal and more absurd ideologues, 'the mantle of destiny' had 'slipped over the broadening shoulders of our party'. Indeed it had 'ceased to become the object of history and become its subject ... not so much the product, as the producer of history'.[254]

It needs to be said again that if what has been at issue in this chapter was merely painful 'unmeaning', then beyond a certain threshold of it, further unmeaning of this kind is of no consequence. It would be wasteful of time and space to subject it to any – let alone serious – scrutiny. But if the issue was not 'unmeaning', but its opposite; and if these meanings can and do have consequences which are true for those who suffer them, and included not only structures of ideological deception, but also blows and sufferings experienced by the body, then to evade them here is an impossible treason.

I think there are, of course, qualitative distinctions to be made between the various components of any political 'culture'. There are layers and depths of corruption, just as there are gradations of them through which the Indian ruling class has passed (to and fro) in its use and abuse of power. They need to be marked and not submerged or subdued, so that finer distinctions do not become blurred and lost in the general welter and whirlpool of a political degeneration.

Thus, there are differences between the embezzlement of state funds and deception about the condition of the people; or between standing on one's head and swearing that black is white (or vice versa, whatever the demands of the moment) and murder, or torture. But their juxtaposition – subject to such distinctions – becomes important when they are interdependent elements in a polity, or in habitual co-existence as the ideology and practice of power.

There is then a justly established nexus between what has passed so far in review, and the lesser, worse, and worst forms of economic corruption. They too must not be dissevered from the theories of 'socialism' and democracy or the concepts of freedom, with which their relationship, however contradictory, is always latent. We can approach this subject, also, by different routes. It is a general class-corruption; it is 'bribery as a demonstrative feature of administration';[255] it is family power shared, as in the India of the Nehrus, the Bangladesh of the late Sheik Mujib or the Sri Lanka of Mrs Bandaranaike, and 'profiting from office'.[256] It can be seen pyramidally, as with other features of the Indian political structure, widely based (or widespread), and concentrated at its apex. But whichever the path, corruption cannot be extricated without distortion and sensation from the explanatory context which is chosen.

Its forms in India are various in type and scale, but help us to draw together threads in this text already present. They can be followed in the footsteps of the bribed policeman patrolling the streets of the brothel. They can be understood in the spending by landlords of that rural surplus which is produced by the labours of millions, on gold hoarding, rack renting, money-lending and conspicuous but untaxed consumption. They can be heard in the assertion that 'a big landlord in Mysore, who is a member of the legislative assembly, spent 48,000 rupees on *ghee* alone for his daughter's wedding. You can imagine from that what must have been the total.'[257]

It is in the massive and continuous evasion of land reform and 'land-ceiling' legislation, whether by transfer within families and other devices, or by violence. It is in the miseries which tell of the landlord who 'says the work is eight acres. But if it is ten acres, can we reckon? How will we know it? We know from the sun, and in our bodies, that we have worked more than eight acres. How shall we argue with him? We must either accept the word of the landlord or accept our hunger'.[258]

It is in the conduct of elections, described in pre-emergency days by Mrs Gandhi's Minister of Health as 'becoming so costly that they can be fought only with black money'.[259] It is in that 'corrupt electoral system', as Subramaniam termed it in 1973 when even dishonest truth on such subjects was less dangerous, which was 'the chief source of the instability of the political apparatus'. 'The political system' he said then, 'is becoming more corrupt, undisciplined, devoid of character and immoral'.[260]

It is in the corrupt record of the Congress Party's trade union movement, the so-called 'stooge unions', battlegrounds of patronage and violence, with their established factory fiefdoms over hiring and firing, under whose rules money has had to pass to trade union officials from the poor, for their sons' apprenticeships. 'In the early 1970s, it could cost 1,000 rupees to be an apprentice, but now it is higher because of inflation';[261] an industrial microcosm of the parent Congress.

It is in the long wretched history of police larceny and looting, during the excuse of civil disturbance, of small shops and poor shanties. 'They stuffed their pockets with my provisions,' he said, 'taking anything they wanted, cigarettes, sweets, seven rupees from my cash box, and biscuits, my glass jars broken, in their eyes the look of the Yamadudargal',[262] messengers of the god of death, the Lord Yama. It is in the hotel manager's testimony that 'they [sc. the police] always squeeze something from us'.[263] It is in the huge totals of 'black money', and in the small change of bribery and intimidation. It is reflected in the judgement of the former Chief Economic Adviser to the government of India – and he should know – that Mrs Gandhi's régime was 'exceedingly corrupt'. 'The victory over Pakistan in the 1971 war,' he has said, 'provided a blanket legitimacy to all kinds of financial skulduggery ... and baser elements usually come to the top in such an environment, which is what happened both in the Congress Party hierarchy and in the civil service.'*[264]

It is to be found in the subcontractor who employs the poor itinerant Rajasthani labourers – men, women (veils drawn across their faces in the dust's blowing, fingers feeling for the veil's edge to draw it closer) and children. From the three or four

---

*Moreover, the general understanding that the political system is corrupt emerges clearly into popular cultural forms, e.g. 'Where did he get all this money from? Rohit's poverty to prosperity drive had for long been a mystery to me . . . These days he has an imported car and a big Green Park bungalow . . . Did he complete any construction project which earned him *lakhs* [sc. hundreds of thousands] in a single contract? Did he get a lottery prize? Did he manage to secure import licences which enabled him to become rich at such a terrific speed? What magic recipe had he discovered?'[265]

rupees they earn each day 'they must give at least one rupee to him each day in return for being hired'.[266] And not only the cheating of the poorest; it is in the Calcutta Metropolitan Development Authority, described by Mitra as the 'lushest arrangement of spoils [partly contributed by the World Bank] to flow in the direction of India's eastern region since the country's independence'.[267] It is in the spending between 1973 and 1976 by D. Devraj Urs, the Chief Minister of Karnataka (where the minimum wage during this period was one rupee per day for the 'unskilled' male worker),[268] of '7,066 rupees on electricity, 18,762 on water, and on furnishing his residence over 100,000', according to an official inquiry reported by the *Times of India*.[269]

So that in both the alleged and the proven corruptions of the Gandhi family and its immediate associates, there is neither exception nor example. In the weight of allegation which attaches to numerous public figures, both the fallen and unfallen, including Mrs Gandhi and her son, ministers of the governments of West Bengal, Karnataka and Haryana, and the ousted Minister of Defence, Bansi Lal (a former Chief Minister of Haryana), there is little unusual, not even in the scale of it. They can be considered only as illustrations of the former Finance Minister's and the former Chief Economic Adviser's judgements of one of the characteristics of the Indian political system.

At this level of state corruption stand the Nagarwala, Mishra and Maruti cases, to go no further. They shed a further illumination upon the meaning during the emergency of corruption's advocacy to others of a scrupulous moral order, an advocacy which stood at the end of the same path trodden by the strolling policeman; and is thus of the greatest relevance to this chapter's context. So too was the enjoining, in accents which masked personal indiscipline and disorder, of a stoical and disciplined obedience in the impoverished millions, and in the name of 'socialism' or 'democracy', 'national interest' or whatever.

Among the questions, therefore, which the fallen leaders would have to answer, was why Rustam Sohrab Nagarwala (a former army captain and private secretary to the Prime Minister) according to his own court confession in May 1971, telephoned and obtained from the chief cashier of the State Bank of India six million rupees in cash. They would also have to answer how, or why, he died in prison in March 1972 'from a heart attack'; already clear was that large funds of 'black money' were being withdrawn to finance the ruling party. The circumstances of the subsequent deaths of other involved people, allegedly including bank officials, would also demand inquiry.[270]

The exact circumstances of, and culpability for, the murder on 2 January 1975 of the Minister of Transport, L. N. Mishra, are questions also widely discussed and considered.* Himself allegedly involved in official corruption and part-responsible for the administration of the brutal response to the 1974 railway strike, he was believed to be ready just before his death, in the then mounting struggle of faction and counter-faction, to reveal the greater corruption of others. Or, he was 'a true soldier of the struggle for freedom and a defender of the democratic values fostered by the Congress ... first martyr in the fight against the disruptive forces of Indian fascism',[274] whichever seems preferable as a temporary interpretation. Temporary it must be, in the absence of any inquiry into his death or any charges following it, and despite the persistent demands made for such an inquiry in the pre-emergency Parliament to clear up the issue. Certainly, the persistent official refusals of action consorted ill with the reiterated determination by Congress leaders that 'the hands that killed Lalit Narayanji [sc. L. N. Mishra] will not be allowed to be raised again'.[275]

The Maruti case, a 'national scandal'[276] centering on the Prime

---

*That both the Nagarwala and Mishra cases are major issues was plain from the frequency of their mention both by innuendo and direct reference in cautious but ordinary discourse, including with senior state officials. Indeed, even if I had not independently found this to be so, Mrs Gandhi within a few minutes of the beginning of my own conversation with her made it plain, raising it *à propos* of a general discussion of the campaign of denigration of her by the British and Western media, by saying ingenuously, 'I am even being accused of murder.'[271] On Mishra, she has said, 'His death was not an ordinary one. It was a calculated political assassination. It is therefore necessary to analyse it from a political angle. He fell a victim to forces opposed to our policies.'[272] Cf. 'Nagarwala's death aroused speculation in Delhi that he had been silenced'; and 'was a secret account of millions of rupees being maintained at the State Bank for the Prime Minister's use? Where did the money come from? What was it being used for?'[273]

Minister's son Sanjay Gandhi – shortly to become the exemplar of political virtue and advocate of the draconian use of state power and violence to enforce it – was debated regularly in the Indian Parliament from 1970 to 1975, until the emergency abruptly foreclosed upon this and other debates. The most persistent and all-party parliamentary critics of what was occurring in this period, and who had sought in vain through questions and emergency motions for official parliamentary or judicial inquiry – the entire opposition walking out of the Lower House of Parliament in protest on 31 March 1973 – were almost without exception or coincidence jailed in the first moments of the emergency being declared.* They included Raj Narain, who called the case 'a disgrace to democracy and socialism';[277] Jyotirmoy Basu, 'corruption and nepotism';[278] Madhu Limaye, 'naked corruption' (and 'the moment I mention Maruti, the Congress Party becomes nervous');[279] A. B. Vajpayjee, 'corruption unlimited' (and 'all the waters of the Ganges will not be able to wash it away');[280] S. N. Mishra, 'India's Watergate' and 'blackmail';[281] with other descriptions 'expunged from the parliamentary record'.[282]

It involved Cabinet discussion, admitted in Parliament[283] by the then Minister for Industrial Development, Dinesh Singh; Cabinet approval, presided over by the Prime Minister, and announced on 31 August 1970;[284] the granting of a licence (or, to be precise, a 'letter of intent') to her own son† on the basis of a paper proposal, with no tenders called for and 'no impartial study',[285] for the 'mass production of 50,000 cars per year' at a 'passenger car unit' to be constructed at Gurgaon in Haryana; whose Chief Minister at the time, Bansi Lal, was to become Minister of Defence in the Gandhi administration. It involved the scrapping of the original state plan to manufacture a small car for India in the public sector which had been announced by Subramaniam, when Minister for Steel and Heavy Industry;

---

*See appendix, p. 405, for Amnesty International's list of Indian political prisoners.

†His associate Madan Mohan Rao of Madras, given approval at the same time for a similar but separate enterprise (perhaps as cover), was not mentioned again, after the early phase of the scandal.

'he might have made the statement', said Mrs Gandhi during her own trial at Allahabad.[286]

It involved the huge capital investment (at first announced officially as '46·5 million' rupees,[287] later described as 'a 170 million project')[288] of millions of private and public funds – from the Punjab National Bank and the Central Bank of India.[289] It involved the grant of unknown sums from the public Industrial Finance Corporation; 'the largest loan for the year was given without security in a record time of one week', so it was alleged in Parliament.[290] It involved private investment by companies and other major shareholders, some of whom were later admitted by the then Minister of State for Home Affairs, R. N. Mirdha, to be 'under pending investigation for economic offences',[291] and whose income tax arrears were alleged in Parliament by parliamentarians subsequently to be imprisoned, to have been written off in return.[292] It was also alleged that as a *quid pro quo* commercial investors received new manufacturing licences and import entitlements. This was 'a type of information' declared D. P. Chattophadyaya, Minister of State for Commerce, under the pressure of parliamentary questions, 'not readily available in the licensing office'.[293]

It involved violations of company law admitted in Parliament by the Deputy Minister of Company Affairs,[294] alleged violations of the 1903 Works of Defence Act,[295] violations of import regulations and of the rules of the Reserve Bank of India.[296] All these breaches of the law were alleged, admitted and denied, while charges of corruption and malpractice were simultaneously admitted and obfuscated by many subsequently promoted ministers, while their critics were to be jailed without trial. To the defence came Subramaniam, with 'the Prime Minister has observed the highest standard of public conduct and decency in this regard';[297] and 'Sanjay Gandhi has laboured hard and caused agony to his dear mother';[298] and 'Maruti is one of the biggest things happening in the automobile industry in India.'[299] V. C. Shukla,[300] Pai,[301] Moinul Haque Choudhuri,[302] H. R. Gokhale,[303] Rhagunatha Reddy ('the allegations are totally baseless and absolutely uncalled for'),[304] Chavan[305] and Chandrajit Yadav[306] all spoke in strenuous defence of scandal.

It involved the allegedly 'improper and illegal'[307] acquisition of land in Haryana by 'unfair means and official pressure',[308] its purchase at one fifth of current market values,[309] and the displacement from it of 1,500 peasant farmers,[310] with the supposed assistance of the then Chief Minister Bansi Lal. Against him earlier corruption charges were pending, together with a chorus of parliamentary demands – signed by 120 members of the opposition – for a commission of inquiry.[311] These charges were, on the one hand, to be described by the Prime Minister at her own trial as of 'no substance';[312] while their suppression, on the other, was considered by the previous Chief Minister of Haryana, Bhagat Singh Dayal, to be 'the shielding of Bansi Lal, because the Prime Minister herself is a party to what is happening in that state, and in her son's Maruti car project'.[313]

Purchase price, design, specification, engine capacity and licensing period; the dates for the 'rolling out' of the pre-production prototype for road trials, for volume production and the volume itself; number of employees, cost of production, company assets and amount of investment; from 1970 to 1975 were announced, raised, lowered, varied, withdrawn or forgotten.* The history of its detail, its apologies, its 'setbacks', its evasions, is a labyrinth; the sums involved of colossal magnitude; entitlement to, and qualification for, such an enterprise and such funds, whether as 'consultant' or 'managing director'[315] – 'taken on for his professional competence'[316] – allegedly non-existent. Or, as Mrs Gandhi put it at the Allahabad trial, 'my son was not an engineering graduate when he applied for the letter of intent'.[317] 'It is true', said a party supporter in Parliament, 'that he has no academic qualifications; suffice to say that Karl Marx and Henry Ford had no qualifications either'.[318]

To proceed further into its recesses brings one wearily to allegedly associated 'dummy firms';[319] to the admitted involvement of other family relations;[320] and to the ultimately 'non-indigenous' nature of the enterprise, contrary to original asser-

---

*For instance, the estimated purchase price of the putative car rose, not surprisingly, from 'incredibly low' at the announcement of the project on 31 August 1970 (that is, about 6,000 rupees) to '25,000 rupees' by 1 April 1975.[314]

tion, since dependent on imported components. It brings one to its alleged covert takeover by the Birla monopoly;[321] and to 'twenty', or even 'forty' million rupees shown as 'dealership deposits'[322] for a car not yet in production. It brings one finally to the announced production by the 'managing director' of 'twenty cars per month' – 'I visit the plant whenever I am in Delhi'[323] – on 20 March 1976, at a price five times the original estimate, and against the 4,000 per month planned and invested for at a cost of unknown and vanished millions. And throughout the period is heard the accompanying language of sycophancy ('we are grateful to Mr Sanjay Gandhi for the development of Haryana'),[324] and familiar – in both senses of the word – explication. Thus, 'When my son has taken a risk I could not say "no" to him. We have got to encourage our young people';[325] 'if a young man wants to do something, the question is whether enterprising young men should be permitted to do something constructive, or whether they should be stifled';[326] and 'nothing wrong has been done. There is no corruption in Maruti. No favour should be, or has been, shown because it is concerned with the Prime Minister. We are just as anxious as anybody else to remove corruption.'[327]

Though this particular labyrinth must now be vacated here, the voices of its corrupted protagonists were not to be stifled by it; on the contrary. As political scandal merely, it is of no more than passing interest; as instrumental test case of the nature of a politics, of more importance. As harbinger of worse to come, it was a forewarning to the victims and imprisoned accusers.

But it is the self-defence of corrupted power and the forms of its Indian expression which continue to haunt and challenge all powers of analysis or description. There is the form expressed through self-pity and special pleading, alternating with aggression; through surrendering self-accusation, followed by denial and accusation of others. It is in intellectual frailty and vague amorphous contradiction, co-existing with the ferocious use of state power. It is in turns of phrase, capricious change of mind, and fluctuating emotion. Though they are (as object lessons, writ large) general paradigms of the insecure responses in crisis of class and faction power, past and present, their meaning contains an unstable resonance when kept and held in their particular place and context.

It could be found in the Prime Minister's complex of repeated personal response, repetition itself conjoined with repeated disclaimer. 'Because the propaganda concerned me personally, I bore it in silence';[328] 'what falsehood has not been uttered? What character assassination has not been done? did I say a word about it?'[329] 'I am not bothered about vulgarity and obscenity and character assassination let loose against me';[330] 'if the intrigue is personal, it does not matter, and I am not bothered about it'.[331] 'All manner of false allegations have been hurled at me. The Indian people have known me since childhood. All my life has been in the service of our people. This is not a personal matter.'[332] 'I have faced ridicules, abuses, allegations and accusation, but I do not heed them';[333] and 'what is essential is to successfully fight any slandermongering against me and the party';[334] reiteration, contradiction and a code of meaning also.

But more than contradiction was at large and more than the reiteration of 'day in and day out I receive press cuttings about the campaign against me, but I do not bother about such petty-minded people';[335] or 'the Indian press thinks it is read and noticed by political leaders, but I do not bother about them'.[336] For there was a beaten path being trodden here. It passed from 'when I myself was subjected to all sorts of insults and accusations, how many came forward to support me?'*[337] to 'I have been threatened, imprisoned, shot at and beaten';[339] from 'nobody has been able to push me around since my early childhood'[340] to 'my attitude of conciliation has led the opposition to think it was a show of weakness';[341] from 'whatever I do, I do after giving serious thought, and very calmly and coolly',[342] to 'if I think that intrigues of a personal nature can have a national consequence, then I have to take whatever action is necessary to prevent it'.[343] This was also the beaten path along which the opponent was being carried, to lose his freedom.

To this, there were different approaches. It might have been

---

*This structure of argument could be extended on behalf of others: cf. '[Krishna] Menon was not only criticized here in India, but he was even hounded out of office.'[338]

directly in personal encounter, face-to-face with an alternating simplicity and complexity of manner. It was vague or convoluted; with a labyrinthine anxiety in the withdrawn glancing, smiling and pallor, a placid silence and an eye constantly twitching; inconsequence and coyness; courtesy and graces. Or, it might have been to seek explanation idly at the lower levels of response (because shorn of context), in 'subterfuge, chicanery and provocation, to keep the ruling party in office';[344] or the journalese, equally idle, of 'the classic suspiciousness of a dictator, who ends up trusting only family and family retainers';[345] or idlest of all, 'the simple charm of an ordinary working housewife'.[346]

Alternatively, a question of manner or impression can be taken on to the higher ground of its real matter and meaning, or be set down among the fixtures and structures of suspicion, falsehood and faction. It can be pursued on the terrain of the people's experience of it, or its expression on the territory of international relations. In the latter case, much of the politics of illusion, self-pity, and aggression has often appeared in foreign policies and diplomatic actions which have duplicated as farce or violence – or both – those I have extracted from domestic Indian practice.

I can give this issue here only the briefest notice; but though it is not the subject of this book, it is a critical one because of the substantial contribution to India's deepening economic crisis of the heavy costs and burdens borne by its impoverished economy as the result of its successive military conflicts with, for example, Pakistan in 1965 and 1971. It is critical also because of the continuities and connections between the internal and external balance of forces, and the modes of action adopted to deal with them.

There is thus an asphyxiating sense of the familiar in the ambiguities and myths of Indian non-violence and non-alignment, which I have already mentioned. More to the point are the specific accounts – painstakingly analysed and recorded – of that 'yawning gap between appearance and reality in the development of the boundary dispute'[347] with China in 1962. In the description of 'the Indian position with all its false premises and opaque casuistry'[348] are terms sought in the struggle to grasp firm hold of evasion and lying; while the 'forward policy' of India on its border with China turns out to have been a suicidal euphemism for Nehru's bellicose (and instantly denied) manoeuvre.

We encounter, now accustomed to it, what would otherwise be bewildering combinations of assertion. Thus 'the seeds of Indian's foreign policy' were to be found growing by the president of the Congress Party 'in the humanist approach of Mahatma Gandhi; but more than anybody else, it was Nehru who endowed India with a world view and foreign policy ... which implies friendliness to all and malice towards none'.[349] But this growth could immediately reappear in chauvinistic mutation as 'the Pakistan conflict, which gave us self-confidence and restored the self-respect of the nation', in the Finance Minister's alternative prospect.*[350] Neither sentiment was politically exceptional, until discovered in peaceful party coexistence with a belligerent (and always denied) practice.

And interwoven in its foreign relations was and is that same warp and weft as in its domestic politics, of deference and defiance, of suspicion and aggression. It is the consequence – but only in part – of the mutilated responses and legacy of reflexes left by the experience of subjection to a colonial power. It is only part, because it presents itself, in theory and in practice, in forms that go beyond such causation. Moreover, it requires the analysis not of a glib psychopathology of power or human nature, but of the political culture of India's ruling class and the embattled political economy of India, to do it justice. Here, there appeared during the emergency those 'external forces waiting for a small mistake to pounce on India';[355] and ('in a voice surcharged with emotion') of 'evil designs out to wreck the political stability of India'.[356] Here was the world both of India-as-Chile, and the 'systematic campaign of denigration all

---

*cf. 'Then we had a nuclear explosion, and our respect in the world went sky-high [sic]', from the same speech;[351] or Arya Bhushan's 'during the short period that Lal Bahadur Shastri was at the helm of affairs, our nation gained tremendous confidence, having achieved singular success in the war with Pakistan in 1965'.[352] cf. 'One of the greatest weaknesses of this country is to run down ourselves';[353] and 'serious attempts have been made to let us down in the world community'.[354]

over Europe and America, not just in Britain';[357] and of 'the suspicion that the J. P. movement received encouragement from outside the country'.[358] It was a world which rotated on its particular Indian axis. The dark night of 'India's freedom and sovereignty ... threatened in a planned manner from all sides'[359] and of 'heavy arms build-up in neighbouring countries'[360] was succeeded by a dawn in which 'foreign countries have failed to create mischief in India and are for the moment keeping quiet',[361] or 'lying dormant';[362] until the reassuring high noon of 'global calculations come to naught, with the success of the amazing Indian experiment'.[363]

In the depths of political, economic, party, factional and personal crisis, external threats ('I have no specific illustrations in mind')*[346] alternated with or displaced internal ones from speech-to-speech, as the more serious to India's political system. The mass-politics of 'facing our enemies with an iron will'[367] changed places with 'Do not think that many nations are against India. Some governments have their own policies, but large numbers even in those countries whose papers criticize us are friendly towards India.'[368] But this was corrected in turn by 'our desire to maintain friendly relations with all countries should not be misconstrued as our weakness'.[369] Denunciation and reconciliation ('I do not think we should get unduly agitated or angry or upset')[370] followed in quick and easy succession.

Here, was the instrumentality, working at many levels, of an elaborated code of reference. There was here both a real and a utilitarian xenophobia; while offered up for the urgent relief of millions was 'nobody has helped us, or wanted to help us';[371] and the encirclement of India, with the 'evil eye cast upon us',[372] for mass-consumption.

---

*Despite the ideological perception of India-as-Chile, of India as target for 'destabilization', the CIA and the United States were conspicuous by the infrequency of their specific inclusion among India's principal enemies, by Congress Party leaders. ('She did not identify these agents of foreign governments';[365] 'she did not want to single out the US' and 'she named no special country'; and, 'it is not for me to give proof of who is doing what against us. It is for them to say what they are doing.')[366] Nor were CIA agents named, proscribed and expelled, as has happened in other countries; and see chapter 8.

The transfer of economic and political crisis thus required many elements, not confined to the attempted political crushing of the people's opposition, the assaults on the trade union and socialist movements, or the overturning of the constitution. It required many other forms of displacement, whether of political realities, of recent historical event, or of the social and economic condition of the people. Some were apparently incoherent, but all were capable of being comprehended in totality. The quickly narrowing paths of escape from a ruling power's crisis must always be widened by the use of force and violence; but indispensable also, is that other force which, with structures of illusion, seeks to arm the mind against all reason.

4 An Eye to India: First Sequence

A crocodile in red blazers, pressed grey flannels, and black well-heeled shoes, with blazing eyes and gleaming black hair, treads the pink-to-rust park paths, the soft dust stifling their scuffing footfalls. There is a bliss in this clear blue heaven and fresh day; the crows floating easy in the sky, the people squatting in silence, unmoving.

On the hard ground before you, are torpid bodies sleeping, dead to the world, undisturbed by boys' voices beneath the flowering trees, heads pillowed upon folded arms, fingers crooked or stiffly splayed, bony knees and bare spindle-shanks bent into a rigid slumber.

It is as calm and mild now as any Riviera morning.

On the park's grey-blackened domes are winged statuary, immobilized; the dark coat on the sparse grass – is it a coat, or a body lying? – stirring and turning, shifting its position. A glossy grey-and-black crow, *Corvus splendens*, with darting eye and black sheen, iridescent with purple, blue and green, hops and struts on the pink pathway before you.

A ragged woman with bare feet, her bird-thin ankles ringed, in a faded green sari, bends in the shadow of the trees, buttocks sharp as blades, and stoops to her small harvest of brushwood, gathered up into thin arms; she straightens up, as the smart boys pass in the sunlight, with their bright polished chatter and formal manner.

A statue, weary to death, stretches its wings on the tip of a cupola, like Eros poised upon a fountain, or an avenging Fury. Beside the little planted flowers, a small child sits in the thin grass, its lips, nose and eyes fly-spotted; a brown-and-cream striped squirrel, sitting up on its haunches, watches for a moment with beady eyes and tiny clasped hands.

You stand still in the warm breeze and gentle fragrance of an Indian idyll.

The poor barefoot boy watches the sleek crocodile passing in its red blazers, grey flannels, and black shoes, you and he listening to the young mannerly voices fading from the gardens; and comes to you, begging, feet padding in pink dust, face pale and with dusty unkempt hair. He stands in front of you, the palm of his hand open, softly saying, 'paise, sahib, paise', the crows cawing in the trees; 'O sahib, paise, sahib, paise'. The vultures, perched and scuffling for a new purchase, fold their wings like sunshades. They sit still as statues, on the hot and derelict domes, blackened with waiting. They are soundless, in the midday blaze; hanging fire.

*

Little Mr Kakubhai, the commercial director, with the cream bone-buttons in his linen jacket (and check handkerchief in his upper pocket) sits cushioned in wicker, on the green lawn, beside the carefully clipped hedges and says, sighing, 'For a worldly being, to set everything worldly aside is so difficult.'

Small arms crooked, with a large silver wrist-watch and heavy gold cuff-links, cocking his head (a black butterfly pulsing, opening and closing its wings on the scarlet bougainvillea), he says softly, 'We must concentrate on the concrete, to reach the meditation of the abstract. You cannot go directly to God.'

Smooth-cheeked and charming, meek-looking as a lemur, jowls pouched like a koala or a chipmunk; with crossed legs and a delicate jewelled finger to his silken ankle, a parakeet squawking, he says, 'You have to make the best efforts with whatever has been bestowed on you from birth, and leave the fruits to God. If you are honest to yourself, the fruits are bound to follow. If they don't come, there is only something wrong with the sincerity of your efforts.'

Eyes closed for a second, sipping an iced drink, seductive; his mouth in a soft upturned smiling, he says, 'Is so deep-rooted this *Karma*, it will take forty or fifty years for the poor people to lose their patience.' There is a silence; of a warm breeze, and birds chirping.

Sitting forward, the wicker creaking, there is a waft of discreet perfume. He says, jewelled finger to his lips, or hand at your sleeve lightly, 'One basic factor is preventing this, shall we say, communism. I will tell you, *Karma* theory is final solution and answer. What is *Karma*? Duty.'

Whispering, eyes contracted to black pinpoints, he says, 'Here the poor man has no envy. Why? He thinks only he should do a better *Karma*, do his duty, in this life, and the next one.' He sits back smiling, relaxing; a delicate Indian miniature. The faint breeze, sighing softly, turtle-doves cooing, stirs the heads of the flowers in the fragrant garden.

*

The incidents of daily life are a text unread in this temple. It stands above the teeming blocked street upon sleek marble, its roof a series of golden recessions to a golden pinhead; upon which an uncertain number of seraphim may be dancing.

Inside, the drums lunge, cascading voices chant, and bells ring the busying worshippers to their ministrations, heads bowed before the smiling or glowering deities; while mooching cows, holy as angels (one with its flank wounds tenderly dressed in lint and bandage), wander the temple precinct. And on the steps in the sun stand the limbless, mewling for pity's sake to the passers-by, stumps pushing at your elbow, fingerless hands searching for the alms-giver.

These steps are a high island. If you turn your back upon the temple, you can see the flowing and drifting tide of life, side-tracked by street works, grudgingly parting – like the waves of the Red Sea in another fable – for the ox-carts, wooden wheeled and grating, which drive slowly into the crowd. You can see the cross-currents cut, and broken, in slow motion; textures re-arranging in the slow sea-change; and the deep street-tide of animals and men closing in upon the dusty wake of each cart's passage; in a tramping mass movement; of shouting and crying, mouths opening and whips cracking.

From here (to the sounds of chanting and drumming) is visible the monstrance and celebration of another host: the quick-change of hands to steady a head-load, head wobbling; a trampling over heaped mounds of earth, neck muscles tensing; the heavy basket's creaking and swaying with the hip's swaying; the worn heel, cracked grey and pitted, lifting from its sandal; the shallow trays of foodstuffs and the flame; figures sitting in sunlight and in shadow.

Only the empty eye of the beggar-girl may not see it, turning herself slowly from side to side, head raised to her whimpers; or the brown goat, sleeping on the temple ledge, snout resting against a white wall, blind to the world. From this vantage-point (to the sound of bells) is to be glimpsed neither a hell nor heaven, and peopled neither by divinity nor devil. Only the woman street labourer, road digging; wincing out of the way of the dry shovelled dust's sudden blowing; her veil drawn across her mouth and nostrils to the anxious eyeline, sweating brow furrowed; the quick turning away of her head and body, her feet and toes bared by the lifting of her sari.

At the temple's waterside the poor washerwomen, legs and arms dripping with slappings and beatings; rolled and sodden cloth wrung and twisted, turned, paddled and pounded; bend to another baptism, whose meaning may be fathomed without benefit of clergy.

*

There is a dusty roar and clamour of flocking crowds on the trodden and rutted banks of the Ganges, in the wide shallows, and on the mid-river spurs and sandbanks, a stadium crowd, like bees swarming (in a dust bowl) and clustered black at the water's edge; breaking and spilling into the muddy water.

Pilgrims in Indian file pass in thousands, not running but walking, with brass pots, grey cloth-wrapped bundles, and fluttering pennants; gossamer and pastel figures standing in fine blown dust, like winged victories; panniered camel-trains in a stately striding, chins up and packs swaying; set upon the goal of the river, like lemmings.

Knotted clouts are clotted and dripping, bodies glistening, nipples dark under soaked green or saffron; rich-dyed or frayed cloth washed in holy water and drying, dark-maroon, dark-blue, scarlet, spread on the sandbanks, colours not of a heavenly, but an earthly rainbow.

Down-river, pigeons are fluttering and wheeling over the pilgrim-city, bells tinkling, moored boats and oars creaking, the sung plain-chant ebbing and flowing, floating and falling to the drum's dry punctuation; clothes slapping in lapping water; backs bending, dressing and undressing, tying and untying, folding and wrapping. Thin flesh, in loin cloths, stands drying itself, rubbed and towelling, amid stacks of shoes and piles of clothing; dugs shrivelled in cold water; hair in a lather; babies carried to the water, thin buttocks in the crook of a mother's elbow; old women, with young girls' gestures, tying up their long hair, bracelets jingling.

Standing phalluses are crowned (poverty atrophies desire) with marigold garlands; saris bend in genuflection, hands folded and eyes gleaming, before black coronae, wreathed in flowers.

The dead body, white garlanded for mourning, is borne, bouncing, on a bamboo stretcher through the narrow streets and dark crowded alleys, the clotted defiles of vegetable sellers and pavement dwellers, mendicants and pilgrims, dwarfs and lepers, holy men and beggars, sitting maimed (with blackened soles like leather). It is laid, streaked with red and bandaged tightly in its cerements and leg wrappings, beside the water, on a mound of ashes and charred kindling, blackened from a previous and still smouldering cremation; waiting.

Eyes closed, faces painted, holy men in G-strings sit, black-bearded, on platforms, under woven wicker umbrellas like meshed toadstools, cross-legged and facing sunwards (flying religious kites soaring or plummeting to the ground); eyes raised in ecstasy, and rolling; or strolling away, come down, in an ambling and easy motion; or, as if stoned, keeled over, bare legs swarming with flies, and sleeping.

River-borne jetsam (floating flowers, sewage and the ash and shank-bones of cremation) sucks at the wooden piers, standing like trestle-tables in water; water merging, fogged and grey, with the skyline; water dark and flowing, or bubbled with exhalations; or bubbles stand, unbursting, resting heavy on unmoving water.

Men and women, young and old, lie near by on their wicker cots; limp and unstirring long after the sun has risen; on trestle beds in a mass of cattle; cows cropping the vegetable droppings; bent old men, barefoot, with glasses, walking with sticks on bow legs, shanks brittle, groping in grubby-white, and white-stubbled; from life to death a stone's throw, or a bare foot's step.

A dog eats a pigeon, wry-necked, down flying; a dog decomposing, teeth bared in a death snarl, or smiling; a mongrel with a large red wound, gnawing and licking; a dog with purple paps, scrounging in white charcoal ashes, biting and crunching; a rabbinical beard (munching), hands gripping a ragbag and brass beaker. There are monkeys leaping and jumping and peeping, walking slowly on all fours, food in hand and tails stiff in air, sitting suddenly, peanut shells cracking; a cow eating a scrap of brown paper, licking the sliver into its mouth, wet snout raised, pink tongue extruded and curling; the slit grey eyes of the brindled goat (glassy as marbles), closing. 'Death', says the *Upaniṣad*, 'is but a taste of life'; but this dog's life is a taste of death, or dying.

*

With his side-to-side rolling motion in the saddle, the rickshaw (with its folded-back pram-hood) pulls and slews to left and right as he pedals into an easy riding and rollercoasting, towards the night-lanes of stalls and counters; and in amongst the carts and barrows, through festoons and billows of curling smoke of wood and charcoal; into the thick of the riddling and roasting and frying, selling and buying, shouting and crying, in the fragrance of allspice and mango, aroma of orange and urine, trodden cowpat and tobacco, paraffin, incense and tallow, and the spittings of betel, like blood-streaks. Here we are caught up among kine, in the tread and crush of flanks and legs, and hemmed in beside the neckfolds and dewlaps of the cows' turning and slow moving; and brought to a braking and creaking standstill in the press of heavily couched oxen, unbudging and bovine, horns whirling.

And then, standing in the saddle (bell tinkling at the road's thumping) he pedals on again, as if on a treadmill or climbing, thin ankle and foot rising and falling, his heavy freight sitting behind him; on worn and bulging red leather, pocked and cracked, brass-studded and banged, rag-shined and flicked with a duster before hiring and starting; past the bridal house at the quietening street corner, hung with a fairground cascade of fairy lights, paper frills and streamers. He pedals through the little litter of yellow, orange and saffron blossom of a wedding's garlands, past the guests parting (bound in silk, dimpled elbows, turbans, and ungathered wisps of hair); gripping the handlebars with fists, knuckles bony, and panting to recover from the sudden setback of a jolting pothole in the deepening darkness (frame shaken and bell tinkling). He gets off, pushing and running, and jumping on again, pedalling on fast, his shirt in tatters, past the poorer and poorest clutter of battered shutters, and signboards, and the small jars, tiny heaps and packets of the barest living.

His toes bare to the pedals, and legs no sturdier than the drumsticks of a plucked chicken, pushing down deep to left and right, he is reduced by darkness to the back of a head as smooth as sealskin, his straining neck nape, and thin shoulders. We pass the last sleepy vendors in their dens and hutches, nodding over their small change in rusting tins, or dozing over their wares to the feeble jetting and flaring of the hanging hurricane-lamps, and the little flickering nightlights: the wizened cobbler, bent over at his last; and the last stitches and pressings of the bespectacled squatting tailor, sitting to his blinding sewing at this hour; and the last café, dark as a cave, with its two long benches and a blackened table, a guttering candle and a picture of Krishna.

And O, then the pitch darkness of the squeaking wheel and creaking wood and leather, and the hard laboured breathing of the pedalling rickshaw-driver. This was a rupee's ride through the backstreets of the night-city; but the clutched coins will make a fist of every hand which receives them.

5 Swinging into Action

We have not been able to give the people the food they need, or shelter or education or many of the other things. But we have given them a new self-confidence, and I think that is a very big thing. We have given them the courage to speak out.

Indira Gandhi, to the Rajya Sabha, 22 July 1975[1]

I am a poor person and India is a desert. I do not know how to arrange the facts for you. But you can let the world know what has happened. It is your duty.[2]

S. Doraiswamy, veteran leader of the Indian Congress Party[3]

Such things did not exist, even under British rule, such atrocity and dishonour, such propaganda, and such lying. It is not for this that Congress fought the British.

The Need of the Hour is Discipline.
Silence is Golden.
Avoid Rumours and Loose Talk. Do Your Duty.

(street slogans)

The new politics of 'swinging into action'[4] was not only to extend the world of illusion, cruelty and corruption, but to enter into headlong collision with reality, as well as with the opposition. An Indian juggernaut rolled forward, from 26 June 1975, and crushed beneath its heavy wheels those who stood in its way – devotee and opponent alike, as in tradition. In this chapter I will single out for attention some aspects of the process; the interaction of institutional change and destruction. I will leave the search for any compensatory and redeeming features in the economic 'new deal', and the effects of the new social policies on the lives and conditions of the people, for subsequent chapters.

To do so, the facts' bare bones must first be patiently exhumed from the burials of lying and rewriting. It is necessary, also, to keep perception steady in the midst of political squalor. For in the motley and ugly political and economic procession which followed, a Trojan horse disgorged fully armed deceit into the political arena, or (perhaps more appropriate) caparisoned beneath a silken and unsteadily swaying canopy of lies; knotted and tasselled, an elephantine deception; and with it a trained servility, bending the knee, and sometimes beguiling to the bystander.

In unsightly and scrambling simultaneity came the politics of the armoured regiment, and the new economic programme; constitutional amendment and the loss of freedoms; the rights of the judiciary, parliament, press and trade unions suspended, curtailed or abolished; and the undoing, reversal and erasure of legal decision. Here were the invalid with a stroke of the pen declared valid and the hitherto illegal made lawful, in the interest of the nation. In the name of the defence of liberty and democracy, came their denial. Opposition was itself opposed, in time-honoured fashion, with the nocturnal visit, the unmarked limousine (the 'Ambassador') or the police wagon. These were the varied mobilizations, however insecure and uncertain – with reality adjusted by force to fit the frame of illusion – of state power, 'swinging into action'.

For what follows the reader will either have begun, or already completed, the assembly of his own structure of reference, whether this text's or some other of his own invention. But, subject to every qualification built into such a structure apart from outright denial of the truth – the method of the Ministry of Information, of Indian embassies and High Commission spokesmen – the depth and scale of the political assault must be regarded as without Indian parallel. Nevertheless, it falls familiarly within the range of understanding accessible to political analysis, or to careful description.

On 26 June 1975 came the declaration of the emergency and

the beginning of mass arrests of the opposition, from prominent political leaders and parliamentarians to the humblest rank and file members of party and trade union, and the banning of twenty-six political organizations from left to right, and back to left again.[5] On the same day there was installed an apparatus of censorship, forbidding among other things mention of the arrests; and there began the strategic presentation of a '20-point economic programme', which I will look at in the next chapter. On 27 June 1975 a drastic executive order was issued under Article 359(1) of the Constitution. With Parliament not in session, and parliamentarians in jail or being hunted; with the reported house arrest of senior army commanders and of alternative inner party leaders of the ruling faction;[6] and, while the cruelties demanded by the imposition of that special form of law and order which defends insecure power with violence accelerated throughout India, the order suspended the rights of citizens under Articles 14, 21 and 22 of the Constitution. I will return to it in a moment. In this period of maximum security, movements of armoured regiments were reported from Delhi,[7] coinciding, on 30 June 1975, with amendment of the feared Maintenance of Internal Security Act (MISA) 'to make it unnecessary to communicate to a person detained under the act the grounds for his detention'.[8]

On 9 July 1975 came the delayed summons to (unarrested) Members for the assembly of Parliament on 21 July 1975.[9] It was preceded on 20 July with the announcement of the censorship of parliamentary proceedings.[10] Parliament's assembly itself brought a collision not only of rhetoric, fear and anger, but the classical accents of older exchanges between the dignity of unarmed truth (banned from publication) and armed deception. On 23 July 1975 came the withdrawal of the opposition; and thereafter the parliamentary deluge. From 1 August the one-sided rump of Parliament, in the shadows cast by the arrest of its members and the loss of their immunity, with report of its proceedings censored, and in the absence of its opposition, began to legislate and to amend the Constitution. Hirelings and turncoats – some traducing all principle – crowded to the parliamentary benches to proclaim their fealty to force and loyalty to liberty. They claimed, too, the spoils of dishonour: that *de facto* immunity which their jailed colleagues, whether themselves men of principle or unprincipled, had simultaneously lost in detention.

On 1 August 1975 constitutional amendment, the 38th since the promulgation of the Constitution, prevented examination of, and challenge to, the validity of the President's reasons for the emergency's declaration. It thus excluded legal petition, on the grounds of the emergency's constitutional invalidity, against summary detention. The 27 June executive order (before mentioned) had already suspended the right to equality before the law (Article 14), the right to life and liberty (Article 21), and protection against arbitrary arrest and detention (Article 22). It denied to any citizen detained – later to include foreigners – the right to move the courts for relief under these Articles of the Constitution also. Conversely, on 5 to 6 August 1975, the Electoral Laws Amendment Act[11] was passed, nullifying retroactively the Allahabad High Court conviction, for corrupt practices, of the Prime Minister. On 7 to 8 August the Constitution was again amended (the 39th Amendment) to deprive the courts of jurisdiction over election irregularities involving persons holding high office, including the Prime Minister – despite the fact, perhaps trivial in this context, that the Prime Minister is not elected as such, but nominated by the President. On 9 August 1975 the Constitution was once more amended (the critical 40th Amendment) in the continuing absence of the opposition, and with the proceedings censored, to give the Prime Minister personal immunity from civil and criminal proceedings.[12] It was retrospective, covering both the periods spent in office and before assuming office. Going far beyond Ford's pardon of Nixon, it was prospective also; extending, in unprecedented fashion unknown to the 'rule of law', the duration of such complete immunity to a 'permanent' protection from all future infractions of the civil and criminal law of India, even after leaving office.

It will be necessary to measure the quality of the further degenerations (or reconstructions) in the polity which accompanied it, in a moment. It is a sufficient caution to say here that the grant of immunity was attended not merely both by rhetoric and violence, but denial of violence, and asseverations of honour. It was preceded and followed by the announcements of the economic 'new deal' to 'ameliorate the condition of the people'; by the further elaboration of censorship regulations and 'press guidelines', and the imprisonment of journalists and academics; by the arrest (and worse) of opposition trade union leaders, and the closure of trade union offices and student unions; by the denial of trade union rights and the construction of a new politics at the point of production. It was lost in the opening and unfolding panoply of repression, deceit and coercion being extended over the face of India, cast into shadow.

On 11 August 1975, the law and the Constitution appropriately amended or crudely manipulated, depending upon judgement, an appeal was swiftly lodged before the Supreme Court against the Allahabad High Court decision. The session of the parliamentary rump was prorogued, its task completed, while the voices of opposition, as we shall hear later, were continuously audible but muted by fear, censorship and detention. The reconstitution – or decomposition – of the body politic was now to proceed by decree and executive order, in grimly repressive and benignly 'reforming' succession and alternation. Thus, as an example of a process, the 'abolition of bonded labour' by decree on 24 October 1975 was preceded the week before (on 17 October) by further amendment to MISA, making it an offence for the prison authorities to disclose even to the judiciary and courts themselves the grounds of a prisoner's detention.[13] On 7 November 1975 came the Supreme Court's reversal (by Chief Justice A. N. Ray, Justices Khanna, Mathew, Beg and Chandrachud) of the Allahabad court's judgement. Under the constraint of the 39th Amendment, they considered themselves to be unable even to question the validity or propriety of its passage – or carriage – through a Parliament whose members were in detention and its opposition absent. The subversion (or 'streamlining') of the constitutional, judicial and political process reached, by 8 January 1976, the suspension by executive decree of Article 19 of the Constitution. This Article contained the remaining (formal) basic freedoms of the Indian people: freedom of speech and expression; the right to assemble peaceably and without arms; to form associations or unions – each cumulatively striking a fundamental blow, as we shall see, against the rights of opposition and of the trade union movement; the right to move freely; to reside and settle in any part of the territory of India; to acquire, hold and dispose of property; to practise any profession, or to carry on any occupation, trade or business.

Two weeks later, on 22 January 1976, arguably the main business in this first seven-month phase of the defence of democracy, or the mutilation by executive excision and parliamentary cudgel of the political physiognomy of India, was nearly completed with another amendment to MISA. It is one familiar to students of the process. It permitted the immediate re-arrest of a detainee upon expiry of the term of detention or release by the courts, on the original grounds of his (or her) detention. That is, it permitted the resumed incarceration for a period of up to one year, extended to two years by further amendment on 16 June 1976 (but exceeded with or without licence, in practice) of a prisoner, who would not know the grounds of his detention. At the same time, the prison authorities were released from 'previous restraints' on the solitary confinement of those in preventive detention. Moreover, the right to review was removed, while every other path of appeal had already been closed by suspension of the residual safeguards inherent in the 'fundamental rights' of the constitution.

As before, approach to such serially described fact can proceed along different routes and for different purposes. It can seek out qualifying factors, or try to create ambiguity from clarity of intent and meaning. It can establish a structure of interpretation, or give the necessary resonance to fact, through the recall of the already established social and economic context.

Response may choose to focus principally upon the depth of the economic crisis and the attempted militarization of the economy. It may be interwoven with the moral suasion not only of reassurance about violence, but about a new politics of equity and justice (to say nothing of the '12-point prohibition programme' of 2 December 1975). It may be set in a context of the attempted extinction of rights of expression and organization.

Apologia can, and did, run along different tracks, usually arriving at a 'cost–benefit analysis', loss of freedom and physical hurt balanced in a calculus against gains in production or 'economic progress', an argument we have to test against fact, later.

Or we may pay attention to the familiar lulling voices, the immediate official blandness. 'The people who have tasted the peace of the emergency will never choose to return to chaos ... the government's writ in the land can now run unhindered.'[14] 'What has happened has been politically met well within the provisions of the constitution',[15] 'undertaken in order not to destroy, but to preserve the constitution',[16] 'neither unconstitutional, nor extra-constitutional, but justified morally, constitutionally and politically';[17] truth or deception, but offering reassurance, as garnish for its violence. No less bland was that language which presented itself in the formal vocabulary of law (and legality), elevated above all taint of suspicion and mayhem. In forbidding the disclosure of the ground of detention – alike of parliamentarian or peasant – it spoke of 'treating such grounds as confidential and ... deemed to refer to matters of state'.[18] Here was the flourish of lawyer's cap and gown and the presidential seal of approval (using the forms of the 'Westminster model') for the foul facts of detention without charge or trial, and the consequential torments to be disclosed and discussed later.

There was, also, the familiar voice of democracy's special Indian invocation; 'the very summoning of Parliament', it said, 'is proof that democracy is functioning in India. The large number of opposition Members present is evidence that not every one of them is behind bars or in detention'.[19]

For those specifically concerned with the uprooting of parliamentary practice, there will be other issues; perhaps, the summons of some members to imprisonment, and others to the new session of Parliament. They would take note that it was followed by the immediate suspension (partially lifted when the job was over) of the rules of procedure, moved on 21 July 1975 by the Minister for Parliamentary Affairs, prohibiting questions and motions by private Members wishing to raise urgent matters on the floor of the house; and followed in turn by swift approval of the emergency proclamation.[20] The introduction and passage through all its readings in two and a half hours (on 7 August 1975) of the Bill to amend the Constitution, and deny the courts jurisdiction over electoral corruption, may have its interest; with the provisions, amongst others, for the requirement of a minimum period of circulation for a Bill, suspended and over-ridden.[21]

For those with an ear for that heroic (or rhetorical) appeal to reason and justice, grounded in the long parliamentary history of 'liberal democracy', and entering into collision with Indian anodyne and apologia, as well as with flail and truncheon, there are other voices. They spoke just before, and at the time of, the opposition's 23 July withdrawal; and though unreported in the press, what they said was circulated beyond the reach of the new parliamentary censor.* There is the voice of downright and most dangerous assertion that 'there are no conditions of emergency in the country and no danger either from internal or external sources'.[22] There are ringing declarations, rising to the parliamentary occasion 'in an extraordinary and most distressing situation, in which thirty-four Members of Parliament are not here, not of their own volition, but because they are in detention'.[23]

'It is as if,' they say, 'under the Constitution, you have a right to subvert the Constitution ... when you cannot answer the people, all the answer that you have is to jail them ... and when we come to attend Parliament, you arrest us.'[24] Or they say 'we know full well that no one is immune from arrest and detention ... [that] any person arrested need not be produced before a court, the news of his arrest, whereabouts and condition can be kept completely secret. He may be physically liquidated by the police and nobody need know anything about it ... I strongly condemn this attempt to create terror ... and let loose the police against the people.'[25] Or, 'what has happened is considered by some of you as the dawn of a new era, while we consider that it is the beginning of a long night of authoritarian rule, of suppression of liberty, and maybe of disintegration of this country.'[26]

* See appendix, p. 378 ff.

They might ask from within the ruling Congress Party faction (and not from the opposition benches) 'how can these two friends, my Congress colleagues Ram Dhan and Chandra Shekhar, turn overnight into "right reactionary" conspirators, with their insistence upon implementing our party programme both in letter and spirit?'[27] Krishan Kant declared that 'I have always been a Congress socialist who believes that socialism in India has to be brought about by the application of Gandhian principle'; and that 'it is not the obstructionist forces ... the forces in our party which were too strong to allow us to implement our programme, who have been arrested'. 'With no free press, nor free speech in parliament, who,' he asked, 'will now criticize its non-implementation? ... Those who brought about this emergency know not what grievous harm they are doing to the nation and themselves. History is replete with bitter examples. It must be realized that all steps have their inexorable inner logic ... into slogan-shouting gimmicks, and total immobilization ... the tyranny of the constable, the clerk and the petty official.'[28]

Or, already detained and released within the first turnover, 'I too was arrested ... I am an old man and cannot speak loudly, but I am not afraid of jail,' said A. K. Gopalan of the CPI–M.

In the last forty-five years I have been in jail for seventeen years, and fought for the freedom of this country ... but we cannot betray the interests of the people and give our assent to the obliteration of all vestiges of democracy in India – freedom of the person, freedom of speech, freedom of association, freedom to approach the courts, freedom of the press, freedom to criticize the government and work for its replacement by a government of the people's choice ... History will vindicate us.'[29]

We hear (briefly) the language, whether rhetorical or stiffly courteous, of parliamentary protest at the burial of the 'Westminster model'; of impotence, ashamed or disbelieving, of those who seek a parliamentary road to socialism. We also hear the tones of a discourse which stood briefly against the debasements of a babel of newspeak, or that swelling harmony of praise in which the sycophant and the servile sang in apparent unison.

But however important or unimportant, these were verbal exchanges merely. Suffocated by the censor, they were at best a shadow play of rebuttal and parliamentary withdrawal. At worst they prospered the glib and the turncoat, awaiting their main chance, when even the semblance of honour is dissolved into that true chaos, to which abasement on the one hand and tyranny on the other lend a precarious structure. And all this was shadow of a shadow against the reality being enacted beyond these encounters, and the statuesque, unmoving condition of the people.

Yet the suppression of a parliamentary or 'bourgeois' democracy, however illusory – and the reinforcement, instead, of other unmediated expressions of state, class or faction power – was one thing. Conjoined with attacks on Constitution, judiciary, press, trade unions and universities it was another. And supposing for the sake of argument, that the weight of the blows were gradually to gather and to fall upon the left, upon opposition organizations of the workers, already bearing the brunt of the economic and social crisis at the point of production. If this were to take place in the name of socialism and the struggle against fascism, then the problems for analysis would become increasingly pressing. This is another item to be placed on the agenda.

And joining partisan issue – and, in general, confusing it further – were friend and foe alike, domestic and foreign, amid the cascade of restriction, coercion and detention. 'Expert' explanation and calculation as to person advantage were bewilderingly interwoven with the general calculus of gains and losses, to the greatest number's greatest happiness. One man's *a priori* assumption, and consequent logic, is another's false premise and even more absurd conclusion; while battle was joined on all sides with reality and opposition, with feints to left and right, and faction within faction, force and farce jockeying for position, until the dust settled and the jails were filled to overflowing.

But if the example of the Indian Parliament be held for a moment, what comes of the closer scrutiny? First, the use and abuse of power – withdrawing behind the arras – had declared itself by executive decree to be ready to remove itself, if it chose, from the parliamentary arena. Where it was necessary, however, to retain the signs and tokens of an elective and legislative procedure then the holding of elections or the swift cynical motion on the nod through Parliament could still be retained to serve the immediate interests of power. Second, and no less important, a forum increasingly used not for the mere expression of dissident opinion, but in order to expose the venality of power, was reduced by censorship and intimidation to a cowed silence, where restored decorum and sycophancy became hard to distinguish. Moreover, the heavy blows struck at Parliament – reducing the days of its sittings per annum, reducing by detention the numbers of its members, and reducing its powers* – testified in themselves to a fear of that parliamentary vigilance we saw in the debates on the Maruti scandal, and which must always be intolerable to corruption.

Third, we also face distillations at their purest of Indian double-think and contradiction (as light relief or further tedium), at the close shearing of Parliament's powers. At the very depth of its loss of function in January 1976, 'Parliament is functioning with full freedom.'[31] In the same month, 'Parliament has a unique place in the esteem and affection of the people, through which they articulate and realize their aspirations and ventilate their difficulties and grievances ... [it is] among the many great achievements of free India';[32] yet at the same time 'Parliament cannot be supreme, because it is only a representative body and not the whole people'.[33] But to the chief censor (H. J. D'Penha), at the very moment of issuing secret guidelines to the press on the reporting and non-reporting of Parliamentary proceedings, 'Parliament is the sovereign body, and therefore its deliberations have sanctity'.[34]

Moreover, because 'the image of Parliament as a voice of the people should in no case be allowed to be impaired'; and because 'no news, report or comment attempting to defile the sanctity of the proceedings of Parliament, or attempting to give

---

*Thus, 'a Member attending the session of Parliament is in no better position than his colleague behind bars, for he is debarred in the House from ventilating a grievance, from raising a debate or putting a question. Even when he speaks in the House on the limited subjects chosen by the government, his speech will not be reported outside. When the Member's right to criticize the government, and publicize these criticisms are suppressed, Parliament loses its importance, basic character and function.'[30]

an inaccurate or distorted version of the proceedings should be published',[35] therefore (if you can follow) 'the speeches of Members of Parliament participating in a debate will not be published in any manner or form, but their names and party affiliation may be mentioned'.* [36] The statements of Ministers however might be published in full, or in a condensed form[38] (though even their contents were not to infringe the wider general rules of the press censor, themselves secret and 'not for publication'). The point requires no emphasis; it has both a name and a local habitation.

These were merely the familiar snares and delusions of a tiresome official deception. Watch more closely and one can see the confused response of the opposition, in alternating boycott and resumption of attendance, taking flight and returning like flocks of starlings. One can listen to the CPI and their fantasts openly declaring, for the benefit of the historian, that they had 'supported in both Houses of Parliament the constitutional amendments, and the amendment to the People's Representation Act because, despite some negative features, their main aim is to assert the supremacy of Parliament'.[39] More, even; they declare correctly that 'our group played a very prominent role in this session of Parliament'. But in the next sentence they complain that 'since there is wholesale clamping of censorship on speeches of Members of both Houses of Parliament, nothing is known outside about speeches of our leading comrades'.[40] One memorable exchange captures the exquisite essence of being hoist on one's own petard; 'it is no use,' said Indrajit Gupta, one of the CPI's parliamentary leaders, 'speaking in Parliament when

*Press protection from the laws of defamation for publishing anything said in Parliament was withdrawn, with the repeal of the Parliamentary Proceedings (Protection of Publication) Act, 1956; doubly gratuitous because of the general censorship, and because the 'presiding officers' of both Houses of Parliament have unrestricted powers to 'expunge scurrilous utterances' of Members of Parliament from the record. It led only to the journalists' cul-de-sac where, for example, 'Mr Shamim Ahmed Shamim (Independent) wanted to know how long the emergency would continue. He made certain remarks, which were objected to by Congress members. The Prime Minister said he was misquoting her.'[37] This was all that could be learned from the press reports of this particular parliamentary exchange, in the blind alley of a suppressed freedom.

speeches are not being fully reported in the press'. 'Speeches,' said the Prime Minister in reply, 'are for the benefit of Parliament. There is a different place for public meetings';[41] but the constitutional right to 'assemble peacably' had gone also, to say nothing of prohibitions on meeting under the Defence of India Rules. That however is a matter yet to be arrived at.

This was instead a familiar echo of the politics of illusion, in that receding wonderland world where the focus of power had swiftly shrunk, and where even Cabinet meetings were no longer needed. Here ministerial protest was conspiracy, and 'Cabinet decisions' could be made in the Prime Minister's secretariat; and Cabinet Ministers had then (reportedly)[42] to read the newspapers to discover what had been decided for them.* We are left then with two kinds of relative political triviality, from which we must remove ourselves. One was exemplified, say, by the futility of formal parliamentary resistance. On 31 March 1976, for example, even the Speaker, B. R. Bhagat, and a swathe of members of the ruling faction joined the opposition to the introduction of a government Bill, which was merely withdrawn for the day, reintroduced in identical form the next, and passed (appropriately on 1 April 1976); the opposition in impotence vacating the chamber.[44] The other was the general circumstance of the coexistence of parliamentary debate and cabal decision, which is not restricted to India.

It is thus necessary to widen the focus for many reasons, if we are to take in this phase of class-power's attempted extrication from its 'accountability' to the people, however attenuated the people's representation may be in Parliament. For it involved, as first corollary, the driving out of Parliament and into the arms of Orwell's licensed criminal, the philistine censor, and the corrupt official – to go no further here into the deeper recesses inhabited by the Youth Congress – of opposition and its expression. For some, however, the primary political issue was a different one. Where balance and calculus are predominant in

---

*cf. 'We just do not know what is happening in the government. We are not consulted by the party bigwigs, and are not to talk of the Prime Minister. We do not even meet among ourselves lest we are suspected of hatching a conspiracy. In any case, nobody is willing to open his mouth.'[43]

the mind of the observer, the suspension (in some cases) and abolition (in others) of the fundamental rights of the person, for example, is not a matter of principle but of political practice. The issue is perceived as one of advantage and disadvantage, a tactical question, and will be weighed accordingly. The answer to that question depended on whether the Indian opposition was perceived to have been only a few, or to be counted in millions. Once that was decided, both the scale and type of measures taken to counter 'conspiracy' or 'subversion' were themselves measured.

For some, then, the question became a judgement as to whether what we are examining was to be counted as sledge-hammer 'over-reaction', or a due minimum of force to restore law and order to a nation threatened by 'fascism' and the forces of 'right-reaction'. For others, the issue was the extent of the damage being done to institutions of state or to the people's organizations or to individuals, by the panic-stricken self-perpetuation of faction power within a general crisis of hegemony or class crisis, and which pointed to a different conclusion.

Alternatively, holding on (or leaning over backwards), it might be possible to argue that there was no real contradiction between professed concern for a principle, and a simultaneous attack on it, because it is not confined to India. That is, what is familiar is tolerable. Or you can place on opposite sides of mental arithmetic's equation, on the one hand the proclamation on 24 October 1975 of the liberation from serfdom of the armies of 'bonded labour', with 'land distribution' to the landless millions; and on the other, the merely temporary suspension of *habeas corpus*. Thus you get not necessarily a 'new deal' but a 'package deal', a *quid pro quo*. And if something should go wrong, and the former turn out to be hollow – little or no *quid* for the *quo* – and its effects vanish into the thin air of the political orator, that will doubtless be quite explicable on other grounds altogether.

There can be no pursuit to its lair of every quarry; some are still too dark even now to see into. But the arbitrary use against political opponents of the Defence of India Rules and the Maintenance of Internal Security Act – as amended and strengthened – was to exceed all previous precedent, both Indian and British in India. Or, if you prefer, 'we stand by the assurance that MISA will not be used against legitimate political activity',[45] and, as the Prime Minister put it to me, 'we don't like to lock anyone up; it is against our traditions'.[46] At the outset, however, what was difficult to force into equilibrium was the political elimination of the rights of the arrested (with even reporting of arrest forbidden) while the right to arrest was given free rein and official licence.

The numbers of 'political prisoners' – as distinct from others such as the 'anti-social', a term covering a multitude of sins and non-sinners – who were arrested and held without trial under the laws of preventive detention were unknown, undeclared, unknowable and complicated by cycles of arrests and releases. The statistics of the turnover of short-term detention are a complex matter. In addition they went to join an already unknown total in detention. 'There are,' said the Minister of Law H. R. Gokhale in Washington (previously encountered speaking in the Maruti scandal) 'only a few hundred prisoners identified with political parties'.[47] Or there were, say, the Home Minister's own '7,000 so far apprehended to prevent the preaching of violence'.[48] But totals of a few hundred or a few thousand must 'somehow' enclose the arithmetic of far larger known totals, to say nothing of the unknown. There were the serving parliamentarians, known by name to Amnesty International; the 13,000 allegedly arrested under MISA and DIR in Madhya Pradesh alone, between June 1975 and February 1976;[49] the 10,000 supposedly removed from the Shimoga district in Karnataka in November and December 1975;[50] the 600 teachers taken in Delhi.[51] Swathes were cut, state by state, through left, right and shifting centre. SP, CPI–M, CPI–ML, Jan Sangh, RSS, the Bharatiya Lok Dal (the Indian People's Party) and the opposition Congress factions. Gandhians preaching peace – including Mahatma Gandhi's grandson, who was arrested in Delhi[52] – and men 'preaching violence' were equally taken.*

*But cf. 'the government's assurance that MISA will not be used against political parties or leaders stands even today', of the Minister of Home Affairs, Brahmananda Reddy, to the Rajya Sabha on 1 April 1976.[53] In

And then, back and forth, the scythe of arrests through the left again (and through the right again, reduced in some cases, as we shall see, by releases into membership of the Congress Party), the treatment of the SP, CPI–M and trade unions severe and often violent.[54] Throughout the whole opposition, leaderships were arrested or hunted, released quickly or more slowly (or not at all). Those released, were released after shorter or longer periods in better or worse conditions, tormented or not in different cases, but torture was to be carefully documented,* and merely continued another fully known tradition. Branches of the CITU and of the CPI–M's national student organization, the SFI, were asserted to have been taken, sometimes lock, stock and barrel, offices sealed or taken over, presses seized, banned and censored.[55] Nor, despite the immunity procured for their leaders by alliance, were the rank and file even of the CPI and its trade union movement AITUC protected, when they joined others in the forbidden dissent of opposition or industrial action.

If both specific and circumstantial evidence are added, and then halved or even quartered for truth's margin of error, in order to establish here a sense of scale and context; and if we avoid, on the one hand, the illusions of an over-magnified underground opposition, and on the other, the scorekeeper's tally, what can be established was the detention, with a turnover of an unknown and by definition much larger figure, of tens of thousands of political opponents. Whether it was the '50,000' of some reports ('it is unlikely that there have been fewer'),[56] or the '100,000' whom the Congress Party's own Krishan Kant 'insisted have now [sc. by November 1975] been imprisoned',[57] cannot be certain. What is also established is that each cautious addition, or exaggerated multiplication of totals, was always countered by the subtractions and divisions ('excepting one or two cases, MISA has been used only against persons who are a menace to the security of the country')[58] of the arithmetic which is employed by power.

---

general the pattern was that the larger political fish were netted with MISA, the smaller with the Defence of India Rules.

* See chapter 8.

What is beyond doubt too was that other total, or net effect, which passed beyond quantity to quality; that is, the consequence for the individual, of ordinance, decree, 'reform' and amendment. Such had been the extent of the operation carried out on the rights of the individual, that by 9 January 1976, it enabled the Assistant Solicitor-General to tell the Indian Supreme Court, correctly, that the citizen had 'absolutely no recourse to any redress or legal or constitutional remedy through the courts to safeguard his right to personal liberty ... even if he is totally innocent and is illegally and wrongfully detained on wrong and false information ... or non-existent grounds'.[59] To put it another way, the asserted need to beat off 'fascism' and 'right-reaction' had not only taken freedom of speech and opinion, but had given the state – that is, the informer and the policeman – an absolute discretionary power over the body of the individual; whether law-breaking or law-abiding a matter of indifference.

The calculus of the apologist had no choice but to weigh the suspension of the constitutional right to 'carry on any occupation, trade or business' as a means of containing 'subversion'. It had to weigh the taking of freedom of speech and opinion not only in defence of freedom in general, that is in the abstract, but also in defence of the *particular* conception of freedom of which these rights are held to be among its leading virtues.* It also had to weigh, for its political meaning, the majority of four to one in the Supreme Court on 28 April 1976 (with Mr Justice Khanna dissenting and whose name should be recorded) which went out of its legal way to confirm the lost liberties of India. It upheld the government's petition to forbid all writs of *habeas corpus*; held that no person could challenge an order for his detention on the ground that it was illegal(!); and went even further to hold, through Chief Justice A. N. Ray, that *since* the con-

---

*e.g. 'The general impression in the public mind,' said the *Indian Express* on 10 January 1976, walking the tightrope of censorship with sub-clause and qualification (excluded here) 'is that internal threats to law and order, and the danger of subversion have been effectively contained by the drastic steps already taken ... suspending the citizen's right under Article 19 of the Constitution would seem to be too sweeping a measure ... the ordinary citizen needs to be assured, because every abridgement of his right to move the courts enlarges the area of discretionary judgement.'

stitution was 'the sole repository of rights to life and liberty', and the Constitution had been effectively amended by decree (on 27 June 1975), the citizen had neither residual rights nor claim to freedom – or even mercy – against arbitrary power. 'The rule of law', said the Chief Justice, in the name of the rule of law over which he presided, was 'not a catchword or incantation'; it was 'not identical with a free society'; and then, in the familiar corrupted accents encountered in a previous chapter, 'no law has been either suspended or altered by the presidential order'.*[60] Thus, with the aid of law, the overthrow of individual right and a constitutional *coup d'état* by presidential order were given their judicial ratification. Assisting Chief Justice A. N. Ray to the decision, were Justices M. H. Beg, P. N. Bhagwati and Y. V. Chandrachud.

Now the 'rule of law' itself, or the concept of *ultra vires*, in a social order such as India's based on misery and unknowing, where it is not based on authorized violence – is arguably neither here nor there, specious. Denial of right is an everyday matter, anywhere; denial of legal right by the law and under the law another, and commonplace also. But denial (arguably shameless) that the law had been changed, when the denial was made possible by the change in the law itself, was circle within circle of equivocation, the creation of another Indian labyrinth which must not – and does not – defeat the patient exploration of its deceptions. It was thus that both lay and legal newspeak came to the aid of embattled power.

Moreover, still straining credulity (though it no longer should) K. M. Nair, the Advocate-General of the CPI-led government of Kerala, intervened at an early stage of these *habeas corpus*

*But Mr Justice Khanna had learned from India's Attorney-General, Niren De, in cross-examination of him, that 'if a district magistrate has a personal grudge against an individual, the former can deprive the latter of his life without redress or remedy'.[61] This exchange may have moved him to dissent from the majority verdict. He held that the Constitution conferred no right to take away the power of the High Courts to issue writs of *habeas corpus*; that the detained could challenge a detention order on the ground that it was illegal; and that the right to life and liberty were rights which existed prior to the Constitution.[62] Mr Justice Khanna, the senior Supreme Court judge, resigned in January 1977 after being passed over for the chief justiceship in favour of Mr Justice Beg (q.v.).

hearings – on 16 December 1975 – to urge his own extremes on the court. He argued that 'the grounds for detentions under MISA were beyond judicial scrutiny'; that the 'satisfaction of the detaining authority as to the grounds of detention was sufficient for the validity of the order of detention'; that 'the detention order was conclusive of the state of mind of the person who passed the order'(!); and that 'the courts could not inquire whether such grounds existed'.[63] At the same time, as we have seen, other CPI spokesmen were complaining that their 'comrades'' parliamentary speeches were unreported by the censor.

In like mode of corruption, only two weeks after the Supreme Court's seal of approval had been affixed to the ending of *habeas corpus*, the Deputy Home Minister, F. H. Mohsin, 'repudiated the charge that fundamental rights are being denied'. 'The government,' he said, 'has only taken away the right of individuals to go to court to enforce them', thus completing the circle of incarceration of mind and body.[64]

This meant various things, and they can be differently expressed. From one point of view it meant, say, that the notorious colonial Rowlatt Act of 1919, which prevented the arrested from approaching the court – '*na vakil*' (no pleader), '*na dalil*' (no plea), '*na appeal*' (no appeal) – had been revived, but with its mode of application excelling the colonial experience. From another, that it was all lost in the perennial miseries of India; or that 'the common man does not read the Constitution, nor study court judgements'.[65]

Or perhaps it pointed to the crowds of the poor, milling and pressing around the entrance steps inside the gates of Madras Central Jail, waiting for hours with their bribes – an apple, or an orange, or money, or biscuits – desperate to discover if their relations were to be found there, and if they were, to see them. And into a cloth bag made of Binny's khaki, held by a deputy warder such as Raj Kumar, the young fellow with the big moustache, tall, with a reputation as a sportsman, go the bribes; the oranges and apples and biscuits to be sold later. If you listened you would hear from a recently released prisoner of the fighting and prison beatings; the open stealing of the prisoners' food by the warders; of the rice mixed with small stones, and fine sand with the millet. In the remand section, the worst section, there were seven hundred prisoners; some of whom would be there for years before being brought to trial, if ever; seven hundred people rushing to the four latrines in the centre of the compound, when the cell doors were opened, and fighting to get to them; kicking up a dust which does not settle. Or, in simplest shorthand, this was the vulnerability of the defenceless; backs bared to the whims of power and dependent upon the smallest mercies.

Only the right (and powers) of the individual provided by Article 31 were now untouched; and despite the CPI's questions and motions for the Article's repeal[66] – all other rights, they argued, having been abolished or suspended – it was left untouched. Still standing, that is, only the right to property; not of the shanty dweller to his shanty, razed by the bulldozer, as we shall see later, but the right to be unequal and the right to the preservation of property-value, still guaranteed by the Constitution. Repeal, said the Deputy Minister of Labour, would 'put an end to the savings habit and affect capital formation'.[67] And as wider context than this, a new politics was simultaneously being articulated; of 'duties to balance rights', a new politics of 'responsibility' in return for 'privilege' urged upon the mass of the people, to dig out and widen the path being taken by emergency India.

But executive decree and faction power had not yet finished with the judiciary. We must also follow further into the labyrinth. 'The basic and incontrovertible fact remains,' said the president of the Congress Party, that 'Parliament represents the will of the people, and the democratic system will lose its meaning unless it [Parliament] is allowed to be fully active.'[68] In order that the same 'parliamentary sovereignty' be protected – which was, as we have seen, being simultaneously subverted – it 'follows as a natural corollary that no court could have the right to declar *ultra vires* any amendment effected to the Constitution by Parliament'.[69] (I will sum up the corrupt implication of the argument in a moment, if it is not immediately visible.) And while the 'independence' of the judiciary – however frail and fallible a bulwark against the abuse of power – was in consequence swiftly being attacked, the Minister of Law was declaring simultaneously that 'the government firmly believes in the independence of the judiciary', but 'at the same time it could not be allowed to strike down progressive legislation'.[70]

Here are the simple outlines of this particular circle: the judiciary is attacked in the name of the 'sovereignty of Parliament' while the sovereignty of Parliament is attacked in the name of democracy and the people; while democracy and the people are being attacked in the name of 'national discipline' and the struggle against conspiracy and subversion.

We must go on, deeper. The Minister of State for Law, as if idly, 'wondered whether judicial review was at all an absolute necessity in a democratic set-up';[71] while the Prime Minister herself was arguing that 'our law which incorporates many of the features of the Anglo-Saxon legal system' ('traditionally used to defend the propertied classes') 'must now be amended, so that the democratic spirit can override our feudal inheritance'.[72] Here we are in a dense thicket of corruption; this was the voice of executive power arguing for its own licence in the name of democracy, and after the constitution and law had already been subverted to protect it from court decision; and with the attempted 'democratic' legitimation of this proceeding still to follow.

And so, dissenting High Court judges – whose voices could also be heard throughout, albeit in a minority, preserving their integrity, while sycophancy and caution overwhelmed their colleagues – began to be 'transferred in the public interest',[73] and 'in consultation with the Chief Justice',[74] from Delhi, Bombay, Calcutta, to remote regions of India, Assam and others.* The CPI again joined in to argue that 'the power of judges be curbed by deleting Article 226 of the Constitution', so that 'parliamentary supremacy be placed beyond doubt', 'by taking away the juris-

---

* They included (according to R. B. Jethmalani, chairman of the Indian Bar Council,' who had to leave India to reveal it) Mr Justice Rangarajan, whose decision in the Delhi High Court in September 1975 freed the editor of the *Indian Express* from detention under MISA; he was transferred to Assam. Additional judge Agarwal, who sat on the bench in the same case, was demoted to district magistrate; and Mr Justices Vimadal and Mukhi, who had been 'upholding citizens' rights', were removed from the Bombay High Court. Jethmalani also referred to 'the collapse of judicial character'. *Guardian*, 10 August 1976.

diction of the courts to sit in judgement over constitutional amendments'.[75] Conventions of State Governors and all-India State Bar Councils, respectively, bent the knee (as at any imperial *durbar*) to proclaim variously that 'the courts' power to issue writs should be suitably modified so that normal administrative work did not get paralysed', and that 'the fundamental rights of the people should not come in the way of the directive principles of state policy' nor be 'used to subvert the democratic structure [sic]'.[76]

Trampled underfoot in the name of curbing 'the reckless folly of writ petitions',[77] was the counter opinion of those few judges (the whole judiciary obviously aware of what was at issue) prepared to express it. 'Judicial review,' said Mr Justice Rangarajan, 'is paramount ... to ensure public good and check individual abuses. The judiciary is perhaps the sovereign form yet known for this purpose',[78] whether true or false, general or special pleading, the subversion of it part of the logic of clearing the decks, so to speak, while 'swinging into action'. And always the familiar voices of official publication and pronouncement, in the running commentary of corrupt power: 'the Supreme Court, High Court, subordinate judiciary are independent of the executive and command universal respect. In maintaining the rule of law this is an important factor.'[79] Or, 'sagacity lies in the avoidance of destructive collisions' between judiciary and executive; 'our people look to the judicial system for the realization of their aspirations for the social, economic and political justice which are enshrined in our constitution'. 'I hope,' said Mrs Gandhi, addressing the judiciary itself after executive order and constitutional amendment had decisively reduced its powers (in this instance, in the speaker's own personal interest), 'the Supreme Court will now fulfil what is expected of it.'[80]

What the decks were being cleared for was further constitutional amendment – arguably gratuitous, because they had already been swept clean by previous amendment and swabbed down by detention. To change the metaphor, the basis had been laid in theory (by lying) and practice (by coercion) to erect a new constitutional structure on the ruins of the old, an edifice in process of assembly throughout our period; or a pack of cards, a speculator's projection, depending on judgement, yet to be arrived at.

The components of the 'new view' of the Constitution are clearly stated even if they emerged from the scramble of competing deception and factional insecurity as to where the line of the constitutional *coup d'état* was to be finally drawn. That is, the 'theory' was plain enough. After nearly thirty years of immobility, with its unfulfilled 'directive principles' in the uninterrupted charge of the ruling party, now, 'the Constitution must be resilient' and 'amended to attune it to changing times'.[81] Moreover – and more ominous – there must be remedy for 'a grave omission on the part of the founding fathers'; namely, the absence of a 'chapter, along with fundamental rights, of "fundamental duties" '.[82] According to the President of India, the people would be 'entitled to press for their rights only after they have discharged their obligations to their nation'.[83] The structure of rationalization was completed, as responsibility for social and economic failure was transposed to the Constitution. Its amendment, it was argued, was above all needed because it had failed the people. So simultaneously with (and in the same speeches as) demands for a 'strong and stable centre', 'constitutional change becomes imperative to meet the people's changing needs and requirements', because 'democratic values are essentially dynamic in character'.*[84]

Woven into this structure – I shrink from the term 'political theory' only because it might serve at this point to dignify deception – was simultaneous retraction, qualification and denial. The Constitution was at once 'well balanced with no need to change it',[87] (with changes already made and others in the offing) and then confused from the same source by 'the spirit of the Constitution was right, and is still right, but in the interpretation we

---

* cf. Amnesty International's Chief Minister of West Bengal, who 'called for a look at the Constitution to find out what changes are necessary for the country's march towards socialism and progress'. 'Can any Constitution bind a nation for ever?'[85] 'With the change in times, human rights, both civil and natural, also change . . . When the rights change there is nothing wrong in changing fundamental rights also . . . The question before the nation today is whether the constitution enables the government to achieve economic emancipation in the shortest possible time.'[86]

find that what comes out is not what was intended . . . and when the interpretation goes wrong, one has to think of making changes'.[88] In the meantime, the plans for radical change to strengthen the executive power still further were explained to the 'common man' with the further deception of their attribution to the opposition, which was 'demanding changes to the Constitution on the ground that its structure is defective'.[89]

Floated early into the midstream of the 'debate' – 'debate', not debate, because being conducted within a faction of the ruling faction, and not in discourse either with the people, Parliament, or even the ruling party – about the desirability of a presidential system, with sweeping and uncheckable powers, were new plans. They went far beyond a ratification of the already established emergency executive practice.

The document in question contained proposals to scrap the parliamentary system entirely. The copy which I have is preceded by a covering letter, headed 'Appeal for Public Debate', dated 9 November 1975 (and over the signature of C. T. Daru, the noted Ahmedabad lawyer), warning that 'drastic changes are proposed without any public debate, and behind the *purdah*'.*[90] The proposals were greeted with wide and slowly mounting opposition, as the documents circulated throughout India. Then only, there was a delayed disclaimer from the ruling faction. The document was described – by authorities on falsehood – as 'false and misleading'; 'mischievous propaganda on the issue of amending the Constitution', and 'trying to create a wrong impression among the people'.[92] The authentic origin of the document itself is clear from simple internal evidence. It contains phrases which were the exclusive coinage and property of members and spokesmen of the ruling junta; the particular forms of rhetoric in use in the emergency period are unmistakable signs of its authorship. Thus, 'the present system of government . . .

---

*And, 'kindly give your thought to this, and raise your voice of protest if you feel that the great democratic constitution of India is sought to be totally destroyed by power-hungry politicians'.[91] C. T. Daru, general secretary of the Indian Radical Humanist Association, and one of the organizers of a convention on civil liberties held in Ahmedabad on 12 October 1975 by Citizens for Democracy, was later arrested. See chapter 8, and appendix, pp. 398–9.

has not come up to the expectation of the common man of our country'; 'the unobstructed working of the executive must be ensured in the interest of the people'; 'the time of the chief executive should not be allowed to be frittered away in fruitless debate and discussion', and so on.[93]

Model examples for the new Constitution of what was soon to be called the 'socialist republic' of India were drawn from other Constitutions (including those of Argentina, France, Greece, Guatemala, Italy and Japan) to provide for what had either already been achieved or was in process, by erosion or enactment. There was to be the further subordination of Parliament and judiciary to executive, the concentration of great power in the hands of a directly elected President, 'more than the USA President', as the document puts it, and including the power to preside over the judiciary, to interpret the laws, and to determine the validity of legislation. It included plans for the complete repeal of the fundamental rights of the citizen; the removal of all safeguards under the laws of preventive detention; the end of federalism; and the power to ban all 'anti-national' and 'anti-social' opposition parties.[94] Or, if you prefer, when the moment came not to disclaim, but to admit, inner-party discussion of such proposals, 'the proposed changes are intended not to dilute democracy but to make it more meaningful and more purposeful to the people'.[95]

And after flurries of announcement and withdrawal, particularly about whether the 'mandate of the people' would be sought before making changes in the Constitution, or afterwards – and with the postponement of the elections due to be held in March 1976* it was reduced to 'ascertaining their opinion'[96] – on 28 February 1976 a party committee was set up by and made accountable to Barooah, the party president. Under the chairmanship of Swaran Singh, the former Defence Minister (and

---

*On 29 December 1975, the Congress Party at its 75th conference decided to put off elections by one year from 18 March 1976; a Bill to this effect was introduced in Parliament on 3 February 1976, and was passed on 6 February 1976, under the terms of Article 38 of the Constitution. For further postponement, followed by the decision to hold elections, see chapter 8.

including the Chief Minister of West Bengal, and the two Ministers of Law who had already spoken much to these questions), its purpose was 'to study and suggest amendments to the Constitution'.[97] We will resume this broadening path later, in order to see in which direction it was designed to lead the people of India.

Once more we have in process and motion numerous interacting and interdependent elements. They are only assimilable at all if given in sequence, and so far have been arranged in no hierarchy of importance. They constituted facets of an entity whose true nature is broken down by analysis, and which must therefore be constantly reassembled in mind, if not on paper, and kept rooted in their twin contexts of the real condition of the people and the realm of ideological illusion. What has preceded, comprehensible as it is in itself, also lacks dimension and meaning without knowledge of the scale of the accompanying attack on press freedom, on the administrative civil service and on the universities; on the remaining non-Congress governments in the states of the federal Indian union, on the trade unions and the rights of independent working-class organization.

The attack on the press ('you know I have always believed in freedom of the press and still do ... but grave mischief has been done by irresponsible writing')[98] was comprehensive. It aroused both opposition – open and covert – and the servilities which we have already encountered. As we have seen, the emergency of 26 June 1975 brought ('not for publication') the imposition of general pre-censorship, under Rule 48 of the Defence of India Rules, 'in order to maintain public order'.[99] It forbade all categories of news, comment and rumour relating to the emergency, to arrests and detentions under MISA, unless pre-authorized in writing by an 'authorized officer' from the Press Information Bureau of the government of India in Delhi, or by a Director of Information of a state government.[100] It was accompanied on the same day by 'general guidelines' ('not to be published') informing editors in language at once careful, lucid and sweeping that 'one of the most powerful aids to the government and the people in an emergency is the press'; that 'in the manner in which information is printed, published or disseminated there can be an accretion of enormous strength to those who are posing a threat to internal security'.[101]

It called on the press for help 'in the fulfilment of the primary task of ridding the nation of the causes of the emergency'; by 'suppressing news themselves';[102] through 'moderation particularly in illustration and headlines';[103] by publishing 'nothing to excite disaffection towards the government established by law in India';[104] 'nothing to promote feelings of enmity between different classes of persons in India',[105] or 'likely ... to cause the cessation or slowing down of work in any place';[106] 'nothing objectionable already published in any foreign newspaper';[107] nothing 'containing false allegations against leaders'[108] or 'denigrating the institution of the Prime Minister';*[109] nothing 'to subvert the functioning of democratic institutions';[111] and nothing 'relating to agitation'.[112] Thus is the image of 'law and order' established.

One month later, on 26 July 1975, editors of all newspapers in India received even more detailed, less literate (and less secure) 'guidelines', as rougher and cruder hands – in the general and necessary degeneration – helped to wield the censor's cudgel. They too were obviously 'not for publication'. News was not to be published which 'contributes to the scare and demoralization about the general situation or public interest in all respects, as determined by the central government';[113] nothing 'which will contribute even in a remote way to affect or worsen the law and order situation';[114] nothing 'which is likely to convey the impression of a protest or disapproval of the governmental measures'.[115] These embargoes were extended beyond news and illustration to advertisements, cartoons, letters to the editor and captions,[116] and justly pointed to the efforts of the more courageous (or incredulous) editors to express their opposition in any way remaining. However, 'positive development stories' and 'official handouts about administrative decisions and policies' were excepted;[117] and 'since news agency messages emanating from Delhi are pre-censored',[118] they too did not need to be re-submitted for censorship.

---

*cf. 'The Congress Party tried to use the [sc. 1961] emergency to stifle criticism of [Nehru] ... those who criticize are traitors'.[110]

And on top of this came executive decree, police action and 'parliamentary' legislation to consolidate and ratify the attack on press freedom. On 8 December 1975, three ordinances simultaneously banned the publication of 'objectionable matter', abolished the Press Council and, as we have already observed, removed the freedom of the press in reporting the proceedings of Parliament.[119] The three ordinances were issued 'by the President', who was on that day – a small matter in a larger context – in Cairo.

The term 'objectionable' was extended beyond all known (or even knowable) bounds. It became an offence, in effect, to publish any material prejudicial to the interests of the government in the opinion of the latter, and passed into statute seven weeks later (on 28 January 1976) by 'parliamentary' enactment, making the decree substantive and permanent law, even if the emergency or the preceding censorship regulations were to be lifted.[120] Its prohibitions included 'inciting . . . any individual or class to disaffection, disharmony or ill-will', or 'causing fear or alarm to any section of the public whereby any person may be induced to commit an offence against the state or public tranquillity'.[121] They included anything defamatory (whether 'by word or sign') 'of the President, Vice-President, Speaker of the Lower House, state Governors, the Prime Minister and all members of the Cabinets of central and state governments', or deemed to be so by them.[122] They applied not only to newspapers and journals, but to 'books, pamphlets, leaflets, sheets of music, paintings, drawings or other visible representation'.[123] The law gave wide powers of search and seizure to police and other petty officials;[124] it provided for forfeitable securities to be lodged with the state by publishers, as sanction against 'objectionable' writing,[125] within a definition itself capable of infinite and arbitrary extension; and it even gave powers to ban *prospectively* publications relating to any particular subject, or class of subjects.[126]

To remove doubt, and to clarify purpose, this was 'to enable the press to be free from vested interest'; 'to prevent irresponsible elements trying to utilize the press for their own ends'; and 'to avoid writings injurious to the intellectual health of society, and which debase the level of public life'.[127] This was arguably the first accurate description of the mode of writing and species (or sub-species) of writer to be protected by the enactment. There was in all this only a shabby progression of excess upon seedy excess; marked with the thumbprints of the corrupt official and the bully, and smudged by an oily sycophancy; but opposed and thwarted wherever it was possible. The list of suppressions was a long and varied one. The Press Council was abolished, from 31 December 1975, because it had 'failed to curb tendentious and provocative writing'.[128] Demands were heard – and heeded – that 'government advertising policy should look not only to a newspaper's circulation, but we should also see if it supports the government'.*[129] Slighting reference to the USA was forbidden, in one place and another, in the name of 'promoting relations with a friendly power'.[131] Criticism of both Amin and Pinochet was censored, for fear of inference and innuendo; Tagore, Gandhi, Nehru (and other writers) in one place or another, forbidden; quotation from Dimitrov disallowed by the CPI's censor in the Kerala administration; and blank spaces themselves forbidden.[132] In sum, this was an apparatus of censorship far beyond anything devised by the former colonial power; and, in the name of a new truthfulness, a seemingly irreversible tidal wave of lying.†

*Even the pro-CPI paper, *Patriot*, reportedly had 'the bulk of its advertisements withdrawn for refusing to join the chorus of praise of Sanjay Gandhi';[130] see chapter 7.

†For example: 'We do not want to have a government news agency', on 13 January 1976.[133] Two days later, consequently, V. C. Shukla, Minister for Information, announced that All-India Radio was discontinuing from 1 February 1976 the services of the two national news agencies, PTI and UNI, already subject to censorship in all their dispatches. They would be 'helped to merge and form a national news agency', 'free from government and monopoly control'.[134] 'The effort is wholly voluntary [as they were squeezed out of existence] and the government has nothing to do with it'; it was 'for the sake of viability and better performance'; because their 'coverage was inadequate', 'their news had proved incorrect', and 'did not reflect in full the life and developments in the country'.[135] Or, if you prefer, 'somehow,' said the Prime Minister, 'we were unable to persuade the owners of the agencies to come together'.[136] 'It is desirable,' said the CPI in addition, 'to have one news agency';[137] finally, 'we never intended or wanted to set up a government-controlled news agency', said Shukla.[138] And by this well-trodden route, such a news agency, *Samachar*, was created in March 1976, 'free from

And thence to 'a code of ethics' (sic).[140] It was announced to Parliament by the Ministers of Information, V. C. Shukla and D. V. Sinha, ostensibly to 'replace censorship'[141] even though censorship law was on the statute book, and emergency regulation was being used while they were speaking; and despite the fact that 'the press was showing great promise'.[142] It was drawn up, among others, by the chief censor H. J. D'Penha, and A. R. Baji, principal information officer to the government of India. It demanded in the preamble 'truthfulness and comprehensiveness in press reporting in a context which gives them meaning', and then, in their name, forbade 'reports which tend to promote tension', and 'news of disturbances and details of members or identity of groups involved in such disturbances, except as officially authorized'.[143] The 'code' spoke in the restrained language of Augean stables already cleaned out and fumigated. It looked to journalists – who were not represented on the drafting committee – for 'high standards of public service', and declared that 'there is nothing so unworthy as the acceptance of a bribe to give or deny publicity to news or comment'.[144] But the 'code of ethics' had been preceded two weeks earlier by Amnesty International's list of imprisoned Indian journalists,[145] and that was another matter entirely, reaching down from illusion to reality, to add injury to insult.

There is a weariness of disgust ('the purpose of censorship is to restore a climate of trust')[146] and tedium, which is a powerful inducement both to stop such an account and then, stronger, to continue. That censorship, in such circumstances and context as I have sought to establish, is necessarily a bad police-measure is no consolation to the fettered and stifled, who know that a voice is a voice only when it is heard. Moreover, in India they had only regression and decomposition to consider, and not a genuine national progress in the condition of the people to describe or foster. That Indian censorship (when it was fought with principle) involved 'a struggle of principle without power,

---

vested interest and monopoly', and 'through the elimination of the duplication of reporting . . . able to serve the people better'.[139] It was then placed in the charge of the *Hindu*'s editor, on behalf of monopoly, vested interest and faction power.

against power without principle', and that such censorship 'does not achieve what it intends, and does not intend what it achieves',[147] is more to the point and will always offer more hope to the censored. Moreover, despite the spreading infections of the disease of sycophancy, and the prophylaxis of self-censorship, opposition continued to express itself in writing; to be noted or celebrated, according to judgement, but not to be exaggerated since it was small against the total of surrender.

Such opposition was both oblique ('in a brief speech, Mr Barooah professed to be overwhelmed by the trust reposed in him by his colleagues')[148] and overt. Some – the most overt – had their papers banned, or went to jail, while the oblique sought to evade the censor's eye and blue pencil. Others tried to erode the confines of their restriction, product of a refusal to betray their profession at all, or too quickly, to the censor, who might also be in covert sympathy with the censored.*[149] As for the reader, he was left to search for and even to imagine he saw when they were not in fact there, the smallest signs of organic life in what was a rising mountain of dead, trivial and repetitious matter, reader and writer together sterilized by the cuts of the censor.

* Commonest of all were accounts of the idiocies of censorship; the following one, from an unimpeachable source, of its workings in the state of Maharashtra:

The censored (pointing to a dozen blue-pencilled pages): Why all this?

Censor: If I allow anything risky to be published, I shall myself be hauled up. I must take care to err on the safe side.

The censored: If you strike out the whole page, how do I know what is right and wrong?

Censor: Go to the Home Secretary, and ask him. I cannot tell you.

(Two days later)

H. S. Gavai (Home Secretary): We could have allowed certain things, but not others. But the law is an ass, and we are the asses who must carry it out. The whole article has to be forbidden.[150]

cf. 'What have the censors told us? You must not write anything against the "20-point programme". You should not write anything against friendly nations, especially the USA. (Laughing) You must not use the word "loot" for profit. And you must not leave any blank spaces.'[151]

Some judges (a minority) tried to stem this tide also, as we have seen them seek to do in another context. But the grip upon principle of the majority could, in most such cases, be released as readily as with the other supposed guardians – in the state apparatus – of the 'separation of powers', civil freedoms, or the ground-rules of parliamentary or 'bourgeois' democracy, when faced with the greater exigencies of class-loyalty, or fear of removal. Thus Mr Justice Madon and Mr Justice Kania of the Bombay High Court ventured on 21 February 1976 to assert – in a 250-page judgement, reversing a decision in favour of the government by Mr Justice R. P. Bhatt – that it was 'not the function of the censor to make all newspapers speak in chorus'. However, they then added (to get the balance right for fear of dispatch to Assam, or even Tripura) that the 'censor is appointed the nursemaid of democracy' and that it was 'certainly his duty to see that dissent and protest do not overstep the permissible limits'.[152]

From one point of view, and for some, the whole of this debate was as nothing when measured against the knife of compulsory sterilization or the shanty tumbling to the bulldozer, ragged children crying in the gutter; not to speak of those for whom both were necessary present pains to be offset by future pleasures; or unimportant compared, say, with the assault on the trade unions. From another point of view, and for others, we see that lies are not established only by decree or ordinance, or by *force majeure* at its most blatant.

We see instead that the new lie – especially where the world of illusion is already sovereign – establishes its dominion over unarmed opinion (whether of judge or jury, teacher or student, parliamentarian or civil servant) by a process of steady percolation into the fabric of institutions. That the majority of judges, civil servants, Members of Parliament, editors, vice-chancellors assisted in the end, or from the beginning, with and without pressure, in the consolidation of the sovereignty of corruption is to the point. More to the point is that the truth can be traduced more easily, because less painfully, by ambiguity, equivocation, inertia or silence; and the process of such decomposition of a political system is arguably an object-lesson for others, especially where class-crisis may be carrying the whole people down with it if resistance is not offered.

But the orchestrated repetition of untruth and delusion, ideological convergence from all quarters, and the removal of institutional safeguards against licence, become dangerously irresistible; above all, making the term 'conformism' inadequate both as reproach and as explanation. Thus, 'in a democratic set-up like ours, the mass media should strive to keep the citizens fully informed about policies and decisions';[153] while 'the working of the press is fast moving towards the system of self-regulation'.[154] Though 'personally, I am not for censorship at all', 'the Home, and Information and Broadcasting Ministers have their own difficulties',[155] and 'the information needs of the common man must be met so as to enable him to live a fuller life ... and to secure his willing participation'.[156] Now, 'editors have themselves come forward to suggest ways to ensure the press's normal functioning';[157] while 'the press and the popularly elected government should function in a manner that would be helpful to each other'.[158] 'The role of the press is not to destroy the moral fibre of the nation';[159] instead, no sooner said than done, 'it is good that our newspapers have been helping to consolidate the new climate of self-restraint and responsible behaviour'.[160]

Before the deluge of police measures, the press had 'only emphasized the negative aspects of life',[161] 'had made it their purpose to denigrate the nation's endeavour',[162] had 'taken a cynically negative approach ... to disrupt the economic and political system',[163] had 'led the opposition'.[164] Then, 'we took the step. What do we find? Once there were no newspapers, there was no agitation. The agitation was in the pages of the newspapers. If you ask why there is censorship of the press, this is the reason.'[165] After the deluge to defend power, 'newsmen must become once again missionaries of a new resurgent India';[166] 'select and integrate the news better';[167] 'help India grow out of intellectual dependence on alien formulations';[168] and finally, the crux of the matter, 'yield place to those with a positive approach and a real concern for the country'.[169] Simultaneously – and here one fears to lose one's senses unless holding on to the guard-rail of reason – 'the commitment to the liberty of the press still stands'.[170] Here, too, was quickly bared the anatomy and process of political devastation, or blueprint for national reconstruction, depending on the reader.

Standing in theory, if not often in practice, between the citizen's liberty (in squalor) and executive licence, beside the judge, the parliamentarian or the editor, were also the 'independent' civil servant of the 'Westminster model', and even the academic. The latter was to be found either in his ivory tower of theory nicely weighing pros and cons in the intellectual balance, or on the somewhat rougher, mind-soiling, ground of practice. We have already heard Mitra's view – not at issue here – of the corrupt hierarchy of the Indian civil service; perhaps true as generalization, as well for university as for civil service. But it was also subject to qualification with greater and lesser degrees of corruption and courage, greater and lesser degrees of fear of detention or dismissal, intimidation and consequent acquiesence; honour and dishonour cohabiting at all levels of ministry, embassy, university and high commission. But that the administrative civil service and the universities contained the 'recalcitrant' – without adducing any other evidence – requires only the testimony of the scale of the simultaneous emergency assault on them.

In the civil service 'efficiency', 'surplus workers', the 'fight against corruption', and the 'public interest' were offered as rationale for sweeping 'compulsory retirements' and 'retrenchments'. Presided over by senior (and often, therefore, the most corrupt) officials, they affected thousands of civil servants of the lower grades. They included the impoverished, and as often overworked as under-employed, clerks and peons whom we have already encountered in passing. Here, as well as the 'surplus' clerk and administrator, were the unintimidated, the 'independent' in an older civil service tradition, and the unpopular, who were swept quietly away from sight or designated as 'malingerers' who required 'screening', 'weeding out' or 'purging'.[171] These were also the escalations of a language passing beyond illusion into (for India) a new vocabulary of politics, whose general meanings I shall discuss in a later chapter.

That there was more than meets the eye here in other ways is obvious. First, the reconstruction of the machinery of the state in the mode we have been witnessing in fact devolves power upon, and does not take it away from, the large and petty corrupt official, and policeman. An extension of executive licence depends upon them, above all, for its enforcement.* Second, there was the balancing act of a plausible real-politik; in exchange for the loss of freedom there was to be, in addition to other benefits, the ending of corruption and malpractice, albeit under corruption's aegis.

Choosing at random from a host of analogous examples, 'the time has come,' said a Health Ministry circular, 'when systematic weeding out of the inefficient and habitually lethargic officials is called for'. [174] The Ministry of Commerce 'in the context of emergency has compulsorily retired sixty officials in the public interest', while 'the work and conduct of some more officials are being watched and their cases will be reviewed some time next year,'[175] ideology become fear as lived experience. There were not only mass sackings of government employees in Andhra Pradesh, Bihar, Haryana, Madhya Pradesh and the Punjab,[176] for instance, but simultaneous arrests also of the sacked,[177] where law and faction moved in joint action. In fact, arbitrary dismissal for 'corruption' (which included 'weeding out inefficient policemen')[178] was also the attempted creation of a 'purged' public service, which would be unanimously loyal to the corruptions of power.

And to seal off all rights, still to come were decree and ordinance to ratify this political process. They would take away the individual public servant's right to appeal or protest to the courts against dismissal; simultaneously reducing again the courts' jurisdiction and function, and vesting them instead in token administrative tribunals where arbitrary power, by being judge in its own case, would be safer from challenge.†[179] With the 'purges' came other administrative reversions, which cannot be

---

*cf. 'The police with more power are more corrupt. Where a bribe was 20 or 30 rupees, small offenders today are paying 100 or 150 rupees to have charges dropped.'[172] The bribe price for job security in the civil service also rose for similar reasons.[173]

†A good example of such a challenge, and response to it, was the protest to the Chief Minister of West Bengal on 12 February 1976 against his ordinance

followed in this text. They included, among others, plans to strengthen the powers of the district magistrate so that he might become – as in the days of the British – 'kingpin of administration at ground level', itinerating with other 'local officials' from village to village.[181] By these means, though in the name of 'acquaintance with the problems of poor rural areas', the writ of national discipline and faction power might be to bear more closely and watchfully on the responses to the steady immiseration of rural India. In sum, the 'administrative process' was being 'streamlined', and 'a more comprehensive programme of revision of basic rules' was 'on the anvil'.[182]

Academic freedom was also placed on the anvil, and suffered in the wake of the emergency a succession of hammer-blows: mass detention of teachers and students, the abolition of teachers' and students' unions, assaults and inroads physical as well as intellectual, entirely consonant with all that has preceded, and governed by the same propulsions. In the balance of assaults, it may weigh lightly; arguably, too, the groves of Indian academe were long ago polluted. A head count of the detainees (teachers and students) arrested on campus, seized from lecture hall, library or hostel – was impossible; suppressed by the censor, fluctuating in continuing turnover, exaggerated by rumour, minimized by rebuttal, and running into thousands.*

We may approach as always by different paths; some academic

---

giving 'arbitrary authority to Calcutta Corporation to enforce premature retirement without assigning any reason'; the reply was 'I am desired to inform you that the promulgation of such an ordinance was keenly felt by the government for toning-up the municipal administration of the state.'[180] ('Toning-up' was a term frequently encountered as euphemism for the abuse of power, and part of a political vocabulary which will be discussed later).

* I myself visited some twenty universities in different parts of India between November 1975 and January 1976; in all of them, faculty members and students – in some cases in large numbers, with departments of politics, in particular, often at half strength – had been detained since the emergency; in others recently arrested, or released on bail. Arrests were continuing, and the police both uniformed and (allegedly) in plain clothes, ubiquitous. cf. D. V. Urs, acting vice-chancellor of Mysore University, 'the universities of the north are not functioning; in effect, they have closed down, frankly'.[183] The national structure of coercion was, of course, being erected at Mysore University also; for further discussion, see chapter 7.

eyes remaining tightly closed – domestic and foreign – to what was happening, others long open, or opened; and, to begin with, listen to individual voices. 'I regret very much', said Professor L. B. Keny, member of the executive committee of the Indian History Congress, writing from Yeravada Central Prison, Poona, on 12 December 1975,

my inability to attend the 36th session of the Indian History Congress, as I was arrested on 1 November 1975, under MISA, though I am not a member of any political party nor any group of 'smugglers'. I was brought here straight from the library of Bombay University; may be that being the president of the Bombay University teachers' union I was given this treatment. Man proposes, and MISA disposes ... if you get my paper for the symposium, and find it worthwhile, kindly arrange to read it.[184]

There was also the voice which said, rightly or wrongly, 'our universities were more free before we gained our freedom'.[185] Or, instead, we could attend to the Minister for Banking and Revenue, Pranab Mukherjee: 'teachers and intellectuals can play a significant role in creating social awareness among the people';[186] or the Prime Minister's 'here the trouble is caused by professors';[187] or the Congress president's 'forces of disruption in universities will be contained and eliminated'.[188] The same voice reminded vice-chancellors that 'the duty of the universities is to create a cadre of meritocracy essential for the survival of democracy, because unless there are enough men of merit, democracy cannot function'.[189] 'Universities', he added, 'should have no objection to police stepping in and maintaining law and order ... a policeman is like a doctor, preventing as well as curing violence.'[190]

And thus, mass arrest, with the response of vice-chancellors and senior academics ranging from the eager and willing, such as vice-chancellors Shrimali and Pande at Benares and the University of Rajasthan respectively, to the querulous and uncertain, or silent; rare (and usually short-winded) the voice in opposition. On 7–8 July 1975, for instance, a few days after the students' union had condemned the emergency, more than one thousand armed policemen in trucks and jeeps surrounded during the night the men's hostels of Jawaharlal Nehru University,

Delhi, sweeping students into detention.*[191] Detained throughout India for interrogation were student union leaders, often associated with the SFI, rank and file students, university employees, and teachers, often named by informers. If unfound, they were to be subsequently hunted until found, the activists and the innocent alike impounded and with no possibility – as we have seen – of appeal, or writ of *habeas corpus*, and with no knowledge of the grounds of detention. Held under the Defence of India Rules, or MISA, they came from universities and colleges – an incomplete list alone contains over one hundred institutions[193] – in Delhi, Bombay and Calcutta; from Amritsar, Gauhati University in Assam, and Aligarh; from the Indian Institute of Technology at Kanpur, and the University of Rajasthan at Jaipur; from Mysore, Bangalore and Indore; from Haryana Agricultural University, and the college at Meerut; from Benares, Lucknow and Ludhiana (where a woman leader of the SFI at Rada College – Charanjeet – was shot dead by police on 2 September 1975, and quickly cremated); from Tripura and Trivandrum in Kerala, from one end of India to another.

In the panic-stricken scramble to quell the student movement (the mass of students hostile) came the pre-dawn swoop, homes raided and the roaming policeman. The Minister of Education himself visited Aligarh Muslim University on 18 and 19 July 1975, to invite the university's 900 staff – of which he had been a member until his elevation – to declare their support for the emergency and for the ending of academic freedom.†[194] Strikes and boycotts followed, *satyagraha* and beatings, baton charges and further detention, the black-listing and expulsion of stu-

---

* 'They knocked at each person's door, scrutinizing the room, asking where was the president of the union [D. P. Tripathi]. They arrested people at random. They said to me, "This person looks innocent. We'll take him." We were taken to Hauz Kaas police station, where there was a man in a mask standing behind a wire mesh. About sixty of us were called in, one by one, and as each person was called, put in to one group or another; this side or that side; the man in the mask signalling to a policeman. I was allowed to go; others were detained.'[192]

† A fleet of buses reportedly attended their decision; thirty-three assented and one bus, half full, took them to a Delhi radio interview, and presentation to the Prime Minister.

dents, teachers dismissed and suspended; the closure of students' unions and in their stead the setting up of students' 'advisory' or 'welfare' councils[195] – or, 'changes in the structure of student unions to make them more democratic'.[196]

In many universities, already admitted students of known affiliation to, or sympathy with, the opposition were prevented from admission (or from returning, particularly where they held union office), as by vice-chancellor Nagchaudhuri at Jawaharlal Nehru University.[197] At Bhopal University a captive students' union made it 'obligatory' for students to attend a Youth Congress rally to welcome Sanjay Gandhi;[198] while in Kerala the CPI Chief Minister indefinitely postponed student union elections 'to instil a sense of the emergency and strengthen discipline'.[199]

Here formal institutional 'change', or destruction, was inseparable – as in the case of press, judiciary and Parliament – from the often impalpable and corrupting effects of coercive pressure (for instance, upon economists to speak in public praise of the 'new economic programme'). It was a matter of hounding and intimidation, the withheld opinion of the already corruptible, the silent or noisy removal of staff and students, the syllabus and reading-list excisions of the newly impermissible. It was a matter of the introduction of 'new structures' in education, meaning in practice enforced resignation and dismissal of recalcitrants; and of 'new contracts' restricting freedom of opinion, with the sanctions of fear and insecurity growing.[200]

The attacks on university teachers' associations and student unions prepare the ground for later analysis of the meaning of more serious attacks on industrial workers and peasant unions. They have in common the displacement or removal of organizations of self-defence, and decisively change the balance of force and vulnerability in favour of vested interest and entrenched power. It makes little difference whether it be at the point of the dissemination of ideas and information, or of industrial production, and whether it be the work of corrupted faction, debased intellect or arbitrary managerial power. Everywhere in the universities some teachers (the small minority) stood openly for principle, with large numbers opposed – though often for different and opposed reasons – to the degeneration or reconstruction. Some by choice and others by necessity remained silent, without alternative employment, ready but unable to leave the country; some, in silence, quickly circulating clandestine literature, others raising funds for the families of arrested colleagues. Another minority (also small) fell immediately to its knees as if in grateful submission, as the practice of their profession was transformed or subverted. At Delhi University, for instance, on 26 July 1975, five university teachers Divendra Kumar, Ravi Chaturvedi, R. A. Qidwai, D. K. Sharma and Kumari Masih welcomed the emergency, on behalf of the Delhi University Teachers' Association, while its president and about one hundred of their colleagues were in detention, and warrants of arrest had been issued for others.[201] There are many dimensions to the *trahison des clercs*; this was merely one of them.

From the centre, recommended by the Sen Committee, adopted by the university grants committee (and supported by the committee of vice-chancellors of the state universities) came yet another set of guidelines for a 'code of conduct for teachers',[202] analogous with that for pressmen. It was to involve, among other things, 'monitoring' of teachers' work (the 'qualitative and quantitative performance of teachers')[203] and the linking of salary increments to the publication of papers. Patna University, however, banned (as safer) the publication by its teaching staff of books and articles, and 'all extramural activities';[204] Calcutta University appointed home-guard invigilators to preside over its examinations;[205] Bangalore University punished its staff (by fining them) for 'errors in tabulation' of the results of examination;[206] while the Governor of Maharashtra state, by ordinance of 13 January 1976, gave himself the power to have done with it all and 'to take over mismanaged educational institutions'.[207] And in the code of practice for Maharashtra's university teachers, there was included – as in other states – a clause stipulating that 'a teacher will not use the facilities of the classroom or library to propagate his own ideas or beliefs for or against a particular school of thought or theory'; subject to this reservation, however, he would 'continue to have freedom of academic thought and expression'.[208]

In the worst of all possible worlds (if this is what it was), where there is no social progress and this time power defends itself in the name of 'raising academic standards' that oblique euphemism for maintaining law and order – two lines drawn from opposite but complementary ends of the academic spectrum happened to meet at a fixed point, and became the lodestar for educational practice. One was marked 'the need for a new intellectual culture',[209] as integrity collapsed in the face of pressure; the other was labelled 'the elimination of the forces of disruption'.[210] Together they provided – and always will – that light by which the policeman may see his way sure-footed on to the campus, whether as informer with his notebook or tape recorder, or 'doctor' with his baton and revolver.

Faction-power had thus assumed multiple and onerous tasks on the declaration of emergency; not only to re-write the Constitution and the newspaper editorial, but to speak (like a ventriloquist) for the parliamentarian and the professor. But it had also to bring to an end, in order to create a 'strong and stable centre', the federal system of government, by ridding itself of – or replacing, in the name of good governance and order – the remaining non-Congress governments opposing it in the states of the Indian union; that is, the DMK government in Tamil Nadu and the coalition front in Gujarat.

By so doing, it arguably did one of two things. It either rationalized and consolidated the political system of India in the interest of democracy and the nation, or sought to bring the 600 millions of India under the control of dynastic licence; either with loins girded *as if* to ameliorate the people's condition, or at last capable of propelling India, with 'writ unhindered', towards a long postponed and overdue national reconstruction.*

Both the governments of Tamil Nadu and Gujarat were removed by the use of unsubtle standard procedures (subject to minor local variation), with consequences equally predictable.

---

* It is also arguable, as we will see later, that these were not necessarily wholly exclusive alternatives, whether in India or anywhere else. Even the most dictatorial régimes are not entirely free; while the maintenance of power – however draconian – always requires a plausible politics of limited benefit to the people, and one form of ratification or another.

The pattern was of sporadic accusations and charges, from the centre, of 'disorder' – accusations confined to those states whose governments were destined for removal. There then followed a gathering crescendo of allegation, by the corrupt, of mismanagement and even greater corruption in others, with a counterpoint of repetitious denial, from the centre, of intent for removal. It could at the discretion of the centre be accompanied by the sudden and unexplained outbreak of riot, with censorship temporarily suspended for the otherwise unprintable news of violence, headlines pointing the reader to the work of *agents-provocateurs* in Gujarat, or to economic failure in Tamil Nadu. It required no subtlety of perception, understanding the Indian ground rules, also to understand what was in each case coming. It meant the imposition on the states in question of 'president's rule' from the centre; troop and reserve-police movements, and mass arrest; with artful strategy and sycophancy's reflex in chorus, proclaiming in both cases an immediate social, economic and political renaissance. The job of consolidation accomplished, there was a gradual return to the silences of censorship, fear and detention, as a new Congress structure of corruption and violence installed itself, 'normality' was resumed, and the federal principle was subverted.

'President's rule' was imposed on Tamil Nadu, for example, on 31 January 1976. It removed a government led by a state-based populist, or 'cultural nationalist' party – the Dravida Mummetra Kazhagam (DMK). In successive elections (in 1967 and 1971) it had won overwhelming majorities in the state Assembly over its political opponents in the state. The DMK had at the time of its removal 160 of the 234 seats in the Assembly, while the state representatives of the Congress faction ruling at the centre, which overthrew it, had 15 seats in total. The DMK government was at once chauvinist, but more important, recalcitrant. A populist government of the state's ruling class in town and country, and thus in microcosm, its local corruptions included, a regional mutation or variant of the ruling party at the centre, it was – crucially – independent of it. The DMK government was able to be critical of a ruling party without a state following; above all it was an exception – with Gujarat –

to the otherwise unhindered writ of ruling power. Moreover, the centre's new apparatus of coercion and violence was superfluous to the DMK's own modes of maintaining law and order over the state's fifty million people.

Thus, on 27 June 1975, immediately after the declaration of emergency, the executive committee of the DMK, under the state's Chief Minister M. Karunanidhi, was 'pained to note the recent approach by the ruling Congress'. It considered, too, that 'the methods practised by the Prime Minister have tended to put out the light of democracy and led the country into the gloom of dictatorship',[211] declarations sealing its own doom and setting in train six months of inevitable reprisal. The DMK spoke both quickly and incautiously (as silence descended on the rest of India) but with sufficiently telling judgement, of 'the image of truth hidden', and 'ludicrous and strange arguments' adduced in justification of the emergency. It spoke of 'schemes for stifling the opposition parties' and of 'casting on 26 June 1975 an everlasting slur on the Indian people'.[212] It spoke of the ruling faction 'going in search of imaginary reasons', 'calling anything and everything conspiracy and reaction', while itself 'standing in the shadows of falsehood'.[213] These were all to seem ironies in view of what was identically to overtake and swamp the DMK itself, by way of explanation for its own removal.

Karunanidhi went further. At a rally in Madras in early July 1975 attended by an estimated 100,000 people, he called for the revocation of the emergency, democracy's restoration and freedom of the press in India; invoking in their name (or as local populism dictated) Gandhian principle, and the tradition of non-violence. On 24 October 1975 he tolerated, without the counter-violence of the centre's norms for maintaining law and order, a general industrial strike in the state.* It involved some 400,000 industrial workers, protesting against India's 'new deal' economic programme, which had scythed down the political and economic rights of the working class of India.

And in response came the familiar motions. First, 'We have

---

* Itself a measure of the opposition in the Indian labour movement (INTUC and AITUC notwithstanding), and here allowed to surface freely.

no intention of enforcing one-party rule in India. Nor is it true that there has been gagging of all opposition. The opposition parties are running governments in Tamil Nadu and Gujarat.'[214] Then, 'I am deeply worried about the poor economic growth of Tamil Nadu ... but I would not have referred to the poor record of the DMK government but for its efforts to mislead the public.'[215] Then, 'the national party [sic] must step in, if the people of Tamil Nadu are to be saved from the misrule of regional parties'.[216] There were other routes and other – equally familiar – movements. They passed from the ominous 'I have been getting from Tamil Nadu Congressmen reports of slanderous personal attacks on me ... let these petty-minded people say what they like ... these attacks are not going to change me',[217] to 'per capita development expenditure under the Fifth Plan in Tamil Nadu has fallen below the national average'.*[218] They proceeded quickly down through the headlines of 'a blistering attack on the performance of the DMK government in Tamil Nadu',[221] and 'it is not my habit to run down any government but I have to do so in Tamil Nadu, because to escape from their own acts of omission and commission they are blaming the central government',[222] and headlong into house-arrest and detention of the DMK government and members of the state's Legislative Assembly.

There are other voices speaking also and as usual, but in monologue. Three weeks before the movement of the para-military to end the DMK's state rule, the CPI 'requests the central government not to extend the DMK ministry's term of office'.[223] There is Karunanidhi's own voice as his fate is sealed, and under mounting pressure: 'I have no plan to resign before the expiry of my term of office'.[224] There is the Chief Minister of West Bengal's 'you are like a drowning man clutching at a straw; you are raising parochial slogans',[225] while Karunanidhi is described as a 'a class fascist of the first order'.[226] And, at the

---

*cf. 'Progress in Tamil Nadu and Gujarat was the same as in other parts of the country since the emergency';[219] or 'the recent Reserve Bank of India study on state government shows an overall decline [throughout India] in the share of development expenditure in total expenditure'.[220] However, the truth or untruth of assertion and counter-assertion were of little account under these rules.

very last, the CPI called out its members in the state to strike – doing so nowhere else – against the DMK's 'failure to implement the 20-point programme',[227] a gratuitous aid, and a national failure.

An accurate head-count of numbers of the arrested was impossible, and unavailable. Many hundreds both of prominent DMK politicians and rank-and-file members were evidently taken in the first wave of detention, or placed under house arrest; 'the smaller fry beaten';[228] people taken from crowded buses by plain-clothes policemen; with Karunanidhi himself facing charges of corruption. Once again there occurred the cycle of arrest, release and turnover, as fear made men turncoats, and bribes unlocked the doors of the prison. The state assembly was dissolved, in the name of a new democratic order and on behalf of its fifteen members of the ruling faction; the Border Security Force and Central Reserve Police were dispatched to Madras and rural Tamil Nadu;[229] there was an army alert on the state's borders;[230] the streets after working hours were quickly deserted; processions and public meetings were banned.[231] Together, they offered the opportunity – gladly seized upon – of simultaneous attacks on other opposition parties represented in the state, on the CPI–M and once more on its trade union organization the CITU, its leadership forced into hiding.[232]

And then, apologia and explanation in a deluge, whose ideological structure corresponds with all the foregoing. The DMK 'was getting substantial financial help from some foreign sources';[233] 'for partisan ends, grossly abusing its power';[234] 'had a veiled objective of seceding from the Indian union'.[235] The state of Tamil Nadu 'had become a sanctuary for all underground people';[236] its 'economic health had sunk totally',[237] and it was 'a hotbed of institutionalized corruption'.[238] And, as *coup de grâce*, the DMK 'had ignored the prevalent feelings in the country and brought about its own downfall',[239] its 'dismissal' 'a natural outcome of its misdeeds', and 'welcomed by the very great majority of the people'.*[240]

---

* cf. 'They say now this DMK government is corrupt. They knew it was corrupt before, and they were not interested. Karunanidhi was not obeying her. That is the reason.'[241]

Familiar, but trivial beginnings; there were deeper resonances. The Congress Party's trade union body in the state (INTUC), for long implicated in 'stooge union' violence, could be immediately observed setting up a committee to 'process specific data regarding ... organized violence against trade unions belonging to other than the ruling [DMK] party'.[242] The pro-CPI *Link* could be heard immediately describing the Prime Minister as 'the saviour of Tamil Nadu', who was 'issuing a new charge sheet against the DMK' for having 'infiltrated party men into the administration' and of 'violating the traditional concept of keeping the administration free of party politics'.[243] Within days, unarrested former members of the DMK government, such as the Minister for Local Administration, S. Ramachandran, were turning their coats inside out in public, quaking at a presumption of guilt by association with former colleagues, and calling for the 'isolation from the party' of the former Chief Minister so that 'the future of innocent fellow party men should not be jeopardized.'[244]

The Prime Minister, also within days of the ousting or 'toppling' of the Tamil Nadu government, was 'lashing out at the opposition', at Aurangabad on 24 February 1976. 'They have tried,' she said, 'to topple democratically elected governments in some parts of the country, and cut the very root of the democratic set-up'; 'if this continues democracy will be destroyed,' she added.*[245] It did of course continue; after Tamil Nadu, Gujarat, but I will come to that in a moment.

First, a brief glance at the consequent renaissance of Tamil Nadu behind the froth of violence and the tedium of detention, from which we should 'constructively' avert our eyes, turning from negative aspect to positive. After all, in the immediate aftermath of rule from the centre – days, not weeks – the administration in general is being 'toned up'; more, 'an entirely new

---

*And cf. 'In the name of democracy, it has been sought to negate the very functioning of democracy. Duly elected governments have not been allowed to function, and in some cases force has been used to compel members to resign in order to dissolve lawfully elected assemblies.'[246]

direction has been given to Tamil Nadu politics, almost over-night'.[247] More specifically, the administration is being made 'honest and clean, prompt and efficient';[248] 'changes are being made in the state's police organization to tone up the working of the department';[249] 'hoarders and smugglers' have been ar-rested;[250] while 'to cleanse the cooperative movement of cor-ruption' 1,500 rural irrigation cooperatives 'have been liquidated [sic]'.[251] The state as a whole 'has been brought back into the *mainstream* of Indian life',[252] another frequently used term, whose implications will be examined later.

The Governor of Tamil Nadu (with vice-regal powers in the absence of elected government) at once perceived that 'prices have gone down, stocks have increased, injustices have been corrected, and the people in all spheres are showing increased enthusiasm'.[253] There was also 'an excellent investment climate'.[254] Moreover, 'disputes between landlords and agricultural labour, frequent in the past, are no longer there, with farm operations going smoothly';[255] and the 'industrial tempo restored, for which Tamil Nadu in the past had a great reputation'.[256]

In the errie silence which followed upon arrest and violence (or, if you prefer, 'the widespread feeling of sudden release from the coils of DMK power')[257] the voice of sycophancy is quickly audible, without need of any censor. 'The real issue puzzling observers of the Tamil Nadu political scene' is 'what has hap-pened to the hard core of the DMK, in the wake of the im-position of President's rule.'[258] 'Although a number of them are lying low' – either 'involved in secret underground operations undermining democracy'[259] or 'gripped by the fear of being out-lawed', according to the pro-CPI *Link*, and 'in utter confusion and panic'[260] – 'it is obvious that the structure of their support was not as solid as many imagined'.[261] The police, moreover, 'have done a neat job in ensuring that there was no collapse of authority, with considerable finesse'; while 'the response of the local bureaucracy is quietly efficient'.[262] Nonetheless, 'it is in-triguing why the DMK strength proved almost overnight to be so hollow'; and, expert in the ways of the absolute corruption of interest as well as power, the writer concluded that 'the

DMK has paid a heavy price by living up to the famous dictum of Lord Acton'.[263]

And before leaving this unctuous state of police finesse, and of bureaucracy quietly efficient, there were other voices to be caught in passing. By 16 April 1976, as degeneration took full hold, Barooah was calling on Congress Party members 'to deal with the DMK', but 'not as a mere political rival'. 'We should', he said, 'fight to eliminate them as a political party', and 'wipe out the DMK in Tamil Nadu'.[264] And then there could be heard the voice of the CPI, tragedy's full circle completed, returning to the scene to complain of 'excesses against the poor people, carried out under the disguise of neutralizing the DMK elements',[265] for which they themselves only a few weeks earlier had been calling.

There is, in fact, little need to cross India to Gujarat merely to witness the same process; that is, to cross a political terrain which no longer requires either map or compass. We need only mark quickly the local variations, and note also that, to the Minister of State for Home Affairs, 'what happened in Tamil Nadu or Gujarat should serve as a warning to others'.[266] The lesson was not spelled out; it was clear enough, however, that a coordinated political apparatus and the expedients required to instal it would take precedence over the principles of federalism and states' rights, as well as the inconvenient facts of locally elected opposition power.

With the government of Tamil Nadu knocked out, the coalition (Janata Front) government of Gujarat – which included an opposed faction of the Congress Party, led by Morarji Desai, until imprisoned – was a sitting target, with little time remaining. There was the score of the pre-emergency electoral defeat there of the ruling faction to be settled; while the associated verdict of electoral corruption delivered against the Prime Minister, although already erased by erasing law and Constitution, still warranted a final *ex post facto* reprisal. In July 1975 the situation was already 'precarious', the centre reported to be 'waiting for the coalition front to deliver the situation into the hands of the government' and the state itself described as 'full of para-military units'.[267] More to the point, the state government – though showing 'extreme caution'[268] – was inexcusably permitting protest meetings and the functioning of democratic institutions.*

This 'caution' obviously was to avail them nothing; nor did the Chief Minister's defensive insistence that the situation was 'completely normal'.[269] For a lesser corruption was here awaiting its defeat, once more, at the hands of the greater corruption of the ruling Congress faction in Delhi. Additionally, unlike Tamil Nadu, the *agent-provocateur*'s violence was ready to be pressed into service, if the expression of genuine opposition of the required kind, and at the needed moment, was not sufficiently manifest.

On 15 December 1975 the president of the Gujarat Congress Party, Hitendra Desai, 'drew the attention' of the Home Ministry to 'the worsening law and order situation in the state'.[270] On the same day, Barooah signalled the centre's decision to commence its preparations to end the Gujarat government's tenure, by telephoning Desai to 'convey his concern at the deteriorating law and order situation in Gujarat'.[271] And if there was no evidence of it, it would have to be created. Thus, on 8 January 1976, the Home Minister announced that 'the law and order situation in Gujarat', which was 'not merely a question of violent incidents but the creation of an atmosphere', was 'under the close watch of the central government'.[272] On 15 January 1976, its close watch completed, a senior Home Ministry official, K. Rustom, 'rushed from New Delhi to have an on-the-spot survey of disturbed areas', as violent incidents and 'rioting', 'stone-throwing', setting fire to shops and looting were suddenly and simultaneously reported in Gujarat – breaking through the rigorously imposed censorship upon 'agitation' – from Nadiad and Petlad, Ladwada, Wadi and Baroda.[273] Blazing headlines referring to 'riot-hit Baroda' pointed the

* Thus, the Gujarat Chief Minister Babubhai Patel inaugurated the 'Save the Constitution' convention in Ahmedabad on 1 January 1976, held under the auspices of Citizens for Democracy. In an extempore speech, later published and privately circulated, he made clear his opposition to the emergency. 'In this state,' he said, 'MISA will not be used against political workers' (*Citizens of India Cherish Democracy*, Navajivan Press, Ahmedabad, p. 7). Patel was later arrested; and see p. 507.

Indian reader's attention not towards the bitter (censored) opposition to the emergency, but towards the necessity to remove the government of Gujarat.

Thus assisted, on 2 February 1976 Desai 'released a party report charging that the state government had been unable to keep order and that political violence was increasing'.[274] On 16 February, V. C. Shukla, Minister for Information, criticized the Gujarat government for its 'failure to protect the interests of the poor, of labour, and of the backward classes'.[275] On 9 March 1976, 'dynamite was discovered in Baroda'. Members of Mrs Gandhi's Congress faction, who were in opposition in Gujarat, promptly accused the coalition government of 'sheltering subversive elements'. There was, they said, an 'inter-state gang of conspirators' in Gujarat 'with the blessings of the front government', which was 'out to destroy the security of the nation'.[276] On 13 March 1976, President's rule was proclaimed in Gujarat, the state government gone, the 'riots' over.

In the round of arrests and detentions which followed – later to include George Fernandes – two journalists, Vikram Rao and Kirit Bhatt, and a municipal councillor, Jaswant Singh Chauhan (all announced to have 'socialist leanings' and later to be 'workers and sympathizers of the Socialist Party'),[277] were arrested, suspected of 'conspiracy and espionage' and of 'crating the dynamite for onward dispatch to Varanasi'. The connection between them and the CIA, said the Home Minister on 17 March 1976 – with perhaps little to learn from the CIA of the art and craft of a government's 'destabilization' – was 'also being investigated'.*[278]

---

* This then left as the outstanding hybrid government – but still marching ostentatiously in step, and even ahead of the column – the ruling Congress/CPI coalition in Kerala. But there had already been straws in the wind for that government. On 30 December 1975, for example, the Prime Minister declared that 'the RSS is finding its foothold in Kerala ... which was bound to be polluted by the activities of the RSS'.[279] In March 1976 there was, despite censorship, widely publicized sabotage of an hydro-electric project in the state, followed by the 'seizure of dynamite' on 29 March 1976, only three weeks after it had been discovered in Gujarat.[280] From such straws, bricks were made in India. But cf. 'the united front government in Kerala received fulsome praise from the Prime Minister' on 11 and 12 February 1976, on her visit to the state, with 'the Achutha Menon ministry

And immediately thereafter there were 'the big relief of rule from the centre' (according to the CPI),[282] 'price increases arrested', and 'the new Gujarat administration fast toning up the machinery of government'[283] to mark the silent surface of the new discipline and order. Beneath it, in the first oblivion of censorship and detention, violence and fear of further violence, the CIA, the guilt of the arrested, the fact and the fiction of opposition, and the government of Gujarat were all temporarily lost from sight together.*

If this further collision with the institutions of India were to be considered only as another violent but minor preparation for national reconstruction, then it was perhaps of relatively little significance. There is, after all, a well-tried principle that without broken eggs (and bodies) there can be neither omelette (nor social progress). With further evidence – still to be summoned – of economic and social achievement, the question of the political nature of such reconstruction might then pale into further insignificance. Alternatively, upon the eventual determination of that question a good deal could depend; and it would not be confined to India.

The scale of the assault, to which we must now turn, on the rights and activities of the working class and the trade unions may have some bearing on the matter. It involved the forcible reshaping of the politics of production; additional vulnerabilities compounding the long history of violence, by the tearing down both of the rights of self-defence, and organized offence, against low wages and other forms of injustice. The rights, for example, to meet, publish and strike were in turn met: with detention and prohibition under MISA and the Defence of India Rules, and by the revocation of the relevant constitutional freedoms under Article 19, as already mentioned. They were met by law and ordinance instituting censorship, and by special regulation

---

hailed as a "pace-setter" for the whole country'.[281] The combination of aspersion, sabotage, the discovery of dynamite, and reassurance was an uneasy one; while excess of all kinds was required in a just-tolerated coalition to prove its credentials to remain in office.

*For the later fate of the arrested and of the government of Gujarat, and for the attachment to the case of George Fernandes, see chapter 8, p. 331.

at the hands of local police authority. They were met by the whim (or licence) of local officials and bullies, to whom the abuse of power over the class devolves in certain kinds of political and economic crisis.

Here context is all important. The minimum necessary is recall of the degree of crisis, of inflation and recession, and of the increasing hardship in the condition of the people; or, to take other accounts, the stagnation of their condition, a word itself pregnant with horror in the circumstance of India. In such a context the removal of the right to strike, a cut in the bonus rate, a decline in real wages, is no abstraction of political or economic theory; nor does fear of detention, as price of wage-demand and protest, constitute a theorem to be found in any textbook of economics. Moreover, to seek to take away the rights of millions to defend themselves (which becomes the right to exist on the very margins of survival) is different in degree, and even perhaps in kind, from the loss by the small literate minority of the population of the luxurious freedom to read and write this or that opinion. If, in addition, it were to be the case that the owners and managers of the means of production need pay a much diminished regard to the claims of those whose labour they purchase, then a new politics is in process of construction. And it is not one which points irresistibly, as we shall see, to a simple 'trade-off' or equation between increased production and diminished freedom.

There are qualities as well as quantities to be observed here, also. They too are capable of measure. It was not only the (laughing) matter of 'we had a strong union two years ago which created a mass struggle. Now, in emergency, they are just helpless',[284] because beyond it was a new and direr view of class and labour. Beyond it was that further licence – whether expressed as dalliance with the notion of a population of millions 'surplus to requirements', or in more sophisticated equivalents to be considered – which flourishes when liberty of protest and organization against it is taken by prohibition, or detention. That makes for another equation, which demands a finer and more careful setting of the balance of judgement.

We can approach closer once more by different routes. We can proceed by the volume of arrests of opposition trade union leaders and rank and file members throughout India, involving 'over 2,000 trade union officials alone'.[285] It mowed through the CITU – taking twenty members of its general council[286] – and other opposition trade union bodies, the CITU 'caught by surprise', 'dazed ... by fear of repression', and 'stupefied'.[287] The working class itself was divided, with the Congress Party's INTUC declaring that the 'role of the working class and trade unions' was 'different during the emergency from its traditional role' and calling for 'increases in productivity and production, without a single machine even for a day remaining idle'.[288] Prohibition orders on meetings and on strikes, charge-sheets and suspension orders, layoffs, lockouts and closures, thus coincided with accreditation and rights of representation being reserved to unions accepting the emergency's restrictions.* So that, while the CITU and other opposition unions were being attacked throughout India, the leaderships of INTUC, the CPI's AITUC and the Hind Mazdoor Sabah (Indian Workers Assembly) simultaneously gained exclusive rights for their officials of industrial representation, while themselves suppressing internal opposition among their own members.

Further elements, many not new, made their appearance. There were the protests to the ILO on 8 November 1975 about 'the grave situation prevalent in India', and on 'the suppression of freedom of association'.[290] There was forcible seizure by the police and Youth Congress members, of opposition union offices and membership registers; and victimization, by dismissal from their jobs, of active trade union workers.[291] There was protest at the arrest of miners' union officials 'after making representations in writing for an improvement in wages', and evidence of intimidation and violence to 'persuade' workers to

---

* 'The workers and the trade unions which aspire to accreditation with the government are required to accept new and special obligations. They are called upon to abjure strikes and agitational methods, to strive for higher production and productivity, and to subordinate their immediate sectional interest for the sake of long range gains for the national economy.'[289]

join INTUC and AITUC[292] – that is, the long industrial history of extra-legal union breaking, at last given full political legitimation. There was the joining of hands of police, management, Congress Party workers and trade unions in familiar Indian alliance. There was complaint to the ILO of the death in custody (in Indore) on 18 September 1975 of the veteran trade union leader, Bhairav Bharati;*[293] and there was the first news of the torture of the arrested, to be discussed later. There was the political meaning of the alternating silence and uneasy protest† of the leadership of AITUC, as the rights and functions of the class and cause they represented were cut, with their aid, from under them.

At no point can this be abstracted from its social and political context, whether it be the new loss of rights of imprisoned trade unionists to approach the courts ('at least the British allowed us to file writs for our members in the courts. But now what can we do?')[295] or to know the reason for detention. It must include the absence of any national social security system; while local provisions to protect workers from arbitrary dismissal, or the consequences of unemployment, illness, or industrial accident are meagre, ineffective or entirely absent. It must include the newly mounting toll of industrial disasters, under the pressures of unprotected fear and demands for increased production, often in satanic conditions and without adequate safety measures. The death toll in the mines after the

---

*'He was arrested on the first day of the emergency – 25 June 1975 – at his native village, four miles from Nagda. Hariprasad Singh, a member of the Congress Party, said "I knew him since his childhood. He was a trusted and ardent fighter for the peasants and workers. We remained friends. There was no serious illness which might have caused his death, but he died in government custody." ' Allegedly, the order for his release came a few minutes before his death.[294]

†e.g. AITUC, on 17 April 1976, protested to the state of West Bengal's joint industrial body (from which opposition unions – the most powerful hitherto in the state – had been excluded) that the jute mill owners in West Bengal had 'arbitrarily reduced wages of workers', 'heavily increased workloads', 'introduced double and multiple spinning operations', 'compelled workers to work on holidays'; that 'the rights of the workers had been unilaterally curtailed' and 'the terms of agreements flouted'. *Economic and Political Weekly*, 1 May 1976.

declaration of emergency, for example, surpassed all previous records,[296] culminating in the huge disaster at the Dhanbad colliery in Bihar on 27 December 1975, of which I will give an account later.

On the question of trade unions, there was a babel of discordant responses, which included eerie echoes of the colonial past, new voices of the present, and tokens of India's future; reassurance, disbelief or anger, depending upon interest and position. 'Immediately after independence there was a total ban on trade unions. Many of us were arrested and jailed, union offices sealed or raided; the right to strike taken, workers tortured. What is happening now is, in the question of repression, what from 1949 to 1951 we suffered under Nehru also. For us, it is not new.'[297] Or, 'the trade union movement had no common aim except to advance their own individual interests at the expense of the nation ... with purposeless parades and demonstrations, frivolous strikes and agitational propaganda'.[298] Or, 'we are gradually stopping industrial action from being taken. The Indian worker, if he is not involved with trade unions, can be persuaded. To introduce into it a political, red or pink, colour kills it. INTUC is doing well. We can make deals with them, since they share our understanding of the position. They know the main thing is disciplining the workforce and increasing production.'[299]

Either, 'organizations critical of the government are virtually prevented from carrying out the ordinary activities of trade unions ... They are not allowed to hold any meetings except for supporting the government ... Such trade unions even if they command the largest membership are excluded from every committee. We request you to appoint an impartial fact-finding committee of the ILO so that the real state of affairs is known to the world, and steps are taken to prevent suppression of trade union and democratic rights in India';[300] or, ' "industrial relations have improved beyond our imagination," the Prime Minister added'.[301]

In economic recession, the displacement and transfer of burdens to the working class is usual. In India, it was accompanied by the politics of an apparent equivalence; that is the prohibition, together, of strikes, lockouts and layoffs. The latter (as we shall see) increased with impunity; the former were met by victimization and dismissal, detention and violence, without redress or protection, and for which there can be neither equivalence, nor real compensation.[302] Moreover, in a 'progressive' struggle directed, in the search for an 'Indian road to socialism', against 'fascism' and 'right reaction', an onslaught not only upon fundamental features of the liberal and social democracy at the centre of the political spectrum, but upon the political rights of the socialist opposition and the trade unions, is critical to any final reckoning of the balance of meanings.

The after-echo of the voices we have heard was a reverberating one; not merely in the silence of detention or the vacuum between economic fact and political fiction, but also in the roar of 'increasing production', or the inundation of the 400 lost Bihar colliers. Thus, we hear that 'indiscipline in industry in this land will never again be tolerated', and that 'workers will not be allowed to sit idle or indulge again in movements, though their rights will be protected';[303] but there was also heard the call to 'rise against the tyranny of the dictator, fight the enemies of the working class and the people',[304] of George Fernandes the railwaymen's leader, 'issuing', according to the resolutions of the CPI's national council, 'rabid leaflets from the underground',[305] until found, arrested and imprisoned. 'He was not interested,' the CPI's Achutha Menon told me, speaking softly, bland or weary, 'in the conditions of the workers. His motives were political only, utilizing every opportunity to bring down Mrs Gandhi. I too have had to warn in Kerala that unreasonable stoppages and irresponsible industrial behaviour would not be tolerated.'[306]

And here, there is another possible route to understanding of this chapter's multiple contents. The expression of the considerable internal strains on the CPI of alliance with a policy which included – and arguably was coming to be dominated by – a political, economic and physical offensive against the working class and its organizations, is informing. These strains were telling, despite what we have just heard, and from time to time they spoke.

To exclude these further discordant voices is to exclude not only political contradiction and evidence of faction and dissension, analogous to that in the ruling party, but also the intermittent surfacing of unease, if not principle. They could be heard despite party discipline and strategy, which dictated CPI participation and acquiescence in the abuse of faction power; and which added their own compressions, at a critical historical moment, to the penal restraints upon real opposition.

CPI responses to the emergency, on closer examination, in fact varied. However judged, they were therefore not exactly the same as outright apologia, nor the simple 'betrayals' castigated as 'left reaction' by the parties to the left of them: that is, the CPI–ML, the CPI–M, the Socialist Party and left-wing Congress factions. Thus, the government was 'urged' by a CPI Member of Parliament 'to allow trade unions to function in a manner in which they can carry on with their work and fulfil their responsibilities'.[307] It was discreetly pointed out that 'taking advantage of the emphasis on discipline, some managements with the help of the bureaucracy have sought to curtail workers' rights and trade union rights', 'raising apprehensions among the working classes'.[308] And though a parliamentary resolution put forward by the CPI–M, 'cannot be supported', the CPI spokesman could be heard 'pleading that the working class should be allowed to hold meetings'.[309]

Moreover, internal party documents and publications reveal differences in their degree of approval for the emergency, from those contained in parliamentary statements and in public. Though it was true that whenever the conflict between the two was acutely presented, an escape from reality and consequence was immediately provided by illusion, the conflict itself was patent. Thus, in public declaration, 'during the recent period, the government has undertaken in response to popular demand significant progressive measures';[310] but in its written variant, 'serious negative factors exist, and new ones have made a recent appearance'.[311] On the one hand the emergency was 'hailed as a bold step';[312] those who were opposed to the emergency were held to be 'objectively supporting fascism' because the emergency in effect was the 'second stage of India's independence struggle';*[313] and, in reply to critics, 'this is not a one party dictatorship because our party is allowed to function'.[315]

On the other hand, in party publication, 'cases of the misuse of the emergency powers against the democratic rights of the common people are continually occurring'.[316] In fact, 'police officers are taking bribes by threatening arrest under MISA. Huts and wayside stalls are being bulldozed, small traders harassed and hoarders not much affected';[317] and 'censorship is working against' or 'playing havoc with' 'the progressive press also'.[318] Moreover, 'the blanket ban on public meetings is hampering our propaganda' while 'the bureaucrats are not even allowing meetings of party members'.[319] On the one hand, in public – in this case S. A. Dange, the CPI's chairman, speaking on 28 February 1976 at the CPSU Congress in Moscow – 'the rightist and fascist forces made a diabolic bid for the seizure of power which was foiled by the bold pre-emptive actions taken in declaring a national emergency'.[320] On the other, in party publication, there appear 'bureaucratic and anti-democratic acts of commission and omission, including the arrest of CPI members'.[321]

But in deep dilemma, when the public convergence of the pronouncements of CPI and Congress then grew too close for comfort, or they became indistinguishable to the the naked eye, the CPI was driven to disclaim any absolute identity. 'If you think that the CPI is a "B" team of the Congress, you will have difficulty';[322] 'the CPI is not dependent on the Congress, nor politically guided by Congress ideology'.[323] On the contrary its 'political existence does not depend upon the mercy of the Congress Party' and it is 'still following the marxist line of action'.†[324]

---

*cf. 'After the state machine was used against fascist and extreme rightist forces, the conditions were never so favourable for the completion of the unfinished tasks of the Indian revolution.'[314] Also, Achutha Menon told me clearly, and then retracted his opinion when I wrote it down in my notebook, that 'there are no significant ideological differences between the CPI and the Congress'.

†cf. 'The fooling of the people is facilitated by the help given to the Congress government by the leaders of the CPSU and the CPI and several other communist parties. They have openly supported this conspiracy to instal a one-party authoritarian government in the country.'[325]

That being so, it was further cornered by the Congress Party's recoil from this 'marxism', and its refusal to engage in joint actions with the CPI to implement the progressive 'new economic programme', stone deaf to the CPI's call for 'the constitution of people's committees'[326] in order to oversee land reform. But since the CPI had been asserting that 'a new stage of popular anti-fascist unity has been reached between the Congress and the CPI at all levels from the national level down to grass-root level',[327] acute forms of unease began to appear in various guises.

They were expressed in an alleviating rhetoric shorn of meaning, its absurd disjunction from reality and practice growing acuter as the CPI was tossed on the horns of its dilemma. 'Let us follow what Lenin said: "Living in the midst of the people. Knowing the people's mood. Knowing everything. Understanding the people. Having the right approach. Winning the absolute trust of the masses, the vanguard never losing touch with the entire army of labour" ',[328] and so on. Or 'negative portents' in the politics and strategy of the ruling faction had to be given impossibly circuitous explanation, image of the CPI's own complicated predicament. Thus 'evil forces are using every instance of bureaucratic misuse of the emergency. Their agents purposefully do things to turn the toiling people against the emergency';[329] 'counter-revolutionary forces are doing it consciously to pour cold water over the enthusiasm of the toiling masses, and turn them hostile to the emergency'.[330] That is, the same right-reaction which made a 'diabolic bid for power' and brought the emergency to India's rescue, was now misusing the emergency's powers to bring it all into discredit.

The struggle of illusion to master or deny reality is of the same order as, and intimately connected with, the force and guile required to master men's bodies. That such a struggle was fully joined on all fronts in the process of 'swinging into action' and was inseparable from it, is self-evident. If illusion was to be successful, then what has preceded must appear the direction of method and order; if not, it was blood spilled and jails filled, heads and laws broken simultaneously.

Arguably – and the matter must be forced to remain open

here despite evidence's accumulations – if illusion was to succeed, it would be a nation's decisive struggle against fascism and subversion. If it failed, it would be a struggle of faction power against the liberties of the people, the brunt of such political crisis in the last analysis being borne by the left opposition, and the economic crisis by the working people of India.

If words alone were counted, particularly those officially promulgated, a complex issue would be easily resolved. The scales were first tilted, and then held down by the censor's fist or finger. Then they were loaded to huge totals, with the 'massive patriotic anti-fascist unity . . . among Congressmen, communists and democratic mass organizations . . . rousing the Indian people towards the fascist danger'.[331] The balance groaned under the burden of the 'enhanced vigilance and all-round strengthening of progressive patriotic forces to safeguard India's national freedom'.[332] 'The struggle of the Indian people against imperialism, fascism and reaction',[333] must be added, and 'the anti-feudal programme of the Indian government in wiping out the social base of the rightist forces'.[334] Weighing in was the additional colossal tonnage of the Soviet Union ('the entire socialist camp is with us'),[335] in solidarity – brought by Alexander Kuzmin to Patna – 'with the fight of the Indian government against fascism's anti-human activities, massacres and oppression of the working classes',*[336] of which we may already have caught fleeting glimpses.

Perhaps, then, what has passed in this chapter is featherweight in comparison with such a barrage. After all, even with the censor's hand removed, we saw that the self-adjusting balance remained unmoving. Is it perhaps that the fight against fascism in a new era of 'destabilization' 'somehow' involves assault on the working class, or trade unions? Could it be that Article 352 of the Constitution was justly invoked to meet fascism's threat to the security of India? Could it be that everything which followed was 'within the framework of the Indian

---

* Other definitions of fascism (for instance, that of 'a whispering campaign') weighed more lightly in the balance. Cf. also, 'it is precisely when a minority tries to convince the people through wrong propaganda and false promises that they will ensure them a decent life that fascism always rears its head'.[337]

Constititution', had had 'no effect upon the rights of law-abiding citizens', who were 'free to pursue their avocations without hindrance', and that there was therefore 'no deviation from democratic values'?[338] Could it even be that what has so far been described did not take place at all, real fact made by the writer's 'reaction', into fiction?

Perhaps, then, we should move away, as from a source which is tainted. When the former Bombay Chief Justice, Washington Ambassador, and London High Commissioner said, 'I wonder whether I am going through a nightmare. I rub my eyes to make sure whether I am awake or asleep',[339] he was obviously dreaming. The Indian suggestion that 'it is possible for them to lie with absolute honesty, because they believe in their own lies and therefore consider themselves honest',[340] was no more (if that) than a reactionary witticism, unworthy of the occasion. The further suggestion that the Indian ruling class have for three decades proved adept at isolating themselves – while trying in turn to isolate large sections of the people – from an awesome social reality, is superficially impressive but too impressionistic to be of value at this juncture, if at any.

And if we kept to the straight and narrow, there would be no need to remind the reader of the warning to the Constituent Assembly in 1949, during debate on the Constitution, that 'if the emergency provisions are adopted, this whole Constitution will be in danger, not so much from those who are agitating in the streets as from those who are in power'.[341] These provisions were similar, said the speaker nearly thirty years ago, to those contained in Article 48 of the Weimar Constitution. If we got on more quickly to the countervailing evidence of social and economic regeneration, we would not be prompted to waste time in thinking there was something else to be noticed in 'the spectre of disorder has been banished',[342] or in 'the opposition had better behave themselves and do a bit of introspection'.[343] There would be no point in following further the path which might (misleadingly) take us downwards; from the Home Minister's 'the element of fear brought about by the emergency is beneficial, for fear when all other means fail can be a potent motivating factor';[344] to 'a man is a performing flea, he can be trained',[345] of the president of the Congress Party. His, we know, was only the voice of the jester, and should therefore be discounted.

It would then be more discreet, as well as less time-consuming, to overlook other outbreaks of candour which periodically appeared to give part of the game away. We should not ask what the Industry Minister, T. A. Pai, meant when he said that 'there are certain problems which cannot be moved on party lines. They require the complete identification of all people who are better off in this country',[346] the abstraction of 'class power' suddenly embarrassingly alive, and speaking of 'safeguarding our own interests, and trying to change the *status quo*'[347] in a political nexus separated only by a comma. Nor should we bother our heads with Subramaniam's 'if we are safe on the food front, we can take risks on any other'.[348]

In any case, there was no violence. It is easy to be in error. In fact, 'since the emergency, we have not used the baton to enforce discipline'.[349] On 5 March 1976, 'there is no show of force whatsoever in the country'.[350] Therefore, we ought probably to discount the announcement on the same day, and from the same source, that there had been 'unnecessary use of force by the police entirely unrelated to security'.[351] Perhaps the Home Minister was misreported when (on the previous day) he urged Chief Ministers to take 'immediate steps to stop police excesses', which he said were 'continuing despite earlier instructions not to indulge in needless violence'. He had received, he added, 'reports of the unbridled use of violence by the police on the public', which they should 'abjure' in order 'to improve their image'.[352]

By 3 April 1976, in any case, 'the police force was being oriented to build up its image as a protection force'; the 'unfortunate feeling about it as a force of repression would be a thing of the past'[353] henceforward. By 19 April 1976, so successful was the reorientation that the Prime Minister had felt able to tell the *San Francisco Examiner* that 'we have not had to use the police at all throughout the emergency',[354] which completed the circle of reassurance, and settled the issue.

The record must then have been wilfully distorted in this

text. 'Magnificent changes have come upon India, with everyone doing their duty of their own free will and unprodded.'[355] There is 'a climate of peace and harmony'[356] with 'no threat to freedom of expression and other freedoms in India';[357] indeed, 'the emergency has been hailed universally within the country and abroad by all the well-wishers of democracy'.[358] 'Profiteering has ended, prices are down, and trains are running to schedule.'[359] 'Workers' legitimate demands are being met and their interests continuing to be protected.'[360] 'The police and defence forces are disciplined and deeply patriotic',[361] the former 'the friends and servants of the people'[362] and 'serving the public politely'.[363] There is 'no ban on holding meetings by political parties for legitimate, constitutional and peaceful activity'.[364] In fact, 'India's people are continuing to be free to express their different opinions',[365] while 'political leaders under arrest are being extended all courtesy and consideration'.[366] Indeed, 'the Prime Minister is not for any kind of imprisonment',[367] and Achutha Menon is 'unaware of any restrictions on academic freedom in India'.[368]

Moreover, 'the working class is agreeing to put up extra efforts and raise production',[369] with 'work going on smoothly and briskly, and as to bribes, no asking for, or giving'.[370] The 'administration in the streets',[371] the 'quality of life',[372] 'railway efficiency',[373] and 'jail administration'[374] are all being 'toned-up' together. Though 'curbs were placed on democracy', it was 'only because it was in danger';[375] instead, 'the most difficult path of each person having to decide for himself or herself has been chosen'.[376] Above all, 'we have given the people the courage to speak out, although we have not been able to give the people the food they need, or shelter, or education'.[377]

Now, 'with opportunists no longer controlling the media, and corrupting the machinery of administration';[378] with 'the Prime Minister engaged in a silent search for men and women of integrity and imagination' ('to act as innovators in enlivening politics by setting a superior example'),[379] the 'time has come to go ahead having removed the mental cobwebs'.[380] Now, 'the forces of hatred having cleared somewhat, we can see our economic goals with greater clarity and urgency';[381] and armed with 'policies which are not Congress policies, but policies voted upon by Parliament'.[382]

Additionally, 'remarkable industrial progress since the emergency'[383] is being reported even in Bihar, which is 'day by day in every way getting better'.[384] 'The face of rural West Bengal is to be changed in the next five years', while 'no state is working so hard for its labouring classes'.[385] Fortunately, 'small farms in India are much more productive than even the big farms which are operated in the USSR and the USA',[386] while 'during the past twenty years in the field of agricultural production, India has surpassed China'.[387] And, at last, 'rapidly moving towards the commanding heights of the economy' is the public sector;[388] together with a new 'people's budget' in the offing, to 'remove the misery of the masses'.[389]

Some apology is obviously owed by the writer to the patient reader. Something must be seriously wrong with the tendency of this, and the preceding chapters; whether product of ignorance, or of the deformed perceptions of the congenital anti-Indian, or both together.

Instead, from the ashes of what we have seen burning in this chapter, we ought now to see arise, at the turning of a page, the phoenix of national resurrection.

6 The New Deal

The new economic programme has generated all-round enthusiasm and new hope among the masses, as it is an expression of the nation's deep and abiding commitment and resolve to rid itself of poverty and inequality. It must be implemented with utmost speed and efficiency.

All-India Congress Committee (AICC)
resolution, 28 December 1975[1]

The 20-point programme is not significant. Great changes are happening in India. We have taken a swing to the extreme right. We will either succeed on a large scale, or fail on a large scale. But it is the political, not the economic, changes which are important.

Ayub Syed, AICC member, 16 January 1976[2]

The economic policy of the government will continue to be left of centre.

Indira Gandhi, 30 December 1975[3]

A fruit seller gave everything she had to the divine child Sri Krishna, captivated by his charming appearance, and the divine imprints on his tender palm. That she would have to starve for the day was totally out of her mind. And in return for the fruits she offered, the Lord blessed her with a fortune; her basket was full of precious stones.

Hindu, 12 January 1976

The crux of the matter has already been stated. Proclamation of the 'new' – a key-word both in political and commercial advertising – was the old but in a renewed paroxysm of the body politic, with its features newly distorted. And it was not so much newness as continuity, and not so much continuity as reversion and regression. And the 'new' spokesmen for India's future were the same as those who had had its bitter past in their custody; the Prime Minister's son representing a new generation and degeneration together.

Economic inflation, with political illusion, have of course had their Weimar and other precedents in history. Novelty here was to lie in the Indian scale of it, and in its consequent meanings; and not only for India. As for the calculus of poverty and riches, they stand facing each other in India in gigantic disproportions. Moreover, a search in the *widening* inequalities of the new economic programme for equivalences between the legions of the poor and the vanguard of riches and power would be immediately defeated. Nor could the 'sacrifices' of the few be matched against the hardships of the many, because the first half of that supposed equation begins to disappear on examination. So that to conduct the debate at all, we are driven to the purest economic and political artifice. We are driven to exclude the bigger disproportions entirely because they will fit with no balance, and to exclude the political destruction wrought by 'swinging into action', because it resists exact quantification.

We are then – by this procedure – left to confine analysis solely to the assessment of profit and loss on the 'dumb millions' account, under the new economic programme. Whether the calculus (as method) is in these circumstances as poverty-stricken as the mass of deprivation it seeks to measure, becomes a minor matter. More important is whether we shall again find fact resist all balance with each new subtraction and addition; that remains to be answered here. If it should turn out to be so, then final questions will arise for determination: if not for the 'poorer and weaker sections', then for whom? And if for 'national revival', for what kind of 'national revival' was the strong and stable centre with its writ unhindered, needed? Beyond it, and the success or failure of 'national revival', the biggest of all political issues lay waiting; for resolution, or revolution, for there will be one phoenix, or another.

The 20-point programme itself had all the marks of inflation. There was a 10-point programme in 1967, a 13-point programme – the Narora programme* – in 1974, and a 20-point programme on 1 July 1975, a week after the emergency's declaration. Were fact and argument to justify the analogy, only five more points of inflation (subsequently to be added by Sanjay Gandhi) would be needed for the 25-point programme of 1920 in Munich. On the eve of the declaration, the people of India were facing the worst recession since the 1930–34 crisis; with rising unemployment, industrial closures, falling prices being paid to peasant producers, overproduction in critical areas of the economy – as in the steel industry – falling demand, and inflation.

And yet, with them, the hardy perennial of a capitalist economy: rising rates of profitability, surviving in the worst of political climates. As the Reserve Bank of India was to show for the pre-emergency (1974–5) period, though the recession was marked statistically by the rise in the value of sales being lower than the rise in the value of production, there were impressive rises both in after-tax profits of large companies in the private corporate sector, and in rates of profit also.†[5] Thus, rising rates of profit went hand in hand, or fist in hand, with stagnant or declining real wages.

It was into this general condition that the new economic programme was inserted, with the special needs dictated by the self-defence of faction adding their own items to make up the 20-points total. None of its content was unfamiliar; indeed among its authors in the planning secretariat were the survivors

* Similar in content to the 20-point programme, it was named after a village some seventy miles south-east of Delhi. It was the site of a '200-acre tented encampment' in late November 1974, when leading figures of the Congress Party 'gathered in secret conclave for three days to discuss the nation's problems'. They were 'heavily guarded by some battalions of the provincial armed constabulary and the military', the costs allegedly met from public funds. Among the principal participants were the Prime Minister and Barooah; 'at the end of these labours, they produced what is known as the 13-point programme'.[4]

† cf. 'The private corporate sector did very well during the Fourth Plan period [1969–74] even though in terms of achieving some of the key Plan objectives, the performance of the Fourth Plan was the poorest of all the plans so far.'[6]

of the disconsolate exodus of Indian planners from Delhi in the 1960s. 'All the points of the programme could have been, but were not, achieved under the *status quo ante*,'[7] during the nearly three uninterrupted decades of single party power; 'all have been invoked as goals in every five-year plan, and indeed featured in Congress programmes even before independence. They will not be implemented now for the same reason that has prevented their implementation in the past – the fact that responsibility for putting such policies into practice rests with the very interests who would suffer from them.'[8]

The promise of their achievement was however expressed with more extravagance, and in a context more drastic and more violent than past programmes. The quickly apparent failure to meet this promise was therefore that much greater than all the previous failures. Certainly novel was that it was the first of India's economic programmes to be 'rendered into a musical score by the Delhi police band' ('the tune based on a song by a drill instructor at the police training school at Mehrauli'),[9] or into 'a Tamil ballet by the song and drama division of the ministry of information' which 'effectively portrayed the import of the 20-point programme'.[10] Because the 'Narora programme', for instance, had done likewise, it was not new that it should 'set the order of priorities for our goal of democratic socialism'; nor that it 'laid down concrete steps to help the oppressed to get up and realize their aspirations'.[11]

So in that same rural India which, 'Mr Barooah admitted', 'had till now remained comparatively unaffected by socialist measures',[12] there was again to be 'implementation of land reforms' (point 2). There was to be the 'provision of house-sites for the landless and weaker sections' (point 3), again 'the liquidation of rural indebtedness' (point 5), the revision of minimum wages (point 6), and again the 'abolition of bonded labour' (point 7). In sum 'the face of rural India would be changed in a truly revolutionary manner.'

But that this revolution was not to take place is not the present point, not even the twenty-first point of the original programme. For these reforms were politically designed to be part of the utilitarian balance being struck between the 'negatives' of the loss of civil liberties and 'curbs on democracy', and the 'positives' of social discipline and economic amelioration. It is a balance which must always be promised, and even notionally delivered, to those in search of an equilibrium of loss and benefit. In like vein there was to be the 'socialization of urban land' (point 11), the 'prevention of tax evasion', 'summary trials of evaders' and 'deterrent punishment of economic offenders' (point 12), and the 'confiscation of smugglers' properties' (point 13).

That these were not to happen either, except as flurry and flourish of 'swinging into action', and as faction power settled to its primary task of self-consolidation, we will see also. That it was greeted both with the soldier Schweik's weary resignation – 'What is this 20-point programme? So many programmes we have had already. It is one more programme only';[13] or 'in buses, trains, planes, wherever you go, I am afraid they are ridiculing the 20-point programme'[14] – and with heraldic fanfares as if at the fall of a veritable Jericho of vested interest, will be obvious.

To the 'pragmatic' Ayub Syed of the All-India Congress Committee the programme was seen as insignificant when compared, as he put it, with 'the building of the mass base of the Congress'. 'I was in the CPI before joining the Congress,' he said to me. 'What was wrong with the CPI? I will tell you. The CPI had no mass base with the people. This we are now achieving. I am a practical man. Without a mass base, we can do nothing in this country.'[15] To the CPI, however, the Congress Party's same rural programme ironically contained 'almost all the main aspects of land, wage and social equality'.[16] To the CPI–M, alternatively, it was 'a cruel hoax to mislead the people'. 'There cannot be,' they said, 'a bigger hoax on the Indian people than this programme, whether it is claimed as an instrument of social change, or as a just relief for the downtrodden sections.' 'The entire controlled press,' they argued, 'is hired to boost the programme, to make fantastic claims on its behalf and to circulate fake tales of its achievements'.[17] But in the view of Barooah (a 'Congress babbler'),[18] 'it would give a new sense of dignity, and a new consciousness to the landless'. 'It will bring about,' he said, 'a qualitative change in social relations, and release for national reconstruction a tremendous reservoir of energy which has remained dormant so far because of soul-crushing poverty and inhuman exploitation',[19] a declaration containing all the political and residual elements we have pondered in an earlier chapter.

But the content of the programme, as well as its context, was this time both more complex and blatant than either apologia or assault at first sight make them. Differences are as critical as continuities. The 'electrifying' speed with which the programme was 'taken in hand',[20] 'with performance increasingly matching promise', and 'the gains' – 'no flash in the pan' – which 'within days were recorded',[21] are not subjects for equally quick dismissal. Their meanings as 'hoax' or substance, in relation to what really happened, have had too many reverberations. As continuity, for example, the abandoned Fifth Plan (1974–9) spoke too of 'the removal of poverty and the attainment of self-reliance'. But as to crucial difference, it also spoke of expanding opportunities for productive employment, meeting minimum needs for elementary education, medical care in rural areas, and nutrition. It spoke – however illusorily – of the reduction of social and economic inequality, restraint on inessential consumption, and extended programmes of social welfare. However these may be incantations, and thirty years have proved them to be so, they at least pointed to India's structural socio-economic problems. Their effective disappearance from the new programme for India's regeneration – thus, to deal with India's vast unemployment there was only 'a new scheme for apprenticeship' (point 20) – must be kept in mind, as the paths of India's emergency economic, fiscal, and social changes are further charted.

So that even before we take up the issue of the non-implementation of India's new deal economic programme, the nature of the Congress Party's balancing act on the high wire of the emergency's political tensions must be considered. For a 'new politics' was adumbrated in the points of the 20-point programme. That is, there was more to them than merely the familiar vacuum of economic rhetoric, or, if you prefer, the new deal's shining promise. In the economic absences was a political balance. Thus, 'accelerated efforts to bring down prices' were joined with 'increases in production' (point 1), and 'more effective workers' participation' (point 15) – together with the abrogation of the rights of the trade unions – was one of the considerations for the 'liberalization of investment procedures' (point 14). And in balance, or part exchange, for 'the improvement in quality and supply of cloth for the common man' (point 10) – which the common man's continuously declining purchasing power simultaneously strips bare of meaning – were the sweeping tax concessions for the middle classes (point 12),* with even larger concessions in the offing.

So the focus of the issue rapidly ceases to be 'why could the 20-point programme not have been carried out in the last twenty-eight years of India's rule by Congress?',[24] for to ask the question was ingenuous. It diminishes interest, too, in the CPI's particular dilemma. First it must laud the programme as the path to social and economic progress; then only to find that 'the official declaration of the implementation of the 20-point programme in most states cloaks the same degree in real terms of its non-implementation'. There is passing relief only in its mixed metaphors; it discerns that the 'regrouping of political and economic vested interests under safe covers has now become the major hurdle'.[25] What we find of substance are, as before, the structure and meaning of the political vocabulary of power; and together with quite other specific, and wholly real, economic interventions, their method of deployment and impact on the actual conditions of the people.

First, the 'moral' component. It was not only present in the strategy of reclaiming for the rural millions their lost dignities while taking most of their remaining freedoms, but a thread present in the 'new' socio-economic artifice in general. It did not pale or relent for a moment, as rhetoric, even in the face of increasingly blatant economic redistribution from poor and

---

*In the first announcements, this was called 'a measure of relief to *middle income* groups';[22] their tax liability [up to the very high figure, for India, of 8,000 rupees per annum] was reduced to nil. Subsequently, the same measure was redesignated in official publications as 'relief to *lower income* groups', and 'those in the *lower income* brackets'.[23] The change was needed as the balance of economic and political advantage under the emergency not only shifted – but was seen in India to have shifted – in favour of the rich against the poor.

poorer, to richer and richest.* It was ubiquitous. It was in the calls for 'stricter codes of austerity to better the life of the nation' and for curbs on 'conspicuous consumption',[28] both before and after sweeping fiscal and other measures restored licence to the wealthy, in the equally familiar (but truer) language of economic incentive and 'demand-creation'.

It was in the language of verbal assaults on corruption, 'smuggling', tax evasion, and 'black money'. It was in the 'socially-conscious private sector', which we saw earlier as a token of a hybrid political inheritance, but which was now additionally 'taking self-corrective measures'.[29] (It was not however in the assaults on 'anti-social elements', since these were physical, not 'moral', and the term was used amongst others to cover the mass detention of political opponents.) It was in the ostensible ethic of the 'new' 12-point prohibition programme of 2 October 1975,†[30] a dead letter in practice but of political significance to Ayub Syed's creation of a 'mass base' for Congress. Under it (point 12) 'leaders of public opinion' would 'set the tone by their personal example'. But there was greater resonance in the 'banning of liquor shops near industrial projects' (point 3) or near 'colonies of labourers' (point 4); with 'pay days to be uniformly dry days' (point 5) in order 'to keep away the workers from drinking', since it was 'rendering the weaker sections still weaker'.[32]

There was initially a seemingly stern puritanism after the declaration of emergency, as after other *coups d'état*. Whether it was to match or to cover the simultaneous assaults on rights to life and liberty, upon the law and Constitution, must be a matter for decision. Thus, 'tax evasion', said the Prime Minister on 1 July 1975, 'is a crime. Punishments will be stern. We are thinking of summary trials.'[33] There were none; the thought was not

---

*Thus, calls for 'the utmost financial discipline', or for 'massive drives for tax collection',[26] or the invocation of the 'obligation' which the state was under to 'prevent concentration of wealth'[27] did not at all cease, even after political and economic decisions, made by the same spokesmen for austerity or equality, had ended the discipline in one case and strengthened the concentration in the other.

†Introduced on that date (Gandhi Jayanti Day) to commemorate Mahatma Gandhi; but on the same day, imprisoned Gandhians were beaten in a *athi*-attack inside Delhi jail.[31]

mother to the deed. Instead, by 30 March 1976, a 'high-powered income tax settlement commission' had been established, in order to enable any assessee to seek a compromise and settlement of income tax proceedings, and be granted immunity from prosecution.[34] Two weeks before, the budget had announced a regressive taxation system; the richer, the larger the relative and absolute tax concession.

Or, within the first ten days of the emergency, at a meeting of the Cabinet committee on anti-smuggling measures on 2 July 1975, orders were issued 'to detain a large number of absconding smugglers'. 'Properties of those absconding,' it was announced, 'are liable to be confiscated'; in another announcement that month, 'the properties of smugglers will be confiscated'.[35] But by 31 March 1976, in the words of the Minister for Revenue himself, 'the government has not so far confiscated any properties belonging to smugglers and foreign exchange racketeers'.[36] And on 19 April 1976, it was announced that the 'settlement commission' would 'deal with compassion in all cases of people connected with smuggling, and their rehabilitation'.[37] Let us pause for a moment and see what can be found.

The number of 'smugglers' arrested was part of that unknown Indian quantity which was masked, not revealed, by announced figures for the detention of 'anti-social elements', making it difficult to decipher by that route much real meaning. It is known that offenders against foreign exchange regulations variously bought their way out of trouble ('embarrassing questions are being asked about the conduct of police authorities')[38] and some in Bombay found sanctuary in the government-run St George's Hospital, at work and in the city during the day and most of the night, but returning to their 'heart ailments' in the small hours of the morning.[39] But that also tells us little which could not readily be anticipated.

There are at least two responses to this. One was that of Ashok Mitra, who should know about this matter also. 'Noises are made from time to time,' he has said, 'about rooting out corruption, but are not taken seriously either by the corrupt officials or by their victims.'[40] This may be true, but does not fully meet the issue. The fact of such threats against 'smuggling',

if not of their serious or thorough-going implementation, re-
tains a more than formal interest. For these were also the reflex
responses of political survival, meeting the political challenge of
that rival pre-emergency populism which had gained ground
precisely by denouncing each entrenched corruption. It was also
residuum – its humbug admittedly discounted – of an older professed morality in Indian politics; but above all, it was political
necessity's Cromwellian pose of even-handed sternness in distributing the pains and pleasures of a resurgent India.*

Thus we can take the 'flying squads' in search of 'black
money', undisclosed wealth, and concealed income in our political stride, just as did those upon whom they (for a while)
descended. The scale of this parallel economy generated both in
the agricultural and industrial sectors was revealed in 1965 by a
government committee (the Wanchoo Committee on Direct
Taxes) to be of huge proportions. Indeed, it was so big that the
report's findings were themselves suppressed. It estimated that
'the money value of deals involving black money may not be less
than 70,000 million rupees (£4,000 million) for 1968 to 1969',[41]
and with commensurately colossal evasions of taxation. But, by
1975, both the planning commission and the executive of the
Congress parliamentary party had received an estimate of 'rolling black money', amounting to 200,000 million rupees (or
about £11,000 million),[42] and so inextricably interwoven into the
fabric of the economy, 'black' with 'white', that the figure was
itself without meaning.

In the exhilarations of a new discipline, it was into this
bottomless deep that the 'tax squads' swooped. But since they
had also been doing this desultorily in previous years (particularly in 1974), on some occasions for a mite of tax revenue to
throw into the widening chasm of the balance of payments, on
others acting in the service of faction power as reprisal against
the out-of-favour, this procedure was not new, though as

---

*Moreover, where 'smuggling' (a generic term) actually means black-
marketeering and hoarding, and where black-marketeering and hoarding
threaten social discontent, and social discontent threatens the tightrope
walk of class power, then 'smuggling' can be perceived as 'anti-social', and
'smugglers' can themselves be threatened.

'austerity' and discipline it was now newly presented. However, now 'no stone,' said Mukherjee on 30 December 1975, 'would be left unturned until economic offences were eliminated completely'.[43] But, 'voluntary disclosure' of concealed income and tax offences had already replaced the grounded 'flying squads'; and on the day after his speech, 'voluntary disclosure' had itself ended also.

What had actually happened – while dawn raids of quite another kind continued – was that from 8 October 1975 (by presidential decree, once more) special and increasingly generous terms were offered to the vast parallel economy, while the countrywide property survey and inventory, originally announced, were quietly abandoned. Black-marketeers, speculators and tax evaders, in return for the voluntary disclosure of 'hidden wealth and income' would be taxed at a concessionary rate of taxation, the delinquent thus being invited to pay substantially less than the law-abiding assessee, who had dutifully declared his income.[44] On 12 November, the Finance Ministry backed off still further. It was now not necessary to disclose the nature or source of the income; the same individual could make any number of declarations on behalf of (and spread among) family members, and even employees, thus further reducing his tax liability.[45] On 25 November it was announced that tax would be levied at the value of the assets at the date when the declarant claimed they had been obtained or purchased;[46] and on 29 November, again by presidential decree, prospective declarants were granted immunity from confiscation, penalty, and prosecution under the Gold Control Act and the Customs Act.[47]

But even the much reduced tariff for permanent conversion of 'black' money into 'white' – described appropriately by the Indian Finance Ministry in ritual terms of 'washing away past sins'[48] – and for immunity from all further inquiry, was still too high for most to pay. The reason was plain. It had become unnecessary to pay it; non-disclosure was cheaper, since it cost nothing. However, the much publicized (and allegedly much inflated) figures of 14,500 million rupees, or £800 million, of voluntarily disclosed black money, undoubtedly false as they were, had more than a simple mathematical dimension. They were part of the topology of politics. They became counters in the complex play and counterplay of simultaneous repression, and the asserted equations of the self-denial of the rich, for the sake of a putative national renaissance. The rich had made their 'sacrifice' to the many-armed deities of the newly disciplined India; it 'balanced' any sacrifice and suffering which might be involved for the poor and the working classes, standing at the real point of stress of the new economic programme.

Woven into this texture was, as always, assertion, disclaimer and lying. On the one hand, 'tax swoops' turn quickly to bribe and barter*, or are 'left to the discretion of the income tax authorities',[50] before fading into the oblivion of the token payment. On the other hand, assertion and evasion declare, from the same source – Mukherjee in this instance – that 'the operation of black money has come to a standstill'[51] by 30 December 1975, but that on 9 May 1976 'black money has not been completely done away with'.[52] (Both were at least partially true; it had by the latter date resumed more openly.) And even when austerity had resumed its original licence, political necessity forbade that appearances be done away with;† while lying provided a welcome sense of the continuous. 'All those,' said Barooah on 27 June 1976, 'who at one stage threatened to upset the economic life with their illgotten black money, however highly placed they may be, are being punished.'[55]

I have gone into detail because this was at the very outset the disruption of the moral equation of equivalent sacrifice; and because it shows how the high flying morality (shadowed by

---

*Evidence of what was happening can be gathered both from direct evidence; and more obliquely. For example, a gang of bogus taxmen in Bangalore, 'posing as income tax authorities', induced house owners to part with large sums of money in return for the dropping of 'further inquiries', until apprehended.[49] For comparable police activity, see chapters 7 and 8.

†e.g. It was revealed on 27 March 1976 that the government of Maharashtra had 'not been able to collect the levy on luxury flats in Bombay' which it had itself ordered, because it 'had no records of the sizes of such apartments'.[53] As another of numerous examples, after the Uttar Pradesh Assembly introduced the Ministers and Legislators (Publication of Assets and Liabilities) Act 1975, Ministers and more than half the legislature ignored its provisions.[54]

violence) of this feature of the 'new' Indian political economy was easily winged and grounded. Since it was vested interest which fashioned the doctrine, it could also (and did) at the same moment fashion its antidote and undoing. But there was a more important and disabling equation beyond it. That is, there was a similarly discoverable unmeaning in the moralities of the new land reform, release from debt and bonded labour, revisions of minimum wages, provision of house-sites for the landless and weaker sections; but similar only in their negation, dissimilar in consequence and signification.

For here we are dealing not with hoarded and undisclosed wealth to be counted in thousands of millions of rupees, but the conditions of life of India's hundreds of millions. And in the latter, worlds collide. On the one hand was the world of the 'release of the tremendous reservoir of human energy', or 'the 20-point programme's anti-feudal orientation', according to the CPI, which would 'open up new possibilities to provide relief to the people', and 'enhance the role of the working class in production'.[56] On the other was the world of entrenched land-lordism, well versed in the arts of negation, and ready itself to swing into action.

Let us, as instance, take point 3 of the 20-point programme: that which was to provide for 'house-sites' for the 'landless and weaker sections'. This points at the outset to a social fact whose enormity we can only pass over quickly: that there are millions of people who live, work and die in the villages of India, who have no 'house-sites'. That is, simply, 'millions of agricultural workers have no house to live in'.[57] That is, after generations of toil for the landlords who own the villages, they are not merely landless, but homeless; or squatters, without right on the land which they till for the landlord, and harvest.

What had happened under the new dispensation? By February 1976, for example, it was alleged that over one million families – perhaps one per cent of India's rural population – had been so provided. From reports by the Kisan Sabhas, and from my own observations, the picture had been somewhat different.[58] Rather, some sites had been 'earmarked', but without physical occupation; sites had been 'earmarked' but without possibility of habitation, and above all without resources for construction; sites had been 'allotted', far from the village and supplies of water. In other instances, sites with habitation were occupied, sometimes to a flourish of trumpets and under the exigencies of the banner headline, sometimes to be evacuated (if necessary, by landlord force) later. Or, in reform's prospectus, 'laws will be introduced to confer ownership rights on landless labourers who have been in occupation of the house-sites of their landlords over a certain period'; and 'resort to evictions will be sternly dealt with'.[59] Political necessity might give a little ground; but it gave greater ground in turn to landlordism's more traditional means of securing rural interest, wherein the villages of India resume an older silence.

It is a silence imposed by an often absolute landlord power which, unless opposed, need house no labour and need pay no taxes. The structure of the rural '*panchayats*', for example, is one of a thorough-going corruption; the fleshy potency of landlord riches and violence presiding over 'the new edifice of socialistic democracy ... concentrating on all-round development of the rural community'.[60] The *panchayat* chairman is, typically, the biggest local landlord; his assistants are his relations, his allies other local landlords. He may be both employer of the village's labour and collector of its taxes. He receives into his own hands, and redistributes as largesse, often among his own family, funds for rural development. Inside his farm compound are his family members and his henchmen, the village's draught animals and its only tractors. In the farm courtyard may be the whitewashed rooms of the rural administration, source of further arbitrary power of grant or denial; and at election, it is he who commands both votes and resources, just as he commands the powers of bribery or violence. The 20-point programme was easily resisted.*

'Agricultural labour is among the worst exploited sections of

---

*As a revealing example, on 13 February 1976, one month before it was ousted by President's rule, the Gujarat coalition government proposed, in order to 'keep the burden on the poor to a minimum', a tax upon rural landlords to 'accelerate the process of rural uplift' and to 'assist the poorer and weaker sections'. Despite the new deal ostensibly in force throughout India, the coalition's proposals were defeated by an alliance of the state's opposition

our society,' said the Prime Minister.[62] Men, women and children stand in the fields, or at the hovel doorway, in accusation for their ragged destitution. Landlessness, homelessness, debt, low wages are one; we have seen that they too stand clustered together. 'A review of minimum wages will be undertaken'; 'action will be initiated for suitable enhancement of minimum wages, *wherever necessary*' (my emphasis).[63] 'Congress headquarters,' said Jagjivan Ram, 'should obtain reports whether all its party members who own land are giving minimum wages to their agricultural labour.' 'They should,' he said, 'be in the forefront of carrying out this decision of the government and the party.'[64] It was, said the CPI, 'a matter of great satisfaction to agricultural workers throughout the country' that there was to be, *inter alia*, a review of minimum wages. After all, as they put it, 'millions have no land to till. They are paid very low wages. Even today, they are paid a rupee or less a day. They get work only for about 200 days a year. Their wages must immediately be increased, and the law implemented. Many of them are half naked.'[65]

Wages were raised; not to a living wage, not based on need, with no limitation on hours, and without machinery for implementation, but in state after state came formal announcement of increases. They were raised from '2.50 rupees' per day in Karnataka to 4.30; from '3 rupees' per day in Maharashtra to 4.50; from '4.65 rupees' to 5.65 in Punjab; from '6 rupees' to 7.25 rupees per day in Bengal; and within these figures were differentially fixed *lower* rates for different skills and types of labour, for women, and for children. All these rates – insufficient for adequate survival – were unpaid even before the nominal increases; they are higher than, and even twice as high as, the per capita daily income of the official statistics earlier cited. (Even at a purely notional figure of 5 rupees a day, it would require a fifty-fold increase to pay for a night's stay in a good Bombay

---

Congress Party and the farm lobby for which it spoke. Hitendra Desai, whom we have already encountered, accused the Gujarat coalition of 'recklessly penalizing all sections of society'.[61] This criticism, in fact, was of an attempted political decision (however cynical its own motive), intolerable to vested interest, emergency or no emergency.

hotel room.) Nonetheless, on the one hand came new rates for farm labourers, bauxite miners and stone breakers, for 'workers who could bring their own implements and oxen', and for those 'who could provide only labour';[66] on the other, the news of non-implementation, greeted with a shrugging resignation or bitter anger.

In Bihar, for example, where it took twenty-two years from the passing of the relevant statute in 1948 to the introduction of a new minimum wages scheme in 1970 (when rural tensions were at their height) there were 'no new measures to enforce the minima'.[67] In Maharashtra, the state legislative council was told of the non-payment to farm labourers of the new minima, and of 'the absence of proper implementing machinery'.[68] In Orissa, a survey revealed that even the state-owned Orissa mining corporation was not paying the new statutory minima.[69] The full list was a long one of the non-payment of 'new' wage rates for a family's subsistence; of accounts unsettled with the poor millions; while in the self-same moments of denial, other accounts were being commuted by presidential ordinance for those other grosser millions, beyond all reckoning, of the totals of huge and undisclosed riches.

Rural indebtedness was to be 'liquidated' under point 5 of the programme. But this was the term used in its popular and populist version (see appendix).* The original prospectus had spoken not of 'liquidation' – an impossible political programme for reasons which reside, as we have seen, in the unreformed structure of rural relations – but of something quite different. There was to be 'a moratorium on suits and execution of decrees against rural debtors'; it 'would be enforced by legislation' and 'give considerable relief to the vast majority of the rural population'.[71] That this did not happen is one thing; that only the day of reckoning was to be postponed, while the accumulating sums of outstanding interest (subject to no limit) mounted, is another.

That the pauperized millions were at the same time for-

---

* Some states, however, such as Karnataka, followed its terms, 'liquidated all debts of the weaker sections of society', and announced 'the dawn of a new era in the history of India'.[70]

bidden to meet or organize to make mass claims, or to take mass action, for their new rights (or 'privileges') against the embedded power of rural landlordism and money-lending is yet another. That freedom from debt today – had it, for the sake of our argument, been intended – would simply lead the moneyless, the workless and the landless back into renewed debt, and into the embrace of the same creditors tomorrow, is another. That only the breaking of the land monopoly of the landlords, their expropriation, and the mass distribution of land financed for peasant production will break the structures of rural bankruptcy and destitution, is plainly more to the point at issue.

But on 24 October 1975, the President of India 'abolished' bonded and forced labour.*[72] As night descended on India's constitutional freedoms, 'every bonded labourer', declared the ordinance, 'stands freed and discharged from any obligation to render bonded labour'. 'Any custom, tradition, contract or agreement shall be void and inoperative ... by virtue of which any person ... is required to do any work or render services as bonded labour.' The bond slave, scot-free, could leave his pharaoh. 'The days of servitude,' said the Prime Minister, were 'over';[74] 'the age-old bonded labour system has ended';[75] 'it has given,' said the CPI, 'new hope to the poorest'.[76] Bonded labour was not merely 'abolished'; although illegal under Article 23 of the Constitution, it was to be doubly illegal henceforward.

Bonded labour was being 'rooted out' by 'vigilance committees'.[77] In state after state, the 'barbarous practice' was 'brought to an end', and declarations made that whole states – such as Maharashtra, Haryana, Kashmir and Tripura, for instance – now had 'no such system'.[78] At the same time, in state after state bonded labour was being 'discovered'. In Orissa, for example, 'the existence of large pockets of bonded labour have come as a shock to the administration ... Nobody thought that the curse existed over such large areas', while 'vested interests are threatening their "slaves" that if they speak out, punishment would be swift since, after all, Delhi is distant'. 'Slave

*The government of Uttar Pradesh was even quicker. It had 'abolished' it by ordinance, on 22 July 1975, within four weeks of the declaration of emergency.[73]

owners,' it was further discovered, 'have their own methods of defending their empire'; while 'the task of freeing the bonded tribals is proving to be tough', and 'no amount of publicity seems adequate to rouse the public conscience'.[79]

But without alternative sources of rural credit, and the demolition of that edifice of usury which has been built by landlessness and landlord rapacity, bondage remains the only form of repayment available to the debtor. His choice is reduced to that between bare survival with forced labour, or starvation in freedom. And thus, on 18 April 1976, the Home Ministry itself announced that 'surveys were being conducted to identify the different forms of debt-bondage which still existed in the guise of ostensibly legal systems'.[80]

Deterrent 'atrocities' and 'reigns of terror' against 'untouchables' and 'tribals' continued,[81] much reduced not by law, but by censorship of their incidence. Delay in freeing bonded labourers was elsewhere ascribed to 'difficulty in identifying both the persons practising this "pernicious" system, and the people in their stranglehold'; while the 'tribals' themselves were 'unwilling to leave their moorings'.[82] The system was discovered – six months after the days of servitude were declared over – to be 'resilient'; with 'an infinite capacity for assuming new forms, such as farm construction and domestic labour on slave wages'.[83] Thus it is that forced and bonded labour must continue throughout India, landlordism riding (as it always has) the reforming crest of every wave until it spends itself and recedes. The unyielding laws of the real political economy of rural India are not so easily diverted from their channels.

And other questions went begging the dusty roads, with the landless, the scavenging and the unemployed 'weaker sections'. 'Will they arrest those guilty of crushing thousands in bondage? Will they confiscate *their* illgotten gains, and distribute them among the wronged ones? Will they confiscate and turn over to the serfs who have worked them for generations, the lands of these slave owners?' But these are different questions. Their answers were not to be found in the 20-point programme; they were in the silence and change of subject which greeted them.

And what finally of the crux of the matter, land reform, or 'land to the landless'? (Not, of course, 'land to the tiller', which would bring down in ruins not only rural oligarchy, but the structures of state and class power which rest upon and express it.) To this 'top priority' was to be given.[84]

But 'land reform' was to mean merely that the 'land ceiling' legislation, long on the statute book and successfully circumvented, was now to be implemented. There was to be 'quicker distribution' *not* of the vast quantities of 'surplus rural land' held illegally, but what was left of it after its wholesale (and retail) reduction by 'absence of land records', collusions and evasions. What was left, was the 'land available for distribution'. In addition, 'ceilings on ownership of urban land' were to be imposed, 'to combat speculation and to achieve social and economic equality'.*[85]

What of this rural land reform? First and most plainly it comes into the fixed category of Indian – and not only Indian – power's commonest reflex responses to social unrest and political crisis. Therefore an ebbing away of the reforming temper might be looked for with emergency power's apparent consolidation. That is exactly what we find. But we find other things also. We find first that the scale of exhortation, 'implementation' and evasion was on a larger scale than with the other measures. We find the politics of Ayub Syed's mass-base coming into sharper collision (if necessary, spilling into violence) both with the realities of rural power and with the 'shifting compromise' between different sectors of an organic vested interest. We find the CPI's credulous expectation of 'people's committees', supervising a rural revolution, of course foundering in the face of both.

There was also far more at stake here. Land reform is historically both totem and intermittently resurrected earnest of political endeavour. It *can* win elections, as can a good harvest, even if nothing of the structure of inequity thereby changes. But in the

---

*It was embodied in the Urban Land Ceiling Act, 1976; immediately qualified by the Prime Minister's statement that in applying the urban land ceiling law to various states, 'the circumstances prevailing in each of them should be taken into account';[86] and was quickly therefore lost from sight in its protective thicket of collusion, evasion and corruption.

end – and it was decisive – the tide of zeal went out as quickly as ever, leaving only the customary tide-mark: a detritus of broken pledges, and another in the barely measurable sequence of sea changes since independence.

The cycle moved swiftly through all its phases, and in an arc which traversed India. It began thus: 'Since the declaration of emergency, almost all the states have accelerated land distribution, and programmes of state land acquisition.'[87] It passed through public threats of police action if 'vested interests obstruct the transfer of surplus land to the landless'.[88] On 28 November 1975, for instance, 'a one-man campaign' of land distribution by the then Chief Minister of Uttar Pradesh, H. N. Bhaguna, was 'bringing sunshine into nearly four million *harijan* homes in U.P.'*[89] By 13 February 1976, it reached the admission by the Agriculture Ministry that there had been 'poor implementation of the ceiling laws almost all over the country'.[90]

On 5 March 1976, eight months after the inauguration of the new economic programme, the Prime Minister observed 'a certain amount of lethargy and hesitation in land reforms'; 'collusion between landlords and officials'; and a 'general lack of appreciation of the vital role of land reforms'.[91] On 12 April the villagers of Sunkadakatte, near Bangalore, were 'reminded' – by the President of India, while he was on a *pada-yatra* – that 'legislation is not an end in itself'.[92] On 10 May 1976, a Bill was actually introduced by the government retrospectively to ratify certain fictitious land transfers by landlords who had earlier evaded ceiling legislation.[93] On 11 May, Jagjivan Ram admitted that 'though most states had enacted land ceiling laws, their implementation had not been satisfactory'.[94] On 30 June 1976, an arbitrarily and suddenly imposed deadline on 'land reform' expired;[95] and with its formal expiry, the dust of minor disturbance and the rural balance also began to settle.

What had happened? Much that was familiar; nothing without

---

*But this was Bhaguna's last stand as Chief Minister. He was dismissed a few days later, as a result of internal Congress Party faction feuds; and the state was under direct rule from the centre until 22 January 1976. Bhaguna's reprisal was to join the newly formed rival Congress faction, 'Congress for Democracy', led by Jagjivan Ram, on 2 February 1977.

its precedent. The facts and figures of claim and counterclaim were in irreconcilable discord; fortunately abated by the failing momentum of the official programme, which sought to ring down the curtain upon this theatre of rural action. What we know first is that the original estimate of sixty-three million acres of land held illegally in excess of the maxima permitted, and thus registrable as surplus, had been reduced to a residual four million as 'target'.[96] We know also that there are fifty or sixty million rural landless.

By 30 June 1976, '400,000 acres'* had been distributed according to official sources, earlier suspect even to the Prime Minister, and with 'pliant officials fudging village records'.[97] Certainly, also, a significant proportion of this small acreage included reserved common land, land unfit for cultivation, and land of even less substance, since not to be found on *terra firma*, but only upon paper.

As instance, in a village which I visited in rural Uttar Pradesh, near Varanasi, were twenty landless families. How much land was available for distribution, I asked the *panchayat* chairman, and biggest local landlord. 'One acre.' 'For twenty families?' 'Then we will get land from the next village.' 'Is there land available in the next village?' There was a silence. 'If there is no land available in the next village, there will be no land reform?' The wind blew the dust of the rutted road into eddies, for answer. 'No,' he answered. And from different parts of India came, as always, reports of the verities and certainties of India's new land reform.

On 15 January 1976, from West Bengal we learn of redistribution 'without possession or occupation' and of clashes between landlords' hirelings and the newly entitled landless;[98] with 'those allotted surplus land prevented from ploughing';[99] of 'ineligible or non-priority categories of people among the beneficiaries', including the 'relatives or nominees of previous owners'.[100] On 22 February there are accounts of 'newly stepped up attacks on the *harijans*' throughout India, which 'are seen

---

*In order to measure meanings of the term 'land reform' in once comparable agrarian economies, cf. the figure of more than 100 million acres distributed, after 1949, among the 300 million 'land-poor' peasants of China.

to be the result of the stress on land distribution ... disturbing to landed vested interests'.[101] From Assam on 18 April 1976, came descriptions of violence and evasion, of 'landlord terror', of harassments and evictions, 'with the connivance of police and revenue officials'.*[102]

And thus 'land to the landless'; with leading Congressmen, including ministers, holding thousands of acres under surrogate transfers.[105] The great landowners of Uttar Pradesh, with their tens of thousands of acres – such as Shiyam Sundar Reddy, and the Ravalapalli Deshmukhs of Nalgonda district – were secure in their huge fiefdoms;[106] while 0·12 acres per head were distributed in West Bengal to a handful of the newly landed, before debt and reversion would restore even this to their original owners.[107]

Moreover and more important, it was time, said the Chief Minister of Punjab, that there 'should be no more talk of land reforms'; attention and energy must now be switched to the 'creation of stability and giving a boost to production'.[108] Land reform, the CPI–M had said on 8 November 1975, would be a 'cruel hoax'; there would be 'some marginal transfers for purposes of propaganda ... some few will no doubt benefit, but the mass will be cheated'.[109] But it was no 'cruel hoax'. It was the politics of rural power, of marginal distribution, and of faction's necessary political motion, at their point of intersection. Its rules were plainly understood alike by smiling benefactor, grateful beneficiary and empty-handed bystander.

Additionally we must hold the widening context steady, and in position. As it became clearer that the main points of the new deal's rural economic programme were not to be implemented, the moral, social and economic arguments implicit in the unwillingly proposed calculus slowly emptied of their meaning. If we look over our shoulders, or back through these pages, we see that on 28 April 1976, for instance, two months before the expiry of

---

*But cf. 'the emergence of the common man as the VIP in every sphere of life,' said the Chief Minister of Assam, in Gauhati, on 21 March 1976, 'is the greatest achievement of our four years in office'.[103] It was also revealed on 1 June 1976 that the new statutory minimum wages introduced in Assam were not being paid in the state; not even to the state's employees.[104]

he land reform deadline, the Supreme Court had pronounced ife extinct in *habeas corpus*. On 16 June 1976, with only two weeks of land reform's propulsions remaining, detention without trial or ground for detention had been extended to two years; in practice and already, unending.

If other meaning conversely became somewhat plainer, it was that of the momentum of threatened faction power returning before our eyes to its old inertia. But it was more selective than ever. It aroused increasing energy to the use of increasing violence. To wrestle the laws and Constitution to the ground, and the opposition into prison, force could find its muscle, while it limply left to their unwanted and uncounted miseries the 'dumb millions'.

Moreover new economic developments were pending, and a new deal *was* being fashioned; a socio-economic reconstruction for which we have been looking, so far in this chapter, in quite the wrong direction. Thus we are already one day too late for it – as I shall show in a moment – by 26 September 1975, and a mile wide of the focus of real economic change, when another presidential decree ostensibly 'ensured equal pay to men and women workers for the same work or work of similar nature'.[110] This, like the rest, came to little or nothing. To go no further, the new minimum wage levels which we have already noticed distinguished between men's and women's minimum pittances, in ways specifically forbidden by official ordinance. Here only further impoverishment and misery was to be discovered; among women plantation workers in North Bengal and Karnataka, for example, from where tea and coffee come, respectively. Here was only the squalid stasis of India; of the ordinance not implemented; of wretchedly underpaid workers, at less than one penny per wicker basket; of sordid circumvention, and regrading of work to avoid equal payment; of implementation in the Minglas, Dalimcote and Ranicherra plantations, but only in return for work norms grossly raised by 20 to 40 per cent (or from five to ten baskets per day), and which exceeded by several times in value of output wage increases measured in denominations of one seventeenth of a penny.[111]

Though in these mites held in the palm of the hand, as in a grain of sand, the world of India is to be found, we must move as we did once before from wasted countryside and plantation to the city, if we are to find what we are looking for. For on 25 September 1975, presidential ordinance cut back industrial wages. The percentage rate of the minimum annual bonus, which possesses formal status as a deferred wage entitlement, and is a vital income supplement which sustains many Indian workers on the threshold of survival, had already been cut.[112] It would not in future be paid except 'upon the availability over a cycle of four years of a company surplus'.*[113] The net effect of the earlier rate cut would be, allegedly, to add hundreds of millions of rupees to the increasing profits of the corporate business sector. Withholding it altogether would add millions more.[114] But these are small additions; a huge new economic equation was in the making.

It did not coincide with the emergency's declaration. The suspension and abolition of many of the rights of the Indian people – and especially of the trade unions – merely made it possible to build the new economic order faster. As early as June 1974 there had been a Wage Freeze Act, which initiated the principle of 'tying up' 50 per cent of cost of living increases and so called 'dearness allowances' in 'compulsory deposits'; another form of concealed wage cutting.† The bonus system, the employers were able to say (as trade union rights were excised, and opposition trade unionists went into detention), was 'irrational and vexatious'.[116] As their confidence grew and the pace of the political offensive on the labour front mounted, the

* Thus, companies henceforward showing a low profit or loss (for this purpose), in notoriously manipulated balance sheets, could effectively cut their workers' wages by withholding the bonus.

† There is also a system of blatant theft from workers' miserable earnings, in the form of often unrecorded wage deductions, themselves made in the absence of a state social security system. These deductions are ostensibly placed (on a factory-to-factory basis) in so-called 'provident funds', which very often have no real existence, and leave the worker cheated in disability or sickness. On 23 January 1976, these funds were admitted by the Minister of Labour to be 'in arrears' to the amount of 286·6 million rupees.[115] This total, never to be repaid, is a compound of pocketed wage deductions and never-to-be-made employers' contributions.

'dearness allowance', bonus and cost of living index were held, for instance, to be 'a poison in Ashok Leyland. It can be done to scrap them. This is the next step. They should be scrapped altogether.'[117] Reddy, the Minister of Labour, whose 'marxist' accents we have heard earlier, actually cited Marx and Lenin in defence of the wage cuts. They had not, he said, written on these questions because in their time these modes of payment were not known to them. *Ipso facto*, they would not have disapproved of this particular bypass taken by Congress on its road to socialism. He did not, however, mention Marx and Lenin when he went on to announce the issue of bonus shares to shareholders, 'in order to add to the capital base, and provide for the stability of production and employment'.[118]

We must now widen once more the scope of attention and information. There is a new economic strategy in articulation; there is, as we have seen, mass unemployment; there is the 'people's budget' still to decipher. There are the economic recession's awesome facts, which we are approaching; there is the massive assault on trade union organization behind us; there is point 15 of the 20-point programme for 'more effective workers' participation' to consider. Apart from the occasions when the attention of the government was drawn, even by its own faction members, to the 'unemployment problem'[119] or 'to the treatment being meted out to the working class',[120] and when strikes lashed back at the new economic order in construction, what was being launched would brook no opposition. Economic structures, first in desperation and then with deliberation, were being bulldozed into rubble; their opponents shovelled into detention. 'Only in the jails,' I was told, 'has there been a real development in workers' participation'.[121]

In the midst of decree and destruction, new industrial deals were struck; we have seen them in passing. In August 1975, for example, in the steel industry, and against what was left of CITU opposition, INTUC, AITUC and HMS agreed to a raised monthly wage (to £16, or $27) in return for four years during which 'they would ensure that no demands were made by workers, and in which they would raise no dispute'.[122] In the attempted construction of a new politics and economics of production, a new balance was in the building. In permutation and combination were lost trade union rights, raised workloads and abolished overtime, holidays cut and hours lengthened, rising production, and jails filling. Even within the participant and obeisant unions who made it possible, there was 'grave apprehension'.[123] At the Prime Minister's demand on 15 November 1975 that the trade union movement discard its identity as a class movement, and learn to subordinate its interests to the interests of the nation, the INTUC general council went so far as to ask for a review of the ordinance cutting wages.[124]

But on all sides there were new and old forms of grim industrial struggle. There was the struggle of the worker, under the compulsions of reduced wages and raised production, to survive physical rigours and preserve his precarious level of living. There was the struggle of the opposition trade unions to rebuild organization decimated by detention. There was the struggle of the Labour Minister 'struggling', as he put it, 'to increase the wages of mine workers'.[125] There was the struggle of the state to erect the scaffolding of a new industrial structure, building both castles in the air and new places of detention, and digging out the foundations of its new economic order.

Workers, having lost their minimum rights of trade union association, were instead given on 30 October 1975, by the *marxisant* Labour Minister, the 'right of association in the production process'.[126] That is, the 'workers' participation' of the original 20-point programme was reduced and confined to the unilateral shouldering among themselves of heavily increased work-loads against recession, and undefended by rights of independent organization. Workers' rights, wages, and conditions were excluded. Excluded were all but 'recognized' unions; and they had the task of policing the new disciplines, at the point of production.*[127]

---

*Or, as the 'new plan' put it, 'the initiative is to be left to each management to evolve a suitable pattern of participation depending on the nature of each unit'. It was to exclude 'participation in managerial decision'; and was to be implemented 'not by law', but 'with all sincerity in every major industry'.[128] The recognized unions themselves (briefly) protested. INTUC called it an 'unfortunate decision';[129] the CPI's AITUC in an official circular called for protest, but warned that 'care must be taken so that we may not fall a prey to, or be utilized by, reactionary and disruptive elements'.[130]

The working class was summoned to be 'realistic';[131] its 're-calcitrant' leaders were imprisoned; it was thanked for 'being ex-tremely cooperative'.[132] It was invited to share a 'national spirit of service to the country by all, especially those involved in indus-trial production'.[133] Obviously absent from the changed terms of debate upon a new industrial order was the question of an ex-tension of trade union rights or of improvement in wages; or of mass unemployment. The reiterations – a catechism not con-fined to India – were of 'realism', 'discipline', 'production' and detention.

The economic sounding-board for these voices, as we shall see in a moment, was of deepening recession; its discords were of destruction and contradiction, in crisis. But it was the realism of class power which continued to impound the workers' 'dearness allowance', reaching a total by June 1976 of 10,000 million rupees.[134] And it was exactly the same realism which, then, re-laxed restrictions on the payments of dividends to shareholders but would not release the 'compulsory deposits' because they 'would be frittered away in consumption'.[135]

As closures, lockouts and layoffs multiplied throughout India, the central government announced that it would 'evolve measures to put an end to such arbitrary acts by management'.[136] It did not; it also did not matter. In recession, such measures would be 'unrealistic'. Wages were severed, by this class realism, from the cost of living index; the standard of living falling further than prices.* 'The trade union movement is critical of the re-strictions put on them,' said Achutha Menon; 'they are resented by and large by trade unions and workers.'[140] No matter; the voice of production met militancy with discipline, trade union opposition with revocation of rights, and strikes with detention.

---

*Thus, e.g. on 7 March 1976, 'Bombay textile workers will get thinner pay packets from 10 March [1976] because of a slide down in the consumer price index'.[137] By 2 May 1976, 'the fall in the price index is misleading, because workers still pay high prices for all essential articles except food grains . . . the real wage of industrial workers in Madhya Pradesh is declining both because of the reduction in bonus and further wage deductions on the ground that the price index has declined';[138] 'real wages of the working people in Bengal have been gradually declining . . . and there is a depression in wages in Tamil Nadu, as in the rest of the country'.[139]

The voice of production, the Minister for Industries, now found the country 'poised for accelerated growth'; with 'western productivity techniques in a developing country like India having great potentialities for application and adoption'.[141]

We should listen carefully to the sounds made by a new economic strategy and by a society in transition. They beckon everyone, far beyond India. They can begin to be gathered up safely and justly from every page which has preceded. The 'hopeless 200 million who should be exterminated' is the wishful thinking of a burgeoning new order also. I began the book with it. Here it begins to find its true context. So does the calling of a halt to land reform, to 'concentrate on production'. So also does 'the price of labour is very low here compared with western standards', of the works director of Ashok Leyland, speaking with coarse reassurance and idly tapping the glass-topped table. 'The price we pay for our chaps is less than one sixth yours' (though it is in fact less still), 'but the difference in efficiency is 15 or 20 per cent only, since labour here is quite skilled and intelligent', he said, smiling but expressionless, and still tapping the table. 'So if we can say over there your humans are used in the factory for 250 days or so each year, the same equipment is used here also, but for one sixth of the price only.' Smiling or grimacing, he said, 'We have now a new discipline also. We don't have your problems. Car workers are always playing up in Britain.' He had a fixed grin, or rictus, with gold-filled teeth; in shirtsleeves, arms folded: K. V. Varadarajan. 'Our British colleagues over here say to us, "it is time the British PM would do the same as yours to the British workers." Is it true what we hear that Ryder is telling them now to work or get out, that he is giving them a good stiff warning?'*[142]

From all the foregoing, it is not difficult to place in position now a provisional working model of India's economic programme. To the general phenomena of the 'political economy of dependence', economic recession and political crisis, we must

---

*British Leyland workers will know the answer. It is not so far from Madras to Cowley and back again, as the economic crow flies. Or as Hancock, the English managing director put it, passing through the office, 'if you ask me, it's bloody sick what goes on at Cowley'.[143]

attach certain Indian particulars. The 'progressive' features of the 20-point programme we have seen quickly come and go, as the necessary radical minimum to make the introduction of the rest possible : that is, on the one hand, an assault on the working class and trade unions and (as we have yet to see fully) other insensate and violent measures of terrorization against the poor masses of India. On the other, there was 'production-discipline', cheaper labour, and above all, a measure of temporary security against working-class resistance. They beckoned India out of recession and down the path not towards 'socialism' or 'self-reliance', but towards a bargain with foreign investment and the multi-national corporation; and towards increasing dependency upon the World Bank and the Soviet Union.

The elements of a provisional political model for India, broad enough to admit the crudities and corruptions of Indian planning, may be sketched in also. We have seen in passing the beginnings of a new redistribution from poor to rich, and a regressive system of taxation. With pressure on wages and the trade unions, tax cuts and – to come – a plethora of incentives, such as the 'liberalization of investment procedures', India was to be made safe again for pillage by monopoly, both Soviet and western. In return, prompted by the blatant subtleties of Indian diplomacy into outbidding each other, the mutual fears and competition of Soviet and western interest would hopefully assist a self-sufficient and non-aligned India to its national resurrection.

Of course, until this happened there would have to be supervision of the economic crisis, and the unalleviated sufferings and miseries of the people. There would have to be supervision of the inflation rate rising and falling amid stagnation, and the turnover of detentions and releases. There would have to be supervision of the state provision of increasing economic subsidy to vested interests (since this is no *laissez faire* economy) as the price of their allegiance in rural and industrial India; and supervision of the whole massive incubus of disease and sorrow. All would have to be supervised by a strong and stable centre, as guarantor for 'democracy's' restoration. That is, it would have to be supervised by the concentrations of executive and para-military power, at the apex of the state system. This power would have to be armed and rearmed at the expense of the people's real rights; inducing 'habits of discipline' in them, in the national and factional interest; and it would have to stand firm until the very day of national resurrection.

By apologists, however, India's economic problems might be differently perceived, and then arranged in different hierarchies of importance. For some, inflation might then be the principal issue; intermittently, it was faction-power's stalking-horse also. In fact, 'inflationary forces raised their ugly heads largely because of the climate of political instability that certain opposition groups had created',[144] a relative novelty in economic explanation, even if the language of it is now familiar to the reader. For others, it was recession as source of India's social and political crisis; with India's helpless millions driven to the sterilizer's knife at the bloody end of a long trail which began, say, with the decisions of middle eastern (or west Asian) oil sheikhdoms. For some, it is the political economy of Indian human nature, and of beggary, slothfulness and a redundant population, which is a self-explanatory cause of causes. For others it is narrowed to problems of economic management and human engineering; of the 'contradictions' of a 'mixed economy', and of trying to reconcile subsidy and tax cut, discipline and incentive, the private and the public interest. For others, yet again, it is a matter of an economy unreconstructed, of structured destitution, unemployment and rural bankruptcy, of the falling purchasing power of the millions without genuine redistribution to put money in their pockets; and of the relative autonomy of vested interest, managing the economy in its own image.

Certain, to begin with, was the continuous recession – called 'sluggishness' by the government's own *Economic Survey* for 1975 – throughout the whole period under review, up to the moment of writing. Certain also, and politically equally important, was 'the poppycock about the buoyancy of our economy and the positive results in containing inflation'.[145] Indeed, the whole emergency period, and in almost every major industry – more drastically in some than in others – was marked by slump, falling demand and stockpiling.[146]

Business leaders and unguarded official sources made recession's extent plain; newly unemployed workers made it plainer. Discordant voices spoke without cease of officially electrifying economic recovery on the one hand, but of an economy in deep recession on the other. Even revenue sources showed a steep fall in collections from indirect taxes 'because of a slowdown in economic activity'.[147] For example, the new president of the Indian Chambers of Commerce (FICCI) V. Arunachalan, on 2 May 1976, and deep into the official period of economic renaissance and the conquest of inflation,* was announcing that 'the recession is not a passing phase or short-term phenomenon'.[149] His predecessor asserted that 'the recession is more widespread even than in 1967';[150] while the industrialist N. H. Tata, president of the employers' federation of India was speaking not only of 'the need to combat recession' but also of 'massive unemployment'.[151]

Tata's term was a just one for the tide of unemployment, rising during the emergency against the 'need of the hour for higher production' and deepening the pre-existing trends and symptoms of recession. To the Rajya Sabha, on 19 March 1976, the Minister of Labour had given figures of a quarter of a million workers laid off in West Bengal alone in the first emergency quarter, between June and December 1975.[152] By 21 June 1976 he was announcing that from June 1975 to April 1976, five million man-days had been lost from lockouts in the private sector.[153] This was almost double the days lost from strikes, which itself revealed that the pinioned unions were fighting on against the new industrial order, while employers fought the recession in time-honoured fashion.

Throughout India the picture of public announcement was uniform. It was of closures of large plants and small, of textile and jute mills, steel plants and tea plantations; of dismissals and 'retrenchments'; and of 'industrial units in almost all sectors laying off workers on a large scale'.[154] Between the unemployed and the exercise of the new impunities of industrial power, stood

*cf. e.g. Sanjay Gandhi, on 4 April 1976, 'nine months of emergency rule have heralded a new era of all-round economic and industrial progress',[148] etc., etc.

only the provision that 'there should be little room for lockouts'[155] in India's resurgence, and the assertion that 'a great responsibility rests on employers to avoid lockouts and layoffs'.[156] On 5 March 1976, as recession – to say nothing of 'rationalization' and the purge of militant workers – cut swathes through the labour force, the government 'withdrew the unfettered rights of an employer to layoff and lockout',[157] as both continued without abatement or redress. No matter; for this too spoke of the making of a new economic order. And so, being swept away in this swollen tide of the existing huge totals of unemployment was the last point of the 20-point programme: for 'new apprenticeship schemes'. As we saw, this was the only reference in the new deal to the massive and growing problem of unemployment, and one which in practice was reduced officially to 'measures to increase employment opportunities for educated young people, by suitable amendment to the apprenticeship act'.[158] Moreover, excluded from the official statistics of recession were the unquantifiable thousands and tens of thousands of 'temporary' or 'casual' workers, who not only live on the margins of Indian life but can also gain no access to the shelter of its official index of unemployment.

The emergency reports from industry speak monotonously of falling demand, under-utilization of industrial capacity and 'sickness among industrial units'.[159] 'Recession has overtaken industry'; 'there is hardly any major industry which is not still in the throes of recession', while on May Day 1976 'capital equipment worth 60,000 million rupees [£3,500 million] is lying idle'.[160] 'They keep on saying,' said Sivasilam of Simpson's, 'that production should be increased, but demand has fallen, so industry is not interested in producing either'.[161] Industrialists thus disagreed openly with the government's analysis that India was not in general recession. It had gripped hard equally on heavy and light engineering and consumer goods industries; on the automobile and textile industries, and in the critical railway and steel industries.[162] There were huge pile-ups of coal stock, chemicals, aluminium, steel and iron ore, to go no further.

In the coal industry, amid the mounting stockpiles at the pitheads and the clamour for the simultaneous raising of production ('government has called upon all sections of industry to work tirelessly to increase production still further'),[163] there was both a rising toll of accidents and 'a year of exceptional performance'.[164] Moreover, there was 'no intention to cut back on even bigger targets'.*[165] And thus, together with rising unemployment, held to be because of 'accumulation of stocks' or 'financial difficulties' or 'trade reasons',[169] the official political celebration of realism and discipline – 'Iron Will and Hard Work Will Sustain Us'[170] – and of Stakhanovite records of unsold and unsaleable production, also passed without pause for breath through its long crescendo.

And what of prices? More precisely, what of the official price index, where the apologist in search of respite, whether faction's spokesman or foreign well-wisher, often rested his case; or, calculus in hand, recovered his balance. On the one hand, there were the 'accelerated efforts to bring down the prices of essential commodities' of 3 July 1975;[171] while on 4 April 1976, 'the prices of all commodities are falling, and consumer goods required for daily use are becoming cheaper'.[172] On the other hand, bland rhetorical assertion must be met with fact, preferably drawn from official sources. At first sight, and indeed at first, 1975–6 showed 'some respite', with the wider the time-scale taken the better; for then it might be set against the massive inflationary rates of 1973–4 which had brought enormous peaks in India's price levels, with 50 to 100 per cent increases between 1972 and 1975 in many basic commodity and other prices.†[173]

---

*cf. 'Dark clouds,' said Gopal Das Nag, the West Bengal Labour Minister, 'are hovering over the industrial scene. Almost every day,' he told the West Bengal assembly in April 1976, 'the labour department hears complaints from employers that because of lack of finance and orders, they will be forced to shut down their units.'[166] His report recorded facts for obvious reasons not prominently publicized in India: a rise in the number of strikes, lockouts, retrenchments, layoffs and closures in the first emergency quarter, over the last pre-emergency quarter. (Also cf. the CPI's 'marked general improvement in the national economy in 1975',[167] on the one hand, and complaints on 2 May 1976 of 'the mounting offensive against the working people',[168] on the other).

†e.g. 'What cost five rupees for a family of four for two days' food now [January 1976] costs twenty-five rupees. But even with the good harvest prices are not coming down to previous years' levels so that people continue to suffer with frozen wages.'[174]

But the 1975 World Bank report on India referred to inflation control as the 'achievement of the past year', that is 1974 – before the emergency altogether.[175] Indeed from March to June 1975 – that is, immediately preceding the emergency – the price index was steady. From mid-July to the end of August – that is, immediately after the emergency – it rose again. From September 1975 to March 1976, good harvests were gathered. With the purchasing power of the Indian people falling, demand reduction by the freezing of wages and the assault on the trade unions, price-cutting to try to stimulate demand in recession, some releasing of hoarded goods by merchants and traders, and what was described as a 'lull in the use of black money in the commodity markets',[176] there was a 7·5 per cent fall in the price index.[177] This fall – and I go into this otherwise unwarranted detail because the indices of price and the volumes of detention existed, for some, in political correspondence – was described alternatively as 'notable', 'seasonal', 'small in relation to previous huge increases' and 'not unusual either in its extent, or in the range of commodities it covered'.[178] (It was also described, as we saw earlier, as 'magical' or 'miraculous'.)

Attached to this are the qualifications of the vulnerable and dependent economy, and the spiralling passage since 1973 of inflation, stagnation and recession, spinning like a dust storm across the arid economy of India. It left in its wake of destruction – behind the blank wall of per capita income growth, officially standing at zero – falling purchasing power, steeply rising rents,* costs of transportation and services; that is, falling real wages, falling faster than all price fluctuations. In an affluent economy, this is belt-tightening; in India, increasing immiseration, with other physical meanings and other dimensions of sorrow, beyond equation.

*e.g. In January 1976, the Maharashtra Housing Board raised the 'service charges' for tenement dwellers in Greater Bombay by 55 to 100 per cent, backdated to 1 April 1974. 'The present living conditions in Goregaon West' [where charges were thus raised] were reported on 12 January 1976 by the *Times of India* to be of 'slush and slime'. The entire colony was 'a stinking slum'; 'the less said about the privies the better'. 'In the monsoon', the paper continued, 'life will be a nightmare . . . the people will have to wade through knee-deep water.' Most of the tenants were reported to be 'in the salaried class'.[179]

And, then, two familiar spectres sat from September 1975 to March 1976 at the feast – in which only some of the people of India can share – of a good harvest. One was that wholesale prices fell further than consumer prices,[180] agricultural commodities fell and not industrial prices,*[181] and manufacturing costs fell further than market prices, as was admitted by the Finance Minister on 21 March 1976 to the Rajya Sabha.[183] Thus the shadow of increasing profit, like that of increasing discipline, also fell across the revellers at their harvest supper. The other is simpler; after March 1976 the price index for basic foodstuffs and industrial raw materials began once more to rise. Landlords and merchant traders, having earlier released their hoarded (and often low quality) stocks for low prices, were making way for the new season and beginning to restore their profit margins, in a 'renewal of speculative activities' and in time-honoured fashion.† By 26 April 1976, inflation was acknowledged to be 'raising its ugly head again'.[185] By 7 May 1976 'the rate of increase and its spread' was 'causing concern to policy-makers', who were promising further 'drastic measures'.[186] Yet in exactly the same period before the emergency, as we have seen, prices were steady.

There are other issues blocking the path of th glib and swift installation of a just economic order for India. Prices paid to the poor peasant producers for their crops of foods and raw materials such as sugar and tobacco, jute and cotton, were falling steeply throughout the period of good harvest. Depressing their precarious condition, forced by debt to sell quickly after harvest to private traders at low prices – as much as 50 per cent below the previous year's prices[187] – these were the perennial 'distress sales' of India's piteous rural history. But the prices of goods and foodstuffs manufactured from their product, as well as the prices of other necessities, were stationary, or falling more slowly. The small arithmetic of mass deterioration is not the mathematics

*e.g. 'The prices of items basic to industrial manufacture have not come down,' said the President of the Andhra Pradesh Chambers of Commerce on 4 April 1976; 'in fact their prices have consistently gone up'.[182]

† The purchase of foreign grain *increased* by 50 per cent in 1975–6 over the previous year, despite the good harvest;[184] rural landlords thus retaining their power to command surpluses and prices.

of rhetoric's economic revival, but of marginal survival. So is the (however slowly or quickly) rising cost in the rural producer's small budget of fuel or fertilizer, coal and kerosene, electricity – if he has it – or rates for irrigation, the latter tripled in West Bengal on 23 March 1976.[188] So, too, is the poor producer's increasing land-tax, doubled in March 1976 in Bihar,[189] for example, and evaded by the richest landlords. The clearest signs of bitter rural hardship assert themselves in such detail, summoning attention behind the blazon of official headlines.

On 11 March 1976, the government gave assurance that it would procure 'all surplus food grains at fixed prices'.[190] But on 4 April come the familiar reports of 'the disheartening spectacle of distress sales' (or rural misery in the midst of harvest plenty), in West Bengal, in Gujarat and other states.[191] Open-market prices were falling, as official agencies left the small producers 'uncared for',[192] non-intervention in the market keeping it depressed and bankrupting the rural producer. The private traders as a result were paying as low a price as they could to the 'hapless producers',[193] as the former hoarded and stocked up again for the returning inflation.* And on 2 May 1976, a new scheme was 'proposed' by the government for 'consumption loans to the lowest stratum of village society',[195] beggared by a free market's good harvest reaped for the landlord and the merchant. It is well known what figure, harvest scythe in hand, stalks among this 'lowest stratum'.

And, similarly, the fall in purchasing power and the unbought stockpiles of cheap cotton cloth were part of the familiar and general crisis of free enterprise's over-production, not in relation to the need but to the effective demand of the pauperized people. Thus, point 10 of the 20-point programme fell also, when the 'common man' in his rags and tatters could not buy the 'improvement in quality and supply of cloth', or the 'More Cloth for More and More!' promised him on huge street hoardings, in part exchange for his lost freedoms.

*cf. 'The big landlords, however, have had no such trouble, as they happened to wield a great deal of influence over the ever-helpful authorities for obvious reasons.'[194]

But it is not at this blinding 'micro-level' of the homeless sleeping in the shelter of house-sized bill-boards proclaiming 'Homes for the Homeless!' that we should be staring. Better to return to that broader and safer vista of industry-wide recession, or the balance of payments; better to return to official responses and 'solutions' to unadmitted recession, and the unregenerated poverties of the 'domestic market'. The new economic order – logically – found them due 'largely to external factors'.[196] The jute industry, for instance, with mills shut in all the jute-producing states of India, certainly wanted no nationalization; 'the government does not consider it necessary to nationalize the industry'.[197] Its socialism was pragmatic. What was required, instead, as we anticipated earlier in our economic model, were subsidized exports. That is, what was needed for India's economic freedom was foreign domination of its economy by capitalist or socialist monopoly.

For, to make its new order, ruling power was travelling a well-trodden and well-beaten path of political economy, as it made tracks from its compound recession of world slump and domestic immiseration, with its crisis of over-production and under-consumption. The emergency route to be taken was to give a retrospective logic to everything so far assembled in the Indian polity (and as verbal shadow, in this text also) of drastic political, economic and social destruction and construction. It drove now towards substantially extended support and borrowing; whether from the Soviet Union, for example, for defence and trade; or from the World Bank for agriculture and irrigation. It sought new investment from multi-national corporations and scanned the world for markets for the sale of the raw materials and foods of its impoverished people. It must turn its back on the small rural producer. It must switch economic resources into subsidy to domestic monopoly, for products of a diminishing social value, on the one hand; and into a sufficient repression of the domestic proletariat and opposition, on the other. It must cut back wages and rights together. The route it sought might take it towards its 'new order', but with a somewhat less new ideology and structure of political power.

We have already seen enough to know that the speed of change (or deterioration) in the period under review was rapid, given the slothfulness attributed to Indian 'human nature'. Vocabulary and practice – like the street hoarding which proclaimed it – were both quickly in position. On 31 July 1975, the Finance Minister announced that 'qualitatively there is now going to be a change in the direction of the economy, in favour of the poorer and weaker sections of the population'.[198] But his own budget* of 15 March 1976 was hailed as 'the best with which industrialists could be provided',[199] with its 'thrust towards accelerated growth',[200] and its big 'concessions to the corporate sector'[201] – concessions in taxes, duties, investments and profits. There was indeed a qualitative change; but in the opposite direction. It was at cross-purposes only with the pose of the official ideology of state power, which continued as it was, unabashed and unabated.† The pace of change itself was merely quickening along a route already chosen.

As early as 13 November 1975 conditions for issuing bonus shares had been relaxed to boost the capital market, and measures introduced to try to stimulate demand.[203] They were greeted by a sharp rise in share prices, and recognition – soon to be vindicated – that the government, despite an even sharper rise in socialist rhetoric, was 'not unduly hamstrung by ideological shibboleths'.[204] These early measures were regarded as positive, but insufficient. The 15 March budget, therefore, brought rises in indirect taxation on the goods and services needed by the mass of the people, to pay for large cuts in direct taxation on the richest; the higher the income, the greater the reduction in tax payable. It brought 'concessions' on profits, capital gains and wealth taxation – cut in order to 'remove a

---

*The word 'own' may need qualification; cf. *The Times* of 10 May 1976: 'it is said that the Finance Minister learned some important taxation proposals only after his secretary was summoned to the Prime Minister's office and told about them. The Minister is said to have felt completely humiliated; a short time later, he suffered a heart attack.'

† Thus, one week after the budget, on 23 March 1976, the Prime Minister told the 'Institute of Democracy and Socialism' that 'where claims of individual privilege clash with those of general welfare, obviously the larger good has to prevail'.[202]

powerful incentive for tax evasion'[205] – and exchanged the pleasures of tax relief for the pains of an earlier 'national discipline'.

It brought the introduction of investment allowances for 'export-oriented' industries, overwhelmingly under the control of Indian and foreign monopoly capital; it gave tax concessions to foreign investors on both royalties and dividends. It brought reductions in excise duties, in response to the demand of Indian capital for a 'quickening of the pace of consumption'. It brought reduction of duties on luxury goods, on television sets, on refrigerators, on cars, to the accusing tens of millions standing or lying in a wilderness of misery and destitution. It brought the continuation of the compulsory deductions from workers' wages. And it brought in its wake, and as consequence, an increased compulsion to rely on foreign borrowing, as we will see in a moment.

The budget had been preceded and was immediately followed by even bigger demands from capital and vested interest, which were yet to be granted.* Moreover, industry had demanded (and got for the first time) detailed and thorough bipartite pre-budget discussions with the government about the former's requirements.[207] It became plain, also, that capital's expectations were implicit in their crescendo of earlier complaints – real though the phenomena were to which they were pointing – about the impact upon them of recession. And as their interests increasingly dominated the emergency economy, so their voices became increasingly strident, particularly in relation to the trade unions and opposition, who were stifled, if not silenced. That it was these voices of vested interest from which the Congress Party was ostensibly protecting the poorer and weaker sections, was no longer the issue. For these were the voices not only which it represented and had always (in fact) represented, but, as the new order was built, it was these interests to which it would now give increasing expression in its political and economic decisions.

* There had been demands by the Chief Minister of West Bengal, for example, for even bigger corporate tax reductions than the 1,000 million rupees given by the budget. This leading spokesman for the interest of the poor, and for providing the people with food and shelter and clothing, also wanted a bigger reduction in duties on luxury consumption which, he said, 'had suffered because of the withdrawal of black money from circulation'.[206]

Thus just as the declaration of emergency had boosted share prices on the Bombay stock exchange,* so the budget drew a huge chorus of approval in the world of domestic and foreign capital, India's marketable value and political stock rising when the message of the budget had been digested. Praise was unanimous from the national chambers of commerce, spokesmen for the right-wing Swatantra and Jan Sangh parties,[210] the Chief Minister of West Bengal,[211] the all-India manufacturers' association,[212] the association of Indian engineering industries,[213] the national alliance of young entrepreneurs,[214] 'industrialists and higher middle-class families in Uttar Pradesh',[215] and the official Soviet news agency, *Tass*.[216] ('Trade union leaders generally remained quiet.')[217]

The budget was 'refreshing'[218] and 'courageous';[219] it was a 'challenge to the ingenuity and sincerity of private entrepreneurs',[220] but also 'pragmatic and balanced'.[221] It was 'truly memorable',[222] 'a bold experiment',[223] 'modern and epochmaking',[224] and 'bound to encourage investment'.[225] It marked 'a definite shift from fiscal theology to fiscal rationality' and 'had brought to an end a twenty-year régime of expropriatory taxation'.[226] There was 'no political motivation behind it,' however, said the economist and Congress parliamentarian, V.K.R.V. Rao; about this, he was 'emphatic'.[227] Nonetheless, 'never before,' said the *Times of India*, on the one hand, as leading industrialists welcomed the ratification of their own proposals, 'has there been a budget with so much cheerful news for industry'.[228] The budget, said *Tass*, on the other, would 'consolidate the country's economic self-sufficiency and independence',[229] inverting its meaning.

For some the good news from India was different. It was also familiar news from that modern battlefield between capital and

---

*The *Economic Times* (Bombay) share index, at low level in recession, had plummeted further downwards after the Allahabad court decision, and the Gujarat defeat of Congress. It soared after the proclamation of emergency.[208] That the 'business climate' was held to have 'improved considerably due to the state of emergency' was thus being asserted *before* the budget, as for example in *Business Week* on 2 February 1976, though with more ardour after it. Or, as A. K. Bahl, Bombay finance manager of Cadbury Fry put it, 'The emergency? I'm all for it'.[209]

labour where state power and the para-military declare a state of siege, arrest the opposition, and declare themselves victors. 'Prime Minister Indira Gandhi may talk socialism,' said New York's *Business Standard*, which can read the economic signs as well as *Tass* can, 'but the pro-business budget demonstrates a pragmatic willingness to employ capitalistic tools to pep up the Indian economy.'[230] According to the *Economist*, under its headline 'Indian Economy: By the Right, Quick March!' ('Mrs Gandhi's government is in a hurry'), there had been 'a basic change of economic philosophy in Delhi'. With 'populism out and profit-making in', 'businessmen are naturally delighted … with its new accent on growth', and 'boost to the capital market'. 'The budget,' said the *Economist*, 'points in the right direction',[231] a direction which would be followed to its logical conclusion.

The CPI, however, was now burdened both with its theory of the 'anti-feudalism' of the 20-point programme and its earlier gratification that, under Congress, India's road to economic progress would 'not be through the capitalist path of development, but through a socialist order', albeit 'different from those followed by other countries'.[232] It was also saddled with an earlier assertion that 'when imperialists sing paeans of praise for something' – as they were doing for the budget – 'it is not out of ignorance. They never take sides out of ethical or democratic considerations', the CPI had said, 'but always in accordance with their class interests.'[233]

And thus when the CPI came to speak, it spoke *sotto voce*; the budget was 'encouraging savings and promoting greater investment'. Equally mutedly, 'the business community and the rich had received undue concessions'.[234] But these concessions turned out, given the rules of the new order, to be insufficient. ('In one budget you cannot do everything,' said Subramaniam).[235] They wanted much more; the stock exchange fell, to prove it. What they wanted were further reductions of corporate and personal taxation, the dismantling of price controls and the freer entry of foreign capital. They wanted 'export income' to be exempted entirely from income taxes, more excise reliefs, and the further relaxation of import policies.[236] Such were the fruits of nine months of cross-class 'national discipline'. And they had less to do with that economic theory under which untrammelled private interest enhances public benefit, than the practical prospect of the private sector being helped by the state to an increasing appropriation of the national wealth, produced by the poor millions of India.

The strident demands of capital easily overrode the formal pleas of Ministers to the business community to make use of its incentives, or even 'to prove itself worthy of the confidence and responsibility reposed in it under the National Resurgence Programme'.[237] Thus, pre-empting by one day the publication on 16 April 1976 of the RBI report for 1975–6, which spoke of 'impressive growth rates in after-tax profits', the private sector was given the first instalment of what it wanted on 15 April: a new 'bold step' in the 'liberalization of imports', including 'simplification of procedures for import replenishment' and a 'more flexible system of automatic licensing'[238] 'hailed' by the national alliance of young entrepreneurs as 'inspiring'.*[239] The struggle against fascism and 'right reaction' was obviously bringing its own rewards.

A second instalment of 'concessions' came on 12 May 1976, seventeen days after the Supreme Court had disallowed *habeas corpus*: new excise reliefs and further tax reliefs on both personal and corporate income. 'The private sector,' said Subramaniam, having done the job demanded of him, 'is on trial.'[241] The tens of thousands who were detained without this last luxury, were less favoured.

The rest was an obvious process. The rhetoric of 'the struggle against imperialism' and the Patna call to 'disband multi-national corporations'[242] notwithstanding, the Indian government now moved quickly to try to encourage foreign investment (CIA or no CIA) to extend its already substantial grip on the Indian economy. It was neither paradox nor ideological contradiction

---

*As the 'business climate' changed throughout urban and rural India – and choosing from a wide range of examples – the post-DMK Tamil Nadu government (under President's rule) decided, on the grounds that 'the public authorities had inadequate storage facilities', to 'adopt a more liberal attitude towards private wholesale traders in food grains', and to 'allow them to step in'. 'Safeguards in the public interest will, of course, be taken to ensure this concession is not misused', the statement of 1 April 1976 added.[240]

that invocations to the cause of a Chinese 'self-reliance' simultaneously intensified, as I will show in the next chapter.

On 18 March 1976, the government welcomed foreign investment 'on a selective basis', where it was 'advantageous to the country's economy';[243] the budget had 'facilitated this by removing procedural difficulties faced by foreign investors'.[244] On 28 March, 'foreign investment would not be allowed in "unlimited areas"'; the government was therefore 'not considering any modification of the present policy'. All proposals, said Subramaniam, 'had to be considered only within the framework of the Foreign Exchange Regulation Act'.[245] On 29 March, asked to comment in the Rajya Sabha about demands made by a visiting US business delegation that India's laws governing foreign investment should be relaxed, H. R. Gokhale replied that India would 'follow her sovereign independent policies irrespective of what they say'.[246] It did not.* On 2 April 1976, the Foreign Exchange Regulation Act was drastically altered 'to accommodate the point of view of foreign investors'.[249]

It permitted them to have both majority shareholding in, and managerial control of, their Indian subsidiaries, provided they could show (by whatever means) that they exported 60 per cent of their Indian production, itself made from India's cheap raw materials and by its cheaper human labour. And so to power's apologia on the one hand and capital's gratification on the other. In the former case, what had been done signified 'foreign participation in the development of the country';[250] 'if India approached the multi-nationals, it was because the country needed their technology'.[251] In the latter case, it meant 'concessions to private foreign investors [led by Britain, the US and West Germany, in that order] who had been made even happier by the overall shift of emphasis in economic policy'.†[252]

---

*The Prime Minister chose 31 March, in the Lok Sabha, to report a threat by IBM – convenient to India's purpose – to leave India unless the rules for foreign multi-nationals were relaxed.[247] As part of the same process, Japan's big new commodity loan to India was – coincidentally – announced on 1 April.[248]

†On 5 April 1976, additionally, came almost complete licence for evasion. Industrial investment in a long list of India's basic industries was to be permitted henceforward to 'non-resident Indians', with exemption from

Arguably all necessary assurances, with or without the budget, had already been given to international capital. As it is, foreign companies in the Indian corporate sector are both more profitable than their Indian counterparts, and certainly more profitable than their parent companies. The typical expected 'pay off' period, often as little as two years, is very short and the rate of exploitation – that is, the share of profit in the value added – therefore very high. The emergency itself, its form and content ('wild conjectures are circulating about nationalization. We have no such plans,' said the Prime Minister. 'Our purpose is to increase production'),[254] and all that was signified by it, would seem to have been an adequate earnest of intention, once the dust had settled and the blood of broken heads had stopped flowing, or being seen and reported to be flowing.

But such additional investment is hard to come by. It requires wooing, and India has many competitors for it where the dust is well settled. Moreover, it is one thing to assert here that 'the goal of self-reliance' or the falsely proclaimed 'domination of the public sector'* in the Indian economy are parts of another residual political debate, even if crucial as ideology or oratorical illusion. They must be seen to be and *repeatedly proven* to the cautious investor to be irrelevant or inoperative, in actual practice. Foreign capital's doubts were easily aroused even by rhetorical CPI demands, say, for 'investigation by a parliamentary committee into the menace of the corrupt activities of multi-national corporations'[256] – there were 202 in India in 1975, with 530 branches throughout the country[257] – or for nationalization of foreign drug firms† or tea plantations.[263] They

---

wealth tax and free remittance of profits; and of capital also, after the unit has gone into production'.[253] For foreign investment in India, see appendix, p. 431.

*For example, even in Subramaniam's 15 March budget, he asserted that 'the public sector has now assumed a really commanding role in the economy' (even though the private sector accounts for four fifths of the value added in industry, and there was to be no further nationalization). 'If the private sector fails to use the occasion,' he added,' and the system does not function, the country might not hesitate to scrap it.'[255]

†The Hathi committee recommended the nationalization of multi-national drug companies, and the setting up of a national authority. On 13 January

were not allayed by the 'pragmatism' of a 'non-doctrinaire approach to nationalization', or the criterion of 'the good of the country', in economic decision-making. What was first required was the physical construction of a politically safe economic order, in which repression played the banker; and election (hopefully) the teller. The Indian government sought to provide it; while class and state power struggled to roll a huge economy of 600 millions on to its back, for the pillage of the hard labour and precious resources of its masses, in the name of mutual and national interest. The political, constitutional, juridical and economic changes not only complemented and reinforced each other; they were the price India was paying for its new order.

Hereon, it was often a model of its kind. American, Soviet, West German, British, Iranian and Japanese official and business delegations, amongst others, from January 1976 – to go back no further – in turn put blatant pressure on the Indian government for political, strategic and economic favours of one kind or another. They offered in return modest political compliance with the emergency (or silence), economic aid, or capital investment. They struck their various hard bargains with a stagnant and dependent economy, in recession. The Indian government bartered its resources and its erased freedoms; that is, its new 'business climate'. Who was uppermost was plain.

Orville Freeman, for example, leader of the US delegation to meetings of the Indo-US business council in February 1976 could contrast, in public, India's poor record in attracting foreign investment with 'countries like Taiwan, South Korea,

---

1976, the government was 'considering these recommendations', though 'since a number of formulations are not being manufactured by Indian units, it is essential that these [sc. foreign] companies continue their production'.[258] On 10 March 1976, 'there will be no takeover now'; but 'the government is planning to give public sector drug units a leadership role'.[259] On 31 March, the government denied in the Lok Sabha a report of the parliamentary committee on public undertakings that foreign drug companies were 'earning huge profits at the expense of the public sector and national interest'.[260] On the same day, the Indian oral polio vaccine production unit at Coonoor was to be closed down. 'It will mean,' said the *Hindu*, 'dependence on imports for polio vaccine for a number of years to come.'[261] On 15 April 1976 the Minister for Chemicals said 'the country has to keep its doors open for import of technology for drugs'.[262] This succession contains its own comment.

Hong Kong and Singapore'.[264] On 10 March 1976 Otto Wolff von Amerongen, the head of a German trade mission, told the Indians that 'with their vast raw material resources and low labour charges, they were an ideal partner for joint ventures and collaboration in third countries'; and that 'a free hand should be given to industry and commerce in India, as it entered into a free market economy, in order to enable it to rebuild its economy'. 'It is on this basis,' he added, 'that German industry [increasingly important in the Indian economy] supports both nationally and internationally the further expansion of the division of labour and, with it, of world-wide free trade.'[265]

With India's new economic order and its political regression together compounding and deepening its dependence, the German trade mission was officially assured that 'there would be no doctrinaire approach', and that 'the regulations were negotiable'.[266] 'Our two countries are large', Freeman was told by the head of the Indian Chambers of Commerce, 'and our economies are complementary. You have sophisticated technology and vast capital resources. We have abundant labour.'[267] Yet this further economic consummation of the marriage of international finance capital with India's abundant labour and vast resources – or, the pillage of the 'third world' – was and is in India's case not the only element in its subordination. But I will come to that in a moment.

Here we will note the characteristic process and progression of only one among several bigamous alliances.* India makes the running, strenuously signalling its intentions and its potential abasements. On 10 January 1976, Chavan wants 'good and healthy relations with the USA',[268] 'external enemies', 'dark forces' and the CIA notwithstanding. On 1 March, the Deputy External Affairs Minister 'would like the USA to cooperate in building highly sophisticated industry not developed in India so far', the 'expansion of economic cooperation' having become 'a new significant facet in India's foreign policy'.[269] On 26 March

---

* e.g. The Indo-Iranian alliance is also worth exploring; for, as the *Hindu* put it on 28 February 1976, 'Indo-Iran economic cooperation now extends over a wide area', and India was 'in a position to meet Iran's requirements for manpower'.

Chavan, pursuing marriage (or at least a liaison), wants a 'mature and constructive relationship with the US based on mutual respect and understand'.[270] On 2 April foreign investors are given their new licence in India. And on 20 April, William Saxbe, the US Ambassador to India, at last indicated 'a thaw in Indo-US relations' and 'a better appreciation in the US government of emergency rule in India'.*[271]

Thereafter, came the part-public resumption of (privately un-interrupted) Indo-US relations. Bought from India was not only American capital's writ unhindered, should the US wish to exercise it, but public support for America's new foreign policy 'initiatives' in Africa, announced unexpectedly by the Indian Commerce Minister at the Nairobi conference of UNCTAD. This was immediately denied on 25 May 1976 in the Lok Sabha as 'unfounded'.[273] It was well founded. Moreover it had been paid for. The tokens of it included the 400,000 tonnes of US wheat and 100,000 tonnes of rice for India at 'concessional terms', but with loans for the purchase repayable to the US in dollars.[274] But the real issues were quite other. They included the promise of enriched uranium for India's (military) nuclear pro-gramme, and the hiring of Indian surplus labour by big US construction companies – such as Kellogg, Bechtel, Marcona and Kaiser – in their industrial investment, construction, and political consolidations in the Middle East†[275] Thus was the international web of the new order being spun. Its filaments were as visible in the meeting between the Indian monopolist G. D. Birla and the President of the World Bank in Washington on 21 April, as in the US Department of Commerce's announcement on 22 May 1976 that 'India's economic situation has improved significantly over the past year', with 'labour peace achieved' and a rise in industrial production.[277]

This immediate pre- and post-budget period, then, was a de-cisive one in signifying the true nature of India's attempted

*cf. T. A. Pai, in London on 10 April 1976 for Indo-British economic talks; 'India's surplus labour force, splendid administrators and technocrats could,' he said, 'be usefully offered to other countries.'[272]

† Indo-US cooperation in 'joint ventures in third countries' was discussed in Delhi on 24 and 25 March 1976.[276]

economic 'reconstruction', and of reaction to it. But if the *speed* of response to the first reassuring sounds of the cracking of heads, and the suppression of freedoms from June 1975, and then to the economic salve applied to its wounds in the spring of 1976, were to be the criterion for distinguishing between the respondents, then the palm would have been awarded earlier to the World Bank's reflexes.

As long ago as on 20 October 1975, and bespeaking its commanding position among India's paymasters of the present and future, the World Bank was recommending India to opt for massive export production during the coming decade, and to substitute imported for domestic manufactures.[278] That is, it had read the political signs aright and seized the moment, if prematurely. India, the World Bank urged, should abandon its wearying effort to build on the backs of its labouring people an industrial infrastructure for its indigenous economic development, and instead tailor its economy, as German industrialists were later arguing, to the 'international division of labour'. But its next intervention was much more timely and more to our immediate point also.

On 16 May 1976 – in a period when news of torture in India was becoming more repetitious – the World Bank kept to the chronology of international capital's extending welcome to the 'new' India. It helped both to redouble India's financial subjugation to unpayable international loan-debt, and to bury fact in half-truth and fiction. A new World Bank report, on that day, 'lauded India's progress' and praised the 'curbing of inflation' – ironically just as prices were again rising. All that we have seen and have yet to see in this book was, transmuted by the newspeak of finance capital into 'vigorous measures' and India's 'adjustment effort'. Likewise the 'reduction of man-hours lost by strikes' was the World Bank's euphemism for the politics of rights denied and the statistics of detention, and all that went with them. For this, it recommended payment to India. It advised the Aid-India consortium of rich nations (which had given $1,775 million to India in 1975–6, and was about to meet in Paris) to sustain – despite their own recessions – aid allocations to India for 1976 to 1977.[279]

No qualitative distinction of time, form or meaning can be made in the simultaneous process of development of Indo-Soviet relations, as India's new order was struggling for consolidation. On 24 February 1976, Leonid Brezhnev expresses 'appreciation of the efforts of India's progressive forces to solve its socio-economic problems'. He 'stresses the importance of further developing relations with India', and declares that 'close political and economic cooperation with the republic of India is our constant policy'.[280] The dates which mark its progress may be exactly aligned (in movement and meaning) with all those that preceded in India's treaty with western capital. On 12 March, the Soviet Union 'will take repayment for a wheat loan in export goods from India'.[281] On 17 March 1976, two days after the budget – which would 'consolidate the country's independence' – a Soviet textile delegation is in Bombay negotiating 'a big deal in cloth,'* while at the same time the Soviet Union is manipulating the rouble–rupee exchange rate in its own favour.[282] On 17 March too, in the exercise of her newly asserted national sovereignty, India was prevented from meeting Egypt's request for Mig-21 spares on the grounds of its 'contractual commitments' to the Soviet Union.[283] What was here being sold and bought by India, and the price the respective purchasers were having to pay for the political and strategic commodities each needed – more, and less, urgently – from the other, cannot be extricated from its economic matrix; while price is a variable term and has many non-economic dimensions.

Thus, on 17 March also, in the budget papers presented to Parliament there was an item for heavy water, critical to India's (military) nuclear programme, to be bought from the Soviet Union by the Indian atomic energy authority.[284] On 18 March 1976 came announcement of a new collaboration with the Soviet Union in satellite communication.[285] On examination, the political, the economic, the technological become one. The collaboration was designed to provide the new order with the equally

---

*Part of the Soviet Union's trade in India's raw materials and basic foodstuffs is said to become made-up and processed goods, which are then resold (at high rates of profit) as Soviet and Comecon exports in the world market.

critical power to bring not economic reform, but television, to the darkest reaches of the people's sorrow; that is, to replace the other programme – whether to distribute 'land to the landless', 'liquidate rural debt' or 'abolish bonded labour' – with a new world of illusions as yet unseen in rural India.

And so, the Soviet Union moved quickly in step and time with western capital's motions. On 24 March, for instance, the Soviet Union was discussing in Moscow plans for 'production cooperation' with India in third countries;[286] on 10 April 1976, what this would mean in practice was again made plain. 'Particularly in those units with labour intensive overtones [sic]' said India's ambassador-designate to the Soviet Union, the 'areas of cooperation could be deepened, to the mutual advantage of both the nations.' 'Our infrastructure has undergone a major change,' he added.[287] And thence to the arrival in Delhi on 11 April of the Soviet Minister of Commerce; and to new long-term trade agreements,[288] themselves the superficial economic ratification of deeper (and uneven) shifts in the very foundations of India's unstable reconstruction. In lieu of self-reliance, India was obtaining deteriorating terms of trade; for sovereignty, a further subordination to the international division of labour; for the further pillage of India's resources, the explanation that in terms of value, 'India can pay back for Soviet hardware by exporting software,'[289] a newer vocabulary for an older practice.

The surfaces only of this simultaneity can be treated. I have also excluded the simultaneous disclaimers that what I have described, which is based upon official sources, was actually happening. Analogously, the government's pre-budget *Economic Survey* of March 1976 admitted, with one of its voices, that 'the burden of external debt is increasing'.[290] With another (or even, in Subramaniam's case, the same) voice, it vigorously denied it. While it denied it, a third and fourth voices – here, the Prime Minister and Finance Minister respectively – 'stress the importance of self-reliance',[291] or insist that 'it is not India's policy to base its relationship with any country on the concept of aid, but on self-reliance'.[292]

Debt, like price, is a term of many dimensions; in every respect, India's has been increasing. It was plain by the time of the 1976 budget that levels of foreign aid coming into the country had risen sharply each year from 1972, balanced only by a rising output of denial. In 1975–6, according to the *Economic Survey*, the inflow of foreign assistance, net of amortization and interest payments, was 9,390 million rupees, surpassing the previous record of 1967–8.*[293] Preliminary budget estimates of gross receipts from external loans for 1976–7 were estimated at 12,060 million rupees; net, after repayments – and judicious political reductions in the figures – underestimated at '8,150 millions'.[296] And on 28 May 1976, in Paris, the rich donor countries† of the Aid-India consortium duly made available to India $1,700 million in loans, 'bilateral aid' and grants for 1976–7, for that adjustment effort which the World Bank had commended. In return, India had to continue to give more of what it had already given; 'expansionary investment policies and appropriate adjustments in its import polices'.[298] For these, and 'effective family planning programmes' – the precise nature of whose operations we have yet to examine – the 'first world' gave its cash and discretion. By so doing, it compounded the coercion of India's people on the well understood international principle of selective non-interference in a nation's domestic affairs.

It is the familiar world of an economy mortgaged. It is also an object-lesson in how a 'new order' may be both sustained

---

*cf. Subramaniam's 'the country has moved away from the position of heavy dependence on foreign assistance of earlier years'.[29] The reverse was true. Official figures for net inflow in 1973–4 were 4,040 million rupees, in 1974–5 7,110 million, and in 1975–6 9,390 million.[295] ('He is counting on more foreign aid,' said the *Economist* on 20 March 1976; moreover, 'the burden of debt service is rising sharply'.) For details, see appendix.

†They include Australia, Belgium, Canada, Denmark, France, West Germany, Japan, Netherlands, Norway, Sweden, the United Kingdom and the United States. On this occasion Britain – which had high hopes of purchasing overflying rights in South India for Concorde – increased its contribution to India's indebtedness; while West Germany and Japan 'softened the terms of their credit'.[297] The volume of comparable direct aid from the Soviet Union, 250 million rupees in 1975–6, is small; instead, India's debt, and domination of her indebted economy, have been expressed through trade, industrial investment and non-aligned alignment.

internally and bankrupted by the forms of debt, investment, trade and manufacture, imposed on the debtor in credit's exercise of political and economic power. And the known world of international finance masks a largely unseen one. For example, while there was a public and official 'cooling' of relations between the US and India, the International Development Agency (IDA) was the largest single donor of aid to India, in the same period; but the IDA is in turn dependent, for the loans which it makes, on US financial resources. Little of all this can be followed here. But in the aftermath of the new 'pro-business' budget which 'pointed in the right direction', it was to take India's central government, industrial development bank, agricultural development corporation, sundry municipal bodies, hydro-electric scheme authorities, and many other public institutions in search of 'fresh lines of credit'. It took them to the World Bank, the IDA, the IMF, the Iranian government credit, the Saudi Arabian development fund, and other sources.[299]

That it should bring the beggared national economy and the 'National Resurgence Programme' to new depths of indebtedness is hardly worth remarking. That it went with new levels of internal repression is perhaps a 'political' rather than an 'economic question'; to overlook it might, after all, be the price of economic progress. That an increase in dependency is, in fact, increasing national sovereignty and self-sufficiency, belongs to India and is less familiar.

But the multiple deteriorations in India's political economy in 1975–6 are not reducible to a matter of debt, even if construed at its widest meaning. The 'liberalization of import policy', the 'new guidelines' of the freed market, the demands of the World Bank's strategy for India, the deteriorating terms of trade and the insistence of debtors, pointed to other consequences for a dependent economy, compounding one dependence with another. They pointed to the 'import surge' which widens the trade gap. They pointed to exports which must be supported by subsidy, induced by incentive, and both at enormous further cost to the economy of India.* They pointed to a new spiral. They pointed,

---

*e.g. The value of direct incentives rose from 4·6 per cent of total exports in 1969–70, to 7·1 per cent in 1975–6 and would rise above that in 1976–7.[300]

that is, to increasingly subsidized exports in order to meet the cost of growing imports, and both in turn inescapable to meet the demands of the creditor, the newly signed trade agreement and of the new 'business climate'. And all of them pointed beyond debt and dependency; beyond the sale of sovereignty and resources; to that deeper depression of the people's fundamental rights and condition, which I will turn to in the next chapter.

To resume: each year since 1972–3, India has had a larger trade deficit,* increased by the burden of raised oil prices, while 'India's capacity to finance huge deficits is diminishing';[302] its gross reserves heavily inflated by borrowing. On 1 February 1976 the deficit stood at its highest ever, the announced ten-month total being 12,350 million; described as 'staggering'[303] even in terms of India's recent economic history, and with imports about to pour into India under the new budgetary provisions to meet corporate and minority demands for the stimulus of production and consumption. Adding to the size of the deficit is the decreasing value of India's exports and the increasing cost to India of its imports, where the terms of trade are dictated in one market by western capital, and the cost of credit in the other by the Soviet Union. That is, as fast as India increases her exports at the expense of the labour of the people, so their relative value against imports from the rest of the world can be made to diminish. This too is a paradigm case; while the expansion of exports, however large and at whatever social and economic cost, cannot offset the declining demand in the impoverished home market. Moreover, the increase in export production itself increases the volume of imports required to maintain it, in an economy receding from self-sufficiency. And, to complete the circle of constriction upon the economy, the creditor waits for repayment, urging India away from import-substitution as part of the interest on the loan to India of his usury capital.

---

*1972–3, 1,640 million rupees surplus; 1973–4, 4,320 million rupees deficit; 1974–5, 11,640 million deficit; for 1975–6, the estimated 13,000 to 14,000 million deficit was suddenly 'revised' downwards, to show a figure of 11,548 million.[301] I have been told on good authority that this was a political falsification of the record.

But that was one half of the emergency equation only. To the Indian industrialist, 'the body politic, which almost became un- workable' had 'come to life again'.[304] What we have seen, then, must be the temporary economic 'disbenefits' – whether or not of the Taiwan or South Korean development model – of a new politics of production and discipline. We have forgotten that 'the main aim of the emergency' was 'maximizing production';[305] 'our purpose is to increase production';[306] 'the people are cheer- fully working harder. Life is normal',[307] and so on. The Stak- hanovite figures of official exhortation, already referred to, were not merely of 'land distributed to the landless', but also of 'unprecedented' growth in industrial and agricultural output.*

There was, then, another world to consider, occupying the same place and time with all that has preceded; where, to the Prime Minister, 'workers must put their heart and soul into increasing production', but 'without asking for any rewards at the present moment'.[314] It was a world in which, to B. M. Birla the leading Indian industrialist, 'labour has begun to realize its responsi- bilities to the nation';[315] or, was 'repairing the sick economy with discipline and devotion'.[316] It was the world of the industrial truce between capital and labour where the pro-government union which 'calls on the management to increase working hours',[317] could be denounced only by the enemies of the people (disturb- ing the unbroken harmony of the new order) as 'the illegitimate progeny of the capitalist class', and 'capitalism's treacherous labour lieutenants'.[318] It was the world we had temporarily forgot-

---

*e.g. 'The [projected] overall rate of growth of *industrial* output' for 1976–7, in the March 1976 pre-budget *Economic Survey*, was given as 'nearly 6 per cent'.[308] For 1975–6, the growth of industrial production was announced by the Ministry of Industry in May 1976 to have been between 4 and 5 per cent, compared with 2·5 per cent in 1974 to 1975.[309] (But this was upon a very low base and was largely confined to the public sector, which was over- producing the stockpiles of recession, while large areas of the private sector showed 'an absolute reduction in output', or a lower growth-rate in 1975–6 than in 1974–5).[310] 'The overall index of *agricultural* production for 1975–6 could show an increase of over 10 per cent.'[311] But cf. the 1976 *Economic Survey*: 'achievements on the production front are likely to fall short of the original draft Fifth Plan target by a big margin'.[312] And, more ominous for the people, despite a good 1975–6 harvest, 'food grain output was only 4 per cent higher than the level attained five years ago'.[313]

ten of equal sacrifice and equal concession; where industrialists tighten their belts, and work not for profits but for the nation; where, seen aright, even 'workers' participation is of self-interest to the management, because it leads to increased production'.[319]

At least, the CPI had done its best to help construct the new order, with its violence, licence and illusion, in the interest of the nation's progress. On 27 December 1975, the 20-point programme was held by its chairman to be an 'agrarian revolution',[320] while to *Party Life* (as to the Finance Minister) the working class was 'responding magnificently to the call of the emergency', and 'doing its maximum to increase production'.[321] True, said the CPI's general secretary also on 27 December, the 20-point programme was being 'tardily implemented in the rural areas'; true, there was 'great resistance from the landlords'; true, that 'authoritarian trends' were developing in state practice; true, that 'in the industrial areas' the programme was being 'implemented sometimes in the reverse direction'.[322]

It was even true, as early as the 22 November 1975 issue of the CPI's *Party Life*, that 'attacks on the working class ... have caused serious discontent among them', and 'the danger of their disorientation from the anti-fascist struggle'.[323] It was true even by November 1975 that 'layoffs, closures and retrenchments' were being 'freely resorted to' and 'arousing working-class anger'. 'Unjustified' – and even 'particularly obnoxious' – 'concessions' were, already by November, being given to the 'Indian monopolies',* which, in turn, were 'hitting both working class and peasant interests'.[325]

As early as November 1975, the CPI was warning therefore that 'anti-working-class and pro-monopoly-policy trends' must be 'reversed', and that 'more active steps' had to be taken 'to curb the profiteers, monopolists and landlords who form the basis of right reaction'.[326] But if the trends were not reversed, the steps never taken, then allowance must presumably be made for what Dange called 'a complicated situation';[327] and for the CPI's sense of priority and interest. On 28 February 1976 in Moscow, as the steps quickened and the trends deepened, the CPI's

---

*cf. the Prime Minister's 'perhaps we are not strong enough in curbing monopoly', to the Rajya Sabha on 22 July 1975.[324]

chairman reported to the CPSU's 25th congress that 'the struggle against reaction's social and economic base is steadily developing in our country'.[328]

Indeed, to persuade the people that India was 'set firmly on the path of self-reliance', according to Jagjivan Ram (who for electoral purposes was later to disclaim his own complicity in the emergency's measures), with its economic policy a 'blueprint for a just social order' and a ' "*mantra*" for establishing industrial democracy',[329] required reality's inversion. Then the brittle and the ragged could be exhorted on May Day 'to mould themselves like steel in to disciplined citizens';[330] and on the same day the Labour Minister could speak of the 'glory of human toil' and the workers' 'moral grandeur'. 'On this day,' he told them – their work increased, hours lengthened, rights curtailed, India's new order at these moments in May being aided from Washington, Moscow and Paris – 'the working class can contemplate its past victories and brace itself for future triumphs'.[331]

The task above all (and one for which labour is peculiarly well fitted) was 'to work tirelessly to increase production still further'.[332] Needed from it was 'sustained hard work, stern discipline and the subordination of sectional interests to the broader goals of the nation.'[333] And if a rise in production is a rise in hard labour, nonetheless to achieve a rise in hard labour without strikes or having to pay increases in wages, is to displace 'economism' at last with the national interest. Already, the 'smart pick-up' in sales in the TV industry, which by 2 June 1976 had 'nearly doubled',[334] car sales also 'picking up' (and 'sales across the counter', 'vanished')[335] was an economic bonus beyond the calculus of a few percentage points in lost wages.

And if these commodities were not for the likes of the worker and peasant in their tens of millions, or for the landless and bonded labourer lost in the silence of rural India, India's 'battle for economic freedom,' said the Chief Minister of West Bengal, 'cannot be won overnight'.[336] Better that the world of Indian labour, armed with its 'moral grandeur', should be producing for export than for its own consumption and survival. And in future, I asked? 'Our workers will be more like the Japanese and

Brazilian concept of the worker in the future'.[337] 'All that is lacking in us,' said the President of India on 13 January 1976, 'is discipline and hard labour.' 'Our average output of work,' he said, 'is not even one fourth that of the American worker.' 'Japan and West Germany,' he added, 'are the two great examples of hard work and discipline' which 'alone could take the country forward'.[338]

The day on which he was speaking was the seventeenth day after the worst mining disaster in India's history, at the 'government-managed' Chas Nala colliery in Dhanbad, Bihar, on the afternoon of 27 December 1975. He spoke on grandiloquently at Panaji on 13 January 1976, of 'the people', who were 'entitled to press for their rights only after they have discharged their obligations to the nation'.[339] Rescuers had still failed to reach any of the bodies of hundreds of miners, engulfed by 110 million gallons of water in a pit known beforehand and declared to be perilous, and where 'even during normal conditions the mine was knee-deep in water'.[340] The lost colliers ('mostly young people')[341] and their weeping families at the pit-heads; the desolated and veiled wives and women – one of whom, the wife of the lost miner Lal Amrud, committed *suttee*, burning herself to death in mourning[342] – eyes and mouths opened in the cries of a Guernica of horror; had discharged their obligation to the raised production and heightened disciplines of the new order.

In the wake of the emergency, throughout the whole of the Bihar coal belt, and naming Dhanbad in particular,* the CITU had complained to the ILO (on 8 November 1975) that trade union representatives of the miners had been arrested, or were in hiding.[344] The complaint, only seven weeks before the disaster, spoke of 'gangster elements at large', of workers and trade unionists 'being attacked with full freedom', of 'terror' against the miners' families, a little later to gather at the pit-head; while

---

*Dhanbad is notorious not only for the violent scale of previous disasters, but for the killings of seven colliery workers early in 1973, shortly after the mining industry was 'nationalized'. They were fired on by police, during a protest over the non-payment of wages. In November 1973, another five miners were shot dead by police during a demonstration in Dhanbad.[343]

the rhetoric of discipline and selfless labour simultaneously roared on unabated, sufficient to swamp in an inundation of words the whole of India.

On 27 December a 'massive rescue effort was under way', the Minister of Labour (Reddy) and the Minister of Mines (Yadav) 'rushing to the site of the accident'; with the central and state governments 'rushing all assistance to the area', and 'rescue efforts swinging into action'[345] for the '372' miners, for all the world as if this were itself the 20-point economic programme. On 28 December Yadav pronounced that 'there were hardly any chances of survival'; there was 'no doubt that only 372 were in the mine'; in a state-managed mine 'proper records,' he said, 'were kept'. Pumping would 'get into full swing' on 29 December. Reddy was 'staying back to supervise the rescue effort';[346] Reddy left the next day.

It was on 30 December also that the Congress Party 'high command' – meeting in plenary session in Punjab for its 75th conference – expressed through Bansi Lal its gratitude to the working class for 'putting up extra efforts and raising production'.[347] On 30 December, the Secretary to the Department of Mines said that there was 'no question of survivors'.[348] On 30 December the Prime Minister, speaking to a small committee of the Congress Party, was 'not sure of how many lives could be saved', but there was 'a chance of saving some'; 'high-power pumps would reach India tonight or by tomorrow'.[349]

And it was on the very same day, 30 December 1975, that the Prime Minister, unstirring to the site of India's biggest mining disaster, called to the workers of India, the 'poorer and weaker sections', 'to put hearts and souls into increasing production without asking for any rewards at the present moment'. 'You should think,' she said, 'not what can be asked for, but what can be given for greater production.'[350]

For days stretching slowly into weeks, pumps were installed, succeeded and failed, claims of gallonage extracted, and its rate of extraction, rising and falling, while the surface of the water remained unmoving; bodies ('hearts and souls') unrecovered, and beyond access or rescue. The former Chief Justice of Patna was to investigate; from local collieries came the huge sum –

possessions sold, money borrowed from the money-lender, savings given – of 200,000 rupees (more than £10,000) for the bereaved families of their fellow miners.[351] And deep in the coils of illusion and violence, insulting the lost and the living, on 10 January 1976 – two days after the suspension of the basic freedoms of the Indian citizen, under Article 19 of the Constitution – the Minister of Health called for 'workers steeped in strains and stresses to take some time off to holiday homes in hills and seasides'.[352]

On 11 January, Reddy called for 'improvements in the working life of the toilers who produce the wealth of the nation.'*[353] On 11 January, 'the place where bodies would be kept for identification had been fenced off', and 'arrangements made for carrying the bodies to burial grounds or crematoria'.[356] On 13 January, it was revealed that the central mining research station had warned the Chas Nala mine management, nine months before the disaster, of the danger of inundation from disused workings – often unreported by the earlier private owners, to evade taxation and inspection – and from the nearby Damodar river.[357] On 13 January, Reddy was 'satisfied with the relief operation';[358] on 13 January, the President spoke of India 'lacking discipline and hard

---

*cf. 'Many Bihar miners are employed on a temporary basis . . . hired or dismissed from day to day. They are housed in rows of one-roomed houses, in the vicinity of the mine. Their pay is not more than 30 or 35 pence a day . . . women workers, who carry the heavy loads of coal in baskets on their heads, from the coal face to the surface, where they load them on lorries, were being paid an equivalent of 20 pence a day in 1975, when the price of a kilogram of rice, their staple food, was from 10 to 12½ pence . . . They worked for 8 or 9 hours a day, seven days a week.'[354] See also, *Times of India*, 3 January 1976: 'miners who evade gangsters at pay offices are pursued in their homes . . . It is useless to turn to the police, who allegedly get a cut from the big money-lenders to look the other way. Some policemen are also alleged to be engaged in the money-lending business. No succour can be obtained from security guards of the mines, who are themselves the roughest and cruellest of the money-lender gangsters. Many of them in the old days were musclemen, hired by private mine owners to subdue labour. After nationalization, they have been given a permanent tenure as security guards.' The official view is, of course, different: 'When we nationalized the mining industry, it was in utter chaos . . . the mines worked very recklessly. All these problems had to be got over . . . well, thanks to the reorganization, etc., etc. . . .'[355]

labour', of India's 'average output not even one fourth of that of the American worker'; on 13 January, 'steps have been taken to ensure that families receiving relief are not harassed or cheated by money-lenders',[359] who had – as is common in India – descended on the stricken community at Dhanbad.

On 14 January, they are 'testing the drained out water for signs of life', with half the pumps 'out of order due to technical problems'.[360] On 15 January, 'the deputy commissioner is giving final touches to arrangements for the assemblage of the families of trapped miners'; and 'the condition of forlorn women is becoming more and more poignant as the day of inexorable reckoning is drawing nearer'.[361]

On 16 January, 'security measures have been unobtrusively tightened to deal with foreseeable contingencies in a distraught mining fraternity'.[362] On 20 January, 'arrangements have been made for burning sandalwood and incense for lessening the stinking of the decomposing bodies as they reach the surface'.[363] On 22 January, MISA was amended to permit the re-arrest of detainees on expiry of their period of detention.

By 26 February (the sixty-first day after the accident), 361 bodies had been recovered; 'the figure includes 296 complete human bodies, 50 torsos, 15 skulls and seven other parts of the human body'. However, said the *Times of India*, 'according to the formula evolved that only complete bodies and trunks are to be counted as one, the total comes to 346'.[364] By 11 March, 416 bodies (of the original '372') had been recovered.[365] By 20 March, according to the official state news agency, reporting from the 'control room' at Chas Nala, there were 431 bodies.[366]

On 30 March, the one-man court of inquiry heard that at 11 a.m. on the day of the disaster, the mine's assistant manager (who had died also) had recommended that because of 'the heavy seepage of water', the miners should be immediately withdrawn from the workings.[367] They were not. Their bodies, instead, were removed later. The miners had gone on strike, too, on the earlier night shift of 26 December, refusing to go on, complaining to the mine management of the dangerous conditions.[368] But the mine management had just decided to raise the daily production target by a further 50 per cent from 1 January 1976[369] in order to register their own contribution, in miners' lives and labours, to the programme of 'National Resurgence'. And on 5 April 1976, five members of a survey team who re-entered the Chas Nala pit under protest – and two of whom were key witnesses still to give evidence to the inquiry – did not return from their survey.[370]

I have gone into the details of Chas Nala. But the new politics of discipline at the point of production, the neglect of safety, the denial of right, and the intensification of effort, did not only take their toll of the lives of miners. This politics was taking precedence in their name, while a new economic order – founded upon and defined by corruption, lying and violence – was, in these very weeks, and on behalf of the poorer and weaker sections, redistributing wealth from miner to monopoly, from poorest to richest.

Against this, the fact illusion now closed over the particular truth at Chas Nala was perhaps as nothing. The tide of 'going all out to increase production', supported by fear and detention, could hardly be halted for a few hundred unfortunate miners. (And with unemployment in millions, there are always more where they came from.) The 'rising trend of disasters' in the pits – in one month alone of the new 'emphasis' on production there were fatal mining accidents on 5, 17, 18, 21 and 27 December, for example – was merely, as the Deputy Minister of Energy put it on 4 April 1976, 'counter-productive'.[371]

We can therefore note only in passing that by 7 April 1976, the figure of the dead had already been reduced in official announcement, by Yadav, to '375', from the 431 miners brought up for mourning and burial.[372] In any case, the 'unobtrusively tightened security measures' had long seen off to their hovels the 'distraught' crowds of weeping women at the pit-head.

By 16 April (the day after those other totals of 'inspiring' concessions to capital, contained in the supplementary budget announcement), a 'fervent plea' was being addressed to miners by the Energy Minister, K. C. Pant, 'not to slacken in their efforts to augment the nation's coal production.'*[373] On 28 April, the

---

*On 9 April 1976, Pant also said (at Neyveli), 'we are seized of the futuristic concerns of landscape saving, and the integrated development of the coal-mining areas. Efforts are already under way to set up a suitable

abolition of *habeas corpus* received its Supreme Court ratification. Discipline, suffering and illusion – the three kings bringing their gifts to the new India – were, together with 'industrial peace and harmony' assuming their dominion in the new economic order; standing out against them, not pity and sorrow, but, as we shall soon see, hatred and anger.

---

authority for this purpose.'[374] But on 2 April 1976, a 'dearth of funds' – announced from Dhanbad itself – was 'posing problems' to the chief executives of Coal India, the nationalized coal board, 'for discharging certain social obligations to mine workers'.[375]

7 Resurgence and Degeneration

A man is a performing flea. He can be trained.

> D. K. Barooah, president of the Congress Party, 12 April 1976[1]

The element of fear brought about by the emergency is beneficial, for fear can be a potent motivating factor when all other means fail.

> K. Brahmananda Reddy, Minister for Home Affairs, 5 April 1976[2]

I saw a beggar being beaten by two policemen and crying, in the street beneath my balcony. I went back into the room. I wanted to interefere, but decided against it.[3]

The Indian people have a terrific capacity to bear their hardships.

> Indira Gandhi, 1 April 1976[4]

Such a political order as India's, emergency or no emergency, is violence; the magnitude of poverty and riches, suffering and privilege, is violence. In addition, the miseries and strengths of the people arrayed and encamped on the land-mass of India, toiling and wasting in their hundreds of millions – at best deceived, inert and pauperized, at worst alert and organized – indict and endanger power. Their presence challenges it to further violence. As they are and as they stand, their very visibility and ubiquity are a source of danger to minority class and faction. The constant and latent fear of the awesome and greater power of the people, both inchoate and focused, arouses – emergency or no emergency – not only the reflexes of paternalism, contempt and hatred, but violence. The instrumental use of such violence is the reflex of power; and redoubled violence, the reflex of power corrupted and additionally embattled.

'Social action' to ameliorate the people's condition in such a cold political climate, when the state's economic prospectuses and programmes are deceptions of the people, must be of a particular nature. Shorn of engagement with the people's real economic needs and therefore of a real sense of justice, it must deal (classically and with increasing desperation) in violence, which in each society generates its own distinctive style and purpose. At best, it is engaged only with socio-economic symptoms, at worst with scapegoats, and not with causes. For causes reside within the very matrix of that structure which is defended by interest and power. That interest is as broadly perceived in theory, as its power is fiercely and narrowly defended in practice. Incapable of reaching a truly reforming utilitarian compromise, and a strategic accommodation with the needs of the people – as must be the case where landed and urban interest are in ultimately irreconcilable ruling alliance – social and economic action must be turned upon the people. It may even be directed in the people's name against them, just as in the name of liberty, liberty may be taken.

Nothing can be extracted from its dense context without distortion. Only in relatedness and juxtaposition, affinity or contradiction can anything be comprehended, and to it some sense and meaning be given. Thus the roar of the slogan 'Marching to a Better Tomorrow!' deafened the stumping beggars; 'Homes for the Homeless!' taunted the sack-wrapped sleeping bodies. 'The Nation is on the Move!', 'Discipline is the Need of the Hour!' stalked a Bedlam. They stood, as markers and islands in the misery of the city's turmoil and running sorrow.

The writer must always walk the streets to find words ('Silence is Golden!', 'Grave Mischief has been Done by Irresponsible Writing!') for the unobserved and the unnoticed, tormented by the rage of movement to find names for the unknown millions, in the anonymous and perpetual struggle of their daily existence. But it was a small burden for the writer carrying notebook and pencil beside the bearers, adjusting the thick hemp ropes knotted across their foreheads, backs loaded ('There is no Substitute for Hard Work!') with crushing weights of coal and railway sleepers ('Discipline Makes a Nation Greater!'). Crossing the boat-strewn and doom-laden city river, pushed fast by the heeling heavy-weight of their loads, the barefoot rickshaw men ('You Too Have a Role in Emergency! Work Hard! Produce More! Maintain Discipline!'), feet pattering, ran before their careening carts and spinning-wheeled rickshaws down the gradient of the grim bridge's teeming carriageway.

They passed in a blur of shouting, rattling, and running ('Punctuality for the Trains Only? No! For You Also!'), the toiling carters and dismounted rickshaw riders, heaving and pulling their brutish and foundered freight ('Economy Has a Higher Growth Rate!') up the slithering incline, scrawny shoulders and arms tugging and straining, struggling feet – heels dug in – gripping and clawing at the polished macadam ('The Most Important Thing in Life is to be Committed to One's Country!'), hurtling carts and rocking rickshaws trampling past them, and pedalling down full tilt into the city, at mid-morning.

Across the city, linked by the simultaneity of the moment and the intricate web of connection and causation, the plump owners of land and labour, sleek and flashy, step from their gliding limousines ('Economic Offences Bring Severe Punishment!'). They lounge deep in the mezzanine, waiting for luncheon and today's *table d'hôte,* or the fleshpots of the *à la carte* menu; plumping down ('the objectives are to fulfil workers' needs and impart dignity to the working classes') into the velvet hotel plush, pulpy pocked noses beginning to bulb. Fleshy, affable and smiling ('forces in the world have never felt happy about our adherence to the trinity of secularism, democracy and socialism'), they are elephant-cheeked and silk-suited, cigarettes in jewelled fingers, jowls hanging.

Here, the mogul spreads the day's paper – 'the programme,' it states, 'will promote equality of opportunity, take the light of freedom to the remotest hamlet, and give a much needed rural force to our socialism, making it real to the vast millions of our toiling peasants' – in a crisp and well-groomed unfurling, in highly polished shoes, slick pomade and unguent ('a call-girl service is available if you want, sir'), to examine stock-movements and futures. Or, slumped in folds of flesh, he is dreaming, and near to dozing; or with raised and crooked beckoning index finger, summons an *apéritif* and an *hors d'oeuvre* – a plate of finger fish, or roasted cashews – from the silent waiters, born servants, moving softly, a clinking glass borne aloft to his service. (A woman, thin as a stick, and racked, bends to her field labour.) There is a gaudy flamingo mural; beaks dabbling down to the flat of the painted water; eyeing and riffling it; craning down, and sifting through its water-coloured ripples, knees kinked and thickening, legs fit to snap, twig-like.

Here are receptions and, *en passant*, assignations. This is no latticed purdah, or discreet *zenana*, but a marble show place, under tiered chandeliers and air conditioned. Here is a brilliantined and moustached smiling at heavily made-up faces (bulbeyed, with brushing black lashes and purple-black mouths, in a wide smiling to muzak), or at blinking *ingénues*. Here are perfumed and shampooed messengers and red-jacketed houseboys ('Michael' and 'Crasto', or 'John' and 'Antonio'), lapels hung with nameplates, white-lettered on shiny black plastic, and with slicked duck's-arse hair styles, sailing the deep-pile carpets. Here are greetings and dimples, wrists and fingers ringed and bangled, and silken gliding saris, heavy ear-rings swinging. Here are youths in shades and stomping platform shoes, round toecaps, curly hair, and flapping trousers, flashy or vicious. Here are girls, emblem of all beauty, in a mish-mash of clipped-quick English and coquettish smiling ('hello boy, hello Johnny, hello Mummy, lots of love from Jennie'), eyes and mouths opening wide together, with glossy hair, flipped plaits, pony tails, slacks and jackets; in cascades of flowers.

In the hotel garden, where 'flower plucking is strictly forbidden', a black snake of hose, a snake in the grass, is dragged scraping and leaking across gravel on the back of a servant; spraying water over his sodden back and shoulder, hand bleeding.

Today's fish mayonnaise stands at eighteen rupees a plate, with an *à la carte* entourage of *canapés* and *vols-au-vent*, *entrées* and *entrecôtes* ('I am being frank', smiling. 'The wolf always eats the lamb. Self-interest prevails, always'[5]), with *fromages à choix*, and *bombes glacées* to follow. The pushing body of a beggar in the press of the city sets up an anonymous clamour.

passing and swept away by the huge crowd's treadings into oblivion. A woman in greyish-green rags and yellow bangles, wolfish or haunted, cocks her head, slapping the slack flesh of her bare stomach, stretch-marked, clutching a baby pale and sleeping. And as a start, here is a fleshy, forking pomp, and pastel folds of lawn at table; and a madrigal of mannered voices ('You can send your man to the post office with this message', or 'I'm flying out tomorrow; for me, it's real cool in London'; or 'a housewife's work is never, never, done, professor'), and light laughter. And, to succeed, a lavish fat grace, with a spotted handkerchief at the lip, or a bib-and-tucker; next, a chomping and crunching, golden ear-rings dangling; and to end, sleek jet moustaches, and teeth-picking over the cigars and brandy ('these days, Rolls-Royces are white elephants, professor'), and a steady bamboozled drinking, voices ('the people are quite happy, I tell you') fading into a haze of smoke and backchat, and the sated smiling and belching of an easy well-being.

Beyond the plate glass and the napery, if you had parted the curtains upon the world 'where claims of individual privilege clash with those of general welfare' and 'the larger good prevails', were the rags and the sacking. For three rupees a day they were laying a sewer; men and women up to their necks in dust and trench-rubble. Their skin was taut and glazed; cheeks as if sandblasted and polished. They stood blackened and haggard, wild-eyed and dazed in the sun's glaring; with dusty bedraggled hair, thin armed and legged, under spilling panniers of sand; nakedness unashamed, and wasted bodies; and the shrunken breasts of old women, working, which self-abandon had uncovered.

The mind's eye of the reader and writer can pass easily enough through this pane of glass, which shuts out (and links) millions. We can travel at will, unlike those with a fixed and unmoving place in its hierarchies of social relations, back and forth, and up and down the inclined plane of the political economy of India. We can speculate idly – from behind security's curtains – notebook in hand, writing, or this book in hand, reading, upon the life of immobilized beggary and hard labour, trying to build a 'new era'[6] and a new nation just like the old one, only with harder labour, more beggared and more violent.

But there were other forces moving about in the teeming city, and other voices, unsilenced by the towering hoardings. And when dusk fell and the homeless – never so 'happy', never so 'contented' – gathered at their pavement fires, there were other flames being blown and fanned from pinpoints of light into life, fitfully burning, doused and extinguished, but lit and relit, and once more burning in their accustomed places. With loss of right came its counter-assertion, followed by assault, detention and resistance. With a new politics at the point of production, the old politics of the struggle between capital and labour was both repressed and regenerated by the dialectic of injustice and opposition. With violence and the new tortures of a new order, and in exchange for the 'flea's' training and fear's 'motivating factor', came older sabotage and counter-violence.

There were other audible sounds and actions, despite the vain suppressions of the pre-censor, the post-censor, the self-censor, the policeman and the jailer. There were the sounds of articulate and inarticulate shame, disgust and dismay for India; exchanged glances of reservation, and the unease of fear and intimidation. In commandeered or holiday applause for the day's political heroine or hero, there was also the anticipatory savour of the tumbrils (as at the passage of the viceroys of another era) when fortunes waver. In despair itself is often anger; and in 'passivity' is to be found, not inertia, but the slow motion of hatred, muted and held by long-suffering in silence, or propelled by torment beyond endurance, and set suddenly on fire.

There were other than the voices of propaganda, its reiterations (trivial, irksome, or violent) falling in tone while rising in pitch and volume, deafening to its sated audience, but deafening also to its begetters. For they imagined that in the echo of their own voices they heard the voices of the answering people. And it was the audience which had the advantage. The continuity of rhetoric and lying contains its own antidote; it is self-cancelling, while the loudest and longest applause can end it. Thus, there were other sounds and voices than the lick of the unctuous sycophant or the hymnody to 'the people once despondent, passive and lethargic', who now – austerely disciplined rich and hard-working poor alike, the halt and the lame, the paupered lepers lying by the wayside and the fleshy gourmands pampered at their tables, alike the quick of the streets, and the streets' dying – were 'all hopeful, cheerful and lively',[7] and changed in the twinkling of an eyelid, or with the blows of a night-stick.

In the same twinkling of the eyelid, as upon the resurrection of the Indian Lazarus at the point of a *lathi*, time may be stopped here by the shutter, upon a held moment in passing, and upon its simultaneities in vertical layer upon layer. In linearity resides causation, but in a selected analytical sequence. There were denser meanings in the moment, say, of 14 January 1976 – very day of observation, in passing, of the spilling trickles of hoisted pannier-sand across the pinched and wasted faces, and of *canapés* and *vols-au-vent* being wolfed behind the curtained windows. Today, to bring down the government of Gujarat, there are riots breaking out in Baroda. They are testing the drained-out waters for signs of life at Chas Nala today, also; and Karunanidhi, chief minister of Tamil Nadu, is accused of clutching at a straw, today, while drowning. Jagjivan Ram tells at this moment of 'miraculous changes wrought by the emergency in the life of the nation', and at St Xavier's Calcutta, Professor John Hicks of Birmingham University will be speaking at 6 p.m. of another reincarnation. (All are welcome.)

The north Indian 'cold wave's' tally of victims is given in today's morning papers; and the lost Bihar colliers are said, at Dhanbad, to be mostly young people. Today, as the trench sand trickles, come the new 'technology data banks' and the new guidelines for the conduct of teachers; and as the white napery is shaken out or carefully unfolded, news of the resilience of bonded labour, and the Prime Minister's 'new forces' creeping in among the *entrées* 'to weaken society and the country'. In Madras, today, the Prime Minister has 'had no time to meet Karunanidhi', his moment held, as the plates are cleared, but their days – and the days of their governments – numbered. She calls instead, in the cigars' exhalations, for a democracy for the whole of the people, complaining (to light chatter and coquettish smiling) of the press cuttings she receives day in and day out – while the old women, skin of their upper arms hanging, bend under the sun to their trench digging – to which she pays no attention, and of the campaign of vilification against her.

And framing the day in the mezzanine, the anxious President of India in the opened rustling paper of the morning, amid the discreet voices, warned of India's lack of capacity for discipline and hard labour. While this evening there is another talk (also at 6 p.m.) for those whose day's labours of 14 January 1976 are over, on 'structuralism' – first of a series – by R. G. Bowers, at the Alliance Française, 24 Park Mansions, Park Street, Calcutta.

There are in this chapter to be grasped other such simultaneities of event, and multiplicities of meaning, level upon level. Thus, embedded in the vertical texture of the stopped moment of emergency India, were varieties of violence against the people; imposed upon them, the deceit and cynicism of their rulers; and capped by that casual and corrupted indifference which is the hallmark of political regression. With its own form of fatalism, and driven from excess to excess and from deception to self-deception, the ruling faction was also imperceptibly approaching the day of its own removal. Deeply embedded also, was intellect traduced in even baser forms, and by men often baser – if possible – than those we have already encountered. Deeper still, and more rooted than the mere raising of fists in self-defence against repression, was the fierce hatred of the millions who were beyond the reach of power.

And at the deepest levels, upon which the polity is grounded and dependent, was that silence – always mis-identified as acquiescence or torpor – which keeps its own counsel until the day of political reckoning and judgement. It bespeaks not the passivities of the Indian nature, but forms of suffering, fear and labour, which can know of no new emergency in its condition. But in that calculating silence, also, was the power of the people, whether dormant or raised from fear to anger, to rural insurrection, or other forms of renewed and organized counter-violence. In this silence, the blue-grey flocks of pigeons (flying fast in the sunlight at Srirangapatnam), beguiled an idle moment; fleeting flocks of grey shadows upon the silent dusty lanes of the village; the thin woman in the lane, hollow-eyed, face veiled by shadow, peeping from her doorway. In the same silence, the man waited for time to go by on the road to Mysore, squatting at mid-morning in the pink dust of the roadside, his back against a tree bole on a New Year's day the same as the old one. He was still there six hours later; but in a different configuration of light and shadow, lying down now, head pillowed on hands, and sleeping through the resurrection of India.

Superimposed on the silence and such waiting, was the shallowest layer where the old order was papered with new programmes. They filtered to its lower depths as renewed promise or torment, brought to the mass rally by the travelling roadshow and the faction-ridden gangsterism of a political leadership in degeneration, armed with always grosser excuses of propaganda and lying. And for each new excess of deceit or violence, level upon level, were either new reasons of state (the crueller the one, the cruder the other), or that other silence supervised by the censor or the official, which spread its hands or shrugged its shoulders, and knew nothing either of the event or the victim or the rights of the inquirer.

Yet to assert a commonplace texture of juxtaposed responses of slogan, lie, evasion, silence, and denunciation, in the wake of complex political crisis and the multi-faceted attempt to found such a 'new order' as we have examined, is insufficient. Moreover, the gamut from sycophancy to hatred is easily explained and traversed, and was no more than would be expected. In any case, when the battered city bus passed, postered with 'Courage and Clarity of Vision, Thy Name is Indira Gandhi!', 'India Succeeds against Inflation!', or 'The Nation Regains the Spirit of Adventure 1975-6!' (the bee swarm of ragged shirts and trousers hanging on for dear life with the tips of its fingers to its slogan-slapped sides, smashed and dented), it was possible to turn away with the crowd, unseeing. While for the clerk in the barber's night shop – a shack on a plinth of bricks by the running drain, for dregs and spitting – with his head pummelled and slapped, head and hair lashed into a frenzy, two heads in the blurring mirror one above the other, ten fingers kneading and a head bobbing, there was neither emergency nor 20-point programme, but only 'you feel sick and tired, when the stomach is empty.' 'This is good for clearing the head,' he said, 'before the morning, when you have not eaten.' The stars he saw in the mirror were not of India's renaissance either. Nor was there any palpable emergency in the viceroy's forgotten summer garden at Simla; only prize roses 'planted by their excellencies' of another era, and cigarette packets dropped by idlers of this one, Blue Moon with Red Lamp, Vienna Charm and a trodden Star, Wills' Virginia and a Royal Highness, cankered.

But there were other resonances underlying and overshadowing the continuities and the silences of India; not merely the 'salutary shock which the people needed',[8] on the one hand, and 'we can be dragged from our beds in the night', 'there is no free press, no free speech, and nothing left to us',[9] on the other. There was more to be listened to than on the one hand 'let us get on with the job of nation building', and 'rumour-mongers are the enemies of the nation';[10] or 'we are afraid to speak, so we ask ourselves who are the fascists';[11] and 'she will be killed for it, she and her family together',[12] on the other. Whether these were the normal exchanges and assertions of prepared positions, the political reflexes of mutual intimidation and bravado, or the colder clarities of opposition is a question I will return to later.

For there is another issue to be resumed first, and set once more in motion. It is for some the 'rational' crux, every preceding fact of this book notwithstanding, of a severely practical political matter. Beggars, pauperism, poverty and over-population – that indistinct, unexamined but sordid incubus, weighing upon the shoulders of the designedly upstanding and resurgent India – demanded drastic and, if necessary, savage remedy in the interest of the nation, and better late than never. The bitterness of cruelty and unavoidable violence, so the argument ran, was the price of the sweet rewards of India's social and economic reconstruction. Better this than that revolutionary insurrection (of which, under the head of another argument, the Indians are congenitally incapable) of the organized people, seeking to seize by violence that marxist phantom, the so-called 'means of production'. For this would terminate in *'dirigiste'* fashion the free choices of the people, rich and starving, to live the lives which suit them, each according to his individual selection. Better by far the lesser violences of the sharp knife of a quick solution. Such a 'solution' has nothing to do with a politics of cruelty and terror, since socialist in intention and socialist in execution; and which (one argument crossed with another) also consorts so much better with the individualism of the Indian character in general and of a free society in particular, wedded to democratic values.

Moreover, before we take up the detail, this is the politics of building a nation and restoring the dignity of the people, with all necessary discipline and vigour, with 'hard work, iron will and clear vision'.[13] In it there were no other echoes – so the argument ran – nothing of the familiar in its content and process, whose manner of efflorescence has been in history the benchmark of a degraded political culture. At most, ridicule might have been made, and in poor taste withal,* of the trivial but necessary excesses, small efficiencies, and assiduous punctualities of a new discipline and order; of the ending of grace periods, say, in reporting for duty,[15] or of 'lightning inspections' of government premises by the painstaking zealot.[16] The critic was welcome (unless expelled from the country) to his analogies with Mussolini and Hitler at the expense of the 'economy's real improvement', and his jests at the repeated official panegyrics – even if they have been heard before – in praise of the punctual running of the trains, as the emergency's vindication.†

And as for that speculative dalliance with the physical elimination of the superfluous and 'hopeless' population – the dreamer's extermination of 200 millions – the judicious temper knows it quickly to have been an atypical excess, zeal also of a

---

*e.g. on 18 December 1975, 'the prestigious Rajdhani express was picked up for a surprise check by Minister of State for Railways, Mohammed Shafi Qureshi. The Minister found everything in order, except a mirror and two chairs in one of the coaches. The mirror's paint had flaked in one spot, and the two chairs had soiled covers'.[14] (Such too was the material of a press neutered and beggared by the censor.)

†The CPI employed the same terms of reference in praise of the 'good results' of the emergency, in contradistinction to its 'negative features'. Thus, 'attendance in offices has become punctual, and work is proceeding properly. *Trains have started running on time also.*'[17] (My emphasis.)

similar order, and equally unimportant. Similarly, to observe here that the pock-marked youth, a salesman, thin legs in grey flannels and wearing built-up shoes, spoke with relish of the 'new iron hand in India',[18] is to vent one's spleen at an excrescence, seen in its worst light, or at an unremarkable dictum. At best, and properly regarded, it was a fit subject for praise as verbal token of loins newly girded, a new determination in the youth of India for the struggle against poverty, taking the path of discipline and order which leads to the goal of the national well-being.

So our argument must have long ago foundered; or, 'derailed' by political logic, have been running in a trackless and over-grown wilderness of the imagination, deservedly forsaken by the shrewdness of the practical politician who knows his own direction. There was a connection, then, which can not only be conceded but welcomed, between the 'iron-handed' discipline of the neophyte trying his puny strength, the 'culture of discipline'[19] of a Barooah, and the emergency 'continuing till discipline becomes a part of national life' of the Congress parliamentarian.[20] This was not fascism by any stretch of the same fevered imagination (and what, anyway, is 'fascism'?), but realism. Moreover, between the restored dignities of the 'weaker sections', and the 'performing flea's' training, there must again have been a logical political connection. By the light of a mature political reason, we would then clearly see that to use fear as a 'motivating factor' is a legitimate exercise of state power, which can make law and order of anarchy and licence, aided by the responsible and selective use of controlled violence.

We can fully understand, now, why on 7 January 1976, the Chief Minister of Maharashtra should announce his 'plan to rid Bombay of the menace of its [75,000] beggars',[21] a total growing daily, compounded by the rising urban unemployment of recession and the propulsions of a profound rural bankruptcy driving the indebted and landless peasant along the dusty roads towards the city, to scavenge in its pitiless streets for survival. They would be 'mopped up',[22] 'rooted out' and 'rounded up',[23] including 'children who had taken to begging',[24] lying and dying on the pavements, or sitting silent, hands extended, fly-spotted and eyes misted; or feet curled and crippled, crawling on hands and knees, (disgustingly) racked, wasted, and broken; the suffering people of the cities of India, offensive to the clearer eye of the fastidious beholder, who was 'requested to cooperate, by not giving alms to the beggars'.

Those who 'jumped the externment order'[25] – and I go into detail, to examine the vocabulary's credentials at closer quarters – would, under state governor Ali Yavar Jung's supplementary executive degree of 17 February 1976 'to check the rising menace of beggars', be imprisoned.[26] Moreover, there would be a 'crash programme for the mass arrest of beggars',[27] but with '*sadhus* and saffron-clad *sanyasis* exempted from the purview of eradication [sic]'.[28] From 1 March 1976 the 'round-ups under the anti-beggary drive' began. The poorest, most hungry and malnourished of Bombay's homeless poor were taken by the truckload from the streets of the city. 'They got off to a good start,' said the *Economic Times*;[29] * with 231 beggars arrested in one day, 'including 31 females, 47 children, 39 infants, 14 disabled persons and 9 lepers.' They were taken first to a 'transit camp' – a cattle shed ('unit 12') at Aarey, as the *Times of India* reported[31] – and thence, having been sorted into categories, the 'able-bodied' (after cursory examination, and worse, as we shall see later) were sent to 'nation-building projects'.[32] In fact, they were taken a hundred miles from Bombay to heavy dam-building work, at the irrigation sites of Kukadi and Jayakwadi.

Thereafter there were more round-ups – for example, of 360 people on 30 April 1976[33] – of the lepers and the homeless, the

---

*Such corruptions were infectious; cf. the *Guardian*'s headline of 2 March 1976, 'Taking the Beggars to the Jobs', above an article by Inder Malhotra, who wrote complaining of 'only 600 beggars rounded up, and that only from the centre of the town' despite 'the government's repeated promise [sic] to rid the city of its tens of thousands of beggars'. He continued, with levity, on the predicament of the special magistrate (whose task was 'not an easy one'), 'foxed by the cases of three members of a family which has been arrested with their two monkeys'; that is, itinerant street entertainers. Finally, 'one unemployed person who despairs of finding a job in Bombay', said Malhotra, with the apocryphal story which makes for a good ending, 'commented that the only way he could earn a living was to start begging outside the Taj hotel, so that he would be rounded up and sent to the dam at Jayakwadi'.[30]

street musicians and the itinerant hawkers. Then came news of beggars fleeing the labour camps, wandering the countryside, hungry and without means of subsistence, of re-arrest and violence;[34] of the setting up of a 'special camp' in Chanda for forced labour;[35] of the state's aim being to 'lead the able-bodied to a life of self-respect, dignity and rehabilitation';[36] of the flight of beggars from the city and from the dignity of rehabilitation, the old and the infirm, the mother and infant, 'the disease-stricken as well as the able-bodied', trying to return to the rural districts from which poverty drove them.[37] And then the fate of the 'mopped up' beggars, men, women and children, was slowly lost in the oblivions of the censor, protecting the interests of the nation both from the beggary of Bombay and its solutions.*

In the vocabulary of headlined 'disgust', 'nuisance', 'evil' and 'menace', in the reiterated calling for 'drives' against 'footpath vendors',[38] 'drives' against 'the beggar nuisance on platforms',[39] 'crackdowns' against 'beggars suffering from diseases, and lepers',[40] there was – to the apologist – neither especial novelty, cruelty nor violence. After all, it was part of a long-standing social history of urban renewal, with its own pedigree to ratify present practice. Moreover, these were now the concerned accents of a civic pride, newly made selfconscious, eyes opened to the human squalors and indignities of the urban landscape, sordidly littered by its human refuse. And if not these, then in the Indian setting, it was trivial. A few thousand beggars are a drop in the polluted ocean of over-population, lost among the millions. And if the argument was callow, it could always be settled by equation : had not economic offenders been put down sternly? Then why not beggars also?

But irony is tiresome. Demolition by bulldozer of slums and 'unlawful encroachments', and the beatings of opponents and bystanders, broke out simultaneously in the cities of India in the wake of the emergency's declaration. This too had its social history, as we have seen already. It should be recalled, and forgotten. The speed and scale of the eruption (and the violence

---

*The Maharashtra government's 'drive against beggars' marked a convergence with the politics of the extreme right Shiv Sena, which in Bombay had advocated for some time exactly the measures adopted.

and counter-violence of opposition) passed all precedent in the mass destruction of the homes of the poorest. Here 'social action' was once more purgation, and surrogate for social justice. And in the distracted women standing amid the domestic utensils of a life pinched to the margin of survival; in children's weeping, hair dusty, the hems of the ragged dresses of small girls unstitched and hanging; in despairing men, watching their shanties crumple and fall in clouds of dust and the tumble of poor timber and ramshackle corrugation, stood – as I saw myself – the victims of that 'cleansing' of the body politic by violence and 'action', which has already been comprehended.

Karnataka set up a 'police wing' to 'deal effectively with the growth of new slums in the city'. 'Civic bodies' were given 'strict instructions' to take 'stringent action' (that is giving licence for arrests, beatings and violence) to see that 'new slums were immediately demolished'.[41] Maharashtra appointed a 'controller of slums', 'armed with special powers' to hound the poor driven from pillar to post in search of shelter, and a 'task force', aided by a special police detachment, to 'protect all vacant lands and summarily demolish any new hutments'.[42] 'Squads of workers', backed up by armed police throughout India, reduced pavement shanties, the last refuges of the homeless, to rubble. Crushed under the caterpillar tracks of the heavy bulldozer were the ramshackle homes of industrial workers in 'unauthorized' colonies of slum housing, as well as the stalls and *jhuggis* of wayside shopkeepers, and the pitches of hawkers. With crowbars and sledgehammers, as I saw myself, destruction was brought to the dense social structure of petty trade and artisan employment of tens of thousands, eking out a small and useful living on the streets of the city.*

Moreover the censor, the sycophantic expert, and the police were quickly in motion together, as tens of thousands of slum dwellers were either driven out of the city, or to rebuild elsewhere in terror before arrest and detention found them; roam-

---

*To get some idea of the speed and scale of this demolition, by 12 December 1975, 34,000 'encroachments' in the Punjab had been 'removed' by local bodies;[43] while a report in *The Times* on 20 April 1976 speaks of 500,000 people in Delhi alone having been 'resettled'.

ing the streets for shelter; or driven to 'camping sites in peripheral areas',[44] and dumped there by the truckload out of sight and reach of the city, without facilities or means of employment, as I shall describe in a moment.

In the clamour of weeping and violence, of ruthless and instant demolition, often without warning, and without remedy or compensation, the ferocity of the urge to 'root out' and 'mop up' was (to the observer, watching) convulsive. Near at hand and surfacing quickly, was the vocabulary not only of urban renewal in official rhetoric,* but also of the palpable social hatred in the politics of action of a 'new order'. The downtrodden were harried not only with the 'new requirements of the civic administration',[47] or the 'expert' language of 'ecological neglect and damage',[48] but with the intonations of physical and class recoil at 'the rickety hovels hugging the disgusted and despoiled earth',[49] and the 'busloads of transient hutment dwellers, sitting four children on a bench with loads of luggage', which was 'telling on the fabric of the social structure of the city'.[50]

But the new misery and suffering was not entirely untold, and this text will add to its record. For there were other voices than those of civic discipline and hatred. They spoke of action 'ill-conceived and cruelly inhuman';[51] of 'children's bitter wailing and the dejection of their parents'; of the rain's teeming down upon the dumped belongings of the newly homeless hutment dwellers, on their bed-rolls, utensils and sacking.[52] They spoke (and we learn) of Chattar Singh the stall owner, who was said to have 'slipped and died' during a 'clean-up operation' and 'clearance by the authorities' of Chandigarh's Shastri market.[53] They

---

*e.g. 'See what's happened in Delhi during the short spell of emergency! Double shift cleaning; new night scavenging service; *encroachments disappear from public places*; Delhi looks greener, cleaner; you the people of Delhi have done it', published by the directorate of information of the Delhi administration.[45] Moreover, benevolence and violence were reconciled by finding a blandly reassuring nexus between them, which awakens the memory of history; e.g. 'Removing encroachments presented some problems. But thanks to the 20-point programme, government machinery moved into action, the encroachers were identified, and removal of encroachments ordered ... Then officials moved into stage two of the operations and demolished the hutments.'[46]

spoke of tens of thousands of roadside shopkeepers and pave-ment-dwellers in West Bengal given six or twelve hours' notice to demolish their own shops and houses, or have them demol-ished at a charge of sixty rupees an hour for their destruction.[54] They spoke of the poor sweepers and scavengers – men, women and children – of Delhi's South Extension, forcibly removed by truck with their few chattels and utensils and dumped five miles from the city, and three miles by foot from the nearest work, or income; without food or means, in a dusty wasteland, without utilities or water.[55]

In old Delhi, they spoke of notice of one hour being given for the vacation of shops and the removal of their stock and con-tents, followed by arrests, police looting, violence and the arrival of bulldozers, crowds held back and beaten, *lathis* swinging (as I saw myself) in the billowing dust and crump of demolition; with the police bribed, and the poor at their mercy; and with premises belonging to local political opponents of the ruling junta earmarked for selective destruction.[56]

This was the politics of action, which, with its violence, arbit-rary or random, selective or programmatic, connected at many points with the lives of the people. It was the familiar politics also of unleashed police riot and sadistic terror; it was the answering politics of despair, of self-defence, and – as we shall soon see – the counter-violence of an affronted and outraged people.

If we move forward a little to that 'greater involvement of the people' in India's renaissance, and which bore even closer upon their bodies, what shall we say of the market town of Barsi, forty-five kilometres north-west of Sholapur in the state of Maharashtra? And of its ten days (with its streets 'unusually quiet') from 25 January to 3 February 1976, which may stand for all the other dates and places? What shall we say of the decision to pick up poor local villagers 'because they could not offer much resistance', come – during those days – to market in Barsi, 'taken away, regardless of age, in prowling municipal garbage trucks for a quick sterilization', and 'dragged by force to the operating table'? Of the fact that they included the old and the young, the newly married and the long widowed, those with children and the childless, and many – such as Krishna

Sopan Mali and Tatya Bondu Pawar and Ganpat Nana Yedke – sterilized already?[57]

What of Shahu Laxman Ghalake, a poor peasant from Kavhe, in Barsi on 31 January 1976? He was 'surrounded by about ten people, thrown into the truck, kicked and beaten'. When he tried to explain that he had already been sterilized, 'the doctor would not listen'. He was held down by two or three people and sterilized again; 'now it had turned septic', and he 'could get no medicine'.[58]

What of sixty-year-old Rambhau Sakharam Pawar, the blacksmith, who lived in a small hut near the Bhogeshwari temple in Barsi? He was picked up by the municipal truck on 1 February 1976, and 'after complications following the operation' could not move out of his hut, received no medical attention and died on 25 February 1976.[59]

What of the poor peasant from the village near Barsi seized while working in the sugar-cane fields by the overseer, and driven to the *panchayat* office and sterilized on an office table?[60]

What of Barsi's ten-day target of 1,000 sterilizations, 'overfulfilled' in days of terror, cruelty and violence, with 1,042 vasectomy and tubectomy operations?[61] What of 'officials straining every nerve to clock in as many vasectomies and tubectomies as possible'?[62] What of 'reaching high targets means a bonanza, since the officials are paid a cut on each operation'?*[63]

What of the voice which said, 'they told us at the mill that unless we were sterilized, we would not get our wages. I was operated nearly six weeks ago. But you see,' he said, pointing, 'what has happened'; his job lost, and his body septic and swollen.[65] What of 'the high-caste village leader' with his eyes on the ten rupees that he was offered (as 'motivator') for each sterilization?[66] Or of the 'doctors' who feared that if they failed to 'achieve the target set for their own area' they would 'suffer in the matter of increments and promotions'?[67] And what of the

---

*The figure for fees and inducements varied. A 'patient' might be paid from 15 to 50 rupees (and sometimes given a blanket or bush shirt also), and in comparison with vasectomy, tubectomy's value was higher. A 'prompter', or 'motivator', might be given 10 rupees for each person brought to the sterilizer, and a 'doctor' from 3 to 5 rupees per 'patient'.[64]

'officials' who 'got wind of the fact that 3,000 Bombay beggars were being assembled at Aarey [see p. 267] to be trans-shipped to the hinterland', and 'rushed to the scene', 'hoping to clock up extra figures'. But they were too late; the local authorities where the beggars were 'to be put to work' had 'beaten them to it, by claiming as their property the 3,000-odd beggars'.[68]

There is no need to tread with the apologist's caution into this brutal collision between the forcible mass-mortification of the defenceless by cruelty and violence, and the problem of over-population;* its solution not new, but reaching new levels of degradation. Between problem and solution was the nexus, not of a participant act of necessity or of the public welfare, but of the political and surgical short cut, armed with a knife, and elsewhere with *lathi* or revolver, sledge-hammer or bulldozer. And between a fistful of rupees for incentives, and the severing of the fallopian tube (for fifty rupees, say), or the excision of the *vas deferens* (for twenty) of the poor peasant and worker, was the driven bargain of the cash nexus between 'patient' and 'doctor', born of the compulsions of fear and need on the one hand, zeal and greed on the other.

But whether with bank-notes or blankets, 'target-oriented programmes'[70] or cash incentives, bandaged wounds septic or healing, a new Jerusalem could not thus be built from a morass of corruption and violence. For these were the sharp and blunt instruments of a politics of action, developing through the decade with increasing momentum, and propelled to faster pace not by the interest of the common weal, but by the gathering degenerations of the political system;† and raised to a pitch of desperation by fear and hatred of the teeming millions of India,

---

*The population of India (at just over 600 million) is estimated to be about 11 per cent of the world's population, rising at the rate of about 2 per cent per annum; this compares with estimated birth rates in Japan of 1·3 per cent, in China of 1·7 per cent, and in Pakistan of 3·6 per cent. Since independence in 1947 the population has risen by about 250 millions. In 1971, the birth rate was 37·2 per thousand. At the end of the Fourth Plan period it had fallen to 35·5 per thousand. A 1·4 per cent birth rate is 'planned by 1984'.[69]

† Or, as the Health Minister put it (obliquely, and in a careful dilution, but confirming this account's correctness), 'some tension is inevitable when one moves from a *laissez faire* situation into an activist position'.[71]

and their unregenerated, unreconstructed and institutionalized destitution.

Moreover, he who held the knife to the body of India had for decades held the whip hand also; first, corruptly commanding the misused resources of the labour of the people, and then commanding the always-more-violent surrogates for solution to the problems of the victim, whether held down by force or by poverty's sorrow.

But there is a different and qualitative relation between poverty, adult illiteracy and over-population, unknown to the thuggery of cudgel and scalpel; between the indices of population growth, and the expenditure of three rupees per head per annum on education in India, in 1976–7. There is a nexus of a different order of magnitude (and quality) requiring a different politics and a different perception, between the poverty of the poorest in rural and urban India and the high mortality rates of their infants.[72] There is a connection between the indigent compulsions of childbearing for work in the harvest seasons, and the exigencies of survival, that frail connection in the human condition where the sterilizer's knife and the peasant seized from the fields (to be held down roughly upon a bare table) is not the control of population, but the bloody severance of a lifeline.

The chronicle of events – until suppressed by the censor – was one of debasement and reversion, not dignity and reason. It pointed not to a new world of national regeneration through the controlled growth of population, welfare expenditure and adult education, but into the lowest depths of the new order and the very basest levels of sadism and degeneration. Above all, the date and motion of event (if the reader wishes to establish his own correlation) were in an exact synchrony with the political and economic reversions of preceding chapters.

Its vocabulary also again forsook much of the rhetoric of promise, for the minatory language of class hatred and mounting violence; moving quickly, from its threats on 30 December 1975 of 'strong steps which will not be liked by all',[73] and their answering chorus of welcome. 'This is the time,' said the *Hindu*, for example, in a first leader, 'to instil in the minds of the poorer sections that they have a responsibility to society for the benefits received by them, and it can be brought home to them by making birth control a condition for eligibility to public largesse'.* [74] Thus on 8 February 1976, the Chief Minister of Maharashtra, S. B. Chavan, addressing a rally of agricultural labourers at Dava, in Akola district, told them that the government of Maharashtra 'would no longer tolerate a situation where the people had the liberty to increase the population'. [76]

On 18 February and 4 March 1976, for instance, the Punjab state government announced a series of punishments and sanctions: prohibiting maternity leave to any female employee after the birth of her first two children, and loan and subsidy for medical aid to third children; prescribing as a rule of public employment that no concessions, such as food loans, would be given – unless 'recourse was taken to abortion' – to employees whose pregnant wives were bearing their third children. [77]

On 7 March 1976, the Uttar Pradesh government announced that April salaries would not be paid to employees who failed, by 1 April, to 'motivate' two people to sterilization and to produce medical certificates that such persons had been so sterilized.† [78] On 20 March, the Maharashtra government announced that 'people with communicable diseases would not be allowed

---

*Also, said the *Hindu*, 'a harsh decision cannot be put off for long . . . some form of coercion suggests itself as the way to solve the problem'. [75]

†This led quickly to new forms of degradation. The poorest and the most beggarly or uncomprehending themselves became the victims of the insecurity of the clerks and servants, in their thousands, of all the state governments – such as those of Andhra Pradesh [79] and Madhya Pradesh [80] – which adopted the example of this particular mode of 'incentive' and 'disincentive'. The result of making payment of salary and annual increment conditional on third-party sterilization included fighting over the bodies of the poor, and the bidding up of the prices of bribes ('the price has gone up as high as 100 rupees') [81] for their sterilization and certification at the gates of the sterilization camps, for example at Chichripur camp, near Delhi. [82] Such auctions secured the salary of the victor, and took the victim, often unknowing, to vasectomy in degrading medical conditions. The Delhi administration (Aurangabad), [83] also) linked school teachers' March 1976 salary payments to 'bringing in people for sterilization', five persons per teacher. Thereafter, came reports from the lower depths that 'many teachers have threatened uneducated men, that they [the latter] would be forced by the police if they did not go voluntarily now, and name them [the teachers] as their motivators'. [84]

to beget children'; 'they would be compulsorily sterilized'; 'sterilization would be immediate'; and 'it would not be conditional on their having children'.[85] The communicable diseases were not specified.* On 23 March 1976, Britain announced a £3 million grant 'in support of India's family planning development'.[87]

At the end of March, the Punjab government approved a Bill under which the having of more than two children could be made a 'cognizable offence', and providing for punishments of fine and imprisonment.[88] On 30 March 1976, the Maharashtra government introduced a Bill providing powers for compulsory sterilization within 180 days of the birth of the last permitted child, the prescribed number to be determined by the government. It further provided for imprisonment of the non-compliant, during which forcible sterilization could be carried out, or the compulsory termination of pregnancy, by abortion.[89] The Minister for 'Public Health', K. M. Patel, 'denied that the Bill infringed Article 25 of the Constitution, and the fundamental right of personal liberty'.[90]

'Incentive and disincentive' slowly grew baser and more oppressive, while the anger of the people was also slowly being aroused to an approaching counter-violence, and bloody riot. On 1 April 1976, the government of Andhra Pradesh told the homeless and the landless that they would get neither 'housesite' nor 'surplus land' allocation without prior sterilization;[91] empty promise mocked by a new violence in which even the poorest applicant for a small loan to buy a bicycle-rickshaw had to produce a certificate of sterilization.[92] On 9 April 1976, the government of Bihar, state of the poorest of the poor masses of India, descended further. Ration cards, it announced, would be restricted to a family's first three children, disqualifying the rest from their slender official entitlement to existence.[93]

---

*cf. 'What are the "communicable diseases" the government has in mind? How are those with such diseases to be identified? And what about communicable diseases which are curable, as indeed most are? Will those suffering from curable diseases also be forcibly sterilized, thereby denying them children even after they are cured'?[86] But these were other questions, they belonged to another form of debate, and they were asked in another political language.

Man was thus additionally set against man, and child against child, deepening the vulnerabilities of the already pitiless struggle for survival, the rich simultaneously luxuriating in the economic redistributions of these moments of assault on the people. Furthermore, moral responsibility for licence and physical brutality was characteristically evaded. On 5 April 1976, 'the question of compulsion,' said the Prime Minister, 'will be left to the states'; 'they will decide whether they want it'.[94] That is, more precisely, the states had been 'allowed to launch programmes of compulsory sterilization'.[95] With knives long ago drawn against the people and bloodied, it was then the hostile attentions of the world's press* and the violence of riot (in Delhi on 19 April 1976) which together furnished strong inducement to further evasion of the truth. The Prime Minister on 30 April 1976 'stressed the importance of family planning, but ruled out coercion';[99] while permitting compulsion. It was thus that violence, cynicism and equivocation made up the (other) trinity – with 'secularism, socialism and democracy' – which upheld the polity of India.

And thence more swiftly still, downwards: to proposals from the Indian Council of Child Welfare, urging compulsory sterilization of 'various categories of unfit parents, including those with lunacy, hereditary diseases, and beggars';[100] downwards on 23 April 1976 (despite the Delhi riots) to denial by the Pune Cantonment Board of admission to its hospitals of women expecting their fourth children;[101] downwards, through news of deaths from septicaemia and haemorrhage, paralytic ileus, toxaemia, and post-operative peritonitis,[102] with low or nonexistent provisions for after-care; downwards, through reports of children taken from the streets to the police station, and the

---

*e.g., on 16 April 1976, the Health Minister Karan Singh told foreign correspondents in Delhi that the 'Western press had been carrying on a campaign of falsification and vilification against India', on the question of its 'family planning programme'. The programme also had what he called 'a lesser known aspect', that of 'helping the infertile beget children'.[96] On the same day, he announced a notional proposal to 'raise the minimum age for marriage from 15 [sic] to 18 for girls and 18 to 21 for boys'.[97] He also warned that 'nothing should be done by over-enthusiastic officials which would have a counter-productive effect'.[98]

price of their return the sterilization of father or mother;[103] downwards along the same route taken by that final (and complementary) loss of *habeas corpus*, ratified by the Supreme Court on 28 April, which extended the state's absolute licence to the whole body of India.

Such accumulation of violence – seen here in no more than a sample, and which by design omits the detail of its grossest cruelties against the people – does not merely challenge step-by-step disentanglement for an intellectual or moral confrontation, but contains its own political dialectic. Whether it was expressed as assaulted dignity's unrecorded reassertion, or the eruptions of an answering violence breaching by its very scale the censor's defences, it contained the same meaning. It interrupts also the reasoner, the reader, the writer, searching all the while (often in company – whether he likes it or not – with the arguments of corrupt and violent power) for the justificatory means and ends of economic necessity, or the 'interest of the nation'.

Indeed, even without the dialectic of action and reaction, there was in the darkest emergency period both compulsive fear as well as hatred in the record of faction's abuse of power. That is, in a politics whether of terrorization or forcible sterilization, of 'disciplined' over-production or the destruction of rights and freedoms, was not only a politics of interest and desperation purging itself against the people, but of that familiar premonitory fear of political failure. And the focus of such fear (both real and apparent) was the fear of an encounter between faction-and fire-power, on the one side, and the mass assertion of the people's anger and its ultimately always greater power, on the other.

It made its appearance, for example, in the continuous record – however reduced by intimidation and the censor – of industrial action and state reaction: the detention of strikers, or the maltreatment of their leaders. It made its appearance again on 19 April 1976 in the riot, police counter-riot and riot deaths at the Turkman Gate, two miles from the Parliament building in Delhi.[104] And was fear as well as hatred which trembled unstably in the eye and the words of the politician, such as Sanjay Gandhi (to whom I will come in a moment). It trembled also on the lips of the shouting policeman, dark eyes in a blackening rage, fist clenched, swinging his *lathi* at the taxi driver* cowering to avoid the swathe of the night-stick, the bludgeon and licence of arbitrary power unleashed against the people, and model for all such cases. Above all, for every verbal violence promised by the thuggery of the political speeches of the newest bearers of the new order, there was somewhere – and even if unrecorded – a matching physical violence, measure for measure, to give it weight and substance.

Thus, 'in the course of a drive for the removal of encroachments and the demolition of unauthorized structures,' said the Home Ministry on 21 April 1976, 'the Delhi development authority took up demolition operations near Turkman Gate, on 14 April', near the mosque of Jama Masjid. The 'drive' had progressed without incident until 19 April when, according to the official version, 'at 10.30 a.m. 500 people, including eighty women, gathered to protest against the demolition operations'. Then 'some leaders in the crowd made inciting speeches'; the crowds 'swelled to 3,000'; 'anti-social elements moved in'; missiles were thrown. 'Mob violence' then increased and 'the police post was surrounded by miscreants'; there was a 'cane-charge' and 'use of tear gas'; police were stabbed, and 'thirty officials and three magistrates injured'. The police 'were thereafter left with no alternative except to fire, to prevent serious harm to life and property'. 'Three persons were killed "on the spot"'; two died later. There would be a curfew until 23 April.[106]

In fact, demolition of the housing of the poor in the walled city ('Delhi's twenty steps to the future') had been going on since the autumn of 1975, the appetite of zeal and excess whetted – as I was to observe myself – by the roar of engines, the sense of power in destruction, by armed police protection, and by the weeping despair of the people.† But the (predominantly Moslem)

---

* 'Now, at last,' said the Bombay University clerk, Remedios, savouring violence with a vicarious satisfaction, and sitting at ease in the back of the halted taxi, 'there is order.'[105]

† 'The travail of the people', reads a Member of Parliament's account of this riot, illegally circulated, 'is indescribable. They are packed into trucks and carried miles away from their demolished houses. They are unpacked,

Turkman Gate area was simultaneously assailed in a convergence of violence from 14 April 1976.[108]

On that day demolition gangs, protected by armed Central Reserve Police, began cutting a wide path of destruction through the people's homes and occupations. It included, as it did in many other cities of India, pulling down permanently and solidly built two-storey buildings. From the first day of demolition, the newly homeless were forcibly transported by truck to dumping grounds in Trilokpuri, Nandnagar and Kichripur localities, 'where there was neither electricity, sanitation, transport nor water'.[109]

Four days later, on 18 April 1976, they were joined by the 'sterilization squads',* who set to work in the same streets around the Asaf Ali road, then being destroyed by bulldozer. They were systematically sterilizing the people at a makeshift 'mobile centre', with sterilization made the qualification for 'suburban re-location'.[111] Taken in alike were Moslem youths and old men, the married men and the unmarried, without rights of protest or redress, and without discrimination.[112] On 19 April, spontaneous demonstration of anger in the streets of the Turkman Gate rapidly turned to violence 'as the police dragged the women, and snatched even the milk-sucking children and threw them on the ground'.[113] As the growing crowd fought back, with unarmed women – according to an eye-witness – attacking fully armed policemen, they were met with *lathi* charges, teargassing, and then firing to kill.[114] In the fierce surge of fighting, numbers of police were killed also, and 'a sub-inspector of police hacked to pieces';[115] resistance spreading quickly through the warren of streets and alleys, as the para-military Border Security Force was moved in large numbers into the area. The numbers of dead are unknown. Eye-witnesses spoke of 'heaps of

---

and the trucks leave them in vacant lots with no amenities, not even drinking water; and miles from their places of avocation, without any alternate work in the areas to which they have been forcibly shifted'.[107]

*'Accompanied', according to the *Economist*, 'by bejewelled members of Sanjay Gandhi's entourage'.[110]

bodies';[116] some counts put the total at over 100.*[117] And by 27 April, 543 people had been arrested.[123]

Demolition at Turkman Gate then 'gathered unprecedented momentum'.[124] An estimated 10,000 people were forcibly evicted.[125] Shops and houses were looted by police, prior to demolition.[126] Moreover, familiar voices of intimidation and accusation spoke in violence's aftermath, and after-echo. They said that 'drastic action will be taken against people interfering with family planning workers';[127] they said, also, that 'many people are missing', that 'the police opened indiscriminate fire from rooftops'; or, they said that 'the police dragged out people from their houses and shot them'.[128] And on 2 May 1976, the Prime Minister and Health Minister, speaking into the censor's deepest silence asserted that 'rumours' of compulsion and coercion were 'false, malicious and totally baseless'.[129]

Response to this, which always had its options, found their possibilities contracting. For whether the issues were that of the decade's alternative practice in Kerala – with a steadily rising literacy and a steeply falling birth rate[130] – or of the principles of Malthus, they were reduced by force to comparisons of the forms and degrees of violence. As the point of the 'new order' was here sharpened to its focus, it was not choice, but polarity which was established in the intensification of the battle between realpolitik and the people. In addition, nothing could stand between the truth of 'during the operation I bled a lot, so they put in three stitches. I was told to go back and have them removed two days later. When I went back the tent had gone, and three days after my wound was septic. Now I have pains in my legs

---

*cf. 'What is certain is that several hours of fighting followed, in which hundreds of people were injured, and perhaps fifty or more killed';[118] and 'one witness said he saw corpses of policemen ("20 to 30") being loaded on to trucks, when the fighting was over'.[119] The Indian government announced on 27 April 1976 a 'death toll of six'.[120] On 3 May the official news agency argued that it was 'insidious rumour', and 'whispers among the credulous' about coercion in sterilization ('without a shred of basis') which had 'caused the violence, destruction and disorder' while 'the reports of death and coercion' reflected 'hostility to the programme of limited families'.[121] So saying, 'rumour-mongers' were also being arrested.[122]

and stomach',[131] and the denial of such truth – except further violence, or silence.*

Both truth and persons may always be violated. But each successive twist and turn of licence – whether by the further dislocation of fact or by a new assault on the people – always begins to tighten the bands which constrict the political system. This is a process, and not an instantaneity. And even though time may be bought by one device or another, it forces action and reaction into profounder confrontation, latent or open, quickly or slowly, and into successively greater suppressions. It is a process also of buckling compression under the weight of state power, as well as of potentially explosive fission, and brings into new proximity and alliance forms of opposition hitherto divided. It brings with it not only the tyrannical and draconian expression of class- and faction-power, but also new and plausible explanations for public and world opinion as political descent, in all its forms of expression, steepens.

In this, however cruel, is the growth of a specific political culture. Its previous historical forms have been various, and will be debated. We have so far seen some of its Indian particularities and forms of excrescence; but also the hallmarks of a common politico-economic genealogy, and aspects of a universal resemblance of appearance. The voices of it began to outshout each other in extravagance of premonition. Not only was 'the multiplicity of parties a threat to a democratic nation';[133] but there would be 'no other party except Congress to go for the next election'. If there were other parties, they were 'fast becoming extinct', would be 'wiped out' and Congress would get 'mass sanction to remain in power'.[134]

The time had come, therefore, 'to announce a scheme of national integration about which no section of society should

---

*There was perhaps one qualification to this: the possibility of a reconciliation between truth, half-truth, and fiction, which became unenviably the CPI's exclusive property. Such a method combined 'misleading motivations', 'over-enthusiasm on the part of the personnel involved', 'improper after-care facilities', and 'unfortunate developments because of the carelessness of some doctors during operations', with 'success stories reported from all over the country', 'undue apprehensions', and the 'overfulfilment of targets'.[132]

have a difference', under which 'the forces of discord' would 'bow out of the national scene', and 'all the parties' would 'fuse their efforts'.[135] 'Awareness of fascism' would 'inspire people to come together',[136] and so armed, the government should (for example) 'use the emergency to implement the policy of having only one trade union in India'.[137] That is, there should be a 'single dynamic trade union movement', in which trade unions would 'shed their political colour'.[138] Or, the National Students' Union of India would henceforth have common membership with the Youth Congress,[139] while elected student unions were dissolved, and nominated bodies set up to replace them. The Congress Party would, moreover, 'play a bigger role in the implementation of government programmes', 'making up for bureaucracy's inadequacies'.[140] It had become their 'duty' to 'intercede in administration on behalf of the people',[141] while 'the rural poor in general should organize themselves under the auspices of Congress'.[142] Likewise, students of Presidency College Calcutta announced that 'our sacrosanct ideal' is 'corporate life', and that 'our political nature does not allow us to protect the interests of all students indiscriminately'; 'in our dedicated drive towards advanced politics we totally refuse to tolerate any opposition'.[143]

Furthermore, in any descent such as this, the necessity of frequent assault in the name of order, and of further assault to restore order, makes for a random violence. Random violence, in turn, paradoxically creates its own forms of convergence, and in the Indian maelstrom was found a democracy of victims, swept by its licence into that forced association which is one of the familiar creatures of political repression.

Thus, such violence made a tormented cross-class community of 'mopped-up beggars' and the weeping children of sweepers, of ruined storekeepers and the distraught wives of miners, of 'weeded out' civil servants and the sterilized childless. It did not distinguish between the Tibetan refugees driven by truck from their roadside encampments in Simla and not seen again, nor their fate questioned;[144] and the 215 advocates of the Tiz Hazari courts in Delhi, who had their offices bulldozed on 27 March 1976, without warning. Next day they marched, black-robed, in a silent procession of protest – called by the Delhi bar associ-

ation – to a High Court surrounded by the Central Reserve
Police, steel-helmeted policemen and tear-gas squads, the en-
trances blocked by police trucks. They marched into the arrest,
also, under the Defence of India Rules, of 163 of their number
on charges of looting and arson and other charges.* [145]

This seeming elision of the distinction of class and interest
between the 'poorest and weakest' sections who were the familiar
scapegoats for political and economic failure, and the privileged
victim who was caught up in violence, was wrought by the compressions of a politics of action. Thus, the prominent business-
man known throughout India, was 'very worried about such
terror';[147] the Delhi editor of a national daily needed to be 'more
cunning to reach the reader';[148] the cautious professor, sitting in
his dark garden, spoke in an undertone of 'the great fear in
India'.[149] Thus it was that the senior civil servant, in the Prime
Minister's own entourage, talked of the 'official demonology, to
keep the crisis and the emergency going',[150] and the shopkeeper
of how 'officials since the emergency are always threatening,
"there is an emergency, you watch what you are doing" ';[151] while
the Supreme Court lawyer spoke of 'dictatorship sprouting
everywhere in this country',[152] and the senior official of the State
Bank of India listened daily to the BBC's shortwave broadcasts
to India.†

This form of convergent response, however – unlike the cross-

---

*On 30 March 1976, the Supreme Court bar association passed a un-
animous resolution in Delhi, 'severely condemning the demolition of
lawyers' chambers without notice, and the indiscriminate arrest and harassment of lawyers thereafter'.[146] After a boycott of the Delhi courts by members
of the bar association, the arrested advocates were released. The motive
for the demolition – as with other acts of intimidation against the legal
profession – is most likely to have been police reprisal against lawyers of the
Delhi courts for their obstruction of the subversion of the rule of law.

† 'Give me his name,' said Ayub Syed insistently, 'give me, and I will
report him.' He repeated the demand several times.[153] Characteristically,
the same state bank official, when I first met him, said at the outset of our
conversation, 'Discipline was needed. There was no use having democracy
for democracy's sake', the familiar first reflex of caution, where fear displaces
the responses of easy discourse. Later he said, whispering, 'India has lost
its freedom'; and 'sycophancy for the ruling family has become nauseating'.
I asked, 'Does anyone believe it?' He replied 'Of course not. But it would be
better to change the subject.'[154]

class satisfactions with the 'iron hand' of India – was crucially barred by the censor. And if they experienced a common victimization, it was because political violence is no respecter of persons. Both were the consequence of the centripetal pressures of a 'new order'; as were the running crowds converging in the streets of Jodhpur (part of it reduced to rubble by demolition) shouting down the swift passage of Rajasthan's Chief Minister, in clouds of funnelling dust, and to the flailing of truncheons.[155]

Likewise, the boundary between truth and fiction was to become increasingly uncertain. With the precarious hold of integrity once loosened and the always slender restraints on licence abandoned, both record and meaning of evasion and lying were themselves erased by further lying and evasion. Moreover, into the vacuum and silence left by repression of dissent, detention and experience of detention stepped those close relations, rhetoric and intimidation. And in the struggle to harness the people's power to the ends of faction by promising, demanding, or seeking to create by ordinance violence and the dissolution of class and the integration of the nation, a political strategy and mode of perception were at work which is not confined to India.

Additionally that traditional populism in the mass politics of India, by which the successions of faction have long sought to embrace the people, now took its place within a new order which was attempting to dismiss or excise most of its other instruments of political mediation. Thus, the range of simplistic political expression employed by class-power and its opposition narrowed to a new focus of confrontation. The familiar rhetorical suggestion by the ruling faction of exclusive or special relationship with one minority group or special interest after the other, came into its political dominion, as a form of the dissolution of separate interest. Moslems,[156] sikhs,[157] punjabis,[158] untouchables and tribal peoples[159] were successively assured of their (separate) primacy in the body politic of India, while each in turn was aroused to the threat of external and internal enemies subverting the security of the organic nation. Political compression not only made unaccustomed bedfellows of its

common victims, but also brought a further quick succession of
identifications by faction-power with its erstwhile mortal rivals,
usually *post mortem*. Thus K. Kamaraj, for instance, was declared – *in memoriam* – to 'belong to us'. 'His guidance' was
always sought, 'his ideals' followed, and more important still, he
was 'close to the policies that we are following'.[160]

Intimidation itself brought other forms of convergence in
which opponents, often merely as price of their physical freedom
from harassment and the risk of detention – and especially on
the right, as ideological distinction with the Congress narrowed
towards disappearance – compressed *themselves* into the mass
politics of action, dissolving simultaneously both political principle and political difference. And as corollary, remaining forms
of opposition violent or non-violent, strikes, other modes of
industrial action, trade union organization itself – heavily assailed by decree and prohibition – came to be seen as 'anti-
national' *per se*. Similarly, the efforts of the 'poorer and weaker'
sections and of vulnerable individuals, whether merely to claim
their promised plots of land or 'house-sites' or to defend themselves against violence, were perceived as further crimes, a
perception which visited the urban 'anti-social' and the rural
'extremist' with further intimidation and violence.

Mass action, mass base, mass rally, and the loudspeaker roar
of the 'unity of the people' sought to swamp the crumbling demolition of their houses. In 'the voice of the peasantry and
workers heard in our programmes'[161] was the evasion of land reform, and the loss of the rights of the trade union. 'Blazing a new
trail of involvement with the masses',*[162] became one with the
knife of compulsory sterilization. Into these lists, also, went the
CPI with the competitive language of its own species of populism. And it was a populism itself convergent with that of the
'new order', because in effect dissolving interest of class into
interest of faction; with 'the entire party and our mass organ-

---

*e.g. on 12 April 1976, 'Indira Blazes New Trail in Mass Contact', during
which, visiting Halur village near Rae Bareli in Uttar Pradesh, 'women fell
at her feet in worshipful admiration'. It was 'for humble folks a great moment
in their lives, and their happiness was writ large on their beaming faces', as
'she entered two houses to the overwhelming joy of the inmates'.[163]

zations taking the initiative and striving for the united mobiliza-
ion of the masses', and 'unleashing united mass initiatives at
grass-root level'.[164]

At mass rallies* were gathered up in tens of thousands those
whom the *lathi* charge (or tear-gas) was elsewhere dispersing;
while 'in an era of mass politics', as the *Hindu* put it, 'the popularity of a leader, or the organizational ability of a party is judged
by the crowds that are drawn on such occasions'.[168] And the
same trucks which elsewhere carried out of the city, for dumping, the victims of demolition and their belongings, brought
back into it that mass audience which bypasses reason and seeks
to overwhelm by force of numbers.

In this desperate effort to compress and depress consciousness
of class interest – always prompted and aided, where it is not
led, by violence – power seeks a compulsory bargain with opponents. It also joins battle obliquely, as well as in direct confrontation, and works towards a final reckoning with the people. That
there is no such final reckoning as power dreams of – the boot
is on the other foot, in the last analysis – is not to the present
point, but neither was it any deterrent to the political compulsions of the national resurgence of a new order.

---

*cf. 'There has to be a magic touch for drawing hundreds of thousands
of people from distant places'.[165] But an eye-witness account of the occasion
of the Madras mass rally on 15 February 1976, after the overthrow of the
DMK government, spoke of 'huge columns of buses coming from all over
the state of Tamil Nadu, for the whole of my journey out of Madras that
morning, travelling past me into the city. Thousands more were in trucks
and lorries, poor agricultural workers, with their pinched faces, enjoying
the drive from the country to the city. As the stream of vehicles passed the
bus I was in, the passengers remained quiet, cautious, even apprehensive,
looking but without comment. At Chingleput, where I was changing buses,
I was told of the curtailment of services because of the commandeering of the
vehicles of the bus companies. When I spoke to people in the convoys who
had stopped there for a brief period, I found that many had never been to
Madras. When I reached my destination in the evening, I heard that everyone in that village had been given five rupees and free transport to Madras
by the village *panchayat* chairman. They would never have another chance
to go there, so poor are they. That is why there were 100,000 on Marina
Beach, Madras, to greet Mrs Gandhi.'[166] Also, cf. 'Popularity? In the old
days for four annas each you could always get a hundred thousand people
together in India. People applauded the viceroys of India also.'[167]

Thus, it characteristically drove hard into the rights of the movement of organized labour; it detained without trial many of its national leaders and local officials; it divided the class (while appearing to unite it), and thanked it for its cooperation. Characteristically, too, what stood out in the opposition labour movement was unpreparednes for the scale of the offensive, defeat, the destruction of organization and a struggle for continuous survival. To understand it, analysis must always be conscious of the internal multiplicities of a class and the heterogeneity of its organization, the variable combativeness and militancy of its sections and fractions, and their varied perceptions of, and responses to, palliation and promise, division and terror. Against this, the swift approach to the threshold of the abolition of the rights of trade unions, and the subsuming and submergence of their specific interest within a political ethic of the organic nation, seek to establish their own overriding uniformity of meaning.

But historical precedent shows that censorship and detention, fear and betrayal, unemployment and violence, cannot between them squeeze out of existence – however near class power may come to it – the indissoluble opposition of the essential interests of the exploited and downtrodden. They are irreconcilable with those of the oligarchies or urban and rural India, whether expressed as faction, caste, class or nation. This truth was in the very expression of 'gratitude' to the oppressed, and 'happiness' at the 'extremely cooperative attitude of the working classes'.[170] It stalked the very words of 'the excellent and magnificent way in which the working population has responded to the emergency which is, in my view, the most encouraging factor in India'.[171] For in the very 'tributes paid to labour for their discipline and devotion'[172] was that special unease – familiar to the working classes as lived experience – of privilege, addressing itself across the chasm of class interest not merely to the 'proletariat' as an abstraction, but to a dangerous power.

Behind the lines were the continuing erasures of censorship, preventing the reporting of industrial opposition. And in the forefront, stood that great necessity – greater always than any other – to move the plethora of the state's power of containment and vigilance, pacification and intimidation, against the working classes. The need to induce between the classes that 'consensus' which is based upon a combination of fear and volition, together with expressions of 'gratitude' for cooperation, are always the hallmarks of the complex relations between capital and labour.

Promise and fear of maltreatment can only with difficulty be resisted once the movement of mass convergence has begun. But whether from Bengal government labour statistics, or the bland euphemisms employed by power ('there have been cases where labour leaders have been able to persuade various unions to go on strike';[173] and 'in several sectors, notably in the textile industry, labour has not fully reconciled itself to the bonus ordinance')[174] or from specific information, came report of the continuities of industrial opposition, every deterrent notwithstanding.

There were for example strikes in Hyderabad on 4 and 5 October 1975 of pharmaceutical workers; in Bombay on 15 and 16 October, and from 9 to 16 November 1975, of woollen workers;[175] and a general strike in Tamil Nadu on 24 October 1975 – in which AITUC and INTUC, despite their leaderships' policies, joined the CITU – of textile, engineering, sugar, cement, plantation, leather processing, rubber, tobacco, fertilizer and foundry workers. In November 1975 there was a strike of power workers in Uttar Pradesh;[176] in Bombay in January 1976 of journalists and newspaper and printing workers;[177] and of plantation workers of CITU, AITUC and INTUC on 26 January 1976 in Kerala.[178] From 18 February 1976, and for thirty-nine days, there was a strike of 12,000 shoe workers in Calcutta and in other centres of India;[179] we know of workers striking at the Steel and Allied Products plant in Calcutta in February 1976, protesting against closure.[180] We know that on 17 March 1976, 800 workers were on strike at the Madras cycle factory, besieging the plant, and bringing armed police to its gates threatening to open fire;[181] we know that on 26 March 1976, tannery workers in Calcutta, also protesting at closure, were teargassed and arrested.[182] We know that from 18 to 25 April 1976, Birla mill textile workers in Delhi, belonging to CITU, AITUC, and INTUC, struck against arbitrarily increased workloads,[183] while 600 garment workers struck in Delhi on 1 May in protest against the compulsion to work on May Day.[184] These were some only of the strikes – which continued to the emergency's last moments, and included textile workers, engineering workers and dockers, among many others – against the bonus ordinance, strikes against the violation of agreements, strikes against arbitrary violence, strikes against the increase of workloads, strikes and protests against industrial closures. And despite the great toll taken upon all forms of resistance to the licence of power, they represented the continuation of such resistance, thinned by detention and fear of detention, and engulfed by denial of right, division and violence.

At the same time, one of the distinctive features of class-violence is that it engages and assaults the working class simultaneously as citizens and producers. In consequence, it magnifies daily the critical necessity for the survival of the independent organization of every democratic interest, above all of the self-defence of organized rural and industrial labour. Simultaneously, it displaces the exercise of such political right, and accelerates the destruction of the separate representation of interest. The trade union movement thus classically faces both violence and a factitious alternative community of interest. Class-power comes armed with the mass rally, the mass base and the mass movement, to replace the trade union with loyalty to factional and national interest, while its members are at the same time caught up in the toils of multiple struggles. There is the first priority of economic (that is, physical) survival; there is the struggle against defection and confusion; there is the struggle for the restoration of rights of communication, meeting and organization; and against the omnipresence of the police and para-military forces.

Thus the process of such convergence reached into the lives of Indian labour not only with an expanding appetite and capacity for violence, but with its own structure of achievement and action, blandishment and promise. It installed itself on the very terrain of the Indian labour movement, and with its wearying rhetorical distractions compounded the already deep exhaustion of effort in the bitter daily struggle for survival, and the daily experience of a numbing deprivation and sorrow.

Moreover, it characteristically brought with it a special vocabulary of political community, negating in the very structure and terminology of its newly minted language the verbal distinctions of separate interest. For without such distinctions, the tyranny of class and faction is more easily established. Thus when the Tamil Nadu government was overthrown, the people of Tamil Nadu came into 'the mainstream of national life'.[185] The Prime Minister called for 'the culture of the tribal people to be brought into the mainstream of national life'.[186] Sikkim upon its 'merger' or annexation, became 'part of the mainstream of national life'.[187] The state of Andhra Pradesh was 'reshaping its economy' so that it could make, according to its information directorate, an 'enduring contribution to the mainstream of national life'.[188] The white-collar trade unions were 'warned' by the Minister of Banking, Mukherjee, 'to fall in line with the mainstream of national thinking'.[189] And the CPI, embedded as it was in the whole process of convergence, signified it plainly by calling upon the CPI-M not merely to abandon 'its blind anti-Congressism', but to 'join the mainstream of national life'.[190]

The 'mainstream' into which were expected to flow one by one, merging their identities, all the separate tributaries of power, was thus counterposed structurally with the dams and breakwaters of dissent. These therefore required dissolution, or violent political removal, if the current of ruling class politics was to run freely in its own channel. The right to strike is traditionally perceived as one such obstruction. Moreover, the state moved directly against the right to the citizen's self-defence, while quickly occupying with its para-military forces that limbo which the rule of law had just vacated.

The further forms of decomposition and attempted reconstitution were various. The gradual evacuation by the ruling class, and selective destruction behind it, of existing mediations of the political process is always a token of it. Some political forms have a harder death or a longer gestation than others; the stages of reversion may be reached more quickly or more slowly, while degrees and forms of resistance conform to no invariant model of the processes of action and reaction. If regression can be progressive (as it can, just as fascism itself contains progressive features), then its progress in India has so far been both long drawn out, and uneven. But its premonitions have been clearly signalled whenever pitched battle has come to be joined in that so-called 'extra-parliamentary' and 'extra-legal' arena, to which the ruling class in India has always had both first, and continuous, recourse. Here there are no mediated rules of conduct; instead torture and state-murder on the one hand, and sabotage, assassination and 'guerilla warfare', on the other, supplant uprooted forms of political struggle.

We have seen enough in earlier chapters to know of their continuous proximity and practice in India. We know that the 'peace' and 'national resurgence' of the emergency period, therefore, represented a continuance of this form of state violence, as well as a further stage in the process of the political decomposition and reconstitution of the forms of class- and faction-power. Conversely, breaking through the calm of India's suppressed disorder and the silences of the censor, lips sealed also on the greater infamies and cruelties of officially condoned violence, were acts of sabotage and jail-breaks, circulated by word of mouth, pieced together, retailed by rumour, and reduced to order by reliable corroboration or oblique admission.

They constituted both solitary acts of forlorn reprisal and the fiercest resource of anger. They ranged in time, place, and nature from, say, the reported engagement at the beginning of July 1975 between 'peasant guerillas' and the Central Reserve Police at Arrah, sixty miles from Patna in Bihar,[191] to the violent jail-break on 26 February 1976 from Presidency jail in Calcutta. But the running theme of sabotage was the most obvious, and the most openly admitted, and must be briefly noted.

On 19 July 1975, for example, the Prime Minister spoke of 'groups at large trying to sabotage essential services';[192] rumour, evidence and admission of railway sabotage were continuous. On 29 December 1975 the Assam Mail, passing through rural Bihar, was wrecked by sabotage;[193] two weeks later, the Hatia–Patna express in Bihar, also.[194] On 30 December 1975, in confirmation, the Prime Minister declared that 'the same type of sabotage is now going on as was witnessed before', and that 'attempts have been made to engineer accidents to trains, which in some cases have succeeded'.[195] Even official statistics, published on 9 March 1976, attributed to sabotage 10 per cent of the year's railway accidents.[196]

Not entirely disconnectedly, on 11 December 1975, the 'growing menace' in Uttar Pradesh, Rajasthan and Madhya Pradesh, of *dacoit*s – that is, 'armed bandits' – was officially reported in Delhi.[197] The term is a term of art. In the past, it has been as often used to cover or mask localized anti-landlord violence and dispossession, as it was now available (like the term 'naxalite') to justify annihilatory violence against the expression of rural misery. 'In the emergency,' said the Minister of State for Home Affairs, 'the aim should not be containment but complete elimination of the "*dacoit*" menace'.*[198] Similarly, on 25 March 1976, after the explosion by sabotage at the Sabarigiri hydro-electric project in Kerala, the Home Minister of Kerala, K. Karunakaran, spoke characteristically in the State Assembly of 'the resurgence of "naxalite" activities in the state'. 'Brought under control in 1970' – by what methods we saw earlier – they were 'again to the fore during the last six months in Kerala', with alleged murders and attacks on police stations by 'armed people'. 'It is not correct to say that there are only poor people in the movement,' he continued; the organizers are 'the children of leaders in society', and the incidents 'not isolated', but 'to be seen in the light of such incidents elsewhere in the country'.[200] The incidents were isolated, but the need of the state to be politically menaced overlapped here with the continuum of violent but sporadic opposition.

In broad daylight, on 26 February 1976, men 'armed with sten guns and hand grenades' made a frontal attack – thoroughly corroborated – on the Presidency jail in Calcutta, which stands in the centre of the city and is reputedly the best guarded jail in India. Eye-witness accounts spoke of the gates being blown

---

*Thus on 3 April 1976, the Home Minister told the Lok Sabha that 'in the last two to three months 117 "*dacoits*" had been killed and a large number apprehended'.[199]

up; of the desperate escape of some fifty prisoners, mostly of the CPI–ML; and of the deaths (in brief but fierce fighting) of several members of the Central Reserve Police force guarding the prison. Other accounts spoke of the escaped prisoners being given refuge by the people, and eluding recapture.* [201]

On this event the censor maintained an absolute press silence. Instead, political response to this dialogue between violence and violence was oblique and cumulative. It spoke for instance of 'the continued attempts made by absconding activists of banned organizations and other anti-national elements operating underground to disrupt public life', announced on 30 March 1976 from Delhi. [203] There were 'underground elements resorting to sabotage on the railways', announced on 1 April 1976. [204] There were 'hardliners not yet reconciled to the emergency', 'forces creating trouble', and 'continuing underground and sabotage activities' announced on 8 April. [205]

Moreover, the very persistence of a hounded opposition, if magnified by the lens of state, justifies increased vigilance by the threatened nation. It justifies the politics of the further closing of the ranks of the people, populist hyperbole in celebration of arbitrary power, and the accumulation of new instruments of violence. At random on 18 April 1976, there was 'a marked increase in the anti-*dacoity* thrust of police operations in Madhya Pradesh', because of 'the fear of certain disgruntled gangs stepping up their activities'. [206] On 5 May 1976, the Home Minister was speaking of 'incidents of extremist violence'. [207] On 5 June 1976, police reinforcements were being dispatched to the area of Durgapur, 'suspected to be the sanctuary of extremists'. [208]

These were no more than signs and tokens, and terse official announcements. They were also the swift running engagements and necessary removals of obstacles on the forced march of the subcontinent; the extraction of the flies in the ointment, other-

---

*There were other jail-breaks; from Delhi jail, for example, and from Bhagalpur jail in Bihar, in April 1976, where most of some eighteen escapees were alleged to have been recaptured and murdered, in reprisal for the killing of a prison warder. [202] On 11 August 1976, the Home Minister told the Lok Sabha that 'police shot dead several political prisoners in Calcutta's Presidency jail last February'. *Daily Telegraph*, 12 August 1976.

wise spreading the balm of its peace across the face of India. They were also the obverse of that 'increasing involvement of the people in the emergency'.[209] They counterposed 'naxalite resurgence' with 'National Resurgence', while 'forces creating trouble' and 'absconding activists of banned organizations' were shown to be trying to waylay and hold up India's trajectory along the road to 'socialism' and justice.

Surging alongside this parodic progress, as if Chiang Kaishek had led the Long March through China, was the continuous use of a parallelism with China. It is complex in origins, as we earlier noticed, and drawn in fantasy from the imagery and vocabulary of the Chinese example. Thus, 'the situation now,' said the monopolist B. M. Birla on 11 May 1976, was 'conducive to a "big leap forward" '.* [210] The state of Haryana announced that it had 'built an economic infrastructure' which had 'made it possible to take a big leap forward'.[212] The emergency, said Subramaniam (who did not himself believe it), was 'a turning point in our history, heralding a big leap forward' towards the 'national objective of a socialist society which is self-reliant'.[213]

The Minister of Industry, as if losing face, was 'ashamed of our shortcomings'.[214] The Prime Minister, whose programmes were the 'programmes of the people', wished 'to serve the people'.[215] The Federation of Indian Chambers of Commerce aimed 'through development to serve the people'.[216] Even the Minister for Information hoped that 'the elimination of the duplication of reporting' – that is the destruction of the independent news agencies, and the setting up of *Samachar* – would 'serve the people better'.[217] And for genuine political and economic progress, the cooptation of a superficial structure of Chinese thought and language was set down in its place, together with Chinese street hoardings dwarfed by the reality in their shadows.

Likewise, in education there should be emphasis on 'learning by doing'.[218] Equipment for classrooms should be 'found locally'

---

*The 'situation' he was referring to, ironically, was the budgetary and post-budgetary redistribution in favour of foreign and Indian monopoly. He added, 'if we are not going to make progress now, I do not think we are going to make it ever'.[211]

or made by the pupils; education was 'not confined to build-ings'.[219] Teachers 'should not confine themselves to the four walls of the classroom'.[220] Their work should be 'related to rural needs and problems',[221] or made 'more relevant to the process of production'.[222] The Prime Minister's own education was re-perceived and re-announced as having been 'entirely in the open'.*[223]

As economic self-reliance, never more distant than it was now, was negated by successions of economic decision, invocation of the virtues of self-reliance was increasingly reiterated in com-pensation. As family planning resorted to compulsion and vio-lence, family planning 'must be made a mass movement'.[225] As rural development and the 20-point programme foundered on the rocks of landlordism and rural stagnation, India must have 'all-round rural development'.[226]

The detail of a close, and sometimes exact, reproduction in fantasy of the Chinese model is very notable, and deserves much more and wider attention than it can here be given. In the cul-tural field, for instance, 'we have to see what is good in the old, and what is good in the new'; 'we should not try to copy what comes from foreign experts. Whatever is good and suits our way of life we should not hesitate in adopting, and whatever is unfit should be discarded'.[227]

Again, the 'Delhi model scheme' (for distributing essential commodities to the people, which it signally fails to do) had eliminated the distinction between urban and rural areas'.[228] The Institute of Engineers drew up plans for the creation of 'a cadre of barefoot technicians throughout the country', 'offering help to villagers and based in rural areas'.†[229] Moreover, not only

_____
*cf. 'When I recommend a "non-formal" education in India, I remember how my grandfather told us all not to bother about examinations, and instead sent us away to the mountains. He said it would be better for us. So I was not harmed by such an education.' And on the question of self-reliance the Prime Minister said to me, 'the trouble is that the people in this country, when they better themselves, always want a brick house. They are never satisfied with local materials. Local materials are not good enough for them.'[224]

†A useful comparison with Chinese practice in the field of technical innovation might be: 'when technology is developed in the laboratories of our Council for Scientific and Industrial Research, the know-how is com-

barefoot technicians and surgeons[231] were urged into the countryside, but professional managers were also called upon – by Subramaniam on 28 March 1976 – to 'move out of their urban settings into the rural areas'. By so doing, they would 'bring the highest levels of managerial competence into rural institutions', and 'inject into the rural economy the kind of dynamism needed to make a massive assault on poverty in rural India'.[232] We will consider further meanings in a moment; but at the outset was visible a Ruritanian – not Chinese – imagination, disjoined from the nature and compulsions of Indian agrarian relations.*

Elsewhere, on 17 May 1976 the Uttar Pradesh Education Minister Ammar Rizvi announced that 'one million students and young people' were to engage in the mass construction of an irrigation canal in the state on the lines of the Red Flag canal, and to be called in parody (but not in irony) the Sanjay canal.[234] It will be in celebration not of the nation's recovered dignity of purpose and sense of direction, but in honour of Sanjay Gandhi; until the programme was abruptly cancelled.

This *'chinoiserie'* was neither farce, nor emulation. Its populism does not fully define it either, though it was one of its elements. Nor were its illusions wholly confined to that realm of the political unconscious in India where China is sovereign. On one level, it was 'advice to city youth to go to villages, because they are two different societies',[235] either in order to 'educate illiterate farmers'[236] or 'not so much for what work you can do, but more to see what it is like in the village' so as to 'achieve a greater integration between the town and rural areas'.[237] On an-

---

municated to our licensing committee', which points to somewhat different procedures.[230]

*And cf. the findings of the Madurai Agricultural College and Research Institute in Tamil Nadu, that 'only 5·55 per cent of agricultural graduates had a positive desire and determination to settle down on their farms and utilize their knowledge for agricultural development'. 83 per cent were 'inclined to take up jobs in government', 25 per cent 'not willing under any circumstances to take up farming'.[233] Obviously even the term 'farming' does not come into correspondence with the actual nature of rural production in India, while it is additionally misleading when transplanted to an affluent cultural perception of its meaning.

other level, it was '80,000 students fanning out into the country-side', and 'settling down in 1,000 camps for a fortnight to carry the message of economic uplift to the villages'.[238] And on yet another, it was 'Youth Congres units at the block level revitalized', at the prompting of Sanjay Gandhi, in order to 'establish contact in the villages with the masses'. [239] That is, it was the attempted creation by the Youth Congress of 'a national movement' to involve 'sophisticated urban youth' in tasks of 'rural reconstruction'.[240]

Though we will come shortly to the question of Sanjay Gandhi and the 'sword-arm' of Congress, we must briefly consider the basic meaning of this rural politics of action. This species of movement was neither new nor confined to the Youth Congress, whose own brand of violent rural politics in Bengal in the early 1970s is well attested. To range no further, in 1973 the National Service Scheme (NSS) sent 65,000 urban youths into the countryside in a campaign then called Youth Against Famine, hard on the heels of rural unrest and having little to do with famine. Indeed, the parliamentary estimate committee's 79th report, issued in April 1975, itself reveals it. The budget allocated to this campaign 'against famine' was only sufficient to support the 65,000.[241]

What is really at issue is the decade's politics of rural pacification, or 'the possibility of unrest, and the steps needed to anticipate it and prevent it'[242] which was itself the primary concern of the estimate committee. Thus, one such NSS programme was 'fanning out' in December 1975 into one of the most turbulent areas of past peasant violence and insurrection in west Bengal – the twenty-four Parganas, and the district of Dakshin Barasat. Supervised by Major B. L. Das, it was triply armed with a programme 'against dirt and disease', a characteristically sub-Chinese objective to 'emphasize the dignity of labour and the need for combining physical work with intellectual pursuits', and the inexplicit compression of 'promoting national integration'.[243]

Much more important to its purpose, the NSS had reached a village – and Major Das was on a tour of inspection – visibly hostile to his jeep's arrival. Its threadbare villagers were living on the margins of survival; the walls of its village buildings were painted with 'CITU *Zindabad*!' while its school was painted throughout with the CPI–ML's hammer and sickle. 'What,' I said to Major Das, 'is the NSS doing here?' 'Here,' he said gesturing, 'the aim is to paint over these slogans. We told them that if you will not do it, we will wipe clean these slogans for you.' And driving his jeep into the school's compound and courtyard, its interior walls covered also in red slogans, he said, 'and if we can get the schoolmasters to us it is very good, because they have the young people.' 'How,' I asked him, standing in the courtyard, 'do you choose your villages for NSS programmes?' 'We go,' he said, 'mainly into CPI–M and CPI–ML areas. Through regular work in such areas, we can bring a change in the pattern of rural thinking.'* Some of the slogans were freshly painted, blood red, others long faded. 'Are they strong here?' I asked. He shrugged. 'They are hiding away now.' 'What will happen when they appear again?' 'We will do like we did before. To set CPI–ML against CPI–M is the best solution.'[244]

But despite the tendency of its practice, this species of half-formed organization of casually privileged or innocently unknowing volunteers, whether led with perception or bravado, is insignificant. And if insufficient for the murderous latency of any renewal of rural violence and insurrection, it was even more so for the exigencies of the political consolidation in the countryside of a 'new order', by all available means.

For the historical moments of the afterbirth of any programme of national resurgence require that its political practice be overtaken from the further right, and across the whole political spectrum. The process may be carried out clumsily or with decision, with puritan rigour or as a flashy and cynically violent crusade, as in India. And it is here that the militant 'youth' movement, national, 'socialist', prepared politically both for real action and violence – and preferably already bloodied by it, as in the case

---

*Also: 'It is difficult in this area. Here they are hostile. In religious areas, it is better. Where there are temples, there is less trouble, because there they feel more for other people.' He told of villagers' recent attacks on the NSS, for example at a NSS camp at Shriniketan; and said, 'we have to give them the feeling this is my village, this is my country, and then we can stop the activity of the anti-social people'.

of the Indian Youth Congress – has a vital role to perform. For its function is to assist in the destruction of the multiple organization and expression of the interests of the people.

The 'youth' wing of the Congress Party, though caught up in that whirling vortex of political regression which can give permanence to no political landmark, was arguably well equipped for a task of this order. In the past, it was (and still is) as corrupt and faction-ridden as its parent Congress Party, and dovetailed well with the latter's mass of intriguing factions, each trying to elevate its own pretender and oust the pretender of another faction. But it had become, as we shall see, something more than a microcosm. Moreover, its use as an instrument for the assumption of power by a family member of the ruling faction, turning his attentions from industrial 'mass production' to the construction of the rhetoric and violence of a populist mass movement, helped to express one of India's moments of deepest political degeneration.

Led by Sanjay Gandhi,* and its internal divisions suppressed with incomplete success by both new and old methods of arbitration and decision, the Youth Congress thus possessed the resources and credentials which were most fitting to its political function. It added them to its record of lumpen and hired intervention in the street politics of West Bengal in the 1970s, and its bloody experiences gained from gang battles in pre-emergency industrial struggles with organized labour. The ground was further cleared for its militantly presented crusading 'idealism', by sycophant and censor, as we shall see in a moment. The captive media resources were thus commanded equally for bland denial, a coarsened rhetoric of engagement with its political opposition, and the mass strategies of the new order. In classical strong-arm combination, it commanded too – as I saw myself – the convoys of unemployed youths brought in tens of thousands to Calcutta. Transported by the open truckload, flag-bedecked, to the mass rally, these 'young turks' of official euphemism can become, when occasion demands it, political

---

*This was the case, even though he was not formally the leader of the Youth Congress movement, but merely a member of its national committee, elected in December 1975.

fiefdom's lumpen private army of volatile fanatics roaring into the city; ready to serve any currently ruling populism, and one faction after the other.

Sanjay Gandhi was very variously misperceived. When a perception of politics was able to get no further than identifying the polity with the individual – the shallowest level of political analysis – then 'the system' was 'no longer functioning ... it's all Sanjay Gandhi and his goon-squads'.[245] Or, little better, he was 'his mother's best political adviser who counselled her to defy the courts, the opposition and even her own party, and to proclaim the emergency'.*[246] His prominence thereafter then became attributable to the political dependence upon him, for its own survival in the moments of pre-emergency disintegration, of family- and faction-power. Thus, just as earlier absence of any visible qualification proved no barrier to a large-scale industrial licence, so lack of political qualification was no obstacle to the assumption and arrogation of a political licence, and one much grosser. Such trivializing arguments, however true, must take their place alongside the accompanying inflations of a chorus of welcoming sycophancy, which would beggar description were it not merely exploring the depths of a now familiar servility and self-abandon. As always, it had its own code of meaning which we must note in passing.† But none of these

---

*Another widely believed assertion, equally peripheral, was that 'he organized hired crowds, paying about four rupees per person, to hold demonstrations outside the Prime Minister's house in Delhi, calling for her not to resign from office'.[247] But cf. 'another canard that was spread and is still being spread is that this whole decision [sc. to declare the emergency] was taken by my son and one of my personal assistants, who have absolutely nothing to do with it ... my family has been very much maligned, and of course my son is not in politics at all'.[248] And 'I would prefer my children not to be in politics, but ultimately you can only guide a person.'[249]

†It also had many variations and emphases. The most informing of the exchanges I had were with Ayub Syed of the AICC, who after speaking of the 'turn to the extreme right' in the Congress Party, spoke as follows of Sanjay Gandhi: 'Two days ago I was with him in Maharashtra. He is the man. He is a great nationalist, and a great patriot. He is more intelligent and a better politician than his mother, father or grandfather. Eventually, he will come to power.' 'Will the people approve of it?' 'They will love it.' 'What if they don't?' 'He will still come.' 'Are you in favour of it?' 'Absolutely.' 'Has he got the capacity?' 'Who else has?'[250]

responses, interesting and even informing as they were, takes precedence over those propulsions in the political economy which deform the political system. In their passage they assault and extinguish some individuals, and protect or aggrandize others, according to that dialectic by which the political elevation of one kind of politics and politician, and the political abasement of another, are connected.

Personal progress and India's political regression were equally steep, the parallelism of its chronology striking. On 9 December 1975, he is unanimously elected a member of the national council of the Youth Congress, and straightaway calls on it 'to take the Youth Congress to rural areas'.[251] By 13 December, after his visit to the bulldozer demolition squads and scene of later riot and killing in the old city of Delhi, the vice-chairman of the Delhi development authority announces that but for the former's 'keen interest' in the 'transformation of the surroundings', the 'task which seemed impossible a fortnight ago would not have been successfully completed'.[252] On 22 December 1975 in Calcutta, the local Minister of State for Food, P. K. Ghosh, ear finely attuned to the correct political wavelength – 'West Bengal youths are being urged to get themselves ready for new responsibilities'[253] – has already 'found in Sanjay Gandhi, a twenty-eight-year-old youth, the qualities of a great leader'. He announces further that that is why he, 'a fifty-nine-year-old man, readily accept[s] Sanjay Gandhi as a leader'.[254]

It was on 29 December 1975 that Barooah described the Youth Congress as 'the sword arm of the Congress Party', and called for the 'active involvement of the Youth Congress in the implementation of the 20-point programme'.[255] The president of the Youth Congress, Ambika Soni, held that the organization had received 'a fresh impetus with his entry'.* [256] And thence,

---

*At the same period, the captive press had also begun to record the ordinary detail of his daily round; absurd, or trivial, were it not for its association with a context of cruelty and violence. e.g. 'Accompanied by his wife he took rice and *dal*, followed by halva as sweet dish, with hundreds of other delegates';[257] or 'today, he had an hour long cross-country joyride in a huge hot-air balloon', 'waved to the cheering people', and 'threw down leaflets containing the photograph of Mrs Gandhi, and copies of the 20-point programme'.[258]

quickly, on 31 December the 'Youth Congress leader' is warning members of the Uttar Pradesh legislature to 'pay less frequent visits to Delhi', and 'go instead to their constituencies and work for the people'.[259]

On 3 January 1976 in Visakhapatnam – and in the presence of most of the Cabinet of the Andhra Pradesh government – the Minister for Parliamentary Affairs, K. Rhaguramiah, finds in him 'the rising sun in Indian politics'. In his own widening *tour d'horizon*, Sanjay Gandhi calls to youth to 'go to the rural areas', denounces 'disruptive forces of the opposition who have waged an undeclared war against the country' ('encouraged by foreign countries'), and claims that 'industrialists who do not want the poor to come up are financing every agitation'.[260] By 11 January, 'the time has come to put aside issues like "rightist", and "leftist"',* 'to work for the poor and downtrodden, without being bogged down by dogmas', and to 'ensure that the interests of the working class do not conflict with the interests of the nation'.[262]

His itinerations not only traversed India, but as they gained ground upon India, his progress was increasingly attended by a political entourage of fulsome place-seekers and personal flunkeys. In addition, his tone of voice and address, magnified as they were by the attentions of the headline writer acting under instructions from the censor, were as unstable in mode and manner as they were absolutely consistent in their poverty of intellect.† Moreover, at work in the form and language of its

---

*cf. 'Sanjay Gandhi, who had nothing to his credit in public life, has been suddenly catapulted into the orbit of Indian politics . . . and is reported to be directly interfering in administrative and other decisions. This person, who on the eve of his open entry into politics, attacked the public sector, voiced the demands of the monopolists, and stated that he had no belief in any "isms", is being accorded the status of a high dignitary of state.'[261]

†Another equally remarkable constant was almost complete consistency – however poverty-stricken – of assertion and reiteration; that is, there were relatively few changes of mind. Where they occurred they were in the direction of immoderation. Thus in Visakhapatnam on 3 January 1976, he was 'in favour of free legal aid, to ameliorate the lot of the village people',[263] but on 28 March 1976 he was against it: 'personally, I am of the view that no free legal aid should be given to anybody'.[264] Cf. Mr Justice V. R. K. Aiyar of the Supreme Court, inaugurating the Bihar state legal aid board in Patna: 'the Prime Minister's people-oriented 20-point programme will not succeed without legal aid to the poor being given'.[265]

populism were characteristic ideological mutations, sometimes matching in date, and sometimes anticipating, the mutations and violences taking place in political practice.

In Bombay on 11 January 1976, he is addressing the Youth Congress, the National Students' Union of India, and the INTUC Youth Front together on the virtues of 'self-reliance', and 'the stopping of wage increases'.[266] By 22 February 1976 in Calcutta, he is 'greeted on a scale befitting a national leader', driving in an open jeep at the head of a fifty-vehicle convoy and receiving a 'tumultuous welcome from hundreds of thousands of people lining the ten-mile route from the airport', 'festooned with banners and punctuated with gaily got-up arches'.[267] Here, the people are urged to 'rise above ideological polemics and think of the emancipation of the poor in the country'.[268] He compares Indian entrepreneurism unfavourably with that of Singapore, Hong Kong, and South Korea, and Indian with Japanese technology,* and assails the idea of nationalization.[270] He 'castigates the marxists for provoking continuous strikes', 'warns youth against involving themselves in the right–left ideological war', and places a 'three-point programme' (later to be raised to five) – to fight illiteracy, fight the dowry, and fight the growth in population – 'before the youth of India'.[271] He 'warns intellectuals not to involve themselves in any ideological controversy',† and 'warns government employees to work with devotion and endear themselves to the masses'.[275]

Quickening, on 26 February 1976 there are 'unprecedentedly large crowds' to greet him in Bhopal.[276] On 6 March, as degen-

---

* He added, 'I can speak authoritatively on this because I have done more than anyone else to develop the indigenous technology of India (!)'.[269] Thus was the truth of Maruti consumed by the new India.

† At Calcutta University, he 'told intellectuals' that 'the uplift of the poor should be the only ideology that intellectuals cherished';[272] cf., also, the widely circulated report of a university students' boycott in Calcutta, and that 'under police auspices' a hired audience replaced them. After he had left, the students *gheraoed* [surrounded and prevented from leaving] the vice-chancellor who had issued the invitation, and demanded that he apologize – as it is alleged that he did – for having called an 'under-qualified non-academic to address them'.[273] Sanjay Gandhi later visited the memorial museum to the nationalist leader of the extreme right, S. C. Bose, and there 'placed flowers on the bed which he used'.[274]

eration deepens, 'the Youth Congress leadership', it is announced, 'has been cleaned up to make way for new and better faces' so that it can 'place itself at the forefront of the implementation of the new economic programme'.[277] On 7 March, he declares that the 'welfare of the poor is the only touchstone of policy'.[278] But on 17 March, the chief executive of the Birla monopoly acknowledged the widely asserted influence of Sanjay Gandhi in the transformation of economic policy, heralded by the new budget. The former expressed his 'happiness at the changes in the government's economic policy', which were now 'in the right direction'; together with 'appreciation of the views of Sanjay Gandhi', and of his 'mature thinking'.[279]

Thus what was being carried in a circling progress around India, from one mass rally to another, was a radical national 'socialism', the opening to the right in the economy, and the last residuum of the 20-point programme, to sycophancy's applause and the roars for mass action. It travelled in convoy through a long tunnel of elaborately festooned and triumphal arches, erected in city after city to greet the epitome and embodiment of a degenerate new order, and passed the vacant lots and mounds of rubble of the route's stall-holders and shanty dwellers, swept away from sight by mass demolition, and lost in an even deeper limbo.*

On 19 March 1976 in the Lok Sabha, his 'voice' is held to have 'created the right climate for economic growth'.[282] On the next day in Andhra Pradesh – welcomed by the Chief Minister and assembled Cabinet of the state government – he is both 'the beacon of hope of an awakened India',[283] and to Raghuramiah, displaying a capacity for assiduous attention if not for extend-

---

*cf. 'Early next morning, all traffic was completely swept from the streets, and all roads leading into the city were lined with gendarmes and troops. Peasants were cleared out of their houses along the road. Some of the more unsightly huts were simply demolished, so that there would be nothing offensive to the eye.' This is Edgar Snow's description of a visit to Sianfu by Chiang Kai-shek in October 1936.[280] Also, cf. the defence by the Chief Minister of Karnataka, Devaraj Urs, in the State Assembly on 18 March 1976, of high levels of expenditure on the visit to the state of Sanjay Gandhi: 'whenever a dignitary visits this state, it is the duty of the state government to make necessary arrangements'.[281]

ing his metaphor, he is again 'the rising sun in the political horizon'. Indeed the Minister for Parliamentary Affairs – stooping lower into the depths of servile bathos – appealed to Sanjay Gandhi 'not to forget the people of Andhra Pradesh, even after assuming higher positions'.[284] In his political responses of 20 March, at Khammam in Andhra Pradesh, strikes and lockouts [both, as we have seen, continuing] had become 'things of the past';[285] while at a 'mammoth public meeting' in Guntur, the opposition parties were 'behaving in the manner of the British of a century ago', and there were 'forces operating in India' whose object was 'to promote conflicts among the people, and to paralyse production'.[286]

At Bikaner in Rajasthan on 24 March 1976, themes combined in even more unstable political mutation. 'The controversy of left and right,' he said, was 'encouraged by the very forces which had supported the British in India.'[287] On 28 March in Lucknow, mind gyrating within the whirling process of political dissolution ('the fifteen kilometre route from the airport decorated with arches and bunting'),[288] 'youth must speak less and work more',[289] and 'leaders must identify with the masses'.[290] 'Camps for youth workers' would be set up throughout India,[291] Youth Congress workers would be 'helped to get jobs in government service',[292] and 'there must be a revival of India's culture, sciences, and old values', including 'Yoga and the medical systems of *Unani* and *Ayurveda*'.[293] On the same day, 'in order to reduce the number of cases pending before the courts' lawyers 'should not entertain weak legal cases',[294] and ('at a huge public meeting' in Lucknow) 'disruptive forces, acting under influences from outside the country, could be compared with those forces which brought slavery to India'.[295] Additionally, 'only the ideology cherished by Mahatma Gandhi – to help the poor – should be adopted by the Congress', and 'we have to identify and root out the fascists'.[296] And as peroration, 'beggars who are rounded up should be forced to go in for vasectomy'; while 'to remove the menace of begging in the country, beggars should not only be vasectomized, but made to work and sent to labour camps'.*[297]

---

*He was also asked 'what his policies would be when he became Prime Minister', and replied 'amidst laughter' (not of irony, but of sycophancy

And thence on 9 April 1976 to a published 'compilation of his speeches to a cross-section of the people' – *The Youth and Sanjay Gandhi* – in which he was re-presented to the people (and in classically heroic language) as 'a true scion of the illustrious house of the Nehrus'. Additionally 'possessing those intense feelings of love and total commitment to the motherland that have characterized the Nehrus', his 'plunge into the politics of India' had 'drawn millions of people to him'.[301] The history of the scandal and corruption of Maruti was, in authorized version, once more reconstructed as 'the politics of prejudice which characterized the post-Nehru period' and which 'presented insurmountable difficulties to his dream of producing the people's car'. More telling, 'the controversy left an impression on his mind', and it was 'not unlikely that his being drawn into politics had remotely something to do with his feelings'.[302] Thus in the midst of the official encomium (and his national campaign as a putative leader of India), a sense of personal grievance made its baleful appearance. It was a sense of both personal inadequacy and of worth unacknowledged, which together were seeking their public and political vindication and quietus in aggression and violence, and at the expense of the people of India.

Thereafter there was a brief hiatus for the inconvenient brutality of the Delhi riots on 19 April, their aftermath of continuing violence, hostile international press attention, and inner faction inquest. And then on to the road again (and under 'a large number of arches') to Agra, on 2 May 1976, to be given 'an affectionate welcome' by the censor.[303] If chastened, he was chastening in turn – and in accord with a clear political logic – attacking 'over-zealous officials' who 'caused harassment to the people', while himself resuming the momentum of excess and resurgence by demanding that 'certain religious leaders who opposed family planning' be 'isolated and eliminated'.[304]

---

according to a member of the audience)[298] that it was 'not possible to look further ahead, since he did not yet know the date of the next election'.[299] As to the circulation of underground propaganda and literature, there was 'no need to get very agitated' – though 7,000 had been officially admitted to have been already arrested for it, as we saw earlier – since to 'remain ignorant of the ideas of certain people would be more dangerous'.[300]

As the rights of India were being systematically assaulted (for this was more than a rake's progress), he was in south India, at Cochin in Kerala on 11 May 1976, 'calling on the working class to keep national cause above sectional interst'.[305] In Uttar Pradesh on 18 May, he was 'besieged with requests' in Amethi, to become its candidate – as he was later to do – for the Lok Sabha. Here, sycophancy, the censor, and the sitting Congress member – Vidyadhar Bajpai – all 'plead with Mr Gandhi' to announce his candidacy for Bajpai's seat, as Bajpai ('it would create a new sense of dynamism among the people') offers to step down before him.[306]

On 23 May he arrives in Calcutta 'on a hurricane visit'. The airport sealed off to the public, he 'takes the salute of a guard of honour from a highly decorated rostrum',[307] and enters the city to the 'tumultuous welcome' of a vocabulary of adulation grosser than any hitherto encountered. Thus, 'to both Sanjay and the people of the state, the visit is going to be a rediscovery of each other'. He is 'a fully fledged national leader', 'a man who cares only for the good of all', and whose 'only ideology is to serve the people'. 'His image shines in its own light', and is 'firmly established in the hearts of the people'. 'Fearless, pragmatic and nationalistic', he possesses 'an unbounded spirit of youth as with all the world's great leaders'. The 'magic of his call' has 'united the youth of the country', which 'stands as a monolithic force solidly behind their national leader'.[308]

In fact Calcutta was in the grip of a welter of faction violence, the installation of a puppet leadership of the Youth Congress, and to sustain it, the intimidatory political culture in West Bengal of gang warfare. The city of the miseries of millions was fortified for the visit by massive security precautions. And to accompany the assault of adulation for 'one of the world's great leaders', there was only that speeding rhetorical vortex of violence, 'whipping up tremendous enthusiasm',[309] in which the (twisting and turning) 'path of Mahatma Gandhi should be followed', and in which 'those who raise frivolous issues like leftist and rightist must be eliminated'.[310] Thence on 24 May 1976 into rural Bengal, recent historical theatre of battle between the power of faction and the power of the people, on a '*pada-yatra*' and 'engendering a new hope in the masses', with an entourage of the servile and the violent. Recorded by the scribe (and insisted upon by the censor), these were 'enchanting and magic moments for the youth leader'. 'Conch shells blowing in welcome' to the 'blithe spirit' on his arrival in Malda, he was 'on the crest of a popular wave'[311] – in front-page headlines – at the tour's ending. It was by these means, disgust deepening also, that the contagious decadence of a Kuomintang politics spread across India, where the 'elimination of rightist and leftist' and 'the hope of the masses' attended one upon the other.

But personal and intellectual inadequacy, and the power to make plain this kind of crude political meaning, are hardly incompatible; history furnishes both analogy and example. More important is that the process of political constriction not only compresses political differentiation (while deepening other forms of contradiction), but tends to dissolve remaining distinction – both of principle and person – in widening areas of the devastated life of a nation. Not only does it propel the gunman on to the campus seeking out the dissident student and teacher for round-up and detention, but it may also clothe the bully's inadequacies in the mantle of the scholar, while upon the readiness for intellectual betrayal – a phenomenon not confined to India – grateful power quickly battens.

Thus, to vice-chancellor K. L. Shrimali of Benares Hindu University (and a former minister of education), with his students and teachers in detention and accompanied on the short journey from his campus house to the university auditorium – to lecture on the 'anti-fascist struggle' – by a jeep of armed policemen, there were 'no negative aspects about this whatever'. 'Do you not regret it all?' I asked him of the lines of club-wielding policemen, guarding access to the auditorium. 'I have no unease about it,' he replied.[312] He received from the then President of India on 3 April 1976 – on the same occasion of investiture as of Satyajit Ray – *Padma Vibhushan*, the high honour of emergency India.

Again, Professor Rashid ud-din Khan of Jawaharlal Nehru University, and a nominated member of the Rajya Sabha, was 'personally very glad that the Prime Minister called a session of

Parliament to ratify the emergency measures'. 'In that way,' he added, 'the rule of law and parliamentary democracy were protected.' (The Patna anti-fascist conference, which he helped to organize but did not attend, he described as 'a racket'.)[313] Malcolm Adiseshiah, Madras University's vice-chancellor, was 'unaware of any constraint upon free discussion and debate in India'. On the one hand, 'I am myself opposed to the emergency,' he said; 'some of its aspects are terrible, and I have taken up certain matters with the Prime Minister and the Minister of Education'. On the other, 'there was before the emergency a general spiritual malaise in India, and a decline in intellectual ferment'; 'constructive dissent' had 'never existed', and 'complaint now about arrest and detention' was an 'excuse from those who were doing nothing for India'.[314] He also was honoured with *Padma Vibhushan* on 3 April 1976.

Or G. C. Pande, Rajasthan's vice-chancellor, a man of piety, other-worldly ('in mystical truth is reached the highest level of self-realization')*[315], a man of gentle meditation, presiding, hands folded, over campus police occupation, arrest and detention;[318] or Surajit Sinha, vice-chancellor of Santiniketan, on 3 March 1976 speaking of the 'new atmosphere of discipline in the country', and extolling his own university as setting 'the ideal standard of healthy, organized behaviour for the nation';[319] or A. L. Dias, Calcutta University's chancellor, speaking on 13 March 1976 of the 'turning of the tide of indiscipline', and of 'normalcy gradually returning to the university'[320] under the aegis of West Bengal's violence and intimidation; or S. N. Sen, Calcutta's vice-chancellor, on 5 April 1976 at Gauhati in Assam – scene of brutal police action against demonstrating students in the early emergency period[321] – 'calling on youth to learn from their past mistakes, and in their lives to maintain the utmost discipline and honesty of purpose',[322] with the example of the contagion of India before them; the list was a long one.

There were many other such voices instrumental to power,

---

*In his book, *The Meaning and Process of Culture* (defined as 'the human endeavour for self-realization'),[316] 'Arjuna', he writes, 'should wield the bow, and his chariot must be driven by Krishna.'[317] Who should wield the *lathi*, and who drive the paddy-wagon, was another and more delicate question.

heads and minds newly lost, or older hands expressing their practised modes of acquiescence, and standing firm upon a secure base of intellectual corruption. (Other voices, whether refusing to be caught up by the betrayal of truth and speaking out, or holding their ground in their own way with whatever diffidence and apprehension, stood out also. About them, silence is here chosen.) They might smile like seraphs, with an 'of course this is a free country'.[323] They might be deaf to all entreaty to their integrity and honour.* They might wilfully see and hear no evil, lying ('the emergency has not in any way told upon the lives of the common people in the country'),[325] or lost in illusion. Or they might be frail before fear in ways from which neither reader nor writer can claim himself immune, in abstract encounter or imaginary anticipation.

But it is nonetheless these voices and acquiescent silences which have always drowned the cries of the detainee and the downtrodden. And whether they tripped delicately around the truth, or kicked the victim after the state had downed him, it was their feet which trampled into an even deeper mire the condition of India. The anglicized wit, mutilated in his own way, might make light of violence, or the heavy-handed and partially Americanized sociologue, mutilated in another, might explain it. But with any of the other variants of inexhaustible obscurantism and absence of moral courage, they entered into an unenviable membership of the community made from the compressions of the body politic.

To it, belonged the corrupt official and his political reflex ('there is a lot of security now in the country, no pickpockets, no hooligans, no cut-throats'), together with the 'iron hand' of the travelling salesman, the policeman, and the censor. To it belonged, also, the faction thug and the political bully: the landlord's henchmen and the company director, with his 'hopeless 200 millions'; the disgruntled clerk seeking 'order' and the

*e.g. In the Rajya Sabha, on 22 July 1975, 'I wanted Professor Dutt [V. P. Dutt of Delhi] and others to raise their powerful voices, and say that while they would like to have an emergency, they would not have this sort of emergency, which is running amok';[324] that the expectation was a vain one, was seen earlier.

elegant cousin of the Maharajah of Jodhpur, speaking fastidiously of the 'salutary shock which the people needed'. It offered a bill of fare of 'disciplines' and 'eliminations' which would 'serve the people'. To its table came the silently passive and the violent as they have always done, and took their places together.

The people, to be served, saved, shocked, or brought to order, are in this dark eddy of streets. They are in the deep flow and passage of bodies, eyes, and faces; of plumping cheeks, and swarthy unshaven faces; of large eyes, and long faces; girls with arching eyebrows, and wistful glances; and deep-set with dark circles, hollow-eyed and haggard faces. Here are aquiline features, and thin-bridged noses; old men walking delicately, as if on tiptoe; bare feet, and feet henna-painted, feet in plastic, feet in slippers, and feet in sandals; grey, black and brown ankles in the gathering darkness; dusty or greying chest-hair, and ragged singlets; grey stubble and dark ageing faces, worn with effort. Here, observer unobserved, there is also a steady glancing both vigilant and knowing; heads held high, eyes dark and blazing; and here a silent guarded hatred, without expression. It is dark, and the people passes, in millions.

8 The Indian Road to Socialism

The victims who talked with me related incidents where they or other political prisoners were hung upside down; were stripped naked and severely beaten with shoes, steel rods and gun butts; had burning candles applied to their bare soles, which were then punctured with nails. The devices for torture which are being used in police stations and jails in India are as varied as they are inhumane and revolting.

Professor Ved Nanda, The Nation, 21 February 1976

We are going to run this country as we think best.

Indira Gandhi, 1 April 1976[1]

Democracy has taken deep root in the country and has come to stay.

D. K. Barooah, president of the Congress Party, 26 June 1976[2]

Your Excellency: It is with deep regret that the International League for Human Rights must submit a communication to the United Nations, evidencing a consistent pattern of gross violations of human rights and fundamental freedoms engaged in during the last year by the government of India ... There are many reliable reports that the government of India has resorted to torture, brutality, starvation and other mistreatment of prisoners arrested during the last year.

The International League for the Rights of Man, to the Secretary-General of the United Nations, 31 May 1976[3]

A sense of fearlessness has developed among the most oppressed sections of the population. They are beginning to realize how to defend their rights.

D. K. Barooah, Link, 27 June 1976

New or old order, order or chaos; reversion or progress; socialism, fascism or stagnation; the issues crowd forward to a conclusion. (Additionally, the travail of India is no new subject for analysis, description, speculation.) Moral argument sets up a clamour for attention; unresolved paradox and contradiction require resolution. Political and economic crisis, the transfer of burdens, the assault on the people, populist real-politik and the constant sorrows of India, once perceived by the beholder, pass and re-pass in the mind's eye. They demand that they be recovered from the disarray of occurrence and experience, be set down, arranged and re-arranged in order. Then, through the artifice of an analytical understanding, comprehension may be arrived at; or only a *reductio ad absurdum* of the new magnitudes of India's emergency humiliations.

For some, the utilitarian calculus was held in suspension over the prostrated nation. They said for example that there could be no real democracy without a surplus, and therefore no room for refinement of method to obtain it, in a race against time and a rising population. Here, for some, was the focus of convergence of political, economic, and 'moral' argument, seeking its own kind of explanation for what has passed and re-passed in these pages.

Certainly there was little refinement of method. 'Stamping on the naked body with heeled boots', 'beating with canes on the bare soles of the feet', 'making the victim crouch for hours in a foetal position', 'slapping both ears with cupped hands till the person bleeds and becomes unconscious', 'beating with rifle butts, causing injury to the spinal cord', 'burning with lighted cigarettes and candle-flames', 'sexual abuses', are common abuses in all senses of the word, and of all the senses. They were not special to emergency India.[4]

What we have already seen contains little enough matter for the exaltation of India. So that if India, to compound its sufferings, passed through the deepest slough of violence, caution intervenes to suggest that enough is enough. That is, beyond a certain threshold – and with a much lower tolerance than that demanded of the victim – it is much better to have done with it, and pass quickly to speculate upon the abstract or the future. It would be better to construct a 'political model' which would explain Indian practice, and cancel observation of the furthest dimensions of the degradation of the people. Moreover, to accompany the descent of India's faction power to the lowest depths, would be to reach down also to an all-too-familiar nadir: finding in a political wasteland an idle sensation only in the sufferings of the tormented.

Indeed, the search for an apposite historical model may also release the writer from the pressure to look steadily, eye-to-eye, with the worst of tyranny's excesses. Furthermore, perception of the repetitious sordidness of India's long decade in the custody – both metaphorical and increasingly literal – of the ruling power, class and party, is distorted by a serial passage from sensation to sensation. It was a decade for which the trial of an historical analogy might begin to shed light on certain aspects of its character and meaning. It was a period arguably reminiscent of other protagonists and another era, of those forerunners 'with their struggles whose first law is indecision, and with their wild inane agitation in the name of tranquillity'. Theirs also were 'passions without truth, and truths without passion'. Their decade also was one of 'heroes without deeds of heroism, and history without events'; 'a course of development ... made wearisome by the constant repetition of the same tensions and relaxations, antagonisms which seem periodically to press forward to a climax but become deadened and fall away without having attained their resolution'.[5]

As with the France of Louis Bonaparte, so arguably with this India: its 'collective genius brought to ruin by the cunning stupidity of a single individual'; while 'the superannuated enemies of the interests of the masses' sought to express the 'collective will of the nation'.[6] As there and then, so arguably in India the 'party of order', 'pretending to see all the horrors of anarchy embodied in them', 'saved society from the enemies of society' in order to 'rule in the name of the people'.[7] By declaring its emergency, perhaps it too sought to 'free civil society from the trouble of ruling itself, by proclaiming the supremacy of its own régime', 'itself half duped and half convinced of the serious character of its own state proceedings', and 'speculating in vulgar fashion on the gullibility of the masses'.[8] The Indian 'party of order', like its earlier counterpart, perhaps also was and is 'a conglomeration of different fractions, intriguing against each other', 'confronting the subjugated classes, and contending with them, without mediation', while 'each of the two great interests into which the bourgeoisie is divided – landed property and capital – endeavours to restore its own supremacy and the subordination of the other interest'.[9]

Indian capital too has its 'retinue of advocates' and its 'characteristic fighting force': 'the scum, the leavings, the refuse of all classes', 'rogues who are supposed to represent the people'. We have watched them too 'improvise a public', 'stage public enthusiasm, shout *"Vive l'Empereur!"*', and insult and beat up their opponents with police protection'.[10] In India also, we have encountered the 'phrases and fantasies of the parties and their real organization and real interests', the disjunction between 'their conception of themselves and what they really are'.[11] We heard from the ruling faction of India the same 'pretentiously paraded exertions', 'useless platitudes' and 'high-flown phrases', in a period 'so poor in events and heroes' that only 'exaggeration could make the former pass for events at all'. We heard too the same 'enthusiastic striving for innovation', with the 'old routine's even more fundamental retention'.[12]

The Bonapartist parallel can perhaps be pressed closer. With a like defeat of attempted impeachment and 'a personal triumph over democratic enemies', corruption was in both cases subsequently reincarnated as 'misunderstood virtue, complaining of the slander of opponents', the 'cause of order identified with the person' of the leader.[13] And we have seen, too, 'legislation muzzling the press, destroying the right of association, and establishing the state of siege as an organic institution'.[14] But even the shabbiest historical analogy (with all its other resonances) serves to dignify the greater shabbiness of what confronts us, for historical retrospect itself can make heroes of the unheroic. Moreover, then, it was the 'red spectre' which was 'continually conjured up and exorcized by the counter-revolution'.[15] Now it was 'fascism' or 'reaction', and it was the counter-revolution which spoke in socialism's language.

Yet historical comparison serves one purpose: it draws observation away from the beguiling and insufficient argument which proceeds from and ends with squalor. It is an argument which harbours within it the false notion of an unchanging India – in which one man's search for, say, beauty, becomes another's discovery of horror, but in which each finds his own separate eternity; or counterposes them in an eternal and immobilized relation. Of course, it is true that the shabbiness of political India appears to have its own staying power, like the sufferings of its people, as if the process of exhaustion and decomposition were capable of a continuous extension, and stasis had its own momentum. Or, as the Prime Minister put the same point on 18 April 1976: 'there is no basic change in our philosophy in India'.[16]

That is, in a political terrain already devastated, further devastation may pass unnoticed. Thus the observer, having peered through the opacities and dullnesses imposed by the censor, might think he saw a political wasteground where only the employment of additional means and methods for the retention of power had scarred its otherwise unchanging surface.

But more was afoot, continuities and constants notwithstanding, paradoxes and unresolved contradictions also. Its trail through the text may be followed. It may be followed from the point at which faction was first discerned battling with its own political failure and economic crisis, custodian of the 'shifting compromise' of class interests of bourgeois and landlord, and presiding with its legacy of ideological ambiguities and illusions over the historic sufferings of the people. That is, there was something more than merely the process of its extrication from the sprung trap, by a constitutional *coup d'état*, or the unfolding procedures of illegitimacy's struggles for legitimation. There was something other than the politics of a new deal and a new authoritarian order; more than a mere sequence of assaults on the liberties and bodies of the people, or an attempt to establish a more acute concentration of faction and junta power within the repressive and ideological state apparatus.

'Fascism' is an over-used term. At its very worst, it loses substance entirely as a term of abuse reserved for those with whom the user is in political disagreement. It may be equally loosely used as a generalized synonym (lacking the critical dimension of analysis of the state's nature) for authoritarianism, cruelty and violence, or the rule of the tyrant and dictator. This usage is little improvement on the first one; while, conversely, those with worked-out diagnostic definitions may confine its appearances to states where the 'rule of developed finance capital' is to be found, and thus exclude its application to India.

The development of previous historical forms of 'fascism' – such as the German or Italian – has, first, been a drawn-out process. Whatever definition of its characteristics is arrived at, therefore, none would be adequate which did not comprehend that they may be exemplified in a polity in embryo, or as tendency,* or as full-term apparition. Second, 'fascism' has 'assumed different forms in different countries, according to historical, social and economic conditions'.[18] Notwithstanding these substantial qualifications, from a historical scrutiny of the particular deformities of state power commonly termed 'fascist', we would need to have found in India a system of political gangsterism; a system of violence against the working class and its organizations; jingoism, demagogy, chauvinism, nationalism and aggression; and the power of capital presiding over part or whole of the economy of the nation.

We would also have to find, specifically mediated by the peculiarities of each nation, some or all of the following: acute economic crisis 'driving the classes off their courses'; the establishment of an 'unrestricted political monopoly by the ruling bourgeoisie, fearing an outbreak of revolution'; the 'suppression of the democratic liberties of the working people'; the 'curtailment of the rights of parliament', and the 'repression of the revolutionary movement'.[19] We would expect – guided by historical example – the substitution of one state form of class

---

*e.g. 'There are already clearly marked fascist tendencies in India's young men and women . . . and the Congress is beginning to reflect them . . . The corporate state with private property preserved and vested interests curbed but not done away with will probably appeal to them . . . If British control were wholly removed, fascism would probably grow rapidly, supported as it would certainly be by the upper middle-class and the vested interests' (Jawaharlal Nehru, *Autobiography*, 1936).[17]

domination, such as that of liberal democracy, by another; that is, the dictatorship of unmediated class power, in a process of consolidation.

Or we might look to see if the ruling class party, serving class interest, presents itself to the people as 'socialist', or depicts its *coup d'état* as a 'revolution'; its demagogy 'taking advantage of the deep hatred of working people for those who exploit them', while bringing nationalism and socialism together in an unholy conjunction. We might not be surprised if the tendency towards 'fascism' was also marked by the 'most corrupt and venal elements' coming before the people with an 'honest and incorruptible government', 'standing above classes', and in the interest of the nation's resurgence or salvation.[20] It might be armed also with an economic and social programme – twenty-five points in 1920 Munich – of promise and part fulfilment.

But with it we would expect an attack on the people, the true *quid pro quo* of another and profounder calculus than the one we have earlier considered. We might find a deepening tendency towards 'more servile forms of labour', robbed of its rights. Analogy would grow close were we to find, for example, the 'plunder of the workers' social insurance funds' and the cutting of wages, a 'new bureaucracy made up of the most submissive followers' of the ruling party, or 'the spreading to an unprecedented extent of corruption and degeneration'.[21] And would we find that in India also 'fascists rummage through the entire history of the nation to be able to pose as the heirs of all that was exalted and heroic'? Or that they represent 'the greatest figures of the past as also having been fascists'?*[22]

*cf. 'In a long speech, studded with copious quotations from Vivekananda, Mahatma Gandhi, Pandit Nehru and others, Mr Barooah outlined the history of the Congress';[23] 'the Youth Congress leader began his address with a review of the country's past glory and said the British had been able to subjugate India and its people only by systematically destroying its industry, its artisans and its intellectuals';[24] 'we have heroes in each and every village, and their stories are part of Indian history. Today the old freedom fighters have a role to play to explain the real motives of disruptionists to the people';[25] 'success has been achieved in ensuring that the democracy established in India by Mahatma Gandhi and Jawaharlal Nehru would not be destroyed, during this first year of war against subversion and the disintegration of the nation'.[26]

And what of fascism's 'penetration into the ranks of the peasantry and working classes', with palliative and intimidation, resemblance to revolution, promise and repression? Or its 'penetration into the ranks of the youth also, by grasp of their need for militant activity', in order to compensate them for the 'full weight of the economic crisis, unemployment and the disintegration of the bourgeois democratic system'?[27] We might look to see, too, if there has been 'a party which systematically calls on the workers to retreat in the face of fascism, leading them to defeat and permitting the fascist bourgeoisie to strengthen its positions'.[28]

Close to the bone, we might find that 'fascism' 'promised the ruined and impoverished peasants to put an end to debt bondage, to abolish rent, and even to expropriate the landed in the interests of the landless', while 'pushing to the utmost limit the exploitation of the great mass of the people by landowners and usurers',* and depriving them 'even of the elementary right to free movement'.[32] And then we might notice, justly because now resumed in proper context – and as Dimitrov put it presciently for our analogy – 'sterilization ... made a method of political warfare', and 'the people ... subjected to other revolting indignities and tortures'.[33]

For in this wasteland there were other figures to be descried, voices stifled, beckoning for attention. They approach like the figures of Hades for their names and places to be recorded, and if they were known, for their assailants and persecutors also to be remembered. Here Hermant Kumar Vishnoi, secretary of the Delhi University union, hangs upside down before us, and is

---

*'And what did the peasants of Germany get? The moratorium cancelled!'[29] cf., also, 'the government's emergency decree issued on the morning after [the Reichstag fire] . . . announced the suspension of various articles of the constitution, particularly those guaranteeing the inviolability of the person, the freedom of organization and the press, the immunity of domicile and so on'.[30] For an alternative Indian view of fascism, cf. 'Allow me to recall what Jawaharlal Nehru said about fascism: in India it takes the form of communalism, regional chauvinism and such other forms. These forces can never be wholly eliminated unless their social base is liquidated. Through the 20-point programme, a nation-wide struggle has been launched to liquidate this basis'.[31]

beaten. Burning candles are applied to his bare soles. Chilli powder is smeared into his nose and rectum.[34] 'The emergency', says a distant voice, 'has been both popular and useful; the economy has improved, and the masses have welcomed it. The trains are running on time, and more work is being done in factories and offices.'[35] The arrested (for putting up posters) – tortured and burned – are borne, 'bodies covered in burns', to hospital in Karimnagar, Andhra Pradesh, on 2 December 1975; the Karimnagar bar association protested to the Chief Minister.[36]

The police beat *satyagrahis* – those offering themselves for arrest in acts of non-violent civil disobedience – in Karimnagar on 14 November 1975, day of the commencement of a national campaign of *satyagraha*.* They beat them also in Vizag on 21 November 1975, in Hindupur on 2 December 1975, and on 4 December 1975 in Kakinada. In the night of 14 November, the policeman Azees is alleged to have brutally beaten the bodies and private parts of Edida Raman and Kraleti Krishna at the police station in Srikakulam. On the same day, it is alleged that Shri Krishnayya and Narsinha Reddy were brutally beaten by Murlidhar Rao, sub-inspector of police at Nalgonda. On the same day, in Kakinada police station, Koka Kurma Rao and Krishna Prasad, *satyagrahis*, were hung by their hair until they became unconscious.[38]

In Belgaum, Karnataka, Ashok Mutgekar who had 'offered *satyagraha*' on 30 November 1975 was allegedly put on the 'aeroplane': that is, suspended by rope from a pulley, dangling by his arms tied behind him. So too was Shri Ravi, arrested on

---

* 'In a typical *satyagraha*, individual demonstrators (*satyagrahis*) – ranging from four to fifty in number – shout slogans against Mrs Gandhi's government and pass out anti-government literature in busy streets. The demonstrators usually wear garlands, people assemble around them, and since the time and place are announced in advance, the police promptly arrest the demonstrators. Each *satyagraha* I saw in Delhi [in the third week of December 1975] had about forty active participants who courted arrest and attracted more than 5,000 spectators. The crowds, predominantly opposition sympathizers, repeatedly shouted slogans demanding an end to the state of emergency, release of political prisoners, and the restoration of civil liberties';[37] and see appendix, p. 400.

2 December 1975 at Mysore, after being kicked and beaten in the Devraj police station; so also Udaya Shankar from Mangalore, in the Bunder police station, at the hands of sub-inspector Uttaiah and in the presence of superintendent of police Chopra. The advocates' association of Bangalore passed a unanimous resolution at 2.05 p.m. on 9 December 1975 protesting to the chief secretary of the Karnataka government at the 'ill-treatment of political prisoners', and at their 'physical torture'.[39]

In Kerala, they 'roll a police *lathi* over the shin-bone', 'with a constable sitting on the *lathi*'; they 'beat on the spine with the elbows'; they 'fist the ear till it bulges', they 'catch both the shoulders from behind and bend the person backward butting with the knee in the middle of the back'.[40] In the police station at Mundiyeruma, Idukki, on the night of 17 November 1975, Thangappan, Prabhakavan and Vasu were allegedly kicked and beaten; Thangappan had to drink his own urine. Purshottam Pai, in the presence of superintendent Sukumaran, was allegedly punched, kicked and beaten at the Kumbara police station of Ernakulam, after 'offering *satyagraha*' on 2 December 1975; he and others had to sit with their legs stretched out, and their soles were caned until the cane was broken.[41]

Of course, there was a wider perspective and horizon than this, beyond these out-of-focus and beaten bodies; the 'control of inflation' and the struggle against 'reaction', or the modernizing industrial interest and the utilitarian calculus. But to make the land safe for democracy and fit once more for its heroes to inhabit, or to build the Indian road to socialism through this political landscape, *satyagrahis* must first be taken to Dewas police station in Madhya Pradesh and forced under extreme duress (on 5 December 1975) to commit acts of sodomy and *fellatio* upon one another.[42] Or, in Rajasthan, while in police custody at Madhopur on 14 November 1975, Jugal Bihari Sharma and Motilal Jat, *satyagrahis*, must suffer electric shocks; and on 21 November at Gangapur, Phulchand, Ramesh Chandra, and Ramesh Sharma the same bitter treatment.[43]

In the same cause, Ghanshayam Tiwari, an advocate of Sikar in Rajasthan who had gone to Jhunjun to try to defend *satyagrahis*, must be 'mercilessly beaten into unconsciousness' at the local police station. The bar association of Sikar condemned this treatment, sent a resolution of protest to the Chief Minister, and demanded an inquiry.[44] In this cause also, must be understood the *lathi* attack and attack by convicts on 2 December 1975 – ordered by the jail superintendent in the presence of Krishan Sarup and Rajender Tanwar, both councillors of Delhi – on political prisoners at the Tihar jail in Delhi, in which more than one hundred detainees, including Mulak Raj Juneja, Krishan Lal and Dayal Singh Bedi, all former municipal councillors of Delhi, were injured.*[45]

To build the new Jerusalem, Satya Prakash must be beaten with rods and shoes at Hauz Khas police station, Delhi on 23 November; his bare soles punctured; his body tied and suspended from the ceiling. O. P. Kohli, president of the Delhi University teachers' association must be made to stand for twenty-four hours in the police lock-up, and when he falls down, must be picked up and forced to stand again. And Om Prakash, *satyagrahi*, must be denied food and water, between 23 and 27 November 1975 at the Timarpur police station in Delhi; beaten, hung upside down, with a rod tied to his neck, and his genitals prodded and beaten with rods of metal.[48]

But we have seen sufficient of the variegated forms of Indian corruption, whose apogee was most purely expressed by this abuse of power, to sense that a general degradation of the people would lead both to excess of cruelty, and a matching excess of denial. That is, as the face of India passed into darker shadow, its political expression was the Rashtrapati Bhavan's mirror reflection, as I observed it: cold, concentrated and sallow; bland and reassuring; melancholy and sombre, the Janus-face of India which we have – in another form – already encountered.

These individuals, whose names are known, must stand for

*The former Mayor of Delhi, Lala Hans Raj Gupta, formally protested to the Home Minister about the attack, on the next day, 3 October 1975.[46] There was a similar attack on political detainees by jail authorities and criminal convicts, on 9 September 1975, at Muzaffarpur Central Jail in Bihar, in which many of the prisoners were injured; some allegedly 'sustained multiple fractures and head injuries', including Professor T. P. Sinha, head of the department of mathematics at Sri Ram Dayal Singh College, Muzaffarpur.[47]

all the thousands of others allegedly similarly beaten and humiliated (' "The world understands only the language of strength",
the Congress president added'),[49] unknown and nameless
throughout India. And against them all was the other speaking
voice of India which expressed its astonishment'. It was aston-
ished that 'the right should be questioned of the freely elected
and popular government of India to take measures under its own
Constitution to deal with a state of emergency created by subversive elements bent on destroying domestic peace and progress';[50] 'elements' with 'faces blackened and forced to parade
in public', or 'forced to stand at night in the open with buckets
of cold water poured on their naked bodies'.[51] Those who are
known must stand for all those unknown, who had their 'thumbs
broken', and their fingers 'crushed and fractured'; for all those
with 'heads bleeding', for all those kicked and beaten.[52] Alternatively, 'most people know the Indian government to be based on
and responsive to the wishes of the people';[53] while 'the care
and concern bestowed by the state authorities upon the welfare
of detainees, who are well-housed, well-fed and well-treated, is
almost maternal'.[54]

But despite the strenuous – or cautious – special pleading of
one kind of vested interest or another, neither dignity nor
honour can be salvaged by the assailants, or those who defended
them, from the incontrovertible evidence of an ignoble brutality.
It may of course be wearying to encounter for the blasé and the
jaded, whose palates have long been spoiled for yet another account of political torture, particularly when practised on the
excessively numerous Indian people; their numbers can evidently be contained only by one form of violence or another. For
others, it may be inconvenient to the careful calculus of political
advantage and disadvantage, the productive and the 'counter-
productive'; or justified by the greatest happiness of the greatest
number; even deserved in the name of law, order and progress.
Whichever the case, however, even the most heroic language of
noble exertion and historic decision,* or the language of the

---

*e.g. 'The magnitude of the impediments and dangers which the emer-
gency enabled us to clear is staggering in its proportions . . . it has marked
the renewal of life for our nation';[55] or, protected the people from the

battle against 'licence', could not dignify licensed thuggery – the struggle, with its 'limited bourgeois content'[57] not of the hero, but the *goonda* – and depravity, gross or furtive. But in such battles of the Bonapartist 'party of order', it was a matter of fighting 'disruption'; and in command of its uniformed and plain-clothes myrmidons (capital's 'characteristic fighting force' of the 'leavings' and 'refuse of all classes'), assaulting in the name of a 'disciplined democracy' a vulnerable people. There were the battles of the 'party of order', which 'saw in every sign of life in society, tranquillity endangered';[58] saw it even in the (limp) shape of the passive protester against India's erased freedoms and redoubled humiliations, who must always provoke the bully – the more insecure, the more provoked – to a gratuitous anger and a random violence.

But this was not all there was to it, large though it was as component. To some kinds of moralist there was a moral argument, and, however attenuated in the teeth of violence, a moral dimension and a saving grace evidently to be found even in the rubble of the shanty and the cries of the tormented. This arose not because 'reaction', 'indiscipline' and 'disorder', 'fascism', 'disruption' and violence, the 'ravages of lawless hordes', 'mobocracy',[59] 'greed and hatred'[60] – all the enemies of the people – had to be fought to a standstill; with in each case their own weapons and arguably by the enemies of the people. It arose because there is a point at which, classically, the utilitarian calculus itself assumes a moral dimension; while its resilience enables it to survive in conditions where other moral notions prove less hardy. What it asserted, simply, was a familiar proposition – always rejected when put by its political opponents – that the means justify the ends: that utility is *per se* a good, providing that the long-term or short-run utility of violence can be vindicated.

In fact, there stood concealed behind this nominally moral argument one of the strengths of emergency India's ruling junta, helping to gain it the encouragement, connivance or silence which greeted its perfectly well understood assaults

---

'ravages of lawless hordes like thugs and *pindaris,* as happened in the declining days of the Moghul empire'.[56]

on the Indian people.* Its very willingness and capacity to establish 'order' and 'discipline' by violence against the people was
perhaps its greatest recommendation; and where the argument
was incomplete or uncertain, racialism or the fear of numbers
could complete it. That is, India's ruling class – which itself
possesses its own forms of hatred of the downcast people of
India – can rely for its support, as it knows from its inheritance
of the colonial experience, on foreign fears and hatreds of its
beggary and teeming population. That this fear and hatred was
presented, both in India and outside it, in the moral disguise of
the people's interest makes no difference to – or strengthens
rather – the force of this understanding.

This is one reason why India's great riches and capacity for
self-sufficiency are discounted; why there was, inside and outside
India, unconcern with the known relation between poverty and
over-population; why forcible sterilization, intolerable to other
people, was ignored, tolerated or encouraged – vicariously – in
the case of India's downtrodden and outcast millions. That is,
it was, to many, a fitting solution; for India, and for Indians.

The 'moral' arguments thus converged in India not upon
the restoration of the dignity and well-being of the people, nor
upon the planned and rational growth of population, but upon
the panic-induced humiliation of the poor and the violation of
the person, working less with minds than with bodies. Here the
stronger, presiding over gross inequity, classically perceives a
Malthusian menace in the numbers of the weaker. Not for the
assailant – who is agent, at however many removes, of a land
wasted – admission that every able-bodied person, as the Chinese
have shown with the largest population in the world, can produce as much value as is needed for subsistence; nor that 'poor
destitute people who constitute a great part of our population
have no other wealth than their own children'.[62] Instead, the

---

*Thus, by 16 June 1976 in Washington ('the US government is sym-
pathetic to India's birth control efforts'), the World Bank was being asked by
India for a further $70 million 'to carry out its ambitious birth control
programme', which in the year ending 31 March 1976, the bank was told,
had 'sterilized 2·65 million men and women', 53 per cent of them women.[61]

By March 1977, and with the aid of such funds, the total of the sterilized
had allegedly risen to more than seven million.

state punishment and intimidation of the poor childbearer or the beggar punished the destitute for their condition, again in classical fashion, whether it was in the name of 'socialism' or national salvation, utility or the struggle against religious obscurantism* and reaction.

In the narrowed eye of the beholder, outsider or Indian, such a proceeding also assumed – as the banned July 1976 issue of *Seminar* put it – that 'human beings living in poor societies are less than human: they may be fed and clothed on condition that they cease to exercise their critical consciousness, cease to be human'.[64] Such a proceeding merely redoubled the political assault upon the people, in a land despoiled by landlordism and defiled by corruption, and whose material condition is of the richest potential. In this politics of coercion, was a surrogate for action; surrogate for land reform, for the breaching of the nexus between illiteracy and fertility, and between exploitation and over-population. Instead 'targets for sterilization' were set in millions, and in conditions and circumstances observed earlier; instead from Uttar Pradesh, for instance, was announced the compulsory sterilization of the leprous (22 August 1976);†[65] instead, 'at crowded railway stations, their favourite haunts, the "family planners" and the "motivators" came to peddle surgical operations'; and there was even a black market in faked certificates of sterilization.[67] And staring the argument from utility in the eye, and out-staring it, was the dire consequence of the emergency's coercion, harassment, and violence. 'Doubts and fears about birth control have been deepened'; 'family planning and compulsory sterilization have become synonymous, and both are feared and resisted'; 'now fear is based not on superstition and prejudice, but on actual experience'.[68] Thus on 7 September 1976, by further amendment to the Defence of India Rules, new powers were given to the censor to forbid 'news reports or

---

*Thus, 'no religious or political group will be allowed to stand in the way of the nation's progress by obstructing the family planning programme'.[63]

† 'The Uttar Pradesh government has decided to intensify its family planning programme under which beggars afflicted with leprosy will be compulsorily operated for vasectomy. Unmarried beggars with leprosy will also undergo sterilization.'[66]

comments on India's family planning programme';*[69] as the Indian road to socialism passed into still deeper shadow.

If this conjunction between utility, morality and violence was in the last analysis mean and threadbare, the reality of India's degeneration was drabber. Even the terms 'Bonapartism' and 'fascism' seem to shed too much light, rather than too little, on its dull recesses and the shabbier protagonists (and often equally shabby antagonists) who commanded its people and re- sources. The bourgeois *parvenu*, as ever, tried and failed to in- vest his motives and actions with dignity and purpose, or 'timidly conjured up the spirits of the past to help him, and borrowed their names, slogans and costumes';[71] but beneath every political surface the texture of political practice both in domestic and foreign affairs thickened, while its personnel (and their morality) coarsened.

Its tracks and traces could be followed in many directions. As instance among many, Bansi Lal, the Minister of Defence, appeared in the 'venerable disguise and borrowed language' of the military virtues, addressing the Indian army without irony in the vocabulary of bravery and honour.† For corrupt faction must always be uneasy in its relations with the military forces, which in the last analysis, if not the first, is custodian of and threat to faction's precarious power. It must seek to mollify its army, as best it may; is 'always happy to be among the armed forces'; and must insecurely 'praise their valour'.[73] It must regularly recall – as residual political virtue withered on the vine – how the 'brave *jawans* had rebuked aggressors in the past with the full backing of the nation'.[74] And not only must a caricature of

---

* Given the nature of the 'family planning programme' this was a necessary but insufficient precaution. On 17 October 1976, for instance, it became known from police reports that eight people died at Sultanpur in Uttar Pradesh, when 'police opened fire on a mob attacking "family planning" officials'. Similar events took place elsewhere in Uttar Pradesh, at Basti and Gorakhpur, and in West Bengal, Bihar and Haryana. Forty people were also reported killed in 'riots against compulsory sterilization' at Muzaffarna- gar, seventy miles north of Delhi on 18 October 1976.[70]

† ' "You, the brave soldiers," he said, "are the symbols of the unity, integrity and honour of the nation . . . You are the best trained, disciplined, dedicated and courageous." '[72]

martial rhetoric be displayed – placing in their hands 'the country's honour' – but money must be expended also; and not only on the armaments of war, nuclear weapons included, but on pay increases and improved conditions, on gratuities and pensions.[75] Moreover, political regression and national humiliation (or the 'rising prestige of the nation') had to be masked by an India 'encircled' and 'threatened'. What Dimitrov in his study of fascism called the appeal of an 'ill-treated nation' must summon the army's attentions to the enemies which surround it; while beneath the surface, and to deal simultaneously both with the threat of the army and the political opposition, faction rule must build its private armies, striking its own balance of power with the military forces and the people.

Together the Border Security Force ('250,000 strong'), the Central Reserve Police, the Research and Analysis Wing ('a major department of state with an annual grant of approximately £30 millions'),* [76] and the street forces of the organized lumpen-proletariat in those other armies of the Youth Congress, had come to constitute the accoutrements of the police state long before the emergency's declaration. Thus, for instance, the 'nearest significant army base of division strength' has been in Ambala, 150 miles from Delhi, while BSF battalions have had 'free access in and out of the capital'.[78] 'This "second army"' both 'frees the regulars from the task, always unpopular with troops, of acting in support of the civil authority'; and freed the Congress decade from dependence on the army when it launched its large-scale coercive or repressive actions'.†[79]

But here too was further precarious balance, when a rival armed force is counterposed to the regular army. The im-

---

*Justifying the overall increase to 1,600 million rupees in the Home Ministry's budget, before the Lok Sabha on 3 April 1976, Reddy said it was 'because of the "coming-up" of several organizations like the CRP, the BSF, and the Central Industrial Security Forces'. 'We push in a lot of money to the states to assist them to modernize their police forces', he added.[77]

†cf. 'Mr Bansi Lal said there was no politics in the army, and that "our army is united and one". He said the army was not used anywhere in the country during the emergency to maintain law and order. Nor was it used to break any strike.'[80] These tasks were instead carried out by the para-military forces.

munities provided by a growing praetorian guard are themselves perilous ones; while against the greater fire-power of the army must be maintained 'a system of informers to which everyone is subject',[81] including the army. Again, after June 1975 the continuing momentum of assault on the left and upon labour was critical for the support of many senior officers of the armed forces; but it was uneasily conjoined with an increasing military dependency upon the Soviet Union. Above all, a new political thuggery was put in charge of the army; against it, stood the mortification of the pride of the professional soldier.

The issues raised here were not confined to the army. For the effort to 'keep up appearances' without straining credulity, and to maintain the 'dignity of the nation', become increasingly problematical in general when regression and decomposition are in power. But more important, the recalcitrant facts of the emergency contained their own compulsions. Thus the Indian road to 'socialism', formerly barricaded by the opposition, had first to be cleared with the bulldozer; such was its political nature, this road could not then be travelled without a paramilitary escort and police violence; and the 'second army' had therefore to preside over the national resurgence, the economic programme, and the relations between power and the people.* Furthermore, in India corruption plays havoc with the assertion of law and order, as does faction with the unity of ruling power. In the former case, where, say, warrants of arrest – or (a cruder process) threats of arrest, without warrant – were used for extortion,[85] or where there was widespread news or experience of political licence, 'keeping up appearances' set faction an increasingly difficult problem. In these repetitions, to create by suggestion new events, purpose, and progress became increasingly strenuous, when the lengthening road being

---

*e.g. 'India will have a national police computer grid by 1980, the closest parallel to which exists only in the US. Work on this ambitious 80 million rupee project has already started';[82] or 'the West Bengal inspector-general of police has instructed state police forces to undertake extensive *padayatras* as a regular practice';[83] or 'the 13th all-India police science congress reflected the growing awareness among the custodians of law and order of their crucial role in the fast-changing socio-economic situation in the country'.[84]

travelled contained diminishingly distinctive or salient features. For the resources both of manipulation and violence are finite; and they are a poor exchange for the infinite resources of the people.

Political impoverishment led to other kinds of reduction. Energy characteristically came to be directed not to purpose but to the tactics of power's consolidation, and to the fine equivocations which dot the 'i's' and cross the 't's' of political degeneration. This political style found, for example, 'over-crowding in many jails because of heavy pressure on the political situation';[86] in the depths of the emergency, the Home Minister could 'visualize the possibility of the misuse of extraordinary powers in an extraordinary situation';[87] as the jails filled, he was 'seeking to dispel misconceptions as regards the use of MISA'; 'could not give the exact figure of detainees', but suggested that 'the numbers of those detained under section 16A of MISA "worked out" to two for every hundred thousand of the population'.[88] In fact, the tide of incoming arrests, and the outgoing tide of releases, assumed its own extra-legal momentum, measure both of political caprice in charge of the liberties of the individual, and of the growing autonomy of India's 'second army'. Emblem of order and administered disorder, it was thus that the known and unknown quantities of political repression slipped away beyond recall or careful calculation.

As further examples of such political style, in July 1976, there was report of the arrest of members of the Cabinet of the former Gujarat government; and of political detentions in order to create artificial majorities in the city governments of Gujarat.[89] There were also factional arrests of Youth Congress members;[90] and, for instance, arrests of 'over 1,100 persons' (announced on 24 August 1976) designated as 'unscrupulous traders' in a 'drive to bring down rising prices'.[91] Vikram Rao, journalist of the Ahmedabad 'dynamite case', was allegedly tortured;[92] George Fernandes was brought to trial before the Delhi High Court on 4 October 1976, in the same matter, for conspiring to 'overawe the central government by violence'.[93] There were arrests of civil libertarians and constitutionalists, such as C. T. Daru, and others associated with the Citizens for Democracy;[94]

and new phases of arrests of trade unionists – even while constitutional amendment was being proposed by the Swaran Singh committee to proclaim a 'socialist republic' – and of serving parliamentarians.*[95] Similarly, despite intermittent releases of prominent political figures,[97] the power to hold political prisoners without remedy or charges was itself extended on 16 August 1976 from one year to two years; while throughout the emergency the 'party of order' sought in vain to consolidate its position with a long series of specific banning orders, warrants and prohibitions.[98]

Random voices continued to be heard speaking, with whatever difficulty, through the darkest phase of the censor's stiflings. They spoke, for instance, of the president of the Punjab and Haryana High Court – Lakhan Pal – who died in detention.†[99] They spoke, for example, of 120 MISA detainees transferred from Tihar Central Jail in Delhi to solitary confinement in outlying jails in Ambala, Bareilly and Agra,[101] and of hunger strikes.[102] They spoke of members of state governments unaware of who was being arrested in their own states, or carrying out orders from the centre which could not be questioned.[103] They spoke of the retention in jail of thousands of rank-and-file Socialist Party, CPI–ML, CPI–M, CITU, and Jan Sangh members;[104] and of oaths of loyalty to faction power having to be sworn by political prisoners, as the price of release from detention.[105] It was possible to hear likewise of the harassment of the families of 'suspects', of wives and even children hounded, of living in fear and under surveillance; of the betrayal of neighbour by neighbour ('because a man has a different opinion from those who overhear him, they report him'); of the police 'becoming vengeful' when the wanted hide, and

---

*Also to be reckoned with were the unknown numbers 'kept in unlawful custody by the police', who 'took care to see that the arrests were not even put on record'. In the case of *satyagrahis*, 'many were then beaten up in the most brutal manner before release a few days later'.[96] For a letter of protest on this alleged practice, sent to the Prime Minister, see appendix, p. 400.

†The International Commission of Jurists in Geneva expressed 'deep concern at his death in detention' in a cable to the Prime Minister on 9 August 1976, and called for an amnesty for all Indian political prisoners.[100]

in reprisal arresting family members, and ransacking houses.[106]

Recourse to this form of dogged intimidation and violence must always set up its own noisy clamour of exertion and fear in both assailant and victim. It exhausted both power and the people, making it difficult for both to attend to anything but their own narrowing circumstances, as the ground shifted beneath them. Thus for the former, an increasingly crude and simple code of devices continued to explain the defence of class interest in terms of the interest of the nation. For the latter, 'Down with the Emergency!', or 'Down with the Dictator!', or 'We will Make a Vietnam out of India!' daubed – and quickly covered over – expressed inchoate threat and reflex, and the first writing on the wall, for faction, of a growing hatred and anger.

Formal opposition, still in disarray, was grouping, disintegrating, regrouping. The political kaleidoscope, its surface patterns precariously balanced, was nudged or shaken into new configurations made from old elements, themselves unchanging. The parties of the 'new' or 'united' formations of the opposition – such as first the Lok Sangharsh Samiti, or People's Struggle Committee, and later the 'combined' opposition front, composed heterogeneously of Congress-(O), BLD, Socialist Party and Jan Sangh – gyrated about each other, just as factions and sub-factions of the ruling power slowly gyrated about the body of India, scavenging for the spoils of office. Thus, for example, released detainees of the Jan Sangh joined the Congress Party; sometimes Congress-(O) and CPI likewise; the CPI and the CPI–M held discussions and lost members to each other, in the taking up of old positions. I will return to this briefly in a moment.

The exhausted populism of the 'JP movement' continued to be harried by the censor and the policeman; it was run to ground long after it had been defeated.* 'The petty bourgeoisie and their

---

*For instance, it was accused of 'continuing to receive foreign funds';[107] and, at a critical juncture, J. P. Narayan's attempt to reach his Bihar 'constituency' was side-tracked.[108] On 25 May 1976, for example, he tried to publicize a programme of united opposition – in association with the disparate party organizations of the People's Struggle Committee.[109] But it was accused by the Prime Minister of 'being bent on worsening the present

democratic representatives' – of another epoch and nation – also had 'made revolutionary threats', like those of J. P. Narayan. They also believed, as he did, in the 'trumpets whose blasts would make the walls of Jericho collapse'. And when, in France, they were 'confronted with the ramparts of despotism', they too 'endeavoured to imitate that miracle', while 'avoiding the means to the end like the plague, and clutching at excuses for their failure'. They also therefore 'ran into a blind alley'. As in India, so in France, the 'blaring overture which announced the struggle died away into a subdued grumbling as soon as it was due to begin', and their action also – like that of the 'JP movement' – 'collapsed like a balloon pricked by a needle'.* [113]

The heyday of *sarvodaya* and *satyagraha* was over; a fool's paradise made, by state practice, of the moralities of a Mahatma Gandhi, or all the pieties of a Vinoba Bhave. Instead, there was the shooting of 'wagon-breakers' (seventy-eight were killed in five months in 'battles between police and railway bandits', announced on 16 September 1976);[115] instead, the warning that 'disruptive forces in the country would be ruthlessly put down if any became active';[116] instead, the hanging of oppressed and stone-poor peasants such as Kista Gowd and Jangam Bhoomaiah.† Against these, the meek call of the pacifist and the

---

system through violence';[110] while the *sarvodaya* movement itself was in process of division.[111] Lastly, the clear imputation from Narayan himself after his release that his sudden kidney failure in detention had been induced by his captors requires to be recorded.[112]

*cf. 'You know I am an old man. My life's work is done. I have given all my life to the country and ask for nothing in return. So I shall be content to die a prisoner under your régime', in J. P. Narayan's letter from detention to the Prime Minister, dated 1 July 1975.[114]

†When Gowd and Bhoomaiah were hanged in Secunderabad jail on 1 December 1975, after three years in the condemned cell – two village poor among twenty-eight arrested for the murder of Lachchu Patel of Adilabad in Andhra Pradesh, a landlord 'notorious' and 'widely hated' for his 'extortions, atrocities, and violence'[117] – the repeated appeals that mercy be shown, made on their behalf by 130 Supreme Court lawyers, six former High Court judges and three former Chief Justices, were overridden. Two amnesties also passed them by; and 'New Delhi displayed an iron determination, appropriate for a better cause, to carry out the death sentence upon them.'[118] Cf., three months after the executions, the Prime Minister's 'Quite frankly,

acharya, uncertainly disfavouring peaceful disobedience and calling on the government to 'follow the path of self-discipline'[120] in the wake of mass detention and violence, fell on deaf ears; additionally inaudible against the rhetoric of national salvation.

Instead, there was the characteristic political style of the 'party of order'. The chained leader of the Socialist Party was accused of conspiracy to 'overthrow the government' and to 'create countrywide chaos', accusing his accusers of 'tyranny and torture and trumped-up charges'.* [121] Armed police ('we don't want to stifle criticism of the government's policy')[122] surrounded and entered the *Indian Express* offices.[123] The *Statesman* was harassed,[124] and there was the defeated closure and banning of presses and journals ('we have no desire to take away the freedom of the press'),[125] such as *Seminar, Opinion, Janata, Mainstream, Sadhana* and *Fulcrum,* which had been battling on to maintain the last integrity of the national press and press freedom.† [126] Instead, there was the process of 'screening newcomers' from the Jan Sangh into the Congress Party on their release from detention, so that they might prove their faith in the ideology of the party'; furthermore, it would be necessary to 'observe them, test them, and keep them under watch for some years to come before we can have faith in them'.[129] Also in process was the 'admission to the Congress fold' of members of banned right-wing organizations, committed to a politics of

---

I am against capital punishment altogether . . . I think that the whole system of justice should not be so much to punish as to cure the person, but unfortunately we do not have it.'[119]

*For the torture of Lawrence Fernandes, his brother, see appendix, p. 416.

† The Delhi High Court (in a judgement unheard in India) held that 'the censorship measures exceeded legitimacy to an unimaginable extent'. 'There cannot be a more draconian assault on people in a democracy than the one which is disclosed by the guidelines issued by the chief censor', the court stated. The judges added that it was 'beyond their comprehension how it could be justified on the grounds of securing public order'.[127] The Delhi High Court likewise opposed an attempt to close down the *Statesman,* after the state had demanded that its 'presses be forfeited', under legislation earlier considered.[128] Similar efforts by the Delhi municipal corporation to sell the property and chattels of the *Indian Express* for alleged non-payment of taxes were also opposed by the court. *Guardian,* 2 November 1976.

extreme nationalism, 'communalism', obscurantism and violence. And thus, despite the 'screening', 'many RSS men who
till the other day were in jail under MISA' had 'suddenly
turned into patriots and active supporters of the Congress',[130]
in order to take their emergency places at the then head of the
political column proceeding towards socialism in India.*

Conversely, consolidation of power constantly re-encountered
not only unresolved political and economic crisis, but the recurring exhaustion of its own momentum; the palling of its own
conviction and purpose. The utilitarian will for palliative reform
– which to carry forward requires continuous re-invigoration,
but is negated by equally continuous preoccupation with the
retention and legitimation of power – was constantly sapped by
the need for recourse to the simpler crudities of coercion. Moreover, in the suppression of the struggle of the classes, the discord
of single-party faction was not abated but re-asserted. The shifting compromise was unable to hold steady as the whole of
India was spreadeagled before it. The 'party of order', once
temporarily freed by detention and violence from the attentions
of formal opposition, was instead subverted by faction and dissension. The saviours of the nation, vying for favour under
internal intrigue's increasing pressures, came to have in common
not a shared sense of political direction, but only the instinct
for self-preservation. Moreover, both the base ('mass base') and
the articulation of power in these circumstances did not widen,
but narrowed: to an unstably contracted junta rule, composed
of the dynasts and, let us say, Bansi Lal, Mukherjee, Qureshi

---

*This continued the long history of overt and covert relations between
the Congress Party and the extreme right parties. In the past, it had included
tactical relations with the RSS – as during the 1965 war with Pakistan,
when they carried out civil guard duties in Delhi. Thus, for example, 'RSS
leader Gowalkar was able to secure open allies among rightist sections of
the ruling party'.[131] As ideological difference between the right parties
diminished and the attack on the left continued unabated, the Jan Sangh
executive in Uttar Pradesh (for instance) as early as 25 June 1976 pledged
its 'full support to all the constructive schemes launched by the government
for the benefit of the people', and called on its followers to 'refrain from
joining any activity which disturbs the peace and security of the state'.[132]
cf. 'She said that not all her party were wedded to socialism. They were not
being thrown out, because they would not be able to go against the stream.'[133]

and Om Mehta, the architects of India's emergency misfortunes.*

There were other Indian alternations: struggling to keep up democratic appearances, and throwing to the winds all caution; maintaining the strictest control and surveillance over dissident and opponent, and allowing the administrative apparatus of coercion itself to slip into disarray and disorder; the pressure for election and the need for repression; the ebb and flow of left and right faction within the ruling party. The Youth Congress riding high was also riven. It was suddenly assailed for 'indiscipline and turbulence', while politicians of the Congress Party attacked each other for 'exploiting the younger generation', and for 'inciting the Youth Congress to take part in activities' for which they were 'not fitted'. And as the struggle to oust it from its usurpation of older vested party interest sharpened, 'youth power', they said, 'was misused with disastrous consequence both for youth and the country'.[134] The Youth Congress reasserted the claims of the sword-arm of Congress to act as 'watchguards for the people',[135] and on 11 August 1976 warned, with the strength of its three million members, and in the accents of Sanjay Gandhi, that 'whoever looks on with folded arms should be branded as an enemy, and should be treated at par with those who obstruct the onward march of our country'.†[136]

Similarly, fingers began to point into the shadows lengthening and deepening across India, and drew attention not to the strength but the growing weakness of the ruling power, unable to continue without elaborate forms of artifice and intimidation. But to the CPI – still then engaged in its own solitary and whirling *contredanse* with the ruling faction of the Congress Party – it continued to be 'the duty of workers to understand

*cf. 'The emergency provided the chance of a lifetime for the unscrupulous and corrupt, especially those whom it brought to political ascendancy at the expense of the legitimate bearers of power and the interests of the people' (Rajni Kohati, *Seminar*, no. 203, banned, July 1976, p. 14).

†On 7 August 1976, Sanjay Gandhi announced that the Youth Congress would 'spearhead a campaign of social regeneration', and increase its membership to five million; he declared that its 'basic preoccupation' was 'not politics', but 'Indian society's revitalization'.[137]

the historic significance of the struggle against imperialism led by Indira Gandhi, the unique anti-imperialist ruler'.[138] In turn, the CPI – its reduced capacity to confuse its working-class constituency a wasting political asset to the Congress – came in for 'strong denunciation by Youth Congress leaders for its role during the freedom movement';[139] its weakness in numbers, ideological conviction and coherence further exploited by the ill-disguised contempt and hostility of the ruling party in the states and at the centre.*[140]

It offered new political anodyne and 'definition'. 'By the term "socialism", we mean a social and economic set-up wherein all our people will be happy and contented';[141] seeking to accompany, in the interest of the Soviet Union, the burlesque and flailing progress towards socialism of one faction or another of the Indian ruling party. 'It is the proud privilege of the CPI', said its General Secretary, 'that with all its moral and human resources, it plunged into the fight against Indian fascism'. Moreover, 'but for the action taken by the Prime Minister, the wheels of history perhaps would have changed [sic]'; while the fact 'that the 20-point programme has not been implemented according to our expectations is indeed tragic'.†[142] Thus, in the face of class violence, there was a continuing drift of members, and a lost sense of direction; continuing support for ruling class interest; confused movement towards the left-opposition on the one hand, and the Congress on the other.

And on the main Congress road to socialism, the failure to secure economic revival by repression, and the failure to control internal division and external opposition, was slowly and fatally

---

*This was later to express itself in a crescendo of fierce attacks on the CPI by Congress Party leaders; for 'policies of duplicity', 'sabotage plots', 'unclean intentions', and for 'shirking its responsibility to the motherland'. *Guardian*, 29 December 1976, *Times of India*, 13 January 1977, and *Hindustan Times Weekly*, 16 January 1977.

† cf. 'Dange concluded that the task before the working class, as before all classes, except for a handful of monopolists, was to fight for the implementation of the 20-point programme, eschew disruptive and divisive tactics, be on guard against the reactionaries who continue to be active, and to prepare for a long and hard struggle, which was certain to culminate in socialism. Whether or not the audience understood Dange fully is difficult to say. By the time he spoke, many had left the meeting.'[143]

increasing the pressure for a renewal of the régime's 'popular' legitimation. And yet, there had also to be installed in the political vacuum created by the partial or total suppression of existing institutions, new and contradictory processes for the ratification of power; for by the very nature of rule by faction it must abhor a vacuum. No régime – and especially not a corrupt and unstable one – can stand its own dissolution of the varied forms of order without their effective replacement. Indeed it stands or falls by its success or failure to instal them; for it must retrench and ratify, after it has abandoned the former positions from which the line of power was defended.

As example, the organization of arrest and the surveillance and selection of the 'anti-social' required at the local – or precinct – level newly elaborated (but not new) political structures. So also, both for purposes of social control and election, did the supervision of local patronage and local violence, urban and rural, much of which had passed into the bloody hands of the Youth Congress. Its general immunity from law or sanction was of course long established; but in the fetid climate of political decomposition, its ranks came to be increasingly dominated not by a cadre of 'sophisticated youth', but by the roughest lumpen elements. As a result, however, consolidation by the 'party of order' was constantly forestalled by the faction violence which entered the lists of the Youth Congress with them; while the autonomous structures of local control which they sought to establish collided with the competing claims of the police, the magistracy, and the civilian administration.

Thus the ranks of Congress, Youth Congress and INTUC were all riven by fratricidal faction-clashes, and for the same reasons. That they always had been is one thing; but that this deepening factionalism (with its deepening violence) at the same time demanded the united loyalty of the people, was another. Between 21 and 25 June 1976 alone, for example, such struggles surfaced publicly in West Bengal, in Gujarat and in Maharashtra.[144] In West Bengal as instance – the most notorious – leading groups of Congress members were suspended from the party and simultaneously arrested, on the orders of the Chief Minister S. S. Ray, whose position was itself threatened. One group at Barrackpore was charged with 'conspiracy to murder'; another at Midnapore with 'terrorizing the people', and 'extortion'.*[145]

The struggle for political consolidation by manipulation of the Constitution was both another world, and the same one. Another because it suggested an orderly and lawful transformation towards the nation's 'unification'; the same, because lawlessness and a constitutional *coup d'état* were seeking legitimation, through the abuse of the law itself and the Constitution. The Swaran Singh committee, whose appointment to 'study and suggest amendments to the Constitution' was noted in an earlier chapter, began to produce its recommendations in May 1976. It recommended that the right of Parliament to amend the Constitution be put beyond the judiciary's challenge. It also recommended the amendment of Articles 226 and 227 of the Constitution, in order to reduce still further the power of the High Courts to issue writs on behalf of a citizen seeking enforcement of the law, or complaining against the executive's otherwise arbitrary powers.[151]

It recommended the abolition of the rights of the courts in industrial and labour matters, and in service disputes, and also in regard to questions of revenue, food distribution and land reform, on the grounds that the judiciary had prevented social and economic reform in India since independence. It sought to carry further that process – described earlier – of weakening the

---

*cf. 'Factional rivalries will not be tolerated in the state', said the Chief Minister on 24 June 1976, in the thick of arresting faction rivals; 'the people of West Bengal have become sick of factional politics', he added.[146] On 13 September, it was reported that 'planeloads of Congress activists, including members of Mr Ray's Cabinet and central government Ministers, have travelled between Calcutta and Delhi in the last ten days almost continuously, and remained locked in discussions all day and often most of the night'.[147] The Orissa, Kerala, Tamil Nadu, Delhi, Uttar Pradesh, Bihar, Punjab, Mysore and Madhya Pradesh organizations were similarly riven by purges and dismissals.[148] In Orissa, they were to reach a climax with the removal of the Chief Minister, Nandini Satpathy. (In West Bengal, there were also other forms of unremitting faction struggle in the Congress Party's trade union movement).[149] In some states, as in West Bengal, rival factions coexisted with separate organizations, each claiming primacy as local representatives of the Congress Party. Cf. 'The challenge of the future can be met only by having complete solidarity in the party.'[150]

judiciary in the name of Parliament, while Parliament's powers were simultaneously eroded in the national interest. It recommended giving the centre the right to deploy its police and security forces in any state of the union; that is providing additional constitutional sanction for the toppling of dissident state governments with the centre's para-military apparatus.

It recommended giving the centre the right to declare an emergency selectively in any part of the country; it recommended the incorporation in the Constitution of an Article laying down the citizen's fundamental duties, to include the promotion of the 'unity and integrity of the nation'. It recommended the provision of punishment for failure to observe such duties. And it recommended that the preamble to the Constitution be amended to declare the India which we have seen, to be a 'sovereign, democratic, secular and socialist republic'.

'The word "socialist",' said Swaran Singh, 'has been added so that there is no doubt or confusion about our objectives'; and, in his further clarification, these were to 'implement the socio-economic policies of the Congress Party'.[152] This proposal was greeted with 'jubilation' by the Youth Congress;[153] to the CPI, it represented a 'big step' which 'responded to the hopes and aspirations of the Indian people';* [154] while to the Chief Minister of West Bengal, it 'did not mean the end of the private sector'.[156] The CPI–M and Socialist Party condemned the proposals as 'totally unacceptable', proclaimed that sovereignty rested with the people, and that basic changes in the Constitution could not be effected by a rump Parliament whose term had been artificially extended. They claimed that the recommendations attacked the fundamental rights of the judiciary, the states and the people, reduced the powers of Parliament, and concentrated such rights and powers in the hands of the Congress Party.† [157]

---

* 'It is true that the mere description of the Indian republic as socialist does not mean it has become a socialist state, but the name does give and spell out the direction of the country, and this we consider as most significant and welcome.' [155]

† In West Bengal, the left-opposition parties convened a public open-air meeting in the Calcutta Maidan on 13 July 1976, on the issue of the constitutional amendments. The gathering was banned (as were others), though some meetings of protest took place in the state during that month.[158]

Initially set a ten-day deadline in August 1976, within which they had to offer their comments before a Bill incorporating the Swaran Singh proposals was introduced in Parliament, the CPI–M, the Socialist Party, the Congress-(O), Jan Sangh, BLD and DMK refused the 'invitation to talks' to discuss the proposals. ('Some parties are not cooperating with us, but some are cooperating').* [159] In the meantime, on 17 August 1976 – during a brief interlude in which other constitutional matters had to be dealt with – President's rule in Tamil Nadu was extended for a further six months from 10 September. 'Because of the drought condition in Tamil Nadu, and the official efforts to meet the situation', said the Home Minister, 'it would not have been possible to hold elections before the expiry of the existing proclamation.'[162] And likewise, on 26 August 1976, elections due under law in Kerala, and already twice postponed, were postponed again by legislative enactment.[163]

When the draft Constitutional Amendment Bill – containing fifty-nine amendments – was published on 30 August, it went 'further than had been expected'. It was 'viewed with alarm by the opposition';[164] the Bill would 'strangle democracy', and 'impose authoritarian rule'; it was either a 'blueprint for dictatorship',[165] or a constitutional mandate for corrupt faction-power. It would prohibit the Supreme Court from reviewing the substance of constitutional amendments; it would bind the President to accept the 'advice' of a council of Ministers; it would permit the prohibition of 'anti-national activities and associations' which 'impaired security', 'created internal disturbance' or 'disrupted

*The CPI 'cooperated'. An 'in-depth examination' of the proposals took place at two short meetings on 13 August and 18 August 1976 between the CPI, represented only by its two parliamentary leaders in the Lok Sabha and Rajya Sabha, and Swaran Singh and Gokhale. Later, Gokhale said that the CPI had 'given their views and made their own suggestions'. They included a request for elections to be held, and the setting up of joint standing committees of both Houses of Parliament to 'supervise the functioning of government'.[160] Earlier, they had 'expressed the hope' that the government would reconsider its decision 'to include the Press Censorship Act and MISA in the ninth schedule of the Constitution'.[161] The government did not reconsider it. The process of formal consultation with the opposition was ended on 18 August 1976, ten days after it had started.

public services', and thus legitimize the banning of political parties and of trade unions.[166]

The 'main thrust' of the proposed Bill was 'to establish a totalitarian rule of one-party dictatorship under the cover of the Constitution', said Samar Mukherjee of the CPI–M; or, less exactly in the event, 'to make an already established constitutional dictatorship permanently in-built in the Constitution', according to H. M. Patel, speaking for the non-communist opposition.[167] Even the CPI objected to the Bill; the opposition's speeches were not reported; the Prime Minister, 'rarely looking up, initialled documents that a messenger brought in every few minutes';[168] the opposition once more vacated the parliamentary chamber in protest; and using its two thirds majority, the Congress Party approved the formal introduction of its own constitutional amendments.* On 2 November 1976, the Bill was passed by the Lok Sabha; and on 11 November by the Rajya Sabha. On 5 November the rump Parliament had already extended for a further year – till March 1978 – the time within which an additional legitimacy by election could be sought by faction-power.

The strenuous attempts at consolidation, by physical, 'constitutional', and 'popular' means – in that order – of domestic faction, the struggles to maintain unity and order, the quagmire of rhetoric and lying, and the dull thud of repeated violence were also refracted in India's foreign relations, by new political compulsions. There was, above all, the need to match the domestic

---

*In fact, the proposals merely re-presented fundamental features of the *earlier* proposals for a presidential system, which had been circulated the previous autumn, before the Swaran Singh committee had been established. This was because the latter's recommendations, after their official welcome was over, began to meet objections from some sections of the Congress Party. For instance, B. K. Nehru – the Indian High Commissioner in London, relative of the Prime Minister and allegedly author of the earlier proposals – did not think the Swaran Singh proposals went far enough. He described them as 'very minor changes'; 'personally,' he said, 'I would have gone very much further in restricting the interference of the judiciary with the will of Parliament',[169] which (decoded) signified – as we have seen – the strengthening of the arbitrary powers of the executive. The ground of his argument was, characteristically, that it would 'prevent our libertarian attitudes going to the extreme'.[170]

'national resurgence' by demonstrating the new dynamism of the nation. It was necessary to find for the régime international understanding for its assault on the people; again to keep up appearances and maintain old relations; to gain a pacific breathing-space from the exertions of its domestic politics of violence and coercion; and to maintain its claims to political primacy in south Asia.

All this merely added a new set of superficially confusing alternations to the existing pattern. We have already examined the cyclical pattern of belligerent denunciation by the threatened or 'ill-treated' nation, and that selective accommodation from which other countries quickly sought their own benefit; or the assertion of political strength and national independence, together with economic dependency and political subordination.

So to the familiar politics of 'some foreign countries want a government in India which is more pliable, but so long as I breathe I will not be pliable to them,'[171] or of the 'evil designs' upon India of other nations and so forth,* the politics of dynamism and of national transformation propelled India into the foreign correlatives of its domestic politics of 'action', or of its new programmes of regeneration. Of India's nearest neighbours, Burma, Nepal, Afghanistan, Sri Lanka, Pakistan, Bangladesh, and China were in turn touched by the alternations I have mentioned. There were continuities and renewals of belligerence with asseverations of good intention, as in the case of Bangladesh and Pakistan; and in the case of Bangladesh, covert forms ('we have no intention to interfere in their internal affairs')[173] of paramilitary intervention. There was tactical accommodation ('mending fences', or a *modus vivendi*) as in the case of China. There was continuing hostility, dependency, and strategic accommodation in relations with the United States and the Soviet Union. There was the reiteration of the principles of non-alignment and pacific purpose, with a rising defence budget and an intensifying nuclear armaments programme.

A structure of ideological repetitions matched both in form

---

*e.g. 'If the government had not taken severe steps, India would have been engulfed in instability and chaos like its neighbours.'[172]

and content the apparatus of domestic assertion. Thus, with 'increased external dangers from all directions' for domestic political purposes, there were also 'purposeful foreign policy thrusts' and 'systematic efforts to strengthen India's relations with neighbours'.[174] 'New content' was being given to the 'concept of bilateralism' and 'peaceful coexistence'; a 'durable peace' was being sought in the sub-continent 'free from the meddling of the big powers',[175] and so on.

But Pakistan was also 'arming itself feverishly' and 'preparing again',[176] the 1972 Simla accord between them 'crumbling';[177] while India was simultaneously seeking to normalize their relations, broken off in 1971, and ready to 'give a crushing blow to any country [sc. Pakistan] that dare violate the territorial integrity of the nation'.*[178] After 'strenuous, friendly and frank' talks on 12–14 May 1976 in Islamabad, India and Pakistan agreed to restore full diplomatic relations.[180] With Bangladesh, which had 'emerged as a friendly neighbour'[181] after its 'liberation' in 1971 into the Indian sphere of influence and Pakistan's brutal division, India had been in increasingly belligerent disputation after the overthrow and assassination of Sheik Mujib.

The ostensible cause is the sharing of the waters of the Ganges,† the real one, hostility to the successor Bangladesh governments. The consequence was, alternately, the 'seeking of the friendliest relations'[184] and 'a policy of maximum possible fortitude';[185] attacks on Bangladesh's 'hostile anti-Indian propaganda', disclaimers of interference, and reiteration of the prin-

---

*cf. 'As a consummate character-actor, who is quite adept in the art of portraying himself both as a strong man and a man of reason, Mr Bhutto has been trying to talk tough and at the same time placate India.'[179] Despite – or because of – two wars in eleven years, it was obvious that the rulers of India and Pakistan, having a great deal in common, understood one another.

† The short-term agreement of 18 April 1975 with Sheik Mujib on the sharing of waters at the Farakka barrage expired on 31 May 1975; since then, it is alleged that India has 'continued to siphon off the water', diverting it from Bangladesh, with disastrous effect, even during the dry season.[182] Cf. 'It is essentially a scheme which benefits India . . . The plan goes back to British days when the idea of switching water from the Ganges into the Hooghly [for Calcutta] was conceived. With the completion of Farakka, India achieved its basic ambitions for the control of the Ganges.'[183]

ciples of coexistence.[186] The familiar movements of Indian patrols on the India–Bangladesh border were followed by the equally familiar bursts of 'unprovoked firing' on them, with Indian fire 'returned in self-defence', as in India's other war with China.[187] And thence, to the accompaniment of protests at the 'continuing Dacca slander campaign against India', followed the well-attested 'aiding of insurgents against the anti-India Bangladesh government' – which is in turn supported by Pakistan – and the 'arming by India of Bangladesh guerrilla forces' on the border, in its pursuit of peaceful coexistence with its neighbours.[188]

More important, in the quadrille of diplomatic relations between India, the Soviet Union, the United States and China, through which Sino-Soviet and Soviet–American conflicts express themselves in their different ways in India, (officially) India's relations with the Soviet Union were 'based on solid foundations', 'finding sustenance from the common endeavour of both countries to work for the reduction of international tension'. With the United States there was 'a mature and constructive relationship and better understanding'; there was 'no conflict between the national interests of the two countries'.[189]

In fact throughout this period – as we have seen – occurred the cautious circlings of the super-powers around the enervated and embattled polity of India, and the manoeuvrings and out-manoeuvrings of political and economic interest in the prostrations and exertions of India's junta. At issue were *inter alia* roubles (and their value), and dollars; Mig fighters, trade and aid, and the delivery to India of American-enriched uranium, which as plutonium is used in the making of India's nuclear weapons; the 'threat of China'; political support for emergency India's new order, and for its suppression of the liberties of the people; and Soviet–American rivalry for influence in south Asia.

Inserted into and bound up with this complex texture, there was agreement in April 1976 to resume diplomatic relations with China, and an exchange of ambassadors in September between Peking and Delhi. There was thus a swift passage in Sino-Indian relations. It moved from 'the sanctimonious Indira Gandhi government' which did not hesitate to discard the last shred of the fig-leaf of democracy and nakedly laid bare its ferocious features' and 'those who bow before her survive, and those who resist perish', of 29 June 1975,[190] to the presentation of credentials fifteen months later.*

The polemics between India and China had continued while India's emergency economic problems had deepened towards the budgetary redistributions of the new economic policy, and the open invitation to foreign monopoly capital to enter India. They continued – though on a diminished scale – as the Soviet Union's abuse of its economic domination in trading relations with India was exacerbating existing Indian suspicions of the Soviet Union. On 5 March 1976, for example, 'the Chinese have never stopped their bid to create disorder in other countries';[192] and on 31 March, the annual report of the Indian Defence Ministry accused China of 'not responding to India's initiatives and efforts to pursue a policy of peace and friendship'. Further, China was 'continuing a propaganda campaign against India', 'continuing to misrepresent developments within India', while lending 'moral and material support to underground elements in India' in order to 'help create an insurgency condition'.[193]

But the report, when published, was already out of step with the necessity of events. That is, the necessity (among others) for India to assert a notional independence of the Soviet Union had already carried it towards the formal resumption of relations with China.† The latter's fierce political criticism of India had already abated; and by 2 June 1976, the Chinese government was 'reiterating' its 'desire to develop better relations with the countries on the Indian sub-continent'.[194] On 21 August the Rajya Sabha was told that the Indian government was 'not aware of any anti-Indian propaganda by the Chinese in the recent

---

*Left behind also was the alleged border crossing into Chinese territory by Indian troops on 20 October 1975, with the familiar counter-allegation that the Chinese had 'intruded well into India'. The Chinese Foreign Ministry protested at the 'sheer reversal of black and white and confusion of right and wrong', on 3 November 1975.[191]

†It also led to a sharp acceleration of the CPI's anti-Chinese polemics; thus, on 18 April 1976, the pro-CPI *Link* was referring to Mao Tse-tung's 'half-paralysed brains', the 'cadaverous Chairman' and the 'doddering Mao', as well as to Wang Tung-hsing, an 'accomplished torturer and for many years the head of Mao Tse-tung's enormous personal bodyguard'.

past'.[195] By 10 September, on the death of Mao Tse-tung, Mrs Gandhi was to describe him as 'a statesman who led the resurgence of the Chinese people'.[196] And on 11 September the new Chinese ambassador Chen Chao-yuan was speaking not of 'the reactionary rule of the Indira Gandhi régime', but of 'fifteen years of friction' as a 'small period in history to two countries whose friendship dated back centuries', on his arrival in India.*[197]

The intersecting points of Sino-Soviet and Soviet–American conflicts and relations thus touched together, and for the first time in a decade and a half, upon the surface of the political economy of India. In the case of the Soviet Union, though its political and economic support for India is ultimately unreliable and coercive, and unable as it is with its own economic problems to underwrite an economy as impoverished and ransacked as India's, it was nonetheless critical to the precarious maintenance of state power by the ruling faction of the Congress Party, its anti-communism and hostility to the Soviet Union notwithstanding. It was therefore critical also to the denial of the rights and liberties of the people of India as they were beaten and cajoled along the Indian road to 'socialism'. The Soviet Union's additional interest in the suppression by whatever means of a left-opposition politically hostile to it, has been fully met for a decade by the Indian state, acting in its own convergent class interest. Paradoxically, this has not helped the CPI – indeed the reverse is true – for the simplest of reasons. Indian governments have no need of the support of the CPI in order to gain the support of the Soviet Union, for it is obviously a support autonomously determined by the latter's own state interest. To the Chinese, in the earlier phase of their criticisms, this was perceived as a matter of 'Soviet social imperialism painstakingly propping up the Indian government so as to scramble for hegemony with the other super power in south Asia.'[199]

However, to any faction of Indian class power presiding over India, the same circumstance gives opportunity for the unsubtle utilization of its political, economic and military relations with

---

*On 13 September, first fruits were being gathered: it was reported from Delhi that 'the Chinese have refused to encourage Dacca in the Bangladesh–India dispute on the Ganges'.[198]

the Soviet Union – that is, its August 1971 treaty of 'peace and friendship' – in order to strengthen its bargaining position with the interests of foreign capital. That this has had a relatively limited success is in part because of the irony that the United States, India, and the Soviet Union share, on the one hand, a common interest in preventing peasant revolt and the next stages of peasant insurrection in India, and a common hostility to the dangerous example of the Chinese revolution. Both the US and the Soviet Union thus continued to carry out covert intelligence operations in India throughout the whole of our period; and both have knowingly contributed to India's nuclear programme.

On the other hand, the increasing domination of foreign finance capital in the Indian private sector and of the Soviet Union in the public or 'state capitalist' sector of the Indian economy, have made a temporarily compatible political and economic combination in India's progress towards 'socialism'. Thus, the potential for exploitation by India of the complex political rivalry and division between the United States and the Soviet Union, has been reduced hitherto both by the degree of their common strategic interest in India's pivotal position, and the greater interest (and fire-power) which the former has so far chosen to display elsewhere in the Indian Ocean and south Asia.

In addition, both American and Soviet interest in emergency India (as we saw earlier) measurably quickened together – 'détente's' other dimension – to the invitation of India's new deal, and the extremism of its repression of the labour movement and the left-opposition. Moreover Indian, American and Soviet interests are all served, however precarious the balance of forces, by a modestly enlarged presence of the United States in India, carefully modulated allusions to the CIA notwithstanding. For it prevents the unchallenged influence of the Soviet Union in India, while foreign capital helps to reduce the economic burden on the Soviet Union of India's multiple forms of dependence (or 'self-reliance'). The admission of China into this balance was also in the mutual interest of China and India, long-term for the former, less long for India. For the latter, it reflected not the dynamism of a resurgent nation but the strengthening of its hand, in straitened circumstances, with the Soviet Union, and the compulsions and improvisations of the 'new' political order. For the former, it gave a resumed diplomatic and political access – on easy terms – to the observation in India of the Soviet Union.

As for emergency India in the Soviet Union, it was a matter of arms supplies, the bitter dispute about India's increasing debt burden, 'excellent relations' (8 April 1976)[200] and 'deepening friendship' (8 June 1976),[201] and of multiple journeys to Moscow. A cross-section sample – choosing from a long list – might include Chief Justice Ray and Justices Beg and Bhagwati,[202] whose earlier appearances in this text can be re-examined with the help of the index; a 'high level defence team' for discussions on the requirements of the Indian navy, air force and army;[203] an official delegation, for the first time, from INTUC;[204] Achutha Menon, for medical treatment; the Prime Minister and the 'illustrious youth leader' of India's lumpenproletariat, on a visit to which the Soviet Union attached 'exceptional importance'.[205] It was a matter of signing a 'new pledge of friendship and cooperation' ('experience', said Leonid Brezhnev, 'has confirmed the foresight of the policy pursued by the Indian Congress Party'),[206] 'long private talks', and the Soviet Union's 'full understanding' of India's resumed relations with China.[207]

As for the Soviet Union in emergency India, it was amongst other things a matter of India's continuing reiteration of a politics of 'non-alignment', which has become a useful and irreplaceable synonym for joint dependency on foreign capital and the Soviet Union. It was a matter of Soviet foreign policy incorporated in India's denunciation of 'outside incitement of interference which might aggravate the situation in the sub-continent'.[208] It was a matter of India's public, though not private, distinction – another *quid pro quo* for arms and aid – between the Soviet navy which was merely 'cruising in the Indian ocean',[209] and America's establishment there of naval bases. Or it was India at the summit meeting of the non-aligned nations in Colombo in mid-August 1976, 'protesting on the Soviet Union's behalf' at the invitation to the conference of Romania.[210] It was also the Soviet-supported

suffering of the people on the Indian road to socialism, and above all the mutilated Indian variant of the politics of 'anti-imperialism' and 'anti-fascism'.

In these two last terms was contained another crucial field of contemporary distortion of political meanings, which deserves extensive exploration for what might be learned from it of the future fate of classes and nations. That is, in their names, the economic exploitation and dependency of India and the indigence and pauperized misery of its millions, expressed itself not in a struggle for the gaining of the dignity and freedom of the people, but in reprisal against them. And it was this assault and repression by ruling class faction and state power, which was then spuriously dignified by 'third world' association with the cause of 'anti-imperialism' and with those who have fought in their own countries for a liberation both real and apparent.

It deserves to be explored, for it would reveal also the masked present and future divisions in the relations between the newly independent and liberated countries, and between them, the Soviet Union, and China. It would give additional resonance, for instance, to the complex attack by Cuba at Colombo on those members of the 'movement of non-aligned countries' who in their own countries – as in India – 'foisted themselves on the people by means of crime and violence, be it to preserve obsolete feudal structures or to prevent revolutionary changes'; and who, by means of 'non-alignment', 'conceal the brutal repression which they unleash against their own peoples'.*[211]

Thus, arms twisted behind them, prisoners were suspended

---

*cf. 'When there is a real desire to free the country from imperialist exploitation, then the people must also be freed from the plunder of the fruits of their labour by the feudal lords, the landholders, the oligarchs and the social parasites of all kinds.'[212] There were many reflections of the adoption of a corrupt 'third worldism' by India. Another was to be found in its advocacy of third world countries 'pooling their news information' on a regional basis through their own news agencies, in order to become 'independent' of the western media. The ostensible grounds were that 'freedom of information is as essential as a new economic order'.[213] For India, a potentially valid notion signified only the extension of press censorship and the further stifling, through the use by India's regional neighbours of controlled *Samachar* information, of the flow of news to and from India about what was being done to its people.

by ropes and pulleys, but it was 'not necessary that all governments must run on the Westminster model';[214] beaten with canes and *lathis*, India was 'desperately trying to find a system of democracy which suits the masses'.[215] Hanging upside down before us in exemplary fashion, 'discipline does not mean regimentation, but in its truest sense, discipline is placing the nation's interest above the individual'.[216] And hanging by the hair, 'the gains of the emergency must be preserved as a way of life, voluntarily chosen'.[217] With his ears slapped with cupped hands, till the head bleeds and the person becomes unconscious, 'only a political illiterate would be opposed to what is happening in India';[218] burned with lighted cigarettes and candle flames, the nation had taken 'a clear leap forward'.[219] With bodies and private parts kicked and assaulted, India was both 'the only major country in the world to have checked inflation' and a country where prices were 'still falling.'[220] With the soles of their feet beaten with canes, 'once the people come to view that discipline pays and conflicts harm their interests, there will emerge an image of a strong India';[221] and with the soles of their feet punctured, 'I should like India to be a much more disciplined country than it has been, a country where the laws, whatever the laws may be, are obeyed by the people'.[222] With the rolling *lathi* pressing down upon the bared shin-bone, 'I would like to see a government that is willing to take unpopular measures';[223] and with police urinating in the mouths of Malik Chand, Satyapal, and Rawan Kumar at Yamuna Nagar in Haryana, the 'spectre of disorder in India' had been 'banished'.[224]

Nor was it ever explained within the terms of the utilitarian calculus 'how the arbitrary and limitless powers given to the forces of law and order, meant to be used only against the enemies of the people' could have been put to such benevolent use 'in the hands of an administration left untouched in the matter of its class composition, its inherited values and habits, and its subservience to politicians in power'.[225] It was not clear either how 'the censoring of news, the detention of the opposition, the imprisonment of individuals could have freed any bonded labourer, conferred ownership rights on any tenants, given any land to landless labour'.[226]

But the Indian state – organ of the class rule of the bourgeoisie and landlords – should not have been disturbed. For overwhelming the original circumstance of the emergency's imposition to rescue faction power from its political crisis, it was now on course towards 'progress', with a 'stable' economy and a 'disciplined' people. Additionally, Mrs Gandhi was 'leading the country to socialism, as Mahatma Gandhi led India to independence.'[227] Or, 'like Chiang and the Kuomintang, Mrs Gandhi and her Congress' had 'moved steadily further to the right by the need to repress opposition, disaffection and resistance'.[228] That is – the same point more modestly made – there was 'marked reluctance in ruling circles to discuss the ending of the emergency, when clearly the impulses which sparked the declaration have faded'.*[229]

Instead on 12 December 1975, for instance, 'the threat to the nation is still alive', for 'foreign forces cannot tolerate the strength of India'.[232] On 4 March 1976, ' "can we say that the dangers which existed are past? Can we say that the opposition has realized that they have no popular support?" she demanded'.[233] On 1 April 1976, 'the emergency should continue until discipline is inculcated among the people';[234] on 5 April, 'every party is entitled to woo and convince the public and come to power, but unfortunately now and in the foreseeable future, there is no alternative to the Congress Party'.[235] On 8 April 1976, there was 'nothing in the present situation to warrant the revocation of the emergency'.[236] On 25 June 1976, the emergency would continue 'until the present gains have been consolidated, and become a part of normal life'. 'Opposition to me', said the Prime Minister, 'has only been subdued, not eliminated'.[237] On 29 June 1976, the 'state of emergency cannot be withdrawn by a snap

*Also to this purpose, the régime intermittently perceived *not* increasing 'discipline', but an 'erosion' of it. Such 'slackening of effort' in turn justified further repression, even if at the (lesser) expense of consistent ideological presentation.[230] A further alternation – especially necessary during visits to India of foreign critics of the régime – was to assert the emergency's gradual 'liberalization'.[231]

decision';[238] and so on month by month, a receding echo, as the ruling faction was moving under pressure towards its gamble with election, and one Ides of March or another.*

The clamour of voices which accompanied them on their journey was of special pleading and wishful thinking, of apologia and incoherence, of defiance and denunciation. To Swaran Singh, the emergency was 'effective crisis management not abrogation or abridgement of freedom'.[242] To Abu Abraham, a nominated member of the Rajya Sabha, 'three hundred years of colonial dominion' had produced 'in vast sections of our people' a 'servility of mind not easy to remove'. The emergency was 'trying to assert the self-respect of the nation'.[243] To T. N. Kaul, India's Ambassador in the United States, the 'economic revolution taking place in India' was 'no less important than the revolution of independence'.[244] To G. V. Shukla, press counsellor at the Indian High Commission in London, emergency India remained 'as always very much an open society'.[245] And to Vishnu Sharma of the Indian Workers' Association, the emergency had 'saved us from an extreme fascist situation'.[246]

As for the legacy of empire and independence, of paternalism and special interest, it spoke for itself and in its own accents. To the British High Commissioner in India, 'obviously enormous advantages have flowed from the emergency, though one does not agree with all its aspects', while 'the BBC and the British press indulge in a lot of anti-Indian propaganda'.[247] Edmund Dell MP was 'glad to hear the excellent economic news about India and [of] its negative rate of inflation';[248] to Eldon Griffiths MP, 'India desperately needed the smack [sic] of firm government'.[249] To Jennie Lee, Baroness Asheridge ('she has shown remarkable perception and understanding of India's problems'),

---

* cf. 'When events were taking place in Bangladesh, I was not afraid, because I knew I had not done anything wrong. I also know I have established this country on a strong footing.'[239] For other versions of uneasy anticipation e.g. 'the jump to dictatorship [may be] accomplished by a threatened practitioner of parliamentary forms, through a quasi-constitutional and para-military *coup d'état*. Sheik Mujib leapt first, and his quick fate suggests that the ending remains the same. Mrs Gandhi . . . has just jumped.'[240] Or 'it is only a matter of time before Mrs Gandhi, or the gang led by her son are called to account. The price in blood could be heavy.'[241]

emergency India was 'fighting for its own form of socialism'. 'Socialists in Britain', she said, were 'looking to Indian [Congress] Socialists for inspiration'.[250] Moreover – speaking in emergency India – 'the consolidation of freedom and the democratic form of government' had been 'a success' and India was 'on the threshold of a second revolution'.[251] To Michael Foot MP, the allegation that Mrs Gandhi 'wanted to be a dictator' was 'a monstrous lie'; to Julius Silverman MP, Mrs Gandhi was 'a passionate believer in democratic principles';[252] to Margaret Thatcher MP, India had 'met with considerable success in tackling problems like world recession and inflation';[253] to William Whitelaw MP, 'the Indian people since the declaration of emergency' had 'shown a new sense of awareness';[254] to Canon Kenyon Wright of Coventry Cathedral, the emergency had 'done tremendous good to the Indian people'.[255]

There was a receding echo in these voices also, lost in the miseries of millions; where other suppressed voices spoke not of the India which was 'only mildly authoritarian',[256] nor of 'the world' 'being taught what democracy really is by Indira Gandhi',[257] but instead of 'the demagogy which is the art of playing on the hopes and the fears, the emotions and the ignorance, of the poor and exploited'.[258] These voices spoke of 'the régime throwing a few crumbs to the people'. They spoke of the 'bourgeois parties not only divided, but their intensified fight leading them to an unprecedented crisis involving the mass of the people'.[259] They spoke too of the 'authoritarian régime with its "socialism" and brazen capitalist system, long-term promises alternating with proclamations to serve the contingencies of the moment, of high moral adjurations with wretched platitudes, the promise of support to the poor and the exploited combined with open intimacy with the big exploiters, and the service of their interests'.[260] Or they said, idly, that 'she cannot turn back now. There will be no way back for this lady; this is bad politics, a very big mistake. This lady will suffer in the end, her sons also';[261] or, that 'indispensability and democracy cannot go hand in hand – no one is indispensable to us';[262] or, that the 'political culture and sensibility of the Nehru era' had 'come to a decisive termination'.[263] They spoke also of the 'common man's support for Indira Gandhi for saving the country';[264] or said 'there will be a revolution in the end. The people will fight for their freedom again. This they will do. It is their duty.'[265]

They asked, 'what do these leftists have in their heads? Nothing. Now their time is nearly finished. When Sanjay comes, they will be eliminated';[266] or said that 'Indian revolutionaries are facing an enemy many times more formidable and sophisticated than the Chiang Kai-shek régime in China';[267] or that 'the situation in India cannot be separated from the political crisis facing the whole of south Asia'.[268] They argued that the régime was 'very vulnerable, resting on insecure social foundations';[269] or that it was 'armed and well-equipped, with nuclear weapons, a satellite communications network and a developed transport system, a million-strong disciplined army, and the million-strong para-military forces';[270] or they said 'you cannot get away with murder, and remain in power'.[271]

And for India's ruling class 'socialism' – emergency, or no emergency – there was its own classical dilemma, beyond solution: its path had first to be cleared of socialist organization. Moreover, the people's capacity to defend themselves had also to be disabled. For it was only then that the people's condition could be taken in hand by class power, while vain efforts were stepped up to 'counter hostile anti-Indian propaganda'.* Elsewhere on the journey, the CPI, similarly plagued, and travelling its parallel and isolated path with its disconsolate outriders,

_____

*Thus, 'Western publicity media have tried to weaken and denigrate the country and our institutions through slander and misrepresentations. Appropriate and effective action to speedily counter this propaganda and to project a correct picture of India in foreign countries continues to be taken by the government and by our missions abroad through interviews, speaking engagements, letters and articles for publication and briefings to suitable persons.'[272] This served (inadequately) to internationalize assiduous deceit about India's political condition. It carried the Home Ministers responsible for the repression and violence to New York and London, took the Indian High Commissioner in Britain to New York and Texas, and brought letters of unashamed dishonesty from Indian press counsellors into recalcitrant newspaper offices. It also exerted pressures – sometimes crude – on editors and journalists outside as well as inside India, while conversely giving widespread publicity in the censored Indian press ('UK leaders appreciate India's great efforts', *Amrita Bazar Patrika*, 26 March 1976) to favourable foreign comment – however trivial – on India.

had beckoned the CPI–M to join them upon it, to join the 'mainstream of the patriotic forces' and 'return to its parent party',[273] accusing it of 'having done a great disservice to the country and to the communist movement'.[274]

In fact, two members of the CPI–M's politbureau – Basavapunnaiah and Namboodiripad – had briefly detached themselves from their own ranks, in an instructive encounter early in May 1976, to canter alongside the column advancing towards Congress socialism, in order to 'explore the possibility of united action with the CPI on one or the other class and mass issues affecting the life of the common people'.[275] Nothing had come of it except recrimination, each continuing to discover disarray and declining membership in the other. The CPI – 'ruling out the possibility of a merger'[276] – had accused the CPI–M of being 'upset by the growing unity of the patriotic and progressive forces', and of 'continuing in the company of counter-revolution'.[277] The CPI–M, in return, disclaimed any intention of 'imposing any such separation between the right CP and the ruling Congress Party, a wedlock forged after years of stupendous effort'.[278] The CPI–M had then clarified its clouded position: distinguishing between an impossible 'united front' with the CPI and tactical 'united actions' to ward off – in particular – the deepening assault on the trade union and working class movement. On the one hand, there could not be 'a united front with the right-CP, so long as they do not give up their class-collaborationist line and their policy of close alliance with the Congress Party'. On the other, 'united actions on specific issues' – such as the deteriorating economic condition of the people, or the political attack on the labour movement – were possible with 'all mass organizations whichever political party leads them'.*

Later, as political attacks on the liberties of the individual, the Constitution, and the socialist and labour movements deepened, and in conclave early in August 1976 in Calcutta, the CPI–M – with numbers of its members and middle-rank cadres imprisoned – had demanded the lifting of the emergency and

---

*But the CPI–M had 'barred a political front with right parties'; and had 'upheld the supremacy of the people'.[279]

the holding of elections. It had also condemned the amendments to the Constitution; decided 'not to set up an underground centre', and chosen instead to 'mobilize the masses in a long-drawn-out process'.* [280] The politicians of the ruling-class and their para-military cohorts were in the meantime able to advance towards their own socialism against this opposition; against the banned CPI–ML,† decimated, its fractions 'in discussions with the CPI–M' and 'regrouping';[284] against the Socialist Party, its detained members and leaders unreleased, or produced manacled for trial and sentence; against the continuing political resistance of the CITU in the labour movement;[285] against jail-breaks, strikes, sabotage and counter-violence.

And at the point and counter-point of production and of industrial labour, were to be heard other and familiar voices. 'The influence of the CITU in India is being gradually eliminated by the Youth Congress.'[286] 'Ninety per cent of the working-class is opposed to the emergency, but they are waiting. And if they strike, what can the government do? Jail everybody? They can do nothing.'[287] 'My brother is a trade union official. He used to be a proud man. Now he has become like a dog with his terror. I am ashamed to see him.'[288] 'This thing can be maintained only by fear, by bribes, by violence. This thing they can do. But they cannot defeat the working class, they cannot end their struggles.'[289]

On this road to socialism, the economic landmarks denoted earlier continued to make their appearance to the emergency's last moments. There were lockouts, closures, retrenchments; strikes, and strikes banned, in some cases for six months from the date of the banning order;[209] rising prices, for example of food

---

*Similarly, on 9 April 1976, five members of the CPI–M's politbureau – Jyoti Basu, Namboodiripad, Gopalan, Ramamurthy and Surjit – submitted a fourteen-page memorandum to the Prime Minister, calling for the 'normalization of the situation, the restoration of democratic rights, and the withdrawal of MISA'.[281]

† cf. 'The future is a more frightening increase in the appeal of the CPI–ML in certain parts of the country';[282] and 'protest by landless labour against their conditions of existence is being treated by landlords and the state as if it were extremist violence, and dealt with on an annihilatory basis'.[283]

grains, edible oils, sugar and cotton, and officially 'inexplicable' or 'disturbing';[291] and as indices of recession, increases in money supply but not in investment.* With them came the continuous 'economic optimism' of official apologia and concealment,[293] together with Reserve Bank of India reports which revealed the nature of India's economic stagnation.† There was a continuing inflow of aid and loan resources; further relaxation in the payment of dividends ('to a hearty chorus of approval by various stock exchanges and industrial organizations')[295] and the further 'liberalization of imports'. There was the continuation of compulsory wage deposits, and of the freezing of 'dearness allowances'.[296] And with these, false official announcement whether of the 'cessation of food-grain imports'[297] or of acreage distributed by land reform; while increasing American investment, according to US ambassador Saxbe, was 'serving notice' that 'we are coming back to India strongly'.[298]

Outside India there was condemnation, credulity, support, lack of interest, confusion or silence – a familiar range of response to another polity plunged deep into coercion, fear and violence. They accompanied the procession and the passing shadows. So also did calls for the release of the imprisoned, calls for an international boycott, for the restoration of civil liberties, for the repeal of repressive legislation. For some in Britain, nurtured on a colonial diet of belief in India's residual Anglophilia, non-violent neutrality, democracy and organizational ineptitude, it took more time to catch up with what had happened. For others again, the communist party – or sympathy with it – enforced its own differently compelled ambiguity or silence, in solidarity with the CPI's dilemma or with the Soviet Union.

But there was international protest at torture; marches to Indian embassies and political rallies; campaigns and confer-

---

*cf. 'The throwaway concessions given to industrial tycoons and business sharks in the hope of wooing them have yielded no results in terms of step-up in investment.'[292]

†e.g. The RBI report published in August 1976, showed that between 1960 and 1975, there were six good years, three years of marginal improvement, and six years of decline in output; 'in the last twelve years, productivity has gone up at a low rate of only 1·4 per cent per annum'.[294]

ences for the 'restoration of democracy' or 'civil liberties' in
India, for the 'release of political prisoners', and the 'halting of
prison killings and tortures'.[299] Representatives of Indian diplomatic missions held bland or disorderly counter-meetings, and
itinerated the host nation, 'projecting a correct picture of India'
and denouncing their critics.* The opponent Indian exile was
harassed and threatened, had his passport removed, or was
placed under Indian police surveillance.[300] India in turn was
placed in the same category of nations with Iran and Brazil,
Indonesia or Chile, for their widespread use of torture, the
form of their 'stability', and the pattern of their 'modernization'.[301]

In India, it was precisely Iran, Japan, Hong Kong, Singapore
and South Korea which were variously invoked by political and
industrial power as exemplars for India's socialist progress. The
last three had succeeded in attracting foreign investment, and
were an example to India. The Shah of Iran was, for instance,
celebrated by 'India's Greatest Weekly: *Blitz*' (its editor, R. K.
Karanjia, the most sycophantic of all the apologists for the
junta) as a 'monarch who has transformed his country's trauma
into a white revolution'. 'So why', asked Karanjia, 'can she not
ditto his achievement?'[302] The Prime Minister on 10 May 1976
spoke of the 'contemporaneity' of the Indian and Iranian situa-
tions; the Iranian Prime Minister, visiting India, not surprisingly
'felt as if he was in his own country'.†[303] Japan also was a new
ideological model. It was held up as an example to India for its
participation in industrial consortia at work in third countries;[305]
while its agriculture suggested, to ruling class advocates of a swift
and selective land reform, the quick distribution of 'small plots'

* Spokesmen for the overseas Congress Party, acting under cover of
Indian missions – as in Britain – did the same. But the strength of local
Indian community opposition to the emergency – as in Birmingham –
often prevented such meetings, or met them in turn with violence, or the
threat of violence.

† Iranian students in India hostile to their own government, and to the
increasingly frequent visits to India of its political, commercial, military
and para-military envoys, were singled out – at the request of Iran's Delhi
Embassy – and deported. Thus, on 8 April 1976, a deportation order was
issued by the Punjab police against Mansoor Najefi Shustari, an Iranian
student at Punjab Agricultural University in Ludhiana. The occasion of it
was the forthcoming visit, on 10 May 1976, of the Iranian Prime Minister.

of land in order to forestall agrarian rebellions.[306] Or it was elsewhere invoked for its 'review of judges' performance by the
people';[307] or for 'hard labour and effort' and 'without the assistance of other countries';[308] or 'for translating its religious herit-
age into techniques of management'; or for 'devotion to duty,
loyalty to the institution, and dedication to the country', and for
'working hand in hand with government'.[309]

But whatever the model, the Indian emergency was a specific
political expression of economic dependency, 'under-development' and hegemonic crisis. It pointed, both when it was at its
most brutally coherent and when it was apparently 'muddling
through with a series of *ad hoc* measures',[310] to the latency –
with or without an emergency – of a specific national socialism
of 'under-development', which is not confined to India. Rooted
in the fear of insurrection, grounded in violence and the miseries
of the people, it was propelled in India by a profound economic
and political crisis in the interests of arguably the most developed
bourgeoisie of an 'under-developed' nation. Such a solution
characteristically seeks, above all, the forced growth – macabre
in relation to the poverty of the rural millions lost in the wilderness of India – of its capitalist industrial sector, at whatever
cost in life, right, or the dignity of labour. And during its emergency phase it sought it by concentration of class-power, compulsion, assault on the labour movement and the rights of the
people, and the Stakhanovite emulation of capitalist models of
economic coercion.

Provoked by political disorder and fearing invasion of its
interest by populist, democratic or violent opposition, class-

---

On 15 April, the Iranian Embassy was taken over in protest, and fifty-six
Iranian students arrested. On 21 April, after a second demonstration, there
were 117 arrests; 94 were detained. Reports from inside Delhi jail alleged
that brutal beating followed. On 22 April, a twenty-four-hour hunger strike
began; on 23 and 27 April police and convict warders attacked the
Iranian detainees, on the first occasion 'directed by an Iranian secret police
officer with his face covered'. On the second, they were attacked with 'tear-
gas and clubs, causing serious injuries from tear-gas shells, and fractures'.
Forty-two Delhi University and JNU professors had earlier protested to the
Prime Minister about the deportation order against Shustari, expressing
'anxiety that this country should maintain its traditions of protecting the
legitimate interests of foreign nationals in India'.[304]

faction – steeped in the corruptions of three decades of power – was awakened from its lethargy and irresolution to attempt the abrupt completion of that 'unfinished revolution' which was the legacy of the freedom struggle and independence. This is turn demanded, as prerequisite, a Caesarist attack by one faction of the threatened ruling class and its leaders upon its faction rivals. By so doing it sought in vain to consolidate once and for all irreconcilable class interests – those of the oligarchies of domestic landlord reaction and modernizing industrial power – by increased violence, the elimination of opposition and radical ('socialist') political reconstruction.

In the attempt, it directed attention to the main features of the development process – or 'development discipline'[311] – of a Brazil or a Uruguay. Such a process demands that an increasing proportion of the national budget be spent on law and order; it demands the invasion of foreign interest, its uncertain appetite for further investment and involvement in India whetted only with the greatest exertion. It demands a 'coherent and sustained new economic policy', in which its functionaries of state gain 'new and valuable experience in managing the economy of the nation'[312] and a cruel sophistication in the service of power. It demands the prohibition of strikes and protests, intimidation through brutality and detention, and a mass clean-up operation of the political, legal and labour systems.*

What has been passing before us, therefore, is the 'socialism' of capital; the 'socialism' of a 'new order'. The head of the column was first glimpsed approaching in India – as we saw – before independence, and in other former colonialized countries also, such as Burma or China, where nationalism, 'socialism' and fascism converged during the 1930s into confused expressions of the political struggles of the exploited to free themselves from foreign domination. We have seen the Indian column, flanked by the para-military forces, carrying the white ensigns

---

*cf. 'What they are eventually all resolute about is keeping the masses down; keeping wages low enough to provide adequate incentives for entrepreneurs; accumulating capital at the expense of depriving the people of their rights. From this may come a step forward in industrialization, with a decline in real wages, and backward agricultural regions remaining poverty-stricken.'[313]

of Iran, the tattered pennants of the Kuomintang, and finance capital's standards; its escorts, the faded red flag of the Soviet Union. We have seen a motley procession, led by a small vanguard of the bourgeoisie and the landlords, and followed by the hopes and despairs of hundreds of millions. And beyond the next (or the next) barrage of political and economic crisis, the army lies waiting in ambush; and the people.

For the spectral shapes of India's miseries haunt the mind's eye, and make a nonsense of all fine calculation falling short of revolution. And while economic and political power remains in the hands of privilege, faction, and corruption, even the most oppressive and tyrannical régime in the history of India could not meet the minimum needs of the people, with or without a 20-point, or 25-point, programme. It is impossible for agriculture to be revolutionized by presidential ordinance, or the people's energies released from their thraldom of misery, defeated toil, debt and violence, without the expropriation of the landlord and the ending of the money-lender's rural dominion. It is not the 'surplus' but the land itself – the primary means of production – which must be, and will be, distributed to the people of India.

It is impossible for the people to produce a surplus for their own well-being, when they are looted by the parasite and the oppressor. It is impossible for the nation to advance along the road to 'self-reliance' (to say nothing of the road to socialism) without the transformation of those social and economic relations which consign the millions of India to a deprivation and beggary devastated by suffering and sorrow.

Instead, on 17 January 1977 (with an 'uncanny sense of timing'),[314] came the announcement of a March election, 'electrifying India'.[315] It would provide, according to the Prime Minister, 'an opportunity to cleanse public life of confusion';[316] that is, under the pressure of deepening internal party hatreds and divisions, and the emergency's political and economic failure, an opportunity to purge party dissentients and silence critics, by appealing over their heads to the Indian people. 'It is the people who are the masters', she added;[317] funds and votes, it was expected, would be gathered in time-honoured fashion. To help achieve this, it would be conducted in the dark shadows of emergency, of sweeping preventive detention regulations, and of a Constitution comprehensively amended – as we have seen – to provide near-absolute executive powers.

In addition, to fight this election sixty days and less was to be given to political detainees who were being freed after up to twenty months in preventive detention. As the prison-gates opened, they were generally held to be 'disorganized, demoralized and divided';[318] among the first releases were Morarji Desai ('We will have a thumping majority'),[319] Mohan Dharia and Chandra Shekhar. In this amnesty, 'detainees belonging to banned political parties would remain in prison'; 'in certain cases, leaders of recognized political parties', such as George Fernandes, 'would also be kept in detention'.[320] As for those released, 'their attitude', said Bansi Lal, in the familiar accents of the Congress Party's restored democratic practice, 'will be watched, and if they try to repeat their past activities' – or 'go back to their old games' – 'the same steps will have to be initiated against them once again'.*[321] Or, as Barooah had said on 19 November 1976, 'the country can do without the opposition. They are irrelevant to the history of India.'[323]

'It will be suicidal', said George Fernandes, speaking of a 'sham', calling for a boycott, and writing from prison, 'for the opposition parties to oblige Mrs Gandhi, by participating in the kind of election she is planning.'[324] But for the legitimation of precarious faction-power, seeking its political vindication, and a renewal of its 'mandate', 'parliamentary government', said Mrs Gandhi, 'must report back to the people and seek sanction from them to carry out programmes and policies for the strength and welfare of the nation'.[325]

Instead, a débâcle. There was no boycott. Both the Socialist Party and the CPI–M took part in the election. The accumulated anger of the people overrode the obstacles of fear and coercion. The election proved suicidal not to the opposition but

*Similarly, the 'press censorship regulations' would be 'lifted' for the occasion, but not the Press Censorship Act, in which these regulations had been embodied. Moreover, 'nothing was to be published', said V. C. Shukla, 'which might undermine the aims of the emergency'; and 'nothing which lowered the standards of public life'.[322]

to the ruling faction, the reaping of a whirlwind. As polling day – from 16 to 20 March 1977 – approached, it was assailed by new internal rivalries unleashed by the election, and brought to the verge of disintegration by Jagjivan Ram's sudden defection from the junta. The CPI, shifting its position on the horns of its own political dilemma, publicly switched its allegiance from Mrs Gandhi to Jagjivan Ram, and from one Congress faction to another, while making electoral deals designed in vain to sustain Mrs Gandhi in office. Neither she nor her son were even elected to the Lok Sabha. They fell, apologizing.

With them, Bansi Lal, Gokhale, Swaran Singh, Mukherjee, and V. C. Shukla, among many others, who days before were bestriding the crown of the Indian road to 'socialism' also fell by the wayside. They were overtaken on right and left by the opposition alliance, the Janata Party, composed of Morarji Desai's Congress faction, the Jan Sangh, the BLD, and Socialist Party, holding together in unwonted solidarity – united by Mrs Gandhi – to defeat the ruling junta. It was the electoral Waterloo which had been postponed by the emergency's declaration; on 21 March 1977, its strategies defeated, the emergency was ended. Political prisoners were transmuted into Cabinet Ministers. But the protagonists of the election – Morarji Desai, chosen to head the new administration, Jagjivan Ram, and Mrs Gandhi – had, once again, been the leaders of (three) opposed Congress factions; fallen government and victorious coalition alike led by Congress rivals.

As the Gandhi administration departed, one acrobat's volte-face succeeded another. Accomplices who had previously bowed the knee to power, and helped (eyes averted) to hold it up in position while it committed its excesses against the people of India, now rose – the better to see where the next main chance might be discovered – fearlessly to disclaim responsibility and implication. Jubilation drowned the emergency's reverberating echo; while others began to slip away stealthily, in silence, or to leap nimbly from one bandwagon to another, as the column following India's fallen leaders halted.

In the emergency dissenting voices had been heard, which leave their own echoes. 'There are thousands in detention', they said, 'and the sufferings and poverty of the people are greater than under the British, or at any time in the history of India. Now it is the Indian oppressors whom the Indian people fight, for the freedom of India.' And in a dingy room, mosquitoes whining, bald head catching the dim bulb-light, in a white linen *dhoti* and sandals, the political leaders asked, 'if tens of millions of the people of India are living in hunger, starving, ridden with diseases, without land, without employment, without shelter, which kind of people will say that the world's biggest democracy is in India?' 'I like to read Marx and Gorki', the teacher said, also. 'But reading for my education was not necessary. From poverty when I was a child, I had malnutrition; and from this, I learned without books about politics and economics in India.' The outriders were out of earshot, though he spoke in a whisper. 'One day there will be revolution, I tell you, the same as in China. Who will be able to stop such a thing in India? Supreme Court? Lok Sabha? Police? Army?'

Not only questions were left behind, as the column's swaying baggage-train of attendants passed, following emergency power on its progress towards a 'socialist' India. 'Every dog has his day in India', said one answer, 'this pack also. When they are gone, no one will mourn them.' 'Keep it up, Stolypin and Co! You are doing good work for us', said another.[326] And by its measures of repression, the Indian polity had declared itself again to the millions in India who already understood it; had clarified understanding of its own nature and of the forces which command and defend its interest. It had declared once again not the emergency of the people, but the emergency of power. In capital's renewed reign of promise and terror, and in landlordism's age-old inertia and violence, were demonstrated in turn the nature of the resistance and the scale of the onslaught required to oppose them.

But the lives of tens of millions lie far beyond the horizons of a bird's-eye view such as this one, or of a vicarious battle fought with words and thoughts from a safe distance; hard and cruel, steeped in resignation and silence, or fierce with hatred and anger, they also lie beyond reach of every declaration of emergency and every 20-point programme.

9 An Eye to India: Last Sequence

The construction-boss (with a speculative turn of mind), legs crossed, with his whisky, and sitting in a warm light, says 'Beggars we don't like. They do not take pains to earn a living.'

Knees, wrists and ankles – bodies bent in three – wrenched, dislocated and shrivelled, are set down upon the pavement. There are varieties of beggary and beggar. In the appartments' long shadows, an extended arm is a pillow.

Sipping, he sits deep in his sofa. Some have had their legs broken and twisted, bent behind them, disarticulated; to move, hopping on their hands, buttocks scraping the ground, rags trailing.

The soda siphon hisses, the servant closing the french windows softly behind him. The philosophical speculator is deep in thought, brow furrowed. His lady-wife joins him, perfumed and charming; hands folded in her lap in repose; a graceful and erect posture, and proud posing.

... the poor haunted girl-child stands before you, blood streaking her ragged skirt, turning and staring, pointing beyond the last circle to a crucifixion, or Golgotha ...

She says, arranging the folds of her sari, 'It is pointless to feel pity'; the speculator pensive. He says, breaking his own silence, and with a Roman stoicism, 'We must have courage to wash them away completely.'

There will be a day of reckoning for this; a balancing of the books and a new equation, though they rise now, the speculator and his brahminical lady, parcels rustling, through twenty floors or more; up, in a swift high-rising acceleration, soaring high over the lolling heads and stumping beggars, and the clotted runnels of the teeming city; and braking softly – doors hissing open, and closing quickly – to a smooth touchdown, and a marble landing.

From their flowered and fragrant roof garden, sanctuary from the stench and exhalation of an Avernus, is a clear vista of the huge ground-swell of the city; from this perspective, the black chimneys of labour stand between fragile penthouse statuary, white as alabaster; flags flying and smoke rising as from a vast battlefield; from such an elevation, the foreshortening of the oceanic struggle of the classes; and a bird's-eye view of the horizon.

The construction-boss, speculating at his parapet, shades his eyes also, as if taking the salute at a troop review and a march-past; or counting the enemy's divisions in millions.

*

They are bringing in the harvest. The paunched landlord is sweating, watching the labour. Huge cart-wheels are large as mill-stones.

To buy food, poor Minu took a loan of five hundred rupees from landlord and money-lender Kundilal of Satta village, and for the last seventeen years has been in bonded labour.

The tethered black beast-of-burden stands nose-tied (led by the nose), mind blanked and head lowered; a man crouching against a wall, waiting for time's passing.

... the debtor agreeing to labour in the creditor's fields in lieu of interest ... and being unable to pay the principal, his sons and sons' sons shall be bonded, until the loan's repayment.

A dense midday silence, as if nothing doing; containing an order which must be found; the fly-whisk flick of a tail, the flicker of an eye-lid; field-hands as if unmoving.

Piled dry stooks; and a hoopoe (*Upupa epops*) standing in the stubble; the ground rutted. Cow-pats drying, with a *suttee's* hand-prints; the cow sitting heavy, front legs bent and fold.

Flailing and beating, sound stifled; the air dust-laden. By the threshing-ground, wheat-from-chaff; winnowed, breeze taken. And a stone-poor gleaning. Men, women and children (in millions) stooping and picking; field hands, landless; or crouching, not speaking, doing nothing (in millions), elbows resting on knees, and fingers plaited.

Squatting and riffling through hair, de-lousing; crouching one behind the other. In eyes hatred, or glances averted. Slender bodies working, shrouded; and in white weeds, widows. In the eyes of the landlord, squat and heavy, the look of the Lord Yama, death's anger.

Arms raised above the head, the riddle tilted and shaken, the saris stirring; arms rising; the crooked arm straightened; arms risen, an exaltation; the chaff blowing.

Feet padding the road; women walking, heads loaded, trudging to the village, or feet flat-planted and proud of this walking; men driving the ox-carts home, in slow motion.

They are bringing in the harvest.

There is a silence as of something pending; as at a hanging; or before an act of violence.

*

The sun is setting; blazing.

Pedals and wheels are turning, spinning; revolving in the roar and trampling clamour at the day's ending; the grinding crunch of gears changing; smashed and broken buses, chassis and superstructure in grating separation, are near keeling over, or overturning.

In stagnant filth by the black sewer (matting and thatch turned sodden and rotting) are gleaming bodies, babies' bellies and navels; dipping hands cupped, scooping and swilling, hair streaming at stand-taps; tipped buckets of running water, dripping and spilling; in trampled mire, children's wet spines, ridged and bending over, naked and shining ('it is life', says the sage, 'which shines in all beings; than he who knows this there is none wiser'); in satanic squalor, washing, pails clanking; in disarray, order; in nakedness, power; and in a miasma, scrubbing.

The sky is on fire, enflaming the city.

Beside the heaps of smoking blown refuse are faces ravaged, hooded by filth, the waste-ground pitted. Where the ground shows bare, turning to broken stone and lengthening shadow, look closer!

A woman in a fiery red sari stoops to her washing and pounding; straightening in the swirl of smoke, the folds of her sari drawn to the shape of a Fury, hands dripping; or bloody.

The day is dying, quickly.

The limping body and unkempt hair (the light of self, *ātman*, near-extinguished) of an old abandoned woman, passes.

The blind beggar sings – *Inquilab Zindabad*! – two metal rods clashed together; a nasal singing, an old mouth; O, puckered. Children born between the legs of the crowd, at the kerb's edge, are crawling into the gutter.

The sky is a dusty darkening violet; the sandal-tree has lost its fragrance, the touchstone its magic. Here are only pot-holes and rubble. Rags are cross-hatched and tattered.

The light is ebbing; failing.

Above a tangle of greying greenery and a rubbishy garden, the fading Victorian lady leans against stucco on an abandoned balcony, arm raised (wrist broken and fingers missing), pointing in a long-lost direction.

Stockaded shacks are of wood, straw and rag; staked fences, cloven; rags upon a bed-trestle, and an awning; hangings; light shining through sacking and wicker.

Night is falling. The harvest moon rains fire; strange this fate, says Vidyāpati.

Smoke spirals from the burning *ghat*'s funeral pyres, over the tumble of a battered commerce, a Sodom and Gomorrah. Night has fallen on hell-fires, or a Valhalla (come Siva, destroyer, arm the people!); on shadows sitting up under sack-cloth, small fires burning, flames licking the darkness; on stretched-out bodies, cinder and ashes.

On sacking, are little grey bundles in hemp, grey on black; small mounds, without adults; arms, legs and sleepy heads in the unlit side-streets; curled up in a foetal slumber, infant hands raised in dense shadow; children sleeping, unnoticed.

The last stalls and street-altars are taper-lit; before them a cross-legged sitting, silhouetted, in the flickering darkness; or heads in hands, night-blackened, waiting.

Appendix: Select Documents

From Members of Parliament to the Speaker of the Lok Sabha,
21 June 1975

New Delhi
June 21, 1975

To the Hon'ble Speaker,
   Lok Sabha,
   New Delhi.

Sir,

We are perturbed that summons for the Monsoon Session of
Parliament this year have not been received so far. It has been
the practice in the past to have the Monsoon Session from the
middle of July and to send the summons by the first week of
June. It is pertinent to invite your kind attention to a decision
taken by the General Purposes Committee of Lok Sabha at
their sitting held on April 22, 1955 and their following recommendation on the time-table of the three sessions of the Lok
Sabha to be held every year:

(1)	(2)	(3)
Session	*Date of commencement*	*Date of termination*
Budget	February 1	May 7
Monsoon	July 15	September 15
Winter	November 5 or four days after Deepavali whichever is later	December 22

The Cabinet also agreed with these recommendations and

as far as possible the sessions are held round about these dates every year.

We are afraid that this time-honoured practice accepted by the Cabinet and implemented hitherto appears to be in danger of being given a go-by.

We are aware that as the constitutional head, the President has to summon the Houses of Parliament to meet. It is also clear that the Constitution only stipulates that a period of six months will not elapse between the concluding day of one session and the first day of the next. But parliamentary democracy functions and flourishes not only on the letter of the Constitution but also on the practices and the conventions evolved. Although the Constitution only lays down that at least two sessions will be held in a year, it was the practice to hold three sessions. When there was a lame-duck session after the elections, we had one more session. This practice, we are afraid, is sought to be given up to meet the convenience of the Prime Minister. There has been a demand, rightly so, that the House should meet earlier than usual to discuss the implications of the judgement given by the Allahabad High Court. Instead of advancing the usual date, there has been a deliberate delay. The tendency to dishonour the practice will, it is apprehended, embolden the executive to override the conventions and subvert the Constitution itself. The appeal preferred by the Prime Minister to the Supreme Court does not affect the issues of morality and propriety raised by the judgement of the High Court. The decision of the Supreme Court in the stay petition is not relevant to these issues. It is inconceivable by any standard of parliamentary democracy that a person who has been held guilty of corrupt practices should continue as Prime Minister. She has every right to appeal to the highest court of the land and obtain its decision. But till the proved charges have not been set aside and she is not absolved of all corrupt practices as proved in the High Court, propriety, rectitude and convention require that she steps down from her office immediately.

As custodian of the rights and privileges of the House and as one who is specially responsible for the proper working of the parliamentary democracy in this country, you, more than anybody else, must be concerned. At this time of crisis, when democratic conventions are being flouted and parliamentary traditions scuttled, and autocracy is being enthroned in the place of democracy with the strange plea that a particular individual is indispensable to our country, we look to you to uphold the traditions of democracy. We are not here to suggest who should be the leader of the party which enjoys a majority in the House. It is the internal affair of that party. But we are of the firm opinion that with such a judgement from a High Court, Mrs Indira Gandhi has lost the moral authority to continue in the office of the Prime Minister. If she wins her appeal in the Supreme Court and if her party so desires she may return to power later. The said order does not absolve nor does it negative the judgement of the High Court. We do not want that the Prime Minister should oblige the opposition, but we feel that she should fulfil her obligations towards parliamentary democracy.

We, therefore, request you to impress upon the President and Mrs Indira Gandhi the need to observe the well-established conventions and practices of democracy.

> Yours sincerely,
> *S. N. Mishra**
> *Era Sezhiyan*
> *Jaganatharao Joshi†*
> *Madhu Limaye‡*
> *V. R. Scindia*
> *Jyothirmoy Bosu§*
> *Samar Guha***
> *Erasmo de Sequeira*

*Arrested 27 June 1975.
†Arrested shortly after declaration of emergency.
‡Arrested 26 June 1975.
§Arrested 9 July 1975.
**Arrested shortly after declaration of emergency.

Guidelines for the Press in the Present Emergency, Press Information Bureau, Government of India, 26 June 1975

NOT TO BE PUBLISHED

Declaration of national emergency to meet the threat to the security and stability of India by internal disturbance will point to the need for extreme caution and circumspection in the handling and surveying of news and comments. The press requires to be advised to guard against publication of unauthorized, irresponsible or demoralizing news items, conjectures, and rumours, and yet the press should be enabled to fulfil its obligation to the public. One of the most powerful aids to the government and the people in an emergency is the press. In the manner in which information is printed, published, or disseminated there can be an accretion of enormous strength to those who are posing a threat to internal security.

In an emergency declared to meet an internal threat, the concern of the government is mainly with the misguided and subversive elements within the country which by their acts may try to prejudice peace and stability of the nation. In a democratic country in which citizens are fully conscious of their duties and responsibilities to the nation, the aim of the government is not so much to rely in every case on the wide and extraordinary powers conferred on it, but as far as may be enlist the voluntary cooperation of all sections of the population, in maintaining an atmosphere conducive to the fulfilment of the primary task of ridding the nation of the causes of emergency.

General Guidance

1. Where news is plainly dangerous, newspapers will assist the Chief Press Adviser by suppressing it themselves. Where doubts exist, a reference may and should be made to the nearest Press Adviser.

2. Where matter has been submitted for examination before publication, the advice of the Press Adviser should be followed.

3. When guidance is being given advising against the publication of news or comments relating to a particular matter, no mention

of or reference to that matter should be made without obtaining fresh clearance, for moderation should always be observed and all sensationalism avoided. This should be observed particularly in illustration of posters and headlines.

4. No publicity to be given for rumours.

5. When any document or photograph is officially issued, care must be taken to retain the sense of the accompanying caption or description.

6. No reproduction of objectionable matter already published in any Indian or foreign newspaper.

7. No unauthorized news or advertisement or illustration to be published in regard to vital means of communication.

8. Nothing to be published about arrangements relating to the protection of transport or communications, supply and distribution of essential commodity, etc.

9. Nothing to be published which is likely to cause disaffection among the members of the armed forces or public servants.

10. Nothing to be published which is likely to bring into hatred or contempt, or to excite disaffection towards, the government established by law in India.

11. Nothing to be published which is likely to promote feeling of enmity and hatred between different classes of persons in India.

12. Nothing to be published which is likely to cause or produce or to instigate or incite, directly or indirectly, the cessation or slowing down of work in any place.

13. Nothing to be published which is likely to undermine the public confidence in the national credit or in any government loan.

14. Nothing to be published to encourage or incite any person, or class of persons, to refuse or defer payment of taxes.

15. Nothing to be published which is likely to instigate the use of criminal force against public servants.

16. A prejudicial report means any report, statement, or visible report, whether true or false, which, or the publication of which, is an incitement to the commission of any of the prejudicial acts mentioned above.

New Delhi, June 26, 1975.
RA/TML/T.no.556.

Guidelines on Pre-Censorship, Press Information Bureau, Government of India, 27 June 1975

NOT FOR PUBLICATION   IMMEDIATE

The following are further clarifications about the guidelines on pre-censorship:

1. Material which has no bearing on internal security or situation need not be submitted for pre-censorship. Thus reports about literary, scientific, cultural activities and other day-to-day developments having no bearing on the internal situation need not be submitted for pre-censorship. Similarly, positive development stories or official handouts about administrative decisions and policies are exempted from pre-censorship.

2. Since news agency messages emanating from Delhi are pre-censored they need not be re-submitted for censorship. The agency messages originating from your centres, however, will have to be pre-censored.

3. Developments in other countries as long as they do not refer to the internal situation in India need not be pre-censored. Reports of newspapers' comments or reactions from abroad relating to Indian situation have to be pre-censored.

New Delhi, June 27, 1975.
RS/BV/T.no.559.

The Twenty-Point Programme, 1 July 1975

1. Accelerated efforts to bring down price of essential commodities, increase production, speed up procurement and streamline distribution of essential commodities.

2. Implementation of agricultural land ceilings and quicker distribution of surplus land.

3. House-sites for landless and weaker sections.

4. Abolition of bonded labour.

5. Liquidation of rural indebtedness.

6. Revision of minimum wages for agricultural labour and their enhancement, wherever necessary.

7. Five million more hectares to be brought under irrigation.

8. Further generation of 2,600 megawatts of power.

9. Special help for handloom industry and protection to weavers.

10. Improvement in quality and supply of cloth for the common man.

11. Socialisation of urban and urbanisable land. Ceiling on ownership and on plinth area of new dwelling units.

12. Prevention of tax evasion, summary trials and deterrent punishment to economic offenders.

13. Special legislation for confiscation of smugglers' properties.

14. Liberalization of investment procedures and action against misuse of import licences.

15. New scheme for more effective participation of workers in industries.

16. Removal of constraints on the movement of goods by trucks – national permit system to be introduced.

17. No income tax up to an annual income of Rs. 8,000.

18. Supply of essential commodities at controlled prices to students in hostels.

19. Provision of textbooks and stationery for students at controlled prices – also book banks.

20. New apprenticeship schemes to enlarge employment and training, especially of weaker sections.

Revised Guidelines for the Coverage of Parliamentary Proceedings, Office of the Censor, Government of India, 20 July 1975

The following guidelines for the coverage of Parliament proceedings should be kept in view:

(a) The statements of Ministers may be published either in full or in a condensed form but its contents should not infringe censorship.

(b) The speeches of Members of Parliament participating in a debate will not be published in any manner or form but their names and party affiliation may be mentioned. When publishing names of Members who participated in a debate, the fact that they supported or opposed a motion can be mentioned.

(c) The results of voting on a Bill, Motion, Resolution, etc. may be factually reported. In the event of voting, the number of votes cast for and against may be mentioned.

Speech of Mohan Dharia* (Cong.-R) to Lok Sabha, 22 July 1975

Sir, the 26th day of June 1975, the day when the emergency was declared, when my colleagues, several political workers and leaders were barbarously put behind bars, when the freedom of the press and civil liberties were surrendered to the bureaucrats, that day will be treated as the blackest day in Indian democracy and in the history of our country.

I would at the outset like to condemn this monstrous operation. I have no doubt that it is the Prime Minister and a few of her colleagues who are responsible for it. I am not charging the whole Cabinet, because I know that even the Cabinet was told about it after the operation was already initiated. I am not charging the whole of them because even though they are not under house-arrest, all of the party is under mouth-arrest, including her Cabinet colleagues. Therefore, I am not charging them.

A systematic propaganda is being carried on that it is because of the opposition parties, it is because of the right reactionary forces, it is because of extremists, that the economic programme could not be implemented. Is it true?

I know things from close quarters. In 1969 in Bangalore, my amendment was supported by 170 members of the AICC, an amendment to nationalize the banks; it was not done. But no sooner was the political life of the Prime Minister at stake, then the banks were nationalized. The party welcomed it. The party did not split on programmes; the party split for personalities. But even then we welcomed it, because we felt that it would accelerate the whole process of the politics of commitment. Unfortunately it did not happen. After the massive mandate nobody prevented us from implementing that. It is we who faltered, and we are the fathers of the situation that is existing in the country today. Why are we forgetting that? So far as the economic programmes are concerned, it is being said that they are the programmes of the Prime Minister.

*Mohan Dharia, ex-Minister, was suspended from the ruling Congress Party; and arrested in December 1975, under the Maintenance of Internal Security Act.

I can understand the programmes of the party in power, the programmes of the government. But why are they creating the personality cult? It is also the way to develop dictatorship in the country. Let us not forget that.

Even then as an ardent admirer of economic programmes, I am here to welcome those programmes. I can assure this House that whatever may be my differences with the government, all my endeavours will be to see that those programmes are a success and that all possible cooperation is given to them. I should like to have that constructive approach. But let me be allowed to say that when I look at the 20-point programme, the basic decisions are not there. All these programmes could have been implemented without declaration of emergency. To say that an emergency was necessary is a blatant lie, if I may be allowed to use that word; no other word could be found for it.

Sir, June 12 was a bad day for the Congress Party. The rude shock came when Mrs Gandhi was unseated and disqualified to contest any elective post for six years by the Allahabad High Court. Though the judgement was unfavourable, it was perhaps the golden opportunity for Mrs Gandhi to establish her moral leadership along with the political leadership in the country. With a view to respect the judiciary by the highest executive personality, and to create ideal conventions for healthy democracy, a voluntary declaration by Mrs Gandhi to step down till the final ruling of the Supreme Court would have raised her prestige sky-high. Sir, I would therefore like to request the government to immediately withdraw the unwarranted emergency, to release the political leaders and workers, and to resume a national dialogue.

I appeal to the Prime Minister to please think of the democratic traditions that her father Shri Jawaharlal Nehru and other great leaders have taught to this country. I have no doubt that if she reconsiders, there are chances of getting the present situation rectified.

Sir, may I appeal to all sections that even today the time is not lost. I can understand taking action against hoarders, black-marketeers and anti-social elements. But so far as political leaders are concerned, please release them. Let us re-think about the emergency. Wherever it is necessary, I shall stand by it so far as the socio-economic transformation and the progress of the country is concerned. That is the way of dealing with it. A national dialogue is necessary. Through this you will evolve a national programme of action. Let us involve the millions of our people in its implementation. By these dictatorial methods, you may get some satisfaction of retaining this power in your hands, but it will not last long. The people are bound to rebel. My call to the millions of people of this country is this: Please be patriotic and express your resentment at these atrocious measures through peaceful, non-violent and legitimate means. My call should reach the people. I hope sanity will prevail and I hope the patriots among the Congressmen will see that our democracy and independence is not destroyed. I am grateful to you for giving me this opportunity.

From the speech of A. K. Gopalan* (CPI–M) to the Lok Sabha,
21 July 1975

I have heard the speech of Food Minister Shri Jagjivan Ram;
I am afraid that these are not the words of the Minister, as I
have seen him also sometimes looking at the Prime Minister ...
I know the reason why he was looking and I sympathize with
him.

I rise to speak in an extraordinary and most distressing situation in which thirty-four Members of Parliament are not here,
not on their own volition, but because they have been detained
without trial, and Parliament itself has been reduced to a farce
and an object of contempt by Smt. Gandhi and her party ...

On behalf of the CPI–M, I totally oppose the new declaration
of emergency and its ratification in this House. We know fully
well that in the present situation no one is immune from arrest
and detention. There are hundreds of persons inside the jails,
including Congressmen. [... Interruption]

There was a rumour – when I was inside the jail – that Shri
Jagjivan Ram and Shri Chavan were under house-arrest. I do
not know how far it is correct or not. Many leaders of opposition
as well as thirty-nine Members of Parliament, including some
Congress leaders, are inside the jail. We cannot betray the
interests of the people and give our assent to the obliteration of
all vestiges of democracy in India: freedom of the person, freedom of speech, freedom to form associations, freedom to approach the courts, freedom of the press, freedom to criticize the
government and work for its replacement by a government of
the people's choice ...

Every day constitutional changes are coming – every day,
every hour. One such suspension means that there is not even
equality before the law. Any discrimination can be practised by
the executive. Any person arrested need not be produced before
a court. The news of his arrest, whereabouts and condition can
be kept completely secret. He may be physically liquidated by

*Arrested and detained for a week on the declaration of emergency.

the police and nobody need know anything about it. That is the position today ...

The camouflage of the emergency being used only against right-reactionary parties, has been fully exposed by the indiscriminate arrests of the thousands of CPI-M and other left and democratic party leaders and workers. The police have been let loose on the people. In Kerala, for example, thousands of political workers belonging to the opposition parties including the CPI–M, the Kerala Congress, the Socialist Party and so on were arrested and large numbers brutally beaten ...

In the name of emergency the police and the CRP and other coercive agencies have been given such brutal power over the people that semi-fascist and autocratic rule has replaced the norms of civilized behaviour. I strongly condemn this attempt to create terror among the people and to let loose the police against them ...

The industrialists in the name of productivity can impose any workload and retrench workers, and any protest will be crushed. Wage cuts can be resorted to; and any resistance will be crushed. Working conditions can be worsened, and the least protest will be met by summary dismissal. No movements against this exploitation will be allowed. In the rural areas, too, agricultural workers fighting for better wages, tenants fighting against evictions, all will meet the same fate. No movements against this terrible exploitation will be allowed. That is why these measures virtually amount to a dictatorship of the bourgeois and landlords, against all other sections of the people ...

Who will believe that by suppressing the popular forces fighting against the monopolists and landlords, by suppressing their agitations and by denying them all democratic rights Smt. Gandhi is fighting right-reaction? ...

The CPI, the wretched traitors to the working class and the toiling people, continues to function as her majesty's loyal opposition. Our party considers it as its foremost task to awaken and organize the people against the grave peril they are facing. We appeal to all democratic forces and men of goodwill, all who cherish the right of the people to struggle for a better life to join with us in this struggle ... The interests of the people demand that the emergency be fought, and the broad-based united struggle against the exploiters be carried on with the strength of the people.

We will never surrender ourselves to the ruling classes, we will never betray the toiling people and democratic forces of our country. History will vindicate us. Thank you.

From the speech of Krishan Kant (Cong.-R) to the Rajya Sabha,
21 July 1975

... It is very difficult to associate my Congress colleagues
Chandra Shekhar and Ram Dhan with rightist conspiracy.
Chandra Shekhar has remained radical and leftist and a fighter
for the poor ... How can these two friends turn overnight right-
reactionary conspirators? I have always been a Congress socialist who believes that socialism in India has to be brought about
by the application of Gandhian principles ...

Nobody stopped the Congress Party from carrying out the
radical restructuring of the economy of the country and taking
measures to eradicate poverty. The rightists outside the Congress were too weak to stop us from carrying out the programme.
It is certain forces in the party which were too strong to allow
us to implement them. Today, unfortunately, it is not the obstructionist forces who have been arrested, but Chandra Shekhar
and Ram Dhan. Chandra Shekhar's leftism and nationalism is
too visible to be recounted here. Ram Dhan, a leader of the
weaker sections, has been fighting for the causes of the downtrodden and poor.

What prevented the Congress and the government to follow
up the bank nationalization and the election manifestoes of 1971
and 1972 with vigorous measures? Which opposition obstructed
the Prime Minister and the government in 1971, 1972, 1973 and
early months of 1974? Even though we had the biggest majority, yet we did not have the will to act and implement radical
measures. Besides passing some legislation on paper and making
some amendments to the Constitution, what else have we
done? ...

I would like to ask, who amongst the Congress leaders have
been punished for sabotaging the Congress programme during
the last few years? Only Krishan Kant, Chandra Shekhar,
Mohan Dharia, Ram Dhan. Their only crime known to the
people in the country was their total commitment to a continuous insistence upon implementing party programmes and
policies both in letter and spirit. If we agitated against malpractices and corruption, it was in the high tradition of the

Congress ... Today, who are the supporters and enthusiasts of the 20-point programme? Read the censored newspapers. The daily retinue to the Prime Minister's house will show that the saboteurs of the Congress economic programmes are now the enthusiastic supporters of the emergency. Those who have profited by inflation and sabotage of government policies have turned overnight into loud-mouthed supporters of the 20-point programme. Let me warn you against such time-servers who are supporting her programmes as the noose supports the persons to be hanged ...

Let us face the question, who are opposed to the 20-point programme? Most of these programmes had already formed the basis of our demands during the national struggle. Jawaharlal Nehru emphasized them, and one can read the Avadi Resolution, the Nagpur Resolution, and find all these points there. The non-implementation of these programmes was due to the vested interests in the Congress itself and I may warn you that not only at the end of emergency but even during the period of emergency, the same vested interests are going to sabotage these national programmes ...

Bereft of ideology, this nation is drifting towards a personality cult, into slogan shouting, gimmickry and into total immobilization. Cabinet colleagues have not been taken into confidence. Senior partymen who have spent their lifetime in the party are not with us today. The men dedicated to the values of Gandhi, Nehru and socialism have been put under arrest. In this situation, who is going to implement the 20-point programme? ...

*From the speech of N. G. Goray (SP) to the Rajya Sabha,
22 July 1975*

... It seems that all of you on that side have come to the conclusion that the best and the safest place for the people like me is in jail. And we have come to the conclusion that an egalitarian democracy is impossible in India unless you are removed from power ... Is this the ideal democracy? Is this the tryst with destiny about which Jawaharlal Nehru had spoken? Let us be very frank and let us admit that what has happened today is considered by some of you as the dawn of a new era while we on our side consider that it is the beginning of a long night of authoritarian rule, of suppression of liberty and, maybe, even of disintegration of this country ... It is as if, under the Constitution, you have a right to subvert the Constitution ...

Now the charge is about violence. I would like to ask you 'How many people have your police and your Border Security police killed by shooting innocent people?' Will you please publish your records and say how many times after independence, police opened fire and how many people were killed? Without any fear of contradiction I will tell you that the British never shot at people like this ... And if a man like J. P. Narayan says that whenever an order is given you to shoot, don't shoot; you try to understand whom you are shooting, try to understand who those people are; don't shoot on innocent people: what is wrong? ...

When you cannot answer the people, all the answer that you have is to put them in jail, throw them in jail and put them behind bars. Is this the answer? And even what we speak here, I know, will not be allowed to go out. When we come to attend Parliament session, you arrest us ... the President calls us here for attending Parliament, and as soon as we come here, we are arrested. You ask us to go to a meeting, and when we go to the meeting we are arrested. My friend Madhu Dandavate was arrested; Mr Advani was arrested, Mr Mishra was arrested. Why? Because they were attending a meeting which you yourself had called. What is this? Is this democracy? ...

Do not think that you will be able to manage India with

only Shrimati Indira Gandhi and your party behind her; it is too vast a country, with so many people, so many shades of opinion, so many religions.

Sir, I know that the contradictions are glaring. I know that we have differed. Still there is no other way for us. If you think that the only way is to shut the mouths of all the opposition, then I tell you you are not only harming the opposition, you

are not only harming democracy, you are harming yourself. And with this appeal I conclude.

*Statement made on behalf of the opposition parties by
N. G. Goray (SP) and Tridib Chaudhuri (RSP) on withdrawing
from the Rajya Sabha and Lok Sabha respectively, 22 and 23
July 1975*

It is after a great deal of deliberation that we in the opposition
parties, excluding of course the CPI and some Independent
members, decided to attend and participate in the present session
of parliament. Our reluctance rose from the fact (1) of the press
censorship, but even more so from (2) the resolution standing
in the name of Shri Raghuramiah/Shri Om Mehta, the Minister of Parliamentary Affairs, asking the House to suspend all
rules relating to questions, 'calling attention', and any other
business to be initiated by private Members. We could not but
take note of the fact that apart from government's business,
Parliament has to perform other duties also, such as debate on
government policy, and exercise effective supervision over executive action in various ways. Only by putting a question, or giving
a 'calling attention' notice, or initiating a debate can a Member
focus the attention of the House and through it of the country
to matters of public importance. And that is why constitutional
authorities have upheld that right of an ordinary Member. If
all these were to be abandoned unceremoniously, we would really
be acquiescing in something that cuts at the very root of the
role of Parliament in its time-honoured functions. Nevertheless,
it was felt that perhaps the proceedings in this session of Parliament will be conducted in a normal manner, and that speeches
made on the floor of the House will be allowed to be reported
freely and faithfully, in spite of the press censorship.

To our dismay, we find that the reporting on the All-India
Radio of yesterday's proceedings of the House is such that it
can only mislead. It mentioned only the names of the participants, whereas Shri Jagjivan Ram's speech was reported fairly
fully and high-lighted. This morning's newspapers' reporting of
the proceedings is also on the same lines. We cannot but protest
most emphatically against such unfair reporting of the proceedings, which tells the country the government's point of view in
regard to the emergency without indicating what the opposition

had to say on the floor of the House on this very vital subject.

It is clear that this has been done in accordance with the instructions issued to the press and the All-India Radio by the Chief Censor on the 20th July, under the heading 'Guidance for the Covering of Parliamentary Proceedings'. It is not indicated if these instructions that 'the speeches of Members of Parliament participating in the debate shall not be published in any manner or form though their names and party affiliations may be mentioned', were issued with or without the approval of the Speaker/Chairman.

We have, therefore, been compelled to ask ourselves the question whether continued participation in the further business before Parliament on these terms would serve any useful public purpose. The decision to amend the Constitution, to make the proclamation of emergency non-justiciable, makes the consideration of this question more urgent and immediate. It is evident that government having already denied the entire people of the country the basic fundamental rights is now determined to ride roughshod over the rights of the Members of Parliament.

Taking all relevant facts into consideration, and bearing in mind in particular the fact that leading Members of Parliament have been incarcerated, we are satisfied now that no useful purpose will be served by our taking part in the further proceedings of this session of Parliament, for it is clearly in no position to discharge the functions of a free and democratic Parliament.

Guidelines for the Press, Office of the Censor, Government of India, 26 July 1975

NOT FOR PUBLICATION

The purpose of pre-censorship is to ensure that no news is published in a manner that:

(a) it contributes to the scare or demoralization about the general situation or public interest in all respects, as determined by the central government
(b) it will contribute even in remote way to affect or worsen the law and order situation, and also news about
(c) any action or statement or event that is likely to cause disaffection between government and the people.

In this connection, the following guidelines may be noted:

(1) All news reports, headlines, editorial comments, leader page articles, letters to the editors, advertisements and cartoons fall under censorship rules, and have got to be cleared by the Chief Censor to the government of India, or by persons on his behalf duly authorized by him.
(2) Nothing should be allowed to be printed which is likely to convey the impression of a protest or disapproval of the governmental measures. The practice of leaving the editorial column either blank or fill it with quotations should not be followed.
(3) The factual accuracy of all news and reports must be ensured and nothing should be published which is based on hearsay or rumour.
(4) Any objectionable matter already published should not be reproduced.
(5) Official releases including photographs should be so published that the accompanying caption or description does not distort its purpose.
(6) No unauthorized news or advertisement or illustration should be published in regard to vital means of communication.
(7) Nothing should be published about arrangements relating to the protection of transport or communications, supply and distribution of essential commodities, industries, etc.

(8) Nothing should be published which is likely to:

(a) cause disaffection among the members of the armed forces or public servants;

(b) bring into hatred or contempt the government established by law in the country;

(c) promote feeling of enmity and hatred between different classes of citizens in India;

(d) cause or produce or instigate or incite, directly or indirectly, the cessation and slowing down of work in any place within the country;

(e) undermine the public confidence in the national credit or in any government loan;

(f) encourage or incite any person or class of persons to refuse or defer payment of taxes;

(g) instigate the use of criminal force against public servants;

(h) directly encourage people to break prohibitory laws;

(i) affect India's relations with foreign countries.

(9) Nothing which is sought to be published should:

(a) attempt to subvert the functioning of democratic institutions;

(b) attempt to compel members of legislature/Parliament to resign;

(c) relate to agitations and violent incidents;

(d) attempt to incite armed forces and the police;

(e) attempt at promoting disintegration of the country and incite communal passions endangering national unity;

(f) attempt at denigrating the institution of President, Prime Minister, governors and judges of Supreme Court and High Courts;

(g) attempt at endangering law and order; and

(h) attempt to threaten internal security and economic stability.

(10) Quotations, if torn out of context and intended to mislead or convey a distorted or wrong impression, should not be published.

(11) For the coverage of the news, comments or reports, relating to the proceedings of state legislatures, Parliament and courts of law, the following guidelines should be kept in view:

(a) The statements of Ministers may be published either in full or in a condensed form but its contents should not infringe censorship.

(b) The speeches of members of legislatures/Parliament participating in a debate will not be published in any manner or form but their names and party affiliation may be mentioned.

(c) The results of voting on a Bill, Motion, Resolution, etc., may be factually reported. In the event of voting, the number of votes cast for and against may be mentioned.

In case of any doubt, the Chief Censor to the government of India or persons authorized by him should be consulted by the quickest possible means and their instructions obtained.

Please note that there should be no indication in the published material that it has been censored. Printing of captions as 'passed by censors' or 'passed for publication' is not permitted.

On political prisoners: letter from leaders of the opposition to the President of India, 5 August 1975

New Delhi
August 5, 1975

President of India,
Rashtrapati Bhavan,
New Delhi.

Dear Rashtrapatiji,

We feel very much concerned at the informations and reports which we are receiving, regarding the high-handed and inhuman treatment of the jail authorities and the executive towards the political prisoners who have been arrested since the second proclamation of emergency, and seek your personal intervention.

The political prisoners are now being treated in a much worse manner than during the British rule. Their whereabouts are kept a closely guarded secret from their relatives. Even in case of Members of Parliament the news of their arrest and whereabouts are being published in the parliamentary bulletins and not in the press, and their relatives also are not being informed.

From the reports which we are receiving, it appears that Shri Jayaprakash Narayan, Shri Morarji Desai, Shri Jyotirmoy Bosu, Shri K. R. Malkani, Chaudhary Charan Singh and many others in different parts of the country have been kept in solitary confinement. Most of them are not even allowed to meet their relatives or lawyers.

The jail codes of various states are not being complied with in respect of political prisoners and they are refused even to have a look at the jail codes and jail regulations.

We are surprised and shocked to receive information and reports, the authenticity of which we have no reasons to disbelieve, that third-degree methods are being employed on many political prisoners in jails and police lock-ups. In this connection the recent statement of Shri Brahmananda Reddy to the effect that police are not to use third-degree methods is significant.

Reading material and other amenities are not being allowed to the political prisoners. In many cases, food in accordance with jail code and regulations is not being supplied to the political prisoners, and letters written by or to them are being withheld for unreasonably long time.

We request you to see that the authorities concerned are prevailed upon to treat the political prisoners in a normal manner, and to notify the fact of their arrest as well as their whereabouts to their relatives within the shortest possible time and treat them in a humane way.

We would further request you to advise the government to allow an all-party delegation of Members of Parliament to visit jails to look into the condition of the détenues.

Thanking you,

Yours faithfully,
Signed by the non-CPI
opposition leaders.

On the amendment of the election laws: letter from leaders of the opposition to the President of India, 5 August 1975

4, Parliament House,
New Delhi
August 5, 1975.

The President of India,
Rashtrapati Bhavan,
New Delhi.

Dear Rashtrapatiji,

We, the undersigned Members of Parliament, on behalf of ourselves and also the various political parties we represent, have to submit this memorandum before you in connection with the Election Laws (Amendment) Bill, 1975, introduced in the Lok Sabha on the 4th August, 1975 and further amendments proposed thereto by the government on the 5th of August, 1975. We request you not to give your assent to the above Bill, if passed by both Houses of Parliament, for the following reasons:

The whole purpose of the Election Laws (Amendment) Bill, 1975 is to prevent the Supreme Court from deciding the Prime Minister's appeal in the pending election appeal according to the law prevailing. The change of law during the pendency of the appeal is obviously for the purpose of helping the Prime Minister to succeed in the appeal. Such a Bill, if passed, is bound to destroy whatever faith the people have in the rule of law. Since the rule of law is the very basis of democracy, it is desirable that the president may not give assent to this Bill.

Moreover, the clauses 2 and 4B of the Bill, if passed, are bound to make fair elections virtually impossible. One of the main reasons which makes the present election procedure unfair consists of the assistance which the ruling party is able to have by utilizing government funds, and government machinery, for furthering its own election prospects. Clauses 2 and 4B of the Amendment Bill will always favour the party in power against the opposition parties, because the party in power will be able to secure both official assistance as well as government machinery for its electoral success. These provisions, therefore, do not deserve to be assented to by the President.

It should be recalled that a Joint Committee of Parliament on Electoral Reforms had made certain recommendations. Thereafter, the government made a definite commitment to discuss with the opposition parties various suggestions for electoral reforms before bringing any Bill for change in the electoral law. The discussion had started, and opposition parties had submitted their written views on the various amendments which were necessary for bringing about reform in electoral process. One of the points emphasized by the opposition parties in their memorandum was that necessary alterations should be made in the law so as to prevent any party from utilizing government funds and official machinery for the success of its candidates. The amendments sought to be made in the Amendment Bill are contrary to the memorandum submitted by the opposition parties unanimously, and also contrary to the promise made by the government to consider the recommendations so made, as well as contrary to the unanimous views of the Joint Select Committee.

Regarding the remaining provisions of the Amendment Bill, and the amendments proposed thereto by the government after introduction of the Bill, they are obviously intended to help the Prime Minister in her pending appeal and as stated above, it is not proper that a law which is otherwise fair and just should be altered merely for the purpose of helping an individual to litigation to success in the court.

In this connection, it may be mentioned that the amendments proposed by the government to section 8A of the Representation of the People Act, particularly the proposed sub-section 3 thereof, which makes it obligatory on the part of the President to obtain the opinion of the Election Commission and also to act according to such opinion, is against the spirit of the Constitution and derogatory to the high position the President occupies.

Thanking you,

Yours sincerely,
Signed by the
non-CPI opposition leaders.

*Excerpts from speech by M. C. Chagla to the All-India Civil
Liberties Conference, Ahmedabad, 12 October 1975**

... When I look at the present situation, I wonder whether I am
dreaming, or, to use perhaps a better expression, I am going
through a nightmare. I rub my eyes to make sure whether I am
awake or asleep, and I find it is not a dream or a nightmare but
it is a stark, grim, ghastly reality ... Anybody like you and I
may be shut behind bars; I do not know whether I will go back
to Bombay, because they may shut me up and they need not
tell me why they shut me up, and might give the reason that I
have delivered this speech today. Most people today in the jails
do not know why they are there, and they cannot defend themselves, because where there is no charge there cannot be any
defence ...

What is the position today? Is anything left of civil liberties
in the country? ... When the Prime Minister says that dictatorship is democracy, you must accept her word. But at least some
of us are not fooled. Those of us who are here know what is
democracy and what is dictatorship, and the mere fact that the
Prime Minister calls a situation today, which to my mind is
nothing short of dictatorship, a democracy, does not make this
country a democracy ...

One of the most serious losses to our civil liberties is the freedom of press. Now democracy cannot function without a free
press ... No paper or news from outside can come into this
country which contains any reference to India hostile to the
Prime Minister, or to the government ... The censorship will
not permit a trial to be reported or the speeches in Parliament
... But you can sing hymns of glory to the Prime Minister, and
they are being sung every day. You can shout 'hosannas' in her
favour, as they are being shouted every day. And they will be

*The speech was delivered extempore to the conference, which was
presided over by the former Chief Justice of the Supreme Court of India,
J. C. Shah. M. C. Chagla was Chief Justice of the Bombay High Court from
1947 to 1958, until his appointment by Nehru as Indian Ambassador in
Washington. He was later chosen to be Indian High Commissioner in
London. Thereafter he held the portfolios of External Affairs and Education
in the Indian Cabinet. He belongs to no political party.

reported in full. I am sickened to read today's newspapers ...

But the curious thing is this: we are accused of being fascists, of being right-revisionists. They are the democrats. I do not think there can be greater limit to this linguistic perversity than to call us fascists and call themselves democrats ... The question I ask myself is: Do I want to live in a police state? ... Because this is a police state, when a man cannot write what he wants and have it published, when newspapers cannot publish any comments, when people can be sent behind bars without any reasons being assigned, there is not much difference between a police state as existing elsewhere, and what is existing here today ...

And remember this. There is no worse form of dictatorship than what is known as constitutional dictatorship. If behind the facade of the Constitution, technically observing the rules that the Constitution lays down and violating its spirit, you build up a dictatorship, then you have a constitutional dictatorship. I would rather have the Constitution abrogated than to pretend that she is constitutional, she is democratic and all that she has done is permitted by the Constitution. This is constitutional dictatorship ...

Today our hands are shackled, our mouths are sealed, our pens cannot write anything because it cannot be published. But, public opinion can still assert itself. Here you are over a thousand people. You have heard what I have said. By word of mouth you can carry this message outside. If public meetings are not allowed, hold the meetings of 200 or 300 called by invitation to discuss the problems. Then gradually public opinion will assert itself ...

I refuse to believe that my country which has had civilization going back to centuries, my country where the Constitution was drafted for a democratic state ... will always remain in the shadow of dictatorship. There is a saying in English that 'when the night is darkest, the dawn is not far'. I see the night very dark. I am an old man and have not got long to live. But, you younger people will see the dawn. The dawn is bound to come. This country cannot go under. For thousands of years we have survived all sorts of troubles and I think that we will survive both Indira Gandhi and her dictatorship.

*From the Lok Sangharsh Samiti (People's Struggle Committee)
to the Prime Minister, 9 January 1976*

January 9, 1976

Chairman: Shri Morarji Desai
Secretary: Shri Nanaji Deshmukh
Treasurer: Shri Asoka Mehta

Dear Indiraji:

You are aware that the *satyagraha* that we launched on the 14th of November has been going on in the different states of our country. You must also be aware that nearly 90,000 *satyagrahis* have been arrested during the last seven weeks. Though batches of our *satyagrahis* have offered *satyagraha* in nearly 3,000 places, and on over 500 occasions, the reports that you have received must have told you that there has been no case – not even a single one – of any kind of violence or disorderly behaviour on the part of our *satyagrahis*. There has been no report – from any state – of even a stone being pelted by any of our *satyagrahis* or any of the millions of sympathizers who have witnessed the scenes of *satyagraha* in urban centres or rural areas. Even in the face of the unprovoked aggression and violence that they had to meet from the police as well as *agents-provocateurs* at many places, they remained absolutely peaceful and non-violent.

2. While announcing the emergency, and later, while justifying the total suppression of all civil liberties and fundamental rights, you have repeatedly accused the opposition of plotting to launch a violent movement to disrupt law and order. We denied your allegations, and asked you to disclose the evidence that led you to this conclusion, to prove our guilt before an impartial judicial forum. You ignored our demands, and denied us an opportunity to prove our innocence. But you have now had an opportunity to see the kind of movement we run. I am sure you must have been impressed by the totally peaceful, non-violent and orderly nature of our *satyagraha*. Perhaps it has helped you, and everyone else, to see how baseless your apprehensions and accusations were.

You are surely aware that our workers have offered *satya-graha* only in four ways : (a) raising slogans demanding the withdrawal of the emergency, the restoration of fundamental rights, the release of political prisoners, etc.; (b) distributing leaflets; (c) breaking the ban on the peaceful assembly of more than four persons; and (d) addressing crowds that gather to witness the *satyagraha*. The *satyagrahis* have not raised a single slogan, uttered a single word, or distributed a single pamphlet, inciting or advocating any kind of violence whatsoever.

3. One would have thought that the totally non-violent and civil conduct of the *satyagrahis* would have met with an equally civil and lawful response from the government as well. But it is a matter of shame and regret that the violence and torture that the police employed in many places were in no way different from what you and I have described as barbarous, inhuman and reprehensible during the days of the British. We were told that one high police official in Hyderabad said that *satyagrahis* should not expect the police to kiss them. We certainly do not expect the police to kiss or garland our *satyagrahis*. Gandhiji has taught us that the *satyagrahi* seeks and welcomes the punishment that the law prescribes for the infringement of whatever law he chooses to defy. We have, therefore, no complaint whatsoever against the imposition of any penalty that is prescribed by law, and lawfully awarded to us by the courts; and if the government had seen that the police adhered to the rules, procedures, and punishments that the law prescribes, we would not have had to write this letter to you.

4. But the reports that we are receiving about the treatment that the police is meting out to *satyagrahis* and prisoners will fill anyone who reads them with shame and indignation. In many places, *satyagrahis* who are peacefully offering themselves for arrest have been subjected to brutal man-handling. Peaceful volunteers have been *lathi*-charged while offering *satyagraha*.

5. Although the law specifically lays it down that every citizen who is arrested should be produced before a competent magistrate within twenty-four hours, many of the *satyagrahis* who are arrested are not produced before magistrates for many days. During these days, they are kept in unlawful custody by the police,

and beaten up and tortured in the most brutal manner, while taking care to see that the arrests are not even put on record. No case is filed. When the next-of-kin approach the police with inquiries about the whereabouts of the arrested, the police flatly deny that they have arrested the person. After a few days of torture, the *satyagrahis* are either let off or produced before a magistrate and remanded to custody.

6. *Satyagrahis* are often handcuffed and chained or dragged with ropes round their waists, although para. 15(ii) of the 'Model Prison Manual' specifically prohibits such handcuffing. *Satyagrahis* who have attained eminent positions in their own profession or public life have been paraded in handcuffs. We have received reports of senior advocates, office-bearers of bar associations, professors, readers, engineers, students and others being taken about with handcuffs in this fashion.

7. In this International Women's Year, we have received reports of women *satyagrahis* being beaten, handcuffed, and chained – at least one instance of a respectable pregnant woman *satyagrahi* being chained to her cot; of senior police officers illegally breaking into the cell of women *satyagrahis* at midnight and threatening, abusing and intimidating them; of women *satyagrahis* or political prisoners being isolated from other women political prisoners and kept in the cells of women criminals convicted for murder, theft, prostitution, etc.

8. We have received many reports of the inhuman torture inflicted on *satyagrahis*; of the same cruelties and revolting indignities that the police of the imperialists perpetuated; of the police stripping *satyagrahis* and using burning candles or blocks of ice on their bodies, of excreta being pasted on faces; of prisoners being subjected to urination on their faces or being forced to drink urine; of the use of burning cigarettes, chilli powder and many other revolting forms of torture that remind one of the Middle Ages. I am not describing them since I am enclosing some reports that give the names of the victims, the places, dates etc. and all other details that you may need to inquire into the truth of these reports. I am sure these reports will shock you as they shocked us when we read them.

9. Nor are the reports of inhuman treatment confined to the

cases of under-trial prisoners. We have received reports of brutal *lathi* charges within prison cells and barracks to 'punish' prisoners who dared to complain about the infringement of the provisions of the jail manual; or hardened criminals serving life terms or long sentences for murder, *dacoity* etc. being incited and let loose into the barracks of political prisoners to 'teach them a lesson'; of prisoners being denied adequate clothing, mattresses, blankets, and even food; of political prisoners being denied the rights and privileges that they are entitled to, etc. – not to mention instances of unwarranted and vengeful solitary confinement and mental torture, against which the courts have had to issue strictures.

10. What is even more shocking is that this pattern of treatment is being followed in spite of the repeated statements that you and the Home Minister have made on the floor of the House, in the Parliamentary Consultative Committee on Home Affairs, and elsewhere, declaring that the government wants the police to treat prisoners with courtesy and decency; that specific instructions have been issued to the police to refrain from torturing prisoners and suspects, and using violence and third-degree methods. We would have liked to believe that the police is perpetrating these atrocities in spite of your statements, and that you are unaware of what is happening.

But many eminent public men and distinguished Members of Parliament like Shri A. K. Gopalan, Tridib Chowdhury, Krishna Kant, Samar Mukherjee, Jagannathrao Joshi, Era Sezhiyan and others, and ex-Chief Ministers and Ministers like Shri E. M. S. Namboodiripad, Veerendra Patil, T. N. Singh and others have written to you many times drawing your attention to the atrocities and torture that are being inflicted on political prisoners – whether they are *satyagrahis* or political prisoners being held under the MISA or the DIR.

11. You are aware that our government is a party to the UN Declaration of Human Rights. Recently, we also voted in the UN General Assembly in support of a resolution that specifically outlaws the use of torture against any prisoner or suspect. Our country voted for this resolution, and we are proud that we did so. But I wonder what the other delegations at the United

Nations would have felt if they knew that at the time our delegation voted for the resolution, our hands were black with the same crime that we were condemning and outlawing.

12. I do not want to make this letter longer. I am enclosing a number of reports that we have received from the different states. These reports speak for themselves. In view of your repeated statements that the government is against torture and third-degree methods, we request you to kindly issue immediate instructions to end these reprehensible practices, and to inquire into the specific instances that we are bringing to your notice.

Yours sincerely,
Sd/ Ravindra Varma,* Secretary.

Shrimati Indira Gandhi,
Prime Minister,
1, Safdarjung Road,
New Delhi.

*List of imprisoned Indian parliamentarians, Amnesty
International, 16 March 1976†*

V. S. ACHUTHANANDAN – member of the legislative assembly
of Kerala for Aleppey, and a member of the state committee of
the Communist Party of India (Marxist); arrested after the June
1975 state of emergency declaration; held under the Maintenance of Internal Security Act; place of detention unknown.

LAL K. ADVANI – member of the Rajya Sabha for New
Delhi state and leader of the Jana Sangh Party; arrested 26 June
1975; detained under the Maintenance of Internal Security Act;
held in Bangalore Jail.

S. C. ANGRE – member of the Rajya Sabha; arrested after
the June 1975 state of emergency declaration; held under the
Maintenance of Internal Security Act; place of detention unknown.

H. BAHINPATHY – former speaker of the Orissa legislative
assembly and member of the Socialist Party; arrested shortly
after the June 1975 state of emergency declaration; held under
the Maintenance of Internal Security Act; place of detention
unknown.

BHAGABAT BEHAR – member of a legislative assembly, and
of the Socialist Party; arrested after the June 1975 state of
emergency declaration; held under the Maintenance of Internal
Security Act; place of detention unknown.

SARLA BHADORIA – member of a legislative assembly, and
of the Bharatiya Lok Dal; arrested after the June 1975 state of
emergency declaration; held under the Maintenance of Internal
Security Act; place of detention unknown.

BHAGIRATH BHANWAR – member of the Lok Sabha, and of
the Bharatiya Lok Dal; arrested 26 June 1975; held under the
Maintenance of Internal Security Act; detained in the District
Jail in Indore, Madhya Pradesh.

*Ravindra Varma was subsequently arrested.

† This list of parliamentarians in prison was correct as at 16 March 1976,
when it was prepared by Amnesty International. It did not pretend to be
comprehensive: it contained the names only of those people who had come
to the attention of Amnesty International.

SONESWAR BORA – member of the legislative assembly of Assam and of the Socialist Party; arrested shortly after the June 1975 state of emergency declaration; detained under the Maintenance of Internal Security Act; place of detention unknown, probably in Assam.

J. P. BOSE – member of the legislative assembly, and member and former secretary of the Uttar Pradesh branch of the Socialist Party; arrested shortly after the June 1975 state of emergency declaration; detained under the Maintenance of Internal Security Act; place of detention unknown, possibly in Uttar Pradesh.

JYOTIRMOY BOSU – member of the Lok Sabha for West Bengal; deputy leader of the Communist Party of India (Marxist) and leader of the CPI–M parliamentary delegation; arrested 9 July 1975; held under the Maintenance of Internal Security Act; originally detained in Tihar Jail where he was kept in solitary confinement; he was transferred to hospital because of poor health following an appeal to the High Court against his detention conditions; subsequently detained in Hissar Jail, Haryana; now detained in Calcutta where he was allowed to attend his father's funeral; the Calcutta High Court have ruled that he remain in Calcutta for medical treatment.

P. K. CHANDRANANDAN – member of the legislative assembly of Kerala for Aleppey, and member of the state committee of the Communist Party of India (Marxist); arrested after the June 1975 declaration of a state of emergency; held under the Maintenance of Internal Security Act; place of detention unknown.

MADHU DANDAVATE – member of the Lok Sabha for Maharashtra, and of the Socialist Party; arrested June 1975; held under the Maintenance of Internal Security Act; detained in Bangalore Jail; his wife has also been detained since June 1975.

MORARJI DESAI – aged eighty; member of the Lok Sabha and former Deputy Prime Minister; leader of the opposition Congress Party; one of the most outspoken critics of Prime Minister Indira Gandhi, he headed the 'People's Struggle Committee' which was to supervise a campaign of civil disobedience as part of Jaya Prakash Narayan's anti-corruption campaign; arrested 26 June 1975; held under the Maintenance of Internal

Security Act; held in solitary confinement in a state hotel in Haryana; was denied visits by his family until 17 August 1975, and on 29 October 1975 the New Delhi High Court overruled government orders preventing friends and lawyers from visiting or corresponding with him.

RAM DHAN – member of the Lok Sabha for West Bengal, and secretary of the parliamentary Congress Party; arrested 26 June 1975; held under the Maintenance of Internal Security Act; detained in Rohtak Jail, Haryana.

MOHAN DHARIA – member of the Lok Sabha for Maharashtra, and member of the Congress Party; arrested mid-December 1975; held under the Maintenance of Internal Security Act; probably detained in Nasik Jail, Maharashtra.

SAMAR GUHA – member of the Lok Sabha for West Bengal, and leader of the Socialist Party; arrested June 1975; held under the Maintenance of Internal Security Act; detained in Rohtak Jail, Haryana.

GADADHAR GIRI – member of a legislative assembly, and of the Socialist Party; arrested after the June 1975 state of emergency declaration; held under the Maintenance of Internal Security Act; place of detention unknown.

MRS MRINAL KASHAN GORE – aged forty-eight; member of the national committee of the Socialist Party and member of the legislative assembly of Maharashtra for the Socialist Party; arrested 21 December 1975; held under the Maintenance of Internal Security Act; detained in the District Prison in Akola, Maharashtra; she is held alone in a barrack in the prison's female ward.

NOORUL HUDA – member of the Lok Sabha for Assam, and member of the Communist Party of India (Marxist); arrested after the June 1975 state of emergency declaration; held under the Maintenance of Internal Security Act; place of detention unknown.

DINESH JOARDER – member of the Lok Sabha for Malda, West Bengal, and member of the Communist Party of India (Marxist); arrested after the June 1975 state of emergency declaration; held under the Maintenance of Internal Security Act; place of detention unknown.

JAGANATHRAO JOSHI – member of the Lok Sabha for Shajapur, Madhya Pradesh, and member of the Jana Sangh Party; arrested shortly after the June 1975 state of emergency declaration; held under the Maintenance of Internal Security Act; detained in Tihar Jail, New Delhi.

HUKAM CHAND KACHWAI – member of the Lok Sabha, and member of the Jana Sangh Party; arrested 26 June 1975; held under the Maintenance of Internal Security Act; detained in Central Gwalior, Madhya Pradesh.

PURSHOTTAM KAUSHIK – member of the legislative assembly of Madhya Pradesh and chairman of the Madhya Pradesh branch of the Socialist Party; arrested shortly after the June 1975 state of emergency declaration; held under the Maintenance of Internal Security Act; place of detention unknown, probably in Madhya Pradesh.

RAM KISHAN – member of the legislative assembly of Rajasthan and member of the Socialist Party; arrested shortly after the June 1975 state of emergency declaration; held under the Maintenance of Internal Security Act; place of detention unknown, probably in Rajasthan.

VIRENDRA KUMAR – member of the Lok Sabha, and member of the Jana Sangh Party; arrested 28 June 1975; held under the Maintenance of Internal Security Act; detained in Central Jail, Indore.

S. K. KURDU – former member of the Lok Sabha and member of the Socialist Party; arrested shortly after the June 1975 state of emergency declaration; held under the Maintenance of Internal Security Act; place of detention unknown.

A. P. KURYAN – member of the legislative assembly of Kerala for Ernakulam, and member of the Communist Party of India (Marxist); arrested after the June 1975 state of emergency declaration; held under the Maintenance of Internal Security Act; place of detention unknown.

HARDIVARI LAL – member of the legislative assembly of Haryana; arrested after the June 1975 state of emergency declaration; held under the Maintenance of Internal Security Act; place of detention unknown.

RAM LAL – member of the legislative assembly of Haryana

and of the Jana Sangh Party; arrested 26 June 1975; held under the Maintenance of Internal Security Act; place of detention unknown.

MADHU LIMAYE – member of the Lok Sabha for Bihar and of the Socialist Party; arrested 26 June 1975; held under the Maintenance of Internal Security Act; detained in Jaipur Jail, Rajasthan.

S. N. MISHRA – member of the Lok Sabha for Bihar, and member of the opposition Congress Party; arrested 27 June 1975; held under the Maintenance of Internal Security Act; detained in Bangalore Jail.

JENESHWAR MISRA – member of the Lok Sabha for Allahabad, Uttar Pradesh, and member of the Bharatiya Lok Dal; arrested 26 June 1975; held under the Maintenance of Internal Security Act; detained in Central Jail in Naini, Allahabad.

PILOO MODY – aged forty-eight; member of the Lok Sabha, a leader of the Swatantra Party and general secretary of the Bharatiya Lok Dal; arrested 26 June 1975; detained in Rohtak Jail, Haryana.

LAXMINARAYAN NAIK – member of a legislative assembly, and of the Socialist Party; arrested after the June 1975 state of emergency declaration; held under the Maintenance of Internal Security Act; place of detention unknown.

RAJ NARAIN – member of the Rajya Sabha and member of the Socialist Party; he successfully brought charges of election malpractice against Prime Minister Indira Gandhi in 1975, which contributed eventually to the declaration of a state of emergency on 26 June 1975; arrested 26 June 1975; held under the Maintenance of Internal Security Act; detained in Tihar Jail, New Delhi, where it has been reported that he and several other political prisoners went on hunger strike in October 1975 to protest against the ill-treatment and beating of political prisoners.

LAXMINARAIN PANDEYA – member of the Lok Sabha for Mandsaur, Madhya Pradesh, and member of the Jana Sangh Party; arrested after the June 1975 state of emergency declaration; held under the Maintenance of Internal Security Act; place of detention unknown.

BIJU PATNAIK – member of the legislative assembly of Orissa and of the Bharatiya Lok Dal; arrested 26 June 1975; held under the Maintenance of Internal Security Act; detained in Rohtak Jail, Haryana.

RABI RAY – member of the Rajya Sabha for Orissa and member of the Socialist Party; arrested June 1975; held under the Maintenance of Internal Security Act; detained in Tihar Jail, New Delhi.

VIRENDRA KUMAR SAKHALECHA – member of the Rajya Sabha for Madhya Pradesh, and member of the Jana Sangh Party; arrested 28 June 1975; held under the Maintenance of Internal Security Act; detained in Central Jail, Indore, Madhya Pradesh.

JAGANNATH SEIN – former member of the legislative assembly of Haryana; arrested 26 June 1975; held under the Maintenance of Internal Security Act; place of detention unknown.

MANGAL SEIN – former member of the legislative assembly for Haryana; arrested 26 June 1975; held under the Maintenance of Internal Security Act; detained in Rohtak Jail, Haryana.

CHANDRA SEKHAR – member of the Lok Sabha and of the working committee of the ruling Congress Party; arrested 26 June 1975; held under the Maintenance of Internal Security Act; detained in Patiala Jail, Punjab, allegedly in solitary confinement.

UGRA SEN – former member of a legislative assembly, and chairman of the Uttar Pradesh unit of the Socialist Party; arrested after the June 1975 state of emergency declaration; held under the Maintenance of Internal Security Act; place of detention unknown.

BHAIRON SINGH SHAIKHAWAT – member of the Lok Sabha and member of the Jana Sangh Party; arrested 26 June 1975; held under the Maintenance of Internal Security Act; detained in Sariska Jail, Alwar, Rajasthan.

MAHADEEPAK SINGH SHAKYA – member of the Lok Sabha for Uttar Pradesh, and member of the Jana Sangh Party; arrested 2 July 1975; held under the Maintenance of Internal Security Act; detained in District Jail, Kota, Rajasthan.

MAHADEEPAK SINGH SHARYA – member of the Lok Sabha,

and member of the Jana Sangh Party; arrested 2 July 1975; held under the Maintenance of Internal Security Act; detained in the District Jail, Kota, Rajasthan.

RAM RATTAN SHARMA – member of the Lok Sabha, and member of the Jana Sangh Party; arrested 2 July 1975; held under the Maintenance of Internal Security Act; detained in the District Jail, Banda, Uttar Pradesh.

BALBIR SINGH – member of the legislative assembly of Punjab, and member of the Socialist Party; arrested 26 June 1975; held under the Maintenance of Internal Security Act; place of detention unknown.

DAL SINGH – member of the legislative assembly of Haryana and member of the Bharatiya Lok Dal; arrested 26 June 1975; held under the Maintenance of Internal Security Act; possibly detained in Rohtak Jail, Haryana.

MUKHTIAR SINGH (MALIK) – member of the Lok Sabha for Haryana and member of the Jana Sangh Party; arrested 26 June 1975; held under the Maintenance of Internal Security Act; detained in Ambala Jail, Haryana.

NARENDRA SINGH – member of the Lok Sabha for Madhya Pradesh and member of the Jana Sangh Party; arrested 20 July 1975; held under the Maintenance of Internal Security Act; place of detention unknown.

K. A. SIVARAMABHARATHY – member of a legislative assembly, and member of the national committee of the Socialist Party; arrested after the June 1975 state of emergency declaration; held under the Maintenance of Internal Security Act; place of detention unknown.

B. TALUKDAR – member of the legislative assembly of Assam and member of the Socialist Party; arrested shortly after the June 1975 state of emergency declaration; held under the Maintenance of Internal Security Act; place of detention unknown, but probably in Assam.

G. S. TOHRA – member of the Rajya Sabha; arrested after the June 1975 state of emergency declaration; held under the Maintenance of Internal Security Act; place of detention unknown.

MAHADEO PRASAD VERMA – member of the Rajya Sabha;

arrested after the June 1975 state of emergency declaration; held under the Maintenance of Internal Security Act; place of detention unknown.

PHOOL CHAND VERMA – member of the Lok Sabha for Madhya Pradesh, and member of the Jana Sangh Party; arrested after the June 1975 state of emergency declaration; held under the Maintenance of Internal Security Act; place of detention unknown.

FATEH SINGH VIJ – former member of the legislative assembly of Haryana; arrested 26 June 1975; held under the Maintenance of Internal Security Act; detained in Ambala Jail, Haryana.

PINARI VIJAYAM – member of the legislative assembly of Kerala for Coimbatore, and member of the Communist Party of India (Marxist); arrested after the June 1975 state of emergency declaration; held under the Maintenance of Internal Security Act; place of detention unknown.

SHARAD YADAV – member of the Lok Sabha for Madhya Pradesh, and a member of the Socialist Party; arrested after the June 1975 state of emergency declaration; held under the Maintenance of Internal Security Act; place of detention unknown.

May Day Manifesto of the CPI-M, 1 May 1976

Comrades! Workers! Employees! Toilers of India!

Raise the flag of working class unity on May Day! Raise the flag of solidarity of the workers of India with the peasants, with the agricultural workers, with all the toiling people!

Comrades! Never since Independence has such an offensive been waged by the big capitalists and landlords against the working class and the people! Never have the people and the working class of India been deprived of every semblance of right by the régime of the capitalists and landlords as after the declaration of emergency on June 26, 1975!

The Indira Gandhi régime has, under the signboard of fighting reaction, launched a wholesale attack on the liberties of all sections of the people, on peasants, on the middle class, on the working class. Its purpose is to ensure the unbridled exploitation of the people of India by the big capitalists and landlords.

The anti-people régime has deprived the people and the working class of the right to hold meetings and demonstrations. It has banned all strikes and trade union agitations. Through the press censorship law and other measures, the régime has brought the entire press under its control. It has stifled every criticism of its anti-people actions. It has banned all news of working-class strikes and struggles, all news of the suffering of the common people. No trade union can issue a leaflet or a poster calling the workers to action, or criticizing the régime.

The authoritarian régime has detained, without trial, thousands of leaders of democratic parties. It has detained, under the Maintenance of Internal Security Act (MISA) and arrested, under the Defence of India Rules (DIR), leaders and activists of militant trade unions, *kisan sabhas*, agricultural labourer organizations, student and youth organizations all over the country. The threat of MISA and DIR hangs, like the sword of Damocles, over every honest person trying to defend the interests of the exploited sections of society, trying to defend democratic and fundamental rights.

Those arrested and detained under the emergency are treated with the utmost callousness and brutality.

The dictatorship of the Congress Party oppresses everyone, whether he is a worker or employee, peasant or agricultural labourer, doctor or teacher, lawyer or judge, artist or writer.

The Congress Party is working brazenly to change the Constitution. It wants to deny the people every right they possess. It wants to perpetuate its dictatorship and arbitrary rule. Already, it has amended the Constitution to raise the Prime Minister and the President to a pedestal reserved for tyrants.

Now, it directs its attack against the powers of the courts, because it cannot tolerate the slightest curb on arbitrary action and on violation of the law by the executive.

Comrades! What has the emergency brought to the workers and employees of India?

A régime which suppresses the people, robs them of their democratic rights, facilitates the designs of foreign imperialists, is undermining national freedom! The Congress régime is undermining national freedom!

The working class and the toiling masses must demand an end to the policy of wooing the multi-national corporations by offering them super-exploitation of Indian labour. They must demand an end to the dependence on foreign 'aid' and borrowings, which mortgage India's economy to the imperialist world. They must demand nationalization of all monopoly concerns. They must demand a policy of self-reliance.

The working class has a special role to play in the struggle of the entire people against tyranny of emergency rule. It is a powerful class, a class which has seen many heroic battles. It must take up the challenge boldly and on a growing scale.

Disunity among the ranks stands in the way of throwing the full strength of the working class into this task. However, it must be noticed that the very leaders who have split the working class in the interest of the capitalist class, who have full-throatedly supported the emergency, are now forced to admit in sundry devious ways that it is the employers who have reaped the benefits of the emergency, and it is the working class which has been systematically attacked.

Notwithstanding the reign of repression, notwithstanding the disunity foisted on the trade union movement by treacherous reformist and revisionist leaders, there have been protests and strikes and other forms of mass action against the emergency. There have been inspiring actions against the Bonus Act in Kerala, in West Bengal, in Tamil Nadu, in many other states. Kerala, West Bengal and Tamil Nadu have seen a number of united actions for immediate demands; workers of unions affiliated to all the central trade union organizations, the CITU, the UTUC, the AITUC, the INTUC, the HMS, the HMP, have joined these struggles ...

On this May Day, let the working class raise high the banner of joint, united action, the banner of the unity and integrity of the trade union movement, the banner of the unity of the entire class. Let it sink all differences of trade union affiliation and raise the urgent common demands of the class – the right to organize and strike; the recognition of trade unions; the withdrawal of the Bonus Act and the impounding of dearness allowance; the need-based wage; an end to all retrenchment, lay-off, increased workload and closure; equal wages for equal work, for men and women; and unemployment relief.

Whilst fighting for its own demands, let the working class champion the struggle of all sections of the people against the tyranny of emergency rule, and for the restoration of democratic rights. Let it inspire all true democrats to form a broad alliance to achieve this prime task. The ruling classes must not be allowed to snuff out and extinguish our precious democratic rights and liberties – this shall be the slogan of the working class, the toiling masses, all democratic people.

Let the workers celebrate this May Day through demonstrations all over the country, in factories and workshops, to protest against the emergency and to demand its withdrawal, to demand an end to the 'India' of MISA and DIR, to demand the release of political prisoners, to establish people's rights. Let it be known in the remotest corner of the country that the people of India led by the working class are determined to defeat the Congress régime's attempt to rob and cheat the people of their rights.

On the day we raise the banner of unity to defend democratic rights, let us remember that this is the day dedicated to international solidarity, the day we proudly raise the war cry, 'Workers of the World, Unite.' ...

Before the High Court of Karnataka at Bangalore; writ petition of 13 May 1976

Between:

Lawrence V. Fernandes, 3 Leonard Road, Bangalore 25, presently detained in the Central Prison, Bangalore ... Petitioner
and:
1. The Government of Karnataka,
   by its Chief Secretary,
   Vidhana Soudha, Bangalore
2. Shri M. L. Chandrashekar,
   Commissioner of Police, Bangalore
3. The Senior Superintendent,
   Central Prison, Bangalore

Petition filed under Art. 226 of the Constitution of India
The above-named petitioner states as under:

1. He is forty-four years old and a law-abiding, patriotic citizen who has not done anything prejudicial to the interest of the nation or of the society or of the state. He engages in social work as a member of the Lions Club, but is not in any political party.

2. On May 1st at about 8.30 p.m. two police officers came to his residence and took him away saying that they wanted to interrogate him about the *habeas corpus* petition lying before this Hon'ble Court of his younger brother, Michael B. Fernandes, a MISA detenu since December 23, '75. He was taken to the COD office, where after some such questioning, they began questioning him about the whereabouts of his elder brother, George Fernandes. Thereafter they began torturing him until 3 a.m. and when he was in a semi-conscious state and appeared to be dying they even talked in terms of throwing him on the railway tracks to be killed by a moving goods train. He was kept in solitary confinement for two nights in the Vyalikaval Police Station lock-up and then at Malleswaram police station. He was tortured on the second day also. On May 9 he was taken to Davangere by car and kept in Davangere extension police station lock-up and on 10th produced before the Magistrate at

the residence in the morning and at 2.00 p.m. in the chambers of the Magistrate's Court there as though arrested there on the same morning. He was tortured there and kept in a closed lock-up till 11th morning. On being brought to Bangalore he was again kept in solitary confinement in the Malleswaram police station lock-up. As part of the torture he was beaten ruthlessly with *lathis* and after as many as five of them broke to pieces due to the form of beating, they used a banyan tree root and rope to beat him with. They also booted him, slapped him and man-handled him. His left side was totally crippled and he was un-conscious on occasions. He was taken to hospital three times, and each time presented under a different false name impersonating a police officer. A doctor was also brought to the COD office at 9.00 p.m. on the third day for treating him. He was taken to Malleswaram and Bowring Hospital for checking his condition. He was so kept until May 20 when he was produced before the 2nd Metropolitan Magistrate at Bangalore in his chambers during lunch-time at 2.30 p.m. and then taken to the central prison where he was put in a cell. During the twenty days in the custody of the police, he was starved without food on three days and not given proper food on other days. He was allowed bath on three days only, and made to live in the same clothes. He was abused with vulgar language most of the time. He was not allowed to contact his aged parents, his seventy-five-year-old father being a heart patient. He was refused permission to contact any lawyer. He was threatened with further dire consequences to himself and his parents if he reported to the magistrate and anybody else about the torture. In spite of his old parents making frantic oral, telegraphic and written inquiries at all levels right up to the President of India and Prime Minister of India, they were not informed about his whereabouts for all the twenty days.

3. In the prison cell he was served on May 22 with an order of detention dated May 21, '76 signed by the 2nd respondent detaining him under MISA as a 'B' class detenu. He is still continued to be kept in the cell where only condemned prisoners, escaped convicts and jail punishment cases are kept in solitary confinement.

4. The petitioner submits that he is in a high state of mental and nervous tension and physically almost crippled. Although he was medically examined soon after he was brought to the prison and in spite of his bad condition he was not given specialist medical treatment. He is unable to walk as his left side is almost paralysed. There is still painful swelling of the left foot and left wrist and pain and weakness of body and limbs throughout left side from shoulder downwards and the right leg and right hand. Only on the ninth day after his detention, on May 29 he was taken to the Victoria hospital where after being X-rayed, his left leg and left arm were put in plaster. He was brought back to the prison and kept in the cell where there are no proper medical and nursing facilities.

5. By keeping him in the cell, the petitioner is not allowed contact with other MISA detenus including his younger brother who is in the same prison as a MISA detenu since December 23, 1975. The cell does not have normal living facilities and no medical attention. The petitioner cannot walk without support of some person. He is physically weak and nervously upset and feels terribly afraid of police and new faces. In this condition his physical and mental health will be impaired if he is not given full medical attention in proper surroundings and proper nutrition and timely food. All this is not possible in the cell of a prison, and his requests for transfer to a good hospital have not been answered favourably.

PRAYERS

The Petitioner prays that:

6. (a) The petitioner may be ordered to be produced before this Hon'ble Court when this petition is taken up for admission and hearing.

(b) He may be ordered to be transferred to a good hospital or nursing home in a special ward and given proper treatment and nutrition to enable him to regain his mental and physical health.

(c) He may be given all the normal facilities 'B' class detenus are entitled to and not kept in a cell.

(d) That he may be kept in Bangalore only and not transferred anywhere and his family may be ordered to be allowed to attend on him in the hospital in Bangalore itself.

(e) The Government and police compensate him for the torture inflicted on him during the twenty days.

(f) That this Hon'ble Court order a thorough judicial probe into the action of the police in kidnapping him, illegally confining him and torturing him, so that all the guilty persons are suitably punished under law.

(g) That he may be granted any other relief this Hon'ble Court may deem fit.

(h) This Hon'ble Court be pleased to issue such appropriate writs, directions or orders as this Hon'ble Court may deem fit.

(i) The petitioner submits that as he is in prison he is unable to pay any Court fee, if required, along with this petition, but he undertakes to pay it through his mother before or when the petition is taken up for admission as required.

Petitioner

Place: Bangalore
Dated: 31st May 1976

Appendix: Statistical Tables

*Table 1   National Income of India, at 1960–61 Prices:
1960–61 to 1974–5*

Year	Net national product (Rs. million)*	Per capita national product (Rs.)	Index no. of NNP, 1960–61 base	Index no. of per capita NNP, 1960–61 base
(1)	(2)	(3)	(4)	(5)
1960–61	132,940	306·3	100·0	100·0
1961–2	137,630	310·0	103·5	101·2
1962–3	140,450	309·4	105·6	101·0
1963–4	148,450	319·9	111·7	104·4
1964–5	159,170	335·8	119·7	109·6
1965–6	150,210	310·4	113·0	101·3
1966–7	152,430	307·9	114·7	100·5
1967–8	166,600	329·2	125·3	107·5
1968–9	170,570	329·9	128·3	107·7
1969–70	179,550	339·9	135·1	110·8
1970–71	190,350	351·8	143·5	115·1
1971–2	192,990	348·4	145·5	114·0
1972–3	191,300	337·4	144·2	110·4
1973–4	197,240	340·1	148·7	111·3
1974–5†	200,400	337·7 (GOI)	150·7	110·3

*'Rs. million' refers here, and throughout, to 'millions of rupees'.
†*Economic Times*, 27 November 1975

SOURCES: *Economic Survey, 1970–71* (GOI), for data up to 1969–70; Central Statistical Organization, cited in *India 1976*, Ministry of Information and Broadcasting, (GOI), Delhi 1976, Table 11.1, p. 142.

The data on net national product (NNP, col. 2), and on per capita national product (col. 3) for the period 1960–61 to 1974–5, show a slow and halting rise; after 1970–71 their significance for the people is a dire one. Note that the per capita national product (col. 3) has actually fallen from 1970–71. Together with Table 2 (q.v.), comparing the trends of NNP, money supply and wholesale prices, they provide the quantifications of India's economic stasis and the trend of inflation.

Table 2　Annual Growth-rates of National Income and Money Supply; with Consumer Price-index for Industrial Workers and Index of Real Earnings from Third Five-Year Plan Period (1961–2 to 1965–6) to 1975–6

Period	Annual rate of growth of net national product (at 1960–61 prices) (per cent)	Annual rate of growth of per capita net national product (at 1960–61 prices) (per cent)	Annual variation in money supply with public (per cent)	Consumer price index for industrial workers (1960 = 100)	Index of real earnings of workers (1961 = 100)
(1)	(2)	(3)	(4)	(5)	(6)
Third Five-Year Plan (yearly)	2·6	0·3	9·6		
1966–7	1·0	−1·0	9·3		95
1967–8	8·2	5·9	8·1		91
1968–9	3·0	0·6	8·0	174	94
1969–70	6·5	4·3	10·5	177	101
1970–71	5·2	2·9	11·8	186	101
1971–2	1·8	−0·4	14·0	192	101
1972–3	−1·5	−3·6	15·7	207	103
1973–4	5·0	2·8	15·2	250	n.a.*
1974–5	0·2	−1·7	6·3	317	n.a.
1975–6	n.a.	n.a.	9·9	313	n.a.

*Not available

NOTE: Col. (6) relates to the calendar years 1966 to 1972; in subsequent years, figures have not been made available because of what they would reveal of the deterioration in real earnings.

SOURCES: Cols. (1) and (2): *Economic Survey, 1975–6* (GOI), p. 59; col. (3): *Report on Currency and Finance, 1974–5*, Reserve Bank of India; and weekly statistical supplement to the *RBI Bulletin*, 1 March 1976; col. (5): Labour Bureau, Min. of Labour, GOI, cited in *Report on Currency and Finance 1974–75*, vol. 2, p. 32; *RBI Bulletin*, May 1976, p. S 369; and Labour Bureau, August 1976; col. (6): *India 1976*, Table 22.3, p. 332.

The rate of growth of money supply from the Third Plan period far outstrips the rate of growth of national income, revealing the degree of inflation in the economy. The rise in the cost of living index, which is itself a manipulated figure, reveals the same trend.

Table 3 Net Availaiblity per day of Cereals and Pulses (Food grains)

		Per capita net availability per day (grammes)		
Year	Population (millions)	Cereals	Pulses	Total food grains
1956	397·3	360·5	70·4	430·9
1961	442·4	399·7	69·0	468·7
1962	452·2	399·0	62·0	461·0
1963	462·0	384·0	59·8	443·8
1964	472·1	401·0	51·0	452·0
1965	482·5	418·6	61·6	480·2
1966	493·5	360·0	48·2	408·2
1967	504·2	361·7	39·7	401·4
1968	515·4	404·1	56·0	460·1
1969	527·0	397·9	47·3	445·2
1970	538·9	403·1	51·9	445·0
1971	550·8	417·8	51·3	469·1
1972	562·5	420·2	47·1	467·3
1973	574·2	383·1	41·4	424·5
1974	586·1	411·9	40·9	452·8
1975	597·9	373·6	41·7	415·3

SOURCE: *Economic Survey, 1975–76* (GOI), cited in *Economic and Political Weekly*, 20 March 1976, p. 478.

These are the statistics of the 'decades of progress', at one of its most basic measures. Additionally, the data on per capita net availability do not reveal levels and disparities of actual consumption (see Table 5) among different classes and sections of the people, and in different regions of India. They show, instead – the 'green revolution' and intermittent years of good harvest notwithstanding – the lack of rural development, in relation to the actual needs of the Indian people.

Table 4   Per Capita Annual Availability of some Key Articles of Consumption

Year	Edible oils* (kilogrammes)	Sugar (kilogrammes)	Cotton cloth (metres)
1955–6	2·5	5·0	14·4
1960–61	3·2	4·7	13·8
1961–2	3·2	5·8	14·8
1962–3	3·1	5·4	14·4
1963–4	2·7	4·9	14·7
1964–5	3·6	5·1	15·2
1965–6	2·7	5·7	14·7
1966–7	2·7	5·1	14·0
1967–8	3·4	4·3	13·6
1968–9	2·6	5·0	14·4
1969–70	3·0	6·1	13·6
1970–71	3·5	7·3	13·6
1971–2	3·0	6·7	12·4
1972–3	2·4	6·1	13·2
1973–4	3·4	6·0	12·0
1974–5†	3·2	5·8	12·9

*Includes ground-nut, rape-seed and mustard oil, coconut oil and sesamum oil, but excludes oil used for *vanaspati* manufacture.

†Provisional.

SOURCE: *Economic Survey, 1975–76* (GOI), quoted in *Economic and Political Weekly*, 20 March 1976, p. 478.

With per capita availability of food grains, these are the indices of annual (not weekly, nor even monthly) availability of key items of consumption to the people of India. Their quantities are derisory; their fluctuations are those of an economy which has not progressed; and their falls – as in the case of cotton cloth – contain their own comment.

Table 5 Percentage Share in Total Consumption by Decile Groups,
1968–9

Decile groups of population (per cent) from poorest to richest	Share in total consumption	
	Urban sector	Rural sector
0–10	2·72	3·29
10–20	4·17	4·79
20–30	5·27	5·87
30–40	6·36	6·90
40–50	7·51	7·98
50–60	8·83	9·19
60–70	10·44	10·63
70–80	12·59	12·50
80–90	15·97	15·37
90–100	26·14	23·48

SOURCE: National Sample Survey, 23rd round (GOI).

	Urban sector	Rural sector
Bottom 20 per cent	6·89	8·08
Top 20 per cent	42·11	38·85

The magnitudes of disparity and inequality are shown here to be greater in urban even than in rural India; while inequalities of income are in fact even larger, as could be expected of an economy such as India's. Moreover, here we glimpse the 'poorer and weaker sections', *before* inflation was to make them poorer still.

Table 6　Landholdings Survey, 1961–2

Size group (in acres)	Percentage of total holdings	Percentage of area operated
Up to 1	17·13	11·40
1–5	44·56	7·90
5–20	33·79	51·60
20–50	3·49	17·50
50 and above	1·03	11·60

SOURCE: Land Holdings Survey, 1961–2, of the National Sample Survey (NSS), 17th round.

Table 7　Distribution of Operational Holdings According to Size, 1970–71

Size group (in acres)	Percentage of total operational holdings	Percentage of area operated
Below 1·235	32·88	3·36
1·235–4·94	36·79	17·50
4·94–24·70	26·41	48·26
24·70–49·40	3·03	17·59
49·40 and above	0·89	13·28

NOTE: The term 'operational holding' is defined as 'the fundamental unit of decision-making' in agriculture; not the same thing as an ownership holding, which was the subject of the 1961–2 survey.

SOURCE: *All-India Report on Agricultural Census 1970–71* (Dept. of Agriculture, Min. of Agriculture and Irrigation, GOI), Table 1, p. 113.

Tables 6 to 9 must be taken together, as expressing – albeit in different ways – the essential features of the patterns of land-ownership and operation in India. The structural congruence between them is unmistakable.

Table 8   Estimated Number of Rural Households According to Area of Land Owned, 1971–2

Land owned (in acres)	Percentage of total households	No. of households
Nil	9·34	7,281,000
0·01–1	34·89	27,193,000
1–5	33·78	26,330,000
5–10	12·22	9,526,000
10–20	6·49	5,053,000
20–50	2·89	2,254,000
50 and above	0·39	302,000
Total	100·00	77,939,000

SOURCE: *Statistical Tables: All-India Debt and Investment Survey, 1971–72,* Reserve Bank of India, vol. 1, table 1, p. 16 (a survey carried out in collaboration with the National Sample Survey, 26th round, of the government of India).

Table 9   Distribution of Assets of Rural Households on 30 June 1971

Asset group (in rupees)	Percentage of total households	Percentage of total assets
Up to 500	11·38	0·23
500–1,000	8·35	0·53
1,000–2,500	15·49	2·30
2,500–5,000	16·09	5·17
5,000–10,000	18·31	11·63
10,000–15,000	9·71	10·47
15,000–20,000	5·69	8·65
20,000–30,000	6·24	13·40
30,000–50,000	4·83	16·22
50,000–100,000	2·94	17·55
100,000 and above	0·96	13·96

SOURCE: *Statistical Tables: All-India Debt and Investment Survey, 1971–72,* Reserve Bank of India, vol. 1, table 6, p. 27.

The statistical quantifications of rural inequality are illustrated (and no more) in Tables 6 to 9. They serve to substantiate, in their own way, argument about the concentrations of wealth and indigence, land-ownership and land-hunger. And within their mathematical hierarchy, resides the pyramid of landlordism. The text indicates sufficiently that there has been no significant change in these orders of magnitude.

Table 10   Direct and Indirect Taxes as Percentages of Total Tax
Revenues of Central and State Governments and Union Territories
1948–9 to 1975–6 (Rs Million)

Year	Direct taxes	Indirect taxes	Total	Percentage of direct taxes to total	Percentage of indirect taxes to total
1948–9	2,390	3,630	6,010	39·77	60·23
1949–50	2,190	3,940	6,130	35·73	64·27
1950–51	2,310	4,280	6,590	35·05	64·95
1951–2	2,430	5,310	7,740	31·39	68·61
1952–3	2,480	4,610	7,090	34·98	65·02
1953–4	2,400	6,730	7,130	33·66	66·34
1954–5	2,370	5,230	7,600	31·18	68·82
1955–6	2,550	5,580	8,130	31·37	68·63
1956–7	2,930	6,460	9,390	31·20	68·80
1957–8	3,230	7,890	11,120	29·05	70·95
1958–9	3,360	8,170	11,530	29·14	70·86
1959–60	3,710	9,140	12,850	28·87	71·13
1960–61	4,200	10,400	14,600	28·77	71·23
1961–2	4,670	11,900	16,570	28·18	71·82
1962–3	5,740	14,080	19,820	28·96	71·04
1963–4	7,070	17,170	24,210	29·20	70·80
1964–5	7,630	19,310	26,940	28·32	71·68
1965–6	7,750	22,730	30,480	25·43	74·57
1966–7	8,320	25,940	34,260	24·28	75·72
1967–8	8,590	27,790	36,380	23·61	76·39
1968–9	9,100	30,130	39,230	23·20	76·80
1969–70	10,430	33,530	43,960	23·73	76·27
1970–71	10,910	38,640	49,550	22·02	77·98
1971–2	12,750	45,150	57,900	22·02	77·98
1972–3	11,830	52,530	64,360	18·38	81·62
1973–4	13,240	60,650	73,890	17·92	82·08
1974–5*	14,600	74,290	88,890	16·42	83·58
1975–6†	15,720	83,540	99,260	15·84	84·16

*Revised estimate.   †Budget estimate.

SOURCES: Commerce, March 27, 1976 for the period 1948–9 to 1971–2;
and Economic Survey 1975–76, GOI, p. 76, for the period 1972–3 to 1975–6.

Direct taxes are taxes on income and corporate profits. Indirect taxes are
excise and customs duties, i.e. taxes on commodities, the burden of which
falls on the 'common people' or 'the poorer and weaker sections'. The
continuously rising level of indirect taxes as a proportion of the total tax
revenue of the central and state governments is one of the most strongly
consistent evidences of the direction of economic development in India.
The trend has been reinforced for 1976–7, as the text makes clear.

Table 11   *Assets, Sales and Profits of Selected Medium and Large Private Sector Companies, 1970–71 to 1973–4*

	Annual increase or decrease (percentages)			
	1970–71	1971–2	1972–3	1973–4
1. Net worth (paid-up capital and forfeited shares, reserves and surplus)	—	6·6	6·7	8·9
2. Gross assets and inventories	—	9·2	7·7	10·8
3. Net assets and inventories	—	8·0	5·8	10·7
4. Sales	—	12·1	11·0	8·7
5. Profits after tax	—	−0·2	5·1	25·0
6. Profits retained as percentage of profit after tax	51·1	48·4	47·1	61·3
7. Profits after tax as percentage of net worth	11·2	10·5	10·3	11·9
8. Gross profits as percentage of sales	10·3	10·0	9·5	10·5

SOURCE: From the study of the finances and working of 1650 medium and large public limited companies in the private sector, *RBI Bulletin*, September 1975, pp. 710–834.

The figures for profit and profitability – such as the five-fold increase in profits after tax from 1972–3 to 1973–4 – may be usefully contrasted with all the indices of the deprivation of the people, the stagnation of the economy and the withholding since 1972–3 of the index of real earnings. Reference to the text of this book (chapter 6) will reveal that the trends exhibited here were fully sustained in 1974–5, and 1975–6.

*Table 12   Percentage of Salaries and Wages in Gross Value Added,
1950–51 to 1972–3 – the Index of Surplus Value*

Period (average annual)	Percentage share of wages and salaries in gross value added*	Percentage share of surplus value in gross value added
1950–51 to 1954–5	63·4	36·6
1955–6 to 1959–60	60·4	39·6
1950–51 to 1959–60	61·5	38·5
1960–61 to 1964–5	54·6	45·4
1965–6 to 1969–70	55·6	44·4
1960–61 to 1969–70	55·2	44·8
1970–71 to 1972–3	53·2	46·8

*The classification 'wages and salaries' includes also the salaries of managers and other non-workers; consequently its share is overestimated in the above table. It follows that the share of surplus value (third column) is correspondingly underestimated.

SOURCE: *Economic Times* Research Bureau: 'Structural Pattern of Factorial Payment', *Economic Times*, 14–15 July 1975. The article is based on data from the RBI study of 1650 selected medium and large public limited companies in the private sector (op. cit.), and on data from the Annual Survey of Industries of the government of India.

Table 13   Outstanding Long-Term Foreign Investments by Source, 1955 to 1969 (Rs. million)

	as at end of December			as at end of March			
	1955	1961	1962	1966	1967	1968	1969
Canada	23	65	73	131	143	146	185
France	—	—	—	261	442	464	513
West Germany	24	107	120	396	846	967	1,040
Italy	—	41	52	194	361	401	734
Japan	2	32	33	422	654	825	761
Sweden	—	44	74	88	118	184	186
Switzerland	57	93	108	227	259	286	324
UK	3,659	4,462	4,822	5,492	6,456	6,283	6,311
USA	396	959	1,062	2,445	3,720	4,207	4,296
Other countries	236	238	269	434	737	841	885
International institutions	27	757	719	692	1,066	980	878
Total	4,424	6,798	7,333	10,782	14,802	15,584	16,113

NOTE: These figures include valuation changes.

SOURCE: *India: Pocket Book of Economic Information 1973 and 1974;* Dept. of Economic Affairs, Ministry of Finance, GOI, Delhi, 1975, p. 113.

These figures can be supplemented with more up-to-date but less comprehensive data given elsewhere. The above data reveal the main sources, trends, and accelerations in foreign investment. The UK and the USA are by far the leading investors. They are followed by West German capital (increasingly important in certain key sectors of the economy), Japanese capital (growing) and Italian capital. The rate of increase of American capital is plainly higher than that of British capital.

Table 14   Outstanding Long-Term Foreign Investment (by Industry), 1955 to 1969 (Rs. million)

	as at end of December			as at end of March			
	1955	1961	1962	1966	1967	1968	1969
Plantation	872	1,024	1,116	1,122	1,297	1,233	1,224
Mining	93	124	130	98	114	107	115
Petroleum	1,040	1,525	1,540	1,709	1,921	1,964	1,957
Manufacturing	1,291	2,950	3,254	5,506	7,434	8,332	8,902
Services:							
Trading	268	293	310	365	570	536	522
Construction, utilities and transport	427	565	609	1,254	2,339	2,240	2,236
Financial	174	124	178	511	908	960	936
Miscellaneous	259	193	196	217	219	212	221
Total services	1,128	1,175	1,293	2,347	4,036	3,948	3,915
Total	4,424	6,798	7,333	10,782	14,802	15,584	16,113

SOURCE: *India: Pocket Book of Economic Information 1973 and 1974*, Dept. of Econ. Affairs, Ministry of Finance, GOI, Delhi, 1975, pp. 115–16.

With Table 13, these statistics are evidence for the proposition that the Indian state and Indian capital collaborate on an increasing scale with foreign finance capital. Emergency developments were intended to give a substantial impetus to this process. There is nothing exceptional about it; except that it refutes – as do other indices – the notion that India is proceeding along its own path of 'non-capitalist development'. Moreover, as on 31 March 1974, there were 752 corporate bodies in India controlled by foreign enterprises, the value of their assets 30 per cent of the entire private corporate sector in India. (*Times of India Year-Book, 1976*, pp. 588–9).

Table 15   Significance of Private and Public Sectors in the Indian Economy

Share of private and public sectors in domestic product (at current prices) (year 1973–4)

Gross domestic product	Rs. 424,430 million
Gross product of private sector	Rs. 355,760 million
Gross product of public sector	Rs. 68,670 million
Contribution of private sector to gross domestic product	83·8 per cent
Contribution of public sector to gross domestic product	16·2 per cent
Net domestic product	Rs. 398,990 million
Net product of private sector	Rs. 335,420 million
Net product of public sector	Rs. 63,570 million
Contribution of private sector to net domestic product	84·1 per cent
Contribution of public sector to net domestic product	15·9 per cent

NOTE: The 'public sector' is made up of three categories: government administration, 'departmental enterprises', and 'non-departmental enterprises'. The largest component of the public sector is government administration.

SOURCE: *India 1976*, op. cit.

The suggestion that 'India has taken the non-capitalist path of development', and that the public sector has 'commanding importance in the national economy' cannot be sustained. Figures are not available after 1973–4, but as the economic developments of 1975–6 have shown, both propositions are now even less valid.

Table 16   Inflow of External Assistance – Gross and Net
(*Rs. million*)

Year	Gross aid utilization	Amortisation payments	Interest payments	Total debt service (columns 3 and 4)	Net inflow of aid (column 2 less column 5)
(1)	(2)	(3)	(4)	(5)	(6)
1966–7	11,320	1,570	1,150	2,720	8,600
1967–8	11,770	1,940	1,220	3,160	8,610
1968–9	9,130	2,070	1,370	3,440	5,690
1969–70	8,370	2,380	1,420	3,800	4,570
1970–71	7,800	2,540	1,580	4,120	3,680
1971–2	8,210	2,710	1,750	4,460	3,750
1972–3	6,050	3,020	1,770	4,790	1,260
1973–4	6,920	3,000	1,840	4,840	2,080
1974–5	8,300	3,310	1,810	5,120	3,180
1975–6*	16,390	4,700	2,300	7,000	9,390

* Economic Survey, 1975–76 (GOI), cited in *Commerce*, 27 March 1976.

SOURCE: *Report on Currency and Finance 1974–75*, vol. 2, RBI, p. 225.
See Table 17.

Table 17   Aggregate External Assistance – by Source (Rs. million)

Country/institution	Authorized up to March 1975		Utilized up to March 1975	
	value	percentage of total aid	value	percentage of total aid
IBRD/IDA	34,930	21·5	24,160	17·2
USA	60,100	37·1	60,100	42·8
USSR	10,330	6·4	7,320	5·2
West Germany	12,180	7·5	11,330	8·1
UK	14,390	8·9	13,030	9·3
Japan	5,540	3·4	4,710	3·4
Others	24,660	15·2	19,670	14·0
Total	162,130	100·0	140,320	100·0

SOURCE: *Report on Currency and Finance 1974–75*, vol. 2, RBI, p. 227.

Table 16 shows, contrary to official assertion, that India is increasingly a debtor country. Its burden of external indebtedness and the rising level of investment by foreign capital make it impossible to corroborate official assertions as to India's increasing 'self-reliance'. Table 17 shows something of the distribution of this economic dependency.

Table 18 Defence Expenditure of the Government of India:
Current Expenditure and Capital Outlay, 1950–51 to 1976–7
(Rs. million)

Year	Total expenditure
1950–51	1,683·2
1955–6	1,898·2
1956–7	2,118·5
1957–8	2,796·5
1958–9	2,788·1
1959–60	2,669·7
1960–61	2,809·4
1961–2	3,124·9
1962–3*	3,860·0 ⎱ (India's China War)
1962–3†	5,045·6 ⎰
1963–4	8,160·0
1964–5	8,060·0
1965–6	8,850·0 (war with Pakistan)
1966–7	9,090·0
1967–8	9,680·0
1968–9	10,330·0
1969–70	11,010·0
1970–71	11,990·0
1971–2	15,250·0 (war with Pakistan over Bangladesh)
1972–3	16,520·0
1973–4	16,810·0
1974–5	21,570·0
1975–6*	24,100·0
1976–7†	25,440·0

*Budget estimate.   †Revised estimate.

SOURCES: *Reserve Bank of India Bulletin*, March 1963, pp. 305 and 307, for the period 1950–51 to 1962–3; Prakash Karat, 'Structure and role of the armed forces in the Indian state', in *India: state and society*, M. Kurian (ed.), Orient Longman, Madras, 1975, p. 283, for 1963–4; budget figures cited in *India 1976*, table 4.1, p. 40, for the period 1964–5 to 1974–5; *Economic Times*, 24 March 1976, for the period 1975–6 to 1976–7.

The defence expenditures of India's impoverished economy have increased sharply in the last fifteen years. Moreover, these (carefully managed) official statistics do not take account of India's accelerating nuclear and paramilitary spending throughout this period. Their full meaning, furthermore, can only be established in closer juxtaposition with the indices which have preceded this one.

Notes

The main abbreviations employed in the notes are as follows:

ABP   *Amrita Bazar Patrika* – the daily paper
AICC   All-India Congress Committee
DAVP   Directorate of Advertising and Visual Publicity
Econ. Times   *Economic Times*
EPW   *Economic and Political Weekly*
GOI   Government of India
Hindu (Int. Ed.)   *Hindu (International Edition)* ·
Hind. Times   *Hindustan Times*
IG   Indira Gandhi
Ind. Exp.   *Indian Express*
MIB   Ministry of Information and Broadcasting
PBEI   *India: Pocket Book of Economic Information, 1973 and 1974*,
   Delhi, Department of Economic Affairs, Ministry of Finance,
   GOI, 1975
PBLS   Pocket Book of Labour Statistics, 1975, Simla, Labour
   Bureau, Ministry of Labour, GOI, 1975
PODS   Preserving Our Democratic Structure, Delhi, DAVP,
   MIB, GOI, 1975
qu.   quoted in
RBI   Reserve Bank of India
TPP   'Torture of Political Prisoners in India, March 1976', compiled
   by the Lok Sangharsh Samiti, for the International League for the
   Rights of Man.

CHAPTER ONE: FROM CRISIS TO CRISIS

1. 1976 World Bank report, qu. *Hindu*, 17.5.76.
2. On 4 Aug. 1975; qu. GOI, *The Turning Point* (DAVP, MIB, 1975).
3. *PBEI*, p. 2; GOI, *India Today: Basic Facts* (MIB, 1974), pp. 10–11; F. T. Jannuzi, *Agrarian Crisis in India: The Case of Bihar* (University of Texas Press, 1974).

4. *Guardian*, 7.7.75 ('Bihar spends 400,000 rupees a month on its security forces, a large sum for India').

5. GOI, *A Hundred New Gains* (DAVP, MIB, 1975), p. 10.

6. Roger Hansen, *The US and World Development: Agenda for Action, 1976* (Overseas Development Council, Praeger, 1976), qu. *Ind. Exp.*, 2.4.76; *PBEI*, p. 255.

7. *PBEI*, p. 253.

8. Hansen, op. cit., qu. *Ind. Exp.*, 2.4.76.

9. *PBEI*, pp. 52–3.

10. GOI, *A Hundred New Gains*, p. 11.

11. Conversation between P. Das and the writer, Calcutta, Dec. 1975.

12. *PBEI*, pp. 10 and 50.

13. GOI, *Years of Achievement: Food* (DAVP, MIB, 1975), p. 1.

14. *PBEI*, pp. 52–3, and RBI, *Report on Currency and Finance 1974–75*, vol. 2, pp. 22–3.

15. Report of Economic and Scientific Research Foundation on the 'Environmental Problems of Developed and Developing Countries', qu. *ABP*, 26.5.76.

16. *PBEI*, p. 158.

17. ibid., p. 50.

18. ibid., p. 27; and, e.g., *ABP*, 24.3.76.

19. ibid., pp. 50 and 54; see appendix, p. 426.

20. To Rajya Sabha, 29 July 1975; qu. GOI, *The Turning Point*, p. 27.

21. Amartya Sen, *Dimensions of Unemployment in India*, Indian Statistical Institute, Calcutta, 1973; at p. 13, he discusses estimates which, by 1971, ranged between 20 and 40·5 million for rural unemployed and 'severely under-employed'.

22. *Economist*, 20.3.76; Ashok Mitra, *Economist*, 24.1.76.

23. *Economist*, 24.1.76; *PBEI*, pp. 59 and 63; RBI, *Report on Currency and Finance, 1974–5*, loc. cit.

24. *PBEI*, p. 147.

25. ibid., p. 65; see appendix, p. 423.

26. GOI, *Economic Survey, 1975–6*; see appendix, p. 424.

27. *EPW*, 6.12.75.

28. *PBEI*, p. 37; see appendix, p. 421.

29. Communicated to the writer in rural Tamil Nadu, December 1975.

30. See chapter 2, p. 41–3.

31. *PBLS*, p. 161. Table 11.9 indicates that the per capita and per day consumption of calories is less in India than in either Pakistan or Sri Lanka.

32. *PBEI*, p. 147.
33. *PBLS*, pp. 141–5; NSS Surveys on consumption expenditure confirm this.
34. *PBEI*, p. 147; GOI, *Economic Survey, 1975–6*, cited in *EPW*, 20.3.76.
35. GOI, *Years of Achievement: Food*, pp. 9–10.
36. *PBEI*, pp. 144–5 and 147.
37. See *Report of the Famine Inquiry Commission*, 1945.
38. *Times of India, Statesman, Indian Express, passim*, Aug.–Sept. 1972; for more recent famine, *EPW*, 30.11.74.
39. GOI, *Years of Achievement: Food*, p. 3.
40. *PBEI*, p. 42; GOI, *India 1976* (Delhi, MIB, 1976); see appendix, p. 433.
41. *PBEI*, pp. 113 and 196. ('80 per cent of heavy machinery production, 60 per cent of oil extraction, 30 per cent of steel production, 20 per cent of power generation derive from Indo-Soviet joint enterprise', *Link*, 22.7.76.)
42. *PBEI*, p. 34; *Economic Survey, 1975–6*; *EPW*, 10.1.76.
43. *PBEI*, p. 23; *PBLS*, p. 1.
44. On 28 July 1975, qu. GOI, *The Turning Point*, p. 31.
45. *PBLS*, p. 34.
46. *PBEI*, p. 37; p. 145. Publication of the official national index of real earnings has been suspended since 1972–3.
47. qu. *Link*, 2.5.76; *ABP*, 24.3.76.
48. To Rajya Sabha, 28 July 75, qu. GOI, *The Turning Point*, p. 31.
49. qu. *Hindu*, 21.2.76.
50. To Lok Sabha, qu. GOI, *The Turning Point*, p. 82; *Lok Sabha Debates, 5th Series*, vol. 54, no. 11, col. 164.
51. *PBEI*, pp. 52–4.
52. ibid.
53. P. C. Mahalanobis' estimates, made for the formulation of India's second five-year plan (1956–61), was based on a ceiling for land-holdings of twenty acres; *EPW*, 3.4.76.
54. Thus, under the 1971 and 1972 land reform laws only about 200,000 acres were distributed; under previous laws, between one and two million acres may have been distributed.
55. Confirmed by national sample surveys of land-holdings in 1954–5, and 1961–2, and of 'operational holdings' in 1970–71; see appendix, p. 426.
56. *Draft Fifth Plan*, qu. *EPW*, 5.6.76.
57. *EPW*, 6.12.75.

58. qu. *ABP*, 24.3.76.

59. GOI, *A Hundred New Gains*, p. 18.

60. T. A. Pai, qu. GOI, *The Turning Point*, p. 30.

61. To Rajya Sabha, 22 July 75, qu. *PODS*, p. 9 (my emphasis).

62. This was politically ingenuous, as this chapter seeks to make clear

63. Privately circulated; see appendix, p. 385.

64. *Radical Review*, vol. 3, no. 3., p. 24.

65. GOI, *Economic Survey, 1975–6*, qu. *Econ. Times*, 9.3.76.

66. Francine Frankel, *India's Green Revolution: Economic Gains and Political Costs* (Princeton, 1971), pp. 33, 192–3.

67. qu., *Econ. Times*, 9.3.76.

68. *W. Bengal State Labour Department Survey for 1975* (Calcutta 1976); qu. *ABP*, 24.3.76; also see the work of P. K. Bardhan e.g. 'The Green Revolution and Agricultural Labourers' *EPW* (special number), July 1970.

69. e.g. *World Bank Atlas* (IBRD, 1975), pp. 7, 28; *PBLS*, p 150.

70. Reserve Bank of India (RBI), *Bulletins*, August 1970, Sept 1975; in many other states, stagnant, and thus falling below the growth rate of the labour forces, *EPW*, 20.12.75.

71. *Ind. Exp.* (editorial), 16.1.76.

72. IG, qu. *Hindu*, 21.2.76.

73. IG, qu. *Econ. Times*, 14.4.76.

74. Harry Magdoff, *Monthly Review* (New York, Jan. 1976), pp. 4–5, which contains a general characterization of the classical features of the 'underdeveloped' economy, and informs much of this passage.

75. e.g. RBI *Bulletins*, Nov. 1974, pp. 2101–44, Sept. 1975 pp. 710–845, and April 1976; *Financial Statistics of Joint Stock Companies in India, 1961–71*, p. 136; also, *EPW* 20.12.75.

76. 14.4.76.

77. 17.4.76.

78. The oldest of the three Indian communist parties, it celebrated its fiftieth anniversary in 1975.

79. *PBEI*, pp. 149–50; *Link*, 25.4.76; *EPW*, 15.5.76.

80. 26.1.76.

81. Neville Maxwell, *Woman on a White Horse*, Reprint Series No 79 (Oxford, Institute of Commonwealth Studies, 1975), p. 366.

82. Amnesty International, *Report on Prison Conditions in W. Bengal* (London, 1974), and Amnesty International, *Annual Report 1974–5* (London, 1975).

83. ILO, *135th Report* (Geneva, Feb. 1973), paras. 27–68, approved at its 189th session by the ILO governing body; ILO, *153rd Report* (Geneva, Nov. 1975), paras. 69–98.

84. Amnesty International, *Report on Prison Conditions in W. Bengal*; Amnesty International, *Annual Report 1974–5*; and ILO, *135th Report*, loc. cit., and *153rd Report*, loc. cit.

85. See, e.g., *EPW*, 22.12.73, for an account of conditions in Calcutta's Presidency Jail.

86. Jawaharlal Nehru, *Autobiography* (London, Bodley Head, 1936), p. 90.

87. qu. Era Sezhiyan (DMK), *Parliament under Emergency* (privately circulated, undated), p. 5.

88. *The Century* (Delhi), 1.11.75; describing itself as the 'journal of the thinking people'.

89. See *EPW*, 26.5.73.

90. See, e.g., Biplab Dasgupta, *The Naxalite Movement* (Delhi, Allied Publishers, 1974).

91. The Communist Party of India (Marxist–Leninist) was formed on 22 April 1969, and banned under the 1975 emergency.

92. *ABP*, 12.3.73.

93. Amnesty International, *Report on Prison Conditions in W. Bengal*; *EPW*, 27.7.74.

94. See appendix, pp. 387–8.

95. GOI, *Why Emergency?* (Ministry of Home Affairs, GOI, 1975), p. 31; and see *Guardian*, 13.9.72, 19.9.72.

96. *EPW*, 18.5.74, 25.5.74.

97. Conversation between railway worker and the writer, Calcutta, December 1975.

98. GOI, *Years of Achievement: Railways* (DAVP, MIB, GOI, 1975), p. 10.

99. The Communist Party of India (Marxist) broke away from the CPI in 1964; its affiliated industrial and student organizations are the CITU and SFI, respectively.

100. e.g. *Econ. Times*, 4.2.72, *Hindustan Times*, 15.3.72, *EPW*, 4.3.72.

101. *The Times*, 6.3.72, 13.3.72, 14.3.72, 17.3.72; *Le Monde*, 12.4.72.

102. e.g. W. Bengal's chief secretary spoke of 'large-scale arrests under MISA', and of 32,000 prisoners held in W. Bengal's jails as a result, qu. *Statesman*, 8.1.72.

103. *Guardian*, 10.7.76.

104. Amnesty International, *Report on Prison Conditions in W. Bengal*, passim.

105. ibid.

106. qu. *PODS*, p. 7.

107. 4.2.72; and e.g. 'Ghoshpukur village in Hooghly district. The evening of March 24. The army appears and cordons off the village. The police begin going from house to house, beating men, insulting women, young and old, looting whatever they can lay their hands on inside the houses. Next morning they come again. Most of the men are away. They begin attacking the women. The 23-year old daughter of Akkel Ali is beaten and when her mother tries to save her, she is also beaten and both are dragged by their hair ... A contingent of the police, led by the officer-in-charge of the station, arrives and takes charge of the attack. They bayonet Akkel Ali's wife ... They kick Arshed Ali's pregnant wife. One of the beasts tries to violate 32-year-old Nurunnahar. She is saved because of the resistance of others ... This happened in Ghoshpukur, but it can be any village in West Bengal, or for that matter any town, even the City of Calcutta' (Jyoti Basu, *Cry Halt to This Reign of Terror*, Calcutta, 1972, p. 1).

108. 15.3.72.

109. 4.3.72.

110. 4.3.72.

111. *PODS*, p. 6.

112. Maxwell, *Woman on a White Horse*, p. 361.

113. Amnesty International, *Annual Report, 1974–5*.

114. *EPW*, 12.5.73; *Le Monde*, 15.6.73.

115. Amnesty International, *Annual Report, 1974–5*.

116. ibid.

117. GOI, *Reason For Emergency* (Delhi, DAVP, MIB, 1975), p. 5.

118. e.g. Maxwell, *Woman on a White Horse*, pp. 357 ff.

119. S. S. Ray, Chief Minister of West Bengal, and D. K. Barooah, president of the Congress Party, qu. *Ind. Exp.*, 30.12.75.

120. Maxwell, *Woman on a White Horse*, p. 361.

121. Barooah, qu. *Ind. Exp.*, 30.12.75.

122. For this terminology also see chapter 3, pp. 101–2.

123. GOI, *Reason For Emergency*, p. 5.

124. In Hyderabad, 18 November 1975, qu. *Ind. Exp.*, 19.11.75.

125. *Times of India*, 26.6.75; GOI, *Reason For Emergency*, p. 4; GOI, *Why Emergency?*, p. 13.

126. M. C. Chagla, 'Civil Liberties in India' (a speech of 12 October 1975, Citizens for Democracy, privately circulated, undated), p. 4.

235297655892

952558364559876

127. Conversation between the Prime Minister and the writer, New Delhi, December 1975.
128. *Times of India*, 13.6.75.
129. *EPW*, 14.6.75.
130. Chagla, p. 4.
131. ibid., p. 4; *Times of India*, 25.6.75, 26.6.75.
132. Sezhiyan, p. 4; 'the opposition parties were trying to come to some understanding, and sought the guidance of J. P. Narayan, who came to Delhi and joined them in their deliberations'.
133. *Guardian*, 20.8.75; cf. the *Times of India*, 25.6.76, which reduced the number to a mere handful.
134. Chagla, p. 4; *Times of India*, 26.6.75.
135. Sezhiyan, p. 3; 'apprehensive that the summoning of the House was being delayed to suit the convenience of the Prime Minister', and wishing to 'discuss the implications of the Allahabad judgement' (ibid., p. 4).
136. *Guardian*, 20.8.75; cf. Rajni Kothari, 'The End of an Era', *Seminar*, Jan. 1976, in which he argued that by June 1975 'the opposition movement had virtually collapsed', and there was 'no serious threat to the régime'; while the emergency itself was 'no answer to the crisis that had been growing during the decade of non-performance preceding it'.
137. Rashtriya Swayam Sevak Sangh (RSS), one of the several components, with the Shiv Sena, and the Anand Marg, of the extreme right.
138. CPI-M, 'On the Declaration of Emergency: For All Party Units' (Calcutta, 3 Sept. 1975).
139. Chagla, p. 5.
140. Maxwell, *Woman on a White Horse*, p. 365.
141. See, e.g., CPI, *Resolutions and Report of the National Council* (which met from 25 August to 28 August 1975, in Delhi), Sept. 1975.
142. ibid., pp. 10–11, p. 20.
143. ibid., pp. 10–11.
144. ibid., p. 20.
145. IG, at Hyderabad, 17 November 1975, qu. *Hindu* 18.11.75.
146. IG, qu. *Ind. Exp.*, 31.12.75.
147. GOI, *Why Emergency?*, preface.
148. IG, qu. *Ind. Exp.*, 18.11.75.
149. GOI, *Why Emergency?*, preface.
150. IG, to Lok Sabha, 22 July 1975, qu. *PODS*, pp. 6–7.

151. IG, *Sunday Telegraph*, 12.10.75, reprinted in *Cross-Section* (Delhi), November 1975, p. 1.

152. IG, qu. *Hindu*, 13.4.76.

153. GOI, *Why Emergency?*, preface.

154. ibid.

155. GOI, *Reason for Emergency*, p. 3. But, cf. '. . . there was a minimum of violence considering the depth and spread of the movement and its intensity . . . in many cases, the violence was provoked by the Congress Party and government themselves', J. P. Narayan, letter to *The Times*, 5.6.76.

156. Ashok Mitra, qu. *Economist*, 24.1.76.

157. IG, qu. *Econ. Times*, 2.4.76.

158. Barooah, qu. *Ind. Exp.*, 30.12.75.

159. ibid.

160. GOI, *Why Emergency?*, p. 50.

161. ibid., p. 13.

162. ibid.

163. S. S. Ray, qu. *Deccan Herald*, 30.12.75.

164. e.g., IG, *Broadcast to the Nation, June 26, 1975* (DAVP, MIB, GOI, 1975), p. 1.

165. IG, to Rajya Sabha, 22 July 1975; qu. *PODS*, p. 8.

166. For 'all-India movement', S. S. Ray, qu. *Deccan Herald*, 30.12.75.

167. IG, *Broadcast to the Nation, June 26, 1975*, p. 1.

168. ibid.

169. GOI, *Why Emergency: Questions and Answers* (DAVP, MIB, 1975), 'published to meet public demand', p. 3.

170. IG, to Rajya Sabha, 22 July 1975, qu. *PODS*, p. 12.

CHAPTER TWO: ON THE CONDITION OF THE PEOPLE

1. *Hindu*, 7.3.76; inaugurating the 25th annual convention of the Travel Agents' Association of India.

2. *Hindu*, 21.2.76.

3. *Econ. Times*, 14.4.76.

4. *Ind. Exp.*, 31.12.75.

5. IG, qu. *Ind. Exp.*, 2.4.76.

6. GOI, *India Today: Basic Facts*, p. 26.

7. GOI, *Years of Achievement: Rural Development* (DAVP, MIB, 1975), p. 11.

8. IG, qu. *Ind. Exp.*, 12.7.75.

9. Prof. Chaman Kashkari, qu. *Times of India*, 15.1.76.

10. Jagjivan Ram, Minister of Agriculture, qu. *Ind. Exp.*, 15.1.76.

11. Directorate-General of Technical Development, qu. *Statesman*, 14.1.76.

12. *Peacock Colours In The Sun: Rajasthan* (Dept. of Tourism, GOI, 1973), p. 10.

13. Sen, p. 13.

14. ibid.; see also S. Mehra, 'Surplus Labour in Indian Agriculture', *Indian Economic Review*, April 1966; *Report of the Committee of Experts on Unemployment Estimates* (Planning Commission, GOI, 1970); V. M. Dandekar and N. Rath, 'Poverty in India', *EPW*, 2.1.71 and 9.1.71; Raj Krishna, 'Unemployment in India', *Indian Journal of Agricultural Economics*, Jan.–March 1973.

15. Dandekar and Rath, loc. cit.

16. Karl Marx, *Wage Labour and Capital* (Moscow, Progress Publishers, 1952), p. 44.

17. As in the case of unemployment, there is a large literature; notably, the work of P. D. Ojha and V. V. Bhatt; Dandekar and Rath; and P. K. Bardhan (e.g. 'On The Minimum Level of Living and The Rural Poor', *Indian Economic Review*, April 1971; 'On the Incidence of Poverty in Rural India', *EPW*, Feb. 1975).

18. Bardhan, loc. cit; Dandekar and Rath, loc. cit; for individual states, e.g. Tamil Nadu, A. Vagiswari, 'Income Earning Trends and Social Statistics' (Madras, Madras Institute of Development Studies, 1972), p. 58; or, for Bihar, F. T. Jannuzi, *Agrarian Crisis in India*.

19. Bardhan, loc. cit.

20. Dandekar and Rath, loc. cit.

21. See, e.g., *United Nations Population Year-Book*, 1974.

22. Joyce Hopkirk, *Daily Mirror Book of Successful Slimming: How You Can Lose 5, 10 or 50 lbs.* (London, Mirror Group, 1976), p. 15.

23. ibid.

24. *S. Standard*, 22.2.76.

25. C. Gopalan, qu. *Hindu*, 12.1.76.

26. Kuldip Nayar, *Ind. Exp.*, 15.1.76 ('where poverty engulfs more and more people liberty ceases to have a meaning').

27. *PBEI* (Oct. 1975), p. 9, under head 'Economic Framework'.

28. ibid., p. 9, under head 'Income and Employment'.

29. *Ind. Exp.* (leader), 8.10.75, which refers to 'the committee under the Minimum Wages Act in Karnataka [which] fixed wages under the Act lower than the cost of maintenance [calculated on "two

meals a day of the cheapest grain in the locality, two sets of clothing per annum and a shed to live in"], on the ground that market wages were lower still'; *Econ. Times*, 7.8.75; and *PBLS*, p. 40.

30. *Asian Drama* (London, Allen Lane, 1968), p. 1065.

31. e.g. *Blitz*, 10.1.76.

32. *Link*, 2.5.76, citing 'farm management studies undertaken in various regions since 1954'.

33. Karl Marx, *Capital* (Moscow, Progress Publishers, 1959), vol. 3, pp. 595–6.

34. *W. Bengal State Labour Department Survey for 1975* (Calcutta, 1976), qu. *EPW*, 1.5.76.

35. See, e.g., RBI's *Statistical Tables: All-India Debt and Investment Survey, 1971–2*.

36. *PBLS*, pp. 141–5.

37. Arvind Narayan Das, 'Where Lender is Lord', *Times of India*, 30.11.75.

38. ANS Institute of Social Studies Survey, Patna, qu. ibid.

39. *People's Democracy*, 13.6.76, citing UNI survey.

40. Indian School of Social Sciences, 'Bonded Labour in India' (Calcutta, 1975), p. 2.

41. *Hindu*, 3.4.76; and referring to the Pania 'tribals', 'most of them seem to suffer from malnutrition, skin diseases, rickets, yaws and enlarged liver'.

42. ibid.

43. *Link*, 18.4.76.

44. e.g., *Econ. Times*, 3.4.76, which refers to the 'letting loose of terror against *adivasis*' in the Shahada tribal belt of Dhulla district, in Maharashtra state, by 'the men of a private army of the landlords'.

45. *Times of India*, 10.10.74.

46. Das, loc. cit.

47. C. Subramaniam, to Lok Sabha, 4 Aug. 1975; qu. GOI, *The Turning Point*, p. 76.

48. For the anatomy of bonded debt, see Indian School of Social Sciences, 'Bonded Labour in India', which gives typical details (p. 18) of the bonded debtors of Satta Village, Purola block, Kashi district, Uttar Pradesh, thus:

Name of Debtor	Loan taken (rupees)	Name of creditor	Purpose of loan	Number of years of bonded labour served
Minu	500	Kundilal	Food	17 years
	300	Lalsingh	Food	17 years
Strmu	220	Thakur Singh	To repay loan	6 months
Banasu	300	Sulku	Food	1 year
Dilsuk	105	Dev Singh	Food	5 months
Sukha	300	Hukma	Marriage	18 years
	35	Thakar	To buy sheep	5 years
	20	Sulku	To buy wooden box	10 years
Nanda	100	Dev Singh	Food	12 years

49. GOI, *The Turning Point*, p. 76.
50. In Karnataka, Uttar Pradesh, Rajasthan, Andhra Pradesh (and Orissa), Bihar, Gujarat, Kerala, respectively, while the last two are additional variant terms in Uttar Pradesh.
51. Indian School of Social Sciences, 'Bonded Labour in India', p. 1.
52. A. N. Das, 'Where Lender is Lord', *Times of India*, 30.11.75.
53. Indian School of Social Sciences, 'Bonded Labour in India', p. 14.
54. M. K. A. Siddiqui, 'Life In The Slums Of Calcutta', *EPW*, 13.12.69.
55. Based on the 1971 Census; *PBEI*, pp. 19, 27–8.
56. A. P. Sharma, Minister of State for Industries, to Lok Sabha, 6 May 1976; qu. *Times of India*, 7.5.76.
57. *PBEI*, p. 23.
58. *Blitz*, 10.1.76.
59. *Ind. Exp.*, 15.1.76.
60. cf. *Hindu*, 5.12.68; C. Bradinath, *Urban Development of Greater Madras* (Report to the Government of Tamil Nadu, Jan. 1970), p. 2; and *Ind. Exp.*, 15.1.76.
61. Bradinath, p. 2.
62. Official Bombay Slum Census (published 4 January 1976), qu. *Ind. Exp.*, 16.1.76; also *Ind. Exp.*, 15.1.76.
63. S. S. Tinaikar, head of Bombay's 'Reconstruction Board', qu. *Times of India*, 15.3.76.
64. *Ind. Exp.*, 15.1.76.
65. ibid.; and Gangadar Jha, *Econ. Times*, 28.3.76.
66. ibid.
67. 'Madras, The Slum City', in *Radical Review*, September 1970, pp. 7 ff.

68. *Econ. Times*, 28.3.76.

69. *EPW*, 13.12.69.

70. The tendencies are well discussed in *Radical Review*, loc. cit., and patent in the Indian press in the late 1960s and the 1970s.

71. V. D. Narayanan, then mayor of Madras, qu. *Hindu*, 12.5.68. On 10 August 1969, hundreds of council labourers, backed up by more than 100 police, destroyed the Madras slum of Gandhinagar, *Hindu*, 11.8.69; and 'trees under which the people gathered were also felled, so as not to encourage the homeless to take shelter under them' (conversation between social worker and the writer, Madras, Dec. 1975).

72. *Parliamentary Estimates Committee Report, 1976*; qu. *Hindu*, 2.6.76.

73. *Times of India*, 30.11.75.

74. P. K. Kunte, Minister of State for Housing, Maharashtra government, qu. *Samachar*, 13.6.76. What evidence there is suggests that there may be an increasing proportion of the employed proletariat among slum-dwellers; cf. 'Social Welfare in the Slums of Madras City' (Madras School of Social Work, 1965), which reported then that 75 per cent of city slum-dwellers were unemployed.

75. *Ind. Exp.*, 9.6.76; the Minister added that 'he was not aware that even the policemen were living in slums'.

76. *Econ. Times*, 25.8.75.

77. Conversation between local trade union official and the writer, Bombay, January 1976.

78. N. Ram, 'Conditions of Working Fishermen in Madras City', *Radical Review*, Jan. 1971, pp. 12–21.

79. Conversation between national trade union leader and the writer, Calcutta, Dec. 1975, referring to events in W. Bengal in 1972.

80. The Indian National Trade Union Congress.

81. Conversation between Ashok Leyland worker and the writer, Madras, Dec. 1975.

82. cf. 'We call stooge unions *bondas*. In a restaurant, they place the *bonda* on your plate. It is sweet and savoury. Then they put gravy curry, *samba*, on it. The server comes and pours *samba* on your *bonda* (laughter). In the same way, the stooge union leader will put out his *bonda*, and the management pours the *samba* on it (laughter)' (conversation with Ashok Leyland workers, Madras, Dec. 1975).

83. Conversation between trade union official and the writer, Madras, Dec. 1975.

84. Conversation with Ashok Leyland workers, Madras, Dec. 1975.

85. During conversation between Sivasilam and the writer, Madras, Dec. 1975; for the alternative version, conversation between local trade union officials and the writer, Madras, Dec. 1975.

86. Conversation, in the presence of the writer, between Ashok Leyland directors, at Ennore, Dec. 1975.

87. All the facts connected with this case, and quotations from the depositions, are taken from the charge-sheets themselves: *In Ennore P.S. Cr. No. 147/72.* The depositions are dated 18 June 1972. R. R. Jones is described as 'playing a leading role in the attack against the workers' (*Radical Review*, April–June 1972, p. 38).

88. J. P. Naik, *Policy and Performance in Indian Education, 1947–74* (Delhi, Orient Longman, 1975), p. 6.

89. ibid.

90. *PBEI*, p. 30. This is, of course, an average; it is 80 per cent of the total population in Bihar, Kashmir, Rajasthan, and Uttar Pradesh, 66 per cent in W. Bengal, 40 per cent in Kerala; ibid, pp. 29–30.

91. Naik, p. 6.

92. ibid., pp. 6–7.

93. IG, qu. *Statesman*, 28.11.75.

94. *EPW*, 20.12.75.

95. *PBEI*, p. 229.

96. V. P. Dutt, qu. *Link*, 18.4.76.

97. *Seventy-ninth Report of Parliamentary Estimates Committee on the Ministry of Education and Social Welfare* (Delhi, April 1975); qu. *EPW*, 20.12.75; the report also reveals that primary education is not available at all to forty million primary school children.

98. In conversation with the writer, Ministry of Education, Delhi, Dec. 1975.

99. *EPW*, 20.12.75.

100. 'Functional Literacy Programme' of the Department of Adult Education, Ministry of Education (Delhi, 1975), *passim.*

101. N. Hasan, Minister of Education, reporting on meeting of states' Education Ministers, qu. *Statesman*, 28.11.75.

102. *PBEI*, p. 20.

103. ibid.

104. Karan Singh, qu. *Ind. Exp.*, 12.1.76.

105. *Blitz*, 10.1.76.

106. GOI, *India Today: Basic Facts*, p. 16.

107. *PBEI*, p. 227.

108. *PBEI*, pp. 212–15 and 226; see appendix, p. 436.

109. C. Gopalan, qu. *Hind. Times*, 12.1.76.

110. GOI, *India Today: Basic Facts*, p. 16.

111. Indian Council of Medical Research, qu. *Ind. Exp.*, 22.2.76, *Link*, 9.5.76.

112. ibid.; also, 'more elderly people fall prey to tuberculosis than did twenty-five years ago', *Hind. Times*, 7.6.76.

113. *Times of India*, 6.6.76.

114. GOI, *India Today: Basic Facts*, p. 16.

115. qu. *Ind. Exp.*, 22.2.76.

116. Conversation between official of Jadhavpur University, Calcutta and the writer, Calcutta, Dec. 1975.

117. *Statesman*, 27.12.75.

118. ibid.; and, for the incidence of deaths throughout a cold wave, *Statesman*, 10.12.75, 13.12.75; *Times of India*, 17.12.75; *Ind. Exp.*, 14.1.76.

119. A. Bujevic, WHO regional officer, qu. *Samachar*, 7.5.76.

120. *Times of India*, 31.1.76.

121. GOI, *India Today: Basic Facts*, p. 16.

122. Gian Prakash, *Times of India*, 27.4.76.

123. *Ind. Exp.*, 1.4.76.

124. ibid.

125. *Times of India*, 27.4.76.

126. *Link*, 2.5.76.

127. *Ind. Exp.*, 2.4.76.

128. qu. *Ind. Exp.*, 12.1.76.

129. *Hind. Times*, 25.2.76.

130. *Ind. Exp.*, 12.1.76; with an 'estimated 136 million people exposed to the risk', *Hind. Times*, 26.4.76.

131. *Hindu*, 1.4.76.

132. *Times of India*, 30.11.75, based on findings of the 1971 census.

133. ibid.

134. ibid.; 'given the fact that there is going to be a big bulge in the population of children below fourteen years of age . . . it is clear that there will be an even greater number of children at work in the future'.

135. *Ind. Exp.*, 29.12.75.

136. *ABP*, 25.5.76.

137. IG, qu. *Times of India*, 28.11.75.

138. *PBLS*, p. 6.

139. *Committee on the Status of Women in India, Report, 1975*, qu. *The Working Class*, March 1976; also see *Link*, 2.5.76.

140. *Committee on the Status of Women in India, Report, 1975*, qu. *The Working Class*, March 1976.

141. ibid. Also, figures for Karnataka (1957–72) showed a steadily falling proportion of women workers in the total trade union membership in that state; see *Econ. Times*, 25.3.76. For prominent participation of women in trade union organization, e.g. see *Radical Review*, April 1973, pp. 13 ff., on the organization of plantation workers.

142. *Committee on the Status of Women in India, Report, 1975*, qu. *The Working Class*, March 1976.

143. ibid. In Bombay only 8·4 per cent of the total female population is in the work force, in Delhi 5·1 per cent, in Calcutta 4·7 per cent; see *Link*, 2.5.76.

144. *The Working Class*, March 1976.

145. ibid.; also, *Link*, 2.5.76.

146. e.g. F. Chakravarty in *Hind. Times*, 19.1.75.

147. *The Working Class*, March 1976.

148. ibid.

149. 'Indian Plantations: Sweat, Hunger and Despair', *Radical Review*, April 1973, pp. 13 ff.

150. ibid.

151. ibid.

152. *Statesman*, 11.4.76.

153. L. de Souza, Minister of State for Public Health, Maharashtra government; qu. *Ind. Exp.*, 6.4.76.

154. S. D. Panekar and Kamala Rao, *A Study of Prostitutes in Bombay* (Bombay, Lalvani Publishing House, 1967), esp. pp. 90–127, which contains extended passages of women's autobiography. I have both learned, extracted, and conflated from it, and record my debt here.

155. 'From The Green Hills of Purola [Uttar Pradesh] to the Brothels of Delhi' in Indian School of Social Sciences, 'Bonded Labour in India'.

156. ibid., p. 39.

157. ibid.

158. *Link*, 18.4.76.

159. Indian School of Social Sciences, 'Bonded Labour in India', p. 39. According to the Association for Social Health in India, 'prostitution seems to be on the increase in Bombay' (qu. *Hind. Times*, 1.12.75).

160. Panekar and Rao, pp. 3–4, chapter 2, *passim*, and appendix 4, *passim*.

161. Indian School of Social Sciences, 'Bonded Labour in India', p. 41. Maya Ram, *sarpanch* of Kuan Village, Uttar Pradesh, Prem Dutt Sharma, a teacher of Purola, and others; also quoted are the words of Janki, an elderly prostitute originally from Kumolagaon, Purola, Uttar Pradesh, interviewed in a Delhi brothel: 'Buy freedom for our men, give them land, only land. It is this land, these green fields, which will contain their girls. Nothing else can' (op. cit., p. 46).

162. ibid., p. 48.

163. Panekar and Rao, *passim*.

164. *PBEI*, p. 229.

165. ibid., p. 29.

166. e.g., 'A poor woman in Raina police area of Burdwan district, West Bengal, sold her ten-month old son for 500 rupees to a rich man living in Khandagosh police-station area of the district. She was without any food for a number of days. Many families in that village are in a half-starved condition' (*Ganashakti*, 17.3.76).

167. Communicated to the writer, Amritsar, Nov. 1975.

168. Conversation between woman rural trade union worker and the writer, Karnataka, Jan. 1976.

169. qu. *ABP*, 16.4.76; suicide 'because of unemployment' is recorded for instance, in *Times of India*, 28.11.75.

170. *North Indian Patrika*, 19.12.75.

171. *Hindu*, 22.2.76.

172. *S. Standard*, 22.2.76.

173. Sign in Bombay's covered market.

174. See M. Blaug, and others, *Causes of Graduate Unemployment in India*, LSE Studies on Education (London, Allen Lane, 1969); it is also 'rapidly increasing', perhaps by about 15 per cent per annum, *Link*, 25.4.76.

175. Conversation between social worker and the writer, Calcutta, Dec. 1975.

176. Conversation between Bombay property-developer and the writer, Bombay, Jan. 1976.

177. In conversation with the writer, Jodhpur, Nov. 1975.

178. As n. 176.

179. Peasant song of rural Kerala, communicated to writer, Cochin, Jan. 1976 (Malayalam original; writer's translation).

180. Communicated to the writer, rural Tamil Nadu, Dec. 1975.

181. Conversation in rural Tamil Nadu, Dec. 1975.
182. Conversation between eye-witnesses of July 1974 South Madras food riots and the writer, Madras, Dec. 1975.
183. As n. 182.
184. I G, qu. *Econ. Times*, 14.4.76.

CHAPTER THREE: THE POLITICS OF ILLUSION

1. I G, *Broadcast to the Nation, June 26, 1975*, p. 1.
2. qu. *Ind. Exp.*, 2.5.76.
3. e.g. Kista Gowd and Jangam Bhoomaiah, hanged in Secunderabad jail on 1 Dec. 1975; Phiroz Rustomji Durawala, hanged in Yerawada prison, Poona, on 1 Jan. 1976.
4. Maxwell, *Woman on a White Horse*, p. 357.
5. ibid., p. 358.
6. ibid.; and, for a literal expression of it, the 'queues of astrologers at her Delhi bungalow' (*Economist*, 29.5.76). Cf. 'The purpose of education is to eradicate superstition', I G, qu. *Econ. Times*, 24.4.76.
7. Prabhat Patnaik, 'Imperialism and the Growth of Indian Capitalism', in *Explosion in a Sub-Continent*, R. Blackburn, ed. (Penguin Books, 1975), p. 58.
8. ibid.
9. R. Gopalakrishnan, in the *Black Liberator* (London), vol. 2, no. 4, Winter 1976.
10. ibid.
11. Premen Addy and Ibne Azad, 'Politics and Society in Bengal', in Blackburn, ed., pp. 107 and 117–18.
12. See chapter 6.
13. This is, justifiably, one of the recurring themes of Nirad Chaudhuri's writings. See, e.g., *The Continent of Circe* (London, Chatto & Windus, 1965).
14. Resolutions of All-India Congress Committee (AICC), May 1929.
15. ibid.
16. Mahatma Gandhi, in *Maratha*, 12.8.34, qu. Blackburn, ed., p. 134.
17. *Maratha*, 12.8.34.
18. ibid.
19. qu. Blackburn, ed., p. 135.
20. AICC Resolutions, 1929.

21. *Draft Outline, First Five-year Plan*, Planning Commission (GOI), July 1951, pp. 3 ff.

22. *Report of 45th Indian National Congress*, Karachi 1931, pp. 139–41.

23. *Draft Outline, First Five-year Plan*, pp. 3 ff. cf. Nehru, to Lok Sabha, 25 May 1956, 'Why should we fritter away our energy in pushing out somebody who is doing it in the private sector?' qu. P. Chattopadhyay, 'State Capitalism in India', in *Towards National Liberation: Essays on Political Economy*, ed. S. A. Shah (Montreal, 1973), p. 68.

24. *Draft Outline, First Five-year Plan*, pp. 3 ff.

25. Nehru, to Lok Sabha, 17 Feb. 1948; see 'Flexible Economic Policy' in *Nehru's Speeches* (Delhi, MIB, GOI), vol. 1, *1946–49*, pp. 107–118.

26. *Mainstream*, 13.12.75.

27. Barooah, qu. *Deccan Herald*, 1.1.76.

28. ibid.

29. IG, qu. *Ind. Exp.*, 31.12.75.

30. Barooah, qu. *Ind. Exp.*, 30.12.75.

31. IG, qu. *Ind. Exp.*, 31.12.75.

32. Subramaniam, to Lok Sabha, 31 July 1975, qu. GOI, *The Turning Point*, p. 55.

33. *Link*, 11.1.76.

34. Dharam Vir Sinha, Deputy Minister for Information and Broadcasting, in Mysore, 14 March 1976, qu. *ABP*, 15.3.76.

35. IG, qu. *Ind. Exp.*, 31.12.75.

36. Barooah, qu. *Times of India*, 30.12.75.

37. IG, qu. *Ind. Exp.*, 31.12.75.

38. IG, to Lok Sabha, 22 July 1975.

39. Barooah, qu. *Deccan Herald*, 30.12.75.

40. IG, to Lok Sabha, 22 July 1975.

41. IG, qu. *Ind. Exp.*, 31.12.75.

42. ibid.

43. IG, qu. *Ind. Exp.*, 31.12.75.

44. Conversation between Ayub Syed and the writer, Bombay, Jan. 1976.

45. Krishan Kant, to Rajya Sabha, 21 July 1975, privately circulated; see appendix, pp. 385–6.

46. Sanjay Gandhi ('addressing a mammoth public meeting') at Guntur, Andhra Pradesh, 20 March 1976, qu. *Hindu*, 21.3.76.

47. Sanjay Gandhi, qu. *Econ. Times*, 7.3.76.

48. Subramaniam, to Rajya Sabha, 29 July 1975.

49. Subramaniam, to Lok Sabha, 4 April 1975, qu. G O I, *The Turning Point*, p. 71.

50. I G, inaugurating a savings scheme in Delhi, 1 April 1972, qu. *Times of India*, 2.4.72.

51. Maxwell, *Woman on a White Horse*, p. 360.

52. ibid.

53. Sanjay Gandhi, qu. *Econ. Times*, 7.3.76.

54. qu. *Deccan Herald*, 30.12.75.

55. Pai, qu. *Ind. Exp.*, 17.10.75.

56. A I C C Draft Resolution on Economic Policy, Dec. 1975, qu. *Ind. Exp.*, 29.12.75.

57. I G, at Loyola College, Madras, qu. *Times of India*, 15.1.76.

58. ibid.; also, qu. *Statesman*, 28.11.75, on the same subject.

59. J. G. Gurley, 'Rural Development in China, 1949–62', in *World Development*, July–August 1975, p. 456.

60. Report of conference of state governors, qu. *Econ. Times*, 20.3.76.

61. ibid.

62. I G, interviewed by Swedish television on 12 March 1976, qu. *Fin. Times*, 18.3.76.

63. *Link*, 18.4.76.

64. Rhagunatha Reddy, at conference of state Labour Ministers, qu. *Ind. Exp.*, 12.1.76; cf. Jagjivan Ram's 'the fruits of labour must be available to all' (qu. *Ind. Exp.*, 31.12.75).

65. ibid.

66. Ashok Mitra, *Economist*, 24.1.76.

67. Barooah, qu. *Deccan Herald*, 1.1.76.

68. ibid.

69. Barooah, qu. *Deccan Herald*, 31.12.75.

70. ibid.

71. G O I, *A Hundred New Gains*, p. 18.

72. Pai, to Rajya Sabha, 29 July 1975, qu. G O I, *The Turning Point*, p. 32.

73. I G, qu. *Statesman*, 28.11.75, at Central Advisory Board of Education, on lack of progress in education.

74. B. C. Bhagabati, at a public meeting in Calcutta, qu. *ABP*, 25.3.76.

75. ibid.

76. Conversation between K. N. Johry, Council for Scientific and Industrial Research (C S I R), and the writer, Delhi, Dec. 1975.

77. As n. 76.

78. Conversation between Johry and the writer, Delhi, Dec. 1975.

79. Conversation between Nurul Hasan, Minister of Education, and the writer, Delhi, Dec. 1975.

80. As n. 78.

81. Report of symposium of Associated Chambers of Commerce and Industry (Delhi), qu. *Econ. Times*, 25.4.76.

82. Arvind Mafatlal, the industrialist, qu. ibid.

83. Kailash Chander, president of Indian Council of Social Welfare (Delhi), qu. *Times of India*, 16.12.75.

84. Conversation between block development officer [sc. rural administrator] and the writer, Varanasi, Dec. 1975.

85. I G, laying foundation stone for Hooghly bridge, Calcutta, qu. *Hind. Times*, 21.5.72.

86. Hasit Hamani, *Statesman*, 14.1.76 (letter to editor).

87. Bansi Lal, qu. *Ind. Exp.*, 31.12.75.

88. I G, interviewed by Anthony Mayer and shown by BBC (hereafter 'Mayer interview'), qu. *Ind. Exp.*, 2.4.76.

89. I G, qu. *Times of India*, 15.1.76.

90. I G, addressing Institute of Democracy and Socialism, Delhi, qu. *Econ. Times*, 24.3.76.

91. Conversation between Rashid ud-din Khan and the writer, Jawaharlal Nehru University, Delhi, Nov. 1975.

92. G O I, *Why Emergency?*, pp. 20–21.

93. ibid., p. 15.

94. Jagjivan Ram, Minister of Agriculture, qu. *Econ. Times*, 10.4.76.

95. 'New Economics: Facts Do Not Fit', *EPW*, 1.7.72.

96. *Ind. Exp.*, 3.5.76.

97. Fakruddin Ali Ahmed, President of India, qu. *Ind. Exp.*, 13.4.76.

98. ibid.

99. I G, qu. *Hindu (Int. Ed.)*, 10.4.76.

100. ibid.

101. Jagjivan Ram, qu. *Ind. Exp.*, 31.12.75.

102. Conversation between Ayub Syed and the writer, Bombay, Jan. 1976.

103. G O I, *A Hundred New Gains*, p. 17.

104. Subramaniam, to Rajya Sabha, 28 July 1975.

105. Barooah, qu. *Deccan Herald*, 1.1.76.

106. S. S. Ray, qu. *Ind. Exp.*, 30.12.75.

107. G O I, *Why Emergency?*, p. 1.

108. Barooah, qu. *Deccan Herald*, 1.1.76.

109. ibid.

110. S. S. Ray, qu. *Deccan Herald*, 30.12.75.

111. S. S. Ray, qu. *Ind. Exp.*, 13.1.76.

112. S. S. Ray, qu. *Ind. Exp.*, 30.12.75.

113. S. S. Ray, qu. *Deccan Herald*, 30.12.75.

114. The song 'Indira Hindustan Ban Gaie' ['Indira has become India'] was sung at the start of the official proceedings of the 75th plenary session of the Congress Party at Kamagata Maru Nagar, 29 Dec. 1975 (*Ind. Exp., Statesman, Times of India*, 30.12.75); cf. 'no individual can be the nation' (IG, qu. ibid, 30.12.75); and 'it is not correct to call me a symbol of India or its future' (qu. *ABP*, 3.4.76).

115. S. S. Ray, qu. *Ind. Exp.*, 30.12.75; and 'those who are criticizing the Congress Party are blindly anti-Congress, anti-India, and anti-Indira' (qu. *Deccan Herald*, 30.12.75).

116. ibid.

117. IG, to Rajya Sabha, 22 July 1975, qu. *PODS*, p. 13.

118. *PODS*, p. 13.

119. IG, qu. *Ind. Exp.*, 20.7.75.

120. Kuldip Nayar, *Ind. Exp.*, 15.1.76.

121. Jaganath Mishra, Chief Minister of Bihar, qu. *Guardian*, 7.7.75.

122. Brahmananda Reddy, Minister of Home Affairs, qu. *Econ. Times*, 6.4.76.

123. IG, qu. *Econ. Times*, 4.3.76.

124. ibid.

125. S. S. Ray, qu. *Deccan Herald*, 30.12.75.

126. G. P. Yadav, qu. *Hindu*, 8.1.76.

127. ibid.; cf. J. P. Narayan, *The Times*, 5.6.76 (see chapter 1, n. 155).

128. IG, to Institute of Democracy and Socialism, qu. *Econ. Times*, 24.3.76; cf. 'Opposition is undermining the democratic system: P. M.' (headline in *Times of India*, 11.12.75).

129. Barooah, qu. *Deccan Herald*, 1.1.76.

130. IG, qu. *ABP*, 3.4.76.

131. IG, Mayer interview, qu. *Econ. Times*, 2.4.76.

132. Jagjit Anand, *Guardian*, 7.7.75 (letter to editor).

133. Barooah, qu. *Deccan Herald*, 1.1.76.

134. Conversation between the Prime Minister and the writer, Delhi, Dec. 1975.

135. Brian Davey, *The Economic Development of India* (Nottingham, Spokesman Books, 1975), p. 198.

136. Angus Maddison, *Class Structure and Economic Growth, India and Pakistan* (London, Allen & Unwin, 1971), p. 95, qu. ibid., p. 198.

137. Krishan Kant, to Rajya Sabha, 21 July 1975, privately circulated; see appendix, pp. 385–6.

138. ibid.; he was expelled, with Chandra Shekhar (Cong.-R), on 9 Jan. 1976 (*Hindu*, 10.1.76).

139. R. K. Karanjia, *Blitz*, 10.1.76.

140. ibid.

141. The title of a biography, published by the Council for Socio-Political Studies, Delhi, and 'released by Barooah' (qu. *Times of India*, 11.12.75).

142. Karanjia, *Blitz*, 10.1.76; he described this as 'an unknown fact'.

143. Barooah, qu. *Guardian*, 26.1.76 ('carried away by his own rhetoric', Inder Malhotra, ibid.).

144. S. M. Banerjee (CPI), to Lok Sabha, 28 August 1975.

145. Karanjia, *Blitz*, 10.1.76.

146. G. P. Yadav, qu. *Hindu*, 8.1.76.

147. Abu Abraham, journalist, *Guardian Weekly*, 1.2.76.

148. Karanjia, *Blitz*, 10.1.76.

149. B. M. Birla, industrialist, qu. *ABP*, 4.5.76.

150. Sheik Abdullah, Chief Minister of Kashmir, qu. *Hindu*, 29.3.76.

151. Om Mehta, Minister of State for Home Affairs, in New York, qu. *Hindu*, 19.4.76.

152. Barooah, qu. *Guardian*, 26.1.76.

153. Karanjia, *Blitz*, 10.1.76.

154. cf. Martin Woollacott, 'Mrs Gandhi and her advisers were far less confident than they pretended about how the opposition and the country would react' (*Guardian*, 10.7.75).

155. Karanjia, *Blitz*, 10.1.76; for 'command-post', cf. 'the High Command's decision to continue the emergency was widely welcomed during the discussion [sc. among Congress Party leaders]' (*Ind. Exp.*, 30.12.75); and 'the High Command were seated in sofas on the dais, whereas traditionally they lounged on mattresses' (*Deccan Herald*, 30.12.75); also 'the sun was shining through a thin curtain of morning mist as Mr Barooah stepped up the podium to unfurl the Congress Party tricolour amidst the sounding of bugles' (*Times of India*, 30.12.75).

156. Barooah, qu. *Times of India*, 11.12.75.

157. qu. *Ind. Exp.*, 31.12.75.

158. Karanjia, *Blitz*, 10.1.76.

159. *Times of India*, 20.4.76.

160. Barooah, qu. *Guardian*, 26.1.76.

161. qu. *S. Standard*, 28.12.75.

162. Karanjia, *Blitz*, 10.1.76.

163. Conversation between senior official of the State Bank of India, and the writer, Dec. 1975.

164. David Holden, *Sunday Times*, 28.12.75.

165. Conversation between managing director of Simpson's, Madras, and the writer, Dec. 1975.

166. Hiren Mukherjee (CPI), qu. Sezhiyan, p. 6.

167. IG, qu. *Hindu*, 15.2.76.

168. *Link*, 22.2.76.

169. Jagjivan Ram, qu. *Link*, 22.2.76.

170. Jagjivan Ram, qu. *Ind. Exp.*, 15.1.76.

171. B. R. Shukla (Cong.), to Lok Sabha, 7 Jan. 1976, qu. *Ind. Exp.*, 8.1.76.

172. Swaran Singh Sokhi (Cong.), to Lok Sabha, 1 April 1976, qu. *Statesman*, 2.4.76.

173. qu. *Link*, 9.5.76.

174. AICC Subjects Committee resolution, 75th plenary session of Congress Party, qu. *Hindu*, 31.12.75.

175. M. S. Qureshi, Minister of State for Railways, qu. *Ind. Exp.*, 29.4.76; cf. K. C. Pant, Minister for Energy: 'nationalization of the mines anticipated the energy crisis in an uncanny fashion' (*Econ. Times*, 10.4.76).

176. AICC Subjects Committee resolution, qu. *Hindu*, 31.12.75.

177. Arya Bhushan, in *Competition Review*, Jan. 1976.

178. cf. S. S. Ray, 'democracy and secularism are our way of life, and socialism is our goal' (qu. *Ind. Exp.*, 30.12.75), and Barooah's 'the main components of the Congress political culture, whose foundation was laid by Mahatma Gandhi, is *nationalism based on secularism*, and democracy based on social justice' (qu. *Deccan Herald*, 1.1.76, my emphasis).

179. Conversation between senior official of State Bank of India and the writer, Dec. 1975; the Valluvar Kottam (temple) in Tamil Nadu was inaugurated by the President of India in April 1976, cost over seven million rupees, and '2000 families were forcibly evicted to make room for the saint' whom it commemorates (*Link*, 25.4.76).

180. IG, qu. *Hindu* (*Int. Ed.*), 6.3.76; and see *Times of India*, 2.3.76.

181. See chapter 7, p. 285.

182. For the emergency convergence between the publicly assailed Jan Sangh and the Congress Party, see chapter 8, pp. 335–6.

183. Barooah, qu. *Deccan Herald*, 1.1.76.

184. IG, to all-India Fighters Federation in Bangalore, qu. *Hindu* (*Int. Ed.*), 14.2.76.

185. IG, addressing troops in Jammu, qu. *Hindu*, 29.3.76.

186. IG, to 'a huge public meeting', Jammu, qu. *Hindu*, 29.3.76.
187. IG, at G. B. Pant University, qu. *Econ. Times*, 3.4.76.
188. Barooah, *Ind. Exp.*, 30.12.75.
189. Y. B. Chavan, in Poona, qu. *Hindu*, 26.12.75.
190. IG, at Kamagata Maru Nagar, qu. *Deccan Herald*, 30.12.75.
191. IG, to freedom fighters, qu. *Times of India*, 15.1.76.
192. IG, qu. *Hindu (Int. Ed.)*, 4.1.76.
193. IG, qu. *Times of India*, 18.1.76.
194. Barooah, qu. *Deccan Herald*, 1.1.76.
195. Press Trust of India (PTI) report, 30.11.75; cf. 'anti-fascist' conference at Pune; also, 'fascist clutches', ibid.
196. V. P. Dutt, to Rajya Sabha, qu. *Ind. Exp.*, 7.1.76.
197. IG, to Lok Sabha, qu. *PODS*, p. 1; cf. 'RSS teaching to young children was criminal. My father was also attacked, but this [referring to 1975 Gujarat election campaign] went beyond the limit' (conversation between Prime Minister and the writer, Delhi, Dec. 1975).
198. Barooah, to 'anti-fascist' conference at Patna, qu. *Ind. Exp.*, 5.12.75.
199. Biswanath Mukherjee (CPI), qu. *ABP*, 27.12.75.
200. IG, qu. *ABP*, 14.3.76.
201. IG, qu. *Hindu*, 29.3.76.
202. Barooah, to Patna conference, qu. *Ind. Exp.*, 5.12.75.
203. Shashi Bhusan (Cong.) to Pune conference, PTI report, 30.12.75.
204. IG, qu. *Hindu*, 29.3.76.
205. Message to Pune conference, qu. PTI report, 30.12.75.
206. Barooah, qu. *Deccan Herald*, 1.1.76.
207. IG, in Calcutta, qu. *Hindu (Int. Ed.)*, 2.3.76.
208. GOI, *Reason for Emergency*, p. 4.
209. GOI, *Why Emergency?*, p. 15; e.g. also, *Times of India*, 15.1.76; interview with Swedish television, qu. *ABP*, 18.3.76.
210. Subramaniam, to Rajya Sabha, 29 August 1975, qu. GOI, *The Turning Point*, p. 28.
211. IG, qu. *Ind. Exp.*, 12.7.75.
212. IG, qu. *Econ. Times*, 26.3.76.
213. IG, qu. *Ind. Exp.*, 8.1.76.
214. V. A. Seyid Muhammad, Minister of State for Law, to Rajya Sabha, 19 March 1976, qu. *Econ. Times*, 20.3.76.
215. J. R. D. Tata, industrialist, qu. *Mainstream*, 13.12.75, p. 10.
216. *Link*, 11.1.76.

217. Syed Ahmed Hashmi (Cong.), to Lok Sabha, qu. *Ind. Exp.*, 8.1.76.
218. H. R. Gokhale, Minister of Law, to Bihar state convention of lawyers, qu. *Hindu* (*Int. Ed.*), 14.2.76.
219. John Jacob, president of Singapore Indian Congress, 'India Then and Now', press release dated 15.3.76.
220. I G, Mayer interview, qu. *Ind. Exp.*, 2.4.76.
221. Chavan, qu. *Times of India*, 26.12.75.
222. J. R. D. Tata, qu. *Mainstream*, 13.12.75.
223. I G, Mayer interview, qu. *Ind. Exp.*, 2.4.76.
224. I G, at Rae Bareli, qu. *Ind. Exp.*, 13.4.76.
225. Chavan, qu. *Times of India*, 26.12.75.
226. I G, to Lok Sabha, 22 July 1975.
227. I G, Mayer interview, qu. *Ind. Exp.*, 2.4.76.
228. I G, in Madras, qu. *Ind. Exp.*, 15.1.76.
229. I G, Mayer interview, qu. *Ind. Exp.*, 2.4.76.
230. I G, in Hyderabad, qu. *Ind. Exp.*, 18.11.75.
231. I G, to Rajya Sabha, 1 April 1976, qu. *Hindu*, 2.4.76.
232. I G, qu. *Ind. Exp.*, 11.7.75.
233. I G, in Moscow, qu. *Guardian*, 12.6.76.
234. Conversation between official of National Physical Laboratory and the writer, Delhi, Nov. 1975.
235. I G, in Patna, qu. *Ind. Exp.*, 2.5.76.
236. qu. *Ind. Exp.*, 30.12.75.
237. S. S. Ray, qu. *Ind. Exp.*, 30.12.75.
238. ibid.
239. qu. *ABP*, 25.3.76.
240. ibid.
241. ibid.
242. qu. *ABP*, 25.3.76.
243. I G, to Rajya Sabha, 22 July 1975, qu. *PODS*, p. 10.
244. I G, to Rajya Sabha, 22 July 1975, ibid., p. 12.
245. Thus, in C P I – M polemic the term 'left-reaction' is reserved for the C P I.
246. See report on political prisoners in Kerala, *EPW*, 7.12.74; it refers to beatings by warders in the Erumeli case (7 May 1974), but also to cruel and sadistic practices during interrogation, described by released detainees.
247. Neville Maxwell, *India's China War* (Penguin Books, 1972), pp. 483–4.
248. C P I, *Resolutions and Report of National Council*, Delhi, 1975, p. 14.

249. ibid.

250. ibid.

251. ibid.

252. ibid., p. 17.

253. ibid.

254. Mohit Sen, *New Age*, 28.12.75; also 'it is almost as if from being a party in itself, it has become a party for itself'; and 'it would be no exaggeration to say that *by the adoption of its programme* [at the seventh congress in Bombay, in 1964], *the CPI has achieved Marxism–Leninism*' (emphasis in original). The same issue of the paper also carried a full-page advertisement for the Oberoi-Sheraton hotel in Bombay.

255. Maxwell, *Woman on a White Horse*, p. 358.

256. ibid.

257. Conversation between university teacher and the writer, Mysore, Jan. 1976.

258. Conversation in rural Karnataka, Jan. 1976.

259. Karan Singh, to parliamentary forum 'for the eradication of corruption', qu. *Hind. Times*, 10.8.73.

260. Subramaniam, to National Students' Union of India, qu. *Commerce* (Bombay), 21.7.73.

261. Conversation between Ashok Leyland workers and the writer, Madras, Dec. 1975.

262. From privately communicated account of aftermath of strike at Neyveli, Tamil Nadu.

263. Conversation between hotel manager and the writer, on a date between Nov. 1975 and Jan. 1976.

264. Ashok Mitra, *Economist*, 24.1.76.

265. *Confidential Advisor* ('for adults only'), Dec. 1975.

266. Conversation between trade union leader and the writer, Uttar Pradesh, Dec. 1975.

267. *New Internationalist*, Jan. 1976; for the Calcutta Port Trust, see *Business Standard*, 27.3.76.

268. *PBLS*, p. 40.

269. *Times of India*, 8.4.76.

270. *Times of India*, 26.5.71, 28.5.71, 29.5.71; Nagarwala was jailed for five years, after a trial of unprecedented brevity, for what he claimed was a 'hoax'. Requests for a judicial inquiry, made to the Lok Sabha on 28 May 1971, were refused.

271. Conversation between Prime Minister and the writer, Delhi, Dec. 1975.

272. IG, qu. *Hindu* (*Int. Ed.*), 4.1.76.

273. Maxwell, *Woman on a White Horse,* p. 364.
274. Barooah, qu. *Ind. Exp.*, 30.12.75.
275. Barooah, qu. ibid.
276. (All references to the Maruti case, unless otherwise specified, have been taken from PTI and UNI agency reports of parliamentary proceedings, in order to illustrate one of the pre-emergency functions of the independent press agencies); Niren Ghosh (CPI–M), to Lok Sabha, 30 March 1973.
277. Raj Narain (SSP), to Lok Sabha, 9 Nov. 1970.
278. Jyotirmoy Basu (CPI–M), to Lok Sabha, 22 Dec. 1973.
279. Madhu Limaye (SSP), to Lok Sabha, 10 Nov. 1970, 31 July 1973.
280. A. B. Vajpayjee (Jan Sangh), to Lok Sabha, 22 Dec. 1972, 16 May 1973; K. R. Malkani, editor of the Jan Sangh paper, *Motherland*, which had investigated the Maruti case, was also arrested, *Guardian*, 14.7.75.
281. S. N. Mishra (Cong. O), to Lok Sabha, 16 May 1973, 22 Dec. 1972.
282. In Rajya Sabha, 18 Nov. 1970.
283. On 9 Nov. 1970.
284. See *Times of India*, *Ind. Exp.*, and *Hindu*, 1.9.70, for the details.
285. D. L. Sen Gupta (Cong. O) to Rajya Sabha, 9 Nov. 1970.
286. The fact that Subramaniam had announced to Parliament in 1962 that the government 'had decided to produce 50,000 small cars in the public sector' was raised at the Allahabad trial on 19 March 1975.
287. On 31 August 1970.
288. Basu (CPI–M), to Lok Sabha, 22 Dec. 1972.
289. Bhai Mahavir (JS), to Rajya Sabha, 19 Dec. 1972.
290. In Lok Sabha, 27 August 1974 and 21 Nov. 1974.
291. In Lok Sabha, 22 Dec. 1972.
292. e.g. O. P. Tyagi (JS), to Rajya Sabha, 14 May 1973.
293. In Lok Sabha, 27 August 1974; the unanswered questioners included Hiren Mukherjee (CPI), who was a persistent complainant during the whole period.
294. Bedabrata Barua, to Rajya Sabha, 15 May 1973.
295. Lok Sabha debate of 16 May 1973.
296. Lok Sabha debates of 31 July 1973 and 16 April 1975; and Limaye (SSP), to Lok Sabha, 18 Dec. 1974. He alleged that questions on this matter put up for parliamentary answer had 'disappeared from the parliamentary secretariat'.
297. In Lok Sabha, 22 Dec. 1972.

298. ibid.
299. ibid.
300. In Lok Sabha, 22 Dec. 1972.
301. In Rajya Sabha, 12 August 1973, 16 April 1975.
302. In Lok Sabha, 25 June 1972.
303. In Lok Sabha, 7 March 1973.
304. In Rajya Sabha, 19 Dec. 1972.
305. In Rajya Sabha, 28 Nov. 1972; in Lok Sabha, 23 Feb. 1973.
306. In Lok Sabha, 8 May 1975.
307. Allahabad High Court trial, 19 March 1975.
308. Basu (CPI–M), to Lok Sabha, 22 Dec. 1972.
309. As n. 308.
310. As n. 308.
311. In Rajya Sabha, 30 March 1973.
312. On 20 March 1975, at Allahabad.
313. In Rajya Sabha, 30 March 1973.
314. Sanjay Gandhi, 31 March 1975.
315. Whichever the case, the post of 'chief executive' was filled in 1973 by Wing-Commander R. H. Chaudhry (retired).
316. Barua, to Rajya Sabha, 14 May 1973.
317. Allahabad High Court trial, 19 March 1975.
318. Amrit Nahata (Cong.), to Lok Sabha, 22 Dec. 1972.
319. Basu (CPI–M), to Lok Sabha, 16 April 1975.
320. 'Indira Gandhi: "The work of Mrs Sonia Gandhi [daughter-in-law] was connected with the Maruti Limited." Counsel: "Was she appointed as an insurance agent exclusively for the Maruti Ltd?"
Indira Gandhi: "I do not know" ' (Allahabad High Court, 19 March 1975).
321. Lok Sabha debate of 26 Feb. 1975.
322. Lok Sabha debate of 31 July 1975.
323. At Guntur, Andhra Pradesh, qu. *Hindu*, 21.3.76.
324. Ranbis Singh (Cong.), to Rajya Sabha, 30 March 1973.
325. IG, in Ahmedabad, 23 Sept. 1970.
326. IG, in Lucknow, 16 March 1973.
327. IG, in Delhi, 27 Feb. 1975.
328. IG, to Rajya Sabha, 27 July 1975, qu. *PODS*, p. 11.
329. ibid.
330. IG, qu. *Ind. Exp.*, 15.1.76.
331. IG, Mayer interview, qu. *Ind. Exp.*, 2.4.76.
332. *Broadcast to the Nation, June 26, 1975.*
333. IG, at mass rally on Madras beach, qu. *Hindu* (*Int. Ed.*), 15.2.76.

334. IG, qu. *Econ. Times*, 1.5.76. ('it is not enough for Congressmen to paste my photographs on walls').

335. IG, in Madras, qu. *Ind. Exp.*, 15.1.76.

336. Conversation between Prime Minister and the writer, Delhi, Dec. 1975.

337. IG, qu. *Ind. Exp.*, 1.1.76.

338. IG, qu. *Deccan Herald*, 11.1.76 ('he was a guide to my generation').

339. IG, at Madras rally, qu. *Hindu* (*Int. Ed.*), 15.2.76.

340. IG, Mayer interview, qu. *Hindu*, 2.4.76.

341. IG, to Lok Sabha, 9 Jan. 1976, qu. *Hindu*, 10.1.76.

342. IG, to Rajya Sabha, 22 July 1975, qu. *PODS*, loc. cit.

343. IG, Mayer interview, qu. *Ind. Exp.*, 2.4.76.

344. Conversation between Delhi editor and the writer, Nov. 1975.

345. *Economist*, 29.5.76.

346. Conversation between Jennie Lee and the writer, London, Oct. 1975.

347. Maxwell, *India's China War*, p. 504.

348. ibid., p. 491; he also refers to 'jingoist passions aroused by the Nehru government' (p. 490).

349. Barooah, qu. *Deccan Herald*, 1.1.76.

350. Subramaniam, to Lok Sabha, 31 July 1975, qu. GOI, *The Turning Point*, p. 52.

351. Subramaniam, ibid.

352. *Competition Review*, Jan. 1976.

353. Pai, to Rajya Sabha, 29 July 1975, qu. GOI, *The Turning Point*, p. 33.

354. IG, at G. B. Pant University, qu. *Hindu*, 3.4.76.

355. IG, qu. *Ind. Exp.*, 31.12.75.

356. IG, qu. *Deccan Herald*, 1.1.76.

357. IG, qu. *S. Telegraph*, 12.10.75.

358. IG, qu. *Ind. Exp.*, 29.6.75.

359. Declaration of 'anti-fascist' conference, Patna, qu. *Ind. Exp.*, 7.12.75.

360. IG, at 'mammoth public meeting', Patna, qu. *Econ. Times*, 2.5.76.

361. IG, in Durgapur, qu. *Econ. Times*, 4.3.76.

362. IG, qu. *Ind. Exp.*, 30.12.75.

363. Barooah, qu. *Deccan Herald*, 1.1.76.

364. IG, qu. *S. Standard*, 11.1.76.

365. *Deccan Herald*, 30.12.75.

366. Senator George McGovern, qu. *Hindu*, 10.1.76; and IG, qu. *Link* 2.1.77.

367. IG, in Patna, qu. *Econ. Times*, 2.5.76.

368. IG, to Institute of Democracy and Socialism, qu. *Econ. Times*, 24.3.76.

369. IG, qu. *Econ. Times*, 2.5.76.

370. IG, to Rajya Sabha, 1 April 1976, qu. *Econ. Times*, 2.4.76.

371. IG, Mayer interview, qu. *Econ. Times*, 2.4.76.

372. IG, in Patna, qu. *Econ. Times*, 2.5.76.

CHAPTER FIVE: SWINGING INTO ACTION

1. qu. *PODS*, p. 12.

2. Communicated to the writer, W. Bengal, Dec. 1975.

3. Communicated to the writer, Madras, Dec. 1975.

4. *Hindu*, 4.7.75; to describe emergency ministerial energy in 'implementing' the 20-point programme.

5. Including the RSS, Anand Marg, the Jamait-e Islami, the CPI–ML, and a number of 'naxalite' organizations.

6. These were said to have included General Manekshaw, Jagjivan Ram, and Y. B. Chavan; and see appendix, pp. 382–4.

7. *Guardian*, 10.7.76, 'according to reliable sources'.

8. GOI, *Thirty Days of National Discipline* (Delhi, DAVP, MIB, 1975), p. 7 (hereafter referred to as *Thirty Days*).

9. Sezhiyan, p. 6; and see appendix, pp. 371–3.

10. ibid; Sezhiyan also states that he wrote to the Speaker and the Minister for Parliamentary Affairs in protest, calling for the release of fellow Members of Parliament, but 'no reply was sent by them' (ibid.)

11. Section one empowered the President, 'in consultation with the Selection Commission', to determine whether any person found guilty of a corrupt practice should be disqualified from office. According to Sezhiyan, 'the contents of the Bill were not allowed to be published in the newspapers the next morning' (ibid., p. 10).

12. Emergency sessions of the state legislatures ('where Congress had comfortable majorities') were also convened on 8 August 1975 to ratify the amendment, as required by the Constitution; see Sezhiyan, p. 8.

13. 'One more effort on the part of the government to keep their actions beyond the scope of the judiciary, beyond the scope of justice' (Sezhiyan, p. 19).

14. GOI, *Thirty Days*, p. 1.

15. IG, qu. *Econ. Times*, 5.3.76.
16. IG, qu. *PODS*, p. 4.
17. S. S. Ray, qu. *Ind. Exp.*, 30.12.75.
18. Presidential ordinance of 17 Oct. 1975, amending sec. 3 of MISA, qu. *Times of India*, 18.10.75; incorporated in Maintenance of Internal Security (Amendment) Act, 1976, s. 4(9)(a).
19. IG, to Lok Sabha, 22 July 1975, qu. *PODS*, p. 4.
20. Sezhiyan, p. 7; and 'even in British days, the prerogative of the question hour was respected when there were emergency sessions of the legislative assembly', as on 14 Sept. 1942. He calls the suspension 'inglorious' (ibid.); and *Lok Sabha Debates, 5th Series*, vol. 53, col. 26–72.
21. Sezhiyan; 'on important legislations . . . no intimation, no public discussion, and no time for a sober and deep consideration by parliament itself' (Sezhiyan, p. 10); and *Lok Sabha Debates, 5th series*, vol. 54, col. 6–72.
22. Sezhiyan, p. 7.
23. A. K. Gopalan (CPI-M), to Lok Sabha, 21 July 1975, *Lok Sabha Debates, 5th series*, vol. 53, col. 92–103; see appendix, pp. 382–4.
24. N. G. Goray (SP), to Rajya Sabha, 22 July 1975; see appendix, pp. 387–8.
25. As n. 23.
26. As n. 24.
27. Krishan Kant, to Rajya Sabha, 21 July 1975, see appendix, pp. 385–6.
28. ibid.
29. A. K. Gopalan, loc. cit.
30. Sezhiyan, p. 10.
31. Om Mehta, Minister of State for Home Affairs, qu. *The Times*, 18.1.76.
32. 'The Indian Parliament: Its Growth and Achievements', in *Competition Review*, Jan. 1976.
33. N. A. Palkhiwala, qu. *Link*, 27.6.76.
34. GOI, 'Guidelines for Covering the Proceedings of Parliament', No. 2/147/75-CC, Office of the Chief Censor, New Delhi, 7 March 1976 ('not for publication').
35. ibid.
36. GOI, 'Revised Guidelines for the Coverage of Proceedings of Parliament', Office of the Chief Censor, New Delhi, 20 July 1975; see appendix, p. 378.
37. *Ind. Exp.*, 8.1.76; Shamim in fact accused Mrs Gandhi of saying 'I will never bow before Mr Morarji's demand for

Gujarat elections'; 'she had to bow', he added. *Lok Sabha Debates*, 5th series, vol. 55, no. 3, col. 198.

38. See appendix, p. 378.

39. CPI, *Resolutions and Report of the National Council*, p. 27.

40. ibid.

41. qu. *Hindu* (*Int. Ed.*), 9.1.76.

42. e.g. *The Times*, 10.5.76.

43. qu. ibid.

44. Lok Sabha, 31 March–1 April 1976; the Bill successfully sought to vary the terms of a legally valid collective agreement between the Life Insurance Corporation and its employees, and was opposed, *inter alios*, by S. M. Banerjee (CPI), V. P. Sathe, R. Kulkarni and C. M. Stephen (Cong.), *Econ. Times*, 1.4.76.

45. F. H. Mohsin, Deputy Home Minister, qu. *Econ. Times*, 9.4.76.

46. Conversation with the writer, Delhi, Dec. 1975.

47. qu. *Statesman*, 3.5.76.

48. Om Mehta, to Home Ministry's parliamentary consultative committee, qu. *ABP*, 18.5.76.

49. *New Statesman*, 13.2.76.

50. Information supplied to the writer, Karnataka, Jan. 1976.

51. Information supplied to the writer at Jawaharlal Nehru University, Delhi, and Delhi University, Nov.–Dec. 1975.

52. Information supplied to the writer, Delhi, Nov. 1975.

53. qu. *Ind. Exp.*, 2.4.76.

54. Information supplied to the writer; corroborating documentary evidence was supplied to the Commonwealth parliamentary conference in Delhi between 28 Oct. and 4 Nov. 1975; then to Amnesty International, the ILO, and the United Nations; and see chapter 8, *passim*.

55. Information supplied to the writer.

56. e.g. *New Statesman*, 13.2.76 ('many allege 100,000 plus'); cf. B. K. Nehru, Indian High Commissioner in London, 'the figure in the British press has been 175,000 to 200,000. The government of India has given out no figures' (*Listener*, 8.7.76).

57. *New Statesman*, 28.11.75; cf. '34,630', Charan Singh, to Lok Sabha, 5 April 1977.

58. Mohsin, qu. *Econ. Times*, 9.4.76.

59. V. P. Raman, qu. *Times of India*, 10.1.76.

60. *Ind. Exp.*, 29.4.76.

61. *Times of India*, 17.12.75; *Seminar*, no. 199, March 1976.

62. ibid.

63. *Statesman*, 17.12.75.

64. To Lok Sabha, 14 May 1976, qu. *Samachar*, 14.5.76.
65. S. A. Aga (Cong.), to Rajya Sabha, 19 March 1976, qu. *Econ. Times*, 20.3.76; 'he is interested only in those elected to authority fulfilling their promises'.
66. Lok Sabha debate of 26 March 1976, on a Private Member's Bill introduced by Bhogendra Jha (CPI).
67. Balind Verma, to Rajya Sabha, 26 May 1976, qu. *ABP*, 27.5.76.
68. Barooah, qu. *Deccan Herald*, 1.1.76.
69. Barooah, qu. *Econ. Times*, 18.4.76.
70. Gokhale, qu. *Hindu (Int. Ed.)*, 14.2.76.
71. V. A. Seyid Muhammad, qu. *Hindu (Int. Ed.)*, 27.3.76.
72. IG, qu. *Econ. Times*, 24.3.76.
73. Gokhale, to Rajya Sabha, 17 May 1976, qu. *Samachar*, 17.5.76, referring to 'five judges'.
74. *Ind. Exp.*, 2.6.76 ('sixteen judges'); cf. *Economist*, 29.5.76, '62 high court jurists'; an unknown additional number of the judiciary resigned, together with additional Solicitor-General Nariman; and see *Guardian*, 8.10.76.
75. qu. *Link*, 27.6.76; Article 226 permits the courts to issue writs to enforce the fundamental rights of the citizen.
76. *ABP*, 20.3.76; *Hindu (Int. Ed.)*, 3.4.76.
77. Inder Malhotra, *Guardian*, 22.3.76.
78. Mr Justice S. Rangarajan, qu. *Econ. Times*, 24.3.76.
79. GOI, *India Today: Basic Facts*, p. 40.
80. IG, laying the foundation of the new Supreme Court, Delhi, qu. *Econ. Times*, 16.4.76.
81. Barooah, qu. *Deccan Herald*, 1.1.76.
82. Shriman Narayan, qu. *Tribune (Ambala)*, 12.12.75.
83. qu. *Ind. Exp.*, 14.1.76.
84. Barooah, qu. *Deccan Herald*, 1.1.76.
85. S. S. Ray, qu. *Ind. Exp.*, 30.12.75.
86. S. S. Ray, to Congress lawyers' council, *Ind. Exp.*, 14.1.76.
87. IG, qu. *Econ. Times*, 1.3.76.
88. IG, qu. *Hindu*, 1.4.76.
89. IG, in Rae Bareli, qu. *Ind. Exp.*, 13.4.76.
90. Ahmedabad, 9 Dec. 1975 (p. 2).
91. ibid.
92. Gokhale, qu. *Hindu (Int. Ed.)*, 14.2.76.
93. *A Fresh Look of our Constitution: Some Suggestions*, Ahmedabad, n.d., [p. 1].
94. ibid.
95. IG, to Rajya Sabha, 9 Jan. 1976, qu. *Hindu*, 10.1.76.

96. IG, qu. *Deccan Herald*, 1.1.76.

97. *Times of India*, 27.2.76.

98. IG, *Broadcast to the Nation, June 27, 1975* (in Hindi) (DAVP, MIB, GOI, 1975).

99. GOI, 'Censorship Order', ref: RA/TML/T.no.558 (Delhi, Press Information Bureau), 26 June 1975.

100. ibid.

101. GOI, 'Guidelines for the Press in the Present Emergency', ref. RS/TML/T.no.556 (Delhi, Press Information Bureau), 26 June 1975; see appendix, pp. 374–5.

102. ibid., 'General guidance', rule 1.

103. ibid., rule 3.

104. ibid., rule 10.

105. ibid., rule 11.

106. ibid., rule 12.

107. ibid., rule 6.

108. GOI, 'General Guidelines for the Press', ref. RS/TML/T.no. 557 (Delhi, Press Information Bureau, GOI), 26 June 1975, rule 6.

109. ibid., rule 7.

110. Maxwell, *India's China War*, p. 481 n.

111. GOI, 'General Guidelines for the Press', ref. RS/TML/T.no. 557, op. cit., rule 1.

112. ibid., rule 3.

113. GOI, 'Guidelines for the Press' (Delhi, Office of the Censor), 26 July 1975, preamble (a); see appendix, pp. 391–3.

114. ibid., preamble (b).

115. ibid., rule 2.

116. ibid., rule 1.

117. GOI, 'Guidelines on Pre-Censorship', ref. RA/BV/T.no.559, (Delhi, Press Information Bureau), 27 June 1975, rule 1; see appendix, p. 376.

118. ibid., rule 2.

119. Prevention of Publication of Objectionable Matter Ordinance, 1975; printed in full, e.g., in *Statesman*, 11.12.75. Part of the ordinance was in fact modelled on the Punjab Special Powers (Press) Act, 1956.

120. Prevention of Publication of Objectionable Matter Act, 1976.

121. ibid., chapter 1, sect. 3(a).

122. ibid., chapter 1, sect. 3(b).

123. ibid., chapter 1, sect. 2.

124. ibid., chapter 4, sect. 22.

125. ibid., chapter 3, sect. 8.
126. ibid., chapter 2, sect. 5.
127. Official release accompanying ordinance, 8 Dec. 1975, qu. *Statesman*, 9.12.75.
128. ibid.
129. S. B. Chavan, Chief Minister of Maharashtra, qu. *Ind. Exp.*, 7.4.76.
130. *Economist*, 29.5.76.
131. See GOI, 'Guidelines for the Press', rule 8; information communicated to the writer by newspaper editor, Bombay, 1976.
132. Information communicated to the writer, Delhi, Calcutta, Madras, Bangalore, Trivandrum and Bombay, Nov. 1975 to Jan. 1976.
133. IG, to pressmen in Madras, 13 Jan. 1976, qu. *Ind. Exp.*, 14.1.76.
134. To Rajya Sabha, 15 Jan. 1976, qu. *Ind. Exp.*, 16.1.76.
135. ibid.
136. qu. *Hindu (Int. Ed.)*, 10.4.76 ('the merger of the news agencies had no direct cause and effect relation with the emergency').
137. Bhupesh Gupta (CPI), to Rajya Sabha, 15 Jan. 1976, qu. *Ind. Exp.*, 16.1.76.
138. qu. *Ind. Exp.*, 16.1.76.
139. Shukla, qu. *Econ. Times*, 27.4.76.
140. *EPW*, 24.1.76; *ABP*, 28.3.76.
141. *Guardian*, 28.5.76.
142. Shukla, to Lok Sabha, 26 April 1976, qu. *Econ. Times*, 27.4.76; Sinha told the Rajya Sabha on 25 March 1976 that pre-censorship was still in force, but had been relaxed 'everywhere except Punjab, Rajasthan and W. Bengal' (qu. *Hind. Times*, 26.3.76).
143. *ABP*, 28.5.76.
144. ibid.
145. *Guardian*, 10.5.76.
146. IG, *Broadcast to the Nation, June 27, 1976*.
147. K. Marx, 'Debates on the Freedom of the Press', in *Marx–Engels Collected Works*, Vol. 1 (Moscow, Progress Publishers, 1975), pp. 159 and 164.
148. *Deccan Herald*, 30.12.75.
149. Information communicated to the writer by newspaper men in Delhi, Calcutta, Bangalore and Bombay, Nov. 1975 to Jan. 1976.
150. Information supplied to the writer, Bombay, Jan. 1976.
151. Conversation between trade union leader and the writer, Calcutta, Dec. 1975.

152. qu. *Hindu*, 22.2.76.
153. J. S. Yadava, *Econ. Times*, 21.3.76.
154. Resolution of all-India newspaper editors' conference, Patna, 28 March 1976, qu. *Econ. Times*, 29.3.76.
155. IG, qu. *Econ. Times*, 5.3.76.
156. *Econ. Times*, 21.3.76.
157. IG, message to editors' conference, qu. *Econ. Times*, 26.3.76.
158. Shukla, address to editors' conference, qu. *Econ. Times*, 27.3.76.
159. ibid.
160. IG, qu. *Econ. Times*, 26.3.76.
161. Yadava, *Econ. Times*, 21.3.76.
162. IG, qu. *Econ. Times*, 26.3.76.
163. Barooah, qu. *Deccan Herald*, 1.1.76.
164. IG, interview with Swedish TV, qu. *ABP*, 18.3.76.
165. IG, to Rajya Sabha, 22 July 1975, qu. *PODS*, p. 13.
166. Sinha, in Mysore, 14 March 1976, qu. *ABP*, 15.3.76.
167. Sinha, qu. *Econ. Times*, 15.3.76.
168. Sinha, qu. *ABP*, 15.3.76.
169. Sinha, qu. *Econ. Times*, 15.3.76.
170. Barooah, qu. *Deccan Herald*, 1.1.76.
171. e.g. Om Mehta, qu. *Hindu*, 1.4.76.
172. *New Statesman*, 13.2.76.
173. Information supplied to the writer, Delhi, Nov. 1975.
174. *Times of India*, 17.12.75.
175. *Tribune (Ambala)*, 12.12.75.
176. CITU protest to the Director-General of the ILO, 8 Nov. 1975, privately circulated.
177. ibid.
178. Mehta, qu. *Reuter*, 17.5.76.
179. Lok Sabha debate of 31 March 1976, qu. *Hindu*, 1.4.76.
180. qu. *People's Democracy*, 4.4.76.
181. Conference of state governments' senior officials, qu. *Guardian*, 10.5.76.
182. GOI, *A Hundred New Gains*, p. 1.
183. In conversation with the writer, Mysore, Jan. 1976.
184. Information supplied to the writer.
185. Conversation between Delhi University professor and the writer, Nov. 1975.
186. qu. *ABP*, 22.3.76.
187. In conversation with the writer, Delhi, Dec. 1975.
188. Barooah, qu. *Ind. Exp.*, 13.4.76.
189. ibid.

190. qu. *Times of India*, 13.4.76.
191. Information supplied to the writer at JNU Delhi, Nov. 1975.
192. Communicated to the writer, Delhi, Nov. 1975.
193. Information supplied to and collated by the writer from numerous sources in India. Because of censorship, it rarely appeared in the press: an exception is *Hindu*, 29.3.76, which refers to the arrests of 'misbehaving students' under MISA at an agricultural college in Indore.
194. Information supplied to the writer.
195. e.g. at JNU Delhi, Benares Hindu University, the University of Rajasthan, and many others.
196. Satish Chandra, chairman of UGC, qu. *Ind. Exp.*, 13.4.76.
197. Information supplied to the writer at JNU, Nov. 1975; a strike took place on 22 Aug. 1975.
198. *Madhya Pradesh Chronicle*, 21.2.76.
199. Information supplied to the writer.
200. Information supplied to the writer; also, e.g., *Free Press Journal*, 22.3.76 ('500 qualified teachers in 190 colleges of Pune University to get the axe') and 8.6.76 ('another 150 to 200 science lecturers ... affiliated to Nagpur University').
201. Information supplied to the writer, Delhi University, Nov. 1975.
202. *Times of India*, 15.1.76.
203. Vice-chancellors met at Lucknow, 23–4 Dec. 1975, for discussions in which this was an item on the agenda (also, *N. Indian Patrika*, 18.12.75); they also discussed 'the future shape of students' organization', and the rules 'governing the admission of students'.
204. *Times of India*, 2.5.76; cf. 'I must be in my place six days a week, yet produce two research papers per annum or forfeit my increment. I have to sign a register to say where I am going, and with whom I have been speaking' (conversation between university teacher in Mysore and the writer, Jan. 1976).
205. *ABP*, 31.3.76.
206. *Times of India*, 12.1.76.
207. *Ind. Exp.*, 16.1.76.
208. *Seminar*, No. 199, March 1976.
209. Satish Chandra, qu. *Ind. Exp.*, 13.4.76.
210. Barooah, ibid.
211. Resolutions of the executive committee of the DMK, Madras, 27 June 1975; information supplied to the writer.
212. ibid.
213. ibid.

214. *Ind. Exp.*, 19.8.75.
215. IG, to Lok Sabha, 9 Jan. 1976, qu. *Hindu*, 10.1.76.
216. B. M. Pillai, President of the Tamil Nadu Congress Committee, qu. *Ind. Exp.*, 12.1.76.
217. IG, to 'a huge gathering of cheering Congressmen' in Madras, 14 Jan. 1976, qu. *Times of India*, 15.1.76.
218. IG, qu. *Ind. Exp.*, 15.1.76.
219. N. G. Goray (SP) to Rajya Sabha, 6 Jan. 1976, qu. *Ind. Exp.*, 7.1.76.
220. *Ind. Exp.* (editorial), 16.1.76.
221. *Hindu*, 10.1.76; cf. 'Indira exposes DMK mess-up', *Ind. Exp.*, 15.1.76 ('the centre has been trying to help opposition governments and not to topple them').
222. ibid.
223. M. Kalyanasundaram, general secretary of CPI in Tamil Nadu, qu. *Ind. Exp.*, 3.1.76.
224. qu. *Ind. Exp.*, 17.1.76.
225. S. S. Ray, qu. *Times of India*, 15.1.76.
226. K. Manoharan (of the Anna-DMK, or rival DMK faction), qu. *Ind. Exp.*, 7.12.75.
227. *Ind. Exp.*, 3.1.76; according to Kalyanasundaram, '10,000 volunteers participated in the agitation'.
228. Information supplied to the writer.
229. UPI report, 3.2.76, qu. *Intercontinental Press*, 16.2.76.
230. Information from Hyderabad, supplied to the writer, Feb. 1976.
231. For three months initially; extended to 31 July 1976, *Ind. Exp.*, 26.4.76; thereafter extended again.
232. Information supplied to the writer; for example, a warrant was issued on 31 Jan. 1976 under MISA for the arrest of the president of the CITU in Tamil Nadu, V. P. Chintan.
233. B. P. Maurya, Minister of State for Industry, at Ootacamund, 25 April 1976, qu. *ABP*, 26.4.76.
234. Om Mehta, to Lok Sabha, 31 March 1976, qu. *Hindu*, 1.4.76.
235. Maurya, qu. *ABP*, 26.4.76.
236. Brahmananda Reddy, at Madras rally, 15 Feb. 1976, qu. *Hindu*, 16.2.76.
237. *Link*, 22.2.76.
238. Barooah, qu. *Hindu*, 16.2.76.
239. Mehta, qu. *Hindu*, 1.4.76.
240. B. Reddy, qu. *Hindu*, 16.2.76.
241. Conversation between newspaper editor and the writer, Bombay, Jan. 1976.

242. *S. Standard*, 8.2.76.

243. *Link*, 22.2.76.

244. qu. *Hindu* (*Int. Ed.*), 14.2.76. Karunanidhi made up for it later. Thus, 'Sanjay Gandhi's five-point programme is essential for the progress of the nation,' qu. *Samachar*, 27.12.76.

245. IG, qu. *Hindu* (*Int. Ed.*), 28.2.76.

246. IG, *Broadcast to the Nation, June 26, 1975*.

247. G. K. Reddy, *Hindu*, 19.2.76.

248. IG, at Madras rally, 15 Feb. 1976, qu. *Hindu*, 16.2.76.

249. Mohsin, to Lok Sabha, qu. *Free Press Journal*, 29.4.76.

250. *ABP*, 27.2.76.

251. *Econ. Times*, 23.3.76.

252. Barooah, in Madras, qu. *S. Standard*, 15.2.76. He visited the city for discussion with local Congress politicians ('Congress being a democratic organization, we believe in the sovereignty of discussions').

253. K. K. Shah, qu. *Ind. Exp.*, 8.3.76.

254. Shah, qu. *ABP*, 23.2.76.

255. *Times of India*, 23.2.76.

256. A. C. George, Minister of State for Industry, qu. *Hindu*, 15.2.76.

257. G. K. Reddy, *Hindu*, 19.2.76.

258. ibid.

259. M. Bhaktavatsalam, former Chief Minister of Tamil Nadu, qu. *ABP*, 18.4.76.

260. *Link*, 22.2.76.

261. G. K. Reddy, loc. cit.

262. ibid.

263. ibid.

264. Barooah, at Thanjavur, 16 April 1976, qu. *ABP*, 17.4.76.

265. *Link*, 18.4.76.

266. Mehta, to Lok Sabha, 31 March 1976, qu. *Hindu*, 1.4.76.

267. *Guardian*, 10.7.75.

268. ibid.

269. *Times of India*, 16.12.75.

270. ibid.

271. ibid. ('he inquired about the health of party-workers allegedly injured in assaults by Janata Front supporters').

272. B. Reddy, to Rajya Sabha, qu. *Hindu* (*Int. Ed.*), 10.1.76.

273. *Ind. Exp.*, *Times of India*, *Hindu*, 16.1.76.

274. William Borders, *New York Times*, 3.2.76.

275. qu. *Times of India*, 16.2.76; on a visit to Gujarat, 'the Minister

assured workers that the centre would always protect their legal rights'.

276. *Econ. Times*, 12.3.76; 800 sticks of dynamite in seven crates ('weighing 114 kgs') had been discovered on a transport company's premises in Baroda.

277. *Econ. Times*, 18.3.76, 20.3.76 and 27.3.76; *Ind. Exp.*, 31.3.76.

278. *Econ. Times*, 18.3.76.

279. I G, qu. *Ind. Exp.*, 31.12.75.

280. *Hindu*, 26.3.76, *Ind. Exp.*, 31.3.76 and 2.4.76.

281. *Link*, 22.2.76.

282. *Link*, 18.4.76.

283. ibid.

284. Conversation between Ramaswamy, director, Ashok Leyland, Madras, and the writer, Dec. 1975.

285. CITU protest to the Director-General of the ILO, 8 Nov. 1975.

286. ibid.

287. 'Report of General-Secretary to CITU Working Committee Meeting', Madras, 10–12 Nov. 1975, p. 23 (mimeograph).

288. e.g. *S. Standard*, 8.2.76.

289. *Ind. Exp.*, 3.4.76.

290. CITU protest to the Director-General of the ILO, 8 Nov. 1975.

291. Conversation between national trade union leader and the writer, Calcutta, Dec. 1975.

292. CITU protest to the Director-General of the ILO, 8 Nov. 1975; also 'AITUC and INTUC local leaderships are using police terror to capture CITU unions in Trivandrum, Ernakulam and Calicut ... the AITUC is using police force to occupy CITU offices in Kottayam in Kerala, for example' (conversation between trade union official and the writer, Cochin, Kerala, Jan. 1976).

293. CITU protest to the Director-General of the ILO, 8 Nov. 1975 ('several trade unions and Members of Parliament demanded appointment of a judicial inquiry into the causes of his death, but the demand has not been accepted by the government so far').

294. 'Report by CITU vice-president [Mohammed Ismail]', Madras, 10 Nov. 1975 (mimeograph).

295. Conversation between trade union official and the writer, Bombay, Jan. 1976.

296. *Hindu*, 3.1.76.

297. Conversation between national trade union leader and the writer, Calcutta, Dec. 1975

298. John Jacob, 'India Then and Now' (press release), 15.3.76.

299. Conversation between Sivasilam and the writer, Madras, Dec. 1975; also, 'in India, compulsion is needed. The worker has to be disciplined and pressured in his own interest'.

300. CITU protest to the Director-General of the ILO, 8 Nov. 1975, p. 7.

301. IG, qu. GOI, *Thirty Days*, p. 2.

302. e.g. *Ganashakti*, 27.3.76: 'the police burst five rounds of tear-gas shells to disperse a crowd of workers in front of the East India chrome tannery in Tanagra, Calcutta, closed after an industrial dispute. Seventy-two arrests were made.'

303. S. S. Ray, qu. *ABP*, 13.3.76, 3.5.76.

304. *Rise Against the Black Ordinance*, undated leaflet, over the name of George Fernandes.

305. CPI, *Resolutions and Report of National Council*.

306. Conversation with the writer, Trivandrum, Jan. 1976.

307. Parvathi Krishnan (CPI), qu. *Link*, 18.4.76.

308. *Link*, 27.6.76.

309. *Hind. Times*, 15.5.76; *Patriot*, 15.5.76.

310. S. A. Dange, CPI chairman, in Moscow, qu. *Ind. Exp.*, 29.2.76.

311. *Party Life* (CPI), 22.11.75.

312. Z. A. Ahmed (CPI), to Rajya Sabha, 6 Jan. 1976, qu. *Ind. Exp.*, 7.1.76.

313. Conversation between Achutha Menon and the writer, Trivandrum, Jan. 1976.

314. *Link*, 11.1.76.

315. Conversation between CPI students and the writer, Presidency College, Calcutta, Dec. 1975.

316. CPI, *Resolutions and Report of National Council*, p. 4.

317. ibid., p. 26.

318. ibid., p. 27.

319. ibid., p. 28.

320. qu. *ABP*, 29.2.76.

321. CPI, *Resolutions and Report of National Council*, p. 17.

322. Indrajit Gupta (CPI), to Lok Sabha, 7 Aug. 1975 (39th amendment debate); information communicated to the writer.

323. Somenath Lahiri (CPI), at public meeting, Calcutta, qu. *ABP*, 27.12.75.

324. ibid.

325. 'Report of CPI–M Central Committee Meeting', 22–8 Jan. 1976, Madras, p. 5 (mimeograph).

326. Gupta, to Lok Sabha, 6 Jan. 1976, qu. *Ind. Exp.*, 7.1.76.

327. *Party Life*, 7.9.75.

328. ibid.

329. CPI, *Resolutions and Report of National Council*, p. 17.

330. ibid.

331. Declaration of Conference against Fascism, Patna, 6 Dec. 1975, qu. *Ind. Exp.*, 7.12.75.

332. ibid.

333. *Ind. Exp.*, 5.12.75.

334. *Link*, 22.2.76.

335. Dange, at Patna, 4 Dec. 1975, qu. *Ind. Exp.*, 5.12.75.

336. UNI report from Patna, 4.12.75.

337. IG, qu. *Ind. Exp.*, 4.12.75.

338. GOI, *Why Emergency, Questions and Answers*, [pp. 3–4].

339. Chagla, p. 3.

340. Conversation between Nirad C. Chaudhuri and the writer, Oxford, March 1976.

341. H. V. Kamath: *Constituent Assembly Debates*, vol. 9, col. 140, qu. Maxwell, *Woman on a White Horse*, p. 365.

342. GOI, *Thirty Days*, p. 1.

343. B. Reddy to Lok Sabha, 2 April 1976, qu. *Econ. Times*, 3.4.76.

344. B. Reddy, qu. *Times of India*, 6.4.76.

345. Barooah, qu. *Times of India*, 13.4.76.

346. To Rajya Sabha, 28 July 1975, qu. GOI, *The Turning Point*, p. 29.

347. ibid.

348. To Lok Sabha, 31 July 1975, ibid., p. 58.

349. IG, qu. *S. Telegraph*, 12.10.75.

350. IG, qu. *Econ. Times*, 5.3.76.

351. ibid.

352. ibid.

353. Reddy, to Lok Sabha, 2 April 1976, qu. *Econ. Times*, 3.4.76.

354. IG, qu. *Hindu*, 19.4.76.

355. John Jacob, 'India Then and Now' (press release), 15.3.76.

356. *Econ. Times*, 1.5.76 (report from Rajasthan).

357. IG, to Rajya Sabha, 1 April 1976, qu. *ABP*, 2.4.76.

358. GOI, *Reason for Emergency*, p. 1.

359. John Jacob, loc. cit.

360. S. S. Ray, qu. *ABP*, 3.5.76.

361. IG, *Broadcast to the Nation, June 26, 1975*.

362. IG, at Mysore, 13 Feb. 1976, qu. *Hindu*, 14.2.76.

363. John Jacob, loc. cit.

364. Mohsin, to Lok Sabha, 1 April 1976, qu. *Ind. Exp.*, 2.4.76.

365. Om Mehta, qu. *ABP*, 18.5.76.

366. IG, *Broadcast to the Nation, June 27, 1975.*

367. IG, qu. *S. Telegraph*, 12.10.75.

368. In conversation with the writer, Trivandrum, Jan. 1976.

369. Bansi Lal, qu. *Ind. Exp.*, 31.12.75.

370. John Jacob, 'India Then and Now' (press release), 15.3.76.

371. F. A. Ahmed, qu. *Econ. Times*, 21.3.76.

372. G. K. Reddy, *Hindu (Int. Ed.)*, 6.3.76.

373. GOI, *A Hundred New Gains*, p. 9.

374. *Times of India*, 16.12.75.

375. IG, to Rajya Sabha, 1 April 1976, qu. *ABP*, 2.4.76.

376. IG, qu. *Econ. Times*, 30.4.76.

377. IG, to Rajya Sabha, 22 July 1975, qu. *PODS*, p. 12.

378. Arya Bhushan, *Competition Review*, Jan. 1976.

379. G. K. Reddy, *Hindu (Int. Ed.)*, 6.3.76.

380. Pai, qu. *Ind. Exp.*, 31.12.75.

381. IG, *New Programme for Economic Progress* (broadcast of 1 July 1975, DAVP, MIB, GOI, 1975), [pp. 1–2].

382. IG, qu. *Hindu (Int. Ed.)*, 10.4.76.

383. *Econ. Times*, 24.4.76.

384. Bihar Government Department of Information and Publications, qu. *Link*, 4.4.76.

385. S. S. Ray, qu. *ABP*, 27.2.76.

386. Subramaniam, qu. *Ind. Exp.*, 30.7.75.

387. A. P. Shinde, Minister of Agriculture, at Indore, qu. *Ind. Exp.*, 12.1.76.

388. Barooah, qu. *Deccan Herald*, 1.1.76.

389. Sankar Ghose, Finance Minister of W. Bengal government, qu. *ABP*, 9.3.76.

CHAPTER SIX: THE NEW DEAL

1. To 75th Congress Party conference, qu. *Ind. Exp.*, 29.12.75.

2. Conversation between Ayub Syed and the writer, Bombay, Jan. 1976.

3. qu. *Ind. Exp.*, 31.12.75.

4. *Everyman's Weekly*, 1.12.74.

5. qu. *ABP*, 17.4.76; total operating profits for 1974–5 were up

41·8 per cent compared with 1973–4, return on net assets was up from 11·5 to 13·5 per cent, profit margin on sales up from 11·7 per cent to 12·9 per cent, return on shareholders' capital up from 11·4 per cent to 14·3 per cent, and rates of gross profit accumulation up from 16·3 per cent to 18·1 per cent; and see appendix, p. 429.

6. *EPW*, 20.12.75.

7. Conversation between senior civil servant and the writer, Delhi, Nov. 1975.

8. Maxwell, *Woman on a White Horse*, p. 366.

9. *Statesman*, 10.6.76.

10. *Hindu*, 2.4.76; a 'gramophone record of the 20-point programme' was also made, *Hindu* (*Int. Ed.*), 28.2.76.

11. Barooah, qu. *Deccan Herald*, 1.1.76.

12. ibid.

13. Conversation between Ashok Leyland workers and the writer, Madras, Dec. 1975.

14. Conversation between advocate of the Delhi High Court and the writer, Nov. 1975.

15. Conversation between Ayub Syed and the writer, Bombay, Jan. 1976.

16. *Party Life*, 7.9.75, p. 19.

17. CPI–M, 'Twenty-point Programme: A Cruel Hoax' (mimeograph dated 8 Nov. 1975).

18. ibid.

19. qu. *Deccan Herald*, 1.1.76.

20. GOI, *Thirty Days*, p. 2.

21. GOI, *A Hundred New Gains*, p. 1.

22. e.g. GOI, *A Hundred New Gains*, p. 29.

23. e.g. GOI, *Thirty Days*, p. 6.

24. O. P. Tyagi (JS), in Lok Sabha, 6 Jan. 1976, qu. *Ind. Exp.*, 7.1.76.

25. *Link*, 4.4.76.

26. IG, qu. *Econ. Times*, 8.4.76.

27. F. A. Ahmed, qu. *Statesman*, 16.5.76.

28. IG, *New Programme for Econ. Progress*, [p. 1].

29. AICC resolution on economic policy, Congress 75th conference, qu. *Ind. Exp.*, 29.12.75.

30. qu. *Hindu*, 2.10.75.

31. Information communicated to the writer, Delhi, Nov. 1975.

32. Vengal Rao, Chief Minister of Andhra Pradesh, to all-India prohibition workers' conference, qu. *Hindu* (*Int. Ed.*), 28.2.76.

33. IG, *New Programme for Econ. Progress.*
34. *Statesman*, 30.3.76.
35. GOI, *Thirty Days*, p. 7.
36. Pranab Mukherjee, qu. *Free Press Journal*, 31.3.76.
37. *Times of India*, 20.4.76.
38. Inder Malhotra, *Guardian*, 11.6.76.
39. *Patriot*, 29.5.76; *Guardian*, 11.6.76.
40. *Economist*, 24.1.76.
41. *EPW*, 11.10.75; *Link*, 11.1.76; and see M. J. K. Thavaraj, 'Fiscal Policies and Inflation: the Indian Experience', *Social Scientist*, Jan.–Feb. 1975.
42. In a report compiled by Vasant Sathe (Cong.), qu. *Blitz*, 10.1.76.
43. qu. *Ind. Exp.*, 31.12.75.
44. *Econ. Times*, 10.10.75 ('on a disclosure of 100,000 rupees, the tax-rate is only 46·25 per cent, whereas a regular assessee has to pay 53·60 per cent'); also, *EPW*, 11.10.75.
45. *EPW*, 6.12.75.
46. Chairman of Central Board of Direct Taxes, in Madras, qu. *EPW*, ibid.
47. *Times of India*, 1.12.75.
48. 'Finance Ministry sources', qu. *Deccan Herald*, 1.1.76.
49. *Deccan Herald*, 2.1.76.
50. *EPW*, 6.12.75 (or 'a matter of negotiation and bargaining').
51. qu. *Ind. Exp.*, 31.12.75.
52. qu. *Hind. Times*, 10.5.76.
53. *Times of India*, 27.3.76.
54. *Samachar*, 5.4.76.
55. qu. *Link*, 27.6.76.
56. CPI, *Resolutions and Report of National Council*, p. 12.
57. ibid., p. 19.
58. e.g. the council of the Uttar Pradesh unit of the CPI–M's Kisan Sabha met on 12 March 1976 to review this question; their report is summarized in *People's Democracy*, 28.3.76.
59. IG, *New Programme for Econ. Progress*, [p. 3].
60. Hira Singh, 'Panchayats for Rural Weak', *Mainstream*, 13.12.75, p. 25.
61. *Times of India*, 14.2.76, 17.2.76; see *Econ. Times*, 27.2.76 for the abandonment on 26 Feb. 1976 of the tax proposals.
62. *New Programme for Econ. Progress*, [p. 3].
63. ibid; and see *Link*, 27.6.76.
64. qu. *Ind. Exp.*, 31.12.75.
65. *Party Life*, 7.9.75, p. 19.

66. *Econ. Times*, 15.3.76.
67. *EPW*, 13.12.75 (instead, 'the relegation of more administrative powers to the . . . district magistrates').
68. *Free Press Journal*, 24.3.76.
69. *Link*, 2.5.76.
70. *Econ. Times*, 4.3.76.
71. GOI, *Thirty Days*, p. 10; e.g. 'relief in rural indebtedness and house-sites to *harijans* have already been provided', Bansi Lal, qu. *Ind. Exp.*, 31.12.75.
72. *Times of India*, 25.10.75.
73. GOI, *Thirty Days*, p. 9.
74. qu. *Ind. Exp.*, 31.12.75.
75. John Jacob, 'India Then and Now' (press release), 15.3.76.
76. *Link*, 27.6.76; the ordinance was made statute law in the Bonded Labour Act, 1976.
77. *Econ. Times*, 4.3.76.
78. *Hindu* (*Int. Ed.*), 14.2.76.
79. *Link*, 18.4.76; bonded labour was also 'discovered', e.g. among S. Indian fishermen, *Hindu*, 29.3.76.
80. Reddy, qu. *Link*, 18.4.76.
81. e.g. *Hindu*, 2.4.76 ('atrocities continue to be reported in "several places" '); *Patriot*, 27.5.76 ('a reign of terror against *harijan* families of Kathpur village by the Bilaspur landlord, and 40 armed persons').
82. e.g. *Econ. Times*, 15.3.76 ('no Panias [sc. tribal people] have yet been freed').
83. *Statesman*, 14.1.76.
84. GOI, *Thirty Days*, p. 8.
85. ibid., p. 9.
86. qu. *Hindu*, 29.3.76; this was regarded as 'gratifying' by, for example, the Madras Urban Land-owners' Association.
87. GOI, *A Hundred New Gains*, p. 21.
88. *Econ. Times*, 14.10.75.
89. *Statesman*, 28.11.75.
90. *Econ. Times*, 14.2.76.
91. qu. *Hind. Times*, 6.3.76; she suggested that in order to show achievement, the figures for distribution were 'not correct figures'. cf. *EPW*, 3.4.76 ('the reforms have been unrecognizably whittled down').
92. *Ind. Exp.*, 13.4.76.
93. *Samachar*, 10.5.76.
94. qu. *Samachar*, 11.5.76.

95. The deadline was announced after a meeting of Chief Ministers in Delhi, 5–6 March, 1976, *Hindu*, 7.3.76.

96. *Ind. Exp.*, 4.3.76.

97. Inder Malhotra, *Guardian*, 30.6.76; (two states, Maharashtra and Rajasthan, 'between them account for the bulk of the land distributed').

98. Sivadas Banerjee, *Times of India*, 15.1.76.

99. *Guardian*, 30.6.76.

100. *Times of India*, 15.1.76.

101. *Link*, 22.2.76.

102. *Link*, 18.4.76.

103. Sarat Chandra Sinha, qu. *ABP*, 22.3.76.

104. *Patriot*, 1.6.76, based on evidence of the Assam Rural Workers' Union.

105. Information communicated to the writer, Delhi, Dec. 1975.

106. Information communicated to the writer, Varanasi, Dec. 1975.

107. *Times of India*, 15.1.76.

108. See *EPW*, 13.3.76.

109. CPI–M, 'Twenty-point Programme: A Cruel Hoax'. The fate of the tribal dispossessed is above all a test case for land-reform, to say nothing of their continuing eviction, by force or stealth, from land which belongs to them. Thus, 'land has been allotted on paper, but they have not been given physical possession' (*Times of India*, 22.12.75); then, 'there were no guidelines laid down for distribution' (*EPW*, 3.4.76); and, *coup de grâce*, 'tribals are refusing to accept land offered to them', because of 'fear of reprisals from non-tribals' (*Patriot*, 4.6.76).

110. *Times of India*, 27.9.75.

111. Reports of the Cha Bagan Mazdoor Union and Karnataka Provincial Plantation Workers' Union, communicated to the writer.

112. From 8·33 per cent to 4 per cent.

113. *Times of India*, 26.9.75; it also made 'excess payments for 1974' liable for recovery.

114. e.g. 2,500 million rupees was cited by Samar Mukherjee (CPI–M) to the Lok Sabha on 6 Jan. 1976, based on figures from the Finance Minister. It was alleged that the Bonus Amendment Act, 1976, would add a further 250 millions.

115. To Rajya Sabha, on 23 Jan. 1976; qu. *Ind. Exp.*, 24.1.76.

116. K. K. Podar, President of the AIOE, qu. *Econ. Times*, 1.5.76.

117. Conversation between K. V. Varadarajan and the writer, Madras, Dec. 1975.

118. qu. *The Working Class*, March 1976.
119. Amarnath Vidyalankar (Cong.), qu. *Link*, 18.4.76.
120. Prasannabhai Mehta (Cong.), ibid.
121. Conversation between national trade union official and the writer, Bombay, Jan. 1976.
122. Information communicated to the writer.
123. *EPW*, 22.11.75.
124. ibid.; the demand was put to the 56th session of the INTUC General Council.
125. To Lok Sabha, 31 March 1976, qu. *Econ. Times*, 1.4.76.
126. *Ind. Exp.*, 31.10.75.
127. See *Econ. Times*, 28.9.75.
128. AICC resolution to 75th Congress conference, qu. *Ind. Exp.*, 31.12.75.
129. *Econ. Times*, 28.9.75.
130. *New Age*, 12.10.75.
131. IG, qu. *Ind. Exp.*, 31.12.75.
132. IG, qu. *S. Standard*, 11.1.76.
133. IG, qu. *Ind. Exp.*, 31.12.75.
134. Subramaniam, to Lok Sabha, 19 May 1976, qu. *ABP*, 20.5.76.
135. ibid.
136. R. Reddy, qu. *Ind. Exp.*, 12.1.76; cf. K. K. Podar, 'justice demanded that the employer be given the right to lay off workers'.
137. *Business Standard*, 7.3.76.
138. Homi Daji (CPI), qu. *Link*, 2.5.76.
139. ibid.
140. Conversation with the writer, Trivandrum, Jan. 1976.
141. Pai, in Bombay, qu. *ABP*, 22.4.76.
142. Conversation between K. V. Varadarajan and the writer, Madras, Dec. 1975.
143. At Ashok Leyland, Madras, Dec. 1975.
144. GOI, *A Hundred New Gains*, p. 3.
145. *Mainstream*, 13.12.75, p. 3.
146. The evidence throughout the period is overwhelming and voluminous; for aluminium industry, e.g. *Fin. Exp.*, 29.9.75, *Econ. Times*, 4.4.76; cement, e.g. *Times of India*, 12.12.75, *Fin. Exp.*, 10.6.76; chemicals, e.g. *Econ. Times*, 11.10.75, *Statesman*, 25.4.76; coal, e.g. *Econ. Times*, 25.3.76, 28.3.76, *Ind. Exp.*, 2.4.76, *Statesman*, 26.4.76, *ABP*, 1.5.76; copper, e.g. *Econ. Times*, 28.7.75; cotton textiles, e.g. *Times of India*, 1.9.75, *Econ. Times*, 9.9.75, 4.10.75, 19.10.75, 20.10.75, 29.3.76, 1.4.76, 4.4.76, 20.4.76, *Hind. Times*, 18.6.76; cotton yarn, e.g.

Fin. Exp., 11.9.75, *Hindu*, 12.1.76, *Econ. Times*, 16.4.76; diesel engines, e.g. *Econ. Times*, 3.4.76, 14.4.76; dying and screen printing, e.g. *Econ. Times*, 11.4.76; electrodes, e.g. *Econ. Times*, 5.3.76; fertilizers, e.g. *Econ. Times*, 19.9.75, 11.3.76, 3.5.76; hosiery, e.g. *Econ. Times*, 30.3.76; jute, e.g. *Statesman*, 13.10.75, *Econ. Times*, 19.10.75, 4.4.76, 9.6.76, *ABP*, 6.3.76, 11.3.76, 13.3.76, 19.3.76, 23.3.76, 23.4.76; machine tools, e.g. *Times of India*, 12.12.75; newsprint and paper, e.g. *Hind. Times*, 13.10.75, *Times of India*, 12.12.75, *Econ. Times*, 2.4.76; plastics, e.g. *Econ. Times*, 14.3.76; railway wagons and automobiles, e.g. *Times of India*, 13.10.75, 12.12.75, *Ind. Exp.*, 16.1.76, *ABP*, 8.4.76, *Econ. Times*, 18.4.76, 7.6.76; rubber, e.g. *Econ. Times*, 2.4.76; stainless steel, e.g. *Econ. Times*, 5.3.76; steel, e.g. *Business Standard*, 26.9.75, *Fin. Exp.*, 4.10.75, 10.6.76; tyres, e.g. *Econ. Times*, 11.10.75, 1.4.76.
147. *Statesman*, 14.1.76.
148. Sanjay Gandhi, at Baruat, Meerut district, qu. *ABP*, 5.4.76.
149. qu. *ABP*, 3.5.76.
150. Harish Mahindra, qu. *Econ. Times*, 3.5.76.
151. qu. *Econ. Times*, 1.5.76.
152. qu. *Times of India*, 20.3.76; and see *EPW*, 27.3.76.
153. qu. *ABP*, 22.5.76.
154. e.g. *EPW*, 3.10.75; *Econ. Times*, 16.10.75; *Times of India*, 12.12.75; *Fin. Exp.*, 18.1.76; *Patriot*, 21.3.76.
155. GOI, *Thirty Days*, p. 11.
156. IG, qu. *Hindu*, 19.7.75.
157. Through the Industrial Disputes (Amendment) Act, 1976, which provided for prior official approval for layoffs. It was ignored from the outset; as R. Reddy revealed, to Rajya Sabha, 19 March 1976, qu. *Hindu*, 20.3.76.
158. IG, *New Programme for Econ. Progress*, [p. 6]; cf. 'much has been said of the success of the apprenticeship scheme. But the claims made on its behalf do not quite fit into the picture' (*Statesman*, 14.1.76).
159. *Times of India*, 6.3.76; *ABP*, 3.5.76.
160. Mahindra, qu. *Econ. Times*, 2.5.76.
161. In conversation with the writer, Madras, Dec. 1975.
162. FICCI conference, qu. *Econ. Times*, 3.5.76.
163. GOI, *Thirty Days*, p. 10.
164. K. C. Pant, qu. *Ind. Exp.*, 2.4.76.
165. ibid.
166. qu. *EPW*, 1.5.76.

167. N. K. Krishnan, *Party Life*, 22.11.75, p. 3.

168. *Link*, 2.5.76.

169. U.P. government report (Jan. 1976), qu. *Econ. Times*, 21.4.76.

170. Political street-slogan.

171. Point 1 of the 20-point programme.

172. Sanjay Gandhi, qu. *ABP*, 5.4.76.

173. *EPW*, 8.5.76.

174. Communicated to the writer, Calcutta, Dec. 1975.

175. cf. *Guardian*, 7.7.75, which reported that 'prices in Bihar had begun to stabilize and even drop' before the emergency.

176. *EPW*, 8.5.76.

177. ibid.; and cf. Bangladesh, where with a similarly good harvest, 'prices which had risen by about 80 per cent in 1974, fell by about 10 per cent in 1975–6' (*Guardian*, 25.5.76).

178. *EPW*, 8.5.76.

179. K. A. Nageswaran, *Times of India*, 12.1.76.

180. *EPW*, 8.5.76.

181. *Ind. Exp.*, 31.12.75; *Econ. Times*, 13.4.76.

182. G. M. Surana, qu. *Econ. Times*, 5.4.76.

183. To Rajya Sabha, 27 March 1976, qu. *ABP*, 24.3.76; he also rightly pointed out that costs of production had fallen due to the withholding of workers' wages.

184. From 4·8 million tonnes of food grains in 1974, to 7·4 million in 1975, mainly from the US (*Patriot*, 2.5.76); this despite the fact that two of India's US grain suppliers, Bunge Corporation and Cook Industries, were admitted, in the Lok Sabha on 29 March 1976 by A. P. Sindhe, Minister of Agriculture, to be currently 'under investigation in the US for "malpractices" '. For US grain suppliers' frauds, see *Econ. Times*, 20.2.76.

185. *Econ. Times*, 27.4.76; *Patriot*, 26.4.76.

186. e.g. *Econ. Times*, 8.3.76 ('prices looking up'), 25.4.76 ('cotton prices have advanced sharply'), *Business Standard*, 7.5.76, *Econ. Times*, 11.6.76, *Samachar*, 15.6.76, *Hindu* (*Int. Ed.*), 14.8.76 ('food grains, edible oils, sugar and cotton').

187. *People's Democracy*, 6.6.76.

188. *People's Democracy*, 11.4.76.

189. *Ganashakti*, 6.4.76.

190. Sindhe, qu. *ABP*, 12.3.76.

191. *Econ. Times*, 29.3.76; *Link*, 4.4.76.

192. *Link*, 4.4.76.

193. ibid.

194. ibid.

195. Mukherjee, qu. *ABP*, 3.5.76.
196. D. P. Chattophadyaya, to Lok Sabha, qu. *ABP*, 13.3.76.
197. ibid.
198. qu. *Econ. Times*, 1.8.75.
199. Pai, qu. *Hindu*, 7.4.76.
200. Subramaniam, to Lok Sabha, 15 March 1976, qu. *ABP*, 16.3.76.
201. Subramaniam, ibid.
202. qu. *Econ. Times*, 24.3.76.
203. *Econ. Times*, 15.11.75.
204. *Times of India* (editorial), 15.11.75.
205. Subramaniam, qu. *ABP*, 16.3.76.
206. *EPW*, 28.2.76.
207. *Econ. Times*, 3.8.75.
208. e.g. *Econ. Times* share price index, 22.3.76, 20.4.76, 5.5.76.
209. qu. *Business Week* (*New York*), 2.2.76.
210. *Econ. Times*, 17.3.76.
211. qu. *ABP*, 18.3.76.
212. ibid.
213. ibid.
214. ibid.
215. *Econ. Times*, 20.3.76; and 'budget pleases India's rich' (*Guardian* headline, 16.3.76).
216. qu. *Econ. Times*, 17.3.76.
217. *Econ. Times*, 20.3.76.
218. S. S. Ray, qu. *ABP*, 18.3.76.
219. J. Sengupta, Bengal Chamber of Commerce, qu. *ABP*, 18.3.76.
220. K. R. Puri, governor of the RBI, qu. *Ind. Exp.*, 1.4.76 ('on all accounts, it is a testing time for them').
221. S. S. Ray, qu. *ABP*, 18.3.76.
222. N. A. Palkhivala, to Forum of Free Enterprise, qu. *Statesman Weekly*, 27.3.76.
223. V. K. R. V. Rao, qu. *Econ. Times*, 19.3.76.
224. Palkhivala, loc. cit.
225. S. S. Ray, *ABP*, 18.3.76.
226. Palkhivala, loc. cit.
227. To Lok Sabha, 18 March 1976, qu. *Econ. Times*, 19.3.76.
228. *Times of India*, 16.3.76.
229. qu. *Econ. Times*, 17.3.76.
230. *Business Week*, 19.4.76 ('foreign investors are generally pleased with the budget').
231. 20.3.76.

232. *Link*, 11.1.76; see appendix, p. 433.

233. *Party Life*, 7.9.75, p. 5.

234. *Link*, 4.4.76.

235. To forum of financial writers, qu. *Samachar*, 28.3.76.

236. e.g. *Ind. Exp.*, 22.4.76, *Econ. Times*, 2.5.76, *Link*, 9.5.76.

237. Subramaniam, qu. *ABP*, 24.3.76.

238. *ABP*, 16.4.76.

239. ibid.; also welcomed by the AIEI as a 'simplification of paper-work' (ibid.).

240. *Ind. Exp.*, 1.4.76; similarly the procedures for the 'disposing of industrial licence applications from entrepreneurs' were 'facili-tated' on 5 April 1976, qu. *Ind. Exp.*, 6.4.76.

241. qu. *ABP*, 18.5.76 (and 'the ball is now in its court'); for details, see *Statesman Weekly*, 15.5.76.

242. *Times of India*, 8.12.75.

243. T. N. Chaturvedi, director of India's Investment Centre, qu. *ABP*, 19.3.76.

244. ibid.

245. To forum of financial writers, qu. *Ind. Exp.*, 29.3.76.

246. qu. *Econ. Times*, 30.3.76.

247. qu. *Times of India*, 1.4.76.

248. *ABP*, 1.4.76 (seven billion yen, or over 200 million rupees).

249. *Ind. Exp.*, 3.4.76 ('it has been known for quite some time that the government would ultimately dilute the provisions of the Act'). The rules were further 'amplified' on 15 April 1976.

250. Pai, qu. *Hindu*, 6.4.76.

251. Pai, to Lok Sabha, 30 April 1976, qu. *Samachar*, 30.4.76.

252. *Guardian*, 26.4.76.

253. *Ind. Exp.*, 6.4.76.

254. IG, *Broadcast to the Nation, June 27, 1975*.

255. qu. *ABP*, 24.3.76.

256. H. Mukherjee (CPI), in Lok Sabha, 30 April 1976, qu. *ABP*, 1.5.76.

257. Gokhale, to Rajya Sabha, 29 March 1976, qu. *Ind. Exp.*, 30.3.76. According to the Companies' Act Report for 1975, there were 510 companies registered under the Act in India, of which 301 were British, 81 American, 20 Japanese, and 12 West German, qu. *Link*, 4.4.76.

258. P. C. Sethi, Minister for Chemicals, to Rajya Sabha, qu. *Statesman*, 14.1.76.

259. C. P. Majhi, Deputy Minister for Chemicals, qu. *ABP*, 10.3.76.

260. Sethi, qu. *Hindu*, 1.4.76.

261. *Hindu*, 18.3.76.
262. Sethi, qu. *Times of India*, 16.4.76.
263. e.g. Chattophadyaya, qu. *ABP*, 18.4.76 ('the government has no intention of asking foreign tea companies to wind up business in India').
264. qu. *EPW*, 21.2.76.
265. qu. *Econ. Times*, 11.3.76.
266. *ABP*, 14.3.76 (he 'got the impression that conditions for new investments were negotiable on a case by case basis', as they were).
267. *EPW*, 21.2.76.
268. qu. *Hindu*, 11.1.76.
269. Bepin Pal Das, qu. *ABP*, 1.3.76.
270. To Rajya Sabha, 26 March 1976, qu. *ABP*, 27.3.76.
271. qu. *Samachar*, 20.4.76; on 21 April, Chavan said 'India is making constructive efforts to improve its relations with the US' (qu. *Samachar*, 21.4.76).
272. qu. *ABP*, 11.4.76.
273. Chattophadyaya, to Lok Sabha, 25 May 1976, qu. *ABP*, 26.5.76.
274. *ABP*, 3.5.76; as Jagjivan Ram put it (qu. *ABP*, 17.5.76), 'import of grains would continue for maintaining trade relations with other countries'; but see chapter 8, p. 359.
275. This activity surfaced, for example, in the *Ind. Exp.*, 14.1.76 and *Hindu*, 9.2.76; involved in this, *inter alios*, are the Bank of America in India, the Indo-American Chamber of Commerce, the Indo-US Business Council, and the Indian Engineering Export Council.
276. *ABP*, 23.3.76; by the 'Indo-US Sub-Commission on Economic and Commercial Affairs'.
277. *ABP*, 23.5.76.
278. *Econ. Times*, 20.10.75.
279. *ABP*, 17.5.76; the report, however, also pointed out the absence of real long-term agricultural growth, and the low level of industrial activity.
280. To 25th CPSU Congress, Moscow, 24 Feb. 1976, qu. *Hindu* (*Int. Ed.*), 28.2.76.
281. *Times of India*, 13.3.76.
282. *Econ. Times*, 18.3.76 (they were purchasing twenty-five million metres of cloth).
283. ibid.
284. *Ind. Exp.*, 18.3.76.
285. *Times of India*, 18.3.76.

286. *Econ. Times*, 25.3.76 (the Russians were being given, at the same time, a 'survey of the hopeful trends in the Indian economy, and of the upsurge in production').

287. I. K. Gujral, qu. *Econ. Times*, 11.4.76.

288. *ABP*, 14.4.76.

289. *Econ. Times*, 11.4.76.

290. qu. *Econ. Times*, 10.3.76.

291. qu. *ABP*, 14.3.76.

292. To Rajya Sabha, 9 March 1976, qu. *ABP*, 10.3.76.

293. *EPW*, 3.4.76.

294. ibid.

295. ibid.; quoting *Economic Survey, 1975–76*.

296. Conversation between senior civil servant and the writer, Delhi, Nov. 1975, on regular 'adjustments' to official statistics. Moreover, the figures for aid in the pre-budget *Economic Survey* and the budget itself did not tally; cf. 'these are undoubtedly record levels of inflow of foreign aid into the country' (*EPW*, 3.4.76).

297. *ABP*, 29.5.76.

298. ibid.

299. e.g. *ABP*, 27.3.76; *Ind. Exp.*, 18.4.76; *Hindu*, 18.4.76; *Business Standard*, 20.4.76; *Hindu*, 20.4.76; *Statesman*, 20.4.76; *Econ. Times*, 26.4.76.

300. *EPW*, 15.5.76.

301. *Statesman*, 17.5.76; on 18 April 1976, before the revision, the deficit was described as the 'biggest trade deficit ever' (*ABP*, 19.4.76).

302. *Economist*, 20.3.76.

303. *Econ. Times*, 10.3.76.

304. Mahindra, qu. *Econ. Times*, 2.5.76.

305. Barooah, qu. *Ind. Exp.*, 31.12.75.

306. IG, *Broadcast to the Nation, June 27, 1975*.

307. GOI, *Thirty Days*, p. 3.

308. Presented to Parliament on 8 March 1976; qu. *ABP*, 1.3.76.

309. qu. *EPW*, 22.5.76.

310. ibid.

311. *ABP*, 1.3.76.

312. qu. *Econ. Times*, 9.3.76.

313. Subramaniam Swamy, *Guardian*, 2.6.76.

314. IG, qu. *Hindu*, 31.12.75.

315. qu. *Hind. Times*, 12.5.76.

316. *Link*, 14.4.76.

317. e.g. Delhi State Electricity Workers' Union, qu. *Econ. Times*, 18.4.76.
318. CPI–M, 'Twenty-Point Programme: A Cruel Hoax'.
319. V. A. Karnik, of Bennett, Coleman & Co., qu. *Econ. Times*, 4.4.76.
320. qu. *Statesman*, 27.12.75.
321. *Party Life*, 22.11.75, p. 4.
322. Rajeswar Rao, qu. *Blitz*, 27.12.75.
323. *Party Life*, 22.11.75, p. 4.
324. IG, to Rajya Sabha, 22 July 1975, qu. *PODS*, p. 12.
325. *Party Life*, 22.11.75, p. 4.
326. ibid.
327. qu. *Intercontinental Press*, 26.2.76.
328. qu. *Ind. Exp.*, 29.2.76.
329. qu. *Ind. Exp.*, 31.12.75.
330. IG, at Bokaro strip-mill, 1 May 1976, qu. *ABP*, 2.5.76 ('caring little for what some people outside speak of us').
331. qu. *Econ. Times*, 1.5.76.
332. GOI, *Thirty Days*, p. 10.
333. AICC resolution to 75th Congress conference, *Ind. Exp.*, 30.12.75.
334. *Business Standard*, 2.6.76.
335. *Econ. Times*, 29.5.76.
336. S. S. Ray, qu. *Ind. Exp.*, 14.1.76.
337. Conversation between K. V. Varadarajan and the writer, Madras, Dec. 1975.
338. Ahmed, qu. *Ind. Exp.*, 14.1.76; *Statesman*, 14.1.76.
339. ibid.
340. Information communicated to the writer; the shaft which was inundated was originally sunk in the mid-1960s by the British International Construction Co.
341. R. Reddy, qu. *Statesman*, 14.1.76.
342. *Hindu*, 31.12.75.
343. Mary Tyler, *India Today*, no. 2, Winter 1975.
344. CITU protest to the Director-General of the ILO, 8 Nov. 1975 ('in Bihar, scores of CITU activists have been arrested in the coal belt including two General Council members, and active workers of Bihar colliery Kamgar Sabha, Dhanbad').
345. *S. Standard*, 28.12.75.
346. qu. *Ind. Exp.*, 29.12.75 (Yadav described the accident as 'most unfortunate').
347. qu. *Ind. Exp.*, 31.12.75.

348. *Hindu*, 31.12.75.
349. ibid.
350. qu. *Hindu*, 31.12.75; *Ind. Exp.*, 31.12.75.
351. *Ind. Exp.*, 3.1.76.
352. Karan Singh, qu. *Hindu*, 11.1.76; these were the accents of the erstwhile Maharajah of Jammu and Kashmir.
353. qu. *Hindu*, 12.1.76.
354. Mary Tyler, *India Today*, no. 2, Winter 1975.
355. Pai, to Rajya Sabha, 29 July 1975, qu. *The Turning Point*, p. 40.
356. *ABP*, 11.1.76.
357. *Fin. Exp.*, 13.1.76.
358. *Ind. Exp.*, 14.1.76.
359. ibid.
360. *Ind. Exp.*, 15.1.76.
361. *Ind. Exp.*, 16.1.76.
362. *Ind. Exp.*, 17.1.76.
363. *ABP*, 20.1.76.
364. *Times of India*, 27.2.76.
365. *Times of India*, 12.3.76.
366. *Samachar*, 20.3.76.
367. *Econ. Times*, 31.3.76.
368. *Times of India*, 8.4.76.
369. Information communicated to the writer.
370. *Statesman*, 7.4.76, 9.4.76.
371. Siddheswar Prasad, qu. *ABP*, 4.4.76.
372. To Lok Sabha, 7 April 1976, qu. *Econ. Times*, 8.4.76.
373. qu. *Econ. Times*, 17.4.76.
374. qu. *Econ. Times*, 10.4.76.
375. *Econ. Times*, 3.4.76.

CHAPTER SEVEN: RESURGENCE AND DEGENERATION

1. qu. *Times of India*, 13.4.76.
2. qu. *Times of India*, 6.4.76.
3. Communicated to the writer, Delhi, Nov. 1975.
4. qu. *Times of India*, 2.4.76.
5. Conversation between K. V. Varadarajan and the writer, Madras, Dec. 1975.
6. e.g. cf. 'A new five-star hotel has come up in the suburbs of Bombay. Named Hotel Sea-Rock, it has five restaurants, including a revolving one, two swimming pools, tennis courts,

badminton courts, bowling alley, skating rinks, water-polo, and even a room where yoga can be practised' (*Ind. Exp.*, 27.4.76).

7. John Jacob, 'India Then and Now' (press release), 15.3.76.

8. Conversation between member of the 'royal household' of Jodhpur and the writer, Jodhpur, Nov. 1975.

9. Conversation between member of Railway Workers' Union and the writer, Rajasthan, Nov. 1975.

10. Street slogans.

11. Conversation between university professor and the writer, Rajasthan, Nov. 1975.

12. Conversation between students and the writer, Bombay, Jan. 1976.

13. IG, *New Programme for Econ. Progress.*

14. *N. Indian Patrika*, 19.12.75 (UNI, 18.12.75).

15. e.g. under rules introduced by the government of Kerala, *S. Standard*, 11.1.76 ('heads of offices have been asked to conduct not less than three lightning inspections in a fortnight to discourage loitering'); see also *Econ. Times*, 27.4.76.

16. e.g. of the Delhi railway-board offices by the Minister for Railways, Qureshi, to 'check the attendance of the staff after lunch' (*Times of India*, 16.12.75).

17. CPI, *Resolutions and Report of the National Council*, p. 25.

18. Conversation with the writer, Calcutta, Dec. 1975.

19. qu. *Deccan Herald*, 1.1.76.

20. B. R. Shukla (Cong.), to Lok Sabha, 7 Jan. 1976, qu. *Ind. Exp.*, 8.1.76.

21. S. B. Chavan, qu. *Hindu*, 8.1.76 ('drawn up for the celebrations to mark the "decade of progress" under the stewardship of Prime Minister, Indira Gandhi', *Ind. Exp.*, 15.1.76.

22. *Econ. Times*, 5.3.76; also 'smoked out', *Times of India*, 25.2.76, and 'eliminated', *Econ. Times*, 2.3.76.

23. Chavan, qu. *Hindu*, 8.1.76.

24. ibid.

25. ibid.

26. The ordinance amended the Bombay Prevention of Begging Act, 1959; *Hindu*, 18.2.76.

27. ibid.

28. *Econ. Times*, 19.2.76.

29. *Econ. Times*, 2.3.76.

30. *Guardian*, 2.3.76.

31. *Times of India*, 25.2.76; Aarey is 25 km north of Bombay.

32. *Econ. Times*, 2.3.76.

33. *Hind. Times*, 1.5.76; they included sixty-two children.
34. Communicated to the writer.
35. *Times of India*, 14.3.76.
36. S. S. Shinde, Maharashtra's Minister for Social Welfare, qu. *Times of India*, 18.2.76.
37. *Free Press Journal*, 7.3.76 ('residents of Thane, Kalyan, Ulhasnagar, Ambarnath, and Bhiwandi are perturbed by the sudden influx of beggars of all ages'); cf. Shinde, 'the idea is certainly not to drive away the beggars' (qu. *Ind. Exp.*, 12.3.76), and 'it is calculated that once the round-up operation goes into full-swing, most beggars will return to the state of their origin' (*Econ. Times*, 19.2.76).
38. *Ind. Exp.*, 29.12.75; in the same period, and using the same vocabulary, similar attention was being paid to the 'stray dog menace', e.g. *Hindu*, 3.1.76, 12.1.76.
39. *Hindu*, 22.2.76; cf. 'emergency has brought forth many deeds of magnitude, and the use of the dog-squad by central railways against unsocial elements is one of them' (*Madras Evening Daily*, 29.12.75).
40. *Hindu*, 31.12.75 ('they are found all over the place on railway platforms').
41. *Times of India*, 8.1.76; *Ind. Exp.*, 16.1.76 ('to demolish huts on roads and footpaths according to the requirements of the civic administration').
42. *Hindu*, 12.1.76.
43. *Tribune*, 13.12.75.
44. *Ind. Exp.*, 15.1.76.
45. *Mainstream*, 13.12.75 (advertisement).
46. *Hindu*, 5.4.76, reporting from Bhopal.
47. *Ind. Exp.*, 16.1.76.
48. P. J. Deoras, qu. *Econ. Times*, 21.3.76.
49. *Ind. Exp.* (caption to a photograph), 4.12.75.
50. Deoras, loc. cit. (and 'the haunting of adolescents at bus-stops and colony roads').
51. *Ind. Exp.*, 15.1.76.
52. *Times of India*, 5.6.76, on 'several thousand hutment-dwellers shifted to Cheetah colony near Mankhurd in Bombay'. For the demolition of Bombay's 72,000-strong Janata colony, see *Times of India*, 17.4.76, 18.4.76; and *EPW*, 3.4.76.
53. *Link*, 4.4.76 ('hundreds of people lost employment').
54. Samar Mukherjee (CPI–M), to Lok Sabha, 6 Jan. 1976, privately circulated.

55. Students and serving staff of Delhi University's school of planning were feeding lines of hungry children here daily in early December 1975, with canisters of hot food brought from the University.
56. Information provided to the writer.
57. M. Rahman, *Fulcrum* (Bombay), April 1976, pp. 12–15; one had been married only four months, another had been sterilized twice before, one man was dumb, and two were aged eighty. For similar accounts from Bihar, including that of the newly wed daughter of an untouchable, see Arun Sinha, *EPW*, 24.4.76.
58. *Fulcrum*, loc. cit.
59. ibid.
60. ibid.
61. ibid.; cf. 'the state of Maharashtra scored a great success this year' (*Link*, 25.4.76).
62. S. Arora, *Fulcrum*, April 1976, p. 15.
63. ibid.
64. *EPW*, 24.4.76, 22.5.76; *Fulcrum*, loc. cit.; *Ind. Exp.*, 1.4.76.
65. S. Arora, *Fulcrum*, loc. cit.
66. *EPW*, 24.4.76.
67. ibid.
68. *Fulcrum*, loc. cit.
69. *PBEI*, pp. 19–20, 23 and 253; Karan Singh, qu. *Ind. Exp.*, 17.4.76.
70. *EPW*, 24.4.76.
71. To Lok Sabha, 29 April 1976, qu. *Econ. Times*, 30.4.76.
72. e.g. see Mahmood Mamdani, *The Myth of Population Control: Family, Caste, and Class in an Indian Village* (New York and London, Monthly Review Press, 1972).
73. *Hindu*, 12.1.76.
74. ibid.
75. ibid.
76. qu. *Hindu*, 9.2.76.
77. *Hindu*, 18.2.76; *ABP*, 4.3.76.
78. *ABP*, 8.3.76.
79. *Hindu*, 5.4.76.
80. *Times of India*, 8.6.76.
81. *Ind. Exp.*, 1.4.76.
82. ibid.
83. *EPW*, 27.3.76; for official denials, *Ind. Exp.*, 21.3.76.
84. *Ind. Exp.*, 1.4.76. In Delhi, those 'bringing 50 cases for steriliza-

tion would be entitled to take part in a draw for television sets and refrigerators' (*Hindu*, 5.4.76).

85. *Econ. Times*, 20.3.76.
86. *EPW*, 27.3.76.
87. *ABP*, 24.3.76.
88. *EPW*, 27.3.76.
89. *Ind. Exp.*, 31.3.76.
90. *Econ. Times*, 2.4.76.
91. *Hindu*, 3.4.76; for similar provisions, e.g. in Himachal Pradesh, *Hindu*, 9.4.76; and Uttar Pradesh, *Times of India*, 6.6.76, and *Hind. Times*, 10.6.76.
92. ibid.; applied also to those wanting loans to buy a milch-cow.
93. *Hindu*, 10.4.76; *Samachar*, 10.6.76.
94. qu. *Ind. Exp.*, 6.4.76.
95. Karan Singh, qu. *Econ. Times*, 17.4.76; the Health Minister was congratulated in the Lok Sabha, on 27 April 1976, by the economist V. K. R. V. Rao (*Econ. Times*, 28.4.76).
96. qu. *Ind. Exp.*, 17.4.76.
97. *Econ. Times*, 17.4.76.
98. qu. *Ind. Exp.*, 29.4.76.
99. qu. *Econ. Times*, 1.5.76.
100. Tara Ali Baig, qu. *Hindu*, 11.4.76.
101. *Ind. Exp.*, 23.4.76.
102. e.g. *Times of India*, 26.4.76; *Link*, 25.4.76; *EPW*, 22.5.76; *Ananda Bazar Patrika*, 21.6.76.
103. Information provided to the writer.
104. This was not the first occasion of resistance to demolition in that area; there were clashes with police in Karol Bagh and Jama Masjid in late summer, 1975.
105. Bombay, Jan. 1976.
106. *Statesman*, 22.4.76.
107. Information supplied to the writer.
108. Information supplied to the writer.
109. Statements of Mohammed Ismail (CPI–M) and Bejoy Modak (CPI–M), both Members of Parliament, who visited the area on 25 April 1976; circulated, May 1976.
110. 29.5.76.
111. See *Guardian*, 21.4.76; *Economist*, 29.5.76.
112. Bulletin of People's Information and News Service, Delhi (report dated 23.4.76), privately circulated; Ismail and Modak, loc. cit. ('people who resisted were beaten up mercilessly').
113. Ismail and Modak, loc. cit.

114. Information supplied to the writer.
115. Bulletin of People's Information and News Service, op. cit.
116. Information supplied to the writer.
117. Bulletin of People's Information and News Service, op. cit.
118. *Economist*, 29.5.76.
119. *Guardian*, 21.4.76.
120. *Guardian*, 28.4.76.
121. *Samachar*, 3.5.76 ('rumours can play havoc').
122. *Samachar*, 30.4.76.
123. Mohsin, to Lok Sabha, 27 April 1976, qu. *Samachar*, 24.4.76 ('the situation in the area is under control'). Sixteen hundred signatures were collected at Aligarh Muslim University and sent to the President of India, expressing concern at the Turkman Gate incident.
124. Ismail and Modak, loc. cit.
125. ibid.: 'most of them are artisans, workers, sweepers, and self-employed poor persons, and are Hindus, Muslims and Christians'.
126. Information supplied to the writer; also Ismail and Modak, loc. cit.
127. Krishnan Chand, Lieutenant-Governor of New Delhi, qu. *Guardian*, 21.4.76.
128. Information supplied to the writer.
129. qu. *Guardian*, 3.5.76; and subsequently 'no religious or political group will be allowed to stand in the way of the nation's progress by obstructing the family planning programme' (IG, qu. *Guardian*, 1.6.76).
130. In Kerala, literacy rose from 46·8 per cent in 1961 to 60·4 per cent in 1971, the highest in India (*PBEI*, p. 29). The birth rate has fallen by a third in the decade, from 37 to 25 per thousand, 'revolutionary judged by any standard in the world' (Mrinal Datta-Chaudhuri, 'Compulsions for the Economy', *Seminar* No. 203, July 1976, banned). Also relevant (as he points out) are Kerala's public health and welfare facilities.
131. *EPW*, 22.5.76.
132. *Link*, 25.4.76.
133. Raj Deo Singh (Cong.), to Lok Sabha, 1 April 1976, qu. *Hindu*, 2.4.76.
134. Barooah, qu. 5.5.76; the West Bengal Jan Sangh 'expressed concern' at this statement, qu. *Statesman*, 11.5.76.
135. B. Reddy, to Lok Sabha, 2 April 1976, qu. *Hindu*, 3.4.76; and *Times of India*, 2.10.76.

136. Y. B. Chavan, qu. *Statesman*, 1.12.75.
137. Jagannath Bharadwaj (INTUC) to Rajya Sabha, 10 May 1976, qu. *Times of India*, 11.5.76; cf. Qureshi's call for one union for railway workers, qu. *Times of India*, 9.6.76, and the CPI's call, through Roza Deshpande, one of their Members of Parliament, for a merger of AITUC and INTUC, qu. *Times of India*, 3.6.76.
138. S. Madhavan, Tamil Nadu Food Minister (pre-fall), in Madras, qu. *Ind. Exp.*, 5.1.76.
139. *ABP*, 7.3.76.
140. AICC report, qu. *Statesman*, 31.5.76.
141. *Hindu*, 3.4.76.
142. R. Reddy, qu. *Econ. Times*, 12.8.75.
143. Leaflet circulated by Presidency College (Calcutta) Chattra Parishad, Oct. 1975.
144. Information supplied to the writer, Simla, Dec. 1975.
145. Information supplied to the writer, April 1976; the lawyers' chambers were built on land provided by the Delhi administration; furniture, books, and legal papers were also bulldozed away.
146. Information supplied to the writer.
147. Conversation between industrialist and the writer, Bombay, Jan. 1976.
148. Conversation between newspaper editor and the writer, Delhi, Dec. 1975.
149. Conversation between university professor and the writer, Jaipur, Dec. 1975.
150. Conversation between senior civil servant and the writer, Delhi, Nov. 1975.
151. Conversation in Delhi (Turkman Gate), Dec. 1975.
152. Conversation in Delhi, Nov. 1975.
153. Conversation between Ayub Syed and the writer, Bombay, Jan. 1976.
154. Conversation between State Bank of India official and the writer, Delhi, Dec. 1975.
155. This took place on 1 Dec. 1975, as the Chief Minister drove towards the Circuit House in Jodhpur.
156. *Ind. Exp.*, 31.12.75.
157. *Times of India*, *Ind. Exp.*, 7.12.75 to 10.12.75, during Guru Tegh Bahadur memorial celebrations in Delhi.
158. *Times of India*, *Ind. Exp.*, 30.12.75.
159. *Ind. Exp.*, 31.12.75.

160. *Ind. Exp.*, 15.1.76, *Hindu* (*Int. Ed.*), 21.2.76; additionally India's highest honour, *Bharat Ratna*, was posthumously conferred on Kamaraj, on 3 April 1976. cf. 'the profuse tributes' to Lal Bahadur Shastri, 'who suggested I return to politics, in his usual and quiet way, so I could not refuse' (IG, qu. *Hindu*, 12.1.76).

161. IG, Mayer interview, qu. *Times of India*, 2.4.76.

162. *ABP*, 13.4.76.

163. *Mail*, 12.4.76, *Ind. Exp.*, 13.4.76; both, however, refer to 'women in distress', and 'sights of sorrow', of attachment of property due to non-payment of debts, and of the non-implementation of land-reform in the Prime Minister's own constituency ('Mrs Gandhi consoled them', *Ind. Exp.*, 13.4.76).

164. CPI, *Resolutions and Report of the National Council*, pp. 3 and 14; cf. the report of the CPI's central executive that 'for the first time in its history, the party went among the rural masses in a big way', and that '44,000 villages were covered by the CPI's *pada-yatra* campaign' (*Link*, 27.6.76).

165. *Hindu*, 19.2.76.

166. Communicated to the writer.

167. Conversation between Nirad Chaudhuri and the writer, Oxford, Feb. 1976.

168. *Hindu*, 19.2.76.

169. Jagjivan Ram, qu. *Ind. Exp.*, 31.12.75.

170. IG, qu. *S. Standard*, 11.1.76.

171. Subramaniam, to Lok Sabha, 31 July 1975, qu. GOI, *The Turning Point*, p. 60.

172. *Link*, 18.4.76.

173. IG, qu. *Deccan Herald*, 11.1.76.

174. *Statesman* (editorial), 14.1.76.

175. Information provided to the writer from trade union sources in Bombay, Jan. 1976.

176. Information provided to the writer, Agra, Dec. 1975.

177. As for n. 175.

178. Information provided by CITU to the writer; they also referred to strikes of toddy workers (5 Feb. 1976), brick workers (9 Feb. 1976), and electrical workers (1 March 1976) in Kerala.

179. *Econ. Times*, 28.3.76; *Ganashakti*, 20.3.76, 27.3.76; bulletin of People's Information and News Service, dated 13.4.76.

180. Information communicated to the writer.

181. People's Information and News Service, loc. cit.

182. *Ganashakti*, 27.3.76.

183. *People's Democracy*, 23.5.76.

184. ibid.
185. Barooah, qu. *S. Standard*, 15.2.76.
186. qu. *Statesman*, 28.11.75.
187. Barooah, qu. *Deccan Herald*, 31.12.75.
188. *Mainstream*, 13.12.75.
189. qu. *Times of India*, 17.4.76.
190. qu. *People's Democracy*, 29.2.76.
191. *Guardian*, 7.7.75.
192. qu. *Ind. Exp.*, 20.7.75.
193. *Ind. Exp.*, 30.12.75.
194. *Times of India*, 15.1.76.
195. qu. *Ind. Exp.*, 31.12.75.
196. *Guardian*, 10.3.76.
197. *Tribune*, 12.12.75.
198. ibid.
199. *Hindu*, 4.4.76.
200. qu. *Hindu (Int. Ed.)*, 27.3.76.
201. Information supplied to the writer; also *The Times*, 3.3.76. On 3 March, the Prime Minister visiting West Bengal spoke at Durgapur of 'the atmosphere all around being full of dangers' (*Econ. Times*, 4.3.76).
202. Information supplied to the writer.
203. *Ind. Exp.*, 31.3.76.
204. Mohsin, to Lok Sabha, 1 April 1976, qu. *Hindu*, 2.4.76.
205. Mohsin, to Lok Sabha, 8 April 1976, qu. *Econ. Times*, 9.4.76.
206. *Link*, 18.4.76.
207. Reddy, to Lok Sabha, 5 May 1976, qu. *ABP*, 6.5.76.
208. *Times of India*, 5.6.76.
209. IG, in Shillong, 23 April 1976, qu. *Econ. Times*, 24.4.76.
210. qu. *Times of India*, 12.5.76.
211. ibid.
212. *Link*, 11.1.76.
213. To Rajya Sabha, 28 July 1975.
214. To Rajya Sabha, 29 July, 1975, qu. GOI, *The Turning Point*, p. 36.
215. IG, at Durgapur, 3 March 1976 (visiting Calcutta immediately after the attack on Presidency Jail), qu. *Econ. Times*, 4.3.76.
216. B. M. Birla, qu. *ABP*, 4.5.76.
217. qu. *Econ. Times*, 27.4.76; on 15 Dec. 1975, he 'stressed the need for rural orientation of the mass media' (*Times of India*, 16.12.75).
218. *Hindu*, 8.1.76.
219. IG, qu. *Statesman*, 28.11.75.

220. IG, qu. *ABP*, 12.4.76.

221. ibid.

222. Nurul Hasan, qu. *Ind. Exp.*, 30.3.76.

223. qu. *Statesman*, 28.11.75 ('her school and college life in Poona and Vishwa Bharati were entirely in the open').

224. Conversation between the Prime Minister and the writer, Dec. 1975.

225. AICC resolution, to 75th Congress Party conference, qu. *Ind. Exp.*, 29.12.75.

226. ibid.

227. IG, at G. B. Pant University, 2 April 1976, qu. *Hindu*, 3.4.76.

228. GOI, *Thirty Days*, p. 3.

229. *Econ. Times*, 28.3.76.

230. Conversation between K. N. Johry of the CSIR and the writer, Delhi, Dec. 1975.

231. Karan Singh, qu. *Ind. Exp.*, 12.1.76 ('surgeons told to take new techniques to villages').

232. qu. *Hindu*, 29.3.76.

233. qu. *Hindu*, 30.3.76.

234. *Hindu*, 18.5.76.

235. IG, qu. *Econ. Times*, 2.3.76.

236. IG, at G. B. Pant University, qu. *Hindu*, 3.4.76 ('they should also try to educate farmers about the advantages of the scientific temperament').

237. IG, qu. *Econ. Times*, 2.3.76.

238. *ABP*, 10.4.76; under the National Service Scheme (NSS).

239. Sanjay Gandhi, qu. *Times of India*, 30.12.75.

240. *ABP*, 19.5.76.

241. *Estimate Committee's 79th Report on the Ministry of Education and Social Welfare* (GOI, Delhi, April 1975); *EPW*, 20.12.75.

242. ibid.

243. 'Guidelines for 1975–6', Jadhavpur University National Service Scheme, Calcutta (mimeograph).

244. Conversation between Major B. L. Das and the writer, Dec. 1975.

245. Lewis Simons, *Guardian*, 14.7.75.

246. *Economist*, 29.5.76.

247. Communicated to the writer, Delhi, Nov. 1975.

248. IG, qu. *S. Telegraph*, 12.10.75.

249. IG, Mayer interview, qu. *Ind. Exp.*, 2.4.76.

250. Conversation between Ayub Syed and the writer, Bombay, Jan. 1976.

251. *Times of India*, 11.12.75; on 3 Dec. 1975, he was still being described as 'the son of the Prime Minister' when he paid a 'surprise visit to Patna', and 'impressed the Chief Minister by his simplicity and concern for the downtrodden masses' (*Ind. Exp.*, 4.12.75).

252. Jagmohan, qu. *Hind. Times*, 14.12.75.

253. Asoke Sen (Cong.), qu. *Statesman*, 23.12.75.

254. ibid.

255. qu. *Deccan Herald*, 30.12.75; the Prime Minister on the same occasion (the 75th Congress Party conference) called for the Youth Congress to 'provide a lead to the country' (ibid.).

256. qu. *Times of India*, 30.12.75.

257. ibid. ('Sanjay gives surprise to delegates').

258. *Ind. Exp.*, *Hindu*, 31.12.75.

259. qu. *Deccan Herald*, 1.1.76.

260. qu. *Hindu*, 4.1.76.

261. CPI–M, 'Report of Central Committee Meeting' 22–8 Jan. 1976, Madras, p. 6.

262. qu. *Deccan Herald*, 12.1.76.

263. qu. *Hindu*, 4.1.76.

264. qu. *Hindu*, 29.3.76.

265. qu. *Hindu*, 8.2.76.

266. qu. *Hindu*, 12.1.76; the son of the Prime Minister of Sri Lanka was also present, and was described as 'President of the Freedom Fighters' Youth League' of Sri Lanka (ibid.).

267. *S. Standard*, 22.2.76.

268. *Hindu*, 22.2.76.

269. *S. Standard*, 22.2.76 (and 'blamed the private sector for allowing a climate to be created where nationalization was resorted to'). Cf. 'Nationalization is only beneficial if it results in a decline in prices. Otherwise, it is simply bureaucratization, and I don't regard bureaucracy as socialism' (qu. *Hindu*, 29.3.76).

270. *S. Standard*, 22.2.76.

271. ibid.

272. ibid.

273. Information from Student Federation of India, supplied to the writer.

274. *S. Standard*, 22.2.76. There was a private rapprochement, ending years of coolness, between the Bose and the Nehru families; the Prime Minister received members of the family in Delhi in Nov. 1975 (information supplied to the writer).

275. ibid.
276. *ABP*, 27.2.76.
277. *Hindu* (*Int. Ed.*), 6.3.76.
278. qu. *ABP*, 7.3.76 ('this is the yardstick with which we can never go wrong').
279. D. P. Mandelia, qu. *Ind. Exp.*, 18.3.76; cf. 'the overall shift of emphasis in economic policy, reportedly at the insistence of Sanjay Gandhi' (*Guardian*, 26.4.76).
280. *Red Star over China* (Penguin Books, 1972), pp. 419–20.
281. qu. *Hind. Times*, 19.3.76.
282. *Ind. Exp.*, 20.3.76.
283. *Ind. Exp.*, 21.3.76.
284. qu. *Hindu*, 21.3.76.
285. qu. *People's Democracy*, 28.3.76.
286. qu. *ABP*, 22.3.76.
287. qu. *ABP*, 25.3.76.
288. *Hindu*, 29.3.76.
289. qu. *Econ. Times*, 29.3.76.
290. qu. *Hindu*, 29.3.76.
291. ibid.
292. ibid.
293. qu. *Econ. Times*, 29.3.76.
294. qu. *Hindu*, 29.3.76.
295. ibid.
296. ibid. ('they could not be any other than Anand Marg, RSS and Jan Sangh').
297. ibid. ('perform vasectomy on beggars caught begging, and that will scare away most of them').
298. Information communicated to the writer.
299. qu. *Hindu*, 29.3.76.
300. ibid.
301. *ABP*, 10.4.76.
302. ibid.
303. *Ind. Exp.*, 3.5.76.
304. ibid.
305. qu. *Samachar*, 11.5.76.
306. *ABP*, 19.5.76.
307. *ABP*, 24.5.76.
308. *ABP*, 23.5.76 ('by a special correspondent').
309. *ABP*, 25.5.76.
310. *ABP*, 24.5.76.
311. *ABP*, 25.5.76.

312. Conversation between K. L. Shrimali and the writer, Benares, Dec. 1975.

313. Conversation between Rashid ud-din Khan and the writer, Delhi, Nov. 1975.

314. Conversation between Malcolm Adiseshiah and the writer, Madras, Dec. 1975.

315. G. C. Pande, *The Meaning and Process of Culture* (Agra, S. L. Agarwala, 1973), p. 13.

316. ibid., p. 1.

317. ibid., p. 118.

318. Conversation between G. C. Pande and the writer, Jaipur, Dec. 1975; and information obtained by the writer at Rajasthan University, Jaipur, Dec. 1975.

319. qu. *Econ. Times*, 4.3.76.

320. qu. *ABP*, 14.3.76 ('a living university in a developing society must not rest on its laurels').

321. Information communicated to the writer; it is alleged that the march was savagely attacked by the police, students were beaten up and arrested, and several hospitalized, including one, a girl student, who had her skull fractured.

322. qu. *ABP*, 6.4.76.

323. Conversation between Professor Gargi Dutt and the writer, Delhi, Dec. 1975.

324. N. G. Goray (SP), to Rajya Sabha, 22 July 1975; see appendix, pp. 387–8.

325. I. K. Sandhu, vice-chancellor, Punjabi University, at Patiala, qu. *Tribune*, 13.12.75.

CHAPTER EIGHT: THE INDIAN ROAD TO SOCIALISM

1. qu. Mayer interview, *ABP*, 2.4.76.

2. qu. *Statesman*, 27.6.76.

3. Covering letter, pp. 1 and 6; the league submitted a seventy-three-page documented complaint (see n. 4) to Kurt Waldheim, accusing India of violations of the UN Charter, and of the Universal Declaration of Human Rights.

4. International League for the Rights of Man, 'Torture of Political Prisoners in India, March 1976' (hereafter TPP), compiled by the Lok Sangharsh Samiti; included in the submissions to the UN by the International League for the Rights of Man, 31 May 1976.

5. K. Marx, 'The Eighteenth Brumaire of Louis Bonaparte', in *Surveys From Exile: Political Writings, vol. 2,* ed. D. Fernbach (Penguin Books, 1973), p. 170.

6. ibid., pp. 170–71.

7. ibid., pp. 155 and 180.

8. ibid., pp. 163, 198 and 191.

9. ibid., pp. 172, 175 and 174.

10. ibid., pp. 197–8.

11. ibid., p. 174.

12. ibid., pp. 155, 182 and 153.

13. ibid., p. 182.

14. ibid., p. 184.

15. ibid., p. 171.

16. qu. *San Francisco Examiner,* 18.4.76.

17. Jawaharlal Nehru, *Autobiography* (London, Bodley Head, 1936), pp. 590–91.

18. Georgi Dimitrov, *Report to the 7th Congress, Communist International, 1935* (London, Red Star Press, 1973), p. 41.

19. ibid., pp. 41 ff.

20. ibid.

21. ibid., esp. p. 45.

22. ibid., pp. 99–100.

23. qu. *Deccan Herald,* 1.1.76.

24. Sanjay Gandhi, qu. *Times of India,* 30.12.75.

25. IG, qu. *Times of India,* 15.1.76.

26. Barooah, qu. *Ind. Exp.,* 30.12.75.

27. Dimitrov, *Report to the 7th Congress,* p. 51.

28. ibid., p. 53.

29. ibid., p. 45.

30. Dimitrov, *Final Speech at Reichstag Fire Trial,* Dec. 1933 (London, Red Star Press, 1973), p. 28.

31. Barooah, qu. *Link,* 27.6.76.

32. Dimitrov, *Report to the 7th Congress,* p. 45.

33. ibid., p. 46.

34. International League for the Rights of Man, TPP, p. 10.

35. Barooah, qu. *Guardian,* 26.1.76 ('all this has been achieved not by bayonets but by popular support').

36. International League for the Rights of Man, TPP, p. 2.

37. Ved Nanda, *Nation,* 21.2.76.

38. International League for the Rights of Man, TPP, pp. 2–3.

39. ibid., pp. 3–6.

40. ibid., p. 7.

41. ibid., pp. 7–8.
42. ibid., pp. 8–9.
43. ibid., pp. 9–10.
44. ibid.
45. ibid., p. 11.
46. ibid., p. 11; leaders of the opposition did likewise in a letter dated 6 Oct. 1975, privately circulated.
47. Leaders of the opposition protested to the Prime Minister in a letter dated 22 Oct. 1975, privately circulated.
48. International League for the Rights of Man, TPP, pp. 10–12.
49. Barooah, qu. *Ind. Exp.*, 31.12.75.
50. *Samachar*, 7.6.76; *The Times*, 3.6.76.
51. International League for the Rights of Man, TPP, p. 12.
52. ibid., pp. 12 and 14.
53. G. V. Shukla, press counsellor at Indian High Commission in London, *Guardian*, 31.7.76 (letter).
54. B. K. Nehru, Indian High Commissioner, *Sunday Times*, 6.6.76 (letter), quoting 'as a matter of interest' an (undated, unascribed) Indian Supreme Court judgement.
55. Barooah, qu. *Deccan Herald*, 1.1.76.
56. ibid.
57. K. Marx, *Surveys from Exile*, p. 148.
58. ibid., p. 190.
59. V. P. Dutt, to Rajya Sabha, 6 Jan. 1976, qu. *Ind. Exp.*, 7.1.76.
60. IG, qu. *Hindu*, 3.4.76 ('resulting in wrongful acts which harmed the entire country').
61. Gian Prakash, qu. *Guardian*, 17.6.76.
62. *People's Democracy*, 11.4.76.
63. IG, to AICC, 30 May 1976, qu. *Guardian*, 1.6.76.
64. Nirmal Verma, *Seminar*, no. 203, July 1976, p. 32.
65. *Hindu*, 23.8.76 ('beggars are being rounded up in important tourist and pilgrim centres').
66. ibid.
67. *New Internationalist*, no. 41, Aug. 1976, pp. 21–2.
68. *EPW*, 22.5.76.
69. *Guardian*, 8.10.76.
70. *Guardian*, 18.10.76, 26.10.76.
71. K. Marx, *Surveys from Exile*, p. 146.
72. Bansi Lal, qu. *Hindu*, 16.8.76.
73. IG, in Jammu, 28 March 1976, qu. *Hindu*, 29.3.76.
74. ibid.; (also 'servicemen were cautioned against machinations of anti-social elements in the country').

75. e.g. *Hindu*, 29.3.76, 16.8.76; *Hindu (Int. Ed.)*, 6.3.76.

76. *The Times*, 26.1.76.

77. qu. *Hindu*, 4.4.76; *Times of India*, 4.4.76.

78. *The Times*, 26.1.76.

79. Maxwell, *Woman on a White Horse*, p. 361.

80. To Lok Sabha, 6 April 1976, qu. *Hindu*, 7.4.76.

81. K. Marx, *Surveys from Exile*, p. 188.

82. *Financial Express*, 9.6.76; also *Hindu*, 2.6.76.

83. *Patriot*, 16.6.76.

84. *Link*, 11.1.76.

85. *Observer*, 18.7.76; and information communicated to the writer.

86. B. Reddy, to Lok Sabha, 3 April 1976, qu. *Hindu*, 4.4.76.

87. ibid.

88. Reddy, to Lok Sabha, 16 Aug. 1976, qu. *Hindu*, 17.8.76; also *Hind. Times*, 21.6.76.

89. *Guardian*, 13.8.76 ('imprisoned in the last week of July').

90. ibid.

91. *Hindu*, 25.8.76.

92. Subramaniam Swamy, qu. *S. Telegraph*, 20.6.76 ('strapped to a chair and given electric shocks').

93. *Times of India*, 25.9.76; *The Times*, 5.10.76; *Guardian*, 5.10.76.

94. *Guardian*, 24.8.76.

95. Amnesty International secretary-general to *The Times*, 3.7.76 (letter); Amnesty International, 'Parliamentarians in Prison as at 16 August 1976' (London, 1976) contains seventy-nine names, twenty more than at 16 March 1976. Also, e.g., *D. Telegraph*, 11.6.76 and *Le Monde*, 10.9.76, for continuing arrests at that time.

96. Lok Sangharsh Samiti to the Prime Minister, 9 Jan. 1976; see appendix, p. 400–404.

97. Such as Charan Singh (BLD) released 7 March 1976; Ashok Mehta (SP) released 16 May 1976; Piloo Mody (Swatantra) released 6 Oct. 1976; Babubhai Patel, former Chief Minister of Gujarat, released 7 Oct. 1976; Chandra Shekhar and Mohan Dharia, released 12 Jan. 1977; and Morarji Desai, released 17 Jan. 1977.

98. e.g. 'processions and public meetings in Tamil Nadu', until 31 July 1976 (*Ind. Exp.*, 26.4.76); 'public meetings, assembly of 5 or more persons, slogan-shouting, speech-making and demonstrations in south Delhi', until 15 Sept. 1976 (*Hind. Times*, 15.7.76); 'prohibitory orders under DIR throughout the district of Patna' (*Samachar*, 15.7.76); and so on across India.

99. Information communicated to the writer; and see *The Times*, 26.7.76.
100. For his death, *The Times*, 26.7.76; and information communicated to the writer.
101. *Information Bulletin no. 8* (Calcutta, CPI–M), 11.6.76.
102. ibid.
103. Information communicated to the writer.
104. Information communicated to the writer; also Amnesty International, 'Parliamentarians in Prison'.
105. Information communicated to the writer.
106. Information communicated to the writer.
107. e.g. Lok Sabha debate, 10 March 1976, qu. *Econ. Times*, 11.3.76.
108. *The Times*, 2.8.76.
109. *ABP*, 26.5.76; it called for the restoration of civil liberties, independence of the judiciary, an 'egalitarian social order', 'elimination of unemployment', and maximization of production.
110. IG, at Red Fort, Delhi, 15 August 1976, qu. *Guardian*, 16.8.76; also 'they do not have love and respect for the nation, and do not realize the consequences of their propaganda' (*ABP*, 27.5.76).
111. *Hindu*, 16.8.76 ('differences with the agitational approach of J. P. Narayan').
112. *Swaraj* (London), 12.2.76 (interview with J. P. Narayan).
113. K. Marx, *Surveys from Exile*, pp. 78–9.
114. qu. *Sunday Times*, 1.2.76.
115. *The Times*, 17.9.76; and, e.g., *Statesman*, 13.1.76.
116. IG, at Patna, qu. *Ind. Exp.*, 2.5.76.
117. *Blitz*, 13.12.75.
118. ibid.
119. IG, in Delhi, 29 Feb. 1976, qu. *Hindu* (*Int. Ed.*), 6.3.76.
120. *Hindu*, 26.12.75; *The Times*, 19.1.76; for Vinoba Bhave's alleged support for compulsory sterilization, *ABP*, 4.3.76.
121. *Guardian*, 24.9.76, 5.10.76 ('Fernandes in chains attacks dictatorship', headline); for an account of his treatment in jail, *The Times*, 20.9.76.
122. V. C. Shukla, qu. *Times of India*, 27.6.76.
123. *The Times*, 26.8.76, 5.10.76 ('because of alleged non-payment of taxes'); *Guardian*, 2.10.76 ('its power supply cut off'), and 2.11.76 ('its property auctioned').
124. C. R. Irani, the managing editor of the *Statesman*, had his passport withdrawn in January 1976; *Guardian*, 14.9.76.
125. IG, qu. *Samachar*, 30.6.76.

126. *Sunday Times*, 5.9.76; a report on the closures was submitted to the International Press Institute. The BBC closed its office in Delhi in August 1976, because it was 'unable to contribute to our programmes' (*The Times*, 6.8.76).

127. *D. Telegraph*, 9.6.76.

128. *Guardian*, 14.9.76.

129. *Hindu*, 15.3.76 (on Gujarat); AICC circular, qu. *Hindu*, 10.4.76; IG, qu. *Hindu*, 31.12.75.

130. *Link*, 4.4.76, 27.6.76.

131. *Mainstream*, 13.12.75, p. 10.

132. *Link*, 27.6.76.

133. IG, qu. *Times of India*, 30.12.75.

134. *Hindu* (editorial), 16.8.76 ('it is not as though this danger has passed').

135. Declaration of Indian Youth Congress, 9–10 August 1976, Delhi, qu. *Hindu*, 12.8.76; the 'explanation of the role of Mrs Gandhi in national integration' was also declared to be one of its tasks.

136. *Samachar*, 11.8.76.

137. qu. *Hindu*, 8.8.76.

138. Dange, qu. *EPW*, 22.5.76.

139. *Business Standard*, 30.5.76.

140. See, e.g., *Times of India*, 13.1.77, for attacks on CPI 'conspiracy'.

141. Achutha Menon, qu. *Hindu*, 16.8.76.

142. Rajeswar Rao, qu. *Link*, 27.6.76.

143. *EPW*, 22.5.76.

144. Maharashtra and Gujarat, *Times of India*, 22.6.76.

145. Barrackpore, *Statesman*, 25.6.76; Midnapore, *Statesman*, 24.6.76.

146. qu. *Samachar*, 24.6.76.

147. *Link*, 12.9.76; *Guardian*, 14.9.76.

148. e.g. Orissa, *Link*, 12.9.76; Kerala, *Link*, 9.5.76, and *Information Bulletin no. 8* (Calcutta, CPI–M), 11.6.76; Tamil Nadu, *Econ. Times*, 18.4.76, and *ABP*, 24.4.76; Delhi, *Ind. Exp.*, 20.3.76; and information communicated to the writer.

149. *Business Standard*, 26.4.76; *Statesman*, 9.5.76.

150. IG, qu. *Ind. Exp.*, 1.1.76.

151. *EPW*, 5.7.76. The Supreme Court bar association called for the proposed changes to be deferred during the emergency, *Econ. Times*, 20.5.76; the Calcutta High Court bar association, in a unanimous resolution of 14 May 1976, declared the proposals 'unacceptable', as striking down the rule of law and giving

'unassailable supremacy to the executive'; information communicated to the writer.

152. *EPW*, 5.6.76.
153. *Hindu*, 12.8.76.
154. *New Age*, 6.6.76.
155. Bhupesh Gupta, qu. *Link*, 27.6.76.
156. qu. *Times of India*, 5.6.76.
157. *Ganashakti*, 19.5.76, 29.5.76; *ABP*, 5.5.76; *People's Democracy*, 6.6.76, 25.7.76.
158. *People's Democracy*, 11.7.76.
159. *Hindu*, 10.8.76.
160. *Hindu*, 19.8.76.
161. *Link*, 27.6.76.
162. Reddy, to Rajya Sabha, 17 August 1976, qu. *Hindu*, 18.8.76; the state of emergency in Nagaland was also extended for six months from 26 Sept. 1976.
163. *Hindu*, 27.8.76; despite the opposition of the Chief Minister of Kerala.
164. *Guardian*, 30.8.76.
165. H. M. Patel, qu. *Guardian*, 2.9.76; *The Times*, 2.9.76.
166. *Guardian*, 30.8.76; *The Times*, 2.9.76.
167. qu. *The Times*, 2.9.76.
168. ibid.
169. qu. *Listener*, 8.7.76.
170. ibid.
171. IG, qu. *Ind. Exp.*, 15.1.76.
172. ibid.
173. Bansi Lal, to Lok Sabha, 6 April 1976, qu. *Econ. Times*, 7.4.76.
174. *Link*, 4.4.76.
175. Inder Malhotra, *Guardian*, 9.6.76.
176. Bansi Lal, to a 'massive public meeting', at Sonepat, 1 March 1976, qu. *Econ. Times*, 2.3.76.
177. S. R. Ghauri, *Guardian*, 12.4.76.
178. Bansi Lal, qu. *Econ. Times*, 2.3.76.
179. *Hindu*, 3.4.76.
180. *People's Democracy*, 23.5.76.
181. GOI, *Years of Achievement: Irrigation* (Delhi, DAVP, MIB, 1975), pp. 8–9.
182. *Guardian*, 9.9.76.
183. *Guardian*, 28.4.76.

184. *Report of Indian External Affairs Ministry*, 1975–6, qu. *Econ. Times*, 4.4.76.
185. Inder Malhotra, *Guardian*, 9.6.76.
186. *Econ. Times*, 27.3.76, 4.4.76, 9.4.76.
187. *Econ. Times*, 22.4.76.
188. *Guardian*, 4.5.76, 9.9.76.
189. *Report of Indian External Affairs Ministry*, 1975–6, qu. *Econ. Times*, 4.4.76.
190. *Peking Daily*, 29.6.75; cf. 'Premier Chou En-lai said . . . that by its doings the Indian government is lifting a rock only to drop it on its own feet and will eventually eat the bitter fruit of its own making, and meet with ignominious defeat' (*Peking Review*, 4.2.72).
191. *Peking Daily*, 4.11.75.
192. IG, interview with Karanjia, qu. *Econ. Times*, 5.3.76.
193. *Report of Indian Defence Ministry*, 1975–6, qu. *Econ. Times*, 1.4.76 ('particularly in the north-eastern region').
194. New China News Agency, qu. *People's Democracy*, 13.6.76.
195. Bepin Pal Das, to Rajya Sabha, qu. *Hindu*, 22.8.76.
196. qu. *Guardian*, 10.9.76.
197. qu. *Guardian*, 13.9.76.
198. ibid. ('recent deeds of Peking have pleased New Delhi, though these have not been publicized').
199. *Peking Daily*, 29.6.75.
200. Y. B. Chavan, qu. *Econ. Times*, 9.4.76.
201. IG, qu. *Guardian*, 9.6.76.
202. *Ind. Exp.*, 19.5.76.
203. *Free Press Journal*, 19.5.76.
204. *Business Standard*, 18.5.76.
205. *Guardian*, 12.6.76.
206. *Times of India*, 9.6.76.
207. *Guardian*, 14.6.76.
208. Indo-Soviet joint communiqué, Moscow 13 June 1976, qu. *Guardian*, 14.6.76.
209. IG, at Moscow press conference, qu. *Guardian*, ibid.
210. *Guardian*, 19.7.76 ('the Soviet Union does not want to see the Romanians at such an event').
211. Carlos Rafael Rodriguez, at 5th summit conference of non-aligned countries, Colombo, qu. *Granma* (Havana), 29.8.76.
212. Fidel Castro, quoted by Rodriguez, loc. cit.
213. Political declaration of Colombo conference, 1976, qu. *Hindu*, 21.8.76; *Guardian*, 14.8.76, 18.8.76.

214. N. K. P. Singh, *Guardian*, 28.7.76 ('India's unfair image abroad', letter to editor).
215. ibid.
216. IG, qu. *Ind. Exp.*, 2.4.76.
217. F. A. Ahmed, qu. *Hindu*, 15.8.76 ('collective action on agreed programmes tends to bring people together').
218. Conversation between Jennie Lee and the writer, London, Nov. 1975.
219. Ahmed, qu. *Hindu*, 15.8.76.
220. John Jacob, 'India Then and Now' (press release), 15.3.76.
221. Y. B. Chavan, qu. *Hindu*, 26.12.75.
222. B. K. Nehru, qu. *Listener*, 8.7.76.
223. ibid.
224. GOI, *Thirty Days*, p. 1.
225. Ashok Rudra, *Seminar*, July 1976, p. 26.
226. ibid.
227. Barooah, qu. *ABP*, 28.6.76.
228. Maxwell, *Woman on a White Horse*, pp. 366–7.
229. *Seminar*, July 1976, p. 11.
230. IG, at state governors' conference, Delhi, 20 March 1976, qu. *Econ. Times*, 21.3.76 ('though there has been much talk, nothing substantial has been done so far about rural uplift').
231. e.g. IG, qu. *Hindu*, 20.2.76; qu. BBC Mayer interview, *Ind. Exp.*, 2.4.76.
232. IG, qu. *Ind. Exp.*, 30.12.75.
233. IG, qu. *Econ. Times*, 5.3.76.
234. *Ind. Exp.*, 2.4.76 (summarizing Congress Party position in Lok Sabha debate, 1 April 1976).
235. B. Reddy, qu. *Econ. Times*, 6.4.76.
236. Mohsin, to Lok Sabha, 8 April 1976, qu. *Samachar*, 8.4.76.
237. IG, qu. *Guardian*, 26.6.76.
238. K. L. Dorji, Chief Minister of Sikkim, qu. *ABP*, 29.6.76; cf. 'you can trust her that she will not continue the emergency a moment longer than necessary', S. S. Ray, qu. *Ind. Exp.*, 30.12.75, and 'nobody, least of all the Prime Minister, wants to extend the emergency beyond the period necessary to maintain peace and stability' (ibid.).
239. IG, at Madras Marina rally, qu. *Hindu*, 16.2.76.
240. Maxwell, *Woman on a White Horse*, p. 358.
241. qu. *D. Telegraph*, 28.6.76.
242. qu. *Guardian*, 24.2.76.
243. qu. *Guardian*, 19.1.76.

244. qu. *Samachar*, 4.8.76.
245. qu. *Guardian*, 31.7.76 (letter).
246. qu. *Time Out*, 23.1.76, p. 5; cf. 'Indians in UK hail emergency' (*Hind. Times* headline, 1.12.75, quoting A. S. Rai of Southall).
247. qu. *Econ. Times*, 28.3.76 ('BBC and press anti-Indian, admits envoy', headline).
248. qu. *Hindu* (*Int. Ed.*), 14.8.76.
249. qu. *The Times*, 25.6.76 ('the Gandhi Raj is more effective ... far less oppressive than predicted and reported').
250. Jennie Lee, qu. *Deccan Herald*, 1.1.76 (and 'socialists should rally to Mrs Gandhi', BBC '*World Tonight*', 20.2.76).
251. In Madras, qu. *Ind. Exp.*, 7.2.76; but cf. 'parliamentary democracy on the Westminster model [in India] has demonstrably failed' (*Observer*, 25.4.76).
252. Foot, qu. *The Times*, 7.1.77 ('the peddling of such lies can do infinite damage to relations between our two countries'); Silverman, qu. *Tribune* (Ambala), 12.12.75 ('he was struck by the relaxed atmosphere in New Delhi, and did not see any kind of police activity').
253. qu. *D. Telegraph*, 23.9.76.
254. qu. *ABP*, 26.3.76.
255. Letter to *The Times*, qu. *ABP*, 18.5.76; and the Archbishop of Canterbury Dr Coggan, visiting India, 'commended the family planning programme' (qu. *The Times*, 28.10.76).
256. David Holden, *Sunday Times*, 28.12.75 ('every train and plane I happened to catch was dead on time').
257. Professor Mark Solomon (US), at Patna 'anti-fascist' conference, qu. *Blitz*, 13.12.75.
258. '*The Dawning of The New Deal*', dispatch no. 7 (CPI–M), 29 Oct. 1975, p. 18.
259. ibid.
260. ibid.
261. Conversation between Calcutta trade unionist and the writer, Jan. 1976.
262. Chagla, p. 5.
263. Conversation between JNU professor and the writer, Delhi, Nov. 1975.
264. Conversation between Ayub Syed and the writer, Bombay, Jan. 1976.
265. Conversation between railway union official and the writer, Karnataka, Dec. 1975.

266. Conversation between BICC director and the writer, Calcutta, Dec. 1975.

267. Biplab Dasgupta, *New Internationalist*, August 1976.

268. Conversation between Bombay University professor and the writer, Jan. 1976.

269. As n. 268; cf. 'her position is essentially fragile', *Daily Telegraph*, 28.6.76.

270. Dasgupta, loc. cit.

271. Conversation between newspaper editor and the writer, Calcutta, Dec. 1975.

272. Y. B. Chavan, to Rajya Sabha, 16 Jan. 1976, qu. *Hindu*, 17.1.76.

273. *Link*, 27.6.76.

274. Biswanath Mukherjee, qu. *Statesman*, 27.12.75.

275. *People's Democracy*, 22.8.76.

276. Rajeswar Rao, qu. *Ind. Exp.*, 28.5.76.

277. *People's Democracy*, 22.8.76.

278. ibid.

279. *People's Democracy*, 4.7.76 and 28.8.76, restating the resolutions of its central committee, Madras, 22–8 Jan. 1976.

280. *The Times*, 27.7.76, 3.8.76; *Le Monde*, 7.9.76.

281. *ABP*, 16.4.76 ('they had a 40-minute interview with the Prime Minister').

282. Kothari, *Seminar*, July 1976, p. 15.

283. Information communicated to the writer.

284. Information communicated to the writer.

285. Marked by reports of significant CITU victories in trade union elections fought against INTUC and AITUC; e.g. *Ganashakti*, 24.3.76 (24 Parganas), *People's Democracy*, 4.4.76 (Durgapur steel plant), 11.4.76 (Nangal); and 20.6.76, for SFI victories in student elections.

286. Conversation between BICC director and the writer, Calcutta, Dec. 1975.

287. Conversation between CITU trade union official and the writer, Uttar Pradesh, Dec. 1975.

288. Conversation in Mysore, Jan. 1976.

289. Conversation between CITU trade union leader and the writer, Calcutta, Dec. 1975.

290. e.g. at the Neyveli Lignite Corporation from 21 June 1976, *Hindu*, 21.6.76.

291. e.g. Shinde, qu. *Statesman*, 16.7.76; Subramaniam, qu. *Hindu*, 11.8.76; and *Guardian*, 15.1.77 ('India moves to peg price rises').

292. *Link* (editorial), 12.9.76.
293. *ABP*, 27.5.76 ('31 per cent rise in annual plan'); Inder Malhotra, *Guardian*, 27.6.76.
294. *Econ. Times*, 6.8.76.
295. *Statesman*, 4.7.76 (dividends); *Samachar*, 29.6.76 (aid and credits).
296. *Link*, 12.9.76.
297. Shinde, to Lok Sabha, 23 August 1976, qu. *Hindu*, 24.8.76.
298. In Madras, qu. *Hindu*, 11.8.76 ('the name of the game is free enterprise').
299. Thus, a convention was held by the Committee for Civil Liberties in India at the Conway Hall, London, on 3 April 1976, sponsored among others by the CPI–M and the Indian Workers' Association; and an 'International Conference for Restoration of Democracy in India' at Alexandra Palace, London, on 24 April 1976, organized by the Friends of India society, and addressed by Subramaniam Swamy of the Jan Sangh. Meetings and protest marches were held by the Alliance Against Fascist Dictatorship in India (AAFDI) with the support of the Indian Workers' Association (GB), and by the Campaign for the Release of Indian Political Prisoners (CRIPP).
300. e.g. Mohammed Hoda, of the International Transport Workers' Federation, and a representative in London of the Socialist Party, had his passport impounded by the Indian High Commission in London, *Guardian*, 5.8.76.
301. e.g. *Guardian* (editorial), 14.6.76.
302. *Blitz*, 10.1.76.
303. *Statesman Weekly*, 15.5.76; cf. 'New Delhi and Paris base their politics on the same collection of principles' (Jacques Chirac, then French Prime Minister, visiting India, qu. *Le Monde*, 24.1.76).
304. Information communicated to the writer.
305. D. C. Kothari, qu. *Econ. Times*, 2.5.76.
306. Subramaniam, to Rajya Sabha, 29 Aug. 1975, qu. GOI, *A Hundred New Gains*, p. 18. Cf. Robert Shaw, *Jobs and Agricultural Development*, Overseas Development Council, monograph no. 3 (Washington, 1970), p. 62, which shows that Japanese and Taiwanese models of rural development have been consistently held up to India by US advisers and World Bank sources. The same report also urged implementation of land ceilings and the slowing of population growth, pp. 62–3 and 66.

307. A. R. Antulay, general secretary of AICC, and secretary of the Swaran Singh committee, qu. *Econ. Times*, 27.4.76.

308. F. A. Ahmed, qu. *Statesman*, 14.1.76.

309. N. B. Grant, general manager, Bharat Aluminium, qu. *Statesman*, 3.12.75.

310. K. N. Raj, 'Growth and Stagnation in Indian Industrial Development', G. L. Mehta memorial lecture, Indian Institute of Technology, Bombay, 1976, pp. 13–14.

311. F. A. Ahmed, qu. *Econ. Times*, 2.5.76.

312. RBI, *Annual Report, 1975–6*, 13 Sept. 1976, qu. *Financial Times*, 14.9.76.

313. Magdoff, *Monthly Review*, Jan. 1976, pp. 4–5 ('Brazil is an outstanding example of what I am referring to').

314. *Financial Times*, 21.1.77.

315. Inder Malhotra, *Guardian*, 19.1.77.

316. qu. *Financial Times*, 19.1.77.

317. ibid.

318. *Financial Times*, 21.1.77.

319. qu. *Guardian*, 21.1.77.

320. ibid.

321. qu. *Times of India*, 8.1.77.

322. Shukla, qu. *Guardian*, 21.1.77.

323. qu. *Samachar*, 19.11.76.

324. qu. *The Times*, 20.1.77.

325. qu. *Guardian*, 19.1.77.

326. Lenin, *Proletary No. 3*, 8 Sept. 1906, qu. *People's Democracy*, 18.4.76.

Select Bibliography

This bibliography is confined to sources cited in the text and the notes.

INDIAN PRESS AND PERIODICALS

Amrita Bazar Patrika
Ananda Bazar Patrika
Blitz
Business Standard
Century
Commerce
Cross-Section
Deccan Herald
Economic Times
Economic and Political Weekly
Financial Express
Free Press Journal
Fulcrum
Ganashakti
Hindu
Hindu International Edition
Hindustan Times
Hindustan Times Weekly
Indian Express
Link
Madhya Pradesh Chronicle
Madras Evening Daily
Mainstream
New Age
North Indian Patrika
Party Life
Patriot
People's Democracy
Radical Review
Seminar
Statesman
Statesman Weekly
Sunday Standard
Times of India
Tribune
Working Class

FOREIGN PRESS AND PERIODICALS

Black Liberator
Business Week
Daily Telegraph
Financial Times
Granma
Guardian
India Today
Intercontinental Press
Le Monde
Listener

Nation
New Internationalist
New Statesman
New York Times
Observer
Peking Daily

Peking Review
San Francisco Examiner
Sunday Telegraph
Sunday Times
Swaraj
The Times

PUBLISHED WORKS

Amnesty International, *Annual Report, 1974–5*, London, 1975.

Amnesty International, *Report on Prison Conditions in W. Bengal*, London, 1974.

Basu, Jyoti, *Cry Halt to this Reign of Terror*, Calcutta, CPI–M, 1972.

Blackburn, R., ed., *Explosion in a Sub-continent*, Penguin Books, 1975.

Blaug, M., and others, *Causes of Graduate Unemployment in India*, London, Allen Lane, 1969.

Chagla, M. C., *Civil Liberties In India*, [Ahmedabad, 1975].

Chaudhuri, Nirad, *The Continent of Circe*, London, Chatto & Windus, 1965.

Communist Party of India, *Resolutions and Report of the National Council*, Delhi, 1975.

[Daru, C. T.], *A Fresh Look of our Constitution: Some Suggestions*, Ahmedabad, 1975.

Dasgupta, Biplab, *The Naxalite Movement*, Delhi, Allied Publishers, 1974.

Davey, Brian, *The Economic Development of India*, Nottingham, Spokesman Books, 1975.

Dimitrov, Georgi, *Report to the Seventh Congress, Communist International 1935*, London, Red Star Press, 1973.

Frankel, Francine, *India's Green Revolution: Economic Gains and Political Costs*, Princeton, 1971.

Gandhi, Indira, *Broadcast to the Nation, June 26, 1975*, Delhi, Ministry of Information and Broadcasting, 1975.

Gandhi, Indira, *Broadcast to the Nation, June 27, 1975* (in Hindi), Delhi, Ministry of Information and Broadcasting, 1975.

Gandhi, Indira, *New Programme for Economic Progress* (broadcast of 1 July 1975), Delhi, Ministry of Information and Broadcasting, 1975.

Government of India, *A Hundred New Gains*, Delhi, Ministry of Information and Broadcasting, 1975.

Government of India, *India 1976*, Delhi, Ministry of Information and Broadcasting, 1976.

Government of India, *India Today: Basic Facts*, Delhi, Ministry of Information and Broadcasting, 1974.

Government of India, *India: Pocket-Book of Economic Information, 1973 and 1974*, Delhi, Ministry of Finance, 1975.

Government of India, *Pocket-Book of Labour Statistics, 1975*, Simla, Ministry of Labour, 1975.

Government of India, *Preserving Our Democratic Structure*, Delhi, Ministry of Information and Broadcasting, 1975.

Government of India, *Reason for Emergency*, Delhi, Ministry of Information and Broadcasting, 1975.

Government of India, *Thirty Days of National Discipline*, Delhi, Ministry of Information and Broadcasting, 1975.

Government of India, *The Turning Point*, Delhi, Ministry of Information and Broadcasting, 1975.

Government of India, *Why Emergency?*, Delhi, Ministry of Home Affairs, 1975.

Government of India, *Why Emergency: Questions and Answers*, Delhi, Ministry of Information and Broadcasting, 1975.

Government of India, *Years of Achievement: Food*, Delhi, Ministry of Information and Broadcasting, 1975.

Government of India, *Years of Achievement: Irrigation*, Delhi, Ministry of Information and Broadcasting, 1975.

Government of India, *Years of Achievement: Railways*, Delhi, Ministry of Information and Broadcasting, 1975.

Government of India, *Years of Achievement: Rural Development*, Delhi, Ministry of Information and Broadcasting, 1975.

Jannuzi, F. T., *Agrarian Crisis in India: The Case of Bihar*, University of Texas Press, 1974.

Kurian, M. (editor), *India: State and Society*, Madras, Orient Longman, 1975.

Maddison, Angus, *Class Structure and Economic Growth, India and Pakistan*, London, Allen & Unwin, 1971.

Mamdani, Mahmood, *The Myth of Population Control: Family, Caste, and Class in an Indian Village*, New York and London, Monthly Review Press, 1972.

Marx, K., *Capital*, Moscow, Progress Publishers, 1959.

Marx, K., 'The Eighteenth Brumaire of Louis Bonaparte', in *Surveys*

From Exile (Fernbach, D., editor), Penguin Books, 1973.

Marx, K., *Marx–Engels Collected Works*, vol. 1, Moscow, Progress Publishers, 1975.

Marx, K., *Wage Labour and Capital*, Moscow, Progress Publishers, 1952.

Maxwell, Neville, *India's China War*, Penguin Books, 1972.

Maxwell, Neville, *Woman on a White Horse*, Oxford, Institute of Commonwealth Studies, 1975 (Reprint Series, No. 79).

Myrdal, Gunnar, *Asian Drama*, London, Allen Lane, 1968.

Naik, J. P., *Policy and Performance in Indian Education, 1947–74*, Delhi, Orient Longman, 1975.

Nehru, Jawaharlal, *Autobiography*, London, Bodley Head, 1936.

Pande, G. C., *The Meaning and Process of Culture*, Agra, S. L. Agarwala, 1973.

Panekar, S. D., and Rao, Kamala, *A Study of Prostitutes in Bombay*, Bombay, Lalvani, 1967.

Sen, Amartya, *Dimensions of Unemployment in India*, Calcutta, Indian Statistical Institute, 1973.

Sezhiyan, Era, *Parliament Under Emergency*, [Delhi, 1975].

Shah, S. A., ed., *Towards National Liberation: Essays on Political Economy*, Montreal, 1973.

Shaw, Robert, *Jobs and Agricultural Development*, Washington, Overseas Development Council, 1970.

Snow, Edgar, *Red Star over China*, Penguin Books, 1972.

Times of India, *Times of India Directory and Year-Book*, Bombay, 1976.

West Bengal State, *Labour Department Survey for 1975*, Calcutta, 1976.

UNPUBLISHED DOCUMENTS

Amnesty International, 'Parliamentarians in Prison as at August 1976', London, 1976.

Communist Party of India (Marxist), 'On The Declaration of Emergency: For All Party Units', [Calcutta, 1975].

Communist Party of India (Marxist), 'Report of Central Committee Meeting', Madras, 22–8 January 1976.

Communist Party of India (Marxist), 'Twenty-Point Programme: A Cruel Hoax', 8 November 1975.

Government of India, 'General Guidelines for the Press', ref. RS/TML/T. no. 557, Delhi, Press Information Bureau, 26 June 1975.

Government of India, 'Guidelines for Covering the Proceedings of Parliament', No. 2/147/75-CC, Delhi, Office of the Chief Censor, 7 March 1976.

Government of India, 'Guidelines for the Press', Delhi, Office of the Censor, 26 July 1975.

Government of India, 'Guidelines for the Press in the Present Emergency', ref. RS/TML/T. no. 556, Delhi, Press Information Bureau, 26 June 1975.

Government of India, 'Guidelines on Pre-Censorship', ref. RA/BV/T. no. 559, Delhi, Press Information Bureau, 27 June 1975.

Government of India, 'Revised Guidelines for the Coverage of Proceedings of Parliament', Office of the Chief Censor, 20 July 1975.

Indian School of Social Sciences, 'Bonded Labour in India', Calcutta, 1975.

International League for the Rights of Man, 'Torture of Political Prisoners in India', New York, March 1976.

Jacob, John, 'India Then and Now', Singapore Indian Congress, 1976.

Raj, K. N., 'Growth and Stagnation in Indian Industrial Development', Indian Institute of Technology, Bombay, 1976.

Glossary

Acharya	spiritual guide, illustrious man
Āditya	the sun, god of the sun
Adivasi	aboriginal, 'tribal' inhabitant of India
Agni	fire, the god of fire
Ahimsa	non-violence
Arjuna	a great warrior, brother-in-law of Krishna (q.v.)
Atharvaveda	the fourth *Veda* (q.v.)
Ātman	the light of self
Ayurveda	the '*Veda* of life', a work on medicine
Bhagavad-gītā	the 'song of the adorable', a poem in the Mahā-bārata (q.v.)
Bidi	cigar, cigarette
Brahman	soul of the universe, divine or absolute essence
Bustee	group of hutments
Chaprasi	messenger, courier
Dacoit, dacoity	armed robber, robbery
Deepavali, Divali	autumn festival of lights
Devadasi	temple attendant, temple prostitute
Dharna	sitting outside the door of someone's house to enforce performance of a duty
Durbar	court, levée
Ghat	landing place, wharf, place of cremation
Ghee	clarified butter
Gherao	picket
Gītā	*see* Bhagavad-gītā
Goonda	gangster, thug, bully
Harijan	'child of god', untouchable

Indra	ruler over the deities of the firmament
Inquilab	revolution
Īsá	one of the Upaniṣads (q.v.)
Jawan	soldier
Jhuggi	slum dwelling
Kalazar	visceral parasitical disease
Karma	act of piety and duty
Khanda	section of a Vedic hymn
Kisan	cultivator, peasant
Kohl	antimony powder, used as eye make-up
Krishna	incarnation of Vishnu, the preserver
Lathi	stick, bludgeon
Lok Sabha	assembly or house of the people, Lower House of Parliament
Mahābārata	epic poem of the Hindus
Mantra	metrical prayer, invocation
Mundaka	one of the Upaniṣads (q.v.)
Pada-yatra	journey on foot
Padma Vibhushan	honorific title awarded by the Indian state (lit. 'one whose adornment is a lotus')
Paise	denomination of currency, worth about one seventeenth of a penny
Pan	areca nut and spices, rolled up in a betel-leaf
Panchayat	council
Pindari	plunderer, marauder
Pūsan	deity of providence, the provider
Rajya Sabha	assembly or house of the states, Upper House of Parliament
Rigveda	one of the four *Vedas* (q.v.)
Sabha	assembly
Sadhu	sage, mendicant
Sanyasi	religious mendicant
Sarpanch	head of a *panchayat* (q.v.)
Sarvodaya	communal welfare
Satyagraha	non-violent resistance

Satyagrahi	non-violent demonstrator
Shri, shrimati	prosperity, prefix of honour
Siva	Hindu deity, the destroyer
Suttee	a faithful wife, widow's suicide
Taitirrīya	part of the second – Yajur – *Veda* (q.v.)
Taluk	subdivision of a district
Titiksā	endurance
Unani	Greek, Graeco-Arabic medicine
Upaniṣad	mystical doctrine of Hinduism
Uṣā	dawn, daughter of heaven
Vanaspati	hydrogenated vegetable oil
Vasus	eight attendants of Indra (q.v.), personifications of nature
Veda, vedas	'divine knowledge', four holy books of Hinduism
Yama	god of the dead
Yamadudargal	messengers of the god of death
Zenana	woman's part of the house
. . . *Zindabad!*	Long live . . . !

Index

References to notes are given in italic numerals